CONTRIBUTORS

ROBERT SOMERLOTT, the editorial consultant for this guide-book, has lived in Mexico for nearly 25 years. The author of 14 books, he has had articles appear in *American Heritage* and *The Atlantic,* among other publications. He is also a regular contributor to the travel section of *The News,* Mexico City's English-language daily.

PATRICIA ALISAU, a resident of Mexico for more than 20 years, is a former Central American war correspondent turned freelance travel editor and writer. Her photographs and articles on Mexico have appeared in several European magazines as well as *The New York Times, Newsweek,* and the *Chicago Tribune.*

ROBERT CUMMINGS, a resident of Mexico for the past eight years, has written numerous travel articles as well as a novella, and is currently working on a novel.

CANDACE LYLE HOGAN, a freelance writer and editor currently living in New York City, has explored Baja California over the last 40 years from her home base in La Misión.

ROBIN LLOYD, a resident of Mexico for 17 years, is a correspondent for *The News,* Mexico City's English-language daily, and *Vallarta Today.* He is the author of five books, and his articles and photographs have appeared in *Life, Time,* and *Newsweek.*

MITCHELL NAUFFTS, a freelance writer and editor based in New York City, writes frequently about Mexico.

JACKIE PETERSON, the travel editor of the *Sacramento Union* for 20 years, has worked as a feature writer for the *San Francisco Examiner* and *The News,* Mexico City's English-language daily newspaper. She lives in Mazatlán.

LARRY RUSSELL, a resident of Mexico City since 1973, is a frequent contributor to the travel sections of Mexico's *Vogue* and *Progreso* magazines. He has also, in collaboration with his wife, produced, written, and performed the musical scores for a number of documentary films about Mexico.

SUSAN WAGNER, the travel editor of *Modern Bride* magazine for 10 years, has worked on the staff of *Travel & Leisure* magazine and has written a series of guidebooks to Mexican resorts as well as innumerable articles on the country. She attended graduate school in Mexico and returns there frequently.

CELIA WAKEFIELD has lived in Mexico for many years, the past 17 in San Miguel de Allende, and travels extensively throughout the country. She has written articles for *The Atlantic, Saturday Review, Newsday,* and *Punch.* She is also the author and photographer of *High Cities of the Andes.*

THE BERLITZ
TRAVELLERS GUIDES

THE BERLITZ TRAVELLERS GUIDE TO MEXICO

Fifth Edition

ALAN TUCKER
General Editor

BERLITZ PUBLISHING COMPANY, INC.
New York, New York

BERLITZ PUBLISHING COMPANY LTD.
Oxford, England

THE BERLITZ TRAVELLERS
GUIDE TO MEXICO
Fifth Edition

Berlitz Trademark Reg U.S. Patent and Trademark Office
and other countries—Marca Registrada

Published by Berlitz Publishing Company, Inc.
257 Park Avenue South, New York, New York 10010, U.S.A.

Distributed in the United States by
the Macmillan Publishing Group

Distributed elsewhere by Berlitz Publishing Company Ltd.
Berlitz House, Peterley Road, Horspath, Oxford OX4 2TX, England

ISBN 2-8315-1703-6
ISSN 1057-4786

Designed by Beth Tondreau Design
Cover design by Dan Miller Design
Cover photograph © Dennis Hallinan/FPG International
Maps by Mark Stein Studios
Illustrations by Bill Russell
Fact-checked in Mexico by Patricia Alisau
Copyedited by Cynthia Sophiea
Edited by Mitchell Nauffts and Lisa Leventer

Printed in the United States of America
1 3 5 7 9 10 8 6 4 2

THIS GUIDEBOOK

The Berlitz Travellers Guides are designed for experienced travellers in search of exceptional information that will enhance the enjoyment of the trips they take.

Where, for example, are the interesting, out-of-the-way, fun, charming, or romantic places to stay? The hotels described by our expert writers are some of the special places, in all price ranges except for the very lowest—not just the run-of-the-mill, heavily marketed places in advertised airline and travel-wholesaler packages.

We are *highly* selective in our choices of accommodations, concentrating on what our insider contributors think are the most interesting or rewarding places, and why. Readers who want to review exhaustive lists of hotel and resort choices as well, and who feel they need detailed descriptions of each property, can supplement the *Berlitz Travellers Guide* with tourism industry publications or one of the many directory-type guidebooks on the market.

We indicate the approximate price level of each accommodation in our description of it (no indication means it is moderate in local, relative terms), and at the end of every chapter we supply more detailed hotel rates as well as contact information so that you can get precise, up-to-the-minute rates and make reservations.

The Berlitz Travellers Guide to Mexico highlights the more rewarding parts of the country so that you can quickly and efficiently home in on a good itinerary.

Of course, this guidebook does far more than help you choose a hotel and plan your trip. *The Berlitz Travellers Guide to Mexico* is designed for use *in* Mexico. Our writers, each of whom is an experienced travel journalist who either lives in or regularly tours the city or region of Mexico he or she covers, tell you what you really need to know, what you can't find out so easily on your own. They identify and describe the truly out-of-the-ordinary resorts, restaurants, shops, activities, and sights, and tell you the best way to "do" your destination.

Our writers are highly selective. They bring out the significance of the places they *do* cover, capturing the personality and the underlying cultural and historical resonances of a city or region—making clear its special appeal.

The Berlitz Travellers Guide to Mexico is full of reliable information. We would like to know if you think we've left out some very special place. Although we make every effort to provide the most current information available about every destination described in this book, it is possible too that changes have occurred before you arrive. If you do have an experience that is contrary to what you were led to expect by our description, we would like to hear from you about it.

A guidebook is no substitute for common sense when you are travelling. Always pack the clothing, footwear, and other items appropriate for the destination, and make the necessary accommodation for such variables as altitude, weather, and local rules and customs. Of course, once on the scene you should avoid situations that are in your own judgment potentially hazardous, even if they have to do with something mentioned in a guidebook. Half the fun of travelling is exploring, but explore with care.

ALAN TUCKER
General Editor
Berlitz Travellers Guides

Root Publishing Company
350 West Hubbard Street
Suite 440
Chicago, Illinois 60610

CONTENTS

MAPS

OVERVIEW

By Robert Somerlott

Robert Somerlott has lived in Mexico for nearly 25 years. The author of ten books, he has had articles appear in American Heritage *and* The Atlantic, *among other publications. He is also a regular contributor to the travel section of* The News, *Mexico City's English-language daily.*

For many visitors the most surprising discovery about Mexico is its foreignness. Travellers from the United States who thought they were just going next door are particularly astonished. Even if they have read books on Mexico, seen films set there, and studied photos of the country, they are seldom prepared for the reality that greets them. Europe, even for first-time visitors, seems familiar by comparison.

The surprise often springs from the vivid colors and odd contrasts that abound in Mexico. You climb into an ordinary taxi in Mexico City, for example, and suddenly notice that the driver has transformed his dashboard into a shrine. The Virgin of Guadalupe, the country's patroness saint, lit by twinkling bulbs, presides over a bed of plastic flowers. When the taxi stops for an ordinary traffic light, an extraordinary quartet of fire-eaters leaps into the street to entertain. Or you get on a modern, unusually handsome subway only to discover as you change lines that the station is built around an Aztec temple complete with sacrificial altar. More remarkable still, it is not a set or reconstruction; the temple was once, centuries ago, just that, and the tens of thousands who pass it daily take this incongruity for granted. Or, driving on a new highway in the middle of nowhere, you suddenly overtake a procession of people walking on the shoulder of the road. Their dark, earthy faces are framed by straw hats and handwoven shawls, and they carry banners and religious icons. Oddly, this procession does not seem to end.

1

You drive on, mile after mile, passing a multitude of men and women, many carrying babies. They are joyous, exalted; they sing, chant, and laugh as they trudge through the dust and heat and rain. You have come upon a religious pilgrimage to one of Mexico's several great shrines, where the pilgrims are counted in the hundreds of thousands and walk for days, sleeping at night in the open. You suddenly realize that the deep and powerful impulse that draws millions of Mexicans across fields, through marshes, and over mountains is far older than the religion whose banners they bear. While today the destination may be a church instead of a sacred well, the force that sets this human river in motion is unchanged and, as ever, awe-inspiring.

The sounds in Mexico are often as unfamiliar as the sights. In the middle of the night in an isolated hill town all the bells of all the churches suddenly begin to clang and peal at once. No, it is not a harbinger of revolution, or even an alarm. More than likely, a festival has just started, or a local *fútbol* team has won an important match, or a dignitary has arrived on an official visit. But what does it matter, really? Bells are made for ringing, and Mexico is a land of thousands of bells speaking to one another. In the same town, the shouts of vendors selling strawberries or crab or fresh asparagus mix with the melody of the scissors grinder and the off-key brass of a ragtag band as it marches down a street for no discernible reason.

Mexico, it quickly becomes clear, is not a European country. It is not even really what is today called a "Western" country. Instead, it is a unique blending of cultures based on a civilization that built great and beautiful cities when northern Europe was a wilderness peopled by barbarians.

Mexicans, a traveller soon discovers, express themselves publicly, in rites, rituals, rallies, and fairs. Every town and every parish has its own saint to honor, its own anniversaries to commemorate, its own special reasons for flying banners. Octavio Paz once asked the mayor of a poor village how the town's income was spent. "Mostly on fiestas, señor," was the reply. "We are a small village but we have two patron saints."

The richness of life in Mexico is evident in its streets and plazas, in a gathering together, in a sense of community that has nothing to do with conforming. Families are close, and clan ties are binding, even when disrupted by hardship and migration. But beyond the family, outside the home, lies another life, a necessary world of public ritual, where people stand close as fireworks shriek and explode in the night. "Viva México!" they shout—though the cheers are not for the government; Mexicans distrust all government. No, the cheers are for the land, for the people, for their families and way of life.

Mexico's Pre-Columbian Past

Mexicans are quite different from their neighbors to the north and south for reasons that are both historical (as you will see throughout this book) and racial. The first human inhabitants of the Americas were nomadic hunters from Asia who followed the herds they depended on over a broad isthmus that has long since been submerged under the shallow Bering Sea. We know little about these first "Americans," migrating as they did tens of thousands of years ago, but the evidence indicates that included in these various migratory waves of prehistoric peoples were many racial types. Later and larger migrations were comprised primarily of Mongoloid racial types, and they played the largest part in determining the physical traits of succeeding populations.

From the time of the last great migration (which ended around 9000 B.C.) until the arrival of the Spanish in the 16th century, there was no meaningful contact between the Old World and the New. The Americas, supporting a very small population relative to the rest of the world, developed independently and in isolation.

Civilization here rose in conjunction with the development of corn (maize), which became the food staple of much of the Americas (as it remains today). The Maya called its kernels the "sunbeams of God." Other Mesoamerican people displayed equal reverence toward this life-sustaining plant. (The picture of a lone man hoeing his mountainside patch of corn is a profound symbol of Mexico.)

Some 3,000 years ago a mighty culture suddenly rose and flourished on an unlikely piece of real estate, the swamps of coastal Tabasco, just west of the Yucatán Peninsula. These people today are known as the **Olmecs**, and in many respects theirs can be considered the "mother culture" of Mesoamerica. While much of their history and accomplishments remain lost to time, we do know that the Olmecs invented the first form of writing used in the Americas, a numerical system later adopted and vastly expanded by the Maya; that they were the first Mesoamerican people to devote themselves to astronomical studies; that they originated many of the religious concepts and customs that came to characterize Mesoamerican civilization; and that they also became accomplished at jade carving and developed methods of transporting huge boulders great distances.

About 2,000 years ago there was a stirring of collective activity throughout Mesoamerica. It was then that **Teotihuacán**, America's first true city, rose and flourished in the Valley of Mexico some 30 miles northeast of the modern capital. Its builders, who erected such imposing monuments as the Pyramids of the Sun and Moon, were in all likelihood descendants of primitive villagers native to the area. Their name for themselves remains a mystery, but today they are called "Teotihuacanos." Within a century these vigorous people had come to dominate a huge region, sending trading parties out in all directions, some as far as present-day Guatemala. (In addition, trade goods, if not the traders themselves, found their way north up the great rivers of what is now the southwestern United States.)

Over the next several centuries various cultures rose and flowered throughout Mesoamerica: Teotihuacán and Xochicalco in the central highlands, the Zapotec centers in Oaxaca, and, most resplendent of all, the Classic-era cities of the **Maya** in the southeast. The Maya, whose ascendancy was roughly contemporaneous with that of Teotihuacán, founded their earliest ceremonial centers on the shelf of land bordered by the Pacific and the uplands of southern Chiapas and Guatemala. They were the first people in the world to develop the mathematical concept of zero, and their use of numbers and a calendar based on astronomical observation was far superior to the cumbersome systems that prevailed in Europe at the time.

The **Classic era**, as this period of widespread culture and knowledge in Mesoamerica is called, began sometime between the second and third centuries A.D., reached its apogee around A.D. 600, and three centuries later had ended completely. The great cities and ceremonial centers were abandoned; no one knows exactly why—although there are theories. A great plague or plagues has been suggested as one possible cause; a series of crop failures—leading to a rejection of traditional religion—is another. Other experts believe that the maintenance of so many priests and temples simply became too much, that these great civilizations were destroyed by nothing more than excessive taxation. At the same time barbarian peoples from the north were roaming the land; yet their presence, according to the experts, seems not to have been the primary cause for the abandonment, which started in the north and progressed to the south and east, of one city after another. In any case, by the end of the Classic era several qualities that would remain constants in the Mexican character were already evident: a devotion to ritual, a belief in the importance of pilgrimage, a fondness for bold color, and a love of exuberant music and dance.

In the tenth century the country suffered the invasion of a warrior people called the **Toltecs**, who bequeathed it an infusion of much-needed vitality as well as new styles of art. The ancient ruins at **Tula**, northwest of Mexico City, and **Chichén Itzá**, in the Yucatán, are their greatest surviving monuments.

The Toltec conquest, however, proved only to be the prelude to the rise of the **Aztecs**, a fierce imperialistic society with a particularly bloodthirsty religion. After only a century of Aztec rule, the stage was set for the arrival of Hernán Cortés in 1519.

From Conquest to Revolution

The saga of the Conquest has been told and retold. Still, one important fact is often neglected: The conquistadors were defeated and put to flight by the Aztecs. Their eventual victory became possible only after they allied themselves with a native army of the Tlaxcalans, bitter enemies of their Aztec neighbors. **Tenochtitlán**, the magnificent Aztec capital (over which Mexico City was built), was surrendered to Cortés on August 21, 1521.

Following the victory of the conquistadors, it was left to the missionaries of the Church to subdue and secure the rest of the country. Employing tactics and rhetoric perfected during the long, grim decades of the Inquisition, the missionaries set about their task—one they were oddly suited for, believing as they did that Satan was a living presence, an insidious enemy who lurked invisibly at the shoulder of every would-be convert whispering foulness into his ear. Native books, art, buildings, and customs were seen as being steeped not just in sin but in even more dangerous magic. In the end, there was not only fanaticism but fear behind the missionaries' destruction of some of the most glorious art ever created.

(Among the Mayan and Aztec materials destroyed were documents, so-called codices, painted or written on strips of pounded bark or parchment. Only three complete and part of a fourth Mayan codice are known to have survived; all are in European museums. Other codices that remain in Mexico are post-Conquest copies of the originals.)

For almost three centuries Spain held sway over her New World colony, imposing on it her religion, art, and institutions—and still Mexico is only superficially Spanish. It is a curious fact, and one that is implicitly acknowledged on October 12, Columbus Day: In Mexico, it is not so much

Columbus who is honored as it is the people of Mexico themselves, the unique Mexican race, or *raza,* and so the day is known here as the Día de la Raza. It is an entirely appropriate holiday, for today's Mexicans are mostly *mestizos,* a mixture of Indian and Spanish. Of course, the proportion of the mix is impossible to determine and varies from region to region. Then, too, there are the purely Mayan or Zapotec people, or those of other native groups, as well as the purely Spanish, or *criollo.* (Other, smaller European admixtures are present as well—French, Irish, and German, most notably. The African influence is relatively small. Slaves from the Indies sometimes reached the Gulf Coast, and a few were imported, but the Spaniards were afraid of black slavery in New Spain, being nervous about rebellions. Chinese were brought into the north as railroad builders; Lebanese entered the southeast first as peddlers and later as storekeepers.)

During the centuries of colonial rule New Spain, as Mexico was called, was an intellectually somnolent land. Education was reserved for the privileged few, and what little was offered to the poor suffered a terrible blow when the Jesuits, the best and most selfless teachers, were expelled by the Spanish Crown in the 18th century. At the same time Spain was careful not to permit the growth of an indigenous governing class. Mexico paid heavily for this after she gained her sovereignty in 1821: Her leaders had no experience in government, and little understanding of compromise and practicality.

The 19th century was a time of violence, hardship, and loss. The United States invaded Mexico in 1846 and walked away with half its territory two years later. The French marched in 16 years later and, with the help of Mexican conservatives, put the puppet emperor Maximilian on a spurious (and wobbly) throne. Throughout the period Church and State battled without mercy.

The modern Mexican state emerged from a bloody, brutal revolution that raged from 1910 into the 1920s, a struggle comparable in its ferocity to the U.S. Civil War. It was a revolt of the poor, the landless, and the disenfranchised, and when Mexicans speak of "the Revolution," they are referring to this total upheaval of society, not the earlier struggle for independence from Spain. The 1920s witnessed a strike by the clergy; the priests and nuns locked up the churches and departed. Parishioners shot the locks off church doors and conducted their own services, which brought the clergy rushing back, only to be expelled again—this time against their will. The subject remains a touchy one.

Today Mexico has laws on its books and articles in its constitution sharply limiting the powers of the Church and clergy. Clerics recently were granted the right to vote, but they may not hold political office. The Church's ownership of real estate is highly restricted, and it may not buy radio or television stations, although "special" religious rites, such as a Mass celebrated by the Pope, may be broadcast. New churches may be built only by special permission (almost never granted), and the Church may not offer primary education. Convents are illegal but a few small ones are tolerated. In recent years authorities have winked at the Church's small violations of the law and constant testing of limits. But the anti-clerical laws remain official and are usually enforced. Oddly enough, the majority of people in this overwhelmingly Catholic country support the restrictions. They recall the clerical abuses of power, and every school child knows that a Pope once declared the Mexican constitution null and void.

The Mexico of today is the product of long and tragic tumult. The sculpted bronze figures you see in public squares across the land are almost always of men who fought for a losing cause: Cuauhtémoc, the last Aztec ruler, tortured and slain; Hidalgo, Aldama, Allende, and Jiménez, martyrs in the struggle for independence at the start of the 19th century, executed or beheaded; José María Morelos, who continued the fight for independence, executed in 1815; Vicente Guerrero, staunch defender of the rights of the people, first against Spain, then against the rich and powerful of his own country, treacherously executed in 1831; Francisco Madero, the first president of modern Mexico and a great liberal reformer, murdered with his vice president in a Mexico City alley in 1913; Emiliano Zapata, land reformer and hero of the peasants, shot in cold blood in 1919; President Alvaro Obregón, early defender of constitutional government, assassinated three weeks after his reelection in 1928. Their ideas and causes ultimately may have triumphed, but they themselves came to tragic ends, most of them believing their cause was lost. They are Mexico's true heroes, and there is a certain melancholy appropriateness to this in a nation too often beset by turmoil and trouble.

Mexico for Travellers

There is a saying here that goes, "Once the dust of Mexico has settled on your heart, you will find peace in no other land." Certainly, the traveller who discovers Mexico for the first time is likely to return again and again. One trip is not enough to comprehend it—perhaps a lifetime is not sufficient, for its character is like a Mayan temple, built layer upon layer, the newest façade hiding but not destroying the earlier ones. Nor do the centuries quietly vanish when their time is up; in Mexico they linger on, the past mixing with the present, complicating judgments and making predictions all but impossible.

Most visitors come initially for the glorious beaches or the magnificent pre-Columbian ruins. We hope that after experiencing the pleasures of those you will prolong your stay or return to see the less publicized attractions we have chosen, such as the romantic streets and alleys of Guanajuato or the Indian color and serenity of Pátzcuaro.

As well, Mexico is a bargain. Prices change and exchange rates fluctuate, so it is more of a bargain some years and in some seasons than others. Still, all things considered, a Mexican vacation is one of the best travel buys in the world. When this book labels something as "expensive," it usually means an amount that would be considered moderate in New York or Paris, and cheap in Tokyo.

Another reason to go to Mexico is the Mexican people themselves. Mexicans, in general, are fond of foreigners, especially their northern neighbors on the continent. Full of a lively curiosity, tolerant and accepting of different kinds of behavior and tastes, they are generally a kind and courteous people.

Often, it's true, Mexican politicians and intellectuals sound as xenophobic as any in the world. The media here ring with screams about imperialism, arrogance, and exploitation. From a Mexican viewpoint, however, there is often good reason for this screaming. Mexico, after all, has suffered grievously at the hands of foreigners. The United States stormed onto its soil not once but several times, and claimed a large part of it as its own. The French also invaded, and the British, although less involved, are not innocent. Alas, Spain's conduct was simply unspeakable. And yet, despite this discouraging record, ordinary Mexicans like their foreign neighbors. No wonder the feeling is usually mutual.

If a visitor makes the least attempt at uttering a few Spanish words, however badly, Mexicans will go to extraordinary lengths to understand and be of help. A few gestures may inspire an entire pantomime. You'll find no snobbery here, no sense that those who do not speak the native tongue are considered little more than savages.

Almost everyone strives to be helpful. If a car is mired on a country road, suddenly half a dozen men appear from nowhere to push it out. When their efforts fail, someone fetches a team of oxen. Strangers will guide you, be infinitely patient in repeating directions, and sometimes even walk you to your destination. (This can lead to a sort of courtesy disaster when an informant doesn't really know the way but won't be so rude as to disappoint you. Truth must not interfere with politeness.)

Mexicans are often surprisingly familiar with the United States and Canada, at least on a second- or third-hand basis. After all, a chief export of the country is its own sons and daughters for labor abroad. Is there anyone, even in the remotest village, who doesn't have at least one cousin who has crossed two or more borders to find work? Or an uncle living in Los Angeles?

Because these temporary laborers and new immigrants are often exploited, the guilty American conscience expects hostility in return from Mexicans. Mexican fatalism usually prevents this: What happened was the fault of the system, the government, or just bad luck. Nothing personal, and all in all it wasn't so bad. *Así es la vida*—such is life! Why nourish bad feelings? This kind of fatalism moves like a tide through Mexican life, softening its hard edges and making bad times and economic failures bearable. Resignation may be an enemy of progress, but it is also a balm for the wear and tear of daily living.

There is one facet of the national character you probably won't understand, and it may ultimately annoy you, so be prepared. The Mexican concept of schedules and punctuality is a pre-Columbian mystery. At times it seems incredible that the ancestors of these people calculated the world's most accurate calendar. What is two o'clock? Well, it's two until it's three o'clock, clearly. Also, it's two when it's no longer one o'clock. Novelist Carlos Fuentes writes of an old man who wove palm hats as he walked from village to village. Thus, a certain village became two hats away, another one three. Each to his own clock, and you cannot expect a person to keep "English time," which is what the exact time is called.

All the jokes and stories about *mañana* are understatements. In part, the answer that your train/letter/money order will be there *mañana* is simple courtesy, a desire not to disappoint. In part, it is optimism. But it also stems from a belief that you will not take such a word as "tomorrow" literally. *Mañana* is a dream, a hope, a kindness—as well as a way of getting rid of an aggressive, impatient person.

In the end, you must simply relax and adopt this Mexican virtue of fatalism.

Touring Mexico

This book, intended as an introduction to a large and varied country, is *selective* rather than complete. Only the best and most interesting places have been chosen. There is no point in muddying its contents with destinations few people would willingly choose. It also omits places—including a few of Mexico's larger cities—that are simply pass-through points en route to somewhere else. **Monterrey**, for example, Mexico's northeastern metropolis, has some attractive neighborhoods and an admirably renovated downtown section, but it remains a place for business, not for leisure or discovery. Many other large and prosperous cities are omitted for the same reason, among them Torreón, Durango, Ciudad Victoria, and León.

A different type of omission is neatly summed up by the famous remark of Dr. Johnson: "Worth seeing? Yes, but not worth going to see." Some places, even though attractive, are too remote or difficult to reach to be considered here. The once-flourishing mining towns of **Real de Catorce**, south of Monterrey, and **Alamos**, southeast of Ciudad Obregón, are examples. They are interesting if you happen to be in the neighborhood but for most people not worth a special and awkward trip, so they are only covered briefly as side trips from border routes. Many archaeological zones also fall into this category. Dedicated ruins buffs will easily find them in more specialized reference publications.

Two colonial silver cities, **San Luis Potosí** and **Zacatecas**, have attractions that are also not described in detail below because they, too, do not quite justify the trip. If you find yourself in their vicinity, however, do not neglect those handsome towns.

On the other hand, the **Copper Canyon** (and its train), also remote from usual destinations, is special. Its breathtaking natural beauty and the opportunity for adventure it affords justify a trip to Mexico's dusty northwest corner, so we discuss this experience in detail.

Our exploration of Mexico begins with the capital, **Mexico City**, the country's hub and crossroads. The world's largest city is full of both annoyances and charm. Its traffic is manic, its pace distinctly un-Mexican. Traditional Mexican courtesy is put to the extreme test here. Individuals in the D. F. (Distrito Federal, as Mexico City is officially known) are usually as kind and courteous as people in the provinces, even though as city dwellers they must be wary. But courtesy is not a usual trait of crowds, of mobs at the subway, of people rushing desperately to board the bus to get home.

For all its problems, there is much to admire and enjoy in the capital. With its cathedral, its fine government palace, and, hidden just around a corner, the once-great Templo Mayor of the Aztecs, the great Zócalo (main plaza) is a masterly achievement in urban design. The National Museum of Anthropology is the country's finest "archaeological zone," and ranks among the great museums of the world. The pyramids at nearby **Teotihuacán** are marvels of ancient engineering. Finally, the city itself is a museum of people and life, filled with quaint neighborhoods, odd little shops, and unexpected vistas.

Mexico City is also the jumping-off point for a number of short trips, five of which are outlined here: flower-filled **Cuernavaca** and the lovely ruins of **Xochicalco** nearby; picturesque **Taxco**, town of noted silversmiths; staid **Puebla** and the huge pyramid in neighboring **Cholula**; a northward loop including the National Museum of Viceregal Art in **Tepotzotlán**, the ruins of ancient **Tula**, and the 16th-century monastery at **Ixmiquilpán**, with its strange Indian murals; and an excursion to **Valle de Bravo**, a wooded and verdant resort on a man-made lake in the mountains west of the capital, with the Aztec shrine of **Malinalco** an added bonus.

That is as much as most travellers will be able to explore from the Federal District. Those with more time may also want to visit **Tlaxcala**, with its fanciful architecture, and the mysterious pre-Columbian ruins of **Cacaxtla**.

Travellers often talk about discovering "the real Mexico," and while every part of the country is equally real, the sort of place they usually have in mind turns out to be in the historic **Bajío**, the colonial heartland located more or less north of the capital. Although the Bajío lacks Mexico's two greatest attractions for foreign visitors—beaches and ancient archaeological ruins—it is indeed "the real Mexico," as well as the best place to discover what the country as a whole is doing and thinking. The Bajío comprises only an eighth of Mexico's land but produces most of its food. And it is here, in the mining towns of **Guanajuato**, **Querétaro**, **San Miguel de Allende**, and **Morelia**, that you'll see the finest colonial architecture and get the strongest sense of Mexico's colonial heritage.

The valley encircling **Guadalajara** blends into the Bajío without any sharp geographical separation, but Mexico's second city lies far enough west of the capital to have developed its own ways and style. Although it is difficult to rate historical suffering, this area, the **Western Highlands**, probably bore the worst of it during the Conquest, with the barbarity of the conquistadors reaching special depths of sadism. Fortunately, the city of Guadalajara and the surrounding Jalisco region were spared from later foreign incursions. The invasion route taken by the armies of the United States lay far to the east, and the struggles with the French were north and south of Mexico City. Guadalajara also largely avoided the depredations of bandits in military uniforms during the years of revolutionary turmoil.

This comparatively benign history shows in its architecture, its style, and its people. Here is a friendly and vital city, one where sightseers will want to linger but not remain too long—its charms are many, but not infinite. Still, the Guadalajara area has the largest English-speaking expatriate colony in the world—one in the city itself and a second in residence in the small towns along the shore of **Lago de Chapala**. An ideal climate is a powerful attraction, it seems.

Mexico's other celebrated lake, **Pátzcuaro**, is east and slightly south of Chapala, situated among rugged mountains rather than in a fertile valley. With the change in terrain there also comes a change in the people—from the cowboys (real or rhinestone) of Guadalajara to the sober Tarascans of Michoacán. Writer and intellectual Andrés Henestrosa has said, "Mexican songs are Indian inside, European outside— Spanish melody and Indian melancholy." Nowhere does that seem truer than in Pátzcuaro. But if the people are sober, their great market is a riot of color. Ultimately, Pátzcuaro seems outside of time, an Indian Brigadoon only superficially affected by passing fancy.

The mountainous route between Pátzcuaro and Mexico City, via Morelia, is scenic country well worth exploring if you have a car, but not otherwise. You'll want to be able to stop, get out, look around, and breathe deeply—a luxury that buses simply don't offer. The towns themselves are not especially attractive, but the trip is lovely.

Far to the southeast lies **Oaxaca**, just as Indian as Pátzcuaro but utterly different in temperament. Whereas the Tarascan people seem reserved and as cool as their mountain lake, the Zapotec folk of Oaxaca are outgoing, lively, warm, and curious. In forested Pátzcuaro you are aware of shadows; the Valley of Oaxaca, on the other hand, is flooded with sunshine. Centuries ago two ancient cultures, the Zapotecs and later the Mixtecs, flourished in the valleys that converge at the city of Oaxaca. Today the ruins of their many ceremonial centers, including the great **Monte Albán** and **Mitla**, stand as a reminder of that former glory. Two thousand years ago at Monte Albán the Zapotecs began to reshape a mountaintop, creating in the process ancient Mexico's only necropolis, a true city of the dead. Later, the Mixtecs added to Monte Albán's vast honeycomb of tombs while creating for their dead some of the most exquisite jewelry ever fashioned, treasures now displayed in Oaxaca's museums. But the charm of Oaxaca is by no means confined to archaeology. Today's city offers fascinating architecture, colorful craft markets, and the pageant of daily life around its welcoming plaza.

The **Gulf Coast** region is the least visited of those discussed here, but also the most varied. **Veracruz** is a burst of marimba music, a city full of gaiety and celebration. Some of the more sober descendants of old, respectable families (Spanish, of course) lock their doors at *Carnaval* time and insert earplugs, but that staid face is not the one that Veracruz—either the city or the state—usually shows the public.

To the north of Veracruz, two archaeological sites deserve special attention: **Zempoala** and magnificent **El Tajín**, the latter considered by many to rival some of the Mayan sites for beauty and mystery.

Our exploration of the Gulf Coast north of Veracruz ends at sleepy **Tuxpan**, a town with no particular beauty—and certainly little in the way of excitement. What it does have is character and a graceful, unhurried river. Farther north lies the modern port of Tampico, which we do not cover. Its attractions are exclusively for sportsmen, especially sportsfishermen, although it does have good hotels and restaurants because of its status as a prosperous center for the petroleum industry.

To the south of Veracruz are the slightly dubious attractions of **Lago de Catemaco**, not one of the more charming destinations in this book. Fortunately, the big lake, nestled among volcanoes, makes up for the somewhat grubby town. At any rate, Catemaco is the start of a beautiful drive or bus ride east to **Villahermosa**, the gateway to the Mayan world and a handsome city with a remarkable outdoor archaeological museum full of Olmec artifacts.

Ancient Mesoamerican culture reached its zenith in the jungles of the **Yucatán** at such magnificent ceremonial centers as **Chichén Itzá, Uxmal**, and others. Oddly enough, the Maya seem to have done best where the soil was poorest and the climate most inhospitable. **Palenque**, in the northern part of the state of Chiapas, while perhaps the most elegant Mayan ruin, is on the edge of a jungle so dense that no one knows what other ruined cities might be concealed there.

Today the Maya, fighting to keep their ancient traditions alive, survive not only near the great centers their ancestors erected but also in the highland fastness of **San Cristóbal de**

las Casas, capital of the state of Chiapas, where the surrounding hamlets remain virtually untouched by the modern world.

They are also found to the southeast, in **Guatemala**, a country with very different traditions. Ancient legend has it that a Mayan miracle took place here at **Tikal**, the largest and in some ways most impressive of the Mayan cities. And while today the Maya struggle to come to terms with modern divisions that are artificial and political—and over which they had no control—Tikal remains a magnificent reminder of the continuity of Mayan culture as well as a natural complement to explorations of Uxmal, Palenque, and Chichén Itzá. Apart from the Mayan interest, Guatamala's crafts markets, exploding with color, dazzle like fireworks. The landscape, too, can be awe-inspiring, as attested to by the sight of Lake Atitlan shadowed by its volcanoes at sunset.

Mexico's beach and saltwater resorts are by far the country's most popular attractions with visitors, their names synonymous with pleasure and sometimes glamour. **Cancún, Cozumel, Acapulco, Ixtapa/Zihuatanejo**, and **Puerto Vallarta** are just the major ones, but we cover a number—**Mazatlán, Manzanillo, Puerto Escondido**—that are more modest in size and some, such as **Isla Mujeres** and **Barra de Navidad**, that are small and/or little known.

Of course, sand and sea are international, and so are the vacationers who flock to find both in Mexico, including Mexicans themselves. Yet each resort has its own special identity and flavor. Cancún, for example, has a close Mayan neighbor in **Tulum**, one of the last outposts of Mayan greatness and a surprising, if overrun, bonus for vacationers. In fact, none of the big resorts we cover is merely a "hotel culture" (though Cancún comes close). Cozumel has a strong island character all its own, and Acapulco is one of Mexico's largest and most vibrant cities. In all of them you'll find more than clear water, warm sand, and palm trees: They also share the warmth of Mexico.

Baja California, a very special place and the subject of many books in its own right (see the Bibliography for two of them), is not covered as is, say, the Colonial Heartland; instead, we describe it briefly as a possible weekend getaway from Southern California and as a route to the **Los Cabos** resorts—which are discussed in detail.

Mexican Cooking

In recent years Mexican cooking has been given its rightful place among the great cuisines of the world. Corn and beans remain the staples of the land, but they are handled with infinite variety, supplemented and spiced ingeniously. Only a few dishes are as fiery as legend claims; much of the pepper (chile) is reserved for green or red sauces served on the side, and can be tasted with caution by the newcomer. The national herb, cilantro (coriander), lends its distinctive flavor to everything from soup to roast turkey, producing the characteristic tang of Mexico. But it is impossible to generalize about the national cookery, for Mexico has at least a half dozen different cuisines: Yucatecan, Tarascan, Poblano, Veracruzana, food of the Texas border and of the Western Highlands.

Travellers who feel that Mexican food is simply not to their taste need not worry. "International cooking" (sometimes with a Mexican accent) is offered in most places where foreign visitors dine.

Mexican Crafts

In the discussions of various regions in this book there is much mention of crafts and shopping. Because we cover the subject piecemeal throughout the book, perhaps a broader look here will be of value.

In many countries travellers find shopping to be incidental. They may well pick up some souvenirs or buy a destination's famed specialties—jades in the Orient or perfumes in Paris, for example.

Mexico, as in so many things, is different, expressing its character in its handicrafts, which are often beautiful and quite fragile. Shopping in the craft markets, or at least browsing, is one of the decided pleasures of visiting the country. (The same is true in Guatemala, where crafts are not far behind Tikal as an attraction. Almost all of highland Guatemala dazzles with handmade or decorated textiles; vendors in open-air markets expect to sell their wares at about one-third the asking price.) But the Mexican scene is often so rich that visitors find it confusing. What to look for?

First, a few words on those things you *cannot* buy. It is illegal to purchase and take pre-Columbian art and artifacts out of the country. Not surprisingly, Mexican authorities hold a very serious view of the matter; such an offense can lead to heavy fines and imprisonment.

Then why, you might ask, are all these vendors jumping out of the bushes at archaeological sites and offering me carvings? Why aren't they arrested? The answer, of course, is simply that they are offering nothing but fakes. If you find an object attractive and reasonably priced, buy it as contemporary art—but don't think of it as old. Reproductions of ancient works, especially ceramics and clay sculptures, are created in studios under government license. Shops everywhere offer them, especially in the resort centers. Often they are lovely, striking, and unusual. Enjoy them for what they are—not what someone *says* they are—and you won't be disappointed.

Nowadays the best handicrafts are quickly shipped all over the country and soon appear on shelves in Mexico City and Acapulco. On the other hand, if you want to search for the best at the source, here are some tips:

- *Silver.* Mexico City, Taxco, Guadalajara, and Oaxaca
- *Tinware.* San Miguel de Allende
- *Blankets and rugs.* Tlaxcala, Oaxaca, San Miguel de Allende, Pátzcuaro, and Guatemala
- *Clothing.* Morelia, Pátzcuaro, Mérida, Guadalajara, San Miguel de Allende, Mexico City, and Guatemala
- *Ceramics.* Oaxaca, Pátzcuaro, Tonalá, Puebla, and Mexico City
- *Hand-blown glass.* Guadalajara
- *Lacquerware.* Pátzcuaro, Morelia, and Uruapan
- *Copperware.* Mexico City, Guadalajara, San Miguel de Allende, and Santa María del Cobre (near Pátzcuaro)
- *Brass.* Mexico City and San Miguel de Allende
- *Woodcarving.* Paracho (Michoacán) and Pátzcuaro
- *Gold filigree.* Mérida

Every region of Mexico has its special character and unique attractions, as you will see in this book. Each traveller will find places that become personal favorites—be they ruins, dazzling beaches, tile-encrusted palaces, or fragrant plazas.

Yet there is something more in Mexico, an elusive quality that makes the whole more than the sum of its parts. Writer Charles Flandrau, after sojourning through the country at the turn of the century, understood this, and no one since has expressed it quite so well: "The most notable sight in Mexico is simply Mexico."

USEFUL FACTS

When to Go

Mexico is a fine year-round destination, but the various seasons have different attractions. Winter—December through March—is ideal because of the generally cool, dry weather. It's an especially good time to visit the Gulf Coast and Yucatán, which can get unbearably hot and humid at other times of the year. On the other hand, it's also the peak tourist season, when demand for all services is greatest. (You absolutely must have confirmed reservations for the Christmas–New Year week, for example.) Discounts vanish, many prices rise sharply despite controls, and major beach resorts get crowded. Archaeological zones are also heavily visited at this time of year.

April and May usually are not crowded, but spring is also the hottest, driest time of year in many places. The highland regions grow dusty and the land turns brown.

Summer, the second most popular season for visitors, brings rains that are usually brief but often torrential. Mornings and early afternoons tend to be clear and lovely. Summer, even on the coasts, is not as warm as spring.

Fall has temperate weather, with the rains continuing until the end of September. October and November are appealing, uncrowded months. This is also hurricane season on the Caribbean coast, so weather there, usually pleasant in fall, is a matter of luck.

Mexico City closes down during Holy Week (the week before Easter), as millions of its inhabitants rush for the beaches. Avoid the resorts at this time. The capital, on the other hand, is an attractive alternative then, even though some businesses will be closed. Throughout the country all forms of transportation are packed at Easter.

Entry Documents

In theory, U.S. and Canadian citizens need only proof of citizenship and a tourist card to enter Mexico. Ironically, as free trade among the three countries moves closer to becoming a reality, immigration requirements, even for short-term visitors, seem to have been tightened. Instances of U.S. and Canadian citizens being threatened with stiff fines for trying to enter Mexico without a passport have become increasingly common of late. As naturalized citizens and Europeans *must* present a valid passport, and all travellers will find that a passport is invaluable for transactions in banks and money-exchanging offices, we strongly suggest that every visitor to Mexico, regardless of nationality, brings theirs along. Tourist cards are issued at Mexican consulates, border crossings, major airports, and by some travel agencies. There is no charge for the card, which is stamped on entry and which must be turned in, along with a departure tax (currently $12 per person), when you leave the country. The length of permissible stay listed on the card is determined by the official issuing it. The time can be extended, not to exceed 180 days, at tourism offices throughout the country.

See "Around Mexico by Car," below, for information on documents needed to bring a car into Mexico.

Arrival at Major Gateways by Air

The major carriers providing direct service to Mexico are Mexicana, Aeroméxico, Continental, American, Delta, United, Alaska Airways (from its West Coast hubs), Iberia (from Miami), and KLM (from Orlando). With few exceptions international travellers will have to make connections in the United States. (Canadian Airlines International, which offers direct Toronto–Mexico City flights three times a week, is an exception.)

Mexicana offers direct service to Mexico City and Guadalajara (with connections from the capital to every major city in the country) from a number of U.S. cities, including New York, Miami, Chicago, Dallas–Fort Worth, Denver, San Francisco, and Los Angeles. It also offers direct service to Cancún from New York and Los Angeles. Aeroméxico offers direct service to Mexico City and Cancún from New York, Miami, Houston, and New Orleans, and to Mexico City only from Los Angeles. Continental flies direct from its Houston hub to Mexico City and Guadalajara as well as most of the major resorts, including Acapulco, Cancún, Cozumel, Ixtapa/Zihuatanejo, Los Cabos, and Puerto Vallarta. American, which routes the bulk of its Mexico service through Dallas–Fort Worth and Miami, offers flights to Mexico City, Guadalajara, Acapulco, Cancún, Cozumel, and Puerto Vallarta. Delta offers daily flights to Mexico City and Acapulco from its Dallas–Fort Worth hub. United flies daily to Mexico City from Chicago and San Francisco, as well as infrequently to Cancún from Chicago and Washington, D.C. The relatively new Aeropuerto de Guanajuato near León (west of Guanajuato and San Miguel de Allende) is serviced daily from Houston by Continental, from Los Angeles by Mexicana, and from Chicago three days a week by Mexicana. Aeroméxico offers a daily León–Los Angeles flight with a stop in Hermosillo, and flies the same route three times a week with a stop in Puerto Vallarta. For further information contact your travel agent or any of the airlines mentioned above.

Taxis with regulated rates are available at the capital's airport. There is metro (subway) service from the airport, but it can be confusing for passengers with little command of the language arriving in Mexico for the first time.

Some hotels in outlying cities will arrange to have a driver meet passengers at the customs exit gate at the Mexico City airport and transport them directly, thus bypassing a stopover in the capital.

Flights leave daily from Mexico City for Guatemala City. See the Getting Around section at the end of the Guatemala chapter for information on travel to that country.

Around Mexico by Air

Mexico City is the air hub of the country, and air service anywhere is often routed through the capital. There is, in addition, good service from the D.F. to all the larger resorts. For the other regions described in this book the airport gateways are: Morelia, León, and San Luis Potosí for the Bajío (Colonial Heartland) region; Guadalajara for the Western Highlands and Pacific coast resorts; Veracruz and Villahermosa for the Gulf Coast region; Villahermosa, Mérida, Cancún, and Tuxtla Gutiérrez for the Maya region; and Chihuahua and Los Mochis for the Copper Canyon.

Around Mexico by Train

Service is relatively limited and tends to be slow. As in most affairs, everything is linked to the capital. There is good but not rapid service from the D.F. to Veracruz, Guadalajara, Querétaro, Pátzcuaro, Monterrey, Nuevo Laredo, and Oaxaca. While the trains are constantly being upgraded, they are not really a practical option for touring the country. If you are not travelling overnight, get a ticket that is first-class special (*primera especial*), which will guarantee you a comfortable seat. For night travel, you want *primera especial* plus an *alcoba,* a sleeping compartment.

Around Mexico by Bus

The bus is the donkey of motor vehicles in Mexico, able to get to the most remote backwater. Good service will be provided on a bus that runs first class (*primera clase*); ask for direct service (*directo*) to avoid too many stops and detours. In either case, be prepared for the toilet to be out of order and dress for the air-conditioning to be likewise—or else working overtime. Bottled drinks are generally available, but on a long trip you should carry some sort of snack; some bus-station restaurants are less than appetizing.

Second-class buses (*segunda clase*) are often identical to first-class vehicles (although some are older and a bit more rickety) except for the number of stops they make. A second-class bus may stop anywhere along the road to load or unload things, including passengers, bundles of newspapers, chickens, goats, or a hundred pieces of hand-made pottery on the way to market. They may also be jammed to the roof: Try to grab a window seat if you can.

Finally, don't get too discouraged; travelling like this can be fun and colorful or simply fast and uneventful.

A new and far superior class of service began operating in 1991. *Premier de lujo,* or *super de lujo,* offers vehicles equipped with rest rooms, reclining seats, and attendants who serve refreshments. Although expanding rapidly, this service now operates only between the largest Mexican cities and the U.S. border. Two good lines are **ETN** (in Mexico City, Tel: 5/368-0212 or 5/273-0251) and **Primera Plus** (Tel: 5/587-5222 or 5/567-8030); inquire before purchasing another type of ticket—this is much the best choice and worth the price difference.

Rest rooms in bus stations are usually called *sanatarios* yet tend to be anything but sanitary; be prepared for at least a twinge of culture shock.

Around Mexico by Car

Travellers driving into Mexico will need car permits, which are issued free of charge by Mexican customs at the border. The document is valid for 90 days and can be extended by any customs office in the country; official tourism offices in major Mexican cities will refer motorists to the proper authorities for extensions. Only the principal driver needs a permit; passengers need only a tourist card.

The driver must also sign a credit card voucher and a pledge saying the car will not be left in Mexico. The $10 charge is payable only with an internationally recognized credit card issued in a country other than Mexico. Cash is not accepted. Proof of ownership and a valid driving license are necessary.

Drivers without a credit card must present other documents: their license plus one copy, the original car title, the current operating registration, a U.S. insurance policy valid for at least two months after the date of the border crossing, and legal proof of citizenship with a copy. (Have any necessary copies prepared *before* you reach the border.) If the car is not fully paid for, the bank or other lien holder must also authorize the use of the car in Mexico for a specific period of time. Because these rules have resulted in such slow crossings (one to three hours), changing them is under consideration; inquire at a Mexican consulate.

Mexican auto insurance is required by law; short-term policies are sold on the U.S. side near all border crossings. AAA and Sanborn's are reliable, but so are others. All insurance transactions are closely regulated by the government and rates are uniform. *On no account should you drive in Mexico without proper Mexican insurance.* Uninsured drivers go to jail if involved in an accident. You may *not* leave Mexico without the vehicle. If for any reason you cannot take the car back across the border, contact the U.S. embassy or nearest consular agency for instructions.

Once you are equipped with a car permit and Mexican insurance, only two more items are essential: a large measure of optimism and another of patience. Optimism is important, as the first few hours driving through northern Mexico may prove disappointing; it is the least attractive region of the country. Patience will be helpful as you encounter poorly marked highways, unexpected *topes* (speed bumps) that force you to slow to a crawl, and free-ranging livestock oblivious to car horns and shouted imprecations. Similarly, the condition of rest rooms in Pemex stations (Pemex is the governmental gasoline monopoly) may range from offputting to appalling. At such moments, remind yourself about cultural differences and then tell yourself that matters will improve— as indeed they will.

There are countless tricks and techniques to driving in Mexico, but essentially everything comes down to common sense, courtesy, and a little more caution than you would exercise on more familiar ground.

If your car develops trouble at any point, the Green Angels may come to your rescue. The "Angels" are government-subsidized crews in green-and-white utility trucks who roam Mexico's main highways looking for travellers in need of assistance. The service is free, but motorists will have to pay for any gasoline, oil, or replacement parts.

If you find yourself in need of a Green Angel, pull off the highway and raise the hood of your car; this will alert any passing repair crew. If there's a telephone nearby, call the national hotline of the **Secretary of Tourism** (Tel: 5/250-0132), which will radio-dispatch a patrol to you as quickly as possible. Passing truck drivers are also good about stopping and placing calls for you or rendering other assistance. In fact, foreign drivers are frequently surprised by the number of good Samaritans on Mexico's highways.

Low-quality gasoline is one good reason to opt for renting a car rather than using your own. If you're taking your own vehicle you'll face the frustration of trying to find the un-leaded gas that most foreign cars use. Pemex has introduced a new unleaded gas called **Magna Sin**, which can be found along all the usual tourist routes but not on side roads. (Signs posted beside major highways announce the availability of Magna Sin ahead.) Regular leaded Nova will do in a pinch, without poisoning your engine, until you can find the higher octane. (Some drivers have their U.S. anti-pollution package disconnected before crossing the border.) Expect coughs and sputters from the lower-octane mix, however.

The prudent driver will get out of the car at gasoline stations and check the pump to make sure it is set at zero before delivery begins. If possible, order the same amount of gas every time you stop (e.g., half a tank, three-quarters of a tank), and count your change.

Getting to the more interesting parts of Mexico can be a long and expensive proposition. Combining means of transportation is probably your best bet: flying in, renting a car and driving to a particular destination, turning it in and taking a train, plane, or bus to the next spot, et cetera. Rental cars from companies with recognizable names are widely available, though they are likely to be considerably more expensive than in North America. If you want a car with an automatic transmission, you must ask ahead; they aren't standard issue.

Readers thinking of driving into Mexico from the U.S.–Mexico border will want to consult the Getting Around sections at the end of the Colonial Heartland, Western Highlands, and Gulf Coast chapters, as well as the Mazatlán section of the Pacific Resorts chapter. Under the "Driving Down from the Border" heading in each of these chapters you will find much useful information concerning preferred routes, accommodations (usually motor inns), and places to eat.

Except within a large city do *not* drive at night. The reasons are legion.

Local Time
Mexico is never on daylight saving time. Most of the country is on central standard time (Winnipeg, Chicago, Dallas), with the exception of the far west—Sonora, Sinaloa, Nayarit (the mainland coast north of Puerto Vallarta)—and southern Baja California, which are all on mountain standard time (Calgary, Denver). Northern Baja California is on Pacific time and is the sole exception to the daylight saving rule: It always keeps the same time as Los Angeles.

Currency
The monetary unit is the peso, indicated by a dollar sign and sometimes the abbreviation M.N. (*moneda nacional*). At the beginning of 1993 the currency system was revised by dropping three zeroes off all coins and bills: Thus 10,000 old pesos became 10 new pesos, called *nuevos pesos.* New pesos are denoted by the abbreviation N\$. New peso bills come in denominations of 20, 50, and 100; new peso coins (brass with a nickel center) are available in units of 1, 2, 5, and 10.

Mexican *centavos,* which were taken out of circulation in the early 1980s, have been reissued in denominations of 5, 10, 20, and 50. One hundred *centavos* equals one new peso. As of May 1993, old pesos with the three extra zeroes were being phased out, though they will continue to be accepted as legal tender. The exchange rate was about 3.2 *nuevos pesos* to the dollar.

Traveller's checks and foreign currency should be exchanged at banks or private exchange offices (*casas de cambio*) for the best rate. Most banks exchange only during early business hours. Airport exchange offices also give good rates.

With the exception of gas stations, major credit cards are accepted in most larger establishments. You will see the familiar logos posted on doors or windows. If you don't, ask before trying to charge.

Room Rates

Hotel room rates listed in this book are for double rooms, double occupancy, for the 1993–1994 winter "high season," that is, from December 1993 through Easter 1994. These rates, which are provided in U.S. dollars, include taxes but not meals, unless otherwise noted. (A 10 percent VAT tax applies to all goods and services, including hotel rates, in Mexico.) Service charges may not be legally added to quoted room rates. At press time some hotels were expecting to raise prices by 10 to 15 percent in 1994, so rates quoted should be used as general guidelines only. Inquire about actual costs before booking. (Note, too, that travellers may get a discount of 10 to 15 percent merely by asking "Hay descuenta?")

Time-shares

Selling time-shares in condominiums has become a thriving business at almost all Mexican resorts. These units offer endless variations concerning length of time involved, price, and quality. One danger to be aware of comes from high-pressure salespeople, usually native speakers of English, who use bait-and-switch tactics to lure vacationers to their sales pitches or stampede customers into hasty or careless decisions. The brevity of a resort vacation may impel people toward imprudent purchases. It is essential to ask thoughtful questions, to consider printed (as opposed to oral) information, and to comparison shop before signing anything.

Electric Current

Electricity in Mexico is supplied at 110 volts, alternating current, as in the United States and Canada. The same type and sizes of sockets and plugs are also standard in all three countries.

Telephoning

The international code number for dialing directly to Mexico is 52. While long-distance calls within Mexico are relatively cheap, international calls are anything but because of taxes. It is easiest to telephone through hotel switchboards, but all towns have *larga distancia* telephone offices where prepaid calls can be put through.

Business Hours

There is no simple answer to this mystery. The day seems to start soon after 9:00 A.M., but it may be an hour later. Most of the country pauses for a two-hour break at 1:00 or 2:00 P.M., which means that business generally resumes between 3:00 and 4:00 P.M. Some offices will close at 5:00 P.M., which is a modern—and foreign—custom. Many establishments in Mexico City ignore the siesta, others keep it faithfully, and so far most attempts to change the old custom in the interest of efficiency have failed. Closing hour for most stores is commonly 7:00 or 8:00 P.M.

Museums and other public institutions that stay open on Sundays usually close on Mondays. Major archaeological zones are open seven days a week; inquire locally about smaller sites.

Holidays

Official holidays, when most businesses and all offices are closed, are: January 1, New Year's Day; February 5, Constitution Day; March 21, the birthday of Benito Juárez; May 1, Labor Day; September 16, Independence Day (but the celebration starts the night before); November 20, Anniversary of the Revolution; and December 25, Christmas.

Not official but close to it are: Holy Week (*semana santa*), the week before Easter (with work slowly grinding to a halt as the week progresses and stopping completely on Thursday); May 5 (Cinco de Mayo), Anniversary of the Battle of Puebla; September 1, the presidential state-of-the-union report (*el informe*)—banks close; November 2, Day of the Dead; and December 12, Feast of Guadalupe, patroness saint of Mexico.

Also important are: May 10, Mother's Day; and October 12, Columbus Day, called Día de la Raza in Mexico.

Every town has its patron saint and takes a day to a week to celebrate his or her feast. Other religious holidays include: January 6, Three Kings Day, the traditional day of Christmas gift giving (but losing ground to Santa Claus); January 17, St.

Anthony's Day, the traditional day for the blessing of animals; February 2, Candelaria, a rite of spring and the day candles and seeds are blessed; Carnaval (Mardi Gras), which is movable, with the best parties in Veracruz, Mazatlán, Mérida, and Guadalajara; Corpus Christi Day, late May or early June, with fairs and rites throughout the country; and December 16–23, the long Christmas prelude, celebrated with processions, parties, much singing, and nativity plays.

Safety

Beware of pickpockets, especially at public celebrations and on public transportation. The metro in Mexico City is a favorite hunting ground for dips and cutpurses; museum entrances are another haunt. Public streets in general are comparatively free of violence, but normal precautions should be taken. Smaller cities are usually so safe that the only danger is in becoming careless. Theft of valuables from automobiles is common, however, so be careful where you park and leave nothing tempting in plain sight. Cameras and the like should be locked in the trunk.

Taxes

The onerous one is the I.V.A., called "Eva," a 10 percent sales tax on almost everything. By law it is supposed to be included in marked prices and quoted rates, but often it isn't. Ask if something is without tax, *sin* I.V.A. (*sin "Eevah"*), or if the tax is included, *con* I.V.A. (*con "Eevah"*).

Health

High altitudes can play strange tricks on your system. Avoid too much exertion, overeating, and heavy drinking while your body is adapting to the change in its oxygen supply. Alcohol seems to work more swiftly and potently in the highland areas, and can sneak up on you if your usual habitat is located at sea level or thereabouts.

In most places tap water is not purified. The old admonition "Don't drink the water" always seems hardest to remember when you have a toothbrush or an iced drink in your hand. Potable water is provided, in jugs or bottles, by all decent hotels and restaurants. In better establishments ice is made from purified water, but when in doubt, skip the ice.

The bulk of medical opinion is against taking any medicine in advance as a preventive for diarrhea. Rest and moderation are the best cure in almost every case. Most major hotels have a house doctor on call if you do get sick. They are usually prepared to treat only minor illnesses, and will recommend a specialist or hospital if necessary. The U.S. embassy in Mexico City also keeps a list of doctors on hand for emergencies; Tel: (5) 211-0042.

If you come to Mexico for a diving vacation make sure your medical insurance includes diving accidents; some dive operations in beach resorts do not carry their own insurance. In any event it's always better to be covered before setting out from home.

Dressing for Comfort

Tennis shoes, running shoes, or the like are strongly recommended. In all highland areas and even on the Gulf Coast a sweater or jacket will be needed on many nights, as will a windbreaker in Mexico City and at similar altitudes in winter. Informality in dress is the norm, but some restaurants in the capital and elsewhere have dress codes: coat and tie for men, cocktail dress or the like for women. Mexico City is the only truly dressy place in the country, and even there casual wear usually prevails, except in business.

It is no longer necessary for women to cover their heads before entering churches. One dress taboo remains, however: Shorts are not acceptable except in a beach or sports situation.

Rainwear will be needed in the late spring, all summer, and most of the fall.

For Further Information

The following is a list of Mexican government tourism offices in several major U.S., Canadian, and U.K. cities: 405 Park Avenue, Suite 1401, New York, NY 10022 (Tel: 800/446-3942 or 212/755-7261, Fax: 212/753-2874); 128 Aragon Avenue, Coral Gables, FL 33134 (Tel: 305/443-9160, Fax: 305/443-1186); 2707 North Loop West, Suite 450, Houston, TX 77008 (Tel: 713/880-5153, Fax: 713/880-1833); 70 East Lake Street, Suite 1413, Chicago, IL 60601 (Tel: 312/565-2778, Fax: 312/606-9012); 10100 Santa Monica Boulevard, Suite 224, Los Angeles, CA 90067 (Tel: 310/203-8191, Fax: 310/203-8316); 2 Bloor Street West, Suite 1801, Toronto M4W 3E2 Ontario (Tel: 416/925-0704 or 1876, Fax: 416/925-6061); 1, Place Ville Marie, Suite 2409, Montréal H3B 3M9 Québec (Tel: 514/871-1052, Fax: 514/871-3825); 60–61 Trafalgar Square, London WC2N 5DS (Tel: 071/734-1058, Fax: 071/930-9202).

For further information on Guatemala contact the **Guatemala Tourist Commission**, 299 Alhambra Circle, Suite 510, Coral Gables, FL 33134; Tel: (800) 742-4529 or (305) 442-0412; Fax: (305) 442-1013.

BIBLIOGRAPHY

MARIANO AZUELA, *The Underdogs* (1916). A sweaty, gritty novel of the revolutionary upheavals between 1911 and 1920, and a book that changed the course of Mexican literature.

JOSEPH ARMSTRONG BAIRD, JR., *The Churches of Mexico* (1962). A knowing survey of the major architectural achievements of New Spain.

BARBARA BALCHIN DE KOOSE, *Guatemala for You*. A detailed handbook to the country, published in 1989.

SYBILLE BEDFORD, *Sudden View*. A sharp-eyed woman's travel memoir of Mexico, originally published in 1954.

IGNACIO BERNAL, *Mexico Before Cortés: Art, History, and Legend* (1963). A capsule history by the former director of Mexico's famed National Museum of Anthropology.

———, *The Olmec World* (1969). An elegantly written introduction to Mesoamerica's first great culture.

EMMET REID BLAKE, *Birds of Mexico* (1972). The abundant avian life of Mexico presented by a distinguished ornithologist. Illustrated.

ANITA BRENNER AND G. R. LEIGHTON, *The Wind That Shook Mexico* (1943). A long-repressed nation violently enters the modern world. Memorable photographs illuminate the text.

FRANCES CALDERÓN DE LA BARCA, *Life in Mexico* (1843). A series of shrewd, gossipy, and witty letters penned by the Scottish-Bostonian wife of Spain's first ambassador to the newborn Mexican Republic. Delightful, and in some ways oddly contemporary.

JORGE CASTANEDA AND ROBERT A. PASTOR, *Limits to Friendship: The United States and Mexico* (1989). Two informed viewpoints—often in disagreement, always thought-provoking.

MICHAEL D. COE, *The Maya* (fourth edition, 1987). A reliable introduction to the ancient Maya by a reputable scholar.

———, *Mexico* (third edition, 1986). A companion volume to Coe's book on the Maya, and a similarly reliable introduction to the highland cultures of ancient Mexico.

MAURICE COLLIS, *Cortés and Móctezuma*. Thoughtful speculation about the history of the Conquest, as well as insights into its two major figures.

MIGUEL COVARRUBIAS, *Indian Art of Mexico and Central America* (1952). The appreciative views of an artist-scholar.

Some theories are now outdated, but the main points remain valid, and the author's illustrations are unsurpassed in the field.

————, *Mexico South: The Isthmus of Tehuantepec* (1946). A colorful visit to a corner of Mexico as it was yesterday and almost is today. Illustrations by an outstanding artist.

NIGEL DAVIES, *The Ancient Kingdoms of Mexico* (1982). An excellent introductory survey of all the major pre-Columbian cultures except the Maya.

————, *The Aztecs* (1973). A political history of the last pre-Hispanic conquerors of Mexico.

————, *The Toltecs* (1979). An account of pre-Aztec conquest and culture.

BERNAL DÍAZ DEL CASTILLO, *The Discovery and Conquest of Mexico*. Also published as the *Bernal Díaz Chronicle*. An exciting eyewitness account by one of Cortés's soldiers. Essential; basic to everything ever written about the era.

HARRIET DOERR, *Stones for Ibarra* (1978). A penetrating novel of life and death in an isolated mining village.

ERNEST EDWARDS, *A Field Guide to Mexican Birds* (1972). For on-the-spot identification, where and how to watch, and what to look for.

ANDRE EMMERICH, *Art Before Columbus* (1963). The best and most concise introduction, one that untangles a complex field.

————, *Sweat of the Sun and Tears of the Moon* (1968). The use and veneration of precious metals in pre-Columbian art.

CARLOS ESPEJEL, *Mexican Folk Crafts* (1978). A wide-ranging survey that is short on text but lavish in photographic illustrations by F. Catala Roca.

CHARLES M. FLANDRAU, *Viva Mexico* (1908). These traveller's tales sometimes cross the line into fiction, but always to the reader's enlightenment.

CARLOS FUENTES, *The Death of Artemio Cruz* (1962). A powerful and complex novel of the betrayal of revolutionary ideals by politicians and businessmen. A novelist, essayist, and diplomat, Fuentes is the strongest voice currently speaking for Mexico.

——, *The Good Conscience* (1959). An intelligent and observant boy grows up in the provincial city of Guanajuato.

——, *The Old Gringo* (1984). A fictional speculation about the last days of celebrated American author and social critic Ambrose Bierce, who vanished into the Mexican revolution. Replete with pointed observations about Mexico, gringos, and life in general.

THOMAS GAGE, *A New Survey of the West Indies*. An account published in 1648 by the first English observer to report on New Spain. He found little to his liking, establishing a British tradition.

CHARLES GALLENKAMP, *Maya* (third edition, 1985). Ancient Mayan life and art, with a postscript about the Maya in modern times.

GRAHAM GREENE, *The Power and the Glory* (1940). After half a century, this novel of the suppression of the Church in Mexico still crackles with suspense. It has been denounced by many Mexicans, who charge that it, as well as Greene's lesser work, *Another Mexico* (in some editions titled *The Lawless Roads*), were subsidized by foreign oil companies wishing to destabilize Mexico.

BERTITA HARDING, *Phantom Crown* (1934). A biographical work about Maximilian and Carlota.

MARIAN HARVEY, *Mexico's Crafts and Craftspeople* (1973). Where and how Mexican popular arts are fashioned and who makes them. Many photographic illustrations by Ken Harvey.

——, *Crafts of Mexico* (1987). A survey, appreciation, and explanation.

MCKINLEY HELM, *Man of Fire* (1953). Mexican muralist José Clemente Orozco is presented in full color in this critical biography.

C. BRUCE HUNTER, *A Guide to Ancient Maya Ruins* (1974). Practical, portable, and now available in a revised up-to-date edition.

——, *A Guide to Ancient Mexican Ruins* (1977). A companion volume to Professor Hunter's book on ancient Mayan ruins. With site maps and halftones.

JONATHAN KANDELL, *La Capital* (1988). A vivid "biography" of Mexico City that breathes with life, color, and the curiosities of history.

DIANA KENNEDY, *The Cuisines of Mexico* (1986). Of the many books on Mexican cookery, this is the most popular with foreigners and the most representative of the country's varied regions.

JOSEPH WOOD KRUTCH, *The Forgotten Peninsula*. A keen and wise observer examines Baja California.

DIEGO DE LANDA, *Yucatán: Before and After the Conquest*. Friar Diego's eyewitness work, written in the mid-1500s, is basic to all Maya studies.

D. H. LAWRENCE, *The Plumed Serpent* (1926). The author redesigned Mexican mythology to fit his own views, but the atmosphere of Lake Chapala and the Mexican characters he evokes make the story rewarding.

————, *Mornings in Mexico* (1927). Lawrence wrote most of these observations and ruminations in Oaxaca; the city's serene atmosphere lends the book a touch of peace uncharacteristic of the author's work.

A. STARKER LEOPOLD, *Wildlife of Mexico* (1959). Much of this work, written for hunters, has been rendered passé by game laws and extinction. Yet the information that abounds in its illustrated pages remains informative.

OSCAR LEWIS, *The Children of Sánchez* (1961). A profound and moving portrayal of slum life in Mexico City. This true account by an anthropologist caused a sensation in Mexico when first published. Now a classic.

————, *Five Families* (1959). A cross-section of Mexican life in readable form.

————, *Pedro Martínez* (1964). The harsh life of Mexico's farms and villages.

MALCOLM LOWRY, *Under the Volcano* (1947). A cult classic for a generation, this disturbing novel of foreigners in Cuernavaca has moved into the mainstream of literature.

SALVADOR MADARIAGA, *Heart of Jade* (1944). Tinged with mysticism and crammed with adventure, this novel gallops across the Mexican landscape during the Conquest.

————, *Hernán Cortés* (1948). A biography of the conqueror.

J. PATRICK MCHENRY, *A Short History of Mexico* (1962). A concise, handy review, from pre-Conquest to 1960; unusually sympathetic to the Church.

THE METROPOLITAN MUSEUM OF ART, *Mexico: Splendors of Thirty Centuries* (1990). With an introduction by Nobel Prize–winner Octavio Paz, this book is a photographic splendor in itself. From Preclassic fertility figurines to Frida Kahlo.

TOM MILLER AND CAROL HOFFMAN, *The Baja Book III: Map Guide to Today's Baja California*. The best overall practical guidebook for someone planning to drive the length of Baja California.

Minutiae Mexicana. This series of pocket-size booklets in English (usually available at tourist centers in Mexico and sometimes in the United States) deals in summary form with everything Mexican, from bird lore to witchcraft. Many titles, all carefully prepared.

SYLVANUS G. MORLEY, *The Ancient Maya* (revised by George W. Brainard and Robert J. Sharer, fourth edition, 1983). A distinguished Mayanist explores the field for beginners.

WRIGHT MORRIS, *Love Among the Cannibals* (1957). A witty novel about the lives of some jaded Los Angeles show-business types after they move down to the Acapulco of the 1950s to find themselves.

PATRICK OSTER, *Mexicans* (1989). A portrait of a people through the profiles of 20 individuals.

HENRY B. PARKES, *A History of Mexico* (1960). A balanced, straightforward work that has become almost standard for English-language readers in this field.

OCTAVIO PAZ, *The Labyrinth of Solitude* (1962). Sharp, sometimes startling insights into Mexican life and character by a great contemporary writer and philosopher. A Mexican monument.

MICHEL PEISSEL, *The Lost World of Quintana Roo* (1963). A young French adventurer's travels and travails along Mexico's Caribbean coastline before it was changed beyond recognition by Cancún and the advent of mass tourism.

The *Popul Vuh*, or sacred writings of the Quiché Maya. Pre-Hispanic history, legend, and theology interwoven into a fascinating literary tapestry. Also known as the *Book of the Tiger Priests* or the *Book of the Counsel*.

WILLIAM H. PRESCOTT, *History of the Conquest of Mexico*. This masterpiece, first published in 1843, has some faulty and doubtful judgments, yet remains the unsurpassed epic of the Spanish Conquest.

JOHN REED, *Insurgent Mexico* (1914). What a "red" gringo firebrand saw, or wanted to see, in the Mexican Revolution.

ALAN RIDING, *Distant Neighbors* (1988). A U.S. journalist turns a penetrating eye on the Mexico of yesterday and today.

JUAN RULFO, *Pedro Páramo* (1955). The living and the dead mingle elusively in this fictional masterwork of Mexican literature.

LINDA SCHELE AND DAVID FREIDEL, *A Forest of Kings: The Untold Story of the Ancient Maya* (1990). A fascinating, revisionist look at ancient Mayan society by a sometimes controversial authority on Mayan hieroglyphs and her collaborator.

EDWARD SIMMEN, ED., *Gringos in Mexico* (1988). Fifteen U.S. authors, including such unlikely companions as William Cullen Bryant, Edna Ferber, and Jack Kerouac, rub elbows in this short-story collection.

JEAN-MARIE SIMON, *Guatemala: Eternal Spring, Eternal Tyranny* (1987). A disturbing report on repression in Guatemala told in strong words and with the help of powerful, moving photographs.

LESLEY BYRD SIMPSON, *Many Mexicos* (1967). Lively and sometimes trenchant essays on Mexican history, from Cortés through the 1960s. Indispensable.

BRADLEY SMITH, *Mexico: A History in Art* (1968). The story of the country from earliest times as revealed by artists both known and unknown. Fine reproductions make this a lovely way to study history.

ROBERT SOMERLOTT, *Death of the Fifth Sun* (1987). This fictional autobiography of Malinche, Cortés's mistress and guide, gives a different view of the Aztec world.

JACQUES SOUSTELLE, *Arts of Ancient Mexico* (1967). A short but solid survey lavishly illustrated with black-and-white photographs.

————, *Daily Life of the Aztecs* (1961). A less-than-vivid treatment is saved by accurate, telling details.

JOHN STEINBECK, *The Pearl* (1942). A timeless story about a Baja California fisherman and his covetous neighbors. The village life is sharply revealed.

JOHN STEINBECK AND EDWARD RICKETTS, *The Sea of Cortés* (1941). A leisurely but interesting journey along the coast of Baja California.

MARIA STEN, *The Mexican Codices and Their Extraordinary History* (1978). Fascinating stories and explanations of the "painted books" of the pre-Hispanic epoch. An introduction to ancient American writing.

JOHN L. STEPHENS, *Incidents of Travel in Yucatán*. Stephens and draftsman Frederick Catherwood were explorers in the Maya region. Their work, published in 1843, was dismissed as Marco Millions exaggerations. Time has made fools of the critics.

FRANK TANNENBAUM, *Mexico: The Struggle for Peace and Bread* (1950). The outstanding foreign work about Mexico's continuing revolution.

FRANCES TOOR, *A Treasury of Mexican Folkways* (1947). As packed as a piñata with sayings, customs, songs, superstitions, and other lore, this is the foremost work in its field.

MANUEL TOUSSAINT, *Colonial Art in Mexico* (1949). This pioneering work is the cornerstone of Mexican art history. Architecture, painting, sculpture, and a glance at popular arts.

B. TRAVEN, *The Bridge in the Jungle* (1938). An ironic parable of cultural collisions in the form of a novel.

———, *The Rebellion of the Hanged* (1952). The author wrote six novels of revolt set in Mexico's jungles. This, the fifth, is the most powerful.

JOHN KENNETH TURNER, *Barbarous Mexico* (1909; reprinted 1969). Early in this century, the author, a muckraking journalist, penetrated slave camps in southern Mexico and exposed the horrors of the Porfirio Díaz dictatorship, causing a furor in the United States.

GEORGE C. VAILLANT, *The Aztecs of Mexico* (1941). An early work in the field, and still the most complete and interesting for the general reader.

VICTOR W. VON HAGEN, *The Aztec, Man and Tribe* (1961). A popular historical survey with informative illustrations.

BERNARD DE VOTO, *The Year of Decision* (1961). The parts of the book dealing with the U.S.–Mexican War provide a brief but incisive treatment of this tragedy.

JACK WILLIAMS, *The Magnificent Peninsula: The Only Absolutely Essential Guide to Mexico's Baja California* (1987). Well, maybe not the *only* guide (see the Miller-Hoffman book), but a practical one; with photographs.

ERIC WOLF, *Sons of the Shaking Earth* (1959). The land, people, history, and culture of Mexico and Guatemala.

BERTRAM D. WOLFE, *The Fabulous Life of Diego Rivera* (1963). This biography of the tempestuous genius fully lives up to its title. Crammed with wine, women, and outrage.

RONALD WRIGHT, *Time Among the Maya* (1989). The ruminations of a thoughtful, articulate traveller as he journeys through Belize, Guatemala, and Mexico.

AGUSTIN YANEZ, *The Edge of the Storm* (1947). A living, breathing, but fictional creation of a Mexican village. Mexico's first major psychological novel.

MICHAEL ZAMBA, *A Guide to Living in Mexico* (1989). Practical, sensible information for prospective retirees and others.
                                                  —*Robert Somerlott*

MEXICO CITY

By Larry Russell

A resident of Mexico City since 1973, Larry Russell is a frequent contributor to the travel sections of Mexico's Vogue *and* Progreso *magazines. In collaboration with his wife, he has also produced, written, and performed the musical scores for a number of documentary films about Mexico.*

Like wagon-wheel spokes to a hub—an immense hub—all major highways in the Republic of Mexico lead to its capital, Mexico City. Officially known as the Distrito Federal (D.F.), the most populous city on the planet is situated in the Valley of Mexico (called the Valley of Anáhuac in pre-Conquest days) on a site that was chosen in the 14th century by the Aztecs for what would soon become Tenochtitlán, their storied capital. Today the D.F. sprawls over a flat, sun-baked plateau that rises 7,347 feet above sea level and covers 573 square miles. It is surrounded by three forested mountain chains, which dramatically set the stage for 17,883-foot Popocatépetl (Smoking Mountain) and 17,338-foot Iztaccíhuatl (pronounced EE-sta-see-watl, and meaning "Sleeping Woman"), the two perpetually snow-capped volcanoes that dominate the valley's southeastern horizon. On a clear day the panoramic views from the city are breathtaking.

With the climatic effects of its semitropical latitude offset by its altitude, Mexico City has a temperate and invigorating climate that can be divided into two seasons: a dry season, which stretches from November through early May, and a wet season, which lasts from mid-May through October. (The tail end of the dry season, when there are few cleansing rains, may be the least comfortable time of year here.)

Temperatures average 60°F over the course of the year, and seldom rise above an average of 75°F in the hottest months (June and July) or fall below an average of 45°F during the coolest months (December and January). Nights are always cool, and there's a marked temperature contrast between sunny and shady places, as well as between the heat of midday and the chill of early morning and evening.

According to the latest census figures, fully a quarter of Mexico's 83 million people lives in the D.F. Whereas the 1930 census counted only a million inhabitants in the entire metropolitan area, and there were fewer than five million in 1960, the net growth rate of the capital's population today is 1,000 residents *daily*. Projections for a decade from now run as high as 30 million inhabitants.

As a result, the D.F. pulsates with a vibrant energy that makes it a compelling place to visit. In countless ways it epitomizes the best of Mexico—except in the quality of its air. Though Mexico City is notorious for its pollution, the seriousness of the situation has inspired determined—if somewhat belated—action on the part of the people in power (and the D.F. is where most of the nation's powerful live). Every vehicle registered in the Republic of Mexico is banned from circulating in the capital one day a week, Monday through Friday. Called "Hoy No Circula," what began in 1989 as a program to reduce car emissions during the winter months (the city's peak pollution season because of thermal inversions and the lack of rainfall) has been extended "indefinitely"—for obvious reasons. According to recent estimates the ban keeps more than half a million vehicles idle each day it is in effect, eliminating in excess of 3,000 tons of particulate matter from the valley's sometimes poisonous stew of pollution.

(After drivers hoping to get around the restrictions began registering their cars in other states, Mexico City's pollution prevention and control department announced that cars from outside the city, and even the country, would be subject to the ban as well. The day on which such out-of-state cars are banned is determined by the last number on the license plate: Cars with plates ending in the number one or two are banned on Thursdays, those ending in three or four on Wednesdays, five and six on Mondays, seven and eight on Tuesdays, and nine and zero on Fridays. As of March 1, 1993, a newly formed branch of the city's police force, exclusively female and called the "Eco Cops," is on the prowl in bright green patrol cars, impounding all vehicles not displaying a valid decal.)

In fact, many of the country's persistent problems are being addressed with renewed vigor by a breed of younger politicians led by 46-year-old Harvard-educated Carlos Salinas de Gortari. A hands-on president nearing the end of his six-year term, Salinas has utilized the virtually unlimited powers of his office to order Pemex, the government-run petroleum monopoly, to immediately supply unleaded gasoline to every gas station in the nation, and to make it mandatory for all auto-assembly plants and public-transportation vehicles to install emission converters. Recently Salinas disbanded SEDUE, Mexico's Urban Development and Environmental Secretariat, which had long been considered a paper tiger, and instigated the creation of a new governmental group answering directly to him. The goal of the group is to "deal a death blow to corruption in governmental bureaucracy and to dedicate all that is necessary to acquire a healthy ecological equilibrium."

When it comes to crime in the streets, on the other hand, Mexico City is safer than New York, Hong Kong, São Paulo, or Rome. (According to government statistics, Mexico City has fewer per capita crimes of violence than any other city in the world with a population exceeding a million people.) Moreover, visitors enjoy a privileged status here, and not only because Mexicans have a long tradition of hospitality to strangers. As most Mexicans realize, tourism represents one of the few reliable sources of foreign currency and nonpolluting employment.

A Fusion of the Old and New

A visit to Mexico City today is like stepping into an enormous melting pot of history and cultures. Sadly, the blending of these cultures was usually forced and involved much bloodshed. Perhaps the plaque at the Plaza de las Tres Culturas in Tlatelolco says it best: "On the 13th of August, 1521, defended by the heroic Cuauhtemoc, Tlatelolco fell under the power of Hernan Cortez. It was neither a triumph nor a defeat, but the painful birth of the mixed race that is the Mexico of today."

One of the legacies of this painful past is the inherent sense of fatalism that seems to lurk within the souls of most Mexicans. In the D.F. this fatalism is nowhere more evident than in the wild and often reckless style of driving that prevails among its residents. (Public-transportation drivers, oddly enough, are usually the worst offenders.) The local saying here is that if you can drive—and survive—in Mexico City, you can drive anywhere.

To those who have spent time here, it is not just macho boasting. In fact, as a visitor quickly learns, if you scratch a typical Mexico City native you'll find a soulful anarchist. Little wonder, then, that the city itself seems to mirror this side of the Mexican character, from its colorful, bustling street markets (*tianguis*), where the distinctive sound of the penny whistle signals the arrival of the itinerant knife-sharpener, to busy street corners where groups of traditionally attired Indians perform their native dances. Elsewhere, shabbily dressed street musicians congregate in residential neighborhoods to perform on their dented saxophones, beat-up clarinets, and toy-size drums while a skinny kid collects the coins that residents rain down on them from their windows; balloon vendors with their fabulous bunches of brightly colored helium-filled *globos* seem to defy the laws of nature by staying earthbound; barrel organists in funky khaki uniforms grind away in front of cantinas; bell-clangers lead the garbage trucks on their daily routes as if they were drum majors leading a parade; and Indian women, squatting on the sidewalk, sell handmade tortillas at twice the price of the government-controlled *tortillerías* ("The sweat from the palm of the hands is the secret ingredient," say the connoisseurs).

The almost palpable energy in the air is enhanced by telling contrasts on every street and around every corner: sleek limousines parked cheek by jowl with unimpressed burros; chic boutiques selling international designer originals as barefoot Indian women hawk handicrafts made the night before on the sidewalk out front; a gourmet dining in an elegant French or Japanese restaurant while, down the street, a gourmand munches on tacos served from a portable grill set up on the sidewalk.

And yet, despite these contrasts, Mexico City is no longer just a great Third World capital. Today it is a cosmopolitan *world* capital, one that need not take a back seat to any of the great metropolises in the quality and diversity of its architecture, museums, art galleries, public parks, and zoos; the variety and exuberance of its cultural presentations; the range of its hotels, restaurants, and shopping; and the efficiency of its public transportation. And, among the great cities of the world, it stands far above the others in one respect: the warmth of its hospitality.

MAJOR INTEREST

Museums
Museo Nacional de Antropología
Museo del Templo Mayor for its Aztec artifacts
Museo de la Ciudad de México
Centro Cultural de Arte Contemporáneo
Museo de Arte Moderno

Museo de Arte Contemporáneo Internacional Rufino
  Tamayo
Museo José Luis Cuevas, especially for its Picasso
  collection
Museo de San Carlos, for its extensive collection of
  European art

Sights
The historic Zócalo area
Palacio de Bellas Artes
Plaza de las Tres Culturas
Central Paseo de la Reforma
The canal rides of Xochimilco
The pyramids of Teotihuacán

Neighborhoods
The Zona Rosa for shopping and café life
Polanco for dining and shopping
Coyoacán and San Angel, quaint colonial villages with
  beautiful vintage residences
El Pedregal for spectacular homes

Parks
Alameda
Chapultepec

Ancient Mexico City

"Mexico City has almost always been the largest city in the world," writes Fernando Benítez, octogenarian Mexican historian and author. "At the height of the Roman empire's glory, Teotihuacán, as Mexico City was then known, was acknowledged to have been more populated and much more splendid than Rome. It was the capital of an empire that stretched from what is today the northern border of Texas beyond the southern boundaries of the country we know as Guatemala."

The Aztecs
In the early 14th century, some 600 years after Teotihuacán had been mysteriously abandoned by its priest-rulers and inhabitants, a nomadic tribe calling themselves the Mexicas (pronounced meh-SHEE-kas) left their ancestral home of Aztlán in search of greener pastures. According to their mythology, they would recognize the site of their new home when they came upon an eagle perched on a nopal cactus with a serpent in its beak.

After years of wandering, the Mexicas stumbled upon this

apparition sometime around 1325, at a spot that is now buried under the Plaza de Santo Domingo, in Mexico City. At the time, however, the future site of Tenochtitlán, as the Mexicas were to call their new home, was nothing more than an uninhabited, snake-infested island located some 30 miles from the fabled pyramids of Teotihuacán in the southern reaches of a vast, shallow lake. Over the next two centuries, the Mexicas—whom their neighbors dubbed Aztecs, or "people from Aztlán"—worked feverishly to expand the limits of their island city, draining portions of the lake, creating landfills, and constructing causeways to the shore. (Only in recent years, with the construction of the underground metro system, have some startling remains of Tenochtitlán been uncovered. See the Templo Mayor section below.)

Colonial Mexico City

By the time Columbus arrived in the New World, the Aztecs had created, in addition to their magnificent city, a far-reaching empire, and were even then engaged in trying to expand it by bringing coastal lands around present-day Acapulco under their control. When, in 1519, a 34-year-old Spanish sea captain named Hernán Cortés led a band of 550 soldiers and 22 mounted horses inland from their landfall just north of what is today the city of Veracruz, he found a city larger and more spectacular than any existing in Europe at the time. Reliable estimates put the population in excess of 200,000, many of whom lived on man-made plots of land connected to the main island by an intricate series of canals. Despite their admiration for the material accomplishments of the Aztecs, however, the self-styled *conquistadores* were appalled by the natives' religion, driven as it was by human sacrifice, and so promptly set out to subjugate and convert the city's inhabitants to Christianity. (Another theory is that the Spaniards greatly exaggerated the human sacrifice factor in order to justify their actions.)

Eventually the victorious Spanish—with the assistance of an estimated 10,000 Tlaxcalan Indian warriors (dedicated enemies of the Aztecs), gunpowder, and a decimating smallpox epidemic—destroyed virtually every visible aspect of Aztec civilization and over the ruins of their great temples and the emperor's palace built their own cathedral and a palace for Cortés. In fact, most of the foundations of the 16th-century structures here were erected using the sturdy building stones taken from toppled Aztec temples.

From the first, the city—which the Spanish named México (after the Aztecs' name for themselves)—functioned as the capital of New Spain. Nevertheless, the city grew slowly in its formative years, and only regained the population levels of Tenochtitlán early in our own century. Physically, however, Mexico City spread ever wider as the great lake, Texcoco, was drained, filled, and built over.

As it turned out, it was not a very practical site for heavy construction, and the old buildings almost immediately began to settle into the soft underbelly of the ancient lake bed—a process that has been continuing for centuries now. Frequent pumping of underground water and periodic flooding since the 16th century have also contributed to the city's "settling"—by some estimates more than 23 feet during the last century alone. Experts claim the situation has been stabilized by the use of modern engineering techniques and the installation of an ingenious drainage system that has permanently eliminated flooding. Still, while the avant-garde skyscrapers that are constantly going up seem to be in fine shape, you'll see many old colonial-era churches and buildings tilting at odd angles, especially throughout the historic downtown area.

The frequent earthquake activity in the region also has done its share of damage to the foundations of many slowly sinking structures. Although dozens of newer buildings were devastated by the 1985 quake, the city's skyscrapers weathered the shocks thanks to their high-tech "floating" foundations. Most of the colonial structures were unscathed as well; some even lean less than they did before the quake.

Mexico City Orientation

It may be difficult for the first-time visitor to form a mental image of the city, what with its rambling vastness seemingly devoid of a sensible street plan, with many of its major thoroughfares crisscrossing diagonally, and with cul-de-sacs punctuating every neighborhood. Once you get your bearings, however, it is surprisingly easy to find your way around the areas of interest.

The two main arteries in Mexico City are the 27-km (17-mile)-long **Avenida Insurgentes** (in-sur-HEN-tays), one of the longest urban thoroughfares in the world, which basically runs north to south; and the 15-km (9-mile)-long **Paseo de la Reforma**, the eight-lane tree-lined Champs-Elysées of the Americas, which starts out by running parallel to Insurgentes in the northeast, curves and intersects the latter just north of the Zona Rosa, cuts through Chapultepec Park—the city's magnificent public space and the site of the Museo Nacional de Antropología and other great cultural institutions—and

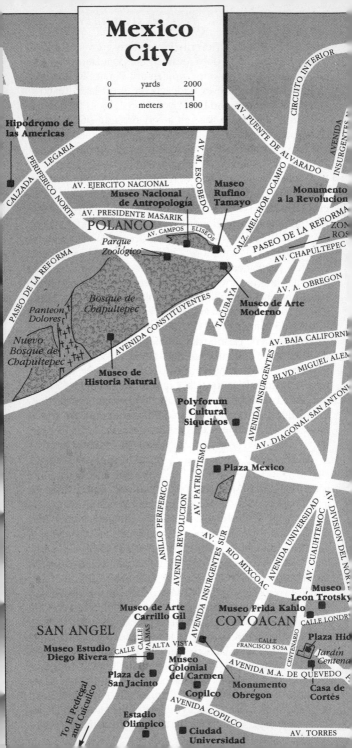

Mexico City

0	yards	2000
0	meters	1800

Hipodromo de las Americas

CALZADA LEGARIA

PERIFERICO NORTE

CALZADA

AV. M. ESCOBEDO

CIRCUITO INTERIOR

AV. PUENTE DE ALVARADO

AVENIDA INSURGENTES

AV. EJERCITO NACIONAL

Museo Nacional de Antropologia

Museo Rufino Tamayo

CALZ. MELCHOR OCAMPO

Monumento a la Revolucion

AV. PRESIDENTE MASARIK

POLANCO

PASEO DE LA REFORMA

ZON ROS

Parque Zoológico

AV. CAMPOS ELISEOS

AV. CHAPULTEPEC

PASEO DE LA REFORMA

Bosque de Chapultepec

AVENIDA CONSTITUYENTES

TACUBAYA

AV. A. OBREGON

Museo de Arte Moderno

Panteón Dolores

Nuevo Bosque de Chapultepec

AV. BAJA CALIFORNI

Museo de Historia Natural

BLVD. MIGUEL ALEM

AVENIDA INSURGENTES

Polyforum Cultural Siqueiros

AV. DIAGONAL SAN ANTONI

AVENIDA PATRIOTISMO

Plaza México

ANILLO PERIFERICO

AVENIDA REVOLUCION

AV. PATRIOTISMO

RIO MIXCOAC

AVENIDA INSURGENTES SUR

AVENIDA UNIVERSIDAD

AV. CUAUHTEMOC

AV. DIVISION DEL NOR

Museo León Trotsky

Museo de Arte Carrillo Gil

Museo Frida Kahlo

COYOACAN

CALLE LONDR

SAN ANGEL

CALLE PALMAS

CALLE ALTA VISTA

CALLE FRANCISCO SOSA

CENTENARIO

Plaza Hid

Jardín Centena

Museo Estudio Diego Rivera

Museo Colonial del Carmen

AVENIDA M.A. DE QUEVEDO

Plaza de San Jacinto

Monumento Obregón

Casa de Cortés

To El Pedregal and Cuicuilco

Copilco

AVENIDA COPILCO

Estadio Olimpico

Ciudad Universidad

AV. TORRES

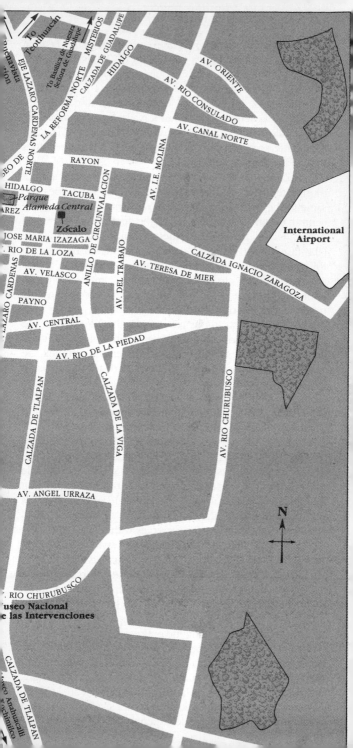

finally turns southwest, where it eventually becomes Federal Highway 15 and continues on to Toluca, 30 miles away. The Zócalo, the Zona Rosa, and Chapultepec Park are all within a 15- to 30-minute walk of the intersection of Reforma and Insurgentes, and it's here as well that you'll find clustered most of the best hotels, restaurants, major foreign embassies, airline sales offices, and other visitor attractions. (The Reforma intersection is also where Insurgentes Norte becomes Insurgentes Sur.)

The Zócalo serves as the eastern boundary of the area of most interest to visitors, and Chapultepec Park does the same to the west. The northernmost point of interest in the central urban area, and one of the first to be discussed below, is the **Basílica de Nuestra Señora de Guadalupe** (Basilica of Our Lady of Guadalupe), which is reached by following Paseo de la Reforma to its beginning at the Tlatelolco traffic circle (about 6 km/3½ miles from the intersection of Reforma and Insurgentes) and continuing north on Calzada de Guadalupe for two blocks.

The **Zócalo**, next in our coverage, is the heart of the old city. Besides the many historical sites, including the cathedral and the excavations of the central Aztec temple complex, the surrounding area is home to the financial district. Colonial in feel and appearance, the narrow cobblestone streets are jammed with all types of shops. It is a bit seedy, perhaps, but picturesque nevertheless and always churning with vitality. The Zócalo itself is off limits to vehicular traffic from 9:00 A.M. to 5:00 P.M., and pedestrian malls are scattered throughout the area, making it ideal for strolling and window-shopping. One of the ancient streets leading west from the Zócalo is Calle Madero. Only a few blocks long, it changes its name as it crosses Eje Central Lázaro Cárdenas and becomes Avenida Juárez. At this point the preponderance of 17th- and 18th-century colonial architecture merges with a dash of the Art Nouveau and other more contemporary styles. The elegant **Palacio de Bellas Artes** (Palace of Fine Arts) is on the right, and to the left, towering above the hustle and bustle, is the **Torre Latinoamericana** (Latin American Tower), a modern 44-story skyscraper with an observation deck on the 42nd floor and a restaurant, the Muralto, with panoramic views from most every table occupying the entire 41st floor.

Continuing west on Avenida Juárez you'll pass the always pulsating **Parque Alameda Central**, abounding with voluptuous statues, bubbling fountains, and young couples courting, before arriving at Paseo de la Reforma. Avenida Juárez continues for another block and ends at the massive **Monumento a la Revolución** in the Plaza de la República, but if you follow

Reforma south and west you'll soon come to its intersection with Avenida Insurgentes.

After passing Insurgentes, Reforma becomes the northern boundary of the **Zona Rosa** (Pink Zone), which is to Mexico City what SoHo is to New York or Chelsea is to London. The U.S. embassy is on the right at the next traffic circle, and straight ahead is the entrance to **Chapultepec Park**, to the north of which is the fashionable **Polanco** district. On the other side of the park Reforma leads into the exclusive residential district known as **Las Lomas de Chapultepec** (*lomas* means "hills" in Spanish), where you'll find a few excellent restaurants and the last of the city's sand castle–like, Art Nouveau mansions surrounded by an ever-increasing number of high rises.

Avenida Insurgentes Sur leads to all the major attractions in the southern part of the city, including the **Siqueiros Cultural Polyforum**; the **Plaza México** (the bullfight ring); the residential colonial neighborhoods of **Coyoacán** and **San Angel**; the avant-garde architecture of the elegant residences in **El Pedregal**; the archaeological sites of **Copilco** and **Cuicuilco**; **University City**, with its famous murals; **Reino Aventura** (Mexico's Disneyland); and the canals of **Xochimilco**. The last, 25 km (16 miles) south of the intersection of Reforma and Insurgentes, is the southernmost boundary of the areas of most interest.

The great pre-Aztec site of **Teotihuacán**, located northeast of the city center, is discussed in a separate section after the coverage for Mexico City proper.

NORTH OF THE ZOCALO

PLAZA DE LAS TRES CULTURAS

Site of the ancient city of Tlatelolco, 2½ km (1½ miles) north of the Zócalo, the plaza is, physically and chronologically, a good starting point for a day's tour that might include La Basilica de Nuestra Señora de Guadalupe, another 2½ km farther north of the plaza, and end back in and around the Zócalo itself.

The Plaza de las Tres Culturas (Plaza of the Three Cultures), inaugurated as such in 1964, is located at the northern end of Paseo de la Reforma (called Reforma Norte at this point) on the corner of Eje Central Lázaro Cárdenas. Examples of pre-Hispanic, colonial, and modern architecture are represented here by, respectively, Aztec ruins, the Templo de Santiago Tlatelolco, and the sleek marble skyscraper housing the Foreign Ministry.

You can get to the plaza on the metro (the number 3 line, Tlatelolco station stop; exit onto González and walk three blocks east; turn right on Lázaro Cárdenas and walk one block south), or you can take the Indios Verdes bus north anywhere along Avenida Insurgentes and get off at the Monumento a la Raza stop, then walk two blocks east. By car, take Reforma Norte to the third traffic circle north of Alameda Park (which is where Reforma Norte ends).

Tlatelolco

Tlatelolco, as the area has been known since pre-Hispanic times, was once an island in an immense swampy lake, and was already inhabited when the Aztecs arrived in 1325. In fact, it was the most important commercial and market center in the Valley of Anáhuac, and the Aztecs, being the Tlatelolcans' nearest neighbors, were its best customers, albeit begrudging ones. (It wasn't until 1473 that the island's inhabitants were forcefully annexed into the Aztec empire.) By the time the Spanish arrived in 1519, much of the lake between Tlatelolco and Tenochtitlán had been filled and built over, and it was here that Cortés and his troops came to marvel at the size and order of the native market. (It was also here, in 1521, that the last Aztec emperor, Cuauhtémoc, made his final stand against the Spanish.)

The Aztec ruins, which are not particularly impressive, are embedded at ground level in the northern outdoor patio of the high-rise Foreign Ministry complex. You can see part of what was once a pre-Hispanic **ceremonial center** as well as the remains of a **palace**, the walls of which were built of basalt and *tezontle,* the reddish-colored blocks of solidified lava characteristic of the native architecture of the period. There are, in addition, two smaller Aztec structures, one of them a square *tzompantli* (wall of skulls) near which thousands of human skulls were discovered, each with holes bored through the temples, presumably the result of having been displayed side by side on poles mounted around the sides of the building.

Templo de Santiago Tlatelolco

The Templo de Santiago Tlatelolco, with a plain façade typical of the fortresslike churches of the 16th and early 17th centuries, was built in 1609 out of materials taken from an old Aztec pyramid. On the pendentives of the cross vault inside there's an interesting Indian carving of the four evangelists. The church, along with the Colegio de la Santa Cruz, which was founded in 1535 by Franciscan missionaries to teach the sons of the Aztec nobility Spanish, Latin, and Christianity, became a center for the study of native culture; it was here that Fray Bernardino de Sahagún wrote *A History of Ancient Mexico*, his famous work on the history, beliefs, and religions of pre-Hispanic Mexico.

LA BASILICA DE NUESTRA SEÑORA DE GUADALUPE

The Basilica of Our Lady of Guadalupe, located north of the Plaza de las Tres Culturas on Calzada de Guadalupe, the continuation of Reforma, is considered to be the holiest Christian shrine in all of Latin America. (Take the number 3 metro line to the Basílica station stop, walk out through the Montier exit, and walk straight ahead about a third of a mile.)

According to legend, Juan Diego, an Aztec who had converted to the Christian faith, was on his way to Mass one cold December morning in 1531, crossing the hill known as Tepeyac, when a vision of the Virgin Mary appeared before him and requested that a church in her honor be built on the spot. When the shaken Diego related this miraculous encounter to the bishop, Juan de Zumárraga, the skeptical bishop asked Diego to show him proof. Three days later the Virgin appeared again and instructed Diego to gather roses, which she then caused to bloom in the frozen ground before him. Shocked at finding roses blooming in winter, Diego bundled them under his cloak and hurried before Zumárraga, where he let the roses tumble to his feet. To the astonishment of both men, stamped upon the peasant's cloak was an image of the Virgin. Needing no further proof, the bishop ordered the church built.

The miracle surrounding the construction of the church was especially significant, in retrospect, for it marked the turning point in the Spanish missionaries' attempts to convert their new subjects to Catholicism. And, as it happened, the apparition occurred on the exact spot where the Aztecs' temple to Tonantzin, their earth goddess, had stood before it was destroyed by the conquistadors.

(It was also here, in the original church, that the Treaty of Guadalupe Hidalgo was signed in 1848, ending the Mexican War; under the terms of the pact, Mexico ceded all or parts of New Mexico, Colorado, Utah, Arizona, Nevada, and California to the United States—reducing her territory by more than 50 percent while, at the same time, enlarging that of her northern neighbor by more than 25 percent.)

The original church was completed in 1533 and subsequently enlarged several times to accommodate the thousands of pilgrims who came in a never-ending stream to worship at the site of the miracle. By 1970, however, the shrine had shrunk so far into the area's spongy subsoil, and had tilted so perilously as a result, that it was declared a safety hazard and closed to the public. In 1976 an ultramodern basilica designed by the great Mexican architect Pedro Ramírez Vázquez (whose achievements include the National Museum of Anthropology in Chapultepec Park) was consecrated on the west side of the same plaza, while the original structure was eventually shored up and opened to the public as a museum of religious artifacts.

The exterior of the new basilica resembles a huge, futuristic circus tent, while the interior is starkly ornate, embellished with glitter but strangely devoid of icons. When its massive doors are opened as many as 40,000 worshipers can participate in the Mass, including those jammed into the immense **Plaza de la Américas** outside, surpassed in size only by the Zócalo. The shrine boasts no paintings, no statues, no cupolas, and just one relic: the miraculous cloak. (No satisfactory explanation has ever been given as to why the cloak itself has not long since deteriorated.) An underpass near the altar allows visitors to view the revered image without disrupting services; moving walkways prevent anyone from lingering too long. The basilica is open to the public daily from 5:00 A.M. to 9:00 P.M.

Outside, the plaza is a constantly changing stage for a steady stream of humanity—worshipers, priests, vendors selling religious paraphernalia, and tourists. Many pilgrims cover the last mile or so of their journey on their knees— which often end up bruised and bloodied—as an act of penance. In addition, the annual anniversary of the second apparition, December 12, is a national holiday, and draws tens of thousands of worshipers to the shrine.

Capilla del Pocito and Capilla de las Rosas

At the end of the plaza and to the right, a winding walkway leads up the hill to a few tiny chapels. One of the more charming is the exuberant, Baroque-style Chapel of the Well, inside of which is a well said to have first bubbled up during one of Juan Diego's apparitions. Built in the 18th century, the chapel is actually two chapels, the larger one distinguished by its blue-and-white tiled domes and its impressive paintings of the Virgin by Miguel Cabrera.

At the top of the hill is the Chapel of the Roses, built to commemorate the place where Diego gathered his miraculous roses. Inside the chapel is a mural by Fernando Leal depicting the legend of the miracle.

PLAZA DE GARIBALDI

This large public square, located on Eje Central Lázaro Cárdenas between Calles República de Honduras and República de Peru, seven short blocks north from the Bellas Artes metro station, is the musical heart of the capital and a must to visit—at least briefly. Surrounded by cantinas, restaurants, nightclubs, and food stalls, you'll know you're getting close when you see dozens of mariachis gathered on the street, all of them ready to offer their musical services for a fee. For better or for worse, it's hard to tell the different mariachi bands apart: Each player wears black silver-studded skin-tight pants and a short brocaded jacket along with his embroidered wide-brimmed sombrero. On cool evenings a serape is added to the costume, each with its own unique woven design and color scheme. Up close, however, there is a touch of seediness to the mariachis—as there is to the neighborhood in general. The plaza at one time was a pickpocket's haven, but this is no longer the case. Just take normal precautions.

In the plaza itself, the cacophonous sounds of trumpets, violins, guitars, and vocalists fill the air. Dozens of bands playing different tunes in different keys simultaneously compete with one another for the attention of would-be customers, and it is quite natural for local businessmen, relaxing after office hours with friends and a few tequilas, to hire a band to accompany them while they sing along. (It could be said that singing is Mexico's national pastime.)

Mariachis are always eager to provide some soulful music announcing one's desire, be it there on the spot or, better yet, under the balcony of the object of one's affection, wherever she may reside. Once a fee is agreed upon (and it is generally rather expensive) the entire group will pile into a taxi, with the *guitarrón* (a large, pregnant-looking guitar that fills the role of the bass) usually propped on the roof and held by an arm extended from an open window. Then, resembling nothing so much as the Keystone Kops, the mariachis will follow your car to the agreed-upon destination. (No matter the hour, neighbors never complain. While the sound of three trumpets, three guitars, two violins, and a choir of voices under your window is bound to get your attention, in Mexico it's exceedingly bad form to protest having your slumber interrupted. In fact, a ban on serenades after midnight was imposed by a mayor of the D.F. in 1960. His successor lifted the ban as his first official act in office, to overwhelming public acclaim.)

Of course, an hour later they'll be back on the plaza ready

Downtown Mexico City

| 0 | yards | 1100 |
| 0 | meters | 1000 |

RIVERA DE SAN COS.

CIRCUITO INTERIOR

AV. EJERCITO NACIONAL

RIO SAN JOAQUIN

AVENIDA MARIANO ESCOBEDO

Monument
Cuauhtém

AV. PARQUE VIA

CALLE VILLALONGIN

POLANCO

AV. PRESIDENTE MASARIK

Plaza
Necaxa

RIO OCAMPO

RIO TIBER

RIO DANUBIO

SENA

AMAZONES

Museo Nacional
de Antropología

MELCHOR

RIO
PANUCO

U.S. Embassy

PASEO DE LA REFORMA

RIO LERMA

PRAGA

HAMBURGO

FLORENCIA

AMBERES

GENOVA

NIZA

LONDR

LIVERPO

PASEO DE LA REFORMA

Museo
Rufino Tamayo

Parque
Zoológico

Museo de Arte
Moderno

AV. CHAPULTEPEC

ZON
ROS.

Bosque de
Chapultepec

Monumento a los
Niños Heroes

DURANGO

PASEO
DE LA REFO

AVENIDA CONSTITUYENTES

Castillo de
Chapultepec

Museo de la
Lucha del Pueblo
Mexicano por la
Libertad

CALZADA J. VASCONCELOS

AVENIDA TAMAULIPAS

INSURGENTES SUR

Mu
Frar
Maye

Parque
Alameda
Central

JUAR

AVENIDA CONSTITUYENTES

EJE 4 SUR

Museo
Nacional
de Artes
Industri
Popular

AV. JALISCO

VIADUCTO RIO BECERRA

BLVD. PRESIDENTE MIGUEL ALEMAN

AYUNTAM

N

To Coyoacan,
San Angel and Xochimilco

ARCC

AV. R
DE LA L

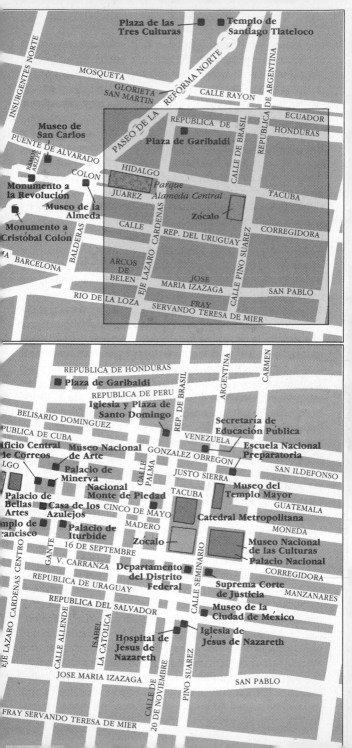

Plaza de las Tres Culturas

Templo de Santiago Tlatelolco

INSURGENTES NORTE

MOSQUETA

GLORIETA SAN MARTIN

PASEO DE LA REFORMA NORTE

CALLE RAYON

REPUBLICA DE ARGENTINA

Museo de San Carlos

PUENTE DE ALVARADO

REPUBLICA DE BRASIL

ECUADOR

REPUBLICA DE HONDURAS

RAMOS ARIZPE

COLON

REPUBLICA DE

Plaza de Garibaldi

HIDALGO

Parque Alameda Central

TACUBA

Monumento a la Revolución

Museo de la Almeda

JUAREZ

CALLE

Zócalo

CORREGIDORA

Monumento a Cristóbal Colón

REP. DEL URUGUAY

'A BARCELONA

BALDERAS

EJE LAZARO CARDENAS

CALLE PINO SUAREZ

ARCOS DE BELEN

JOSE MARIA IZAZAGA

SAN PABLO

RIO DE LA LOZA

FRAY SERVANDO TERESA DE MIER

REPUBLICA DE HONDURAS

Plaza de Garibaldi

REP. DE BRASIL

ARGENTINA

CARMEN

REPUBLICA DE PERU

Iglesia y Plaza de Santo Domingo

BELISARIO DOMINGUEZ

VENEZUELA

Secretaría de Educación Pública

PUBLICA DE CUBA

Museo Nacional de Arte

GONZALEZ OBREGON

Escuela Nacional Preparatoria

ificio Central de Correos

Palacio de Minerva

JUSTO SIERRA

SAN ILDEFONSO

LGO

Nacional Monte de Piedad

CALLE PALMA

Museo del Templo Mayor

Palacio de Bellas Artes

Casa de los Azulejos

TACUBA

GUATEMALA

CINCO DE MAYO

Catedral Metropolitana

mplo de ancisco

Palacio de Iturbide

MADERO

MONEDA

16 DE SEPTIEMBRE

Zócalo

Museo Nacional de las Culturas

GANTE

V. CARRANZA

Palacio Nacional

REPUBLICA DE URUGUAY

Departamento del Distrito Federal

CALLE SEMINARIO

CORREGIDORA

EJE LAZARO CARDENAS CENTRO

REPUBLICA DEL SALVADOR

Suprema Corte de Justicia

MANZANARES

CALLE ALLENDE

ISABEL LA CATOLICA

Museo de la Ciudad de México

Hospital de Jesús de Nazareth

Iglesia de Jesús de Nazareth

JOSE MARIA IZAZAGA

CALLE 20 DE NOVIEMBRE

PINO SUAREZ

SAN PABLO

FRAY SERVANDO TERESA DE MIER

for more good-natured competition with the other mariachis assembled there. Even at the height of the tourist season there are usually a dozen musicians for every visitor, so it is a buyer's market. (The going rate is NP 20 for a song, NP 50 for three songs.) Don't hesitate to bargain during negotiations; it's expected.

Of the four nightclubs around the plaza, **Tenampa** is the most authentic and least exploitative. The energy level inside this huge and sleazy two-room establishment is always high, with three circulating quartets offering serenades. Fortunately, the service is swift and bouncers are placed strategically inside and out to discourage undesirables, so don't worry about giving it a try.

The same kind of energy prevails throughout the rows of taco, torta, and tamale stands jammed together on each side of a narrow paved corridor north of the plaza. Delicate digestive tracts will best be served, however, by limiting the experience to looking and savoring the smells.

Diagonally across Eje Central Lázaro Cárdenas from the plaza is the famous old **Teatro Blanquita**, where top Mexican entertainment is presented nightly. Singers and musical groups, who normally would command fees ten times what they earn at the Blanquita, keep in touch with the grass-roots segment of their public by appearing here between engagements at the more expensive nightclubs in the D.F. and provinces. The government-controlled admission charge makes a night at the Blanquita one of the capital's great bargains. (Many people choose to attend the 7:30 P.M. performance at the Teatro and then visit the plaza afterward.)

PLAZA DE SANTO DOMINGO AREA

Legend has it that the Plaza de Santo Domingo was the spot where, in 1325, the Aztecs saw an eagle perched on a nopal cactus with a serpent in its beak. According to Aztec lore, just such a sight—the central image on the modern Mexican flag—was supposed to mark the place where these nomadic warrior people were to settle down and build a great city.

Located two blocks south and three blocks east of Plaza de Garibaldi, between Calles Belisario Domínguez and República de Cuba, this beautiful old colonial square is steeped in history. Most of the materials used in the construction of its old buildings were taken from the remains of the emperor Moctezuma's two palaces, which stood in the middle of what is now the plaza until the Spanish under Cortés demolished them in 1521. It was also the site of the first Dominican monastery in the Americas, built in 1539. Today, in the fountain in the center of the square, there is an attractive statue of Doña Josefa Ortíz de Domínguez, better known as La Corregidora, the most famous heroine in Mexican history. (See the Querétaro section of the Colonial Heartland chapter for a more complete description of her role in the Mexican struggle for independence.)

The square itself is bounded on the north by the church of Santo Domingo, on the east by the Casa Chata (the former courthouse of the Inquisition) and the Antique Customs House, on the south by a number of rather run-down colonial-era homes, and on the west by the famous arcade known as the **Portal de los Evangelistas** (Arcade of the Scribes), where public scribes set up their tiny portable desks and chairs and, for a fee, pound out anything from legal forms and students' theses to love letters on their ancient typewriters, thereby carrying on a centuries-old tradition. (Seventeenth-century evangelist missionaries were the first scribes here, and hoped by offering their services to win the confidence—if not the conversion—of the local populace.) Flanking them on the sidewalk are a dozen antique printing presses churning out posters, business cards, wedding invitations, and what not, all offering same-day service and decent quality at very reasonable prices.

The Baroque-style **Templo de Santo Domingo** was built between 1716 and 1736 on the site of the original monastery and convent. The Neoclassical main altar within, constructed in 1798, was designed by Manuel Tolsá, and is considered one of the prolific Spanish master's best works.

The **Casa Chata** was locally infamous as the headquarters of the Inquisition from its arrival on Mexican shores in 1571 to its abandonment in 1820. During these bleak years the building was known as the Palacio de la Inquisición. A major renovation of the structure was completed in 1736, elevating it to one of the city's most elegantly sober Baroque buildings. In 1822 it became a military academy, then, from 1855 to 1954, it served as the Escuela Nacional de Medicina. When the school moved to larger quarters, the **Museo de Historia de Medicina** was established here, and today is one of the historic zone's interesting, albeit lesser known, attractions. The history of medicine in Mexico is illustrated here from 13th-century native herb lore to modern science. Note the still-prominent crest at the top of the façade commemorating the original occupants—the Tribunal de la Inquisición—as well as the engraving above the main gate, which translates as "Rise, Lord, and judge your house." Open weekdays 10:00 A.M. to 6:00 P.M.; closed weekends.

The **Antigua Aduana de Santo Domingo** (Antique Customs House) now serves as office space for the Secretariat of Public Education, and inside has a fine David Alfaro Siqueiros mural entitled *Patricians and Patricides*. The three-story building is constructed of *tezontle,* the Aztecs' favorite construction material and the closest thing to an earthquake-proof building material.

Secretaría de Educación Pública

Walk one block east on Calle Luis González Obregón (a continuation of Calle República de Cuba) until you come to Avenida República de Argentina, then turn north. At number 28, on the left side of the street, is the entrance to the impressive Ministry of Public Education building. Once an elegant cloister for nuns of the rather liberal Conceptionist order, it has two interesting patios within surrounded by mural-covered galleries.

Following the Mexican Revolution, poet-philosopher José Vasconcelos, the newly appointed Minister of Public Education, was directly responsible for commissioning a number of native-born artists and encouraging them to make their creative statements on the walls of government buildings in order to promote the development of Mexican cultural values. In the process a powerful Mexican artistic tradition was born.

To his later credit, Vasconcelos turned over most of the wall space at the Ministry of Public Education to a young artist by the name of Diego Rivera, who was just back from years of study in Paris, and who proceeded to paint some of his most important early works here. The results are striking. All the murals in the ministry (with the exception of one or two each by Montenegro, Charlot, O'Gorman, Mérida, de la Cueva, and Amero) are by Rivera, and, taken as a whole, create an epic visual poem of Mexican life, from pre-Hispanic times to the future—or, at least, Rivera's vision of the future. The emphasis of the 235 separate panels is (as would become the artist's trademark) on social struggle, and together they reveal an extraordinarily talented young artist who had not yet succumbed to the bitterness and cynicism that colored his later work.

Escuela Nacional Preparatoria

As you leave the Ministry of Public Education turn right and head back to Calle González Obregón and then left (east) at the corner, where the street's name changes to San Ildefonso. Closed to traffic, the street is part of the old university area and is dominated by the block-long 16th-century former Jesuit seminary that once housed the National Preparatory School. Now part of the National University, it is still known by its earlier name.

To enter one notably beautiful building in this enormous complex go south on Calle Cármen for one block, then take a right on Calle Justo Sierra and look for number 16 in the middle of the block. Restored in 1982, the ancient *tezontle* façade frames an elegant entrance that leads to the cradle of the modern Mexican mural (*muralismo*) movement (follow the signs marked "Anfiteatro Boliver"): Minister Vasconcelos's initial commission was given to Ramón Alva de la Canal, who, in 1921, painted the first true Mexican fresco on one of its walls. José Clemente Orozco painted some of his best early murals here between 1923 and 1926. But the building's most notable work was created by Rivera over the stage in the auditorium. Begun in 1921 and completed two years later, *La Creación,* Rivera's first mural, is hardly recognizable as his by those acquainted only with his later murals, in which he developed his distinctive style of caricaturing well-known historical figures as either villains, victims, or heroes. The anfiteatro is open to the public Tuesdays and Fridays from 3:00 to 5:00 P.M.

The charming pastel-colored **Casa de Tlaxcala**, a renovated 18th-century town house with clean public rest rooms, a small shop selling Tlaxcalan arts and crafts, and a restaurant serving such hard-to-find regional specialties as *gusanos* (maguey cactus worms, fried or broiled), is across the street at number 40. The insular tendencies of the Tlaxcalans, bitter enemies of the Aztecs and reluctant allies of Cortés, are evident in their ceramics and sculpted swagger sticks, the latter unique among Mexican handicrafts. In contrast, the building's graceful central patio is a welcoming oasis from the sometimes oppressive colonial architecture of the surrounding neighborhood. Once the residence of Cuban patriot-writer José Marti, the property was bought by the Tlaxcalan state government three years ago and now houses its tourism offices in addition to the restaurant and gift shop.

When you're ready to move on, head west on Calle Justo Sierra for half a block and take a left on Calle República de Argentina, which becomes Calle Seminario just beyond the fenced-in Aztec ruins on your left. The Zócalo is straight ahead.

THE ZOCALO

Although no longer the geographical center of Mexico City (the growth of the D.F. has been to the west and south), the Zócalo site still is the capital's heart—and for good reason. Perhaps nowhere else in the Western Hemisphere has so much history been enacted as on the stage of this huge square.

On the spot where the great Catedral Metropolitana now dominates the Zócalo, majestic Aztec temples once stood, upon the high altars of which human sacrifices were performed wholesale. After the surrender of Tenochtitlán, Cortés ordered the pyramids razed and the Aztec idols broken into chunks. On a portion of the ruins he then had the foundation for a cathedral laid. The huge plaza in front of the cathedral—today the second largest public square in the world after Moscow's Red Square—was modeled after Madrid's central plaza and has remained basically the same for nearly five centuries.

As it has been throughout its existence, the Zócalo is Mexico City's political and religious center. It is surrounded by, in addition to the cathedral, El Sagrario Metropolitano, an appendage to the cathedral, on the north; the Palacio Nacional and the Suprema Corte de Justicia on the east; the Departamento del Distrito Federal buildings (city government offices, including the office of the mayor of the D.F.) to the south; the entrance to the Portal de los Mercaderes (Merchants' Arcade), between Calle Madero and Calle 16 de Septiembre to the west; and the Nacional Monte de Piedad (government-run pawn shop) at the northwest corner, where Calle Cinco de Mayo meets Calle República del Brasil. The fascinating Templo Mayor and its adjoining museum, the site of recently uncovered Aztec ruins, are located a block north and east of the Zócalo behind the cathedral.

While Plaza de la Constitución is the square's official name, everyone simply calls it the "Zócalo." (*Zócalo* is the Spanish word for "pedestal." In 1843 the mountebank General Santa Anna commissioned a statue of himself here, and a *zócalo* was subsequently constructed in the middle of the great square. For various reasons, the project never materialized, and the pedestal was finally removed in the waning years of the 19th century—but by then the nickname had stuck. Today every main square in every provincial Mexican town is also called the "zócalo," in imitation of the capital's grand public space.) Unemployed tradesmen congregate daily along three sides of the cathedral looking for work. Each displays a hand-lettered sign stating his specialty. There are usually also a few groups of strolling native performers or costumed families dancing in circles, playing wooden flutes, and shaking their ankle castanets while the youngest member of the troupe passes the hat, usually some sort of feathered receptacle.

Every evening at 6:00 you can watch the presidential guards march out of the National Palace and ceremoniously lower the national flag from its gigantic flagpole in the center of the square. An especially fine vantage point for viewing this patriotic scene is the seventh-story rooftop restaurant of the **Hotel Majestic**, the entrance to which is located at the corner of Madero and República del Brasil, across the square. Another good spot is the fourth-floor balcony café of the **Howard Johnson Gran Hotel**, one block south of the Majestic on Calle 16 de Septiembre.

CATEDRAL METROPOLITANA

Tilting this way and that after centuries of settling into the soft subsoil of the Zócalo, the Baroque-style Catedral Metropolitana—the oldest and largest ecclesiastical structure in Latin America—symbolizes as much as any single building in Mexico the brutal suppression of native culture by Cortés and his conquistadors. The original structure, begun in 1525, was built by Aztec survivors of the Conquest under Spanish supervision, with many of the original *tezontle* foundation stones salvaged from their ruined temples. (It wasn't mere coincidence that the site chosen for the cathedral lay directly on top of the leveled foundations of demolished temple bases.)

Political strife and fire halted construction of the cathedral often over the years, and it wasn't until the early 19th century that it was finally completed. As a result, generations of architects and artisans contributed to the final product. And yet despite the combination of seemingly incompatible architectural elements—ranging from ancient Greek to Spanish Baroque to French Neoclassical—the exterior of the cathedral is a remarkably harmonious synthesis of these different styles and impulses. The contributions of Manuel Tolsá certainly helped knit these styles together. Tolsá, a brilliant Spanish sculptor/architect, created the elegant main façade of white marble and gray sandstone as well as the domed stained glass ceiling within, both completed in 1813.

As was so often the case with early colonial-era structures, the indigenous artisans, attempting to follow the instructions of their Spanish supervisors, unconsciously created a new style—a sort of "Indian Baroque"—that was, and remains, unique to Mexico. Today it is most brilliantly evident in **El Sagrario Metropolitano** (The Metropolitan Sacrarium), the annex attached to the cathedral that was designed as a depository for consecrated relics. A creation of Spanish architect Lorenzo Rodríguez, the annex was begun in 1749 and completed 30 years later. The end result is an exterior that qualifies as one of the best examples of the ornate Churrigueresque style and an interior that exhibits a pure Neoclassical sensibility—with one or two noteworthy exceptions, including the baptismal font, to the left of the main altar, with its embedded golden rays.

The interior of the cathedral, on the other hand, is so dark and gloomy that it actually comes as a relief to visit the basement crypts, which are interesting for the 16th-century Gothic ribbing around their vaults (they weren't completed until 1623). This is where you'll find the remains of most of the archbishops of Mexico City, including those of Juan de Zumárraga, the first prelate of New Spain (and the man responsible for ordering the destruction of all Aztec codices that crossed his path, as well as the construction of the original shrine built in Guadalupe's honor).

The cathedral and its adjoining chapel are illuminated at night on national holidays, creating truly startling shadow-and-light effects. On these occasions the Mexican flag flies from its façade and, despite the ostensible separation of Church and State, the ardently nationalistic churchgoers of the D.F. join in the noisy celebration. The cathedral itself, like all religious buildings in Mexico, is owned by the government.

THE TEMPLO MAYOR

The Templo Mayor, or Great Temple, once the ceremonial heart of the Aztec capital of Tenochtitlán, is located behind the cathedral at the corner of República de Argentina and República de Guatemala. It was here, over a period of 80 years, that the Aztecs erected a 150-foot-high pyramid in honor of Huitzilopochtli, their bloodthirsty god of war, and Tlaloc, the age-old Mesoamerican god of rain, at the summit of which countless human sacrifices were offered. Prisoners of war were the usual victims, but if a military campaign failed to produce a sufficient number, slaves would be purchased from Aztec slave-owners to fill the priests' quotas. Convinced that the sun would not rise and the world would end if the gods were not satisfied, their scribes recorded sacrificial statistics that, even by today's jaded standards, are mind-boggling. Bernal Díaz recorded a conversation between Móctezuma II and Cortés on the latter's first visit to Tenochtitlán (at which point the Spaniards were still being treated as honored guests) in which the Aztec emperor boasted that, on the occasion of the dedication of the most recent incarnation of the Templo Mayor, his priests had sacrificed 20,000 individuals.

Little wonder then that the Spanish, despite their own deviousness and greed, had no trouble recruiting other Indian tribes as their allies. With the help of an estimated 10,000 Tlaxcalan warriors, sworn enemies of the Aztecs, and a smallpox epidemic, Tenochtitlán, the chief stronghold of the Aztec empire, was forced to surrender in 1521, after which the victorious Spanish quickly went to work razing the magnificent architectural accomplishments of their Aztec enemies, including the Templo Mayor. (Ironically, the very first colonial structure on the site of the razed temple was the public gallows, completed in 1522. Given their loathing of human sacrifice, the victorious Spaniards had a curiously casual attitude toward capital punishment, with even common thiefs seen fit to hang.)

Over the ensuing centuries the rubble from the ruined Aztec city sank deeper and deeper into the subsoil under and around the Zócalo. Then, on August 13, 1790, 269 years to the day after the final defeat of the Aztec empire, a construction crew working on a restoration project at the cathedral unearthed the famous **Aztec calendar stone**. Weighing 24 tons and measuring nearly 12 feet in diameter, this basalt marvel of pre-Hispanic artistry depicts the Aztec concept of the cosmos, and is now proudly displayed at the National Museum of Anthropology in Chapultepec Park.

In 1900 and again in 1913 additional Aztec artifacts were unearthed in other excavations. But this door to the Aztec past wasn't completely opened until February 1978, when workmen from the city's light and power company, digging just six feet below ground level, uncovered the massive stone disk—ten feet in diameter and weighing eight tons—of Coyolxauhqui, the Aztec moon goddess.

With this discovery experts were forced to agree that, contrary to the long-held belief that the Templo Mayor was buried forever under the nearby cathedral, the actual site of the central temple complex had indeed been found. The light and power company's project was immediately halted and excited archaeologists took over. After five years of careful excavation work, all four sides of the Templo Mayor were exposed; several other temples were also uncovered, along with thousands of statues and relics, some in a remarkable state of preservation—though many of the artifacts (some of them 600 years old) had to be given immediate treatment to prevent them from crumbling into dust upon contact with the air.

The quantity and quality of the finds unearthed at the Templo Mayor site far surpass anything previously found from this period of Mesoamerican history, and new discoveries continue to be made almost daily. The whole site probably will never be explored completely, however; the massive cathedral itself is adjacent to what archaeologists speculate could be some of the most impressive discoveries, but the cathedral site is, and will remain, off limits.

The uncovered ruins of the Templo Mayor are located at Calle Seminario 8, an outdoor museum complex that is far more extensive than archaeologists had originally dared dream. Look, in particular, in the stage 2 area for the *piedra de sacrificios* (sacrificial stone); the nearby chac-mool, to date the oldest piece discovered at the site, reclines calmly with its receptacle for human hearts held snugly against its belly.

Museo del Templo Mayor

Adjacent to the eastern boundary of the excavated area is the Museo del Templo Mayor, a masterpiece of the versatile architect Pedro Ramírez Vázquez, whose achievements include the National Museum of Anthropology and the Basilica of Our Lady of Guadelupe. Objects of all sizes and every description are displayed in the cool, muted interior here, including several life-size ceramic figures known as Eagle Warriors; giant stone serpent heads; obsidian knives (which were used by Aztec priests to remove the hearts from their sacrificial victims); sacrificial altars; and, the pièce de résistance, the stone disk of the moon goddess Coyolxauhqui, the discovery of which was responsible for this extraordinary exhibition. (Also on display is a wooden club about the length of a standard-size baseball bat with a doughnut of black obsidian blades ringing its thicker end. According to one Spanish scribe, a strong man swinging this weapon could decapitate a horse.) Additional exhibits feature ancient cultures that existed in the Valley of Mexico long before the arrival of the Aztecs, and one section of the museum is devoted to the country's geology, flora, and fauna.

The museum is open 9:00 A.M. to 6:00 P.M., daily except Mondays; the ticket office closes at 5:00 P.M. On Sundays and holidays closing time is one hour earlier. English-language tours can be arranged in advance; Tel: 542-1717 between 9:00 A.M. and 4:00 P.M. to make reservations.

Also on the Zócalo

Museo Nacional de las Culturas

One block south and another block east of the Templo Mayor site, at Calle Moneda 13, is the Museo Nacional de las Culturas, otherwise known as the Antigua Casa de Moneda (Ancient Mint), which was built on the site of one of Móctezuma's palaces. Rebuilt in the early 18th century to house the Royal Mint, the structure became the National Museum of Natural History in 1865 and the National Museum of Anthropology in 1940. When the latter moved to its present location in Chapultepec Park in 1964, the National Museum of the Cultures was established in its place. Its building painstakingly restored to its former colonial glory, the museum contains a variety of ethnographic displays from all over the world, including traditional ceramics, artwork, crafts, costumes, and tools. A Rufino Tamayo fresco graces the entrance to the museum. Open 9:30 A.M. to 6:00 P.M., Tuesday through Saturday, and 9:30 A.M. to 4:00 P.M. on Sundays; closed Mondays. Guided tours in English can be arranged by calling 542-0422, ext. 266.

Palacio Nacional

The dominant structure on the Zócalo is the National Palace, the elegant façade of which, handsomely set off by the wrought-iron railings of its many balconies, is made of gray sandstone and rose-colored *tezontle* and stretches nearly the length of the eastern side of the plaza. More than a magnificent architectural creation, the palace is the official residence of the executive power of the government, with the president of the Republic making his most important pronouncements from its center balcony.

The first known structure to occupy the site was the palace of Móctezuma II, who reputedly had an elaborate aviary installed as the centerpiece of a huge garden that took up the entire inner courtyard. After the Conquest, Cortés had Móctezuma's palace destroyed and, as reward for a job well done, was given the deed to the land by the king of Spain. He then had a new palace built from the rubble of the old that, upon its completion, became the seat as well as the symbol of the Spanish Crown's power in New Spain.

Cortés himself lived in, as well as governed from, the palace. In 1529, upon his return from a journey to what is now Honduras, his friends staged a bullfight in the patio (which more or less coincided with the dimensions and location of Móctezuma's splendid patio)—allegedly the first bullfight staged in the Americas. In 1562, years after Cortés had sold the deed back to the Crown, the palace became the official residence of the viceroys who ruled New Spain. A public riot touched off by an increase in grain prices badly damaged the structure in 1692, and what you see today is mostly the result of extensive renovations carried out in the early 18th century. After Mexico gained its independence from Spain in 1821 the palace became the official residence of the president of the Republic, a function it served according to the whims of the titular head of state until 1884. (Both Agustín de Iturbide, the fledgling republic's self-appointed emperor, and Maximilian of Austria, who was appointed emperor by Napoleon III after France invaded Mexico in 1860, chose to live elsewhere.)

In 1884 luxury-loving President-for-Life Porfirio Díaz moved the official presidential residence back to Chapultepec Castle (which had been renovated by Maximilian after his temperamental wife, Carlota, was attacked by bedbugs on her first night in the palace), and the historic old building was converted into government offices. (A restored colonial hacienda in Chapultepec Park, Los Pinos, has served as the official presidential residence for the past half century.) Although renovations have altered its interior considerably over the years, and a third story was added in 1927, the National Palace continues to serve as the working headquarters of the executive branch.

Access to the main patio is through the palace's massive entrance, high above which hangs the famous church bell struck by Father Miguel Hidalgo in his home town of Dolores to proclaim Mexico's independence in 1810. Ornate arches surround the patio; to the left an elegant staircase leads up and past a memorable **Diego Rivera mural** depicting his interpretation of modern Mexican history. Rivera often linked contemporary events with incidents and episodes from different eras. Easily recognizable in this particular work are such leading figures of 20th-century capitalism as J. P. Morgan, John D. Rockefeller, and Cornelius Vanderbilt—all menacingly portrayed. Not surprisingly, given Rivera's political inclinations, the heroically drawn figure of Karl Marx stands out among the "villainous" capitalists. The mural on the northern wall of the patio, also by Rivera, depicts Mexico's history from pre-Hispanic days through the Revolution. The Rivera murals can be viewed from 9:00 A.M. to 6:00 P.M. daily.

The **Museo Recinto Homenaje a Benito Juárez**, located on the first floor of the palace, displays a small collection of memorabilia belonging to Mexico's great reform leader. Juárez, who died on the premises in 1872 while serving his second term as president, carried on an extensive correspondence with his U.S. counterpart, Abraham Lincoln (with whom he is often compared), and their letters to each other are on view as well. The entrance to the museum is through the door on the northern, or Calle Moneda, side of the palace. It's open 9:00 A.M. to 7:30 P.M., Tuesday through Friday.

Departamentos del Distrito Federal

At the southern perimeter of the Zócalo, opposite the cathedral, are the twin buildings containing the offices of the city government, including the office of the mayor of the D.F. The older of the two, on the southwest corner, dates to 1532 and originally was a town hall. Over the years it has served years as a grain exchange, a city jail, and the national mint. Part of the building was destroyed in the civil uprising of 1692 and then rebuilt between 1720 and 1724. The third and top floors were added much later. The indigenously flavored Churrigueresque façade features a number of ornately carved coats of arms, including those of Christopher Columbus and Hernán Cortés. The adjacent structure, inaugurated in 1948, was designed to be a replica of its much older neighbor.

Portal de los Mercaderes

The Merchants' Arcade, located on the west side of the Zócalo, still retains its old pillars but no longer has the stalls where merchants once sold their wares. Built in 1524, the arcade was constructed after local merchants petitioned the newly established colonial government to erect a portico over the broad sidewalk as protection against the morning sun and bad weather. During the arcade's first two centuries of existence, public scribes would set up their portable shops here (before they moved to the arcade of the Plaza de Santo Domingo).

Today the cramped, narrow stalls of the past have been replaced by cramped, narrow shops selling jewelry—perhaps the most visible vestige of a guild system (in which a neighborhood consisting of several blocks confines itself to selling one particular product) that prevailed among the Aztecs. According to local lore, the system is the only indigenous custom adopted by the founders of New Spain. Ambulatory vendors displaying their wares on the sidewalk change daily, with everything from cut-rate "genuine" Rayban sunglasses to cures for intestinal worms vigorously hawked here.

Most of the commercial establishments in and around the Zócalo offer a ten-percent discount off the listed price if you pay in cash rather than with a credit card. You should also be aware that, in general, prices are much lower here than elsewhere in the city.

Nacional Monte de Piedad

Located on the northwest corner of the Zócalo, between Calles Cinco de Mayo and Tacuba, is the imposing Nacional Monte de Piedad (National Pawnshop, translated literally as "National Mountain of Mercy"), occupying the site of a former Aztec palace where the conquistadors were first housed as guests by Móctezuma II. (It was on the roof of the palace, nothing of which remains, that Móctezuma was said to have been stoned to death by his furious subjects as he attempted to calm their anger over his acquiescence to the Spaniards. Because the only documentation ever uncovered pertaining to Móctezuma's demise came from Spanish scribes, some historians feel the story might have been made up to hide Cortés's complicity in the emperor's murder.) Today the National Pawnshop (all pawnshops in Mexico are government owned) offers myriad unredeemed goods for sale. Chandeliers, antique books, office machinery, dentist chairs, artwork, antique jewelry—just about every item imaginable is available in this huge colonial building, which during business hours always seems to be teeming with humanity. Every so often public auctions—at which great bargains supposedly are available—are held to clear out the merchandise.

Suprema Corte de Justicia

The seat of judicial power in Mexico is located at the corner of Avenida Pino Suárez and Calle de la Corregidora, on the southeastern corner of the Zócalo. During the viceregal period (1535 to 1821) the site was occupied by the Mercado del Volador, an open-air market to which fresh fruits and vegetables were brought along the Acequia Real (Royal Canal) from Xochimilco's floating gardens, 16 miles to the south. The present structure, with its somber Baroque façade, was built in 1929 and completely remodeled in 1940.

Inside are three murals by José Clemente Orozco and one by his U.S. contemporary George Biddle. Orozco was commissioned in the early 1940s to paint a series of murals in the building, but his third, *Injustice,* a powerful presentation of judges snoozing in court executed in vivid colors on the landing of the second floor, was considered highly inappropriate by his sponsors and the rest of the proposed series was unceremoniously canceled. You'll find the Biddle mural at the entrance to the library. Open 9:00 A.M. to 2:00 P.M., Monday through Friday.

On the stretch of Corregidora between the National Palace and the Supreme Court you can see a reconstruction of a segment of the walls that used to surround the old Acequia Real.

The **Museo José Luís Cuevas**, the historic center's newest art museum, is housed in a beautifully restored 16th-century building at Calle Academia 13. (To get there, walk two blocks east from the Supreme Court on Corregidora and turn left on Academia.) Originally a convent, the building later served as headquarters for Emperor Maximilian's troops. Today it holds one of the best collections of modern art in Mexico while at the same time honoring Cuevas, considered by many to be the country's finest contemporary painter. Of particular interest is the Sala Picasso, featuring 32 of the Spanish master's finest works. (Cuevas, who has a well-deserved reputation as an *enfant terrible,* denies any outside influence on his work—though he begrudgingly admits his admiration for Picasso.) The museum is open noon to 8:00 P.M. on weekdays, 10:00 A.M. to 6:00 P.M. on weekends; closed Wednesdays.

South of the Zocalo

Museo de la Ciudad de México

Three blocks south of the Zócalo at the corner of Avenida Pino Suárez and Calle República del Salvador is one of the area's more interesting landmarks, the Museum of the City of Mexico. Built in 1526 as a residence for Cortés's cousin, the mansion was remodeled in the 18th century for the count and countess of Santiago de Calimaya and carried their name until it became a museum early in 1964.

The building alone, built of dark red volcanic stone, is worth a visit. The centerpiece of the façade is the count's family crest, decorated with ornately sculpted cannons and gargoyle-like figures. The cornerstone, salvaged from an Aztec ruin, is a sculpted plumed serpent's head that peers menacingly at the passing scene. (Legend has it that Cortés placed the stone here with his own hands.)

The museum's displays cover the history of the city from earliest pre-Hispanic times to the present, although the emphasis begins with the founding of Tenochtitlán. Especially interesting are the models of the ancient Aztec capital, with people going about their work, shopping in the markets, or simply watching as Aztec nobles are carried by in ornate chairs. Depicted in another model is the colonial capital of New Spain, complete with miniature versions of many still-extant buildings, including the one housing the museum. As is the case downstairs, the second-floor exhibits should be viewed counterclockwise, following the city's progress from the 16th century through the Revolution. The southernmost wing of this floor chronicles contemporary Mexico City up to and including the recent extensions to the metro system, the ongoing excavations at the Templo Mayor site, and the ultra-modern high rises that today dominate the city's skyline. The adjoining wing features an impressive collection of 19th-century lithographs. Open 9:30 A.M. to 6:30 P.M., Tuesday through Saturday, and 9:30 A.M. to 3:30 P.M. on Sundays.

Iglesia y Hospital de Jésus

Diagonally across the street from the museum is the fortresslike Iglesia de Jésus, with its entrance on Calle República del Salvador. The church's early Baroque-style façade is topped by a tile-faced cupola, while the plaque on the outside wall of the apse commemorates the first meeting between Hernán Cortés and Móctezuma II—an encounter that, according to Bernal Díaz del Castillo, took place here on November 8, 1519, when it was still the site of an Aztec temple.

Inside is a superb but unfinished mural by Orozco depicting the Conquest, and another by him, entitled *Apocalipsis,* that covers the walls and ceiling behind the dome. (Work on the former was interrupted by Orozco's death in 1949.) The remains of Cortés are also, allegedly, interred here, in an urn identified only by a small bronze plaque on a wall of the tallest altar.

Adjacent to the church is the Hospital de Jésus, which was founded by Cortés in 1524 and completed in 1535. Believed to be the first hospital established in the Americas, it is worth visiting if only to see its inner courtyard. Permission to enter this serene 16th-century patio will be granted graciously at the admittance desk; walk straight into the hospital and take your first left.

An Aztec Temple

One block south on Avenida Pino Suárez is the Pino Suárez metro station, where an Aztec temple was uncovered during construction on the metro in 1968. The temple, which dates from the 14th century, has been preserved as an integral part of the concourse. There is also an entrance here to a subterranean pedestrian walkway that leads back to the Zócalo. Expect lots of activity in this tunnel at all times—everything from wall-to-wall art exhibitions and sidewalk entrepreneurs to droves of people simply going about their business.

West of the Zocalo

Palacio de Iturbide

Located at Francisco Madero 17, four blocks west of the Zócalo, the Palacio de Iturbide is the most elegant structure in the neighborhood, its architecture a curious fusion of indigenous Baroque and Italian touches. The façade is constructed out of *tezontle* and gray sandstone, and the massive, beautifully carved doors open onto an equally striking courtyard. Designed by Francisco Guerrero y Torres and completed in 1780, it was for many years the residence of a Spanish marquis and, later, a count. Then, in 1822, it became the "palace" of its most famous occupant, Agustín de Iturbide, a successful army colonel who won control of the government after Spain granted Mexico its independence the previous year. No stranger to megalomania, the victorious Iturbide had himself crowned emperor and from his palace ruled the country for ten months, during which time he managed to alienate most of his "subjects." A "sabbatical" in Spain followed, but an attempt by the Spanish government to renege on its agreements with newly independent Mexico prompted the Spanish-born Iturbide to again offer his services to his adopted countrymen, who had already had quite enough of him. Needless to say, Iturbide was surprised upon his return to find that the provisional government had condemned him in absentia to death by firing squad, and so it was that he met his maker in February 1824.

In the decades that followed the palace became a hotel, an office building, and a shopping plaza. In 1965 the interior was restored and turned into the administrative offices of a branch of the Banco Nacional de México. Rotating exhibits of a variety of national products are installed on the ground floor.

Templo de San Francisco

As you leave the Palacio de Iturbide continue west on Calle Madero; between Calle Gante and Eje Central Lázaro Cárdenas you'll see what remains of an immense Franciscan monastery, built over the site of what had been Emperor Moctezuma's botanical garden and menagerie. Cortés personally supervised construction of the project, which covered several city blocks when it was completed in 1524. As the headquarters of the Franciscan order, it was the largest ecclesiastical complex in the Americas during the 16th century. In 1856, during a period of intense anti-clerical sentiment in Mexico, the government of Benito Juárez demolished most of the complex, leaving only the shell of the church—the Templo de San Francisco—standing. Rebuilt in 1716, the façade is a magnificent example of the merging of the Churrigueresque and Indian styles, and inside are some lovely Baroque touches. Sadly, the church has sunk so deeply into the marshy soil over the centuries that the building's original ground floor is now the basement.

Casa de los Azulejos

The House of Tiles, across the street from the church of San Francisco at Calle Madero 4, was built in 1596 as a palace for the count of Orizaba. Legend has it that one of the later counts had a son who did not measure up to his father's standards. One day the father reproached his son for his lack of ambition and ended by telling him, "Son, you will never have a house of tile." Stung by his father's criticism, the boy went on to marry a wealthy woman and then tiled the palace from top to bottom with glazed blue-and-white Puebla *azulejos*—to match the sky, as he later told the curious.

In 1904 two brothers from the United States, Walter and Frank Sanborn, opened the first soda fountain in Mexico a few doors away. The enterprising brothers then installed a piano and hired a pianist who specialized in Viennese waltzes, and Mexico City's elite responded to the novelty. Ladies who rarely entered commercial establishments were soon stepping out of elegant horse-drawn carriages to refresh themselves at **Sanborn's** with those amazing concoctions called ice-cream sodas. Walter, a licensed pharmacist, set up a pharmacy in the rear of their large store, arranged so that customers had to pass the tempting beverages and piles of sandwiches (then unfamiliar to Mexicans) in order to reach it.

By the end of the First World War the Sanborns had taken over the Casa de los Azulejos and spread an enormous amber-colored glass roof over its patio and installed a grand piano. What had been a popular drugstore soon became the most elegant public establishment in the city. In time the Sanborns added a perfume department, silver shop, and fur department to cater to their ritzy clientele.

Nowadays a property of Walgreen Pharmacies, Sanborn's is a comfortable place to relax after a morning spent exploring the Zócalo area. The coffee is good, and there's even a 1925 Orozco mural winding up the wall of the stairwell.

Torre Latinoamericana

Diagonally across the street from Sanborn's, on the corner of Madero and Lázaro Cárdenas, is the 44-story Torre Latinoamericana, at 594 feet Mexico's third-tallest skyscraper (the PEMEX building and Hotel de México, both in the capital, now rank one and two, respectively). The enclosed observation deck on the 42nd floor affords panoramic views of the entire Valley of Mexico (on a clear day), and the **Muralto**, on the floor below, is an adequate restaurant. The building's innovative "floating" foundation, designed by Frank Lloyd Wright, has withstood numerous earthquakes while preventing it from sinking into the soft subsoil underlying much of the city. The observation deck is open 10:00 A.M. to 11:00 P.M. daily.

Edificio Central de Correos

Before you cross the avenue and begin to explore the Alameda Park area, there's another interesting cluster of buildings two blocks north on Lázaro Cárdenas. The elegant mansion at the corner of Lázaro Cárdenas and Calle Tacuba is home to the D.F.'s Central Post Office. Designed by the Italian architect Adamo Boari, whose masterpiece, the Palacio de Bellas Artes, is directly across the street, it was built between 1902 and 1907 and opened a year later. As post offices go, you'd be hard-pressed to find a more elaborate one. Particularly noteworthy are the sumptuous details of the building's exterior and the carved woodwork and bronze handrails of the main stairwell inside.

Palacio de Minería

The beautiful Neoclassical building next door at Calle Tacuba 5 is the former Palace of Mining, a creation of the multitalented Spanish émigré Manuel Tolsá. Begun in 1797, it took 16 years to complete, and served as a school for mining engineers until 1945. (It continues to house the Faculty of Engineering.) In addition to its stately façade, the palace boasts a splendid patio and an exquisitely carved staircase. There's also a good 19th-century mural inside by the Spanish artist Rafael Ximeno y Planes, and rotating art exhibits featuring mostly contemporary Mexican works are staged in the lobby.

Plaza Manuel Tolsá

Directly across narrow Calle Tacuba at number 8 is the ornate three-story **Museo Nacional de Arte**. Designed by another Italian architect, Silvio Contri, the building was inaugurated in 1910 as the Palace of Communications and Public Works, later became the repository for the National Archives, and finally, in 1984, assumed its present function. The exhibition rooms, which are reached by climbing a magnificent marble staircase, contain more than 700 works of art, most dating from the 14th century to the mid-20th century, including a number of the finest paintings by the Mexican landscape artist José María Velasco. The museum is open 10:00 A.M. to 6:00 P.M., daily except Mondays.

The Plaza Tolsá in front of the museum is the location of Manuel Tolsá's most famous sculpture, the 29-ton, 15½-foot-tall "El Caballito." Cast in 1803, the massive piece—considered by many to be the finest equestrian statue in the world—depicts the despised Bourbon king Charles IV (1788–1808) astride his horse, and was placed in the Zócalo opposite the cathedral while Tolsá was creating the cathedral's magnificent Neoclassical dome. The odyssey of the "Little Horse" didn't begin in earnest, however, until after independence was achieved in 1821. Then, in order to protect it from the anti-Spanish sentiments of the people, Tolsá had it encased in a wooden globe and moved to the relative safety of a courtyard on the old university campus a few blocks away. There it sat until 1852 (the wooden globe was removed in 1824), when it was painstakingly moved—15 days to travel a little more than a mile—to the intersection of Paseo de la Reforma and Calle Bucareli. It arrived at its present—and, let's hope, final—destination in 1978, and today is one of the capital's more popular attractions.

THE ALAMEDA PARK AREA

THE PALACIO DE BELLAS ARTES

Located at the corner of Juárez and Lázaro Cárdenas, this huge, opulent building designed by Adamo Boari is a Mexico City landmark as well as the nation's foremost cultural center. Eclectic in design—the building itself is a fusion of Neoclassical, Art Deco, and Art Nouveau elements—the Bellas Artes (bay-yas AR-tays) is noted for its excellent acoustics and is home to both the world-famous Ballet Folklórico and the National Symphony Orchestra.

Construction of the building, which was begun in 1904, was halted by the Revolution, and its plans were subsequently modified a number of times before its completion in 1934—hence the mixture of styles. Today the ground floor contains nine spacious galleries that are used for temporary exhibitions, while the second floor has a permanent gallery featuring the works of 19th- and 20th-century Mexican masters. (The Bellas Artes has served as the head-quarters of the National Institute of Fine Arts since 1946.)

But it is the murals in the **Museo Nacional del Palacio de Bellas Artes** on the second, third, and fourth floors that make this such a fascinating and worthwhile stop. Here you'll find the most extensive display of Mexican *muralismo* anywhere in the world, with works by Rufino Tamayo, Juan O'Gorman, José Clemente Orozco, David Alfaro Siqueiros, Jorge Camarena, and Diego Rivera lined up one after the other. Rivera's reworked version of *Man at the Crossroads* (1934), the original of which was commissioned for New York City's Rockefeller Center but was painted over after the artist's sponsors got a look at its graphic political message (they objected, among other things, to John D. Rockefeller being depicted as a devilish capitalist), is just one of the treasures here. Open from 10:00 A.M. to 6:00 P.M., daily except Mondays. Guided tours in English are available dur-ing the same hours, but not on Sundays. Tel: 510-1388 or 520-9060, ext. 3324, for reservations. Admission is free.

Unfortunately, it is estimated that the Palacio de Bellas Artes has sunk more than 16 feet into Mexico City's soft subsoil since it was opened, and it continues to sink at the rate of about three and a half inches a year, despite a number of innovative engineering schemes that have been implemented to halt its downward progress. The principal building material, extremely heavy Italian marble (the type used by Michelangelo), has so far defied modern technol-ogy, and the prognosis is that by the turn of the century the original second floor will become the first floor.

Ballet Folklórico de México

Lovers of dance—which includes most Mexicans—will tell you that the richness and diversity of Mexican culture is nowhere more apparent than in their favorite art form. While most regional folk dances have remained unchanged since the 14th century, the Spanish influence, as exemplified by flamenco and the Dance of the Moors and Christians, has also figured prominently in this rich tradition. Perhaps the best way to experience the full spectrum of dance in Mexico is to see a performance by the Ballet Folklórico de México, which takes the stage three times a week at the Bellas Artes. Authentic costumes, superb dancers, outstanding choreogra-phy, and masterfully performed traditional music all com-bine to make this an unforgettable experience. The Bellas Artes's 22-ton Tiffany crystal curtain, its stained glass portray-ing the snow-capped volcanoes of Popocatépetl and Iztaccíhuatl at dawn and dusk—effects achieved with special lighting—is displayed prior to Sunday matinées.

Performances are held Wednesdays at 9:00 P.M. and Sundays at 9:30 A.M. and again at 9:00 P.M. Reservations should be made in advance through your hotel, a travel agency, or at the box office on Calle Violeta, which is open 11:00 A.M. to 3:00 P.M. and 5:00 to 7:00 P.M., Monday through Saturday, and 8:30 to 11:00 A.M. and 5:00 to 7:00 P.M. on Sundays. Tel: 709-3111, ext. 29. You'll get the best views from seats on the first (lowest) balcony.

PARQUE ALAMEDA CENTRAL

Bordered by Avenida Hidalgo to the north, Avenida Juárez to the south, and Bellas Artes to the east, the park is a pleasant four-block stretch of greenery in the midst of the perennially clogged streets of the capital. Filled with ornate fountains, Neoclassical marble sculpture, wrought-iron benches, courting young lovers, ice-cream and balloon vendors, and towering poplar trees (the park's name is derived from *álamos,* the Spanish word for poplars), it's a good place to relax after a morning spent sightseeing.

Dating back to 1596, it is also the capital's oldest public park. The western section, known as the Plaza del Quemadero (Square of the Burning Stake), was where heretics were burned during the Inquisition. Later, in the 19th century, the park became *the* fashionable place for Sunday promenades (see Diego Rivera's *Dream of a Sunday Afternoon in the Alameda* in the nearby Museo Mural Diego Rivera). Since the Revolution, however, Alameda has been a people's park. Families and couples, mostly working class, congregate for picnics under the poplars, enjoying the free weekly concerts of classical, jazz, rock, folk, and martial music.

During the Christmas season, and especially in the days before the Day of the Three Kings (January 6), the normally lively park becomes even livelier, as dozens of Santa Clauses line up next to their plush crimson chairs set on gaily decorated portable stages and wait to pose with passersby for a small fee. Each Santa brings his own photographer with a shoe-box camera, and traditionally one Santa is always on stilts.

Much of the park's voluptuous statuary was brought from Italy by Porfirio Díaz during his long tenure as president (1872 to 1911). The large semicircular marble monument to Benito Juárez that faces Avenida Juárez was also commissioned by Díaz.

Museo Nacional de Artes y Industrias Populares

The National Museum of Folk Arts and Crafts, housed in the former church of Corpus Christi (inaugurated in 1587 and renovated a century later) at Avenida Juárez 44, directly across from the park's Juárez Monument, is a government-run shop and museum that displays and sells traditional arts and crafts from different regions of the country. The museum section is on the second floor, with its entrance at the rear of the building, and is open 9:00 A.M. to 3:00 P.M. on weekdays. Displayed pieces are for sale on the first floor and mezzanine at prices comparable to what you would pay in the villages of their origin. Among the items for sale are sweaters and ponchos, hand-carved masks, onyx chess sets, hand-blown glassware, bark paintings, and a variety of ceramics. The silver jewelry here is less expensive than it is in Taxco, where it is made, and the wooden toys from the state of Michoacán are especially charming. Also of interest is the ceramic Tree of Life, a traditional wedding gift fashioned in the shape of a candelabra and characterized by intricate decorative motifs featuring angels with trumpets, assorted biblical characters, and flowers. The most ornate come from Metepec, in the state of México. Beautifully carved wooden chests from Olinala, Guerrero, and the hard-to-find Huichol Indian yarn paintings from Nayarit are available here at reasonable prices and can be counted among the best buys in folk art anywhere in Mexico. The retail section is open 10:00 A.M. to 6:00 P.M., daily except Sundays. Tel: 521-6679.

FONART

If you follow Avenida Juárez three and a half blocks to the west you'll come to FONART, a branch of the immense government-run operation that sells native arts and crafts at just about wholesale. Here you'll find handicrafts in precious, semiprecious, and garden-variety materials such as silver, onyx, glass, shell, leather, clay, wood, wax, papier-mâché, and even sugar. The government coordinates the manufacture, distribution, and sale of these goods, and also regulates their prices. The rural artisans are, in effect, subsidized—which is an absolute necessity if these craft traditions are to survive.

Museo Mural Diego Rivera

Just north of FONART on the corner of Calles Balderas and Colón, the Museo Mural Diego Rivera is the new home of the recently restored Diego Rivera masterpiece *Dream of a Sunday Afternoon in the Alameda*. Most certainly the capital's smallest museum, it was built for the sole purpose of housing the mural after its previous home, the landmark Hotel del Prado, was all but leveled in the 1985 earthquakes. (The hotel has since been torn down.) When the mural was first unveiled in 1948 it created an uproar because of a placard carried by one of its figures that stated *"Dios No Existe"* ("God Does Not Exist"), a quotation from a lecture given by the Mexican philosopher Ignacio Ramírez. As a result of the outcry, the mural was covered and remained so until 1956, when Rivera, a devout Communist, finally consented to paint over the objectionable words, substituting in their place the phrase *"Conferencia de la Academia de Letran de 1836"*—a reference to the lecture in which the controversial words had been pronounced. (The chubby young boy with the bulging eyes standing in the front row is a self-portrait.) Open 10:00 A.M. to 2:00 P.M. and 3:00 to 5:00 P.M., daily except Mondays.

PLAZA DE LA SANTA VERACRUZ

Located one block north and two blocks east of the Museo Mural Diego Rivera on Avenida Hidalgo, the Plaza de la Santa Veracruz was built in 1522 on land reclaimed from drained Aztec-built canals, making it one of the first projects completed during the construction of Mexico City. Over the centuries the plaza has sunk some 12 feet into the marshy subsoil and only recently have modern engineering techniques halted its slow descent. The plaza's two ornate fountains are favorite meeting places of the city's pigeons, which drink, bathe, and procreate to their heart's content as the life of the city swirls around them.

Templo de la Santa Veracruz

Under the direction of Cortés a small hermitage was built here in 1527, making this one of the first Catholic sites of worship in New Spain. The hermitage was replaced at the end of the 16th century by the larger church of Santa Veracruz. Today the venerable structure, Mexico's answer to the Leaning Tower of Pisa, tilts precariously forward and to the left under the weight of its twin towers. With their elaborate 18th-century Baroque trimmings, the front and side entrances show evidence of a partial restoration. Inside, note the impressive image of a crucified Christ over the altar, a gift from Pope Paul III to King Charles V of Spain, as well as the many beautifully tiled walls, especially those of the "Lady Chapel," to your left as you enter. The remains of the master artist/architect Manuel Tolsá are also interred here.

Museo Franz Mayer

Housed in the 16th-century Hospital de San Juan de Dios next door to the church, the Museo Franz Mayer boasts an extraordinary collection of mostly applied antique art, including ceramics, crystal, furniture, clocks, and Talavera ware. Mayer, a German-born financier who lived most of his life in Mexico as a Mexican citizen, bequeathed this collection of 16th- and 17th-century antiques from England, China, Spain, and Holland—considered one of the finest collections of its kind in the world—to his adopted country upon his death in 1976.

The museum's noteworthy library houses mostly collectors' items, including 770 different editions of *Don Quixote,* as well as many books whose binding, typography, and illustrations are more valuable than their text. There are also numerous reference works on the particular applied arts that Mayer collected as well as books on painting, engraving, and sculpture. Photographing without flash is permitted. Open 10:00 A.M. to 5:00 P.M., daily except Mondays.

Museo Nacional de la Estampa

The peach-colored town house at Hidalgo 48, directly east of the museum, now houses the National Prints Museum, featuring rotating exhibits drawn from the more than 10,000 prints and engravings owned by the National Institute of Fine Arts. Items on display run the gamut from pre-Hispanic clay seals used for printing colored designs on cloth, leather, and paper to reproductions of contemporary works by the likes of Francisco Toledo, Luís Nishizawa, and Alberto Gironella. Among the most popular items are the engravings of José Guadalupe Posada (1852–1913), whose *calaveras* (skeletons) commemorating the annual Day of the Dead celebration have become cultural icons. The museum is open 10:00 A.M. to 6:00 P.M., Tuesday through Saturday.

Iglesia de San Juan de Dios

The church on the eastern perimeter of the plaza is known to local worshipers as "the church of the hopeful hearts." The statue of Saint Anthony inside is covered with metal hearts, most of them brought by females who visit the church on June 13, the saint's birthday, to pray for success in romance. (The line of believers waiting to enter the church on that day usually stretches for miles.) As well, the table in front of the statue is crowded with fresh gardenias, gladiolus, and daisies brought as offerings by the impatient lovelorn who prefer not to wait for the saint's birthday. For those secure in their loved one's affections the best time to visit is early morning, when the slanting sunlight beautifully illuminates the stained glass in the church's cupola.

Museo de San Carlos

Before you head down Reforma, make a short detour to the Museo de San Carlos, located at Avenida Puente de Alvarado 50 (Puente de Alvarado is the continuation of Avenida Hidalgo), two major intersections west of the Plaza de la Santa Veracruz. Housed in a beautiful Neoclassical structure designed by Manuel Tolsá in 1806 as an aristocrat's residence, the building itself is noteworthy for its unusual two-story oval patio and elegant stairway. The museum's permanent collection on the second floor includes works by Rafael, Rembrandt, El Greco, Rubens, Bosch, Goya, and Van Dyke. Open 10:00 A.M. to 5:00 P.M., daily except Mondays.

Monumento y Museo Nacional de la Revolución

If you walk two blocks south on Calle Ramos Arizpe you'll come to the square known as the Plaza de la República and, in the middle of it, the nation's largest monument, the Monumento a la Revolución. Originally, this massive arch was designed to be the ceremonial entrance to a lavish legislative palace in which President-for-Life Porfirio Díaz was to hold court. By the time the arch was completed, however, the Revolution had begun and Díaz had fled into exile. Today the monument is the final resting place for five of Mexico's most revered revolutionaries: Buried in crypts under the monument's immense pillars are Francisco "Pancho" Villa; President Francisco Madero, who succeeded Díaz only to be assassinated two years later; President Venustiano Carranza, himself a victim of modern Mexico's bloody birth; President Plutarco Calles, founder of the ruling PRI party; and President Lázaro Cárdenas, the man responsible for nationalizing the oil industry and implementing agrarian reform on a large scale.

The Museo Nacional de la Revolución, located in the basement of the monument, presents a well-organized permanent exhibition entitled "50 Años en la Historia de México (1867–1917)." Open 9:00 A.M. to 5:00 P.M., daily except Mondays. Weekday evening hours are from 5:00 to 8:00 P.M., Tuesday through Sunday.

The huge peach-colored building forming the northern border of the Plaza de la República is the **Frontón México**, a 4,000-seat arena featuring professional jai alai every evening except Mondays at 8:00 (7:00 on weekends). There is a dress code.

CENTRAL PASEO DE LA REFORMA

One long block south of the Monumento a la Revolución via Calle Ignacio Ramírez is Mexico City's great thoroughfare, the seven-and-a-half-mile Paseo de la Reforma. Originally called the Paseo del Emperador, after Maximilian, who during the course of his brief and ill-fated reign ordered this grand boulevard built along the lines of the Champs-Elysées, Reforma was completed in 1865 and renamed in 1877 in honor of the great reforms in government and civil rights initiated by Benito Juárez. Once exclusively residential, today it has become *the* chic address for everything from elegant hotels and foreign embassies to the sleek new office towers of national and multinational corporations.

It's also at this point that Reforma, as it proceeds on its stately way to Chapultepec Park and the southwestern environs of the D.F., becomes a veritable open-air museum of monumental statuary. The four principal monuments here are located at *glorietas* (traffic circles) spaced about a half mile apart and serve as the hubs of major intersections. The first of these, where Calle Ignacio Ramírez intersects Reforma, features the **Monumento a Cristóbal Colón** (Christopher Columbus), created by the French sculptor Charles Cordier and donated to the city by Don Antonio Escandon in 1877. The second *glorieta,* at the intersection of Reforma and Avenida Insurgentes, holds the **Monumento a Cuauhtémoc**, the last Aztec emperor, who is portrayed complete with plumed robe, feathered headdress, and spear in hand. The monument itself was designed by Francisco Jiménez and completed in 1887 by Ramon Agra (the figure of Cuauhtémoc was sculpted by Miguel Noreña).

The third *glorieta* is dominated by Mexico's most celebrated monument, the **Monumento a la Independencia**, better known as "El Angel," a 150-foot column surrounded by sculpted figures and surmounted by a golden-winged angel. Begun in 1901 under the direction of Antonio Rivas Mercado and completed in time for the centennial of the Republic in 1910, this startlingly beautiful landmark has become the most recognized symbol of the city. (According to historian Fernando Benítez, the monument's nickname is a misnomer: "Angels are traditionally sexless, and the golden figure is definitely female and was originally referred to correctly as 'La Victoria.' ")

The final *glorieta* before Chapultepec Park is at the intersection of Reforma and Río Mississippi to the north and Sevilla to the south. For the last dozen or so years the circle had featured the Fuente Plan Cutzamala, an avante-garde structure that served as a fountain. The *glorieta* was originally occupied by a bronze sculpture of the Roman goddess Diana; first displayed in 1943, Diana became a bonafide landmark in 1964 when the local version of the League of Decency protested her "immoral nakedness" and demanded that a skirt be placed on the lower part of her body. The fastening of a loincloth caused a successful public protest the following year and the loincloth was removed, but she was shunted off to a less conspicuous spot where she remained until, mysteriously, she disappeared a few years ago.

But now Diana's back, unveiled with little fanfare on July 5, 1992. At an estimated 110 feet tall, the gleaming sculpture is a beautiful addition to the city's skyline. The capital's ongoing intrigues with its statues continue, however, as the Fuente Plan Cutzamala is now among the missing.

The Zona Rosa

"Zona Rosa" ("Pink Zone") is the unofficial name for a roughly triangular 29-block area southwest of the Alameda Park neighborhood. It is bordered by Paseo de la Reforma to the north, Avenida Insurgentes to the east, Avenida Chapultepec to the south, and Calle Florencia to the west. An exclusive residential district from the late 19th century through the 1950s, today the Zona Rosa is home to some of the nation's best art galleries, boutiques, antiques shops, bookstores, hotels, restaurants, discotheques, bars (including gay bars), and nightclubs. Not surprisingly, just about every type of item imaginable is for sale somewhere within its borders, including clothing and jewelry of the highest quality (with prices to match). It is also the location of the **Mercado Artesanías Insurgentes**, an old-fashioned market that houses more than 200 stalls selling a variety of native handicrafts, silverwork, leather goods, onyx, and earthenware. Situated at the corner of Calle Florencia, between Calles Londres and Liverpool, the market is accessible from both those streets as well. Every Saturday the **Plaza del Angel**, a shopping mall located between Calles Londres and Hamburgo, features a flea market specializing in antiques.

In the years after the Second World War a smattering of small cafés began to infiltrate this neighborhood of luxurious two-story residences. Writers and artists such as Octavio Paz, Carlos Fuentes, and Rufino Tamayo soon were spending leisurely afternoons and evenings in these cafés enjoying each other's conversation and company. (One of the regulars from the old days, writer Luis Guillermo Piazza, is given credit for coining the name Zona Rosa. In Mexico, areas designated for legalized prostitution are called "Zonas Rojas," or red zones. Because some of the first cabarets to open in the area in the early 1950s offered entertainment bordering on the risqué, Piazza came up with the name "Zona Rosa." The rest is history.) The Pink Zone's first hotel, El Presidente, opened on the corner of Calles Hamburgo and Amberes in 1956, after which it was just a matter of time before most of the residents sold their properties and fled to the peace and quiet of the suburbs. Many of their homes were converted into chic business venues. (El Presidente was seriously damaged in the 1985 earthquake, and is still undergoing renovation.)

The buildings throughout the Zona Rosa reflect the turn-of-the-century taste for Art Nouveau, a style known in Mexico as "Porfiriato" (after Porfirio Díaz, who was president during the period in which the neighborhood came into its own). These elegant survivors of modern urban planning are appreciated today as nostalgic reminders of the neighborhood's formerly genteel character. Most of the Zona's north–south side streets are now off limits to vehicular traffic, creating lovely pedestrian malls lined with welcoming cafés. In fact, umbrella-shaded tables prevail to such an extent that it is sometimes difficult to determine where one café ends and another begins. During lunchtime the eateries and bars are crowded with tourists and local business-people, who eventually give way to the evening crowd. But the Zona hardly ever sleeps. As the last revelers are wandering home in the early morning light, the local businesspeople are returning to the neighborhood for their breakfast *juntas* (meetings).

BOSQUE DE CHAPULTEPEC

Spread over 40 square miles just west of the Zona Rosa, Chapultepec Park is one of the largest and oldest public parks in the world. Once an island in a swampy lake of dozens of islands, the park has ancient *ahuehuete* trees that were already a hundred years old by the time the Aztecs made their way to the Valley of Mexico in the early 14th century. In the two centuries that followed, Aztec emperors used the virgin forest as a hunting and recreation ground, only to give way to the victorious Spanish viceroys, who constructed vacation homes throughout the forest during the three centuries of the colonial era.

Today Chapultepec Park is a people's park, a place where tens of thousands of Mexico City residents come daily to decompress from the hustle and bustle of the world's largest metropolis. The great branches of the *ahuehuetes* meet high above wandering pathways to form lush green arcades; elsewhere, grassy stretches of open space attract sunbathers and picnickers (although in many areas of the park the grass has taken a beating). Signs prohibiting this and that are nowhere to be seen; the residents of the capital have a magnificent public space to live up to, and, for the most part, they do so with respect and appreciation.

The park itself is divided into three sections. The first (*primer*), or easternmost, section is home to the Museo Nacional de Antropología and the Museo de Arte Contemporáneo Internacional Rufino Tamayo, both of which are located on the north side of Paseo de la Reforma. On the other side of Reforma, due south of the Museum of Anthropology, are a number of attractions: Lago Menor, where ducks and swans vie for the right-of-way with rowboats rented by the hour; Lago Mayor, where the National Ballet performs *Swan Lake* every April; the Museo de Arte Moderno and the Monumento a los Niños Héroes (Monument to the Boy Heroes), both due east of the lakes; the Castillo de Chapultepec (Chapultepec Castle), perched on a steep hill and looking like something out of an illustrated book of fairy tales; the Parque Zoológico de Chapultepec (the zoo), where the first pandas outside of China to be conceived naturally and in captivity were born, and the Jardín Botánico (Botanical Gardens), both due west of the lakes; and Los Pinos, the presidential residence since 1938, at the extreme southern portion of this section where Avenida Constituyentes meets Calzada Molina del Rey.

The newer, middle section of the park, the *segundo sección,* is bordered by the Anillo Periférico Sur to the east, Avenida de los Constituyentes to the south, and Reforma to the north and west. In addition to an amusement complex dominated by a huge roller coaster, this section of the park is home to two other museums, the Museo de Historia Natural and the Museo Tecnológico de Comision Federal de Electridad, as well as the Lerma Terminal de Agua, an exhibition hall for a number of Diego Rivera murals.

The third (*tercer*) section of the park, less crowded than the other two, is bordered by the huge Panteón Dolores (Dolores Civilian Cemetery) to the east, Avenida Constituyentes to the south, and the lovely residential neighborhood known as Lomas Virreyes to the north and west. Characterized by hilly, forested terrain and green pastures carpeted with wildflowers, it is crisscrossed by bridle and foot paths that meander through great clumps of ferns, and is a favorite with the capital's equestrian crowd. (Public stables here rent horses by the hour.) The pastoral clearings host frequent *fiestas de cumpleaños* (birthday parties), which are easily identified by the vividly colored balloons strung between trees to mark the boundaries of the party. It is also home to the Atlantis Dolphinarium, where superbly trained dolphins and sea lions delight the relatively few spectators who find their way here.

FIRST SECTION

Museo de Arte Contemporáneo Internacional Rufino Tamayo

The best way to see Chapultepec Park is to start early in the day with a visit to this museum, which houses the personal collection of one of the greatest Mexican painters of the 20th century. Tamayo, an orphaned Zapotec Indian, is credited, along with Diego Rivera, José Clemente Orozco, and David Siqueiros, with bringing international attention to 20th-century Mexican art. An exile in the United States during much of the 1940s and 1950s, when he refused to join the politically oriented *muralismo* movement led by Rivera and Siqueiros, he returned to Mexico in 1959, where he continued to create paintings—and later prints and sculpture—true to the tenets of the modernist movements that dominated the international art world for most of this century. He inaugurated the museum bearing his name, the first in the country to be financed by private corporations, in 1981, and passed away, at the age of 91, in the summer of 1991.

To get to the museum follow Paseo de la Reforma into the park. After you pass Mariano Escobedo there will be a large signboard with the latest information on the museum's temporary exhibitions on the corner to your right. Take a right on Calzada Mahatma Gandhi and walk the few hundred yards to the strikingly modern building that houses the collection. The Sculptors' Patio at the front entrance is graced by a large Henry Moore. Inside, the first thing to catch your eye will be a major Picasso—part of the museum's permanent collection. While the Tamayo Room is limited to some of the master's lesser efforts, the other nine galleries are filled with splendid works by his contemporaries, both foreign and Mexican, including Marc Chagall, Max Ernst, Joan Miró, and José Chávez Morado, and frequently host travelling exhibitions. Open 10:00 A.M. to 5:45 P.M., daily except Mondays.

To continue your exploration of the park, walk back to Reforma, which runs in a straight line through the northeastern corner of the park, and follow the sidewalk to your right or take your pick from a steady flow of public transportation vehicles heading in the same direction. All buses will stop in front of the National Museum of Anthropology, the next stop after the first traffic light.

Museo Nacional de Antropología

The National Museum of Anthropolgy is one of the great museums of the world, and in itself is reason enough to visit Mexico City. At the very least it deserves the better part of a day of your time.

Designed by Pedro Ramírez Vázquez, this deceptively simple rectangular structure is generally considered to be the greatest achievement of modern Mexican architecture, and certainly is one of the most harmonious settings ever conceived for the exhibition of antiquities. The exterior of the second floor, for example, is dominated by a window lattice reminiscent of traditional Mayan ornamentation. And, of course, no truly "Mexican" building would be complete without a patio. In the case of Ramírez Vázquez's design, the patio is surrounded by almost two dozen exhibition halls and is dominated by a huge inverse "umbrella." Resting on a single reinforced-concrete column decorated with reliefs depicting the history of Mexico and stabilized by special steel stays, this massive concrete cover is designed to catch rainwater and then channel it into the reed-filled pond at the opposite end of the patio.

Standing permanent sentry duty on a marble plinth at the entrance to the museum is a huge, unfinished basalt monolith representing either Tlaloc, the god of rain, or his sister, the water goddess, Chalchiuhtlicue. By all accounts the largest single-piece sculpture (weighing in at 165 metric tons and standing 23 feet tall) created in Mexico before the arrival of Columbus, this massive monolith was uncovered in a riverbed near the town of Coatlichán, some 30 miles northwest of the capital, and dates back to the heyday of Teotihuacán. Transported to its present site with great logistical difficulty (it made the trip on a specially constructed tractor-trailer that was escorted by the Mexican army), the statue was greeted by thousands of passersby as it finally rumbled through the downtown area on the afternoon of April 16, 1964. Then, almost a month before the rainy season usually begins, the skies opened up and a tremendous downpour drenched the astonished onlookers—rain, as it turned out, that continued intermittently for three days.

The exhibition rooms inside are laid out in such a way that you can visit them in any order you choose, but to appreciate fully the treasures of this great museum you should probably start with the **Orientation Room**, straight ahead as you walk through the reception hall, where a 15-minute overview of Mesoamerica's ancient cultures is offered along with guided tours in English, Spanish, German, and French at half-hour intervals. Although the tours cover just a small portion of all there is to see, they provide a valuable introduction to the pre-Columbian history of the region as well as the museum itself.

(As is the case in most museums throughout the country, all signs in the Museum of Anthropology are in Spanish only. A well-stocked bookstore on the left as you enter the reception hall has a good selection of illustrated guidebooks in English, however.)

To the right of the Orientation Room is a **Rufino Tamayo mural** depicting the eternal struggle between good and evil. (Other Mexican painters whose works are exhibited in the museum include José Chávez Morado, Matías Goeritz, Carlos Mérida, and Pablo O'Higgins.) Near the Tamayo mural are the temporary exhibition halls, where recent discoveries from ongoing excavations are displayed. These new additions to the museum's collection arrive on a regular basis; the Templo Mayor site near the Zócalo, for example, recently has produced a series of important pre-Hispanic relics.

The rest of the ground floor is divided into collections classified by either region or culture. These include rooms devoted to **Teotihuacán, Tula,** the **Mexica** (Aztec), **Oaxaca,** the **Gulf Coast,** and the **Maya.** What is probably the most popular piece in the museum is on display in the Mexica Room: the famous **Aztec calendar stone** (which is reproduced in miniature and sold in almost every souvenir shop in Mexico). This 24-ton basalt disk was unearthed during a restoration project on the Metropolitan Cathedral back in 1790, and then for years was left propped against one of the cathedral's walls. More recently, experts have concluded that it was probably carved in the early years of the 16th century and is not so much a calendar as a vision of the Aztec cosmos.

Other well-known pieces in the museum's collection include **El Luchador**, an Olmec wrestler, and a huge Olmec head from the Late Preclassic period (about 200 B.C.). The famous Aztec **obsidian monkey**, one of the 140 priceless artifacts stolen during the Christmas Eve robbery of 1985, was recovered in 1990 and is now back on display (along with a new state-of-the-art alarm system installed as a safeguard).

Outside the Maya Room a small temple in a lovely garden

contains three striking murals depicting Mayan warriors engaged in battle. The murals are reproductions of the originals, which were discovered in 1947 in the jungles of southernmost Mexico at a site known as Bonampak, and are considered to be some of the best preserved specimens of their type unearthed so far. Painted sometime around A.D. 800, the murals depict Mayan warriors as aggressors in a violent confrontation and further discredit the long-held belief that the Maya were dedicated pacifists.

The second floor is devoted to ethnology exhibits illustrating the lifestyles of Indian groups in Mexico today, and is arranged so that its rooms relate as closely as possible to those below. Exhibits on this floor include maps, photographs, examples of arts and crafts, religious objects, farm and fishing implements, everyday wear, native costumes and ceremonial dress, and a number of life-size replicas of traditional shelters created by Indian craftsmen.

The Museum of Anthropology has a passable **restaurant/cafeteria**. Large weekend crowds make the best time to visit a weekday (other than Mondays, when it's closed). Open 9:30 A.M. to 6:00 P.M., Tuesday through Saturday, and 10:00 A.M. to 7:00 P.M. on Sundays and holidays. English-speaking tours are conducted from 10:00 A.M. to 2:00 P.M.

Parque Zoológico and Jardín Botánico

Directly south of the museum and across Reforma is the entrance to the main body of the park. Immediately to the left is a children's zoo; you can rent rowboats at Lago Menor, the large man-made lake to the right. Nearby is another man-made lake, Lago Mayor, where the National Ballet performs *Swan Lake* on weekends in April. At the southwestern corner of the lake is the **Casa del Lago**, a colonial-era mansion-cum-theater that presents concerts, plays, readings, films, and round-table discussions on a variety of topics; admission to all events is free. Daily workshops in painting, music, dance, drama, and arts and crafts, also free, are conducted on the large patio in front of the theater's entrance. The chess and checker boards set into stone tables and scattered about under the ancient lichen-covered *ahuehuete* trees are yet another popular draw.

Nearby is the entrance to the **Parque Zoológico de Chapultepec**, which first opened in 1923. The credit for creating the first public zoo in history goes to Móctezuma II, who caged six jaguars sent to him as tribute and installed them on this very site at the beginning of the 16th century. He later moved the large aviary from his palace in the center of Tenochtitlán here in order to keep the jaguars company and then began to add other species to his collection. Eventually he allowed his favored subjects to visit the compound, and thus was born the concept of a public zoo.

For quite a while the zoo's most celebrated inmates have been the resident pandas. A gift from the Chinese government, the first pair arrived 19 years ago, and produced the first panda cub conceived naturally and in captivity four years later. The zoo is open 9:00 A.M. to 4:45 P.M., Wednesday through Sunday.

Just outside the entrance to the zoo is a depot from which a miniature train departs for its leisurely trip around the entire first section of the park. Tickets are sold at the depot itself, and a complete round trip takes about 45 minutes.

On the western side of the zoo is the **Jardín Botánico**, the origins of which also date back to the reign of Móctezuma II, who is supposed to have puttered around an herb garden on the site. West of the gardens is a small park that has one requisite for admission: You must be at least 50 years old. Inside its fenced-off confines are comfortable benches, beautiful tropical flora, and an ever-present choir of songbirds.

Calzada de los Poetas

South of this small park-within-a-park a pathway known as the Poets' Walk is lined with statues of some of Mexico's greatest writers and poets. At the end of the walk, to the east, is the Móctezuma Ahuehuete Tree—with a circumference of almost 50 feet, the largest tree in a park filled with large trees. Besides being a natural wonder, the tree is an inspiration to all the health-conscious joggers who jam the path that winds past it. The grassy knoll nearby serves as a workout area for fledgling matadors, who cape imaginary bulls under the tutelage of their trainers as the sun rises to warm the always chilly morning air.

Continuing in a southerly direction, you'll come to the **Monumento Nezahualcoyotl** (nez-a-wahl-COY-o-tal) on Avenida Heroico Colegio Militar, the favored route for the capital's hordes of joggers. Nezahualcoyotl, the 15th-century poet-king of Texcoco, is the man most often credited with supervising the planting of the area's *ahuehuete* trees. Nearby you can see the remains of an ancient **aqueduct**, another civic improvement reputedly instigated by Nezahualcoyotl. On the other side of the aqueduct you can either enter a tunnel and wait your turn for the elevator to Chapultepec Castle or follow the winding pathway to the top.

Castillo de Chapultepec and the
Museo Nacional de Historia

The hill of Chapultepec has been the site of one kind of fortress or another since the days when the Toltecs occupied the valley, almost 1,000 years ago. In 1521 an anonymous Spanish chronicler wrote: "The Emperor Moctezuma gazes every sundown at his canalled capital surrounded by lakes ... from his fortress high on the hill. Here he is borne in his jewel-encrusted litter after dinner to smoke tobacco treated with amber and to feast his eyes on the great temples of the pagan gods in the city plaza, washed with the colors of sunset." By the end of the 18th century a combination fort, granary, and summer residence for the Spanish viceroys had been built on the site. That structure was converted into a military college in 1840, almost 20 years after Mexico won her independence from Spain, and in 1847, with U.S. troops threatening to overrun the college, six cadets—soon to be known to posterity as the Niños Héroes (Boy Heroes)—provided the young Mexican republic with its newest martyrs by leaping from the precipice wrapped in Mexican flags rather than surrendering to the invading troops. (If you head south and east, you'll soon come to the six towering marble columns of the **Monumento a los Niños Héroes**. Inaugurated in 1952, the columns frame a large statue of a defiant Mother Mexico holding a dead son in her arms; another son at her feet is alive and ready to defend her. The remains of the young martyrs are buried within the monument.)

The Neoclassical design of the present-day castle dates back to France's short-lived (1864–1867) domination of Mexico. Austrian Archduke Maximilian and his wife, Carlota, sent to rule Mexico by Napoleon III, almost immediately took up permanent residence in the castle, rather than in the National Palace, after Carlota was attacked by bedbugs on her first night in the latter. Maximilian then ordered a complete remodeling of the castle, with results that today can be seen in the design of its gardens, winding stairways, and intimate patios.

After Maximilian was overthrown and executed, the new president, Benito Juárez, reestablished the presidential residence in the National Palace. His successor, President-for-Life Porfirio Díaz, moved the presidential residence back to the castle, where it remained until the populist Lázaro Cárdenas ascended to the presidency in 1934. Cárdenas viewed living in a castle as "undemocratic" and had the presidential residence moved to Los Pinos, an abandoned hacienda nearby, where it remains to this day. At the same time Cárdenas ordered the castle converted to its present function: home to the **Museo Nacional de Historia**. Today the museum houses a collection of memorabilia dating back to the days of the Conquest—blood-stained uniforms, swords, and the like—along with a number of outstanding examples of Mexican *muralismo,* including Orozco's *Benito Juárez and the Reform,* David Alfaro Siqueiros's *The Revolution,* Jorge Camarena's *The Constitution,* and Juan O'Gorman's *Themes of the Revolution.*

Upstairs are exhibits featuring period furniture and clothing, clocks, coins, and jewelry. Perhaps the most interesting pieces, however, are the two horseless carriages—one an ostentatious coach designed especially for the ill-fated Maximilian and the other a stark black coach favored by Benito Juárez (the latter was literally the seat of the provisional government for a short period following Maximilian's demise).

Before leaving the museum be sure to take a stroll around the outside patio for a look at the opulent French-style furnishings left behind by Maximilian and Carlota. The panoramic views of the city and, on good days, Popocatépetl and Iztaccíhuatl, are well worth the climb. The museum is open 9:00 A.M. to 6:00 P.M.; daily except Mondays.

Museo de la Lucha del Pueblo Mexicano por la Libertad

Located just below the castle is the Museum of the Struggle of the Mexican People for Liberty, also known as the Museo del Caracol, after its snail-like shape. You enter this glass-walled structure, which is tucked into the hillside, from the top and then walk down a winding ramp past a variety of three-dimensional models depicting historical events from Mexico's revolutionary past. At the bottom of the hill you can rest on one of the chairs in the small circular garden known as the Audiorama while listening to recorded classical music. Open 9:00 A.M. to 5:00 P.M., Tuesday through Saturday, and 10:00 A.M. to 4:00 P.M. on Sundays.

Museo de Arte Moderno

Turning north and heading in the direction of Paseo de la Reforma, you'll soon see the unmistakable silhouette of the glass-faced Museum of Modern Art. The building itself is actually two low, circular buildings connected by a short corridor and surrounded by a fenced-off sculpture garden. The well-lit interior is dominated by a white marble staircase and an elegant glass dome. One section of the museum is devoted to contemporary art trends of the past two decades and includes photographs, engravings, and sculpture. Another area displays Mexican fine art from the late 19th century through the 1960s. On permanent display are the works of Diego Rivera and his wife, Frida Kahlo; Rivera's mentor, José María Velasco; and such celebrated contemporaries as Tamayo, Orozco, and Siqueiros. Open 10:00 A.M. to 6:00 P.M., daily except Mondays.

THE SECOND AND THIRD SECTIONS

The newer sections of the park, although not far as the crow flies, are difficult to get to on foot. Your best bet is to walk to Paseo de la Reforma and then take any bus marked "Reforma" or "Satelite" heading west. The last stop before the bus leaves the park will be Plaza Petroleos, where the imposing Fuente de Petroleos stands as a monument to President Cárdenas's nationalization of the oil industry in 1938.

Museo de Historia Natural de la Ciudad de México

If you'd like to do more exploring in the park get off here and follow the long paved path south to the Museo de Historia Natural de la Ciudad de México. After the inspired architecture of the museums in the older section of the park, this series of ten drab-appearing domes will come as a bit of a letdown. Inside, however, a modern design and effective lighting enhance the displays of dinosaur skeletons, as well as exhibits on the creation of the universe, the evolution of aquatic and terrestrial life, and an illustrated breakdown of Mexico's mineral wealth, flora, and fauna. Open 10:00 A.M. to 5:00 P.M., Tuesday through Saturday, and 10:00 A.M. to 6:00 P.M. on Sundays. Closed Mondays.

Other Attractions

Just outside the front entrance to the museum is another miniature railroad depot. Although the tracks crisscross the middle section of the park, you'll soon discover that everything of interest in this section is easily accessible on foot. To the southeast, on the other side of a small artificial lake, is the entrance to the **Parque de Juegos Mecánicos** (amusement park), with its awe-inspiring roller coaster known as "La Montaña Rusa" ("The Russian Mountain"), and the **Museo Nacional de Tecnológico de la Comisión Federal de Electricidad** (Federal Electrical Commission Technological Museum). Modern achievement in communications, transportation, and industry, and an explanation of the electromagnetic theory, are some of the subjects presented in dioramas in this roomy, contemporary museum. The museum's fine **planetarium** offers presentations at 11:00 A.M.,

1:00 P.M., and 4:00 P.M., Tuesday through Saturday. Regular hours on those days are 9:00 A.M. to 5:00 P.M. and on Sundays from 9:00 A.M. to 1:00 P.M. Closed Mondays.

Also in this section of the park is the **Lerma Terminal de Agua**, a large nondescript building that serves as an exhibition hall for a number of Diego Rivera murals depicting the importance of water. His best work here, though, is a mosaic at the bottom of the outdoor fountain in front of the terminal, with its dominating figure of Tlaloc, the rain god of the central highlands. On the same traffic circle as the fountain is **Lago Chapultepec**, a restaurant with panoramic views of the lake from every table, adequate food, and live dinner music. (See Dining, below.)

The paved paths to the west and south of the fountain will lead you to sights of interest having to do with water, that most precious of commodities in this often parched land. The **Fuente de Nezahualcoyotl** and the **Fuente de los Dioses** are long stone walls carved with bas-relief murals of Aztec gods and symbols submerged by cascading water. To the south of these fountains, the **Cárcamo**, or municipal waterworks, boasts a rare Rivera sculpture dedicated to Tlaloc.

Still farther south, Avenida Constituyentes is filled with a constant stream of taxis, both private and collective. If you'd like to visit the third, and least developed, section of the park, take a taxi about half a mile west to the Dolores Civilian Cemetery. From there, follow the road due north and you'll soon find yourself in the heart of this urban oasis. The path to the left leads to the **Dolphinarium** (open 10:00 A.M. to 6:00 P.M., daily except Mondays), the one to the right to the **stables** and equestrian areas. If you've had enough park exploring for the day and want to head back into town, cross Constituyentes and hail a taxi heading eastward; it's a five-minute ride to the Zona Rosa.

Polanco

The *colonia* (neighborhood) of Polanco stretches along the northern perimeter of the first section of Chapultepec Park (the section that includes the National Museum of Anthropology and the Rufino Tamayo Museum), and extends as far as Avenida Ejército Nacional to the north, Avenida Mariano Escobedo to the east, and Avenida Molière to the west.

Soon after the Conquest mulberry trees were imported from Spain and planted on what became the Hacienda de los Morales, the first silkworm farm in the Americas. Most of the area remained relatively undeveloped until after the Second World War, when a new generation of wealthy Mexicans began to carve up the empty fields for their mansions and estates. Many of the homes were built in the classic Art Nouveau "sand-castle" style, with carved stone trimmings proliferating around windows and façades. As was the case throughout the D.F., preparations for the 1968 Summer Olympic Games led to urban expansion and changed considerably the character of the four main east–west avenues in the neighborhood: Campos Elíseos, Presidente Masaryk, Horacio, and Homero.

Although it is still an exclusive residential district, the graciously opulent homes and colonial-style mansions here (which tend to be clustered on the tree-lined streets running north to south across the avenues) have been joined by sleek, modern high-rise office buildings and condominiums; fashionable hotels and restaurants; one of the capital's largest department stores; a variety of nightclubs; and, of all things, an authentic Jewish shopping district where the choicest fruits, vegetables, and kosher products are available (though at slightly higher prices than you'll find elsewhere in the city). The **Deportivo Chapultepec** (Chapultepec Sports Club), well known for its elegant tennis facilities and open to the public, is located in Polanco's northwest corner. The **Conservatorio Nacional de Musica** is about 1 km (½ mile) south and east on Avenida Presidente Masaryk.

On Avenida Campos Elíseos, next to the rear entrance of the Stouffer Presidente Chapultepec, the **Centro Cultural de Arte Contemporáneo** houses rotating exhibitions of 20th-century painting on its two lower floors. The upper two floors contain the **Centro Cultural de Arte Prehispanica**—more than 400 art objects dating from 1000 B.C. to A.D. 1521—and the **Centro Cultural de Arte Fotografía**, whose permanent collection spans the entire history of photography, including works by Henri Cartier-Bresson, Man Ray, Edward Weston, and other greats. Open 10:00 A.M. to 6:00 P.M., daily except Mondays, and until 9:00 P.M. on Wednesdays.

It's just a matter of time, though, before the above-mentioned Polanco attractions take a back seat to the burgeoning number of boutiques opened by the fashion world's leading couture houses—among them Christian Dior, Ungaro, Fendi, Cartier, and Nina Ricci. Generally speaking, prices at these huge Art Nouveau temples of fashion—most of which are located on the 300–400 blocks of Avenida Presidente Masaryk—run 15 to 40 percent lower than what you'd pay in the United States and Europe, with the quality and selection every bit as good.

HIPODROMO DE LAS AMERICAS

The Art Deco–style Hipódromo, Mexico City's only thoroughbred racetrack and one of the most charming racetracks anywhere, was built in 1943 after the Second World War shut down U.S. tracks, and was a hit right from the start. The track, located just north and west of Chapultepec Park, is unique in that it operates year-round (except for Easter Week and the last two weeks of the year), with the caliber of thoroughbreds on a par with all but the best tracks in the United States. Favorites win about 35 percent of the time. The track's oval is seven and a half furlongs, and the fountains and ponds of the beautifully landscaped infield are home to dozens of flamingos and swans. Pari-mutuel betting, state-of-the-art tote boards, and numerous TV monitors make the Hipódromo a very comfortable place to make your contribution to the betterment of the breed.

If you're going to spend an afternoon here, you might consider a table at one of the track's five first-class restaurants. At the elegant **Derby Club**, NP 25 (per person) will get you a table with a glassed-in bird's-eye view of the finish line. Another possibility is the equally elegant **Jockey Club** (men must wear ties). The real bargain here, though, are the plush sky boxes, which go for NP 100 and have room for up to 16 people; food and drink service is available, and each box has a color TV for monitoring the action. And, as in all the restaurant areas, betting windows are just a few feet away.

You can make reservations for any of these alternatives by phoning 557-4100; an English-speaking agent will handle your request. Tourists are permitted to enter the general admission section upon presentation of their tourist card and purchase of a program. There are 11 races a day on Tuesdays, Thursdays, and Sundays, and 12 each on Fridays and Saturdays; the track is closed Mondays and Wednesdays. Post time is 5:00 P.M. on Tuesdays, Thursdays, and Fridays, and 2:30 P.M. on Saturdays and Sundays.

A steady stream of collective taxis leaves from the metro's Tacuba station or passes westward along Paseo de la Reforma marked either "Hipódromo," "Legaria," "San Isidro," or "Defensa Nacional." Any of these will drop you near the main entrance. If you're driving, take the Periférico Norte and exit on Calzada Legaria. Turn left at the stop light; straight ahead is the massive Hipódromo parking lot. Taxis are always available during the last three races.

THE SOUTHERN DISTRICTS

There are a number of things to see and do along Insurgentes south of its intersection with Reforma. Down past the Polyforum Cultural Siqueiros and the Plaza México bullfight arena are two colonial neighborhoods to either side of the Monumento a Alvaro Obregón: Coyoacán to the east and San Angel to the west. Both neighborhoods, besides being good for walking, offer small museums, historical sites, cafés, and a glimpse of the good life, Mexico City style.

Farther south on Insurgentes is University City, with its powerful murals and architecture; the archaeological sites of Copilco and Cuicuilco; and Mexico City's version of Disneyland, Reino Aventura. Finally, beyond Reino Aventura to the southeast—but still accessible by public transportation—is the canal district of Xochimilco.

POLYFORUM CULTURAL SIQUEIROS

In 1965 Mexico's famed patron of the arts, Manuel Suárez, commissioned David Alfaro Siqueiros, the equally famous muralist, to create the world's largest indoor mural on a 50-acre tract he happened to own near the Plaza México bullfight ring, 4 km (2½ miles) south of the intersection of Insurgentes and Reforma on Insurgentes Sur.

Suárez was a self-made millionaire who had ridden with Pancho Villa during the Revolution, introduced the cement industry to Mexico, built the first highway from the capital to Acapulco (where he subsequently made a fortune from his real-estate holdings), and fathered 23 children. Siqueiros had been an officer in the Spanish Civil War and then had led a mob in an abortive attempt to assassinate Leon Trotsky in 1940. After spending a few years as a political prisoner in a Mexican jail for his outspoken criticism of the government, he received a presidential pardon in 1964 and agreed to take Suárez's commission with the understanding that he would have complete artistic freedom.

Siqueiros soon had drawn up plans for an elliptical 12-sided structure and went about painting it with the help of some two dozen apprentice-disciples. Suárez took exception to the participation of the assistants, however, as well as to the rather violent anti-capitalistic messages suggested by the design of the mural. The clash of their titanic egos eventually prompted Siqueiros to insist that the developer stay away from the work-in-progress. Suárez's response to this arrogant demand was to order the construction of a tower right next door—from which, upon its completion, he continued to spy on the artist at work below. Fortunately, Suárez allowed the work to continue, and in 1971, after six years of intensive labor, the Polyforum Cultural Siqueiros was inaugurated.

The 12 walls of the structure, each measuring some 820 square feet, are covered with huge, vividly painted human figures that seem to leap out with brutal vitality at passersby. (The sculptured iron fence surrounding the Polyforum also was designed by Siqueiros.) Inside, the mural entitled *The March of Humanity on Earth Toward the Cosmos* is said to be the largest in the world (Siqueiros painted this one entirely himself). The oval-shaped stage is, in actuality, a huge turntable on which more than 1,000 people can stand, inspecting Siqueiros's creation around and above them, as the platform slowly revolves 360 degrees (a full circle takes 15 minutes).

Downstairs is a multi-use theater, the outer corridor of which serves as a sort of museum for the display of native arts and crafts, while on the level below there is a branch of FONART (see Shops and Shopping, below) and a number of art galleries. The Polyforum is open 10:00 A.M. to 7:30 P.M. daily; a sound-and-light show in English is presented every evening at 6:30.

Hotel de México

Nearby, the 51-story Hotel de México—known to locals as "El Elefante Blanco"—stands as a monument to one man's ego and vanity. After a few months of spying on Siqueiros from his lofty vantage point, Suárez, who was none too anxious to become the laughingstock of the capital, decided to enlarge his tower, surely believing that nothing would be more fitting than to build the world's tallest hotel next door to the world's largest indoor mural. The result of this logic is a monstrous structure with more than 1,300 rooms that, until recently, seemed destined never to be occupied. Under construction for 24 years, it was finally sold by the Suárez estate in 1988 (Suárez himself died at the age of 95 in 1987) to a group of businessmen. It seems as though El Elefante Blanco is indeed cursed, however, and it continues to be known to some as the tallest eyesore south of Houston. Still, the top floor of the building, which has been functioning as a revolving restaurant for the past 23 years, affords terrific views of the city on a clear day (especially if your visit coincides with the monthly window washing). There is also a nondescript restaurant on the ground floor.

PLAZA MEXICO

Traditionally, one of the few public events to start on time in Mexico is the weekly presentation of the bullfights at the 60,000-seat Plaza México, located 2 km (1¼ mile) south of the Polyforum on Insurgentes Sur. Promptly at 4:30 P.M. every Sunday a lone horseman in medieval costume prances his steed across the ring and follows the ancient custom of requesting permission of the authorities to conduct a "running of the bulls."

The Plaza México, reputedly the world's largest bullring, has been the principal bullring in the capital since 1946. During the dry season (November through May) the best matadors in the country appear here; the rainy season, on the other hand, is the time for *novilleros* (amateurs) to fight younger, smaller bulls, and for spectators to take their chances with the weather as well as the caliber of the artistry.

A good way to attend the bullfights, especially on Sunday, when it's always difficult to get a taxi in the D.F., is on a tour conducted by an English-speaking guide. The standard Sunday tour includes a morning performance at Bellas Artes by the Ballet Folklórico, followed by a gondola ride in Xochimilco, lunch, and then the bullfights in the afternoon. (If you're on your own, have lunch at **Las Cazuelas**, two short blocks east of Plaza México; see Dining, below.) All travel agencies and most hotels can make arrangements for you. The fee includes transportation and a reserved seat on the shady side of the ring, which should keep you out of harm's way of beer showers generated by disgruntled fans, most of whom seem to prefer the sunny side. If you decide to go on your own, purchase tickets in advance at any local travel agency. By metro, take the number 7 line to the San Antonio station, two blocks west of the plaza.

Coyoacán

The Monumento a Alvaro Obregón is about 4 km (2½ miles) south of the Plaza México on Insurgentes Sur. To the right as you head south is the San Angel area; to the left, or east, is the Coyoacán area. First, Coyoacán.

The quickest and least expensive way to get here from the Zócalo area is by metro; take the number 3 line from the Zócalo's Pino Suárez station to the Miguel Angel de Quevedo station, one stop south of the Coyoacán terminal. As you exit you can turn west on Avenida M.A. Quevedo and walk 15 minutes to the **Monumento a Alvaro Obregón**, which marks the site of Obregón's assassination in 1928. The appeal of this monument has been diluted somewhat now that its main attraction—Obregón's severed hand and wrist, amputated following a battle during the Revolution and pickled in a glass container—has been removed. If you choose to bypass the monument, head north on Avenida Universidad upon leaving the metro and then take the first right onto Avenida Francisco Sosa for the most scenic entrance to Coyoacán.

The tiny 18th-century Baroque-style church on the north corner of Universidad and Francisco Sosa, the **Capilla de San Antonio Panzacola**, looks entirely out of place among the modern structures lining both sides of Universidad. But then the scenery begins to change: As narrow, cobblestoned Francisco Sosa heads toward Coyoacán center, the architectural creations of the 20th century give way to moss-stained stone walls hiding low-slung colonial mansions from prying eyes. Over the entrances to most of these mansions you'll find the centuries-old coats-of-arms of their former aristocratic residents. Coyoacán has always attracted the elite of Mexican society.

The settlement of Coyoacán can be traced back to the ninth century, when Toltecs moved into the area. They were followed, in turn, by Chichimecs in the 12th century and Aztecs in the 14th (the Aztecs built their vacation homes here). Later, Cortés established Coyoacán as the provisional capital of New Spain while the ruined Tenochtitlán was being rebuilt as the Mexico City of the Zócalo area. Today it is a mellow, unspoiled oasis filled with colonial buildings and peaceful gardens. At times it seems as if an ocean separates the serene ambience of Coyoacán from the intensity of the urban sprawl surrounding it.

After some distance cramped Avenida Francisco Sosa suddenly opens up onto the large and attractive **Plaza Central**, which consists of the Jardín Centenario and Plaza Hidalgo. The largest building on the plaza is the so-called **Delegación Coyoacán**, which houses the offices of this quaint municipality. Constructed in 1522, the building originally served as Cortés's first residence, from which he governed the colony until his palace (an earlier version of today's Palacio Nacional) was completed. His coat-of-arms can still be seen embedded in the façade. The 16th-century **Templo de San Juan Bautista** overlooks the plaza, its plain, fortresslike exterior providing no indication of just how lavish and ornate the reconstructed interior is.

Museo Frida Kahlo

From Plaza Hidalgo walk north for half a mile along either Aguaya or Centenario and then turn right on Calle Londres. The Museo Frida Kahlo, Londres 127, is located in the house where the eminent painter was born in 1907 and later lived with her husband, Diego Rivera. The house became a popular gathering place for artists, writers, poets, and intellectuals in the 1930s and 1940s: Among its more illustrious guests at one time or another were Leon Trotsky and D. H. Lawrence. Neither its lively history nor its bright blue exterior prepare the visitor for the ethereal and sometimes macabre self-portraits by Kahlo displayed within, however. Kahlo, who was afflicted by polio as a young girl and later was involved in a serious trolley-car accident, lived much of her life in pain—a fact that is clearly reflected in her art. A number of Rivera's drawings and mementoes of their life together are also on exhibit. Open 10:00 A.M. to 2:00 P.M. and 3:00 to 5:00 P.M., daily except Mondays.

Museo León Trotsky

Two blocks north and two and a half blocks east of the Kahlo museum, at Calle Vienna 45, the Museo León Trotsky is where the great revolutionary lived in exile and was eventually murdered by an assassin in the employ of his archrival, Joseph Stalin. Here, first impressions do tell the whole story, with the house resembling nothing so much as a fortress. The high bare walls are broken only by an equally tall and stark steel door; even the doorbell is hard to find. (It's to the left of the entrance, obscured by ivy.) Keep ringing. Once inside the compound you feel surrounded by a melancholy gloom that hangs heavily over the weed-choked garden and the small moss-covered monument to Trotsky designed by his friend Juan O'Gorman (Trotsky's ashes are interred within along with his wife's, who died in Paris in 1962).

Inside, the rooms have been left much as they were at the time of the assassination. Dozens of large bullet holes—courtesy of a prior attempt on his life allegedly led by the painter David Alfaro Siqueiros—pockmark the walls of Trotsky's bedroom. On August 20, 1940, Jaime Ramón Mercader del Río, an agent of Stalin's posing as the boyfriend of Trotsky's secretary, appeared at the door with a request that Trotsky read a paper of his. Granted admission to Trotsky's study, he then proceeded to smash the founder of the Red Army across the skull with the blunt end of an alpine ice pick he had concealed under his coat. Trotsky's shattered eyeglasses still lie on his desk where they fell. Open 10:00 A.M. to 5:00 P.M., daily except Mondays.

Museo Nacional de las Intervenciones

To get to the Museum of Foreign Interventions, head south on Calle Morelos for three blocks, turn left (east) on

Xicoténcatl, and continue in the same direction across División del Norte until you come to the museum, which is housed in the former convent of Churubusco on the corner of Calle Vicente de Agosto. The Franciscans were responsible for building the original structure on this site in the years immediately following the Conquest, and it later became the base for their missionary activities in China, Japan, and the Philippines. It was renovated in 1768, and 79 years later became the scene of the so-called Battle of Churubusco, where badly outnumbered Mexican troops were overwhelmed by the U.S. army as it closed in on Mexico City.

Today the museum houses eight exhibition rooms filled with the memorabilia of Mexico's anti-colonialist wars, including captured weapons, blood-stained uniforms, documents, photographs, drawings, and a tattered 1847 version of the "Stars and Stripes" captured by Mexican troops. The emphasis throughout is on the bravery of the Mexican soldier rather than the villany of the various aggressors. One of the rooms has a 19th-century carriage that belonged to General (later President) Santa Anna, who led the attack on the Alamo. There is also a lovely garden inside the walls of the former convent with a monument to the fallen defenders of the Battle of Churubusco. Open 9:00 A.M. to 6:00 P.M., daily except Mondays.

Museo Anahuacalli

Back on División del Norte there are usually plenty of cruising taxis. To complete your tour of the Coyoacán area, flag one heading south and have it drop you off in front of the Museo Anahuacalli (now officially called the Museo Diego Rivera), the towering pyramid-shaped structure on Calle Museo, about 2 km (1¼ miles) south of the Museum of Foreign Interventions. (This is a bit off the beaten path; either have your taxi wait for you—a half hour on the meter will cost about NP 12—or backtrack to División del Norte to catch a taxi for the 20-minute ride back to the hotel zone or Zócalo after your tour of the museum.)

Taking its name from the Aztec word for the Valley of Mexico, the Museo Anahuacalli was designed by Diego Rivera and built out of *tezontle*. Much of its ornamentation is derivative of Toltec and Mayan designs, and the overall effect is at once impressive and appropriate. The museum is filled with well-preserved artifacts—many dating back to the Preclassic period—from Rivera's own collection. For the most part these artifacts fall into three broad categories coinciding with the three most important cultures to arise from the Valley of Mexico: Teotihuacano, Toltec, and Aztec.

The largest room in the museum, on the second floor, served as one of Rivera's studios toward the end of his life and is preserved just as it was at the time of his death. On one long wall there is even an unfinished mural with the likenesses of Stalin and Mao Tse-tung charcoaled in. The museum is not without its controversy, however. Serious rumors persist about an anonymous craftsman who churned out excellent replicas of ancient Mesoamerican artifacts for the actress Dolores del Rio, a close friend of Rivera's, and who was later introduced to the great muralist himself. (The extensive collection of vaguely pornographic artifacts is particularly suspect.) Nevertheless, the museum is well worth a visit, if only to appreciate Rivera's achievement as the architect of the building. The artist died before he could realize his vision of designing a cultural complex. The upstairs terrace of the museum affords a view of the staked-out plan for the structures that were never built. High weeds engulf the whole area, which resembles a barely excavated archaeological site after 35 years of neglect. Open 10:00 A.M. to 2:00 P.M. and 3:00 to 6:00 P.M., daily except Mondays.

San Angel

This beautiful neighborhood just west of the Monumento a Alvaro Obregón was known in pre-colonial days by the Indian name Tenanitla, meaning "at the foot of the stone wall"—an allusion to the vast lava field to the south now known as El Pedregal (discussed below). Later, Spanish aristocrats built their gracious walled mansions here, and the area experienced its glory days in the 17th and 18th centuries. After Mexico gained its independence in 1821, San Angel continued to be popular, especially with writers and artists, who spent their leisure time in country residences here. Today, despite having been engulfed by the rapidly expanding D.F., San Angel retains much of its small-town charm and character.

Museo Colonial del Carmen

Taxis aside, the easiest way to get from Coyoacán to San Angel is to take the number 56 or 116A bus, both of which can be boarded at the prominently marked *parada* (bus stop) just west of the Plaza Hidalgo on Avenida Hidalgo. The buses make the trip in less than 15 minutes, stopping right in front of the Exconvento del Carmen, which houses a small museum and an adjacent church. Located on the east side of Avenida Revolución, just north and east of the Plaza de San Jacinto (the site of the Bazar Sábado; see below), the structure, which was built between 1615 and 1628, is a fine example of the ecclesiastical architecture of the period. Inside the main entrance is a beautiful garden graced by a lovely tile fountain and a number of ancient fig trees planted by the convent's founding friars and nuns.

The frescoes in the museum are in various stages of disintegration. In a number of instances the topmost layer of paint has faded to reveal a totally different mural below it and yet a third below that, with probably a century elapsed between the first application of paint and the last. The basement crypt is the most popular attraction here, however. If you've seen Guanajuato's mummies and were favorably impressed, then you're in for a treat. If not, view at your own risk the horrified expressions on the mummified skulls of the 18th-century monks and nuns who were victims of a severe earthquake. The small room in which they had congregated was hermetically sealed by the violent upheaval, and more than a century later their well-preserved remains were discovered by a workman. The adjoining church also has some excellent 18th-century religious paintings by the Spaniard Cristóbal de Villalpando. Open 10:00 A.M. to 5:00 P.M., daily except Mondays.

Museo Carillo Gil

A few blocks north of the Museo Colonial del Carmen, on the same (east) side of Avenida Revolución at number 1608, is the sleek, modern **Museo de Arte Alvar y Carmen T. de Carrillo Gil**, named for the Yucatecan doctor, and his wife, who befriended Orozco, Siqueiros, and Rivera. The museum houses an outstanding collection of the artists' earlier murals and mounts exhibitions of the work of some of their foreign counterparts, including the likes of Picasso, Rodin, and Klee. The Gil Museum has earned a reputation for consistently exhibiting only the finest art. Open 10:00 A.M. to 6:00 P.M., daily except Mondays.

PLAZA DE SAN JACINTO

From the museum head south on Avenida Revolución back to the Museo Colonial del Carmen and then climb the short hill to the Plaza de San Jacinto. Mounted on a wall on the western side of the plaza is a plaque that reads: "In memory of the Irish soldiers of the heroic Battalion of Saint Patrick, martyrs who gave their lives for the cause of Mexico during the unjust North American invasion of 1847." The San Patricio Battalion was made up of deserters, most of them Irish-Catholic immigrants, from General Winfield Scott's army. Brutalized by the harsh treatment dispensed by their officers and lured by

Mexican promises of citizenship and free land, they switched sides and fought against their former comrades-in-arms at the Battle of Churubusco. Eventually, superior discipline and firepower resulted in victory for Scott's troops, and the 71 members of the battalion were summarily tried and hanged in the plaza. Today, besides being a delightful public space, the plaza is the site of a very busy open-air art show every Saturday.

Bazar Sábado

In the northwest corner of the plaza, an artisans' cooperative known as the Saturday Bazaar takes up two floors of an 18th-century mansion. Here you'll find dozens of small shops arranged around an oval-shaped patio offering every kind of handcrafted item imaginable. Many of the artists are immigrants from Europe and the United States who have been drawn to Mexico by the richness of its folkloric heritage. The bazaar is open 10:00 A.M. to 8:00 P.M. every Saturday, and visitors can partake of an excellent afternoon buffet in the patio featuring traditional Mexican cuisine for non-Mexican palates (i.e., not too spicy). A marimba band in the native costumes of Chiapas adds just the right touch to this lively scene.

Outside the entrance to the bazaar you'll encounter Indian women squatting on the sidewalk selling their handicrafts at about half the cost of what you would pay inside. They expect—and look forward to—haggling over prices; the prices inside are fixed. (See also Shops and Shopping, below.)

Museo Estudio Diego Rivera

From the intersection of Avenida Revolución and Calle Altavista, just north of the plaza, it's a ten-minute walk (seven blocks) up the latter to the Diego Rivera Studio Museum (entrance on Calle Palmas). Designed by architect-muralist and longtime Rivera friend Juan O'Gorman in 1933, the artist's studio was opened to the public as a museum in 1986, on the 100th anniversary of Rivera's birth. This rather bizarre studio-on-stilts, which actually consists of two studios—Rivera's blue one was connected to his wife Frida Kahlo's crimson-colored one by an overhead bridge—sticks out like the proverbial sore thumb in this neighborhood of discreet colonial mansions, and has been the cause of more than a few arguments. The continually changing exhibitions of the master's works, on the other hand, are almost always greeted with enthusiasm. Open 10:00 A.M. to 6:00 P.M., daily except Mondays.

San Angel Inn

Diagonally across the street is the landmark 18th-century hacienda that for years has been one of the capital's most elegant restaurants. It was perhaps inevitable, given its outstanding architectural elements and colorful history (the San Angel served as headquarters for General Antonio López de Santa Anna during Mexico's war with the United States and was used for the same purpose by Emiliano Zapata and Pancho Villa 64 years later), that the inn would become a stop for tour buses. As a result, the quality of the food and service has dropped considerably. Still, a stroll through its grounds will give you a little taste of what hacienda life must have been like for the privileged few who enjoyed it during the long centuries of Mexico's colonial domination. (The management of the inn frowns upon blue jeans and sneakers; if you plan on stopping here, wear something a little less casual.) Open 1:00 P.M. to 1:00 A.M. daily; Tel: 548-6746.

There is a taxi stand right outside the entrance to the inn. Taxis also cruise Avenida Revolución.

Copilco

The Preclassic archaeological site of Copilco is located about 1 km (½ mile) south of the Insurgentes Sur turnoff for the Plaza de San Jacinto, just north of University City. A sea of petrified lava, its frozen flow black and lavender, is the graveyard of the ancient Copilco culture, which was buried by a catastrophic eruption of nearby Xitle (Little Smoking Mountain) sometime around the beginning of the Christian era. Ten feet below the lava, excavations here in 1917 uncovered several tombs, pottery, clay figurines, and stone implements dating back as far as 1200 B.C. Today three tunnels created by the original excavations have been converted into a museum, and several of the tombs are displayed in the same position and condition in which they were found, complete with the ceramic, stone, and bone objects found with them.

The site is open 9:00 A.M. to 5:00 P.M., daily except Mondays. The trip on the number 3 metro line from the Zócalo area (get off at the Copilco stop) is 20 minutes, quicker than most taxis. If you prefer to drive, take the "Copilco" exit off Avenida Insurgentes Sur (about 2 km/1¼ mile south of the Monumento a Alvaro Obregón) and turn left onto Avenida Copilco. Turn left again almost immediately and follow the signs. The entrance to the site is at Calle Victoria 54.

Ciudad Universitaria

Four decades ago, after 20 centuries of abandonment, the same lava-strewn moonscape that supports Copilco was transformed into a marvel of architecture, artistry, and urban planning. Today it is the setting for one of the largest and most modern universities in the world.

The Universidad Nacional Autónoma de México (UNAM) is also the oldest university in the New World, dating back to a September 21, 1551, edict of King Phillip II of Spain. Officially opened in 1553, it became a unified entity in name only as its facilities were soon scattered throughout the ever-expanding city. Miguel Aleman, one of Mexico's most productive presidents (1946–1952), instigated a concerted national project in which every building was planned to complement the whole, setting a local precedent for organization and teamwork. Ten thousand laborers worked under the direction of 150 architects and engineers, and in 1954 University City was inaugurated. Today more than 300,000 students are taught by 18,000 professors, who in turn are assisted by 2,000 researchers.

One of the most impressive cultural complexes anywhere in the world, its five square miles contain 80 university buildings; the acoustically innovative, ultramodern **Sala Nezahualcóyotl Concert Hall**; and the Estadio Olímpico, a 100,000-seat stadium inaugurated in time for the 1968 Olympic Games and site of the 1986 World Cup Soccer final. In traditional Mexican fashion, no decent-size wall has gone unpainted, and the work of every great 20th-century Mexican muralist painter can be found somewhere on campus.

With such an overwhelming amount of color and form commanding your attention, the ten-story **Central Library**, built in the shape of a rectangular prism, is the structure that catches the eye before all others. Juan O'Gorman utilized a combination of stone, colored cement, tile, and blown glass to create this startlingly dramatic architectural masterpiece.

Southwest of the library is the low-slung administration building called **La Torre de la Rectoria** (rectory). The wall facing Avenida Insurgentes is covered by a boldly executed three-dimensional mural by David Alfaro Siqueiros, combining painting and high-relief sculpture and creating a perspective-in-motion when viewed from a moving vehicle.

The **Estadio Olímpico**, built to resemble the crater of a volcano, serves as Diego Rivera's canvas: striking reliefs evoke the spirit of athletic competition from pre-Hispanic times to the present.

Other significant murals to look for around campus are those by Francisco Eppens, José Chávez Morado, Matías Goeritz, and Federico Silva. A mass of volcanic rock next to the Sala Nezahualcóyotl features sculptural forms carved out of the frozen lava by Ignacio Asunsolo, Manuel Felguerez, and Helen Escobedo.

To get to University City take the number 3 metro line to the "Universidad" stop. By bus, walk to Insurgentes Sur and take either the 17, 17A, or 17B bus; from Coyoacán take the number 19A bus west on Calle Centenario. A university-run bus swings by the city bus stop to pick up passengers interested in making a circuit of the campus, with stops at all the major buildings. Service daily, including weekends.

El Pedregal

To the west and south of the stadium, extending over an area bounded by Avenida Universidad, Boulevard de la Luz, the Periférico, and Calle Zacatépetl, you'll find the exclusive residential neighborhood of El Pedregal ("the field of stone"), where some of the finest examples of contemporary Mexican residential architecture hide behind an encircling wall. While the ancient lava field itself spreads to the east and south under University City and Coyoacán, it is here in El Pedregal where it is most noticeable. Formed almost 2,000 years ago when nearby Xitle erupted with tremendous force and devastating consequences, the area was a stark and almost surrealistic moonscape. About 40 years ago the architect Luis Barragán began to encourage wealthy clients to purchase land here and then built them innovative, elegant residences that were adapted to the irregular and dramatic terrain. Other architects began to follow Barragán's lead, and in time the neighborhood became one of the most desirable addresses in the city. Today the overall effect is stunning: El Pedregal can hold its own with the world's most exclusive neighborhoods.

The best way to see El Pedregal is by taxi. If you're going to drive, head south on Insurgentes Sur to Avenida Universidad, just before the stadium. Follow Universidad until you come to Paseo del Pedregal, then take a left. Courteous guards at the entrance to this walled-in community will screen visitors briefly—usually no more than a glance into the car—and then wave you in. A leisurely tour of the neighborhood takes about 15 minutes.

Cuicuilco

The earliest evidence of true civilization in the Valley of Mexico was uncovered at the archaeological site of Cuicuilco, just southeast of El Pedregal, during the construction of dormitories to house athletes participating in the 1968 Olympic Games. To everyone's surprise, under the almost ten feet of lava that had engulfed much of the surrounding area construction workers discovered a circular temple base that, when it was finally uncovered, proved to be almost 60 feet high and 41 feet in diameter. Further excavation and study revealed evidence of irrigation canals at the site and established that work on the platform had begun as early as 500 B.C., predating the first civic structures at Teotihuacán (see below) by some 300 years. The artifacts found here suggested that the inhabitants of Cuicuilco had combined farming with subsistence activities such as hunting and fishing, and had abandoned the site in the first century B.C., just prior to the last volcanic eruptions. Everything else about these early inhabitants of the valley remains shrouded by the mists of time. The small **Museo de Sitio y Zona Arqueológica de Cuicuilco** exhibits samples of the pottery uncovered here, as well as a map detailing all the Preclassic sites that have been discovered in Mexico to date. Open 9:00 A.M. to 4:00 P.M., daily except Mondays.

Cuicuilco can be reached by following Insurgentes Sur south (follow the "Cuernavaca" signs) to the "Villa Olímpica" exit; make a U-turn back on to Insurgentes and head north. The site is enclosed by a green wrought-iron fence; the temple base is a short hike down a winding gravel path.

Reino Aventura

Reino Aventura, a recently renovated 100-acre amusement park on the southern edge of the city, is Mexico's answer to Disneyland. Reopened on July 4, 1992, it is now an ecological and cultural theme park that compares favorably with its U.S. and European counterparts.

State-of-the-art innovations include robots that serve refreshments and a most creative computerized maintenance plan. There are 23 rides in all; four water shows a day featuring trained dolphins and Keiko the killer whale; and five ethnic villages (Mexican, Swiss, French, Polynesian, and African).

The park's official address is Carretera Picacho-Ajusco km 1.5. Located about 26 km (16 miles) south of the Zona Rosa, it is easily accessible via the Periférico Sur. If you're driving, turn right just before the Cuicuilco archaeological site; the park is set in a wooded area another 1½ km (¾ miles) down the road. The 30-minute taxi ride costs about $15. Open Thursdays and Fridays from 10:00 A.M. to 6:00 P.M. and Saturdays and Sundays from 10:00 A.M. to 8:00 P.M. The $16 admission fee covers rides and performances.

XOCHIMILCO

The perfect way to experience both grass-roots Mexico and the feeling of Aztec Mexico, when Tenochtitlán was spread out over islands connected by a network of canals, is to treat yourself to a Sunday afternoon gondola ride in Xochimilco (so-che-MEEL-ko), on the southern outskirts of the city.

Migrant Toltecs took refuge here after the fall of Tula, about 900 years ago. These Toltecs, renowned for their craftsmanship in stone, continued to speak their own dialect even after their settlement came under the domination of a Nahuatl-speaking Chichimec tribe known as the Xochimilcas in the 13th century.

In time, the Xochimilcas intermarried with the Toltecs, and together they devised a system of cultivation that established Xochimilco as the main source of produce for the Valley of Mexico (hence the Nahuatl name "Xochimilco," meaning "the sowing place of plant life"). Planting their crops on *chinampas,* small mud-covered nursery beds anchored to the bottom of Lake Texcoco (which here was fresh water) by interwoven reeds, the Xochimilcas exploited the valley's temperate climate, the fertilizing effect of the lake mud, and the abundant supply of water to produce up to seven crops a year.

Faced with a growing population in their capital, Tenochtitlán, 20 miles to the north, the nascent Aztecs initiated hostilities against the Xochimilcas in the mid-14th century and, after decades of resistance, finally achieved control of the area's agricultural output early in the 15th century. Almost immediately the Aztecs increased the number of *chinampas* and established a water route from Xochimilco to the market and sacred precinct at the heart of Tenochtitlán (today's Zócalo). Ironically, in light of the water shortages that now bedevil the D.F., the horse-loving Spanish had little use for a water-based transportation system, and within a century and a half of the Conquest had drained and filled most of the erstwhile Tenochtitlán's canals.

The Canals

Today only five canals from the once-great Aztec city remain—all of them in Xochimilco—and the traffic on them is so heavy (especially on weekends) that at times they resemble nothing so much as bumper-car rides. But don't let that discourage you. Even though the waters are as murky as those in Venice, there are no unpleasant aromas emanating from them. Rather, the soft afternoon breezes—scrubbed free of the capital's notorious smog by prevailing winds—carry the aromas of freshly rolled tortillas, tacos, and a dozen other delicacies sold by Indian women out of their crude flat-bottomed canoes. Elsewhere, gondolas filled with mariachi or marimba bands glide by, auditioning for a chance to serenade you for a small fee as you glide along the waterways.

A standard-size gondola, with room for eight, costs the same regardless of the number of people in your party. Each *remero* (licensed gondolier, of which there are more than 300 in Xochimilco) provides a cooler filled with beer and soft drinks (you have to supply your own wine or Champagne). At the conclusion of the ride you pay the *remero* for his time as well as the beverages consumed—and, of course, you should tip him. A few hours and a few beers cost the equivalent of about $25. You can also rub shoulders with the locals on one of the larger gondolas, which hold about 50 people. An hour's cruise on one of these costs NP 3 (the official government-set rate), and they're not tourist traps; in fact, on weekends, nine out of ten of the larger gondolas are filled with Mexican families out for a picnic or lovers sharing a bottle of wine.

For those who prefer to cruise the canals in relative solitude, the gondolas at Xochimilco are for hire every day of the week, at all hours. Still, it is well worth investigating the Sunday tours, which are offered by all the major travel agencies and many of the city's hotels. These tours usually include a morning performance of the Ballet Folklórico at Bellas Artes; a few hours in Xochimilco, with lunch and a gondola ride included; and either an afternoon bullfight at the Plaza México or a tour of the murals at University City.

The Market and Zócalo

Xochimilco has more than its gondola rides to recommend it, however. The public market here is always bustling with activity, and the fruits, vegetables, and flowers for sale are probably the freshest and cheapest in all of Mexico. In fact, most of the produce and flowers for sale in the hundreds of markets throughout the capital are grown right here, as they have been since pre-Hispanic times, when they were transported by boat along the canals and later the Acequia Real (Royal Canal) to the Zócalo area. (You can still see a portion of the Acequia Real at the southeastern corner of the Zócalo, between the National Palace and the Supreme Court; see the Zócalo section, above.)

Xochimilco's zócalo is one of the most charming in the entire country, its delicate *huexote* trees providing a lovely contrast to the more conventional species planted throughout the square. The 16th-century **Parroquia** (parish church) **San Bernardino**, with its fortresslike appearance and an elaborate altar canopy inside, is well worth a visit, as is the **Escuela de Bellas Artes de Xochimilco**, in the Barrio de la Concha at Avenida Constitución 600, with its murals by Manuel Tolsá (*Apotheosis*) and Acevedo Navarro (*Romantic Muses*).

Museo Arqueológico de Xochimilco

A cab ride of a few minutes will take you to the village of Santa Cruz Acalpixan and the Xochimilco archaeological museum, which is built into the side of an ancient pyramid at Avenida Tenochtitlán 17. (You'll recognize it by the white wall enclosing a large garden.) Inside, a fine collection comprising an estimated 800 pre-Conquest artifacts are on permanent display. Another permanent exhibit features prehistoric fossils. Open 10:00 A.M. to 5:00 P.M., daily except Mondays.

DINING IN XOCHIMILCO

Los Manantiales, an immense restaurant—it has seating for 1,000 diners—with an outrageously ugly exterior but surprisingly good international-style food, is a few minutes' walk from the gondola docks over a short bridge. It caters to tourists, which simply means that the hygienic standards here are superior to those maintained at the many food stands and smaller restaurants scattered around town. (In general, the food in Xochimilco is highly regarded by the locals.)

Xochimilco is easily accessible via the metro. Take the number 2 line to the Tasqueña stop, locate Gate J, and board the number 140 bus, which will drop you in the heart of the Xochimilco market after a 30-minute ride. Or you can take one of the *peseros* marked "Embarcaderos" lined up outside the Tasqueña station at Platform L and be at the gondola docks in 20 minutes. A regular taxi from the downtown area takes approximately 40 minutes and costs the equivalent of $20.

TEOTIHUACAN

If you were limited to visiting only one archaeological site in Mexico, Teotihuacán (tay-oh-tee-whah-KAHN) would not be a bad choice. Situated about 50 km (31 miles) northeast of downtown Mexico City, Teotihuacán was once the religious and commercial center of a great highland civilization (also known to us as Teotihuacán) that predated the Toltecs by 1,000 years and the Aztec empire by almost 1,500 years. In fact, the Classic period of Mesoamerican civilization in Mexico's central highlands was dominated by Teotihuacán, whose influence was felt as far away as Oaxaca, the Yucatán Peninsula (the Classic Mayan civilization there was roughly its contemporary), highland Guatemala, and, to the northwest, Zacatecas. And yet, even as late as the early years of our own century all this had yet to be discovered and Teotihuacán was considered merely a local culture roughly contemporaneous with the Aztecs.

Today the evidence indicates that Teotihuacán developed from villages that made their initial appearance in the Valley of Mexico sometime around the middle of the first millennium B.C. By 300 B.C. a small township had been established on the site, and for the next 800 years Teotihuacán flourished, reaching an estimated population of 150,000 by A.D. 600, making it perhaps the world's first true urban center. Then, for reasons still unknown, the city was abandoned during the eighth century. For years the most popular theory concerning the demise of Teotihuacán held that it had fallen to marauding northern tribes, but a more recent theory maintains that its demise was probably the result of what today would be called poor resource management; in other words, it simply outgrew its available resources.

"Teotihuacán" (in the Nahuatl language, "the place where men became gods") was the name the Aztecs gave the ruined city more than five centuries after it was abandoned. By then most of the ceremonial structures—thought to have been brightly painted—had been buried under a thick layer of dirt and debris. The Aztecs believed that the mounds of earth lining the main avenue at the site were actually the tombs of the deceased giants responsible for building the city in the first place, and named this central axis the *Miccaotli,* or Street of the Dead. (The Aztecs also helped themselves to the art treasures left behind by the Teotihuacanos—many of which are among the objects being uncovered in the ongoing excavation of the Templo Mayor site in the heart of downtown Mexico City.)

To date only an estimated one-tenth of this ancient city has been uncovered—a remarkably low percentage when you consider that several hundred murals, more than 2,000 residential complexes, 80 temples, and more than 700 workshops have already been discovered. (There are several "archaeological" Teotihuacáns, numbered I to IV, with the most recent dating to A.D. 650 and lasting less than a hundred years.)

As was the case elsewhere in Mesoamerica, the pyramids of Teotihuacán originally were built as platforms for ceremonial temples. However, no tombs have yet been linked to these structures—which distinguishes Teotihuacán from Palenque and Monte Albán. In fact, Teotihuacán is unique, as far as ancient Mesoamerican ceremonial sites go, in that the murals uncovered to date do not contain the slightest hint of thematic violence. Instead, the religious symbolism of the artwork found at Teotihuacán revolves around the stars, the rain god Tlaloc, and the benign plumed serpent-god, Quetzalcóatl.

VISITING TEOTIHUACAN

A good starting point for your visit to Teotihuacán is the **Unidad Cultural**, a small complex at the southernmost entrance to the site (opposite the Ciudadela and Temple of Quetzalcóatl) that contains shops, rest rooms, a second-floor restaurant, and a good museum offering concise overviews of what is to follow. You might consider having lunch before you begin, as restaurants in the area are few and scattered. **La Pirámide**, located on the second floor of the Unidad Cultural, offers adequate, moderately priced Mexican and international-style cuisine. If you're looking for better fare, with prices to match, the best can be found at the nearby **Villa Arqueológica** (follow the signs on the access road ringing the site), one of a chain of fine Club Med–operated hotels at Mexican archaeological sites. In addition to its fine food, the Villa Arqueológica has an excellent archaeological library with books in several languages, tennis courts, and a swimming pool. (The other advantage of the place, should you decide to stay there, is that you can start your exploration of Teotihuacán early in the morning, before the tour buses from the capital arrive. See the Accommodations section for Mexico City, below.)

Pirámide Charlie's, a branch of the popular Carlos 'n' Charlie's chain, is a five- to ten-minute walk north of the Villa Arqueológica. For a more romantic setting try **La Gruta**, a restaurant built inside a massive natural cave. To get there, walk to the Pyramid of the Sun, turn east and walk through Parking Lot D to the access road, then turn left. Signs for the restaurant soon appear on the right-hand side of the road.

Both the food (Mexican geared to tourist tastes) and music, which is enhanced by the cave's great acoustics, contribute to the charm of the place. Open 11:00 A.M. to 6:00 P.M. daily.

The most typically Mexican restaurant in the area, **El Gran Teocalli**, is located about 2 km (1¼ mile) from the Unidad Cultural in the village of San Juan Teotihuacán (follow the signs to the "México Libre" highway). Chicken enchiladas are the specialty here, and they live up to their reputation. The marimba music in the background is also good. For real grass-roots cuisine (tacos, tortas, and the like) there are numerous food stands—some of them quite charming—set up across from the southernmost entrance to the site.

Museo Unidad Cultural

With lunch out of the way, begin your tour at the Unidad Cultural museum. In the vestibule stands a full-size copy of the colossal statue of Chalchiuhtlicue, the goddess of rivers and lakes, the original of which, now on display in the National Museum of Anthropology, was unearthed near the Pyramid of the Moon. While you're here, look especially for the ornately decorated stone death-mask inlaid with jade, garnets, and other gemstones—one of the finest examples of Mesoamerican art ever uncovered.

Outside the entrance to the museum is the beginning of the mile-long **Calle de los Muertos** (Street of the Dead), a kind of Via Sacra that serves as the axis around which the site was planned. The reasons behind its almost exact north–south orientation (it's actually aligned 15°30′ east of true north) are still debated, though it's generally agreed they had to do with astronomical alignments (including the rising of the Pleiades on the days of equinox).

The Ciudadela

Directly opposite the Unidad Cultural is the Citadel, one of the most interesting architectural groupings at Teotihuacán. This immense quadrangular complex is bounded by four platforms (three of which have two stories) surmounted by smaller temple platforms. Entrance to the complex is via a broad staircase, which leads down to a sunken patio. It was quite common in Mesoamerican cultures for already existing structures to be covered over and built upon rather than demolished. In the case of the Citadel, excavation revealed that its main pyramid had been erected over an older (c. A.D. 200), more impressive structure, the **Templo de Quetzalcóatl**, now partially revealed at the rear of the complex. To reach the temple, walk across the patio to the squat temple platform with a staircase. On the far side of the platform you'll come upon the façade of this masterpiece of the early Classic period, with its sculpted stone heads of the feathered serpent-god, Quetzalcóatl, and the even more stylized figure of the rain god, Tlaloc.

Pirámide del Sol

From the Citadel proceed up the Street of the Dead to the massive Pyramid of the Sun, which, together with the Pyramid of the Moon, dominates the site. Believed to have been constructed during the first century B.C., the pyramid has a base only ten feet shorter on each side than the Pyramid of Cheops but is less than half as tall. Nevertheless, it is the largest pre-Columbian structure in the New World to survive relatively intact (the great pyramid in Cholula being larger but in ruins).

The pyramid itself consists of five superimposed platforms and is ascended by a double staircase that merges to form a single staircase two-thirds of the way up. Although the climb to the summit is a strenuous one, the view once you get there is breathtaking—if you have any breath left. Spread out below with a startling geometric exactness is all that remains of this more than 2,000-year-old city. Unfortunately, the mammoth gold statue that used to stand at the summit of the pyramid (it may have been placed there by the Aztecs) was ordered removed by Juan de Zumárraga, the first archbishop of Mexico City. In its stead is a stone "cap" placed there by the archaeological team that reconstructed the pyramid more than a half century ago.

Pirámide de la Luna

The next major attraction to the north is, aesthetically speaking, the most striking at Teotihuacán: the **Plaza de la Luna** (Plaza of the Moon). An imposing patio surrounded by a variety of even more imposing platforms, the plaza is a worthy lead-up to the Pyramid of the Moon, located at the end of the Street of the Dead. Consisting of four sloping superimposed platforms situated on a rise (which makes it appear as if it's the same height as the larger Pyramid of the Sun), the Pyramid of the Moon is the most harmoniously designed structure in this ancient city. Archaeologists have reconstructed the façade and massive staircase of the pyramid, which was built around the same time as the Pyramid of the Sun, so that at least an impression of its original splendor remains.

Other Structures at Teotihuacán

On the west side of the plaza is the **Palacio del Quetzalpapálotl** (Palace of the Quetzal Butterfly), to date the only roofed structure to have been uncovered at an archaeological site outside of the Maya region. First discovered in 1962 and subsequently restored, the building's rooms are arranged around a patio whose elaborately carved pillars feature stylized representations of birds and owls, as well as the butterflies that lend the palace its name.

Two other half-buried structures in the plaza area are also worth a look. The **Palacio de los Jaguares** (Palace of the Jaguars), due north of the Palace of the Quetzal Butterfly, has a portico with some well-preserved murals depicting jaguars in plumed headdresses blowing into plumed conch shells. As you exit this courtyard a modern tunnel to the right leads you to the second- or third-century **Palacio de los Caracoles Enplumados** (Palace of the Plumed Shells), distinguished by its bas-reliefs of feathered seashells with mouthpiece-like devices (presumed to be instruments) and red and green parrots ejecting streams of blue liquid, presumably water. (The overall effect is best viewed from the southeast exit to the Street of the Dead.)

Tepantitla

To get to the last worthwhile stop at Teotihuacán, turn left (east) at the Pyramid of the Sun, walk through Parking Lot 2, and turn left onto the ring road, which leads to the ruined residential quarter of Tepantitla, about 1 km (½ mile) from the Pyramid of the Sun. En route you'll pass a room adorned with a mural depicting elegantly dressed priests in headdresses, before coming to the walls of what was once an atriumlike structure. Here you'll find the remains of the most famous mural of the Teotihuacán III period (A.D. 350–650), *The Paradise of Tlaloc,* which depicts human figures sunbathing and chasing butterflies—the Teotihuacanos' vision of a state of grace.

GETTING TO TEOTIHUACAN

You'll need an early start to enjoy this day away from the hustle and bustle of the city. Teotihuacán is about a 100-km (62-mile) round trip, but unquestionably worth the effort. Buses leave the D.F. at 30-minute intervals from the terminal across the street from the Indios Verdes metro station, line 3. The buses are marked "Pirámides-Teotihuacán." The last bus back to the capital leaves at 6:00 P.M. from the main entrance to the site, west of the Unidad Cultural. There is also regular bus service to Teotihuacán from the Terminal de Autobuses del Norte, which can be reached via the number 17 or 17B bus, or on line 5 of the metro. Tickets ($5 per person) can be purchased inside the vast terminal at Sala #8.

All major travel agencies and most hotels offer tours to Teotihuacán, with prices varying depending on the itinerary involved. You might also consider hiring a car and driver for the day. (If you do, expect to pay around $100—which, split three or four ways, is a very reasonable price for the added convenience.) The best place to do so is in front of either the Sheraton María-Isabel or the Hotel María Cristina (see the Accommodations section, below).

If you are driving, head north on Avenida Insurgentes and follow the signs to Highway 85D. At the 15-km (9-mile) mark take the toll road rather than the free road toward Pachuca. At the 25-km (16-mile) mark, bear right for Teotihuacán after paying your toll. Follow the signs to Highway 132.

Tepexpán

You may want to turn off at the 34-km (21-mile) mark and follow the signs to Tepexpán, where a small **museum** (open from 10:00 A.M., daily except Mondays) houses the fossil remains of mammoths unearthed nearby that have been dated to approximately 8,000 B.C. The most amazing remains on display, however, belong to what is reputed to be the oldest human being ever discovered on the continent, remains that were unearthed from under a layer of saltpeter and are thought to correspond to a period of drought that occurred some 10,000 years ago, during the waning stages of the last Ice Age.

San Agustín Acolman

From Tepexpán return to Highway 132 and continue another 4 km (2½ miles) for the next side trip. Exit to the right and follow the road to the towering fortresslike walls of the monastery and church of San Agustín Acolman, now a museum (open from 10:00 A.M., daily except Fridays).

Among the first New World communities founded by the Augustinians, the monastery and adjoining church were begun in 1539, completed in 1560, and restored in 1735. As a result, they are a stylized mixture of the Gothic and Baroque. At the end of the vast nave and around the cloister are unsigned murals depicting a group of monks, probably the dignitaries of the order. The murals themselves are believed to have been painted toward the end of the 16th century. The main altarpiece, Baroque in design, has paintings dating from the 17th and 18th centuries, while the side altarpieces are typical of the Churrigueresque style.

The second floor has two arcades enlivened by paintings from the 19th century, a library with a collection of theological works, and an exhibition room displaying pre-Hispanic artifacts uncovered during 20th-century excavations.

To the right of the church, level with the first floor of the monastery, is a small open-air chapel with a picturesque arch framing its entrance. Inside, a well-executed fragment of a mural portrays Saint Catherine. The monastery itself, with its cramped cells, gives you a feeling for the austere life led by the monks.

After San Agustín Acolman it's back to the highway for the final 13 km (8 miles) to Teotihuacán.

GETTING AROUND

The Metro

Mexico City has an outstanding public transportation system, with the sparkling metro one of the capital's pride and joys. Belgian-designed and -built, the trains run on rubber wheels from one brightly lit station to the next; the entire network covers a distance of 126 miles, and is still being expanded.

As of this writing the fare is 40 centavos. It's best to buy tickets in blocks of five, to avoid long lines. The maps posted in every metro car are quite comprehensive, and a symbol/color system is employed so that it is not necessary to understand Spanish. To change lines follow the signs that say "Correspondencia" and look for the name of the terminal station that is on the line you want as well as in the direction you are going. Avoid rush-hour trips (7:00 to 9:00 A.M. and 5:00 to 9:00 P.M.) if at all possible. During these hours cars are segregated by sex, although a female may accompany her male companion on a "male only" car. Cumbersome luggage is not permitted during rush hours and smoking is prohibited at all times. Maps and general assistance are provided at all major stations.

On Saturdays all lines operate between 6:00 A.M. and 1:30 A.M. On Sundays and holidays all lines operate between 7:00 A.M. and 12:30 A.M. On weekdays all lines operate between 6:00 A.M. and 12:30 A.M.

Microbuses

A fleet of new 30-seat "microbuses" now crisscrosses the capital, replacing the collective taxis (usually Volkswagen *combis*) known as *peseros*. They charge 55 centavos a person minimum, and extra if you travel beyond a certain point: 70 centavos for anything over 10 km (6 miles), and NP 1 for any distance over 17 km (11 miles). They stop whenever hailed (as opposed to the conventional Ruta 100 buses), and you can get off at any point along the set route. Say *"Baja, por favor"* when you wish to get off.

Buses

Take the Ruta 100 buses at your own risk. There is no maximum capacity, so they often resemble cattle cars. And although the fare is an extremely reasonable 40 centavos (have exact change ready before boarding, as drivers do not make change), buses are a pickpocket's paradise. Still, they're an efficient way to travel if you know precisely where you and the bus are going (the drivers tend to be reckless, however). Buses only pick up and discharge passengers at *parada* signs, and will stop only when the buzzer at the rear exit is pressed or someone bangs on the roof.

Taxis

Volkswagen Beetle taxis are the least expensive. Make sure the driver turns on the meter after you get in. If there is no meter reading at the end of the trip, by law you owe nothing. As well, a photo I.D. of your driver must be pasted over the glove compartment; if you don't see one, leave the taxi at once.

While *sitio* taxis (radio cabs that are not allowed to "cruise") charge more, their drivers are also usually more knowledgeable about the city. (Private limousines, with commercial license plates and hooded meters, are found parked outside major hotels. They charge about three times the normal fare, but most of their drivers speak some English. They will also hire out by the hour.) In general, fares for private taxis are about a third of what you'd expect to pay north of the border, and drivers do not expect a tip. Nighttime prices are about 10 percent higher. A *libre* sign in the window means the taxi is available. Strangely enough, a lighted front beam at night indicates the taxi is occupied, while no beam means it's available—but good luck distinguishing a "no-beam" as a taxi in the dark.

Any taxi is authorized to take passengers *to* the airport, although only those belonging to the airport concession are permitted to bring passengers into the city *from* the airport. In other words, don't be lured into jumping from your place in line to flag down an empty city taxi as you're waiting to get out of the airport.

Car Rentals

Renting and driving a car in the capital is not recommended unless you are a veteran Mexico City driver and do not mind paying twice what the same car would cost to rent in the United States or Canada. Consider only the major international agencies. Vehicles from private agencies often are mechanically unreliable, and road service, in the event of a breakdown, is unpredictable.

Long-Distance Buses

Mexico's long-distance bus network is both excellent and inexpensive. All first-class buses—usually called *autobuses de lujo* to distinguish them from *primera clase,* which in Mexico means second class—have co-pilots; most have rest rooms and air-conditioning (many, in fact, are *over* air-conditioned, so be sure to bring a light sweater or jacket along).

Indeed, so popular is this mode of transportation with Mexicans themselves that it is almost always necessary to make reservations in advance. (This is especially true over long holiday weekends, during Holy Week, and from December 15 to January 6, when schoolchildren and bureaucrats have vacation.) In Mexico City travellers can make reservations and purchase tickets (*boletos*) in advance through one office: **Greyhound de México**, Paseo de la Reforma 27; Tel: 535-4200. A number of the major travel agencies, including **Central de Autobuses** (Plaza del Angel, Calle Londres, Zona Rosa; Tel: 533-2047), will make the reservations for you and even deliver the tickets to your hotel. This is a great service, as the major bus lines and their ticket desks are all located on the outskirts of the city in one of four immense terminals, each servicing a cardinal direction. These are (clockwise from the north): the **Terminal Central de Autobuses del Norte**, Avenida de los Cien Metros 4907 (metro line 5 to the Autobuses del Norte stop); the **Terminal de Autobuses de Pasajeros de Oriente** (or TAPO), Calzada Ignacio Zaragoza 200 (metro line 1 to the San Lázaro stop); the **Terminal Central de Autobuses del Sur**, Tasqueña 1320 (metro line 2 to the Tasqueña stop); and the **Terminal Poniente de Autobuses**, Avenida del Sur 122 (metro line 1 to the Observatorio stop).

The major long-distance bus lines are:

- **Autobuses de Oriente (ADO)**, with service to Matamoras, Reynosa, Pachuca, Puebla, Tampico, Teotihuacán, and Tula from the Terminal Central del Norte (Tel: 587-8233); and Campeche, Cancún, Mérida, Oaxaca, Palenque, Veracruz, and Villahermosa from the Terminal de Oriente (Tel: 542-7192).

- **Estrella de Oro**, with deluxe nonstop service to Acapulco, as well as service to Cuernavaca, Taxco, and Zihuatanejo from the Terminal Central del Sur (Tel: 549-8520).
- **Omnibus Cristóbal Colón**, with service to Oaxaca, Salina Cruz, Tapachula, Tehuantepec, and Tuxtla Gutierrez, as well as connections to Guatemala and Central America, from the Terminal de Oriente (Tel: 542-7263).
- **Omnibus de México**, with service to Chihuahua, Ciudad Juárez, Durango, Guadalajara, Guanajuato, Morelia, Querétaro, San Luis Potosí, San Miguel de Allende, and Tampico from the Terminal Central del Norte (Tel: 567-6756).
- **Transportes Chihuahuenses**, with Pullman express cruisers to El Paso, Texas (connecting with Greyhound), as well as service to Chihuahua, Ciudad Juárez, Durango, Querétaro, and Zacatecas from the Terminal Central del Norte (Tel: 587-5377).
- **Transportes del Norte**, with direct express service to Laredo, Texas (connecting with Greyhound), as well as service to Durango, Matamoras, Monterrey, Saltillo, and San Luis Potosí from the Terminal Central del Norte (Tel: 587-5511).
- **Tres Estrellas de Oro**, with direct express service to Guadalajara (continuing on to Mazatlán and Tijuana), as well as Irapuato, Puerto Vallarta, and Querétaro from the Terminal Central del Norte (Tel: 567-8157).
- **ETN**, with service to San Miguel de Allende, Guadalajara, Guanajuato, León, Querétaro, San Luis Potosí, and Morelia, from the Terminal Central del Norte (Tel: 368-0212). In addition to some of the above cities, ETN also services Toluca, Colima, and Manzanillo from the Terminal Observatorio (Tel: 273-0251).
- **Primera Plus** services many of the same cities as ETN from the Terminal Central del Norte (Tel: 587-5222 or 567-8030).

The Mexican National Railway

Although it's not a well-known fact, Mexico's national railroad, the Ferrocarriles Nacionales de México, offers direct rail service to 16 major cities and three border towns from the capital, and vice versa. In other words, it's possible to traverse the country by rail from north to south and coast to coast in relative comfort and safety (although some trains offer vendor food service only).

The Estación Central de Buenavista, located on Avenida Insurgentes Norte, a few blocks north of its intersection with Paseo de la Reforma, is the *only* station with connections to all 19 destinations. For those with limited finances and the luxury of time (punctuality has not yet been elevated to a virtue by the National Railway), it's a great way to travel.

To ensure your comfort, buy a *primera especial* (first-class) ticket, which not only guarantees you a seat in an air-conditioned or heated car (not always the case with second class), but makes you eligible to purchase a berth on a *coche dormitorio* (sleeping car). If you're travelling alone and don't want to share a cabin with a stranger, ask for a *camarin,* a stateroom for one, or an *alcoba,* a stateroom for two (be advised that a "stateroom" in this instance means a Murphy bed that swings down over the toilet, completely filling the small cabin); a *compartimiento* is the same but slightly roomier. A *gabinete* is as good as it gets: three beds, a bath, shower, and room service.

You can purchase tickets for any destination at any of the windows in the Buenavista Station, or from most travel agencies in town. The ticket office at the station is open daily from 6:00 A.M. to 11:30 P.M. Try to avoid waiting until the last minute, as long lines are the rule. For information in English, Tel: 547-6593.

The English-language *Official Railway Guide,* issued by the Ferrocarriles Nacionales de México, is revised on an annual basis (or whenever fares change). For a free copy, write to: *Official Railway Guide,* 1500 Broadway, Suite 810, New York, NY 10036.

ACCOMMODATIONS

Most of the best hotels in the D.F. are centrally located and within walking distance of each other; they range in style from elegant contemporary to intimate colonial. With two exceptions (the Fiesta Americana Aeropuerto and the Villa Arqueológica at Teotihuacán), the ones recommended here can be found within an area bounded by the Zócalo to the east and Chapultepec Park to the west. Generally speaking, the more moderately priced accommodations will be found north of Paseo de la Reforma in the neighborhoods around the U.S. embassy. The "Big Four"—the Sheraton María-Isabel Hotel & Towers, the Westin Camino Real, the Nikko México, and the Stouffer Presidente Chapultepec—each with more than 600 rooms, are all west of the U.S. embassy. The Stouffer Presidente, farthest west, and the Sheraton, right next door to the embassy, are less than two miles apart, and all are within walking distance of the first section of Chapultepec Park, the chic Polanco shopping area, and the Zona Rosa. Expensive by local standards but with rates about 20 to 30 percent lower than what you would expect to pay for comparable accommodations in New York or London, they offer everything a seasoned traveller expects from a luxury hotel. Just as luxurious are two smaller, more sedate hotels located geographically in the middle of this cluster: the Clarion Reforma, with fewer than 100 rooms, and the Marquis Reforma, the city's newest luxury hotel. Both specialize in pampering their guests.

The better hotels in the D.F. all have air-conditioning, but it's usually not needed here except for a few days in early May just before the rainy season commences. The months of peak occupancy are December through March (especially Christmastime) for the luxury hotels, and July and August for the more moderately priced establishments.

The rates given below are *projections* for December 1993 through the spring of 1994. Unless otherwise indicated, rates, which are given in U.S. dollars, are for double rooms, double occupancy; the 10 percent VAT has been added. As rates are subject to change, it's a good idea to double-check before booking.

The international telephone code for Mexico is 52; the area code for Mexico City is 5 (calls made within the D.F. do not require the "5").

Chapultepec Park Area

The ► Camino Real—one of Mexican architect Ricardo Legoretta's masterpieces—is a stark two-story structure that covers a city block facing the eastern perimeter of Chapultepec Park. Outside, the Camino Real is one of the best examples of "Mexican minimalism," a term coined by Legoretta himself when asked to describe his austere designs. Inside, the parquet floors in the huge lobby provide an ideal background for a mural by Rufino Tamayo and a Calder stabile in yellows, purples, and shocking pinks.

The Camino Real's 677 rooms and 36 suites are spacious and comfortable, and each is equipped with a marble bath. The hotel is also home to two of the D.F.'s finest restaurants: **Fouquet's of Paris** (arguably just as good as the chain's Paris flagship establishment) and **Azulejos**, featuring one of the best Sunday-brunch buffets in town. In addition, the hotel has four other restaurants, a 24-hour coffee shop, the very popular **Cero Cero** discotheque, a nightclub, four bars, four swimming pools, and rooftop tennis courts. The Camino

Real is within walking distance of the outstanding museums in Chapultepec Park and is only a ten-minute cab ride from the shops and cafés of the Zona Rosa or the shopping district known as Plaza Polanco, making it an ideal site from which to explore and enjoy Mexico City. For visitors planning to explore a wider area, the hotel has a garage and in-house travel agent; valet service and car rentals are also available.

Avenida Mariano Escobedo 700, 11590 D.F. Tel: 203-2121; Fax: 250-6897; in the U.S. and Canada, Tel: (800) 228-3000. $253.

The 38-floor Japanese-built and -operated ▶ **Hotel Nikko México** opened its doors in 1987. Like the other major luxury hotels in the D.F., it is a huge affair, with 729 rooms and 21 suites, two bars and four restaurants (featuring excellent Japanese, Mexican, and French cuisine), a nightclub and discotheque, an in-house travel agent, laundry and dry-cleaning services, a jogging track and fully equipped gym (complete with sauna), three tennis courts and rooftop swimming pool, and a heliport. While the lobby resembles a modern, ostentatious shopping mall, and the hotel's overall atmosphere is somewhat impersonal, the rooms are large and tastefully decorated. The top floors of the hotel are reserved for those who desire the royal treatment, or a reasonable facsimile: Private registration, an exclusive clublike lounge, and private secretarial services are among the extras. There are also two authentically decorated, and very costly, "Japanese" suites in this part of the hotel. The 37th floor is reserved for women only and has 24-hour security and a special concierge.

Avenida Campos Elíseos 204, 11560 D.F. Tel: 280-1111; Fax: 203-0655; in the U.S. and Canada, Tel: (800) 645-5687. $266.

As you enter the modern, 30-story ▶ **Stouffer Presidente México**, next door to the Nikko, you find yourself in a beautiful five-story pyramidal lobby with a skylight ceiling and a luxurious garden. The Presidente has 617 rooms and 40 suites decorated in a colonial style with modern touches. Some offer panoramic views of Chapultepec Park. Of the hotel's five restaurants, **Maxim's** is the best. The live music in the lobby bar attracts a young singles crowd most nights, and a number of exclusive boutiques line the mezzanine. The hotel also has a nightclub featuring top entertainment, a popular disco, banquet and convention facilities, a travel agency, and a parking garage.

Avenida Campos Elíseos 218, 11560 D.F. Tel: 327-7700; Fax: 327-7730; in the U.S. and Canada, Tel: (800) 472-2427. $264.

The pastel-hued Art Nouveau façade of the ▶ **Hotel Mar-**

quis Reforma, a 20-minute walk east of the Presidente, does not prepare you for its subdued, tasteful interior. In fact, the Marquis Reforma recently was honored as the only Mexico City member of the prestigious "Small Luxury Hotels of the World" registry. The hotel's 115 rooms and 85 suites, many of which overlook Paseo de la Reforma, feature rich woodwork, polished brass, and chrome finishings. Other amenities include a small, modern fitness center with an indoor jogging track, personal facsimile machines and computers on the club floor, and closed-circuit surveillance. The service, too, is admirable; there are two English-speaking employees for every occupied room, and the staff is quite knowledgeable about Mexico's history as well as the best places to visit in the D.F.

Paseo de la Reforma 465, 06500 D.F. Tel: 211-3600; Fax: 211-5561; in the U.S., Tel: (800) 235-2387. $215.

Also on Reforma, a five-minute walk east of the Marquis Reforma between the Monument to Independence and Chapultepec Park, the ▶ Clarion Reforma offers 16 comfortable rooms and 68 beautiful suites, most with sauna or Jacuzzi, and all with great views of the park. The rather hip decor is so understated that the superb amenities might take you by surprise, and Bellini's, on the second floor, is one of the nicest Italian restaurants in the D.F.

Paseo de la Reforma 373, 06500 D.F. Tel: 207-8944; Fax: 208-2719; in the U.S. and Canada, Tel: (800) 228-5151. $232; with sauna, $291; with Jacuzzi, $345.

Zona Rosa

The ▶ Hotel Aristos, which gradually has been upstaged in luxury and popularity by newer hotels, has 360 large, nicely decorated rooms; those on the upper floors afford great views of Paseo de la Reforma. Other amenities here include two restaurants, a bar, a nightclub, a disco, an in-house travel agent, laundry service, and a garage.

Paseo de la Reforma 276 (entrance on Calle Copenhague), 06600 D.F. Tel: 211-0112; Fax: 525-6783; in the U.S. and Canada, Tel: (800) 223-0888. $148.

The ▶ Century Zona Rosa offers marble baths and private balconies in each of its 110 rooms and 32 suites. A heated swimming pool, two restaurants, car-rental desk, garage, and an African safari–style bar that's a bit garish but fun round out this likable establishment.

Calle Liverpool 152, 06600 D.F. Tel: 726-9911; Fax: 525-7475. $122.

A member of the Westin Hotel chain, the 433-room ▶ Westin Galería Plaza has an attractive lobby with a splashing fountain as its centerpiece. Facilities and services include a rooftop swimming pool, a sundeck, three restaurants (gourmet French, Mexican, and international), a lobby bar, a disco, a shopping arcade, and a travel desk.

Calle Hamburgo 195, 06600 D.F. Tel: 211-0014; Fax: 207-5867; in the U.S. and Canada, Tel: (800) 228-3000. $165–$205.

The recently refurbished ▶ **Krystal Zona Rosa** has 330 large and comfortable rooms, a swimming pool, a restaurant, a bar, a nightclub, a shopping arcade, and a Japanese restaurant that's very popular with businesspeople at lunchtime.

Calle Liverpool 155, 06600 D.F. Tel: 211-0092; Fax: 511-3490. $214.

The ▶ **Royal Zona Rosa** is a pleasant family-style hotel with 162 comfortable rooms, two restaurants, a piano bar, a nightclub, a movie theater, shops, an in-house travel agent, laundry service, a swimming pool, and a garage.

Calle Amberes 78, 06600 D.F. Tel: 525-4850; Fax: 514-3330. $225.

The ▶ **Plaza Florencia**, a comfortable ultramodern hotel facing one of the busiest streets in the Zona Rosa, has 150 spacious (and soundproof, according to management) rooms, a restaurant, nightclub and bar, and a garage.

Calle Florencia 61, 06600 D.F. Tel: 211-0064; Fax: 511-1542. $114.

When it opened as an Art Deco showpiece in the late 1950s, the Geneva, as it was then known, was *the* hotel for foreign tourists and visiting dignitaries in Mexico City. After slipping a bit in subsequent decades, it was purchased by the Calinda chain, which spruced up the deteriorating old landmark and restored much of the charm of its heyday. Today the 346 rooms of the ▶ **Calinda Geneve Mexico** encompass a range of styles and decor (a pre-registration check of the room you have been given is advisable; rooms overlooking the street can be noisy), and the "jungle bar," located at the back of the lobby in an area that resembles a giant greenhouse, is a popular meeting place for locals. The facilities and services here include two restaurants and a jazz bar; tobacco, beauty, and barber shops; an in-house travel agent; a car-rental desk; and laundry service.

Calle Londres 130, 06600 D.F. Tel: 211-0071; Fax: 208-7422; in the U.S. and Canada, Tel: (800) 228-5151. $127.

For those who prefer to have cooking facilities in their rooms, the following Zona Rosa establishments are recommended.

The seven-year-old ▶ **Marco Polo** offers a sophisticated

European atmosphere in a sleek, modern structure with 64 beautifully designed rooms. The four penthouse rooms, which are larger and have better kitchen facilities, are well worth the extra cost. The Marco Polo also has a restaurant and piano bar, a number of small meeting rooms, laundry service, and a garage.

Calle Amberes 27, 06600 D.F. Tel: 207-1893; Fax: 533-3727. $182; penthouse suites, $199.

The charming seven-story ▶ **Suites Amberes**, located in the heart of the Zona Rosa, offers 28 large suites, all with kitchenettes and balconies. There is also a good restaurant and piano bar on the premises.

Calle Amberes 64, 06600 D.F. Tel: 533-1306; Fax: 207-1509. $94.

Around the U.S. Embassy

Comfortable, modestly priced accommodations are the rule north of the Zona Rosa in the vicinity of the U.S. embassy. Though this area is a bit farther from the shops and great restaurants in the heart of the Zona Rosa, for most people the added savings will more than make up for the slight inconvenience.

The ▶ **Sheraton María-Isabel Hotel & Towers**, next door to the U.S. embassy, is conveniently located a few minutes' walk from the heart of the Zona Rosa. The gaudy, block-long lobby, with lots of polished wood and brass and ornate chandeliers, is a good example of how a space ought not be used. There are 747 spacious albeit minimally decorated rooms and suites in the hotel as well as three restaurants, one of which, the **Veranda**, offers great views of "El Angel" and rather offbeat entertainment while you dine. The hotel's bustling **Bar Jorongo**, which often features strolling mariachis, is popular with locals and singles. Other amenities and facilities include a rooftop pool, two tennis courts, an in-house travel agent, two bars, a nightclub, a garage, laundry and valet service, a fully equipped gym, banquet and convention facilities, and a variety of shops.

Paseo de la Reforma 325, 06500 D.F. Tel: 207-3933; Fax: 207-0684; in the U.S. and Canada, Tel: (800) 325-3535. $298.

The moderately priced and always full ▶ **María Cristina** is an oasis of charm just a few blocks from the embassy. Chairs and tables are set out for relaxing on the lovely, grassy grounds, and there's a central patio with a fountain as well. The 150 rooms are on the small and plain side (ask for one overlooking the courtyard or the lawn), but the bathrooms are bright and modern and all rooms are equipped with cable TV. In addition, the hotel has a restaurant and piano bar, a tobacco shop, an in-house travel agent, laundry service, and a garage.

Río Lerma 31, 06500 D.F. Tel: 546-9880; Fax: 566-9120. $60.

The ▶ **Bristol**, though not much to look at from the outside, has 92 plain but pleasant rooms and 42 comfortable suites, and offers good value for the money. Facilities and amenities include a restaurant, a lobby bar, a garage, and laundry service.

Plaza Nécaxa 17 (at the corner of Río Panuco and Río Sena), 06500 D.F. Tel: 533-6060; Fax: 208-1717. $77–$184.

The ▶ **Hotel del Angel** has 100 comfortable if modest rooms, and also offers good value for the money. Facilities and amenities include a rooftop restaurant with a view of the nearby Monument of Independence, a video bar, an in-house travel agent, a garage, and laundry service.

Río Lerma 154, 06500 D.F. Tel: 533-0160; Fax: 533-1027. $63.

The Zócalo Area

A beautiful Art Deco–style lobby with a stained glass Tiffany dome and old-fashioned cage elevators is the pride and joy of the ▶ **Howard Johnson Gran Hotel**, conveniently located on the Zócalo. The 101 rooms and 23 suites here, on the other hand, are not nearly as elegant as the lobby. (Try not to get a room with a view of a brick wall.) The hotel does offer adequate and friendly service, however, as well as great views of the Zócalo from the rooms on its upper floors, an in-house travel agent, a restaurant and bar, and a garage.

Avenida 16 de Septiembre 82, 06000 D.F. Tel: 510-4040; Fax: 512-2085; in the U.S. and Canada, Tel: (800) 654-2000. $115.

The ▶ **Best Western Hotel Majestic** offers pleasant colonial decor in a 16th-century building overlooking the Zócalo. Some of its 85 rooms are rather cramped, so a pre-registration check is advisable. There are sweeping views of the historic Zócalo area from the rooftop restaurant, and the hotel also has two other restaurants, a lively bar, an in-house travel agent, and laundry service. Many guests reserve rooms overlooking the Zócalo well in advance of the 15th and 16th of September, when Independence Day celebrations draw thousands to the square.

Avenida Madero 73, 06000 D.F. Tel: 521-8600; Fax: 518-3466; in the U.S. and Canada, Tel: (800) 528-1234. $109.

The ▶ **Montecarlo**, a spotlessly clean hotel housed in an 18th-century monastery, is very popular with visiting foreign students. (D. H. Lawrence lived here for two years during the late 1920s.) For about $25 a night you can get one of the

60 large, airy, no-frills rooms surrounding the hotel's courtyard. The Montecarlo is only a few minutes' walk from the Zócalo and offers free parking for guests.

Calle República de Uruguay 69, 06000 D.F. Tel: 521-2559. $26.

The ▶ **Hotel Isábel**, yet another pleasant establishment housed in a beautiful 18th-century building, has been a favorite of young U.S. and European tourists since the 1960s. The friendly, competent management; clean, spacious rooms; and very reasonable rates make the Isábel one of the best hotel bargains in the capital. Located a few minutes from the Zócalo on Calle Isabel la Católica.

Calle Isabel la Católica 63, 06000 D.F. Tel: 518-1213. $25.

Other Choices Downtown

Located just north of Alameda Park and one block west of the Franz Mayer Museum, the ▶ **Hotel de Cortés** is housed in a 16th-century convent that in the 18th century was used as a hospice; today it is a national monument. Behind its fortresslike façade, the 22 rooms and seven suites, all clean but sparely furnished, are clustered around a truly lovely tree-shaded patio. The Cortés stages a great folkloric show in its courtyard every Saturday evening. (See Dining, below, for more on the Cortés.)

Avenida Hidalgo 85, 06030 D.F. Tel: 518-2181; Fax: 518-3466; in the U.S. and Canada, Tel: (800) 528-1234. $104.

The modern, 25-story ▶ **Fiesta Americana Reforma** is always pulsating with activity—usually because it's hosting yet another convention or tour group. Located halfway between the Zona Rosa and Alameda Park on Paseo de la Reforma, the hotel has 583 rooms, 24 suites, and five nightclubs that often headline top-quality entertainment (see Nightlife and Entertainment, below), which makes it a focal point of nightlife in the D.F. Other facilities and amenities include a swimming pool, three restaurants, two bars, a disco, an in-house travel agent, a solarium, and a garage.

Paseo de la Reforma 80, 06600 D.F. Tel: 705-1515; Fax: 705-1313; in the U.S., Tel: (800) FIESTA-1. $176.

The ultramodern ▶ **Sevilla Palace**, also on Paseo de la Reforma, was built by local businessmen and has a very Spanish flavor. It has 415 spacious rooms, a number of expensive boutiques, a rooftop pool, a health club, a gym, restaurants and bars, and a garage. The lobby is especially pretty, with lots of plants and a bubble elevator.

Paseo de la Reforma 105, 06030 D.F. Tel: 705-2800; Fax: 535-3842; in the U.S. and Canada, Tel: (800) 732-9488. $155.

The original decor of the ▶ **Emporio México**, on Paseo

de la Reforma near the Zona Rosa, was early Space Age. Some of the rooms were left more or less intact during renovation a few years ago, and "garish" is the only word to describe them; a pre-registration check is advisable. All the rooms have first-rate Jacuzzi baths, however, and the price is right. The hotel also has a restaurant, a bar in the lobby, and a garage.

Paseo de la Reforma 124, 06600 D.F. Tel: 566-7766; Fax: 703-1424. $94.

The ▶ **Vasco de Quiroga**, across the street from the Benjamin Franklin Library (an excellent English and Spanish library affiliated with the U.S. embassy), about a ten-minute walk from the Zona Rosa, offers 50 comfortable rooms and lovely colonial decor. It also has a restaurant, spacious bar, and laundry service.

Calle Londres 15, 06600 D.F. Tel: 546-2614; Fax: 546-4202. $70.

The 270-room ▶ **Hotel Casa Blanca**, right off Reforma a block south of the Monument to the Revolution, is a modern high rise with clean, well-furnished rooms, two restaurants, a rooftop pool and sundeck with large-screen TV, and four bars, three with live entertainment.

Calle La Fragua 7, 06030 D.F. Tel: 705-1300; Fax: 705-4197. $122.

Located in a quiet residential neighborhood across the street from the back entrance to the first section of Chapultepec Park, about a ten-minute cab ride from the Zona Rosa, the two-story colonial-style ▶ **Park Villa** offers 44 clean, comfortable rooms, a nice garden area, a decent restaurant, handy parking, and reasonable rates.

Gomez Pedraza 68, 11560 D.F. Tel: 515-5245. $72.

Outlying Areas

Reached directly via overhead ramp from the international airport terminal, the seven-year-old ▶ **Fiesta Americana Aeropuerto** advertises itself as "the only hotel with its own adjoining airport." Whether or not you consider that an advantage, there are 443 large rooms and 33 suites here, an inviting lobby usually filled with business travellers, a nightclub featuring live entertainment, a bar, a number of restaurants, a gymnasium, an in-house travel agent, and a garage.

Fundidora Monterrey 89, 15520 D.F. Tel: 785-0505; Fax: 785-1034; in the U.S. and Canada, Tel: (800) 223-2332. $263.

Northeast of the city at the Teotihuacán archaeological site (a five-minute walk from the Pyramid of the Sun), the Club Med–operated ▶ **Villa Arqueológica** is a small but comfortable hotel with 40 cozy, tastefully decorated rooms, a good restaurant and bar, a library well-stocked with archaeological titles, a swimming pool and tennis court, pleasant grounds, and a one-of-a-kind location.

Club Med, San Juan Teotihuacán 55000. Tel: (595) 6-0750; in the U.S., Tel: (800) 258-2633; in Canada, Tel: (514) 937-7707. $78.

DINING

Mexico City offers more than 30,000 registered restaurants, among which you will find not only regional *restaurantes* featuring exquisite native delicacies (and, often, live regional folkloric music from various corners of the country) but superb international-style dining rooms as well. At the same time, on almost any street corner in the D.F. you will find women selling *carnitas* (chunks of roasted pork), tacos, and enchiladas. (Resist the enticing aromas: It's definitely risky to eat street food in Mexico if your digestive system is not primed.) Many people say that the best Mexican food is found at the tiny stalls, or *fondas,* in neighborhood markets, but going out to a special restaurant is a national pastime.

Many of the best restaurants in the D.F. were created by folks who had never run one before but who liked to eat, happened to own a prime location for a restaurant, and ventured to learn the business through trial and error. Other bistros are manned by European chefs who came to Mexico to direct the kitchens at the large international hotels and then fell in love with the country and decided to try their luck with their own establishments. The dining-out scene in the capital has been enriched by their daring. Most owners of the better restaurants have in common a passion for food, people, and a flair for showmanship. As Jane Pearson Fernández, the owner of the Piccadilly Pub and Sir Winston Churchill's, puts it: "Every day you have to put on a show that appeals not only to taste but to all the senses."

The sheer number of dining establishments in the D.F. guarantees a virtually unlimited range of culinary experiences. You can, for example, feast in former haciendas and 19th-century French-style mansions complete with lush gardens and exotic peacocks. Or you can embark on a gastronomic journey of the country by eating in the city's *fondas,* where you can sample such regional specialties as *cochinita pibil* (roast pork in barbeque sauce) from the Yucatán, *enmoladas de mole negro* (chicken with black *mole* sauce) from Oaxaca, or *albondigas de armadillo* in *salsa de huitlacoche* (armadillo meatballs in a sauce made with a rare and exceptionally flavorful black fungus). Often the menus will sound like the lyrics to a song in an ancient language:

garnachas (fried tortillas covered with sour cream and chile sauce), *pambazos* (a fried roll filled with beans, hot sausages, and chiles), *pelonas* (a *pambazo* made in Puebla), *totopos* (the original nacho), or *chicharrones* (fried pork rinds). Even the foreign chefs here have been influenced to some extent by traditional Aztec and Mayan fare. As a result, certain ingredients will show up on the menus of trendy international eateries with some frequency, among which are the aforementioned *huitlacoche* (sometimes spelled *cuitlacoche*), which grows on corn; *cilantro* (coriander), sometimes referred to as Chinese parsley; and *flor de calabaza,* the flower of the yellow squash plant.

There is an old Mexican saying that goes, *"Todo se aregla en la cama o en la cantina"*—"Everything can be fixed in the bed or in the bar"—which in practice means that in the D.F. more important business deals are closed over lunch tables in the Zona Rosa than are concluded in the glass skyscrapers lining Paseo de la Reforma. Recently, these "business" lunches (which often used to wind up as wild soirées, with the tequila being shared liberally with members of the strolling mariachi band) have been replaced by working breakfasts—one reason you may find yourself standing in line for breakfast at your hotel at 8:00 A.M.

The better Mexico City restaurants also tend to be on the snobbish side. You can almost always count on excellent service at these establishments, but many will insist on relatively formal dress. When in doubt, phone the captain and ask about the dress code—it's better to get this information over the phone than at the door.

The prices of most dishes in exclusive restaurants will be lower than they would be in comparable restaurants in big cities in the United States, Canada, or Europe. Imported wines, on the other hand, are pricey and can cost more than your entire meal; most restaurants will have a local wine list, however. Major credit cards are accepted in all D.F. restaurants unless otherwise noted. (Most will attempt to avoid American Express but will acquiesce if it's the only one you offer.)

A final word: Margarita aficionados should be aware that it's almost impossible to get a frozen margarita in Mexico City, where margaritas are usually served in champagne-style glasses with bits of ice floating around on top. Many Mexicans dining out like to down a couple of tequilas straight instead, with a *sangrita* (spicy tomato juice) as a chaser. They say it "opens the appetite." Remember, though, that the effect of alcohol on your system is accelerated in the D.F.

because of the altitude; new arrivals in the city also should be careful not to eat much.

The restaurants listed below all cater to international guests. They claim to use purified water in all drinks as well as in their ice cubes, and also maintain that all vegetables and fruits on their menus are disinfected. This claim notwithstanding, it's best to avoid iced drinks—and fresh strawberries, even though they taste as good as they look.

Most restaurants in the D.F. open from 1:00 P.M. to 1:00 A.M. The locals start to pour in from 2:00 P.M. on; to guarantee a table for lunch, get to the restaurant you've chosen by 1:00. Dinner crowds peak at about 9:30 P.M. Many restaurants are closed Sunday evenings, and are listed accordingly. Generally speaking, it's best to call ahead for reservations; the area code in Mexico City (when calling from outside the D.F.) is 5.

Zócalo Area

They say you don't really know the people of Mexico City until you have crowded into a traditional dining room such as the one at the **Hostería de Santo Domingo**, which claims to be the oldest restaurant in the country. (In the 18th century the building served as a Dominican seminary.) The service at this perennially popular establishment is almost always swift, but on Sunday afternoons you'll still have to wait in a line that stretches around the block. A perfect chow stop for those who have been busy touring the central historic district, the Hostería is located north and west of the Zócalo at Belisario Domínguez 72. Open 9:00 A.M. to 11:00 P.M., daily except Sundays, when it closes at 6:00 P.M. Tel: 510-1434 or 526-5276.

For sightseers looking for a bite to eat in the immediate vicinity of the Zócalo, the **Hotel Majestic**, Avenida Madero 73, offers some of the best views of the capital's main plaza from its rooftop restaurant. Its Sunday lunch, which begins at 1:00 P.M., includes a splendid buffet of Mexican dishes served casserole style. Tel: 521-8600.

Del Centro, located in the Howard Johnson Gran Hotel, the Art Nouveau landmark adjacent to the Zócalo, offers tasty Mexican and international dishes as well as a Sunday brunch that you might want to precede with an English-language tour of the nearby Templo Mayor site and National Palace. Open from 7:00 A.M. to 11:00 P.M. on weekdays, and 1:00 to 11:00 P.M. on weekends. Tel: 521-5325.

Located three blocks west of the Zócalo at the corner of Motolinia and Cinco de Mayo, **Bar Alfonso** occupies the second floor of a stately old building facing a street that has recently been converted into a pedestrian mall. The high ceilings, brass chandeliers, wood paneling, and superb service are a perfect complement to the delicious Mexican-Continental fare served here, which includes such traditional favorites as *cabrito,* paella, and *camarones* (shrimp) à la vinaigrette. If you're planning on stopping for lunch, go early: The place is jammed with businesspeople most days of the week. Open 1:00 P.M. to midnight daily. Tel: 512-7598.

Café de Tacuba, housed in a colonial-era building that originally was a Dominican convent at Calle Tacuba 28, recently celebrated 80 consecutive years in business at the same location. The Tacuba is renowned for *enchiladas al horno* (stuffed rolled tortillas baked in a hot sauce) and its freshly baked *pan dulce* (assorted pastries), which locals munch on with a *café con leche* in the evenings. Part of the café's charm undoubtedly comes from its efficient, rather matronly waitresses, dressed a bit coyly in colorful regional dress, complete with outsize bows in their hair. Open 8:00 A.M. to midnight, daily except Mondays. Tel: 518-4950. There's also a branch in Polanco, at Calle Newton 88.

El Danubío, a few blocks south of the Zócalo at República de Uruguay 3, is a serious eatery with an emphasis on huge portions of seafood at reasonable prices. Popular with middle-class Mexicans, El Danubío also has an impressive cold counter featuring lobsters, crabs, clams, and baby eels. Open 1:00 to 10:00 P.M., daily except Sundays, when it closes at 6:00 P.M. Tel: 518-1205.

Southeast of the Zócalo at Regina 159, **Fonda Don Chon** is famous for such pre-Hispanic palate teasers as *iguana en salsa verde* (iguana in pumpkin-seed sauce), *león en salsa de ajonjali* (puma leg in sesame sauce), and *albondigas de armadillo en salsa de nuez* (armadillo meatballs in walnut sauce), as well as delicacies like *tepexcuíntle* (prairie dog), stuffed chrysanthemums, ants' eggs, wild boar, snake, and venison. For the less adventurous, the *quesadillas de flor de calabaza* (squash-flower quesadillas) or the *tacos de salpicon de venado* (deer-salad tacos) are unforgettable. Open 10:00 A.M. to 7:00 P.M. daily. Tel: 522-2170.

Located one block south of the Torre Latinoamericana on Avenida 16 de Septiembre near the corner of Eje Central Lázaro Cárdenas, and first opened for business in 1892, **Prendes** is a huge, stately establishment with antique black lacquer chairs and a black-and-white tiled floor. The waiters look as though they were sent over by Central Casting, and the walls are adorned with murals of celebrated clients past and present: ex-President-for-Life Porfirio Díaz, Walt Disney, Frida Kahlo, Pancho Villa, and Gary Cooper. Leon Trotsky had his last supper here, and Señor Sánchez, the father in Oscar Lewis's classic *The Children of Sánchez,* worked here as a food buyer for the last 30 years of his life. The always-fresh seafood is the specialty. The place is usually packed at lunchtime but thins out considerably after 5:00 P.M. Open 2:00 to 10:00 P.M.; closed Mondays. The refurbished, upscale Fronton México has a branch of Prendes that is open 2:00 P.M. to 2:00 A.M.; closed Mondays.

Built soon after the Conquest, the building that houses the **Hotel de Cortés**, Avenida Hidalgo 85 near Alameda Park, originally served as a convent and then later as a hospice for the needy. Declared a national monument a few years ago, it's now a regular stop on the local version of the Grey Line Tour. Nonetheless, it's worth a visit. An oasis in the midst of urban blight, it provides a welcome respite from the rigors of museum-hopping, with a pretty tiled patio rimmed with flowers and a gushing fountain as its centerpiece. The patio also serves as a stage for a twice-nightly folkloric show featuring dancers and musicians in regional dress. The flickering candlelight creates such a romantic atmosphere that the restaurant's "typical Mexican menu," not much better than your average airline fare, often goes unnoticed. Tel: 512-2181.

If you're looking for something different, you'll find it at **Mesón del Cid**, a little bit of Old Spain located two blocks west and south of Alameda Park at Humboldt 61. Dishes such as charcoal-broiled Cornish hen with truffles, Costa Brava salad, and a superb gazpacho earn raves from contented customers. The fun happens on Saturday night, however, when a memorable medieval-style feast is offered along with live entertainment supplied by a robe-clad *estudiantina* (student's choir). Open 1:00 P.M. to midnight, daily except Sundays. Tel: 512-7629.

If hot, spicy food doesn't agree with your stomach but your palate craves the exotic, **Circulo del Sureste**, offering the best in Yucatecan cuisine in a very informal setting, is just the ticket. *Cochinita pibil* and *pollo pibil,* two of the delectable specialties of the house, are marinated overnight in a sauce made from *naranja agria* (sour orange) and *achiote* (a spice made from the seeds of the annetto tree). To top it off, try a glass of Xtabentun (shtah-ben-TOON), a Yucatecan liqueur flavored with honey and anise. The restaurant is located slightly off the beaten path at Lucerna 12, five blocks south of the large traffic circle where Bucareli,

Juárez, and Paseo de la Reforma intersect. Open 11:00 A.M. to midnight, daily except Sundays, when it closes at 6:00 P.M. Tel: 546-2972.

That many artists, intellectuals, and restaurant operators flock to "La Casa Paco," as the locals call it, is all you need to know about the **Fonda de San Francisco**. The fresh flowers on the tables and in the wall recesses are changed daily, and the *sopa de flor de calabaza* (squash flower soup), the *crepas de jaiba* (crab crepes), and the delicious *sopa de queso* (cheese soup) are as good to look at as they are to eat. Located about ten blocks west of the Monument to the Revolution at José Vásquez de León 126, near the phone company building, La Casa Paco is open 1:00 to 10:00 P.M., daily except Sundays. Tel: 546-4060.

The Zona Rosa

José Loredo, the creative chef-owner of **Loredo** (and the son of the restaurant's founder, the late José Ines Loredo), prepares traditional Mexican dishes with a special flair. To start your meal, try his *sopa mixteca,* a savory vegetable soup flavored with bone marrow, and then move on to the *carne asada a la tampiquena* (grilled strips of beef), one of Mexico's best-known dishes and one that Papa Loredo is said to have invented when he lived in Tampico. If you're really hungry, the *fuente de mariscos,* an immense cold platter of shellfish, will satisfy all but the murderously ravenous. Hamburgo 29, at the eastern edge of the Zona Rosa. Open 8:00 A.M. to midnight, Monday through Saturday, and 1:00 to 6:00 P.M. on Sundays. Tel: 566-7114.

Focolare, at Hamburgo 87, is known as "the Restaurant of the Three Suns" because it features gastronomic specialties from three distinct regions of the country: Veracruz, Oaxaca, and the Yucatán. It also serves a breakfast buffet (as a marimba band plays in the background) and a different kind of *mole* sauce every day of the week. Things pick up on Friday and Saturday nights, when there's a Mexican folk-dancing show and a simulated cockfight. (The restaurant is full of tour groups on Saturdays, so you may want to come another day if you're hoping for an intimate meal.) On either side of the restaurant as you enter are two smaller rooms: **El Trumpo**, an English pub–type bar, and **La Pirinola**, a piano bar. Open 7:30 to 1:00 A.M. weekdays and from 9:00 A.M. on weekends. Tel: 511-2679.

Alfredo's, located in the arcade between Londres and Hamburgo, is the best of the many restaurants strung out along this always-bustling alley. Sicilian-born Alfredo, 29 years at the same location, personally supervises the kitchen and is justly famous for his alleged namesake specialty: fettuccini Alfredo. Open 1:00 to 11:00 P.M., daily except Sundays. Tel: 511-3864.

Shirley's, in the Plaza Comermex on Calle Londres, between Calles Niza and Génova, is a sure bet for tourists with queasy stomachs. In business for half a century, Shirley's always draws a lunchtime line for their famous buffets, featuring traditional Mexican cuisine (not too spicy) as well as U.S.-style dishes (including the city's best homemade apple pie). The friendly, efficient service and impeccably clean premises should dispel any lingering homesickness. Shirley's other locations are at Paseo de la Reforma 108 (near the Fiesta Americana Reforma, formerly the Holiday Inn Crowne Plaza) and the corner of Periférico Norte and Reforma in Polanco.

Bellinghausen was owned by the Austrian restaurateurs of the same name until 1962, when Chef Enrique Alvárez took over the management of this bustling steak-and-seafood establishment at Londres 95. Sizable servings of crayfish spiced with paprika and olive oil, shrimp in garlic sauce, and a notable red snapper in a light chile sauce are among the specialties that make this a favorite meeting place of Mexican businesspeople. Open 1:00 to 10:00 P.M. daily. Tel: 207-6149.

Located at the corner of Londres and Niza in what was once the official residence of the U.S. ambassador, **La Calesa de Londres** is a fine restaurant with the stately atmosphere of days gone by. It's especially recommended for beef lovers: The restaurant's owner raises his own cattle on a ranch in Chihuahua, an area famed for its quality beef. A string trio performs nightly in the cozy wood-paneled bar. Open 1:00 P.M. to 1:00 A.M., daily except Sundays, when it closes at 6:00 P.M. Tel: 533-6625.

The two-story **Chalet Suizo,** Niza 37, is the place for Swiss-Bavarian cuisine. The portions are generous and the waitresses in their pretty peasant dresses along with the ethnic decor combine to create an atmosphere reminiscent of an Alpine chalet. A Zona Rosa landmark, the Chalet Suizo is open 12:30 to 11:45 P.M. daily. Tel: 511-7529.

Named for Luis Buñuel's first film, *An Andalusian Dog,* **El Mesón del Perro Andaluz,** at Copenhague 26, used to cater to the capital's filmmakers and other artists. Now it's one of a trio of affiliated outdoor eateries, each with its own front-row seats to a colorful parade of Mexican streetlife. Next door, **El Mesón la Marisqueria del Perro Andaluz** serves tempting seafood. Across the alley, Italian chef Mario Saggese prepares the pasta dishes at his **El Perro d'Enfrente.** All three are open 1:00 P.M. to 1:00 A.M. daily. Tel: 533-5306.

Chez Pascal, located on block-long Calle Oslo, between Calles Niza and Copenhague, is an unheralded but superb French restaurant. Owner-chef Pascal Brunereau takes pride in carefully selecting the ingredients needed for his very individual concoctions, and he makes a point of greeting each and every customer. State your preference—meat, fish, or other—and allow Brunereau to order for you. Rotating art exhibits carefully selected by the maestro "to enhance the culinary experience" are an added bonus in this plain but intimate setting. Open 1:00 P.M. to 1:00 A.M., Monday through Saturday, and until 6:00 P.M. on Sundays. Reservations advised; Tel: 525-8907 or 0947.

A number of restaurant critics put **Estoril**, at Génova 75, among Mexico's finest restaurants. Oaxacan chef Pedro Ortega learned to cook from his Indian mother, who taught him the recipe for his divine *crepas de huitlacoche* (corn-fungus crepes) and chicken in black *mole* sauce, which he makes every Thursday and Friday. His *perejil al Estoril* (fried parsley) is rumored to have aphrodisiacal qualities and the *huitlacoche* mousse is memorable. Open 1:30 to 11:00 P.M., daily except Sundays. Tel: 208-3284 or 3451. There's a branch of Estoril in Polanco in an elegant old mansion at Alejandro Dumas 24. Reservations, jackets, and ties are required. Open 1:30 to 10:30 P.M., daily except Sundays and Mondays. Tel: 531-4556.

Champs-Elysées, across Paseo de la Reforma from the U.S. embassy at Amberes 1, serves a kind of Mexicanized French cuisine in an otherwise typically French atmosphere. Whether by design or accident, the combination works. Tables up front (*"una mesa en frente, por favor"*) offer great views of the passing scene on Reforma. Open 1:00 to 11:00 P.M. on weekdays; closed weekends. Tel: 514-0450.

Popular with business executives for the past 34 years, **Passy**, a garden restaurant with French decor at Amberes 10, is housed in a 19th-century mansion on the Zona Rosa's most elegant street. The crab pancakes, seafood in a shell, and coq au vin are so good that Passy will, in all likelihood, be serving them for another three decades. Wear a tie. Open 1:00 to 11:00 P.M., daily except Sundays. Tel: 208-2087 or 207-3747.

Honfleur, at Amberes 14A, is one of the handful of truly worthy French restaurants in Mexico. Tasty delicacies in subtle sauces are prepared in genteelly elegant surroundings by Cordon Bleu chef-in-residence José Rodríguez, who creates poetry with his soufflés. The service here is as fine as the cuisine. Open 1:00 to 11:00 P.M., daily except Sundays. Tel: 533-2115 or 1181.

Yug, on the western edge of the Zona Rosa at Varsovia 3, is a neighborhood-type vegetarian restaurant that offers a variety of meatless Mexican dishes. Yug's baker makes fresh brown bread daily, and papaya, carrot, orange, and alfalfa juice are available year-round. There's also a whole-grain bakery on the premises. Tel: 574-4475.

La Lanterna, a few blocks west of the Zona Rosa at Paseo de la Reforma 458 (between Calles Burdeos and Lieja), features traditional Italian food and great pizzas. The pasta is made fresh on the premises daily. Open 1:00 P.M. to 1:00 A.M., Monday through Saturday. Tel: 207-9969.

Near the U.S. Embassy

The embassy district is north of Paseo de la Reforma, opposite the Zona Rosa.

·Housed in a beautiful 19th-century mansion at Río Sena 88, its patio framed by classical sculpture and lush greenery, **Les Moustaches** is one of Mexico City's most stunning restaurants. It offers more than elegant decor, however; you quickly get the feeling you have walked into another world as you are ushered to your table. At Les Moustaches everyone is treated like a visiting dignitary. Start your meal with the smoked-salmon soup or spicy shrimp bisque, and end it with flaming baked Alaska or the amaretto soufflé. Jackets and ties are required, and reservations are recommended. Open 1:00 to 6:30 P.M. and from 8:00 P.M. to 12:30 A.M. on weekdays; closed weekends. Tel: 525-1265.

Grass-roots cuisine at its best can be enjoyed at **El Caminero**, one block north of the U.S. embassy at Río Lerma 138. Although it looks suspiciously like a greasy spoon, don't be put off by the cramped, no-frills interior. The lunchtime crowds in business suits come for one thing and one thing only: tacos in every conceivable variety. You'll probably have to stand as you're munching yours, though; there are only a few stools at the counter in this landmark eatery. Open 1:15 P.M. to 1:00 A.M. daily. Tel: 533-3390.

Las Fuentes, at Río Pánuco 127, two blocks north of the Monument to Independence, is a roomy, comfortable, and sparklingly clean vegetarian restaurant—the best of its kind in the capital. French-American owner Monsieur Philipe, who somehow manages to greet every customer, takes pride in personally purchasing his produce every day at dawn in the Merced market. The result is the absolutely freshest food in town—and the largest helpings. Breakfasts are great (served from 8:00 A.M.), and prices are very reasonable. Las Fuentes is crowded at lunchtime, but the service is so good you shouldn't have to wait more than a few minutes, even if the line winds out the door and onto the street. There's also a retail shop here that stocks a wide variety of top-grade health foods. Open 8:00 A.M. to 6:00 P.M. daily. Tel: 525-7095.

Bangkok, a small, unpretentious place, brings gourmet Thai cuisine to Mexico City. Tucked away on the second floor of the Centro Comercial Galerías, a shopping mall six blocks north of the U.S. embassy, it's difficult to find but worth the effort. Enter the mall via the main entrance (Melchor Ocampo 192), take the escalator to the second floor, turn right, and look for the inconspicuous plaques identifying the myriad shops. Bangkok is Local #3. Start out with sopa goong, a shrimp broth, and move on to woon sea goong, noodles fried in a base of corn, shrimp, and egg. Open 1:00 to 10:00 P.M. daily. Tel: 254-4460.

Polanco

You can enjoy the atmosphere of "a thousand and one Arabian nights" and dance until dawn with Mexico's Middle Eastern community at **Adonis**, Homero 424. The food here—falafel, raw and fried kibbe, tabouleh, fish with nuts, stuffed grape leaves dipped in tahini, date pie, and other Middle Eastern favorites—is the real thing. Open 1:00 P.M. to midnight, Wednesday through Saturday, and 1:00 to 6:00 P.M. on Sundays. Tel: 531-6490.

Chef Jacques Bergerault came to Mexico in 1957 to open the kitchen of the famed Las Brisas in Acapulco. Today he and his sons, Jacques and Federico, run the **Café de Paris**, Campos Elíseos 164, one of Polanco's more courtly establishments, and one especially dedicated to pleasing its customers. In fact, Bergerault himself goes to the market twice a week to find the best available ingredients for his daily specials. Begin with *croustade d'oeufs de caille palois* (tart stuffed with quail's egg) and follow it with the *pato al cilantro* (duck cooked in fresh coriander). The original Café de Paris, now in its fourth decade of continuous operation, is hard to find. Tucked away under the Río Mississippi overpass at Parque Melchor Ocampo 14, just a few blocks north of the U.S. embassy (and so always packed at lunchtime with embassy administrative personnel), the restaurant is housed in a rather run-down centuries-old building (whereas the Polanco location would appear very much at home in a chic Paris neighborhood). The quality of the cuisine and service is impeccable at both Cafés de Paris. Open from 1:30 P.M. to midnight, Monday through Saturday, and until 6:00 P.M. on Sundays. Tel: 531-6646 (Polanco) and 528-8997 (original).

El Parador de José Luis, long an institution in the Zona Rosa, has now brought its Mediterranean food (try their *tapas*) and Spanish decor to Campos Elíseos 198. El Parador is also a good place to rest after a strenuous day of shopping in Polanco's expensive boutiques, or to indulge in a serious paella (but give the chef an extra 45 minutes to prepare it). Tel: 533-1840.

El Fongoncito is the name and tacos are their game. With two locations on opposite sides of Calle Leibnitz at numbers 54 and 55, a block from the rear entrance to the Camino Real, El Fongoncito draws taco aficionados from near and far who gorge themselves on the legendary *tacos al pastor* (barbecued beef). In fact, the constant activity requires a permanent crew of four policeman to control the traffic. If you beat the house record for the most tacos consumed in a two-hour period, the tacos are free. Open 1:00 P.M. to 2:00 A.M., Sunday through Thursday, and 1:00 P.M. to dawn on Fridays and Saturdays. Tel: 208-7849.

Just as the Camino Real can claim to be the best hotel in the D.F., the hotel's **Fouquet's of Paris** can legitimately claim to be one of the best French restaurants in the city. Superb service at lunch as well as dinner, live music, and spectacular flaming dishes make this a favorite with socialites, diplomats, and members of the Mexican communications industry. An excellent choice for a special occasion. Open 7:30 to 10:00 A.M., 2:00 to 4:30 P.M., and 8:00 to 11:00 P.M. on weekdays; 8:00 to 11:00 P.M. on Saturdays; 2:00 to 4:30 P.M. on Sundays. Tel: 203-2121.

Meals at the Camino Real's **Azulejos** restaurant are served on an enclosed terrace overlooking a swimming pool. The Sunday brunch here is one of the best in the city. Open 7:30 A.M. to 11:00 P.M. daily. Tel: 203-2121.

Piccolo Suizo, diagonally across from the Camino Real at Mariano Escobedo 539, resembles an Alpine log cabin. It's been a popular meeting place for the neighborhood's many business executives for more than 30 years. The house specialties are *fondue de queso* (cheese fondue) and *pato al orange* (duck in orange sauce). Open 12:30 P.M. to 1:00 A.M. daily. Tel: 531-1298.

Las Mercedes, located one block north of the Camino Real at the corner of Darwin and Leibniz, is the place for hearty, traditional Mexican breakfasts, tasty meat dishes, and delicious hand-made tortillas. The portions are huge and the service impeccable, which explains why it's popular with local businesspeople during the week and families on the weekends. Tel: 250-5000.

The **Hacienda de los Morales**, on the western edge of Polanco (technically in Colonia los Morales Polanco) at Vásquez de Mella 525, celebrated its 25th anniversary in

1993. Originally the site of Mexico's first silkworm farm, the restored 17th-century hacienda is worth a visit for its architecture alone, with colonial-era fountains, chapels, paintings, and furniture. Considering all the bustling activity created by the conscientious, fast-moving staff as they serve hundreds of diners, the food is exceptionally good. The cold walnut soup especially is to be savored. A string quartet creates a soothingly elegant mood in the comfortable lounge. Reservations, jackets, and ties are required after 6:00 P.M. Open 1:00 P.M. to midnight daily. Tel: 540-3225.

Located in a neo-colonial home at Molière 50, not far from the Polanco hotels, **Isadora** is usually packed for lunch and dinner. Chef Carmen Ortino named her restaurant after the flashy, rebellious dancer because she, like the great Duncan, is a passionate performer—of the culinary arts. Reservations are advised, especially if the lovely Carmen is orchestrating one of her seasonal food festivals. A great choice in any season, however, is her ravioli stuffed with *huitlacoche* and covered in a light chile and corn sauce (*raviolis relleno de huitlacoche en salsa de chile poblano*). Open 1:30 to 5:00 P.M. and 8:30 to 11:00 P.M., Monday through Saturday; closed Sundays. Reservations advised; Tel: 280-5586.

The **King's Pub**, an authentic Irish pub where informality reigns, is within walking distance of the Nikko México and Stouffer Presidente Chapultepec at Arquímedes 31. Irish-Mexican owner Pepe Meehan makes all his guests feel at home with his personal brand of blarney. Count on enjoying the best prime rib south of Kansas City, or try one of his "McMeehan burgers," the safe salad bar, and the draft beer. There's also live dinner music upstairs in the evenings. Open 1:00 P.M. to 1:00 A.M., Monday through Saturday, and until 10:00 P.M. on Sundays. Tel: 254-2655.

If you have to limit yourself to just one Mexican restaurant, make it the **Fonda del Recuerdo**, Bahía de las Palmas 39, where four strolling bands play *veracruzano* folk music—simultaneously. Not a place to propose marriage, perhaps, but a terrific spot where the fiesta never seems to end. Known for its giant portions (truckloads of fresh seafood arrive daily from Veracruz), the house offers specialties that include a drink called the "torito"—guanabanana and mamey juice mixed with *aguardiente*. The Fonda del Recuerdo has menus in English and features everything from tortilla soup to crabmeat turnovers. There's also a babysitter on hand in a tot-lot to entertain your children. Open 9:00 A.M. to midnight, Monday through Saturday, and until 8:00 P.M. on Sundays. Tel: 203-0095.

The Argentinian steak house **La Tablita**, at Presidente

Masaryk and Torcuato Tasso, serves choice cuts of meat prepared with special herbs and red-wine sauce. Dining here is something like eating in a greenhouse; the smell of steak cooking on individual braziers fills an atrium alive with the chatter of shoppers and well-dressed businesspeople. And the service, like the cheese turnovers (*empanadas*), is superb. Tel: 250-2522.

There are also branches of La Tablita in Coyoacán and San Angel, both good choices for a quick, satisfying lunch while visiting either of these interesting colonial neighborhoods. In Coyoacán you'll find it on the corner of Avenidas División del Norte and Hidalgo; Tel: 544-0031. In San Angel it's on the corner of Calle Altavista and Avenida Revolución; Tel: 248-2362.

El Buen Comer, Edgar Allen Poe 50, a small French bistro in the garage of a private home where the customers all seem to know each other, specializes in quiches and fondues. French Cordon Bleu chef Roger Marcellini, the founder of this intimate hideaway, and his son and daughter attend to the cuisine. Their beef bourguignon is made with tender morsels of steak, and the house wine is from the vineyards of Tequisquiapán, Querétaro. Open 1:00 to 6:00 P.M., daily except Sundays. Tel: 203-5337.

At Temístocles 12, a short walk from the Nikko México and Stouffer Presidente hotels, **La Palma** is an excellent choice for a typical Mexican meal. Tastefully decorated in elegant but unpretentious colonial style, this little restaurant offers a variety of exotic, hard-to-find dishes. Especially recommended are *tacos de jaiba* (crabmeat-filled tacos), *huauzontles en anchol* (mixed greens in red chile sauce), and *sopa criolla La Palma* (bean soup with vermicelli). The delicious handmade tortillas are reason enough to eat here. Open 1:00 P.M. to midnight, Monday through Saturday, and until 6:00 P.M. on Sundays. Tel: 250-9881.

Rincón Argentina accepts no reservations, but nobody seems to mind. The wooden benches installed on the sidewalk for patient patrons, many of them business executives, are always filled at lunchtime. Rincon Argentina's wide variety of meats is outstanding, and the restaurant's interior, featuring mahogany paneling and framed photos of Argentinian soccer teams, is a bit cramped but cozy. Try the *pascualina*, a pastry tart filled with ham and spinach, and the *morcilla*, a black pudding. The Chilean Santa Marta Cabernet Sauvignon is the perfect accompaniment to a meal here. Open 1:00 to 11:00 P.M. daily. Tel: 254-3750 or 3964.

Sir Winston Churchill's, in the western part of Polanco at Boulevard Avila Camacho 67, is not just for those needing a quick fix of bangers and mash. Housed in an old Tudor mansion, this culinary oasis is one of the finest, as well as most attractive, eating places in the city: The walls are paneled with mahogany; the tables are set with fresh flowers and cranberry-glass goblets; and the fireplace may be roaring. In this regal setting you can indulge in a tender rib eye, a rare piece of roast beef, or a flaming skewer of shrimps in herb butter. Among the many sinful desserts is a cappuccino mousse with whipped cream. The Irish coffee is great and the wine cellar well stocked. If you don't have time for dinner, go for tea. Private dining rooms are available for up to ten people. Coats and ties required. Open noon to 1:00 A.M., Monday through Saturday; closed Sundays. Reserve; Tel: 280-6829 or 3217.

Lago Chapultepec is a large glass-walled restaurant on the shore of Lago Mayor in the second section of Chapultepec Park. A landmark for years, when it was called Restaurante del Lago, it was closed for more than two years due to a labor dispute. Now reopened under new management, the food, service, and background music are adequate, the beautiful setting superb. Caviar and smoked salmon are staples on the international-style menu, and the wine list is extensive. Casual clothing is acceptable until sundown, when jackets and ties are required. Open 8:00 A.M. to 2:00 A.M., Monday through Saturday, and from 11:00 A.M. to 4:00 P.M. for brunch on Sundays. Tel: 515-9585.

Lomas de Chapultepec

Lomas is a luxurious residential neighborhood in the western D.F. that begins where Paseo de la Reforma swings south and west beyond Chapultepec Park. Magnificent trees and beautiful old mansions line the boulevard here, and it's just 20 minutes by taxi from the Zona Rosa (your restaurant will be happy to call a cab for you after dinner).

Colombian-born Guillermo Gomez fell in love with his beautiful partner and wife, Elizabeth, in Victoria, Canada; then, in a daring moment, they decided to move to Mexico City and try their luck as restaurateurs. The result of their decision is the romantically chic **Isla Victoria**, located at Monte Kamérun 120 in a small mansion on a tree-lined residential street. The menu offers daily specials such as Colombian chicken soup served with capers, cream, and avocado; or *marminto,* a cream of mushroom and shrimp soup served in a bowl covered with a puff-pastry dome. Dress is semiformal (chic semiformal, of course); if you manage to look as if you've stepped out of a fashion magazine you will be treated as an honored guest. Children are not allowed. Open 1:00 to 11:00 P.M., daily except Sundays. Tel: 520-5597.

Insurgentes Sur, San Angel, and Points South

Located on Torres Adalid, two blocks east of Insurgentes Sur near the Siqueiros Cultural Polyforum, **Suntory** is the oldest, most elegant, and most expensive of the capital's many Japanese restaurants. Authenticity reigns in this lovely setting: Rock gardens and cascading fountains surround the private dining rooms, and kimono-clad waitresses and *teppanyaki* chefs contribute to the feeling you've somehow been transported to the Far East. Open 1:00 to 5:00 P.M. and 7:00 to 11:00 P.M., Monday through Thursday; 1:00 to 11:30 P.M. on Fridays and Saturdays; and 1:00 to 6:00 P.M. on Sundays. Tel: 536-9432. There's another Suntory on the corner of Paseo de la Reforma and Monte Urales 535 in Lomas de Chapultepec, just west of Polanco. The hours are the same; Tel: 202-4711.

Mazurka, the one and only Polish restaurant in the city, is located at Calle Nueva York 150, four blocks west of Insurgentes Sur in the neighborhood of the Polyforum, but it's hard to find; taking a taxi will save you a lot of aggravation. The Polish owner, Tadeusz Podbereski, is a gracious host who speaks passable English and takes great pride in suggesting the ethnic specialties of his Polish-born chef, including *ges* (duck baked with wild-rice stuffing) and *kaczka* (goose baked with sour-apple stuffing and topped with blueberries). Señor Podbereski is also certain to tell you how much Pope John Paul II loved his *bigos* (sweet-and-sour cabbage stuffed with smoked meats and sausage) when he visited Mexico a few years ago. The restaurant's Old World atmosphere is enhanced by Art Deco touches, slightly frayed red velvet drapes, and a chamber group that performs mostly Chopin in the evenings. A branch has opened recently near University City at Copilco 3. Both are open 1:00 to 11:30 P.M., Monday through Saturday, and until 5:00 P.M. on Sundays. Tel: 523-8811 or 548-7471 (Copilco branch).

For a genuine slice of Mexican life try **Las Cazuelas**, two blocks east of the Plaza México bullring at Avenida San Antonio 143. Delicious home-style cooking at reasonable prices accounts for the line of customers waiting to be seated during peak hours. The trick is to get there before 1:30 P.M., when most Mexicans are still digesting their *almuerzo* (the "snack" eaten between breakfast and lunch). In business since 1916, Doña Emilia Perez de Sotelo, the original owner, began her career as a taco street vendor, selling her wares from a *cazuela* (casserole). She was so successful she soon added more casseroles and eventually progressed to this sit-down restaurant with colorful, hand-painted tiles and furniture and strolling mariachis singing their hearts out. Lined up on both sides of the entrance are about two dozen huge, steaming earthenware *cazuelas* filled with various stuffings for tacos. The *machitos de carnero* (lamb sweetbreads) and *pipian con pollo* (chicken drowned in a squash-seed sauce) are worth the wait, and fruit-flavored pulque—the fermented juice of the maguey plant (before it's distilled to make tequila)—is the beverage of choice. Moderation is advised, however, as this delicious concoction tends to sneak up on the unwary. Open 1:00 to 7:00 P.M. daily. Tel: 563-3956.

Located off the beaten tourist track (it's best to take a taxi) on Calle Mercaderes, a narrow, winding street one block west of Avenida Insurgentes Sur, the **Fonda del Factor** is a 59-year-old landmark widely reputed to serve the best authentic Mexican food in the D.F. A charming colonial ambience, swift, attentive service, and delicious hand-made tortillas are a perfect complement to what is perhaps the best *mole* in the country, Puebla notwithstanding. The restaurant's owners maintain a close relationship with the nuns of the Carmelite order, whose secret *mole* recipes have been passed down for more than 240 years, and as a result the Fonda del Factor is the only restaurant in the D.F. where the public can enjoy these rare dishes. Especially pleasing is the *mole verde de pipian,* prepared with summer squash seeds. Among the other unusual and delicious specialties on the menu are *nopalitos guisados* (braised prickly pear cactus leaves) and *pollo relleno horneado con picadillo estilo Factor* (roasted chicken stuffed with hash à la Factor). Open 1:00 to 8:00 P.M. on Mondays; 1:00 to 11:00 P.M., Tuesday through Thursday; 1:00 P.M. to midnight on Fridays; and 8:00 A.M. to midnight on weekends. Although the restaurant's legal address is Calle Mercaderes 21, taxi drivers are more familiar with the back entrance address, Calle de Factor 34. Tel: 660-2628.

With a quaint brick fireplace as its centerpiece, **La Casserole**, Insurgentes Sur 1880, near the San Angel area, serves Mexico City's best French provincial cuisine in an intimate setting. Some of the delectable specialties of the house include *huachinango papillote,* squab, partridge, and fresh-baked garlic bread covered with melted cheese. And their chocolate mousse is sinful. Open from 8:00 A.M. to midnight, daily except Sundays. Tel: 524-7190.

Located between Avenidas Insurgentes Sur and Revolución at Avenida de la Paz 45, a few blocks east of the Plaza de San Jacinto, **Los Irabien** is one of the very best restaurants in the capital, as well as a convenient stop for breakfast, lunch, or dinner on your way to or back from Coyoacán and San Angel. The Irabien family is dedicated to excellence and caters to more than just your taste buds. Beautiful works of art, including originals by some of Mexico's finest painters, are discreetly interspersed among the spectacular potted plants, antique Mexican furniture, and carved wooden statues. Walls colored in unusual, subdued hues serve as the perfect background for these visual treats. The dining area itself is very comfortable, with every seat offering a fine vantage point from which to eye the rest of the room; a pianist performs at lunch and dinner.

Los Irabien's kitchen is under the supervision of inventive master chef Enrique Estrada. One of his many delicious creations is a liver pâté presented atop a sculpted gelatin, itself a work of art. His *sopa de mariscos* with Pernod is memorable, as are two dishes from the nouvelle cuisine section, both featuring *huachinango* (red snapper): *huachinango en nopalitos al mojo de ajo* (prickly pear cactus leaves filled with filet of red snapper and fried in garlic) and "El Rey del Caribe" (red snapper topped with *huitlacoche* and *flor de calabaza*). Open 8:00 A.M. to 1:00 A.M., Monday through Saturday; 9:00 A.M. to 6:00 P.M. on Sundays. Tel: 660-2382 or 0876.

Two blocks west of Insurgentes Sur at Pedro Luís de Ogazon 102 in San Angel, **Dos Puertas** (Two Doors) comprises several comfortable dining areas surrounded by enclosed gardens. The kitchen here puts out an amazing variety of fine Mexican and international cuisine, starting with breakfast; rotating art exhibitions enhance the elegant atmosphere of the place. Open 7:30 A.M. to 11:00 P.M., Monday through Saturday, and 8:00 A.M. to 6:00 P.M. on Sundays. Tel: 550-7489.

King's Road, located a block east of the landmark San Angel Inn at Altavista 43, serves some of the best beef in the D.F. The prime rib and the U.S.-style steaks at this English pub–type restaurant are excellent, as are the breaded frog's legs. A pianist provides appropriate background music for all meals. Open 1:00 P.M. to 1:00 A.M. daily. Tel: 660-0883.

An ideal place to have lunch en route to University City or Xochimilco is the award-winning **La Cava**, Insurgentes Sur 2465, just south of the university and the Avenida San Jerónimo exit. Diners can choose from its extensive menu of Mexican, Spanish, and international-style entrées in an enclosed dining room overlooking a patio with a cascading fountain, or on the patio itself. There are, in addition, a number of private dining areas able to accommodate up to eight people—the perfect place to have a small celebration. Open 1:00 P.M. to 12:30 A.M., Monday through Saturday, and until 6:00 P.M. on Sundays. Tel: 660-3133.

Mauna Loa, San Jerónimo 240 (the main avenue leading to El Pedregal), is about a half-hour's taxi ride south of the Zona Rosa, but it's worth the trip. Equally delicious Szechuan, Cantonese, and Temujin specialties are brought to your table by attentive waiters, and the nightly entertainment (shows at 10:00 and 11:30) features Hawaiian music, hula dancers, and potent tropical drinks. Open 8:00 A.M. to 1:00 A.M., Monday through Saturday, and 9:00 A.M. to 6:00 P.M. on Sundays. Tel: 548-6884.

Another good choice for lunch in the southern D.F. is the **Antigua Hacienda de Tlalpan**, at Calzada de Tlalpan 4619. A restored 18th-century hacienda surrounded by two acres of beautiful gardens, it was once a stagecoach stop on the Acapulco road and, later, a weekend retreat for President-for-Life Porfirio Díaz. Today it's more likely to be filled with shoppers who have spent the morning at PERISUR, the capital's largest shopping mall, just a five-minute cab ride to the east. The food, mostly international, is better than average, but the grounds alone are reason enough to stop while you're exploring the surrounding area. Open 1:00 P.M. to 1:00 A.M., Monday through Saturday, and until 6:00 P.M. on Sundays. Tel: 573-2361.

NIGHTLIFE AND ENTERTAINMENT

Mexico City after dark can be exciting, but selectivity is the key factor. Keep in mind, moreover, that the mile-and-a-half altitude in the D.F. tends to make each cocktail about twice as intoxicating as it would be at sea level.

Most nightclubs, like many restaurants, are closed Sunday evenings.

The *Tiempo Libre,* a very informative weekly publication, lists all the current events in the D.F.; the latest edition is available at newsstands every Friday.

Cocktail Lounges and Hotel Bars

Live music in most lounges commences at 8:00 P.M. and continues until the 2:00 A.M. closing time (a few remain open longer). Most of the best cocktail lounges are located in the major hotels.

If you visit only one bar in Mexico City, make it the **Bar L'Opera**, located at Cinco de Mayo 14, one block east of the Palacio de Bellas Artes. In business at the same site since

1905, this historic tavern is worth a visit even if you're a teetotaler. It's an old-style cantina, admitting only men as late as 1975, when Mexico passed a law allowing women to patronize cantinas. The velvet-covered booths, garish wallpaper, antique chandeliers, and hand-carved wood paneling were allegedly purchased lock, stock, and barrel from a New Orleans bordello just after the turn of the century. True or not, the generous drinks and free-wheeling camaraderie have prevailed ever since the days when Porfirio Díaz would drop in to down a few tequilas with his cronies. Other celebrated customers have included Pancho Villa, who, peeved at his merrymaking troops, rode through the swinging doors one day in 1911 and allegedly put a bullet in the ceiling; the muralist Diego Rivera; and, more recently, the Nobel Prize–winning Gabriel García Márquez, who, according to the waiter Santiago, nurses a beer for hours while gobbling the bar's famous *botanas* (assorted snacks). "But he's a good tipper." Open noon to midnight, daily except Sundays.

The **Jorongo Bar** is a perennially popular night spot in the Sheraton María-Isabel, featuring the best in ethnic music (mostly mariachi) and jammed nightly in and out of season. It is also the closest thing to a singles bar in the D.F. Next door to the U.S. embassy at Paseo de la Reforma 325, across the street from the Zona Rosa. Open 6:00 P.M. to 2:00 A.M. daily.

The **Majestic Bar**, on the seventh floor of the hotel of the same name at Madero 73, opposite the Zócalo, offers superb views of the cathedral and the National Palace, especially on weekends, when both are floodlit. With the sounds of mariachi music always swirling through the bar, the Majestic is not the place for intimate conversations, however. Open 10:00 A.M. to 2:00 A.M. daily.

Don't be dissuaded by the sleazy appearance of **Tenampa**—if it's a slice of Mexico City life you're looking for, this is the place. The three or four strolling trios get an early (1:00 P.M.) start at this huge establishment, often playing simultaneously as they circulate among the hundreds of tables, and usually wait until the last customer is gone, sometime around dawn, before wrapping it up. Believe it or not, the constant cacophony is tolerable, and as the tequila flows the camaraderie gets mellower. Bouncers prevent undesirables from entering, so it's a safe scene. Credit cards are not accepted, however. North of Alameda Park on the Plaza de Garibaldi. Open 1:00 P.M. to 3:00 A.M. daily.

Club 25, in the Fiesta Americana Reforma, is a rooftop bar with panoramic views from every window, making it an especially popular place for sunset watching. Open 5:00 to 9:00 P.M. daily. Paseo de la Reforma 80.

The always crowded **Gatsby's**, in the Stouffer Presidente Chapultepec, is both chic and cozy, and features live ethnic music played through a well-modulated sound system. Open 9:00 P.M. to 3:00 A.M., daily except Sundays. Campos Elíseos 218, Polanco.

The Nikko México's most popular meeting spot is **Shelty**, a wood-paneled bar on the mezzanine that resembles a traditional English pub. Open 2:00 P.M. to 1:00 A.M. daily. Campos Elíseos 204, Polanco.

Discotheques

If you are fairly sober and presentable, you'll have no problem getting into any of the capital's discotheques. The normal cover charge ranges from NP 60 to NP 120, and major credit cards (with the exception of American Express in some places) are accepted. Most discos open at 10:00 P.M., but the real action generally doesn't begin until midnight. Closing time in most cases is 4:00 A.M.

The newest "in" disco for young *chilangos* is the **Rock, Stock Bar & Disco**, located in the eastern Zona Rosa at the corner of Calle Niza and Reforma. Once the snooty doorman nods you in you're given a metal-detector examination. Then you're led through various air-locked doors, up a bleak-looking stairway, and—*voila!*—into a huge, surreally fluorescent ballroom. A rotating black lightbeam illuminates walls painted with hand- and footprints, and the place is usually packed. Open 8:00 P.M. to 1:00 A.M. on Thursdays; 8:00 P.M. to 3:00 A.M. on Fridays and Saturdays.

Cero Cero, in the Camino Real hotel, has been one of the most popular discos in the capital for the last 19 years, and features live as well as recorded music. The psychedelic lighting alone is worth a visit. Open 9:00 P.M. to 4:00 A.M., daily except Sundays. Reservations necessary on weekends; Tel: 203-2121. Mariano Escobedo 700.

The intimate **Disco Club 84**, in the Stouffer Presidente Chapultepec, has a good sound system and sleek, modern decor. Frequented by youthful locals and tourists alike, it's at Campos Elíseos 218. Open 9:00 P.M. to 4:00 A.M., Thursday through Saturday only.

A familiar Oriental touch—hot towels at every table—distinguishes **Dynasty**, the Hotel Nikko's popular nightspot. Ultramodern decor, classic rock music, and tasty canapes attract a mixed-age crowd of locals and tourists. Best of all, the decibel level is tolerable, which means you can carry on a conversation even when the joint is jumping. Open 10:00 P.M. to 4:00 A.M., Tuesday through Saturday. Campos Elíseos 204, Polanco.

Bar León, at Calle 33, a few blocks north of the Zócalo, recently celebrated its 41st year as the center of Latin music in the D.F. Behind its sleazy, no-frills exterior, three and sometimes four rotating *conjuntos Latina* (Latin ensembles) play "musica tropical"—better known as *salsa*—for their enthusiastic fans. Most nights, throngs of dancers crowd the huge oval dance floor and the energy level is extraordinary. Bar León does not charge a cover—in fact, management's credo seems to be "There's always room for a few more!"—and plainclothes bouncers make it safe enough for women to visit unescorted. Open 10:00 P.M. to dawn, daily except Sundays.

Magic Circus, north of the central historic district, is a bit off the beaten path, so it's best to take a taxi. The design and lighting are state of the art, and crowds of young locals congregate here nightly, but those with sensitive eardrums might consider visiting the disco, under the same management, connected to it. **Privilege** is a bit more upscale than Magic Circus, and insists on a dress code: Men must wear jackets but need not wear ties; no slacks are permitted for women. Open 10:00 P.M. to 4:00 A.M., daily except Sundays. Calle Rodolfo Gaona 3.

News, very similar in decor and ambience to the disco of the same name in Acapulco (it's operated by the same people), is the hippest and largest disco in the D.F. Open only on weekends, from 10:00 P.M. to 4:00 A.M., it's near the El Pedregal neighborhood at Avenida San Jerónimo 252, next door to Mauna Loa (see Dining, above), about a half-hour's taxi ride south of the Zona Rosa.

Nightclubs with Floor Shows
Located on the mezzanine level of the always bustling Fiesta Americana Reforma, **Barbarella** offers two shows nightly, Thursday through Saturday, featuring nationally known headliners. Popular with both locals and visitors, this modern, comfortable room has a relaxed, friendly atmosphere. You can dance to live music between shows, and snacks are served. Open 9:00 P.M. to 3:00 A.M.; closed Sundays. East of the Zona Rosa at Paseo de la Reforma 80. Tel: 705-1515.

Las Sillas, also in the Fiesta Americana, means "The Chairs" in Spanish, and there are more than a hundred in this intimate, friendly room—no two alike—for your sitting pleasure. You can dance to live music before and after the midnight show. Open nightly 10:00 P.M. to 3:00 A.M.; closed Sundays.

Stelaris, on the top floor of the Fiesta Americana Reforma, is considered by many to be the best supper club in Mexico City. The superb food, excellent entertainment (often internationally known headliners), and spectacular views of the city make this a popular choice. There is a dress code. Open 10:00 P.M. to 3:00 A.M.; closed Sundays.

El Corral de la Moreria, at Calle Londres 161 in the Zona Rosa, is an intimate dinner club featuring top-quality Spanish music and flamenco dancing. Skip the authentic Spanish cuisine, though. Shows are at 11:00 P.M. and 2:00 A.M. nightly; open 9:30 P.M. to 3:30 A.M. Tel: 525-1762.

El Patio, a massive landmark nightclub at Calle Atenas 9, near the Zócalo, features national and international headliners every other month or so. Shows here (two a night) are done on a grand scale. The Patio's neighborhood is a bit seedy but not dangerous; it is hard to find, however, so it's best to take a taxi. The normal schedule, between headliner bookings, offers dinner and dancing from 9:00 P.M. to 2:00 A.M. Closed Sundays and Mondays. Tel: 535-3904 to check on upcoming events.

A few blocks south of the Zona Rosa and one block west of Avenida Insurgentes Sur at Calle Oaxaca 15, colorful **Gitanerias** has been a favorite of flamenco devotees for some time now. Two shows nightly, at 11:30 P.M. and 2:00 A.M.; closed Sundays. Tel: 511-5283.

Huge, very popular, and always crowded **Marrakesh** is actually four clubs in one: Valentino's for dancing, the Morocco bar for a tame singles scene, Casablanca for top-quality entertainment, and La Madelon for dinner and after-dinner dancing to live music. Frequented by wealthy locals and visitors alike, Marrakesh is open 9:00 P.M. to 3:00 A.M. nightly. In the Zona Rosa at Calle Florencia 36.

The **Plaza Santa Cecilia** is a traditional Mexican nightclub with four folkloric shows nightly. The room is huge and the food good, but patience is needed, as the service is not especially swift (to put it mildly). Shows at 9:30 P.M., 10:30 P.M., 12:30 A.M., and 2:00 A.M. Located north of Alameda Park on the Plaza de Garibaldi. Tel: 526-2455.

The entrance to **Señorial,** across the street from the Westin Galería Plaza in the Zona Rosa, resembles an enormous upended milk container. Its Sugar Bar, which features live rock music, is very popular with local businessmen, who often arrive in groups, and there is a dress code. Open 10:00 P.M. to 3:00 A.M., daily except Sundays. Calle Hamburgo 188.

Maquiavelo, in the Krystal Zona Rosa at Calle Liverpool 199, offers two floor shows nightly, at 10:00 P.M. and midnight, followed by very danceable music provided by a live orchestra until 3:00 A.M. A friendly ambience and attentive service are staples of this popular nightspot. Open 9:30 P.M. to 3:00 A.M., daily except Sundays. Tel: 211-3460.

Dining and Dancing

Fun always seems to prevail at **Chez 'Ar**, a brightly colored nightclub in the Zona Rosa. You can dance to a combo here from 9:00 P.M. to 2:00 A.M., nightly except Sundays. Located in the Hotel Aristos, Paseo de la Reforma 276. **Yesterday's**, a comfortable, friendly ballroom also in the Hotel Aristos, is frequented by lots of young to fortyish singles four nights a week. The live music starts at 8:30 P.M. and continues until 1:30 A.M. (3:00 A.M. on Saturdays); closed Sundays.

The **Torre de Oro** (Golden Tower), on the 22nd floor of the centrally located Sevilla Palace hotel, offers terrific evening views of the capital's skyline, including the Bolsa (stock exchange) building. Live music, great for dancing, is served up by a good orchestra with an extensive repertoire of American "oldies but goodies." Crowded on weekends with both locals and tourists. Paseo de la Reforma 105. Tel: 566-8877 for reservations.

The great views offered by the **Muralto**, which occupies the entire 41st floor of the Latin American Tower, sometimes extend as far as the surrounding mountains and the Valley of Mexico, and are reason enough to drop by. In the evening the city spread out below appears at its best. The live music begins at 8:00 P.M., and there's a strict dress code for men (tie and jacket). Open 1:00 P.M. to 1:00 A.M., Monday through Saturday, and until 10:00 P.M. on Sundays. Tel: 521-7751.

SHOPS AND SHOPPING

Mexico City, which generates an abundance of artwork, high fashion, and handicrafts, is also the major market in the country for all types of traditional arts and crafts from outlying regional centers. Glassware and ceramics, for example, are only two of the many types of great buys that are available throughout the D.F.

Large stores and open-air markets devoted exclusively to regional handicrafts are scattered throughout the downtown area, with the products of the various states and regions usually separated into sections in each. At many of the markets Indian women wearing traditional garb work their looms on the sidewalks while waiting for customers. This should come as no surprise. Since Aztec times, the *tianguis* has been the economic heart of the Mexican pueblo, at once a place to barter goods and services, eat local dishes, and visit with friends. Traditionally, markets are the cheapest places to buy arts and crafts, regional clothing, foodstuffs, herbs, leather bags, and silver.

Only a few of the *mercados* in the D.F. have English-speaking shopkeepers and accept credit cards, however. If you possess a sense of adventure but just don't have the time to travel into the interior of the country, you can pay a guide to take you around some of these; you'll be able to pay for his time and car on the money you save. More important, you'll take home the memory of a real Mexican shopping spree.

The shops below are discussed first by type and then by neighborhood.

Crafts and Antiques Markets

The easiest market to shop is the **Centro Artesanal Buena-vista** at Aldama 187, just off Insurgentes Norte near the Buenavista metro station and a few blocks east of the Guerrero station. The Centro is more like an American supermarket than a Mexican crafts market, and the prices are higher than in other markets; the vendors here welcome major credit cards, and there's even a place for your guide to sip coffee while you browse through the mammoth warehouse containing more than 80,000 items. Regional specialties such as carved lacquered chests from Olinala (in Guerrero), black pottery from San Bartolo Coyotepec (in Oaxaca), and copperware from Santa Clara del Cobre (in Michoacán) are available in abundance and at fair prices, and the selection of blown glass, brass, ceramics, silver jewelry, tablecloths, regional clothing, and gold (by the gram) is as good as in the Zona Rosa shops. Prices are fixed, and the vendors at the market will pack your purchases efficiently and get them to their destination safely. English is spoken. Open 9:00 A.M. to 6:00 P.M., Monday through Friday, and 10:00 A.M. to 2:00 P.M. on weekends.

If you're looking for a little adventure and have time to bargain, you will do better at **El Mercado de la Ciudadela**, at the corner of Balderas and Ayuntamiento, just a few blocks south of Alameda Park. Built in a former fortress, the market has two *fondas* where you can take a break and drink a beer or order a *comida*. Oaxacan Indians dressed in red *huipiles* sit on the ground, their offspring crawling around their feet as they work diligently on backstrap looms weaving bedspreads, tablecloths, and serapes. In the dozens of workshops inside the peach-colored walls, everything from silver baubles and hand-blown glass to Huichol beaded jewelry and rugs is being crafted as you wander among the more than 250 stalls brimming with native handicrafts. Some shop operators will accept Visa or MasterCard, none American Express; most will honor traveller's checks and U.S. dollars. English here is limited to the basics, but nowhere else can you find such a well-priced and varied selection of masks (stall 65), copper (stall 80A), handmade guitars (stall 81), lacquerware (stall 60), traditional native clothing (stall 77), leather products (stall 85), Oaxacan black pottery (stall 145), and silver (stalls 30 and 82). The market is two short blocks north of the Balderas metro station. Open 11:00 A.M. to 8:00 P.M. daily.

In the Zona Rosa itself is the **Mercado de Insurgentes**, with more than 200 vendors who know what travellers like and are eager to accommodate them. (The entrances to the market, which is bordered to the west by Calle Florencia and to the east by Calle Amberes, are on Calle Liverpool and Calle Londres.) This is an especially reliable bazaar for purchasing silver jewelry and native clothing. Bargaining is expected, and many stalls accept credit cards. Open 10:00 A.M. to 7:00 P.M. daily.

El Mercado de Antiquidades Sábado (Saturday Antiques Market) sets up shop once a week in the patio of the Plaza del Angel, a cluster of antiques shops and art galleries at Calle Londres 161, diagonally across the street from the Mercado de Insurgentes. (There is also an entrance on Calle Hamburgo, one block north of and parallel to Calle Londres.) As a rule, antiques are overpriced in Mexico, but there is always the possibility of coming up with an unexpected treasure that makes the hunt worthwhile. Open 10:00 A.M. to 6:00 P.M., Saturdays only.

The **Mercado de Antigüedades de la Lagunilla** (Sunday Thieves' Market) is located two blocks east of Paseo de la Reforma Norte and the equestrian statue of José Martí, beginning on Calle Rayón and stretching east for dozens of blocks. Amid the tangle of booths selling imported video and audio cassettes, foreign cheeses, hair spray, U.S.-made candy, blue jeans, Ray-Bans, and offbeat items too numerous to mention, you'll find some genuine antiques. Beware of pickpockets, especially on Sundays, the busiest day, and feel free to bargain for anything that catches your fancy.

Clinging to the walls on either side of this labyrinth of stalls are Indians who have brought their wares—masks, bark paintings, wooden fish with pastoral scenes sketched on their sides, and the like—from their villages to sell to the buyers of the various crafts shops. The prices for these goods are generally very reasonable.

The **Bazar Sábado**, in an old colonial mansion on the northwest corner of the Plaza de San Jacinto in San Angel (see the main narrative above), was founded in 1960 by two imaginative entrepreneurs who wanted to give U.S. and European expatriate artists, sculptors, jewelry makers, and dress designers an arena in which to display their unusual creations. At first staged in a small house in the neighborhood, the venture quickly outgrew its original setting as it mushroomed into a collective embracing more than 200 individual operations. Eventually the founding partners purchased the building in which it now resides, renovated it, and opened a new and improved Bazar Sábado in 1965, initiating in the process a Saturday tradition that has delighted countless visitors to the D.F.

The bazaar sprawls around a jacaranda-shaded patio where delicious Mexican cuisine geared to tourists' tastes is served buffet style. There is, in addition, a very good brunch served from 10:00 A.M. to noon and a more elegant sit-down lunch starting at 1:00 P.M., the latter accompanied by an excellent marimba band.

Inside, the bazaar is a two-story maze of cramped stalls. For the first-time visitor it's all but impossible to get oriented, and the polite but determined crowds of browsers leave many people feeling as if they'd gotten stuck in a revolving door. Don't despair; the bazaar is not as big as it sometimes seems, and the patio is never far away. Open 10:00 A.M. to 7:00 P.M., Saturdays only.

Government Arts and Crafts Stores

To promote the production of regional arts and crafts as well as to help artisans finance their work, the federal government and some state governments run their own shops. **FONART** shops (FONART is an acronym, in Spanish, for "National Fund to Promote Arts and Crafts") can be found throughout the country, as well as at five locations in Mexico City: Avenida Juárez 89, Centro; Londres 136, Zonà Rosa; Insurgentes Sur 1630 (in the basement of the Siqueiros Cultural Polyforum); Avenida de la Paz 37, San Angel (within walking distance of the Bazar Sábado); and a very well-stocked warehouse store at Patriotismo 691, Mixcoac. (Mixcoac is a middle-class neighborhood a few blocks from the Plaza México bullring. There's not much here other than the FONART shop, so you'll probably want to take a taxi if you go.) The items for sale vary, but normally there is a good selection of ceramics, jewelry, indigenous clothing, silver, papier-mâché, and glassware. FONART shops accept all credit cards. Open 10:00 A.M. to 7:00 P.M., daily except Sundays.

Located directly across from Alameda Park at Avenida Juárez 44, in a 16th-century structure that was originally the church of Corpus Christi, the **Museo Nacional de Artes y Industrias Populares** has a section open from 10:00 A.M. to 2:00 P.M. and again from 3:00 to 6:00 P.M. where you can choose from among the best for-sale display of regional clothing in town. You can also find wonderful toys, jewelry, and seasonal arts here; at Christmastime an assortment of *nativitas* is for sale in ceramic or tin versions, and in November the museum has the best *calaveras* (skeletons) in the D.F. (See also the Alameda Park Area section above.)

CASART, Avenida Juárez 18C, was specifically set up to promote the artisans of the state of Mexico. This is one of the better places in the D.F. to purchase a set of unleaded ceramic dishes from Valle de Bravo or to find original items from Metepec, where villagers produce charming ceramic pieces.

Arts and Crafts Stores

Located at the corner of Calles Ayuntamiento and Dolores, four blocks south of Alameda Park, the **Mercado de Curiosidades Mexicanos San Juan** is a modern city-run arts and crafts market, and an especially good option for travellers who have grown weary of the communication barrier, as most of the vendors speak a passable English and are willing to bargain. Stall 50 has the much-coveted Olinala lacquerware at very reasonable prices; stall 142, on the second floor, sells silver by the gram and semiprecious stones by the carat; and stall 160 offers a huge selection of easily packed bark paintings. Good buys in leather products, silver jewelry, and hammocks also abound.

Feder's, at Lago Murítz 67, about a 15-minute cab ride north of the Zona Rosa, is difficult to find on your own, but most taxi drivers will know the spot. A restored 19th-century mansion houses this factory outlet, which offers a good selection of beautifully colored hand-blown glass and intricately designed wrought-iron vases, lamps, goblets, candelabra, and tables. Felipe Derflingher, the congenial owner-designer, has received numerous international awards for his creations. Expert packers, Feder's ships worldwide. (Feder's also has a stall at the Bazar Sábado; see Craft and Antiques Markets above.)

Located at Carretones 5, a 20-minute taxi ride north of the Zona Rosa and a bit off the beaten path, the large **Avalos** factory (taxi drivers sometimes refer to it as "Carretones") is well worth making an extra effort to visit. This is where most of the hand-blown glassware you'll see in the better Mexico City shops and restaurants is made. The brothers Avalos, Francisco and Camilo, along with their sister, Estela, who manages the retail shop on the premises, are heirs to a tradition started by their grand-uncles in 1889. Estela will gladly arrange a free tour of the factory for interested visitors; she will also see to it that your purchases are well packed and shipped safely to the destination of your choice.

The Popular Markets

If it weren't for these *tianguis,* where every shopper gets a wholesale price, it would be impossible for most Mexicans to weather their country's ongoing financial crisis. Although they appear to enjoy making crafts, most Mexicans don't buy them. Instead, they prefer to decorate their homes with imported foreign items.

The **Mercado de Sonora**, at Avenida Fray Servando and Calle San Nicolas, about 6 km (4 miles) due east of Chapultepec Park, sells all you need to cast or uncast a spell, which is why it's affectionately known as "the Witches' Market." Vendors at some 30 stalls here hawk amulets, dried bats, good- and bad-luck candles, soap to make you rich, wreaths of garlic to protect your home against the dreaded *envidia* (envy), dried hummingbirds to make a man irresistible to the opposite sex, live animals for sacrificial purposes, medicinal herbs, and decks of tarot cards. The market also abounds with cheap ceramics, toys by the dozen, chickens, ducks, geese, songbirds, iguanas, baskets, and party supplies.

The **Mercado Cuauhtémoc**, at Río Lerma and Río Danubio, behind the Sheraton María-Isabel, is a small neighborhood fruit and vegetable market where you can sample Mexican cheeses and choose from a great variety of seasonings, among other things.

Inside the enormous **Mercado de la Lagunilla Unidad de Ropas**, located at República de Ecuador and Allende, a few blocks northwest of the Zócalo, you'll find enough clothing for sale to dress a regiment, including a variety of regional headwear, serapes, flamenco dresses, and authentic peasant skirts and blouses (not to mention such necessities as a chicken suit, complete with papier-mâché mask). You can also purchase tutus and tulle butterfly wings for your ballet-student daughter, as well as Superman, Batman, or Spiderman outfits. If you wish, Señor José Alducin (booths 89 and 90) will outfit you as any bird, complete with real feathers. He also makes normal clothing to order. At Typicos

Estelita, in the same market (booth 87), you can transform yourself into a mouse, skunk, elephant, or mariachi musician. Esperanza Garcia (booth 134) sells all kinds of dresses, including eye-catching tango and Charleston outfits. (She also makes clothing for dolls.) Be sure to bring your measurements and a translator, however.

Nearby at Calle Allende 84 between Repúblicas de Honduras and Ecuador is the famed Mexican mask store, **Galería Eugenio**, a treasure house of dragons, goblins, religious statues, antique carvings, and, of course, masks. Señor Eugenio claims to have 10,000 in stock, and even if he's exaggerating a bit, it would take you a few days just to sort through those on display from floor to ceiling in the various rooms here. You can't miss the entrance. Just look for the life-size wooden lion standing guard at the door.

Department Stores

There are only two department stores in the D.F. worth mentioning. Puerto Liverpool is less trendy than the Palacio de Hierro, but both are hipper than the American entry, Sears. The block-long **Puerto Liverpool**, with entrances on Avenida Horacio and Mariano Escobedo, the eastern boundary of the Polanco district, is a 10-minute walk north of the Camino Real hotel. Other branches are found in the PERISUR shopping center, Periférico Sur 4690; at Avenida Insurgentes Sur 1310; and, the oldest (opened by a French firm in 1847), at the corner of Calles 20 de Noviembre and Venustiano Carranza, two blocks south of the Zócalo. The downtown **Palacio de Hierro** (Iron Palace) is located on the corner of 16 de Septiembre and Isábel la Católica, a few blocks west of the Zócalo, in a landmark Neoclassical building. Their other stores are found at the corner of Calles Durango and Sevilla, three blocks south of the Zona Rosa; in the Plaza Coyoacán shopping center, Avenida Coyoacán 2000; and in the PERISUR shopping center, Periférico Sur 4690. Both stores cater to people of some means, and international credit cards are welcomed. English-speaking salespeople are available upon request at both.

PERISUR is the largest, most modern shopping mall in the country. It's located just north of the Cuicuilco archaeological site, about a 30-minute taxi ride south of the Zócalo via the Periférico Sur, the main highway to Cuernavaca.

Gifts for People With Everything

Yarn paintings created by the Huichol Indians of northwest Mexico make great one-of-a-kind gifts. Following the outlines of traditional designs (with plenty of leeway for personal expression), lengths of brightly colored acrylic yarn are glued to a base of plywood covered with beeswax. Shooting stars, shamans, blue cows—the subject matter is uniquely Huichol and as fascinating as their culture (which, among other things, embraces the use of natural hallucinogenics such as peyote and "magic" mushrooms).

The Huichols also turn out a variety of ceremonial masks distinguished by their intricate beadwork. Generally speaking, masks are a plentiful folk-art item in Mexico, and enterprising itinerant middlemen roam the countryside buying the barely "used" masks of various indigenous people. (In keeping with age-old beliefs, most native people believe that once a mask is used in a ritual it loses its magical properties.) These, in turn, are sold to shops catering to tourists throughout the Republic.

The **Tapetes Mexicanos**, in the Zona Rosa at Hamburgo 235, is the place to buy the world-renowned Temoaya rugs. Created by Otomí Indian artisans using an ancient technique, these hand-knotted wool carpets are known as "Mexican Persian rugs." Each rug draws its pattern from a different family tradition, which accounts for the more than 300 variations in size and color. Made of pure wool and washable, Temoaya rugs are heirloom souvenirs that will last for generations.

Art Galleries

The **Zona Rosa** is the hub of the D.F.'s many outstanding art galleries, all of which remain open until 8:00 P.M.

Galería Arvil, Hamburgo 9 (between Florencia and Amberes), sells works by Mexico's finest artists, including Tamayo, Zuniga, and Toledo. Contemporary originals and prints, and a good art bookstore as well.

Galería del Circulo, Hamburgo 112, has works by Tamayo, Siqueiros, and Clement, as well as prints by Dalí and Picasso, among others.

Galería Tere Haas, Génova 2, is staffed by knowledgeable personnel, and specializes in paintings, graphics, and bronze sculptures. Zuniga, Castañeda, Amaya, Montoya, Nierman, among many others.

Galería Hardy, Génova 2J, is filled with contemporary art by talented unknowns and has an excellent art bookstore.

Galería de Arte Misrachi, Génova 20, features the masters—Tamayo, Siqueiros, Zuniga, Toledo, Coronel—as well as works by contemporary sculptors. There is another branch in Polanco, at the corner of Homero and Calle La Fontaine.

Galería Lourdes Chumacero, Estocolmo 34, has a fine

collection of contemporary paintings, sculpture, and ceramics.

Galería Solaris, Estrasburgo 19B, sells paintings, sculpture, etchings, and tapestry by the likes of Bustamante, Sebastián, Griza, and Alcántara.

The **Asian Art Gallery**, Amberes 11, is noted for its fine collection of Oriental artwork, sculpture, jewelry, and handmade crafts.

Galería Honfleur, Amberes 14, sells contemporary paintings, sculpture, ceramics, and silver.

Galería Aura, Amberes 38, sells contemporary paintings and sculptures by well-known artists.

Near the Zona Rosa: Galería de Arte Mexicano, Milan 18, three short blocks southeast of the intersection of Reforma and Insurgentes, is one of the most prestigious galleries in the city. The owners choose their artists carefully and have their favorites, including such young Mexican artists as Pedro Friedenberg and Luis López Loza.

Galería Pecanis, Durango 186, a half dozen blocks south of the Zona Rosa, is a fine gallery featuring the work of lesser-known (but very good) Mexican artists. Contemporary paintings, engravings, and drawings make up the collection.

Casasola, Praga 16, a few blocks west of Calle Florencia at the western edge of the Zona Rosa, features a great photography collection of old Mexico, especially the Revolutionary period. You can have your purchases mounted while you wait.

Galería Summa Artis, on the mezzanine level of the Stouffer Presidente Chapultepec, is a chic gallery featuring the works of old Mexican masters as well as aspiring young artists. Paintings, sculpture, graphics, and signed and numbered lithographs fill out its impressive collection.

Galería Estela Shapiro, Victor Hugo 72, one block south and east of the Camino Real, features works by internationally celebrated artists. The gallery also sponsors occasional shows by up-and-coming contemporary artists.

Galería Juan Martín, Dickens 33, in Polanco, has a large selection of strictly modern paintings by a variety of international artists.

Coyoacán: You can find celebrated Mexican bullfight sculptor **Humberto Peraza Ojeda**'s works for sale at his Coyoacán studio, Cerra Blanco 14, Pedregal de San Francisco, about a half-hour's cab ride south of the Zona Rosa. The maestro has ranked among the world's elite artists for more than half a century now, and his sculptures have been given as gifts to a number of heads of state, including Ronald Reagan, Emperor Hirohito, and King Juan Carlos. By appointment only; Tel: 554-9963.

The Zona Rosa

Calle Amberes, one of the city's loveliest streets, is the location of several fine French restaurants as well as practically being an outdoor mall for designer boutiques: Guess? by Georges Marciano, Express, Aca Joe, Ruben Torres, and Ralph Lauren are just some of the well-known names you'll find here. Also here is Noi, a sophisticated dress shop for petites, and the ubiquitous Benetton. (At most of these boutiques international designer fashions are available for less than half their cost in New York or London.)

Tane, Amberes 70, with branches in the Camino Real, Nikko México, and Stouffer Presidente hotels; the San Angel Inn; at Edgar Allen Poe 68 (in Polanco); and in the PERISUR shopping mall, is Mexico's most elegant jewelry and art shop, and a veritable museum of silver treasures. Tane specializes in handmade reproductions of antique pieces from around the world, and also sells sculptures by outstanding Mexican and international artists.

Los Castillo, with stores at Amberes 41, Londres 132, the Calinda Geneve Mexico, and Palmas 50 (next to the San Angel Inn), is the retail outlet of the famous Taxco silver dynasty, and offers quality merchandise at reasonable prices. Original designs in silver, gold, copper, and tin, as well as ceramic ware and furniture, make it an ideal choice for unusual gifts.

Joyería Peyrelóngue, an exclusive jewelry store located right off the Reforma at Amberes 5, offers beautiful gold, silver, and crystal gift items, including Rolex, Cartier, and Mercie watches.

The place for onyx is Muller's, at the corner of Florencia and Londres. Guy Muller, owner and raconteur *extraordinaire,* will serve up interesting anecdotes about the role of onyx in Mexican history as you browse through his well-displayed selection of chess sets, book ends, tables, and sundry other items—all guaranteed not to stain. Muller's creations can be shipped safely to any U.S. or Canadian destination, and his is one of the few Zona Rosa shops open Sundays.

Girasol, Génova 39A, has been setting trends in women's fashion for more than two decades. Designer-owner Gonzalo Bauer utilizes appliqués and hand embroidery in bright colors. Also featured are his unusual, eye-catching leather accessories. There are branches in Polanco (Presidente Masaryk 318) and the PERISUR shopping mall.

An old converted mansion at Hamburgo 203 is home for the **Mexican Opal Company**, where you can observe the opals being transformed into a variety of beautiful merchandise at the workshop on the premises. The well-trained sales staff speak English, Spanish, and Japanese. Tel: 528-9263 for an appointment, be punctual, and ring the bell to the right of the always-locked entrance.

Flamma, in a restored Art Nouveau town house at the corner of Hamburgo and Florencia, sells only one product: candles. There are thousands of them, in a colorful, creatively designed array featuring superb craftsmanship with prices to match.

Coloniart is for the discriminating antiques collector only. Located at Estocólmo and Hamburgo, Coloniart offers no hidden bargains, only exquisite furniture, paintings, and sculpture, and all worth the exquisite prices. By appointment only. Tel: 525-8928.

Polanco

The chic shopping district here on Avenida Presidente Masaryk only recently has come into its own. Nevertheless, the temples to designer clothing now number in double figures and include such notable establishments as **Hugo Boss**, **Christian Dior**, **Ungaro**, **Nina Ricci**, **Cartier**, **Esprit**, **Ferrioni Collection** (a Mexican operation that uses little Scottish terriers on everything in its line, from shoes to umbrellas), and **Amarras** (meaning "to tie" in Spanish and referring to the shop's practice of using the knot as the basic element of design in everything from its bathing suits to shorts and shirts).

For sophisticated leather goods in Polanco check out **Regina Romero**, at the corner of Presidente Masaryk and Julio Verne.

Rodrigo R. Rivero Lake, at Campos Elíseos 199, opposite the rear entrances to the Nikko México and Stouffer Presidente hotels, is the most unusual of the capital's antiques shops. Señor Rivero, who speaks English, is a man with a mission: He searches the world for the rarest of collectibles. A love seat from India and ancient porcelain from China are two of the many eye-catching treasures on display. By appointment only; Tel: 250-8673.

One of Mexico's most celebrated contemporary artists is Sergio Bustamante, the creator of stylized animal and bird sculptures in bronze, copper, and papier-mâché. He maintains a retail shop, the **Galería de Sergio Bustamante**, on the mezzanine of the Nikko México hotel, Campos Elíseos 204, and another in the Sheraton María-Isabel, Reforma 325. Consider his costly creations investments.

San Angel

Three of the most elegant shops in the D.F. can be found in this southern neighborhood near the San Angel Inn, where Altavista meets Diego Rivera and Santa Catarina: **Carlos Demicheles**, perhaps the most exciting Mexican designer on the international fashion scene today; **Aries**, for leather bags, valises, wallets, and portfolio cases; and **Tane** (see also the Zona Rosa), for exquisite silverware. Though they all can be found at other locations throughout the city, it is only here that the shops themselves are treasures of contemporary Mexican architecture. Other shopping meccas on Altavista are **HB Galería** for contemporary art; **Galería Kim** for contemporary art and sculpture; **Farre** for decorator housewares; and **Frattina** for women's designer originals.

Calle Madero

The D.F. is the nation's jewelry-making center. Today the old Calle de los Plateros (Street of the Silversmiths) is known as Calle Madero, but it remains faithful to its 16th-century origins: Shops specializing in custom-made silver and gold jewelry line the street from the Zócalo to Alameda Park.

Bazar del Centro

An old colonial mansion at Calle Isabel la Católica 30, just south of Calle Madero and a few minutes' walk from the Zócalo, is now a very pleasant three-level shopping center called the Bazar del Centro. **Aplijsa**, a prestigious jewelry store from Guadalajara, has opened a branch here and offers an outstanding assortment of jewelry in all price ranges. Other shops ringing the central patio feature quality silver, leather goods, ceramics, and a great variety of expertly crafted products from all over the country.

Salvador Sandoval, owner of both the Bazar del Centro and Aplijsa, purchased the building in 1985 and redesigned and refurbished the old mansion, retaining as much as possible of the original late-17th-century decor, including the entire façade, the iron railings, the exposed beams, and the brick walls. As a result, there is a dramatic contrast between the rather seedy neighborhood and what awaits shoppers behind the Bazar del Centro's massive doors. Tiled benches under graceful laurel trees dot the central patio, and often, during the day, artists work at their easels in view of the curious. In a rear patio more shops offer an assortment of arts and crafts, and a very comfortable pub, the **Cueva de Emiliano**, beckons the foot-sore with a colorful setting and a decent margarita.

SIDE TRIPS FROM MEXICO CITY

CUERNAVACA, TAXCO, PUEBLA, TULA, VALLE DE BRAVO

By Robert Somerlott

The area around the capital has so much to offer that the problem becomes one of choosing among its many archaeological sites, villages, museums, caves, and colonial towns. In deciding, be aware that growth has smudged the luster of some places that once were more attractive.

Toluca, to the west, is one such example. Its famed market is commercial and common now, the modernized city itself of little interest. Not so the nearby pottery village of Metepec, which retains interest for its traditional ceramics, especially its *pulque* jars, trees-of-life, and earthen casseroles. South of Toluca, Malinalco, an Aztec temple site carved out of volcanic rock, draws archaeology buffs. And the scenic Valle de Bravo, though without archaeological sites and the like, is exceptional for an outdoorsy getaway vacation.

Cuernavaca, once an automatic choice, still has attractions, though it has its drawbacks, too, as we shall see. Likewise the famous old silver town of Taxco. The old spa town of Tehuacán can be crossed off your itinerary altogether now that its resort hotel is shabby and neglected. The same can be said of the city of Pachuca, which is simply uninteresting.

Perhaps the most rewarding side trip in the area east of Mexico City, on the way to Veracruz on the Gulf coast, is Puebla, an early colonial town with very attractive ecclesiastical architecture, and nearby Cholula, a pre-Hispanic religious center.

Tlaxcala, while not of the highest interest, is nonetheless an appealing jaunt from Puebla for visitors who have the time. The archaeological zone of Cacaxtla, a short drive southeast of Tlaxcala, is noteworthy for its pre-Columbian murals.

The Museum of the Viceregal Period at Tepotzotlán and the archaeological zone at Tula can be visited either as a side trip from the capital or while you are en route to Querétaro and other northern colonial cities. Both are of somewhat specialized interest. North of Tula, and perhaps not appealing to everyone, is Ixmiquilpán: Though the town is unattractive, its ancient monastery contains some of the most unusual and fantastic murals in Mexico. Like Tula and Tepotzotlán, it is of special, rather than general, interest.

MAJOR INTEREST

Cuernavaca
Scenic beauty on the trip from Mexico City
Hotels and resorts
Pyrámide de Teopanzolco

Xochicalco ruins
Grutas de Cacahuamilpa

Taxco
Picturesque town scenes
Parroquia de Santa Prisca y San Sebastián
Silverwork

Puebla
Scenic beauty
Colonial buildings
Talavera ware
Imposing archaeological site at Cholula
Folk art church at Tonantzintla

Archaeological site of Cacaxtla, near Tlaxcala

North of Mexico City
Museo Nacional del Virreinata at Tepotzotlán
Toltec archaeological zone at Tula
Ixmiquilpán monastery

West of Mexico City
Scenic beauty
Picturesque town of Valle de Bravo
Folk pottery at Metepec
Aztec temples at Malinalco

Cuernavaca and Taxco are easy to combine in one swing south of the capital. The route can be varied by returning to Mexico City via Highway 55, Ixtapán de la Sal, Metepec, and the Toluca bypass. The small but unusual Aztec temple at Malinalco, an interesting sidelight, is also on this route. The trip, often done in one day, actually crowds two.

CUERNAVACA

The journey by car or bus to Cuernavaca from Mexico City takes from an hour and a half to two hours each way— depending on traffic—using the toll road, a route that passes through spectacular mountain scenery; the roadside settlements, on the other hand, look interesting from a distance but are unappealing on closer inspection. You'll want to make frequent stops to take in the views as the road first rises to magnificent heights, then plunges into the semitropical valley enfolding Cuernavaca.

Cuernavaca, now an industrial city of more than a million people, was a winter refuge that beckoned Aztec nobles, Cortés, Maximilian and Carlota, and a legion of their peers and admirers. Malcolm Lowry brought Cuernavaca's expatriate community vividly to life in *Under the Volcano*.

Today Mr. Lowry's famous title is much less appropriate: The great, beautiful volcano of Popocatépetl is obscured by a haze of pollution—not terrible, but becoming ominously frequent and serious due to industrial fumes and exhaust. Every weekend hordes of Mexico City residents flee to this verdant valley to draw breaths of air still relatively fresh. The weekend trippers arrive by auto, jamming the broad highways and overloading all facilities. Cuernavaca should therefore be avoided on weekends.

Along with traffic and industrialization, other menaces to charm have burgeoned: Kentucky Fried Chicken restaurants, electronic hullabaloo, a babel of signs, a glare of chrome and glass-box architecture. The so-called City of Eternal Spring can grate on all the senses at once. Yet there are attractions here, too, though often muffled or camouflaged.

Cuernavaca presents a paradox to the traveller: Two days here can be too much, and yet two weeks might not be enough, depending on how you approach this annoying city—and how you retreat from it.

The "eternal spring" of tourist brochures is almost true. In this Edenesque climate, a colony of retired Americans enjoys its comfort barricaded behind walls of high-priced real estate. Their affluent Mexican neighbors, who outnumber them by far, sip Scotch, not tequila, in residences where petals float on swimming pools and the servants are well trained.

Visitors will see no more of this than a cascade of bougainvillaea tumbling over the outside of a garden wall. Yet a few of the town's inns give a credible imitation of *la dolce vita*—and this is the reason for lingering. Rental houses and apartments, most of them attractive though high-priced, are available on a monthly or seasonal basis. Away from the congestion, life in Cuernavaca can be balmy.

Around in Cuernavaca

THE CENTRAL PLAZA AREA

The main square, or zócalo, is a small park with venerable shade trees and a graceful bandstand inherited from a more serene era. This is an inviting spot on weekday mornings or evenings, but bedlam when weekend visitors claim it. Adjacent is a more ample park that's alive with vendors and, sometimes, musicians. (The crafts displayed nearby are not local, and the markup is steep.)

Palacio de Cortés

Buildings facing the two public spaces range from ugly to acceptable; one of them, the Palacio de Cortés, is the city's most famous structure. This grim pile has been patriotically renamed the **Museo de Cuauhnáhuac**, recalling the original Aztec name of the city. (Spanish conquistadors found the word as unpronounceable in 1525 as modern travellers do today. Cuernavaca, which means "cow horn," was a stab at it.) The palace has been reconstructed so many times that it's hard to guess what it once looked like, although some old photos are displayed inside.

Hernán Cortés ordered the building's construction in 1527, having just received Cuernavaca as part of his personal fief. Expropriated after Mexico won its independence from Spain, the old palace served as the state legislature's chamber for much of the 19th century. In the late 1920s Dwight Morrow, the U.S. ambassador to Mexico, who had a Cuernavaca residence, hit on the happy idea of commissioning the great Diego Rivera to paint murals in the building. Rivera took advantage of the commission to portray Mexico's history from the earliest days of its habitation through the Revolution of 1910, with an emphasis on the events of the Conquest. The results, exuberant and bold, are a national treasure; the rest of the museum—with the exception of a number of exhibits from the archaeological zone of Xochicalco—pales in comparison.

Templo de San Francisco

One long block west of the plaza stands the Templo de San Francisco, begun in the mid-16th century. Here again we have a story of antiquity, destruction, and rebuilding. As in the palace, the murals inside the cathedral outshine the building itself. Very early and naïve frescoes show Spanish missionaries bound for Japan in a skiff, as perplexed sea creatures regard them with curiosity. The friars are also shown at their later martyrdom in Nagasaki.

El Museo Robert Brady, at Netzahualcóyotl 4, was established by the late artist Robert Brady in his former residence, itself once part of the cathedral complex. The Brady collection includes paintings, antique sculpture and furniture, and textiles, all presented as elements of a beautifully decorated home. The museum is open Thursdays and Fridays from 10:00 A.M. until 2:00 P.M. and from 4:00 to 6:00 P.M., and on Saturdays from 10:00 A.M. until 2:00 P.M.

For a simple lunch while exploring the downtown area, **Marco Polo**, a checked-tablecloth pizzeria facing the cathedral at Hidalgo 26, is a good choice.

Close at hand, the **Jardines de Borda** survive as a relic of the demolished palace of 18th-century silver king José de la Borda. The design is formal and attractive: Fluffy ducks preside at a pool, along one side of which is a porch with paintings portraying the love affair between Maximilian and a local beauty known as La India Bonita. Empress Carlota also resided here at the time, but neither gossip nor history has revealed what she thought of her husband's indiscretions.

Pirámide de Teopanzolco

Near the railroad station is the Pirámide de Teopanzolco, a small but interesting pre-Columbian structure that may well be 1,200 years old. Built by the Tlahuica people, who were later conquered by their distant cousins, the Aztecs, the temple was covered with earth by inhabitants of the area at the time of the Conquest in order to prevent its destruction at the hands of the Christians. Almost four centuries passed, during which time the hill became part of the landscape.

Then, in 1910, artillery supporting the rebel Zapata was placed on top of the hill. The repeated firing of the artillery caused a mini-earthquake, dirt and rocks slid away, and the ancient temple was found—except that it was actually two temples, for one had been built over the other in the traditional pre-Columbian manner.

STAYING IN CUERNAVACA

Cuernavaca is replete with just-adequate hotels offering basic rooms to weekend visitors at inflated rates. A few places, none of them inexpensive, are special, however.

The luxury inn ▶ **Las Mañanitas**, a few blocks from the zócalo at Calle Linares 107, is famed for its food, its rooms, and a glorious garden adorned with flamboyant birds. The restaurant is so popular that on weekends it causes traffic jams in the surrounding streets. The suites, with unnecessary but attractive fireplaces, are admirable.

The ▶ **Clarion Cuernavaca Racquet Club**, partially hidden on Calle Francisco Villa in the hills known as Rancho de Cortés, about a 15-minute drive north of the center of town via Avenida Morelos, appears at first to be a posh country club in the colonial style. The nine tennis courts, four of them lighted, attract an international crowd, but the occupants of the 33 ample suites (with living rooms and fireplaces) are by no means all tennis addicts. The dining room, open to non-guests, is quite good, the service at night late and leisurely.

The ▶ **Hostería las Quintas**, much closer to town on Avenida las Quintas but still too far to walk, is less costly than the Racquet Club, less sporty, and even more beautiful in its tropical garden setting. The fine public restaurant is a lovely bower of blossoming shrubs.

DINING IN CUERNAVACA

Three of Cuernavaca's finest restaurants are in the hotels mentioned above; Las Mañanitas is especially recommended.

One of the best restaurants outside the above-mentioned hotels is **La India Bonita**, at Morrow 6. Mexican food is so well presented in simple but attractive surroundings here that the place has become a Cuernavaca tradition. The prices are as pleasing as the savory spices. Tel: (73) 12-1266.

Harry's Grill, at Gutenberg 3 on the main plaza, is part of the Carlos Anderson chain that specializes in collegiate humor and hearty fare. Moderate prices, good service. Closed Mondays. Tel: (73) 12-7679.

A café, ice cream parlor, and gift shop rolled into one,

Sanborn's, at the corner of Juárez and Abasolo, is another bland but reliable link in a national not-so-fast food chain.

Sumiya, in the area called Juitepec, 5 km (3 miles) south and west of town off the Cuautla road, bills itself as a replica of the Japanese imperial palace. Actually, it's the former mansion of Woolworth heiress Barbara Hutton and was once (briefly) the home of the Shah of Iran. The restaurant serves modified Japanese and international cuisine in surroundings that outshine the food. There's also disco dancing on Friday and Saturday nights. Reservations required; Tel: (73) 15-3055.

Tepoztlán

The village of Tepoztlán, with its twisting cobblestone streets, ancient ruins, and Aztec temples clinging to a steep slope, is about 24 km (15 miles) northeast of Cuernavaca by a good highway (115D). Tepoztlán kept its pre-Columbian heritage and language far longer than most villages in Mexico. In fact, as recently as a few decades ago it was still a magnet for anthropologists hoping to study the elements of the earlier culture that survived here. Today, Tepoztlán's isolation has been shattered by the outside world, yet despite the intrusion of souvenir shops the hamlet remains both antique and primitive.

The **Templo y Exconvento de la Natividad de la Virgin María** (1559), a severe Dominican monastery dominating the center of town, is worth inspecting, especially the stone carving around the church portal. A small **museum** behind the monastery on Calle González displays some fine pottery and figurines, gifts from the noted archaeologist Carlos Pellicer.

On a steep hill above Tepoztlán the ancient temple of **Tepozteco** commands the heights and a sweeping panorama of mountains and valley. To get there follow Avenida Tepozteco, northeast of the municipal market, as it climbs the hill before dwindling to a rocky trail. Allow an exhausting hour for the ascent. The temple, which seems to have been dedicated to the bibulous god of pulque, a brewed alcoholic drink, is late Postclassic, built by people who were relatives and, later, subjects of the Aztecs. The zone closes at 4:30 P.M. sharp.

The ▶ **Hacienda Cocoyoc**, a few minutes' drive southeast of Tepoztlán on the Cuautla highway, is a big, sprawling resort set amid landscaped gardens, an old aqueduct, and falling water. Once a thriving sugar plantation, Cocoyoc was burned by Zapata during the Revolution, and was restored in the 1960s by the family that now owns it; amenities include a nine-hole golf course. Prices in this tropical retreat are just moderate enough to attract weekend crowds from the capital, but it is lovely on weekdays. Make sure your room or suite has good ventilation; Cocoyoc is warm.

The Ruins of Xochicalco

The words "pretty" and "delightful" are not ordinarily applied to pre-Columbian ruins. At Xochicalco no others serve so well. The site is beautifully situated in slightly rolling country ringed by rugged mountains that are vivid green in the rainy season, brown and severe in the dry season—but always impressive no matter what time of year.

Xochicalco looks upon the heights of Mount Ajusco some 39 km (24 miles) southwest of Cuernavaca in the direction of Taxco, more than half the distance over a toll road and all of it paved. Take Mexico 95D toward Taxco and exit at the turnoff marked "Alpuyeca." Then follow signs (which are not prominent) to Las Grutas and Alpuyeca. Twelve kilometers (7½ miles) from the exit is the Xochicalco sign, where you turn left and climb the hill to the ruins. In Nahuatl, the Aztec language, the name means "House of Flowers"—highly appropriate, although what the original builders called their city (or themselves) is unknown.

This was not just a ceremonial center, but a true city of at least 10,000 people, and possibly twice that. Although much studied, the ruins remain shrouded in mystery. How did Maya-like figures, carvings, and glyphs arrive in this remote region so far from the main centers of Mayan culture? What kind of people lived here and left their sculptural calling cards? One important point is certain: Xochicalco was in flower at a time, about A.D. 700, when northern ceremonial and religious centers had been abandoned by elites, and the flame of culture and learning had all but sputtered out in Mesoamerica. The comparison to European monasteries during the Dark Ages is irresistible. Was this the place where tradition and culture were preserved while barbarians ranged the land? It seems likely. The inhabitants of Xochicalco adopted the religious and intellectual traditions of earlier cultures, including Teotihuacán and El Tajín (north of present-day Veracruz), changed them somewhat, then passed on these modified traditions as part of the foundation of a new culture that reached its full flower at Tula, quite a bit north of here, in the tenth century.

The **Pirámide de la Serpeinte Emplumada** (Pyramid of the Plumed Serpent), the site's finest monument, displays superb relief sculpture—flowing lines in stone that are indeed as lithe as a serpent as they curve, coil, and finally rear up in fierce, dragonlike heads. An aristocratic figure, instantly recognizable as Mayan, sits crowned with a panache that blends perfectly with the long rhythms of the whole sculpture.

The site also boasts one of the finest ancient **ball courts** in Mexico, laid out in the usual shape of the letter I and more than 200 feet long. From the top of a partly excavated mound known as La Malinche, the view down toward a line of circular platforms is striking. A residential section elsewhere on the grounds comes outfitted with a steam bath. Walls and fortifications protect the impressive area now called the Acropolis.

Grutas de Cacahuamilpa

Between Taxco and Cuernavaca, and easily reached from either, is Cacahuamilpa (kah-kah-wah-MEEL-pah) Caves National Park. The park's enormous corridors and chambers form the largest known cave system in Mexico, and are comparable in extent to the Carlsbad Caverns in the United States.

The entrance to the *grutas* is an awesome mountainside gap that eerily resembles a gigantic architectural structure. The halls and connecting corridors beyond it unfold like a lunar landscape amid fantastic formations of stalactites and stalagmites.

The empress Carlota visited these caves in 1866 and wrote on a wall, "Maria Carlota reached this point." Eight years later a man instrumental in driving her from Mexico, President Lerdo de Tejada, added to the same wall, "Sebastian Lerdo de Tejada went farther." Today conducted tours, in Spanish and lasting about an hour and a half, leave frequently from the entrance. Admission is restricted to escorted groups, but those suddenly struck by claustrophobia can turn back at any time and find their own way out.

To reach the caves from Cuernavaca, a distance of 74 km (46 miles), follow the route to Xochicalco (see above), then continue past the archaeological zone on Mexico 166 for 25 km (16 miles). The caves are just before the junction of Highways 166 and 55. The trip, once you are past Cuernavaca's urban sprawl, is pleasant and scenic. For bus service, take the Zacatepec–México line leaving Cuernavaca's Pullman bus terminal every hour from 6:00 A.M. to 7:00 P.M. Bus service from Taxco (two buses an hour, daily) is provided by Tres Estrellas del Centro and the Flecha Amarillo lines, both using that city's Central de Autobuses terminal at Avenida John F. Kennedy 104.

TAXCO

Located about 80 km (50 miles) southwest of Cuernavaca, Taxco (TAH-sko), a picturesque and photogenic colonial silver town, has been rendered much less appealing to visitors by its very attractiveness and proximity to the capital. Tour buses belching exhaust bear down on its tiny plaza like predatory monsters. Day trips from as far as Acapulco, where tourists are misled by promises of exploration of a "colonial gem," fill its streets with bewildered shoppers. What they get instead is hours of travel and about 45 minutes at their destination. The bus driver is bribed to halt at a certain silver shop, then the herding—soon followed by the roundup for departure—begins. The town somehow manages to accommodate these day-trippers, who are, after all, its bread and butter, but much is lost by the crowding.

Another evil effect of living on tourism is the sense one gets of a town too spiffed up, too conscious of its own image. Taxco, with its white paint and black signs, has an unnatural uniformity akin to the waxy quality of a film set; it does not seem to be a living town. Still, it is undeniably picturesque, even romantic. And while this is especially true of the downtown area—things loosen up away from the town center—downtown is what everyone goes to see. In fact, that really is all there *is* to see, except for strolls through old neighborhoods that are quaint but unimposing. Such a stroll quickly makes it clear that Taxco's silver wealth did not stay in Taxco, but instead went to erect mansions elsewhere.

Taxco's Parish Church

Besides silver, Taxco has another treasure: the **Parroquia de Santa Prisca y San Sebastián**, which lifts its magnificent spires to the glory of God and God's self-proclaimed partner, a French miner named José de la Borda.

Taxco is the oldest mining town in North America and dates back to the days when Mixtec craftsmen hammered its silver into ornaments for Aztec nobles. Of course, the conquistadors were overjoyed to seize its mines, and the serpentine, corkscrew byways of today's town are a reminder of the meandering mining village that tumbled haphazardly down the mountain slope in the 16th century.

The output of silver during those years was substantial but hardly fantastic. Then, in 1716, José de la Borda wandered into town and struck it rich. Grateful, Borda presented the Almighty with the most opulent temple he could concoct. "God gives to Borda, and Borda gives to God," he announced, marking the score even. The church was begun in 1751 and completed in 1758, with the best Mexican architects, painters, and carvers of the day kept busy on it.

Ever since, Santa Prisca has been hailed as the apogee of 18th-century Mexican architecture. In 1945 Manuel Toussaint, Mexico's pioneer art historian, wrote: "A homogeneous work of art, and of a beauty which cannot be described, the church of Taxco dominates the delightful town . . . the interior is an astonishing Churrigueresque work of art, madness is held within bounds . . . reason inexorably controls the effect, and fantasy develops just so far as the restraints of reason permit." In 1991 Santa Prisca was burglarized and religious art valued at $2 million stolen. The thieves left behind many of its finest treasures, however, and first-time visitors will be unaware of the tragic loss.

Over the decades the silver in the mountains was steadily mined out. Although Taxco still mines some silver, its modern connection with the metal dates from the 1930s, when William Spratling, a North American writer and artist, introduced silversmithing as a local art and industry. The **William Spratling Museum**, at the corner of Avenidas Delgado and El Arco, behind Santa Prisca, commemorates his contributions to the town's continued prosperity.

BUYING SILVER IN TAXCO

Taxco's centrally located silver shops are reliable; buyers will not have to worry that some base metal has been palmed off on them. Still, as with anything expensive, you should be cautious; check that the product bears the ".925" stamp, the government's requirement for purity in silver.

Silver as metal is sold by weight, the price set on the world commodity markets. All costs above weight should involve design and *real* overhead. Some shops on Taxco's Avenida John F. Kennedy add a guide or bus driver's commission without mentioning it. Among the better shops in the zócalo area, though, there is little difference in price above weight, and the advantage of buying in downtown Taxco is not price but the range of options, with more than 100 silver outlets to choose from. **Emma**, Calle Celso Muñoz 4, gleams with a wide selection of smaller gifts and remembrance items. Larger works of quality will be found at **Los Ballesteros**, Calle Soto la Marina 5, and **Los Castillo**, Plazuela Bernal 10. Many other good establishments are sprinkled throughout the area.

Agua Escondida, William Spratling 4A, is convenient for lunch or snacks when you're shopping or visiting the sights downtown.

STAYING IN TAXCO

The cottages at the ▶ **Hacienda del Solar** perch atop a mountain in rustic but definitely aristocratic surroundings. Each fireplace-equipped cottage has a balcony affording lovely views, and the furnishings have been selected with care. Two meals a day are served in its dining room—the city's best restaurant—which is open to the public. The view is magnificent, and the cuisine features accents of Italy. The Hacienda is located 3½ km (2 miles) south of town just off the Acapulco road, Highway 95, which makes a U; near the tourism office is a short street leading to the hotel. You'll need a car or taxi to get there from the center of town. Cab fare is about the equivalent of $1.50.

The ▶ **Hotel Santa Prisca** is conveniently located one long block west of the famous church in the center of town. Simple, inexpensive, but attractively colonial, this pleasant inn also houses a commendable dining room.

The **Restaurant La Taberna** serves good international cuisine at reasonable prices. It's located next to the post office on the main street, a thoroughfare whose name changes often and arbitrarily.

PUEBLA

In Puebla you feel close to the sky, a sensation that stems from more than being in one of the highest cities in the world. Happily, despite the fumes from the city's ubiquitous traffic, the air here is still unusually clear. But it's really the four great volcanoes towering above the plain—especially Popocaté-petl, the Aztecs' "Smoking Mountain," and Iztaccíhuatl, their "Sleeping Woman"—that do the most to create this perception of elevation. Their perpetually snow-covered summits do indeed inspire that familiar fantasy of being able to reach out and touch them.

The 95-km (59-mile) drive from Mexico City east to Puebla via toll road 150 winds gently through pine-clad slopes and rugged outcroppings affording spectacular vistas. Puebla stands at the head of a fertile valley along the main trade route to Veracruz and the Gulf of Mexico. The location is strategic; every invading army—whether Spanish, French, or American—has had to storm the town on its way to the capital.

The people of Puebla are called *poblanos,* and the adjective *poblano* is especially linked to their tile-encrusted buildings, a style of architectural decoration gone joyously mad with color. They are just as proud of their *poblano* dress and style,

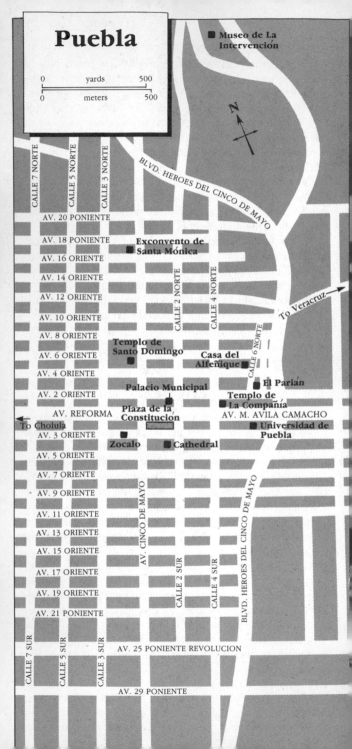

and will boast to anyone who will listen that *mole* sauce, made with chiles and rich but not sweet chocolate, was invented here. Pride is also taken in the city's grid design, in which *avenidas* run east and west, *calles* north and south. This checkerboard of streets was made possible by the fact that there was no native city here before the Spanish arrived—an anomaly in the history of the Conquest—as well as by the fact that the land was flat. Puebla also has more churches than any other place in Mexico, which is either the cause of or the direct result of *poblano* solemnity.

Yes, this is a serious town, where eyebrows are frequently raised. Despite the city's apparently staid demeanor, however, a current of passion runs through *poblano* life. The thousands of students at its large university are second to none in the vehemence and violence of their protests. The workers at the auto factory, the largest Volkswagen plant in the world, belong to a voluble and fierce union. The *poblanos,* like the volcanoes around them, are dignified and quiescent—but not always, and certainly not below the surface.

Visitors to Puebla should be prepared to see an abundance of ecclesiastical architecture, impressive and opulent rather than beautiful. There is fine ceramic work here as well, especially the glazed Talavera ware, and some residences flaunt tile work—gleaming and gay, a flash of fantasy—as exterior decoration. The museums are worth visiting but not worth lingering in. Puebla and nearby Cholula reward the visitor who spends a day between them, but only merit more time if you have a car and can explore a larger area.

Downtown Puebla

The Zócalo

The city's main attractions lie within walking distance of the zócalo, the **Plaza de la Constitución**, a central square that ranks among the most spacious in Mexico. It was planned, as was the whole downtown, by a Franciscan, Fray Julián Garcés, the first bishop of Tlaxcala, who had been assigned the task of locating a new city. According to legend, His Grace was blessed by the nocturnal visit of two angels whom he watched pace off with pole and line a plain ringed with volcanoes. Thus the city was positioned, and so acquired its full name, Puebla de los Angeles, in honor of its angelic surveyors.

American visitors walking through the plaza usually have no idea they are crossing a spot that should be hallowed ground in U.S. history. It was here, in 1847, that General Winfield Scott seized the city after the battle of Cerro Gordo. While Scott's main force moved on to attack Mexico City, Colonel Thomas Childs was left behind in Puebla's zócalo with a small group of U.S. wounded. Colonel Childs, with foresight, rounded up some cattle and a flock of sheep, then spurred his injured men to barricade their camp. Their work was hardly finished when the Mexican general Santa Anna attacked with 2,500 men, employing artillery and posting snipers on roofs that still overlook the plaza today.

The local populace was jubilant at the imminent destruction of the invaders, cheering the besiegers and wildly ringing the bells of the city's 60 churches and convents. But the staunch Americans held their terrible position for 30 days, until the approach of a relieving army put Santa Anna to flight.

The bluish-gray **cathedral** looms over one side of the zócalo, a grim shadow on an otherwise lighthearted space. Twin towers, too far apart, impart a stumpy look to the structure. The gloomy exterior hides a splendid nave replete with marble, lovely wrought iron, and admirable woodwork. The **Palacio Municipal**, the second most impressive structure on the zócalo, was built at the turn of the century in the Spanish Renaissance style—yet another example of the city's long-lived admiration of Spanish models.

Casa del Alfeñique

It is a relief to leave the sternness of the palace and cathedral and discover the totally delightful Casa del Alfeñique, at Avenida 4 Oriente and Calle 6 Norte. The "House of Almond Cake" is indeed a confection, with red tiles accented by black iron work, the whole tied together with sugar-colored masonry to create a *poblano* fantasy. Inside is a regional museum with an emphasis on pre-Columbian history and the indigenous costumes of the area, including *china poblana* dress, the most famous garb of the city.

El Parián, a market across the street from the Casa del Alfeñique, is a cobblestone mall where crafts and almost-crafts are sold. Ceramics are a good buy here, but you should be cautious about the displays of onyx boxes, figurines, bookends, and chessboards—most of the work is imitation and mass produced. The greens and shades thereof, sometimes palmed off as jade, are colored by dye, not nature.

Two Churches

A Churrigueresque riot of decoration at Calle 4 Norte and Avenida M. Avila Camacho, the Templo de la Compañía is also the tomb of the original *china poblana,* a not especially fascinating character, but one who looms inordinately large in the city's collective consciousness. She was perhaps a princess, perhaps Chinese, and perhaps kidnapped by pirates who sold her in Acapulco in 1620. Bought by a Puebla merchant family that later adopted her because of her beauty, sweetness, and virtue, she taught sewing in the Chinese manner, invented the embroidered peasant dress named after her, and was denied her wish to become a nun. Eventually, she devoted an already virtuous life to care of the poor and sick.

The **Capilla del Rosaro** in the **Templo de Santo Domingo**, two blocks north of the zócalo at Cinco de Mayo and Avenida 4 Oriente, is the high point of *poblano* religious ornamentation: Lustrous gold leaf, brilliant tiles, and enamel dazzle the eye. The sculpted Virgin on the altar, spangled in jewels, seems dressed by Tiffany's.

Exconvento de Santa Mónica

The Exconvento de Santa Mónica, six blocks farther north along Cinco de Mayo, was built in the early years of the 17th century as a sort of retreat where noble matrons could be properly chaperoned when their husbands were out of town. The women of Puebla rejected the idea, however, and the building, ironically, became a reformatory for prostitutes. Later it was turned into a convent-college.

The convent went "underground" after passage of the Reform Laws abolishing Church property in 1857, with the nuns remaining secluded in their 39-room establishment. Entrance to the convent was through a secret door in an adjoining house. It was closed by the government in 1934, and is now a museum devoted to religious art and sculpture, as well as to the lives of the sisters. Despite the hocus-pocus of the hidden door, the "secret" was doubtless more widely known in Puebla than is generally admitted today. You can visit the convent daily except Monday at Avenida 18 Poniente 103, just off Cinco de Mayo.

Museo de la Intervención

The Museum of the Intervention, a military museum housed in the Fuerte de Loreto, a 30-minute walk northeast of the downtown area, is mainly of patriotic interest to Mexicans, but military and history buffs will find an interesting di-

orama of the famous battle fought here on May 5, 1862. On
that day badly outnumbered Mexicans, some armed with
guns that had seen service at Waterloo almost 50 years
earlier, turned back a heavily armed spit-and-polish French
army. The battle itself, part of an involved and fascinating
story, is remembered throughout Mexico every year on the
fifth of May (Cinco de Mayo), a legal holiday. To visit Loreto
and its sister fort of **Guadalupe**, take a cab from the zócalo or
a "Fuerte" bus at Calle 16 de Septiembre and Avenida 9
Oriente. It's a short trip, and the fare will be inexpensive.

TALAVERA WARE

Talavera ware, both as dishes and as tiles, is almost synonymous with the Puebla area of Mexico, although it is also
made elsewhere.

The product, unlike most folk pottery, is durable—a quite
un-Mexican quality. Fragility, after all, is part of the national
fatalism: Dishes will be broken anyhow, so why worry too
much or fight too hard to prevent it? Investing in Talavera,
on the other hand, demands faith in the future and optimism
about the human condition.

Real talavera is made of a mix of three clays, which used
to be kneaded together for days by men dancing barefoot in
clay pits. Today machines have replaced the Talavera jig in
more populated areas. Either way, the mixed clay is ripened
for six months, kept under a damp cloth, and rekneaded
every few days. (This, too, goes against the national grain—
witness the quick methods of wine- and cheese-making
generally used in Mexico.)

Finally, the clay is wheel-thrown or molded, and the tile
or vessel allowed to dry in the shade for days. Slow, low-
temperature firing comes next. Prayers are chanted before
and during the opening of the kiln, and the Blessed Sacra-
ment is invoked, even in today's highly commercial operations. Every piece is tested to ring true, and those with a
faulty tone are thrown away. The glaze applied includes
honey; the final product is cream-white. Traditionally, only
two colors are used to decorate the piece: always white, with
blue or yellow in older works, and a bolder color in modern
pieces. •

Puebla's Talavera factories usually will not admit visitors,
but a few have found on-premises sales to be profitable.
Inquire about admission at the tourism office, Avenida 5
Oriente 5, beside the cathedral. Or simply try the **Casa
Rugiero**, 18 Poniente 111, or **La Guadalupaña**, 4 Poniente
911.

An especially interesting place to see fine Talavera is in the

Exconvento de Santa Rosa, Calle 3 Norte 1203. The **Museo de Arte Popular Poblano** housed in the former convent is devoted to arts, crafts, and the kitchen—surprisingly fascinating displays. Not all the pottery is Talavera, but some of the best is. Any Puebla church will also have its own fine examples.

A score of shops in Puebla sell the ware, though not all of it is of high quality. Remember: The whiter the base, the better the work. Any piece with smoke marks should be rejected.

STAYING AND DINING IN PUEBLA

▶ **El Mesón del Angel** is Puebla's most attractive hotel, with beautiful grounds, balconied rooms, and a very good dining room open to the public. Its bold beams and rock-and-glass walls give it a California feeling, while its location northwest of the city center at Hermanos Serdan 807, almost at the toll gate entrance to Highway 190D (the highway to Mexico City), makes it especially appealing to motorists passing through as well as to business executives visiting the industrial zone. For other visitors, however, it is a long way from the center of town.

The ▶ **Hotel Lastra**, also of the first rank but older and less expensive than El Mesón, is in a quiet neighborhood about 3 km (2 miles) northeast of the zócalo at Calzada de los Fuertes 2633. The roof garden is lovely, but the rooms vary in quality in this traditional though much-remodeled inn. Its good restaurant is open to the public.

On the zócalo itself, the ▶ **Hotel Royalty Centro** is a convenient, comfortable, and pleasant choice—depending on which rooms are available. Some are cramped and stuffy; the suites are worth the higher rate. At its best the Royalty is quite nice, and the indoor-outdoor restaurant offers a satisfactory breakfast.

The ▶ **Hotel del Portal** is another pleasant if unpretentious hotel with an excellent plaza location. The rooms at the rear, though smaller, are quieter, and the ambience throughout is colonial. The Del Portal also has a bar and restaurant.

Poblano food is the specialty of the simple, attractive, and popular **Fonda Santa Clara**, Avenida 3 Oriente 307. The *mole* here is outstanding. Tel: (22) 46-1952.

The fare at the **Restaurante del Parián**, Avenida 2 Oriente 415, rises above the threats of the "quaint" decor and menus printed on pieces of wood: The coyness, thankfully, does not extend to the fine *poblano* cuisine, with the *adobo* and *pipian* sauces especially noteworthy. (*Adobo* is a tangy blend of cumin, sour orange, chile, and other spices, as inspiration dictates; *pipian* also varies but starts out with a base of chiles and sesame seeds.) Tel: (22) 46-4798.

Regional cooking in Puebla is usually tasty and tangy, but "Continental" dishes seem beyond local abilities. Visitors hungry for international fare should go to the Lastra or El Mesón del Angel, whose rather elegant restaurants are not limited to regional selections, although these are well prepared, too.

Cholula

The town of Cholula adjoins Puebla, the two now virtually one as a result of growth. In its pre-Hispanic heyday, however, Cholula was a center of trade as well as an important religious center, both a holy city and a place of pilgrimage dedicated to Quetzalcóatl, the Plumed Serpent. Its settlement dates back to 500 B.C., and a city-state (probably a satellite of Teotihuacán, though a very important one that outlived Teotihuacán by centuries) flourished here between A.D. 200 and 300. Various native conquerors ruled the city in later centuries.

Cortés, often mistaken for the god Quetzalcóatl by the indigenous people of Mexico, passed through Cholula on his way to Tenochtitlán in 1519 and ordered a merciless slaughter. He may have misunderstood the intentions of the local people—undoubtedly he was under intense pressure. Whatever the reason, the Spaniards and their Tlaxcalan allies perpetrated a bloodbath.

(Cholula means "place the waters spring from." When Cortés was threatening the city, its inhabitants appeared to believe that native priests could open the sides of the massive pyramid here to release an avenging water monster, perhaps a flood.)

Because of Cholula's sacred status among the local Indians, the Spaniards saw to it that Christian shrines were erected at almost every other corner of the town. One writer has described Cholula as "blistered with churches"—an inspired description. Churches were angrily laid across Cholula like the welts from a lash.

Tepanapa

Today these squat domes and boxy towers cluster around the largest pre-Hispanic structure in Mexico: At least three immense temple bases, one atop another, and four lateral additions were erected here over the centuries, each built at the end of a 52-year religious cycle, according to custom. The result is known as Tepanapa, and although not as tall as Egypt's Pyramid of Cheops, it's almost twice as large at the base.

From a distance the structure appears to be a steep, oddly shaped hill, certainly not man-made. A church perched at the top, the **Iglesia de la Nuestra Señora de los Remedios,** is dwarfed by this mini-mountain. It is meant to look triumphant; it doesn't. Steps and a trail lead up the side of the "hill" to the church, but despite its pretty white-and-gold interior it is not worth the climb. What *is* worth it are the views in every direction—they are magnificent.

The **Plaza de las Estelas** (Patio of the Altars), in the archaeological zone itself, is enclosed on three sides by curiously modern-looking façades typical of Cholula: Broad stairways flank plain balustrades that are balanced by handsome walls. Bold fretwork designs support large panels, and on two stelae carved in bas-relief there are designs clearly derived from the religious center of El Tajín in northern Veracruz state. Wandering through the three main patios of Cholula, a visitor gets a sense of cosmopolitanism, of ideas and elements brought by pre-Columbian pilgrims who came great distances—though no one knows exactly what attracted these pilgrims to Cholula.

Much of the construction is of adobe brick, with pebble facings overlaid by stucco. This inexpensive technique, still used all over Mexico today with slight variations, does not ensure lasting results without constant upkeep. Thus, the method of construction itself has caused some of the deterioration and shapelessness of Cholula's pyramid. The adobe bricks are believed to have been made at a place about 30 miles distant. According to legend, 20,000 prisoners passed them along to Cholula hand-to-hand, bucket brigade style.

Miles of tunnels were cut into the great temple base in the 1930s, revealing even older construction. Feeble lightbulbs allow you to find your way, although it's best to carry a flashlight as well. Here and there you'll notice traces of murals on what were once the exterior walls of older temples. Visitors may enter on their own, but a guide, who can be engaged at the entrance to the site, will certainly help to clarify this puzzling place.

A small **museum** (open daily) in a red building across the street from the entrance to the site contains artifacts and an illuminating cutaway model of the pyramid. Studying this before actually exploring the tunnels of Tepanapa is helpful.

In Cholula itself, the ▶ **Villa Arqueológica,** several blocks south of the pyramid, is a very good hotel, with a pleasant, informal atmosphere and a reliable restaurant. This is also the only really good choice for lunch while exploring the ruins, although **Los Portales,** a shady café on the zócalo, will do for simple food and bottled drinks.

Around Puebla

The little parish church in the village of **Tonantzintla**, 4 km (2½ miles) south of Cholula, is perhaps the most delightful building in all of Mexico. The modest exterior gives little hint of the rich displays of craft and imagination that await the visitor inside. Local artisans, working in the finest native traditions, decorated the interior with such a blaze of folk art that entering the church is like stepping into a kaleidoscope. Sly cherubs with Indian features peer from the polychrome murals and gilding, and the power of undiluted primary colors makes the nave radiant, its angels in miniskirts complemented by an abundance of grapes and flowers.

The façade of **San Francisco Acatepec**, an example of Rococo *poblano* style gone mad, glistens just half a kilometer beyond Tonantzintla on the same road. Every inch of the exterior of this amazing church is covered with green, yellow, blue, and red tiles worked in intricate patterns. The building is as ornate inside as out, a white-and-gold fantasy sculpted in a rarely used Arabian mode—sand and calcimine combined to produce a surface with the hardness and texture of extremely fine cement. The church was gutted by fire decades ago, and what now dazzles the eyes is a modern replica, though perfect down to the last detail.

Travellers with their own vehicles can continue on the same road and arrive in Puebla without returning to Cholula.

Tlaxcala

Mexico's smallest state, Tlaxcala, lies 30 km (19 miles) north of the city of Puebla via Highway 19. Its borders follow almost exactly the frontiers of the ancient Republic of Tlaxcala, chief ally of Cortés in the conquest of Mexico. The tiny state is walled in by high mountains; views of La Malinche in particular are spectacular here.

The capital city, which shares the name of the state, has two buildings of unusual interest. Once a Franciscan monastery, the **Exconvento de la Asunción**, a short walk south of the zócalo, may be the oldest church extant in the Americas. The cedar beams and inlaid wood below the organ loft are remarkable examples of carving and decoration, and very Moorish in their design and execution.

At the eastern end of town, 3 km (2 miles) from the central plaza, stands the famed **Santuario de la Virgen de Ocotlán**, frosted with ornately shaped and molded white plaster. The church was built in 1745 to commemorate a purported appearance of the Virgin on the spot two centuries earlier. The interior boasts polychromed and gilded wood carving, the work of Francisco Miguel Tlayotehuanitzin, an Indian sculptor who devoted 25 years of his life to this glorious achievement.

Cacaxtla

The archaeological zone of Cacaxtla is found near the village of Nativitas, 18 km (11 miles) southwest of Tlaxcala. Watch for a turnoff to the west about a mile north of the town of Zacatelco. (A sign says "Ruinas.") The site, newly roofed, is remarkable for its murals, which were painted with a realism unknown in ancient Mexico outside the Mayan region some time during the ninth century A.D. The murals were discovered in 1975; excavation has been slow, and so scholarly disputes about their provenance still simmer. In one remarkable fresco divided into two sections, a battle rages between magnificently garbed Eagle and Jaguar Knights; the fresco's border, decorated with sea creatures, suggests a Gulf Coast heritage. The zone is open daily, 10:00 A.M. to 5:00 P.M.; the small museum near the entrance to the site is closed Mondays.

NORTH OF THE CAPITAL

For an interesting and very full day of sightseeing by car, head north from Mexico City and make a loop that includes the Museum of the Viceregal Period at Tepotzotlán, the Toltec archaeological zone at Tula, and the monastery at Ixmiquilpán, with its strange, almost bizarre murals. (Because Ixmiquilpán is of less interest than the other two, it can be dropped to shorten the trip.) Both the museum and archaeological zone are on the way to Querétaro, so visitors planning to explore colonial Mexico might choose to include both places on their itineraries as they travel northwest.

Tepotzotlán

Tepotzotlán (teh-pote-so-TLAN) is practically a suburb of Mexico City, lying as it does just north of the Federal District on the west side of Highway 57. (It should not be confused with Tepoztlán, a town with a similar name located near Cuernavaca.) In 1584 the Jesuits established the Seminary of San Martín here, which thrived as both a school and missionary center. In the middle of the 18th century the original church and some of the monastery were replaced with the present structure, one of the most impressive examples of Churrigueresque architecture in the Americas. Both the façade and interior are nothing short of magnificent.

The Churrigueresque

Churrigueresque, sometimes called ultrabaroque, is an ornate style of architectural decoration named for the Spanish designer José de Churriguera, who worked in the early 18th century. Transported to Mexico, his style instantly took root and flourished, the elaborateness of the Mexican versions wildly exceeding the first Spanish examples. This purely ornamental form, which dominated Mexican façades throughout most of the 18th century, is marked by riotous impulses. The law of gravity is defied by columns narrower at the base than the top, and open space is abhorred, except at the sides of a structure; these are left blank. Another Churrigueresque delight is the transmutation of materials, with stone and tile often imitating cloth or wood. While beloved by the Mexican people, clerical and academic authorities were embarrassed by the style's excesses. Aware that European visitors thought the Churrigueresque "unrefined," the powers that be put a damper on its use near the end of the 18th century.

Museo Nacional del Virreinata

In 1767, shortly after the glorious new seminary was completed, the Jesuits were expelled from Mexico by royal decree. The immense complex they had built at Tepotzotlán was put to various uses before it finally became the National Museum of the Viceregal Period. Having been restored to their 18th-century brilliance, today the great corridors and chambers are filled with the finest examples of colonial art, including paintings, sculpture, furnishings, ceramics, and ornaments. One room is a treasure house of ivories brought by galleon from the Far East. The gilded nave of the church, which gleams like Aladdin's cave, has been criticized for its "barbaric splendor," and for good reason. Equally splendid are two smaller gold-encrusted rooms of the adjacent Holy House of Loreto, to the right of the nave. The whole bewildering spectacle is at once pagan and Catholic, and a treat for the senses.

There's a restaurant in one of the ancient patios, but its service is too leisurely if you are hurrying on to other destinations; a number of small cafés across from the church atrium are better for quick refreshments.

The Ruins of Tula

Tula, once the proud capital of the Toltec empire, lies 80 km (50 miles) north of Mexico City off Highway 57, the same road that leads to Tepotzotlán. At Tepotzotlán Highway 57 becomes a toll road; from there, follow it to the Tula exit, which is clearly marked to the right. The exit road, Highway 126, will take you through the modern town of Tula. Follow the signs to "Las Ruinas"; the turnoff is marked by a towering stone warrior sculpted in Toltec style.

Centuries before the Spanish had even imagined there might be such a thing as a New World, Tula was a fabled city. Legend has it that during its golden age the walls were bejeweled; songbirds would land on your shoulder to serenade you; squashes grew so big that a single one would feed a family for days, and cotton grew in a variety of brilliant colors, so there was no need to dye the cloth later. Though you will find no trace of such wonders today, what remains is nevertheless impressive.

Some time around A.D. 900, a nomadic tribe of people entered what is now Mexico from the north. This was a period that has since become known as Mesoamerica's Dark Ages, and it is likely that the northern invaders hastened the decline of the existing civilization. These warrior people, who were later dubbed the Toltecs by their spiritual descendants the Aztecs, began to intermarry with the vanquished tribes of the region, and in A.D. 968 they established their capital at Tula. Over the next three centuries the Toltecs exerted a dramatic influence on the cultures of Mesoamerica. In fact, the Toltec culture is considered to be one of the greatest of Mesoamerica, the successor to Teotihuacán and the predecessor of the Aztec.

Templo de Tlahuizcalpantecuhtli

Today only hints of this bygone glory are evident at the Tula archaeological zone. After leaving the parking lot, passing the museum, and following a dusty path a few hundred yards, you come to the back of the Temple of the Morning Star, with its giant warrior figures exposed to the sky. (The temple is also named for Quetzalcóatl, the legendary Mesoamerican god-hero, who was most often worshiped in the guise of a plumed serpent. Many experts believe he achieved his apotheosis in Tula.) While they once served as huge columns supporting a roof, today these so-called *atlantes*—each more than 15 feet tall and carved in four sections—stand stiffly at attention in full military regalia, their butterfly-shaped shields held closely to their chests. The workmanship is rough and rigid, which only adds to their considerable power. (One of the columns is a replica; the original is on display in the Museum of Anthropology in Mexico City.) Pieces of columns at the base of the temple are all that is left of what was probably a meeting hall. The front of the temple base features a set of steep stairs, and from the top you'll get a bird's-eye view of the whole site.

Other Structures at Tula

The ruins spread out below were the inspiration for Chichén Itzá in the Yucatán, and the similarities between the two are everywhere—from the type of sculpture commissioned to the architectural design of various buildings to the motifs characterizing the relief carvings. At right angles to the temple bulks the **Templo del Sol**, Tula's most ambitious structure. Here, too, the climb to the top affords striking views of the site, especially the giant statues on the platform of the Temple of the Morning Star.

You will also find two spacious **ball courts**, a ruin known as the **Palacio Quemada** (Burnt Palace), and several other structures at Tula. The relief carvings depict stealthy jaguars with outsized claws, eagles, serpents, and skulls and bones. Every detail typifies Toltec civilization; this was, after all, a military society, fierce, ruthless, and enamored of human sacrifice.

The small **Museo de Tula** (open daily except Mondays) has a collection of ceramics and carvings, but the major pieces here are located outside, not in.

Bottled soft drinks are sold at the site, along with a variety of trinkets, but you'll have to go elsewhere for food. The best choice (apart from a picnic lunch) is the **Restaurant Tollan Campestre**, 4 km (2½ miles) past the statue marking the turnoff to the ruins on the way back to the toll road. You'll recognize it by the covered wagon on its roof.

Ixmiquilpán

Ixmiquilpán (eesh-mee-keel-PAHN) is about 50 km (31 miles) northeast of Tula. To get there, follow Highway 126 along the Río Tula; a few minutes past the little town of Tlahuelilpan you take a turnoff to the north. (You don't want to go to Pachuca.) This road ultimately joins the old Pan-American Highway 85. Ixmiquilpán is just north of the junction, and the **Exconvento de San Miguel Arcángel** (Monastery of the Archangel Michael) is in the center of town.

In 1555 Augustinian friars founded a church and monastery here in what had once been one of the capitals of the Otomí people. Nothing out of the ordinary was known about these missionaries until two decades ago, when the white paint was removed from a church wall and something truly extraordinary came to light.

As the paint came off, it became apparent that the friars had allowed their church to be frescoed with pagan murals. On panel after panel, Indians were depicted much as they had been in the ancient codices, engaged in life-and-death struggles against monsters. At least one of these dread creatures was a sort of centaur, a horse with arms, hands, and a bow. Elsewhere, twisting vines and other vegetation seemed to be part of the battle.

These murals were painted at a time when convents in Mexico were usually decorated with solemn monochromes. The only subjects deemed fit for display were grim portraits of saints and martyrs accompanied by a few lifeless flowers copied from prayer books. But at isolated Ixmiquilpán the walls had been allowed to blossom into life.

To this day there is no explaining these murals. When the Inquisition came to New Spain in the middle of the 16th century, the daring missionaries who allowed them to be painted must have had second thoughts and quickly covered the walls with whitewash. Apparently, they could not bring themselves to destroy the heretical works completely—and so some of the very few examples of 16th-century native art managed to survive. Today the murals delight the few travellers who know about this out-of-the-way monastery.

Restaurant Savino, by far the most attractive place for lunch, is on Highway 85 (Calle Insurgentes), 2 km (1¼ miles) east of town where a bridge spans the Tula river. A broad terrace overlooks the tree-lined stream.

The most direct route back to Mexico City from Ixmiquilpán is Highway 85. The capital is 155 km (96 miles) south over a very good road.

Pahuatlán

Travellers with an extra day or so who want to explore a truly off-trail spot will be rewarded in the Nahuatl-Otomí town of Pahuatlán and the neighboring village of San Pablito. From Ixmiquilpán take Highway 105 southward to Pachuca, turning off on the Pachuca bypass to Tulancingo via Highway 130 east. The Pahuatlán road turns north 37 km (23 miles) east of Tulancingo, passing through the little mountain town of Honey (named for the Englishman who founded it) on its way to mountain-locked Pahuatlán, which itself seems frozen in an earlier century. The modest but appealing ► **Hotel San Carlos** on the main street has a swimming pool, terraces, magnificent views, and a restaurant featuring good regional specialties amid amiable confusion. The best rooms are at the rear of the second floor, and the finest of these is suite 201.

Ten kilometers (6 miles) north of Pahuatlán over an unpaved but adequate road is the charming village of **San Pablito**, home of the simple and gracious Otomí people, who make *amati* paper. This tough, fairly stiff material is produced by endlessly pounding the boiled inner bark of wild fig trees. In the village, vats bubble over open fires and the sound of hammers on pulp provides a constant background accompaniment to life in this untouristed Indian hamlet. The end products of all this labor are decorations, bookmarks, mats, and envelopes.

WEST OF THE CAPITAL

As millions of Mexicans and a few foreigners have discovered, **Valle de Bravo** and its lake offer the visitor serene charm, a restful atmosphere, and relief from a hurried sightseeing pace. Located in a mountain valley 145 km (90 miles) west of Mexico City, it's a fine place to contemplate the view, admire the lake, and simply relax. For those who can't sit still, there's boating, horseback riding over mountain trails, a good golf course, and tennis courts. Still, most visitors will assign the trip a lower priority than the other side trips discussed in this chapter, as the area lacks many of the features that travellers in central Mexico find most appealing: major archaeological sites (though Malinalco, while small, is nevertheless fascinating), lofty colonial monuments, and extensive handicraft or folk art centers. The landscape, with a few exceptions, is pretty and romantic rather than spectacular.

In addition to Valle de Bravo, there are two spots of interest south of Toluca. The Aztec shrine at **Malinalco**, 104 km (64 miles) from the D.F., while not a major ruin, is a delightfully unusual one. **Metepec**, just south of the Toluca highway and 92 km (57 miles) from the capital, is justly famous for its pottery, even though it's unlikely to hold most visitors' interest for long.

An indefatigable traveller could cram all this into a single whirlwind day. A better plan is to spend a night in Valle de Bravo, then visit Metepec and Malinalco on the return trip to Mexico City; alternatively, the region can be explored in two one-day trips, returning to Mexico City each night. Two other possibilities: Stop in Valle de Bravo while en route to Morelia (see the Morelia section in the Colonial Heartland chapter that follows); or visit Metepec and Malinalco on the back route to Taxco and Cuernavaca. Highway 55, which winds south almost all the way to Taxco, passes through scenic countryside and the pretty spa town of Ixtapán de la Sal.

In each case, a car is essential, whether your own or rented (hiring a car and driver for the day is another option, though an expensive one). Bus service in the region is slow and roundabout, and especially erratic to Malinalco. Travel agencies in the capital offer organized trips, though not with any frequency. Such group travel is a poor second choice, especially to Valle de Bravo, where a true appreciation of the town depends largely on being free to wander, linger, and dally as you explore.

The Valle de Bravo part of this excursion is also much less desirable on weekends, when Mexico City residents seeking the relatively pure mountain air and clean waters of the lake crowd the limited facilities and stall traffic on the two-lane highway. Weekdays remain tranquil and untouristed.

The Route West

To explore the region west of the capital, follow Paseo de la Reforma through Chapultepec Park and the Polanco neighborhood. The handsome avenue then meanders through the elegant Lomas section, where embassies and opulent private residences line its way. Finally, after a less attractive area of urban sprawl, it merges with the Toluca road, Highway 15.

From here the route winds upward through pine forests onto one of the highest populated plateaus (8,400 feet) in the world. (Ice forms rapidly on the road surface in winter; use caution during cold weather.) Among the trees dotting the slopes at this elevation are pitch pines, Mexico's answer to the sandalwood tree, whose fragrant wood was so treasured by the Aztecs that great quantities of it appear on ancient tribute lists. Everywhere along the road, both before and after the junction with Highway 130 (which heads southwest into Valle de Bravo) stretch scenic vistas dominated by the snow-capped peak of Nevado de Toluca, an extinct volcano towering some 6,200 feet above the surrounding plain. The road threads itself among mountain meadows lined with stone walls and dotted by small farms. The appearance of the people along the roadside also changes remarkably: These are dark-complexioned descendants of Mazahua Indians, who became vassals of the Aztecs in 1432. Today their clothing still has a homemade look, the women's skirts long and heavy. The area is famed for its fine wool, and traditional woven designs can be seen in the shawls and serapes often worn by the local residents in cool weather.

The immediate approach to Valle de Bravo is marked by homes and a few businesses that, with their steeply pitched tile roofs, decorated eaves, and generous use of wood and dressed stone, seem to have been transplanted from the Swiss highlands. Then, after more piney copses and mountain meadows, the town and its mountain-locked lake appear suddenly.

Created in 1947 as part of a huge hydroelectric project, the freshwater lake today is known as **Presa Miguel Alemán**, in honor of a former national president (the word *presa* refers to both the dam and the lake behind it). With a surface area just over 7½ square miles, the lake is not large; set off by steep slopes and rocky ridges, it is lovely, however, and the comparison to Alpine lakes is irresistible—which explains much of the area's newer architecture.

Valle de Bravo

The town of Valle de Bravo itself antedates the lake by at least six centuries, although none of its earliest structures remains. The first European to make his way to this Mazahua Indian center was a Spanish friar who established a mission here in 1530; it wasn't until 1850 that the settlement was elevated to township status. Eleven years later the name Valle de Bravo was adopted in honor of the patriot Nicolas Bravo, who commanded a troop of men from the region in defense of Chapultepec Castle during the U.S. invasion of Mexico. Growth has been rapid over the last two decades, as Valle de Bravo and the nearby residential community of Avándaro became popular weekend and vacation destinations for Mexico City dwellers, but strictly enforced zoning and architectural codes have preserved much of their charm.

Drivers who stay on the continuation of the highway into town will soon come to the zócalo, with its fanciful bandstand. This is the place to park, get out of the car, and stretch your legs as the leisurely life of Valle de Bravo passes by. It's a pleasant, welcoming spot, with arcaded buildings and a typical village church to the north.

The main street, which runs along the east side of the zócalo, is Calle Bocanegra, but as you follow it north and east its name will change to Calle Toluca without warning. Not to worry: The compactness of Valle de Bravo offsets its confusing lack of street signs. The best way to explore the town is on foot, starting with the arcaded buildings (*portales*) on Calle Bocanegra. Here you'll find the **Restaurant El Portal** (Tel: 72/62-0288), a comfortable establishment with an abundance of tile, bricks, and greenery, and fine for a snack or light meal. A block north on the same street is the courtyard of **El Vegetariano**, a restaurant filled on weekends with a Mexico City set that of course eschews meat.

Up and down the length of Bocanegra (and all around the zócalo) are a number of small shops specializing in carved and painted furniture, rustic home accessories, and, occasionally, antiques of dubious age but attractive design.

Mercado Artesanías

The crafts market is an easy stroll from the center of town over cobblestone streets. Just follow Bocanegra three blocks north of the plaza, turn left (west) onto Durango, and walk to the second corner; immediately to your right will be the market. Getting there through the town's picture-postcard streets is really more rewarding than examining the merchandise, most of which is ordinary. However, the traditional Mazahua embroidery, from small pillowcases to large bedspreads, merits inspection. Much of the work is done by machine; nevertheless, embroidery remains a home industry of good quality. You'll also find durable pottery here, though it tends to be more modern than traditional in design.

After you've eaten and had a chance to amble through the market, you'll probably want to fetch your car and drive down to the municipal pier. The lake is visible from many street corners in the center of town, and if you can't see it, you'll find it simply by heading downhill; the return trip is a fairly steep climb, however.

The Waterfront

The *muelle municipal* juts into the water from the southern edge of town. From here you can catch a boat ride on a launch that accommodates 25 passengers; hire a motorboat; or rent "water cycles," untippable paddle contraptions especially popular with youngsters. Water skiers can also hire speedboats at the pier, although the skis themselves are not always available; you'll want to inquire of the boat man before putting money down. The lake is not a great spot for swimming, partly because of the weeds that grow up from the bottom, and partly because the water is cold, particularly during the summer rainy season. The standard launch trip around the lake, on the other hand, is memorable, and offers delightful views of the mountains, forests, and picturesque towns along the shore. Sailboats and the occasional windsurfer add their own splashes of color to the scene.

The restaurants **Los Pericos** and **La Balsa**, which are almost identical in quality, have been built on pontoon rafts and are moored near the pier. Both have bars, passable fare, and refreshing views of the lake. While fish would seem to be the appropriate choice, the menu offerings do not include anything caught locally. (Although both restaurants advertise a local catch, the fish is of the saltwater variety.) Still, sitting at a table in either one, as the restaurant rocks gently on the waves, is a pleasant way to spend an hour or two.

Restaurant Taberna del León, firmly planted on the shore at the head of the pier, is a better choice in terms of food than either of the two raft restaurants, as are the dining rooms in the town's main hotels, as long as you don't mind passing on the views.

Avándaro

The beautiful residential community of Avándaro ambles along the lakeshore southeast of Valle de Bravo. Although the official distance from the Valle de Bravo zócalo is 7 km (4 miles), the only way you'll know you've left one and entered the other is by the prevailing architectural style, which changes from the merely picturesque to affluent-romantic.

To get to Avándaro from the public pier in Valle de Bravo, follow the shore road south to its end at Calle Ameyal, then turn left (east). A block farther on is the **Iglesia Santa María**, an imposing structure housing a famed Black Christ. This life-size statue is celebrated as a miracle worker by the tens of thousands of the faithful who make their way to the church every May 3 to honor the image. Except for the statue, the interior of the church is bare nowadays, its walls scraped of paint in preparation for major restoration work.

Continuing on Calle Ameyal, follow the signs for Avándaro to **La Cascada**, a frothy waterfall gushing over boulders and ledges on its way to the lake. A rocky path leads to the top of the cataract and a fine view of the extinct volcano known as Cerro Gordo.

From here the road, which becomes the Ruta del Bosque (a name no one seems to recognize), winds and curves among groves of pine, affording superb views of the lake at several points along the way. You'll pass an establishment that rents saddle horses by the hour a short distance before you reach the entrance to the Hotel Avándaro Golf and Spa Resort (discussed below). Called "mountain ponies" locally, a name that belies their tameness, these mounts provide an ideal way to spend a few hours exploring the loveliness of the area.

STAYING IN VALLE DE BRAVO

With tennis courts, a well-kept golf course, a large swimming pool, and a restaurant that maintains the area's best kitchen, the ▶ **Hotel Avándaro Golf and Spa Resort** possesses a pleasing combination of luxuriousness and rustic charm. Located off the area's main drive, the cabin-style accommodations (doubled to 130 units three years ago) at this decidedly first-class establishment do not come cheaply, and that's before the cost of massages, saunas, herbal wraps, and a variety of exercise programs are added to the bill. (The owners of the hotel installed a very compact high-tech spa facility around the time the hotel expansion began.) Greens fees at the 18-hole course, sometimes praised as the most beautiful in Mexico, are also extra.

The ▶ **Hotel El Parador**, about 3 km (2 miles) north of the Hotel Avándaro on the same Ruta del Bosque, occupies a large grassy clearing in the woods. While its large bungalow suites have fireplaces that sometimes smoke and rooms that tend to be a little dark despite their big windows, it's a comfortable inn with reasonable rates, a swimming pool and tennis courts, and a fair restaurant. Note, however, that on weekends the Parador is a vacation mecca for some of the world's noisiest families.

You'll find the moderately expensive ▶ **Loto Azul Hotel-Club** at the other end of the lake. To get there, follow Calle Toluca north and east through Valle de Bravo, continuing on as it becomes a dirt road, until you come to the hotel's cabins spread over a forested hillside. Built as a retreat by an Asian religious sect, the Loto Azul still has a touch of the Far East about it, although it is hardly monastic in its comforts. The unusually ample bedroom suites in the main hotel have fireplaces and large windows that either look into the woods or, in a few cases, toward the lake. The lake-view units, which are located on the second floor, must be requested, however. The restaurant is good, there's a swimming pool on the grounds, and, for an extra charge, you can use the steam baths.

Located at Juárez 101, in the center of town near the zócalo, the two-story ▶ **Casa Vieja** is a very simple family-style posada whose rates appeal to travellers on a budget.

Metepec

The pottery center of Metepec lies some 6½ km (4 miles) south of Toluca off Highway 55. While the burgeoning urban sprawl of the latter has almost swallowed the former, Metepec is still the source of delightful earthenware that is shipped all over Mexico. In fact, shops competing for the dollars and deutsche marks of visitors line the road from the highway turnoff all the way to the center of town.

First inspired by the ceremonial needs of the Church, the pottery designs of Metepec were gradually transfigured by local craftsmen, becoming gayer and gaudier. That evolution has continued to the present day, and what you'll find as a result is a polychrome riot in clay: skeletal mariachis, gaudy "Last Suppers" attended by jolly devils, flamboyantly glazed and painted creatures of both flesh and fantasy. The most famous ceramic creations of Metepec are its Trees of Life (*Arboles de Vida*), which can show almost anything as long as it has a vague connection with Adam and Eve and resembles, at least somewhat, a tree. Most of these elaborate pieces end up serving as candelabra, but they really have lost all function except as delightful decoration.

Apart from its pottery and some woollen goods from nearby towns, Metepec will not hold a traveller's interest for long.

Malinalco

While Metepec is merely a shopper's pause on the highway, Malinalco offers the traveller both a sense of mystery and a fleeting glimpse into the Aztec mind, making it among the most memorable archaeological sites in all of Mexico.

Leaving (or bypassing) Metepec, continue south on Highway 55. At the outskirts of the village of Tenango turn left onto the road to La Marquesa. Road signs for Chalma will begin to appear after you have driven 19 km (12 miles); follow the signs until you come to the directional markers for Malinalco. The road is narrow and frequently blocked by slow-moving vehicles; allow about an hour and a half driving time from Toluca. The ruins themselves are situated high on a hillside above the archaeological zone's parking lot. It will take you an additional half hour to climb the 400 feet to the site.

Temple of the Eagle and Jaguar Knights

The Temple of the Eagle and Jaguar Knights (Templo I, or Templo Principal) is, in essence, a single sculpture—including stairs, balustrades, altars, and figures—hewn from the solid rock of the hill. A broad stairway leads to the temple platform and its only entrance, the latter flanked by a large serpent's head and the carving of an eagle knight. (The Eagle and Jaguar Orders were the two principal warrior societies of the Aztecs.) A huge drum with a pseudo–jaguar skin top sits on the opposite side of the door along with the remains of a carved jaguar knight. The doorway itself is carved to resemble a serpent's head, its tongue stretched out on the entry platform. This odd carving has been compared by guides and not a few wags to a doormat, but it seems far more like a predatory limb ready to scoop up anyone with the temerity to step on it. In Aztec legend, it represented the jaws of Tepeyolotl, the earth monster, and was meant to overawe and even terrify the young warrior acolytes who worshiped here. It is easy to believe it did.

The gloomy interior of the circular room is 19 feet in diameter, with half of that given over to a stone bench running along the wall. Eagle and jaguar sculptures dominate, and the same fierce motifs are etched into the floor of the chamber. A modern roof, made of thatch, is an accurate copy of the original covering. Like all pre-Hispanic ceremonial structures in Mexico, the temple once was covered with stucco and painted in brilliant colors—a suitable setting for the painful rites endured by the young Aztec nobles who were initiated into the Order of the Sun here. At the climax of the induction ceremony, the septum of the initiate's nose was pierced, then a jaguar fang or an eagle claw was inserted as a badge of honor and kinship.

Other Structures at Malinalco

Templos II and III, nearby, have not fared as well as their neighbor, primarily because their removable stones were carried off and used in the construction of a Christian church below the site. Templo I, an unbreakable monolith, offered no such readily available building materials.

Templo IV, just north of Templo I, fared better because it, too, was partly hewn from the solid rock of the hill. In the temple itself you'll find two altars in a spacious chamber, with a bench on three sides. As in Templo I, part of the dramatic effect comes from the realization that the surrounding structure was painstakingly chipped from the living rock with stone tools (the ancient Mesoamericans never discovered the secret of metal tools). In the presence of such a labor-intensive achievement, one can't help but think of the Indian *kivas* of the southwestern United States or, even, of certain Egyptian tombs.

With the exception of bottled drinks and some questionable tacos, neither the archaeological site nor the village below has any real services for the visitor. But the site, with its magnificent views of mountainous countryside, is an ideal spot for a picnic.

Travellers heading back to Mexico City can save themselves time and mileage by avoiding Toluca and returning, instead, via the La Marquesa route described above.

GETTING AROUND

Cuernavaca

Several bus lines serve Cuernavaca from Mexico City, all departing from the Terminal del Sur on Calle General Vicente Guerrero. Autobuses Pullman de Morelos is the most convenient choice because of its downtown Cuernavaca depot. The second-class line, Flecha Amarilla, also goes to the center of Cuernavaca. All other bus lines stop at the edge of town, from which passengers must then take a taxi. Both Pullman and Flecha Amarilla offer several departures hourly. Travelling time is just over an hour on weekdays, but less predictable on weekends due to traffic. Seats on the right side of the bus afford better views on the ride from the capital.

A car is a nuisance in the center of Cuernavaca, though you'll need one for exploring outlying areas. A wider selection of rental vehicles is available in the capital, but Cuernavaca itself has half a dozen agencies, including Hertz.

Taxco

Regular bus service to Taxco is offered by several commercial lines from both Mexico City and Cuernavaca. Driving is also easy, and a new road has speeded up the last quarter of the journey. From the capital the trip takes a little more than 2 hours each way. Taxco is about 50 minutes from Cuernavaca.

Tour buses also depart frequently from Mexico City; the booking is usually done at the travel desks of hotels. Be sure to ask how much time is allowed in Taxco before reserving or paying for a tour.

On any bus going to Taxco or Cuernavaca from Mexico City, the right-hand side as you face front offers a much better view of the scenic mountains south of the Federal District.

Rental cars for Taxco trips are available in Mexico City and Cuernavaca. A car opens up a much wider range of possibilities, but is not needed in Taxco itself.

Puebla and Cholula

There is good first-class bus service from Mexico City to Puebla. Autobuses del Oriente, usually shortened to ADO, has several buses an hour leaving from the Terminal del Oriente (TAPO). If you're taking the metro to the station, get off at the San Lázaro stop. The trip to Puebla takes about 2 hours, and, again, you should try to get a seat on the right-hand side of the bus for the best views of Iztaccíhuatl and Popocatépetl. A car is not needed for enjoying downtown Puebla, but bus service to Cholula can be confusing to newcomers. From the Puebla bus terminal, a prepaid (by zone) taxi to Cholula is your best bet.

Tonantzintla is a short taxi ride from the zócalo in Cholula. A car is best for visiting Tlaxcala and its environs.

West of Mexico City

Most travellers headed in this direction will be driving. The road for Toluca and Valle de Bravo descends swiftly into a fertile valley a little less than an hour from the capital. Before Toluca proper there's a prominent sign for Highway 130 and Valle de Bravo to the southwest. Follow Highway 130 for 40 km (25 miles), and then turn right at the well-marked turnoff; Valle de Bravo is another 33 km (20½ miles).

Highway 55 heads south from Toluca through Metepec, and then on to Malinalco and other small villages on its way to the Taxco region. The junctions, coming from both Mexico City and Valle de Bravo, are well marked.

Those who want to visit only Malinalco, omitting Valle de Bravo and Metepec, should follow the Toluca road, Highway 15, to the village of La Marquesa, 35 km (22 miles) from downtown Mexico City, and turn left (south) at the Chalma turnoff. Chalma is 60 km (37 miles) distant, and Malinalco (follow the signs) is another 11 km (7 miles) beyond it.

ACCOMMODATIONS REFERENCE

The rates given below are projections for December 1993 through Easter 1994. Unless otherwise indicated, rates are for double rooms, double occupancy; the 10 percent VAT has been added. As rates are subject to change, it's always a good idea to double-check before booking.

▶ **La Casa Vieja.** Juárez 101, **Valle de Bravo**, México 51200. Tel: (726) 2-0338. $27.

▶ **Clarion Cuernavaca Racquet Club.** P.O. Box 401, Francisco Villa 100, **Cuernavaca**, Morelos 62120. Tel: (73) 11-

2400; Fax: (73) 11-5493; in the U.S. and Canada, Tel: (800) 228-5151. $130.

▶ **Hacienda Cocoyoc**. Carretera Federal, km 32.5, **Cocoyoc**, Morelos 62740. Tel: (735) 6-2211; Fax: (735) 6-1212. $85.

▶ **Hacienda del Solar**. P.O. Box 96, Calle Paraje del Solar s/n, **Taxco**, Guerrero 40200. Tel: (762) 2-0323; Fax: (762) 2-0587. $145.

▶ **Hostería las Quintas**. P.O. Box 427, Avenida las Quintas, **Cuernavaca**, Morelos 62440. Tel: (73) 18-3949; Fax: (73) 18-3895. $128.

▶ **Hotel Avándaro Golf and Spa Resort**. Fraccionamiento Avándaro, **Valle de Bravo**, México 51200. Tel: (726) 6-0303; Fax: (726) 6-0122; in Mexico City, (5) 536-7389. $136 (junior suites); $67 (cabins).

▶ **Hotel Lastra**. P.O. Box 649, Calzada de los Fuertes 2633, **Puebla**, Puebla 72290. Tel and Fax: (22) 35-1501. $78.

▶ **Hotel El Parador**. Ruta del Bosque, **Valle de Bravo**, México 51200. Tel: (726) 2-1173. $124 (includes two meals).

▶ **Hotel del Portal**. Camacho 205, **Puebla**, Puebla 72290. Tel: (22) 46-0211; Fax: (22) 46-7511. $86 (with parking); $69 (without parking).

▶ **Hotel Royalty Centro**. Avenida Portal Hidalgo, **Puebla**, Puebla 72290. Tel and Fax: (22) 242-0204. $57; $78 (suites).

▶ **Hotel San Carlos**. Calle 2 de Abril 26, **Pahuatlán**, Puebla 73100. Tel: (775) 3-1910. $51; $69 (suites).

▶ **Hotel Santa Prisca**. P.O. Box 42, Cena Obscuras 1, **Taxco**, Guerrero 40200. Tel: (762) 2-0980; Fax: (762) 2-1106. $49 (includes breakfast).

▶ **Loto Azul Hotel-Club**. **Valle de Bravo**, México 51200. Tel: (726) 2-0796; Fax: (726) 2-1192. $110 (includes breakfast).

▶ **Las Mañanitas**. P.O. Box 1202, Ricardo Linares 107, **Cuernavaca**, Morelos 62400. Tel: (73) 14-1466; Fax: (73) 18-3672. $100–$250.

▶ **El Mesón del Angel**. Hermanos Serdan 807, **Puebla**, Puebla 72100. Tel: (22) 24-3000; Fax: (22) 24-2227. $155.

▶ **Villa Arqueológica**. 2 Poniente 601, **Cholula**, Puebla 72760. Tel: (22) 47-1966; Fax: (22) 47-1508; in the U.S., Tel: (800) 258-2633; in Canada, Tel: (514) 937-7707. $87.

THE COLONIAL HEARTLAND

QUERETARO, SAN MIGUEL DE ALLENDE, GUANAJUATO, MORELIA

By Robert Somerlott

North and west of the capital lies a pleasant and usually gentle land ringed by mountains. This is the traditional Mexico, where tile-domed churches rise from almost empty fields; where bandstands and fountains shaded by Indian laurels and pepper trees invite the weary to stop and rest a minute. This is picture-postcard Mexico, the Mexico of song and film. At the mention of such towns as San Miguel de Allende and Guanajuato, a Mexican listener is apt to toss his hands in delight and exclaim, "*Ay, que preciosa!* How beautiful!" At the same time, and perhaps not surprisingly, the cities of the colonial heartland tend to be conservative, wary keepers of a heritage.

Charles Flandrau wrote at the start of this century: "Superficially, Mexico is a prolonged romance. For even the brutal realities—of which there are many—are the realities of an intensely pictorial people among surroundings that, to the Northern eye, are never quite commonplace." Such are the colonial highlands.

This is also where the nation's patriotic soul is enshrined (in Mexico it is easy and customary to speak of the soul), as well as where the bitter struggle for independence was

launched. Half a century later, the final siege against Maximilian was waged here, and then, in 1915, one of the bloodiest battles ever fought on the North American continent took place at Celaya, ending in the destruction of Pancho Villa's army.

MAJOR INTEREST

Colonial architecture and history
Scenic beauty
Handicrafts

Querétaro
Historic sights and buildings

San Miguel de Allende
Largely preserved colonial town
Handicrafts, especially metals
Houses and gardens
Study of Spanish language and arts and crafts

San Miguel environs
Spas
Santuario de Atotonilco
Templo de Nuestra Señora del Carmen in Celaya
Augustinian monastery at Yuriria

Guanajuato
Visual drama
Teatro Juárez

Morelia
17th-century architecture
Handicraft marketing centers

The cities of the colonial heartland ring an area known as the Bajío, a vast fertile basin. Multinational companies such as Campbell Soup have built packing plants in recent years, but it's not unusual to see strawberry fields crowding the houses in some towns.

The Food of the Bajío

The abundance of fresh farm products in the Bajío has not, unfortunately, fostered an outstanding regional cuisine. Perhaps this is because its agricultural abundance came late, and only with irrigation. It also might be that Mexicans in the area are as traditional in their diet as they are in their religion. Except in Morelia, where there is a Tarascan touch to the menu, no ethnic group has been able to preserve its special ways of cooking. (The true center for Tarascan cooking is west of the colonial region covered in this chapter.)

As a result, the food of the region is very much an amalgam. The better restaurants—and even some inspired cooks in market stalls—hold their own with any in the country, but the traditional dishes lack the variety and dash of those in other parts of Mexico. Visiting Mexicans often complain, and the more affluent end up patronizing foreign-style restaurants.

You will discover a few culinary specialties, however. Celaya, equidistant from San Miguel and Querétaro, produces *cajeta,* a thick, syrupy caramel confection made of goat's and cow's milk that is packed in wooden boxes and shipped throughout Mexico and abroad. Querétaro cooks work with the *camote,* a relative of the sweet potato, candying it with sugar and lemon juice.

To praise a dessert a Mexican might exclaim, "Good as if made by a nun's fingers!" In the old days the best sweets were made in convents, which preserved Spanish rather than Mexican traditions. Nuns in the larger convents produced almond-paste candy, shaped and colored like little fruits and similar to marzipan. Today the same recipes are cooked up in home kitchens and appear for sale at fiestas throughout the year. Desserts and chicken dishes enhanced with walnuts and almonds have also slipped out of the convents into private kitchens. *Pollo en nogado* is a holiday treat made with chicken, walnuts, chiles, and cinnamon. *Ate de Almendra* is a sherry-and-almond glorification of sponge cake.

Chile sauces tend to be less fierce here than in other parts of the country, but it is not macho to admit it; besides, the next restaurant may slip you liquid fire. Beef, except when ground, stewed, or thinly sliced (as for *carne asada*), is often disappointing.

Beverages in the Bajío are not distinct from those in the rest of Mexico, though nonalcoholic *licuados* and *aguas* here rely a little more on strawberries, which are abundant. The state of Querétaro produces wine, and so does the Dolores Hidalgo neighborhood, but neither area is famous for it.

The Historic Heritage of the Bajío

This fertile region supported a sparse population in pre-Hispanic times. Pottery-making villages flourished as early as 500 B.C., but despite the high art they achieved in clay, they failed to progress to higher levels of civilization.

When the Spanish arrived they found the land occupied by civilized Otomí Indians in the south, but encountered fierce semi-nomadic Chichimecs a little farther north. Far to the west the Tarascans, who in time might have rivaled the Aztecs, had established outposts beyond their traditional base on Lake Pátzcuaro.

Silver accounts for the lightning thrust of the Spanish northward. Their hunger for ore from Zacatecas and, later, Guanajuato propelled soldiers and prospectors still breathless from destroying the Aztecs into the Bajío. Simultaneously, missionary priests who had reaped a harvest of souls in the west moved quickly eastward. As would happen throughout the vast area that came to be known as New Spain, sword and cross marched together, impelled by different motives.

Silver barons and hacienda owners, often one and the same, multiplied their wealth in the 17th century. Native workers were recruited from afar and, as they mixed with local folk, lost their identity as Aztecs, Tlaxcalans, or Mixtecs. Intermarriage between Indian and Indian, as well as Spanish and Indian, produced the population that today characterizes the heartland. When a Mexican from the Bajío says he is of a certain descent, he is probably no more accurate about his ancestry than the typical sixth-generation North American.

Prosperity in the 1700s allowed the cities of the Bajío to embark on ambitious building programs; most of today's great structures date from that century. The same prosperity fanned the flames of independence, however, and in 1810 a revolt plotted in Querétaro and San Miguel blazed forth from tiny Dolores, now Dolores Hidalgo. During the violence-filled decades that followed, construction nearly ceased, leaving a virtual architectural blank from 1810 until about 1880. With the ascendancy of Porfirio Díaz to the presidency, a period of relative calm ensued. Once again, municipal governments turned their attention to dilapidated infrastructures, and a period of zealous rebuilding followed that lasted until soon after the turn of the century—when a new and different kind of revolutionary violence halted everything but destruction and bloodletting.

THE CITY OF QUERETARO

Querétaro, prosperous capital of the small state of the same name, is an oft-bypassed beauty. Motorists heading north for the U.S. border or south to Mexico City usually skirt it, sighing as they pass its unattractive industrial suburbs. The impression from a train is little better.

Tourists' neglect of the city cannot be blamed entirely on unfavorable first impressions. Though worthy and historic, Querétaro lacks the impact of other colonial cities. It can offer a rewarding two days, but seldom engenders a passionate attachment. Yet Querétaro, in its somewhat staid fashion, has attractions to offer.

The first clue that something special awaits is given to travellers approaching from the usual direction, south, on the Mexico City Highway 57 bypass. At the city's edge traffic abruptly ducks under an 18th-century **aqueduct** towering incongruously above the freeway. It comes up so quickly, in fact, that most people are oblivious to the extraordinary structure looming over them. The aqueduct, built between 1726 and 1738, has more than 70 arches, some soaring to heights of 76 feet. Once the town's chief source of water, and, at 4,200 feet in length, reputedly the seventh-largest such structure in the world, the aqueduct still supplies the Fountain of Neptune at the center of the city.

Querétaro once stood astride a vital trade route to the Bajío and the silver-rich mountains protecting it. The Otomí people settled here at least 1,000 years ago; Aztecs assumed loose control of the city in 1446, turning it into their northernmost allied outpost against the hostile Chichimecs.

The conquistadors swooped down on it in 1531, making a quick alliance with an Otomí chief named Conin, but then had to deal with the more formidable Chichimecs. Legend has it that the newcomers and natives agreed to settle ownership by man-to-man combat, a bare-knuckle fistfight. There are variations of what happened next. In one version there was a melee. In another, even as the champions of either side stood ready, an astounding red-and-gold cross carried by Saint James mounted on horseback flared across the sky; the local population reportedly converted on the spot. Querétaro has been a bastion of Catholicism ever since.

La Corregidora

In the early 1800s the traditionally cautious town became a den of conspiracy. At the center of the plot to overthrow Spanish rule was Josefa Ortíz de Domínguez, wife of the *corregidor* (mayor). In September of 1810, Doña Josefa, already under house arrest, managed to warn her fellow plotters that their sedition had been discovered and that the Spanish authorities were ready to pounce. Her message, which, according to legend, was passed through a keyhole, ignited the revolt. Doña Josefa, usually called La Corregidora,

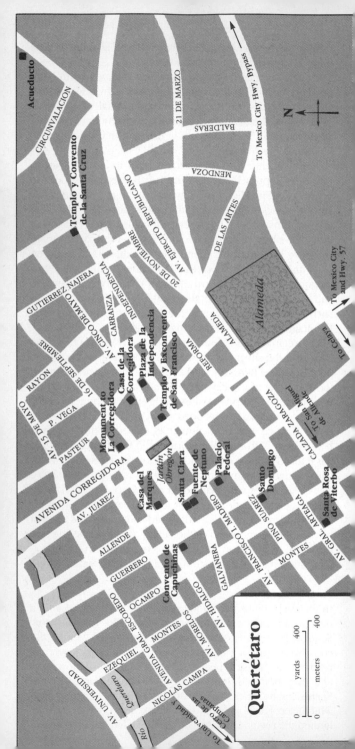

is today the greatest female figure in the history of a country with few acclaimed heroines.

In 1848 Querétaro became the provisional capital of the nation while the U.S. Army was occupying Mexico City. The Treaty of Guadalupe Hidalgo, which ceded almost half of Mexico's territory to the United States (what are now the states of California, New Mexico, and Arizona, and parts of Nevada, Utah, and Colorado), was signed here later that year.

Nineteen years after that national disaster, the beleaguered Emperor Maximilian, along with the remnants of his army, was cornered at the edge of town. After a three-month siege, Maximilian was captured, tried, and executed (an event recalled in a painting by Manet). On a happier day in 1917, the constitution that is still in force in Mexico was written and adopted in Querétaro.

The latest incursion into the city has been quite different from the hostile ones of the past. After the earthquakes of 1985, thousands of Mexico City residents sought solid ground and new lives here, enlarging and changing the city even as they adapted to its peculiar rhythms. In return, these newcomers have brought with them a tonic of sophistication, a delight in the performing arts, and a generally faster-paced lifestyle.

PLAZAS OBREGON AND INDEPENDENCIA

As a major link between the provinces and the capital in colonial days, Querétaro came to dominate the artistic tastes of a huge area, developing a gay, exuberant style that was flashier and more sentimental than the capital's. For two centuries it supplied even faraway towns with painters and artisans.

Today touches of this antique extravagance are everywhere to be seen in Querétaro, from its grillwork and balconies to its cornices and doors. The old section of town is especially delightful for strolling and discovering these architectural details.

Traffic has been banished from the downtown area, which, while a blessing, also causes many a snarl in outlying areas. Parking lots are hidden from the uninitiated, so the best course is to walk or take a taxi to the main plaza.

Jardín Obregón

The spacious and pleasant Jardín Obregón, in the center of town, is adorned with a bronze statue of the Greek goddess Hebe, swans, gargoyles, and curlicues—all the mandatory signs of civic chic at the turn of the century (other Bajío towns were not nearly so stylish). The character of the city becomes apparent in this square, which is suspiciously tidy and well-ordered. There is a strange paucity of vendors here, a lack of the usual confusion and sprawling disorder. It's as if it were saying, This is a tightly governed town, a slightly gentrified town, a town aware of its image.

On the east side of the square looms the **Templo y Exconvento de Francisco**. Built in 1545, it has endured so much expansion and cosmetic surgery that what remains is little more than a hodgepodge. Still, the dome and tower are splendid. Inside, the nave harbors some dreadful sculpture and one exceptional statue, a polychrome Saint James by the local master Arce, who worked at the start of the 19th century. A glance at the organ loft reveals a fine iron grille (*reja*) enclosing the choir.

The 17th-century Franciscan monastery next door has become a regional museum that includes the former **Museo Pío Mariano**, with exhibits of war relics, several fine paintings (including two by the famed Baroque master Juan Correa), and a variety of colonial furnishings, among them chairs identical in design and discomfort to those sat upon in conservative Querétaro today. Elsewhere in the museum, huge music books are emblazoned with hand-drawn notations big enough to be read over the choirmaster's shoulder from the loft above.

While the museum's contents may be scant, the building itself is an exhibit, especially the central patio, with its carved arches and domes in the Moorish (*mudéjar*) style. The smaller Patio of Novices and the Orange Garden evoke a sense of antiquity and the monastic life. The building as a whole is typically Franciscan, strong and practical, handsome but never extravagant.

Plaza de la Independencia

Leaving the museum and walking east along a very pretty pedestrian mall, you pass attractive shops with quite ordinary merchandise. This shaded and flowering street leads to the tiny but charming Plaza de la Independencia. Here, in bronze, stands Marqués de la Villa del Villar del Aguila, the benefactor who financed the Querétaro aqueduct. The marqués was also a keen hunter, as evidenced by the lean stone hounds that cling to his monument. These particular animals are replacements; the original bronze canines were dognapped.

On the east side of the plaza the riotous façade of the onetime mansion of Don Tomás López de Ecala displays Querétaro exuberance run amok, with a pair of vulturine eagles signifying the owner's high rank, stone draperies, and tangles of wrought iron. Don Tomás appropriated part of the park in order to erect this astonishing edifice.

At least a score of other attractive colonial buildings, both religious and residential, enrich downtown Querétaro. For the visitor who chooses to explore on foot there are countless touches of charm—including a statue of La Corregidora in a vaguely Greek costume but wearing long drop earrings for an added touch of elegance. (The statue is one block north of the Jardín Obregón on Avenida Corregidora.) And although sitting and strolling are the town's chief pleasures, Querétaro does have four additional sites of special interest.

SANTA CLARA AND SANTA ROSA CHURCHES

Santa Clara stands gracefully behind its own atrium one block west of the Jardín Obregón, with the **Fuente** (Fountain) **de Neptuno**—the modern terminus of the Querétaro aqueduct—lending it an air of distinction. The fountain, for many travellers, is their introduction to Francisco Eduardo Tresguerras, the Renaissance man of Mexican art. Born in Celaya, about 30 miles west of Querétaro, in 1759, Tresguerras, with one year of formal art training, became an architect, painter, sculptor, etcher, woodcarver, poet, and musician, leaving a legacy of work that remains the pride of the region. His prestige is so great, in fact, that dozens of buildings in various cities are proudly, and falsely, attributed to him by local boosters. As the fountain demonstrates, he possessed a particular talent for warming the cold, often sterile Neoclassical style in which he was forced to build by government decree. (The ruling clique of his day had become embarrassed by the flamboyant decoration of the Mexican High Baroque, or Churrigueresque, style and sought to tame and refine Mexican buildings by making them look vaguely Roman. Artistic strangulation generally resulted; Tresguerras saved many new structures from what would have been an otherwise arid fate.)

Templo de Santa Clara

At Santa Clara he designed the fountain, although he did not create the sculpture. In the last years of the 1790s he redid the dome and tower of the church, and probably created the main altar and interior vaulting as well. The rest of the church, dating from its original construction in 1633, features Baroque ornamentation that is majestic to the point of being sublime.

The church itself is the only surviving structure of a huge religious complex that once stretched all the way to the Jardín Obregón. At one time 8,000 nuns and their servants found shelter here, in what was one of the richest religious communities in the world. Evidence of that wealth is abundantly obvious in the church's ornamentation and sculpture, the most famous piece of which is the beautiful *La Piedad* by Mariano Arce. That there were hundreds of such communities throughout the country explains in part the genesis, in the mid-19th century, of Mexico's anti-clerical laws.

Templo de Santa Rosa de Viterbo

Southwest of the center of town on Avenida General Arteaga, a rather long six-block walk from the main square, stands the imposing church of Santa Rosa de Viterbo, the most unusual of Querétaro's many ecclesiastical monuments. In 1670 three pious young sisters were granted permission to construct cells for their religious devotions. Other aristocratic girls immediately demanded the same fashionable seclusion, and thus began the convent. In time the nuns became teachers and the convent a college. (Of Mexico's tens of thousands of nuns, most were simply women in retirement and seclusion, "extra" women in a society that had no use for unmarried ladies of gentility. The teacher-nuns at Santa Rosa were among the exceptions.) The college was eventually housed in its present building, which was completed in 1752. The dome is so ponderous that special flying buttresses had to be added to support it, creating in the process a strikingly theatrical exterior.

Tresguerras was employed to rebuild and redecorate the structure at the end of the century, but it is hard to say how much of the building is his. Certainly he did the outer ornamentation, the dome and tower, and the carvings in the sacristy. In the same room you'll find one of the best murals painted during the colonial period, often attributed to Tresguerras but probably the work of José de Páez. The mural depicts nuns and their pupils in an enclosed garden while lambs carry white roses that turn red upon contact with the blood of the Savior.

Convento de la Santa Cruz

Some distance east of the Jardín Obregón, at the corner of Carranza and Acuña, the Convent of the Cross commands the highest ground in the city, the alleged spot where Saint James stopped the fight between conquistadors and Chichimecs, thereby settling the future of Querétaro. Nowadays the view of the town's roofs and many church towers is almost as dramatic.

The church was for many years headquarters for the missionary priests who went forth on foot to Christianize the area of New Spain that is now the southwestern United States. Among them was Father Junípero Serra, whose missionary activities (he founded the California missions of San Diego, San Luis Obispo, San Juan Capistrano, Santa Clara, and San Francisco, among others) have virtually assured him of sainthood while earning the condemnation of Native American rights activists. In the late 1600s the church was also home to more than 7,000 mostly scientific volumes—what was probably the largest library in the New World at the time. A century and a half later Maximilian used the adjacent convent as a barracks, only to have it become his temporary prison. Today mementos of the emperor are on display there.

The Convent of the Cross itself is a labyrinth of seven patios and rooms that are literally countless due to the fact that many are sealed and buried. The present structure, with expansions and rebuilding, dates to around 1650. Historically and spiritually it is the most important edifice in Querétaro and, as the site of a famed miracle, attracts pilgrims from all over the country.

According to legend, Fray Antonio Margil de Jesús Ros (1657–1726) was an exceedingly devout missionary who, among other feats, walked barefoot from present-day Guatemala to Texas. In a garden at the church he reportedly plunged his staff into the ground, where, like Aaron's rod, it took root. A tree soon sprang up that bore cross-shaped thorns—a tree that continues to thrive in the same courtyard alongside some of its offspring. Supposedly, this type of tree will grow nowhere else—which means it not only has to be protected from the usual souvenir hunters but also from seekers of holy relics, who would shred it to its last root if given the chance.

Cerro de las Campanas

Whether or not the Hill of the Bells is worth visiting depends on your sense of history and romance. Outwardly it is not much, and the whole site has been called ugly by some. But those fascinated by the story of Maximilian and Carlota will want to stand on the spot where their tragedy came to an end and modern Mexico began—or at least was reassured about its survival.

The hill rises between the university and the industrial

zone at the western edge of town. The first thing to arrest the eye is a stone colossus of Benito Juárez, harsh and rough, appropriately made of unyielding granite. His words are inscribed below: "Between individuals as between nations, respect for the rights of others is peace."

The memorial to the ill-fated emperor is down the hill at the spot where he was executed. In death as in life the two leaders do not meet. The Austrian government has erected a chapel here as well, and near its altar are three stone plinths marking the spot where Maximilian, with his two Mexican generals, faced the firing squad. (Juárez once observed that Maximilian was honored to die beside two gallant Mexicans who loved both their church and their country.) The chapel is poorly maintained, however, and from the beginning was cheap, even mingy, somehow suggesting that the emperor, for all his glamour, was as great an embarrassment to Austria as he was a plague to Mexico.

SHOPPING FOR OPALS

East of the city is one of the world's major veins of opals, a source of every grade of this lovely stone. The mines have been worked for more than a century now, and their yield is not as abundant as it was a few decades ago, when opals were offered on almost every corner of the city. But the mines continue to be worked, and Querétaro remains a cutting and marketing center for them—as well as for amethysts, topazes, and aquamarines from elsewhere.

Evaluating opals is a tricky business. Buyers should always avoid street vendors who have just made "wonderful finds." Perhaps the first dealer you should consult is José Ramírez, owner of his own opal mine, who for many years has had an outstanding shop, **Lapidaria Querétaro**, at the corner of Pasteur Norte and 15 de Mayo, north of the monument to La Corregidora. Both loose stones and stones in settings are offered, and lovely imported amethysts and topazes may also be inspected here.

To compare prices and quality go to **El Rubí**, a few steps west of the Jardín Obregón at Avenida Madero 3. This is a family affair run by three gracious sisters who are both welcoming and knowledgeable. Again, both set and unset stones are displayed.

The **Sociedad Cooperativa Otomí**, in the center of town at Cinco de Mayo 29, has a much smaller collection, as does **Opalo** at Corregidora 13 Norte, near Sears.

Opals and other stones at these (as well as other) established stores are the only Querétaro specialty worth the attention of shoppers. A better selection of art and craft products will be found elsewhere in Mexico.

STAYING IN QUERETARO

Most of the modern Querétaro hostelries are strung out along Highway 57 to attract motorists travelling to or from Mexico City, and therefore tend to suffer from typical motel monotony, limited service, and isolation. An exception is the attractive ▶ **Holiday Inn Querétaro**, a very well run establishment two miles west of the center of town (on an access road east of Highway 57) that more than justifies its slightly higher prices with comfortable rooms, pleasant decor, and facilities such as lighted tennis courts. The Holiday Inn also has a fine Mexican/international restaurant with an ample selection of wines, gentle lighting, and music in the evenings. The cheerful coffee shop, La Capilla, serves good breakfasts.

Less complete in its offerings but perfectly acceptable is the ▶ **Real de Minas**, part of a chain of motor inns popular with Mexican business and government travellers. It, too, is near the highway, about a mile from the center of town.

Visitors arriving by bus or train may want a more central location (although the Holiday Inn is especially helpful about arranging transportation). On the Plaza de la Independencia in the historic district is the ▶ **Mesón de Santa Rosa**, an elegant and unusual colonial building that has been restored and adapted with taste. The dining room is rather formal, with both food and service seeming more European than Mexican.

Five blocks west of the main plaza at Guerrero Norte 10A is ▶ **El Señorial**, a conveniently situated and modern hotel with protected parking.

The ▶ **Hacienda Jurica**, 13 km (8 miles) northwest of the city off Highway 57, is a fashionable resort hotel that is particularly popular with vacationers from Mexico City. It offers an 18-hole golf course, squash and tennis courts, even a roller-skating rink. Not all rooms in this 17th-century hacienda are excellent, but most are.

▶ **La Mansión Galindo**, another elegant resort, is located some distance to the southeast on the way to Mexico City. Take Highway 57 east for 37 km (23 miles) to the Amealco exit, and then follow Route 120 another 6½ km (4 miles). After the turnoff, the directions will be clearly marked. The hacienda dates from the 16th century, but not even the viceroys of that era imagined the luxury that the Galindo offers today: lighted tennis court, posh nightclub, and more. The Galindo is popular with the capital's film, TV, and political folk.

DINING IN QUERETARO

Querétaro's most fashionable restaurant is also its best. Situated near the northeastern entrance to the city, on the service road of the Mexico City–San Luis Potosí bypass just west of the aqueduct, **Gitano's** is gently lit and offers impeccable service. Lobster and crayfish are featured on a varied menu, and violin music adds to the refined atmosphere. Open for lunch and dinner until 1:00 A.M. Expensive. Tel: (42) 13-7033.

The **Parilla Argentina Fogon Pampero**, near the entrance to the country club on Boulevard Las Américas, opposite the bullring, packs in local businessmen for afternoon feasts of, usually, beef. This rather plain place serves large (but not cheap) portions of hearty food. Tel: (42) 16-0685.

For a simpler meal or snack while downtown, the **Flor de Querétaro**, a family spot at Juárez 9, off the Jardín Obregón, offers an inexpensive menu for a set afternoon dinner (the *comida corrida*), as well as à la carte Mexican dishes. Tel: (42) 12-0199.

The **Fonda del Refugio**, a somewhat fancier restaurant and sidewalk café, is located in the historic zone at Corregidora 26. The café is popular with the more affluent students from the local university, and outdoor tables here are at a premium. Traditional dishes are satisfactory, the attempts at international cuisine a bit riskier.

The dozen or so hole-in-the-wall counter-in-the-front spots scattered throughout the Jardín Obregón neighborhood are all right for tacos, tortas, and the like. One is much the same as another, but out-of-towners should confine themselves to bottled beverages.

SAN MIGUEL DE ALLENDE

The usual approach to San Miguel de Allende is from the southeast, by car or bus from Mexico City via Querétaro. Above the town the cobbled road suddenly widens into a balustraded *mirador* (overlook), where most drivers pause to admire the view. After shooing away the vendors of flimsy rugs, you gaze across a valley toward a pale lake and distant mountains. The town lies directly below, its domes and towers clinging to the slope of the Hill of Moctezuma, a pastel collage.

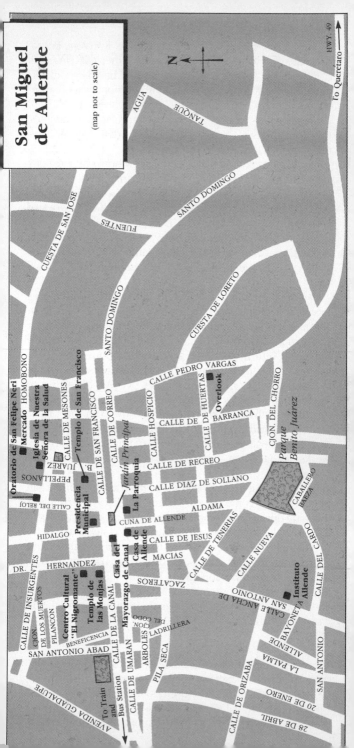

San Miguel de Allende

(map not to scale)

N

To Querétaro
HWY. 49

AGUA
TANQUE
SANTO DOMINGO
FUENTES
CUESTA DE SAN JOSE
SANTO DOMINGO
CUESTA DE LORETO

CALLE PEDRO VARGAS
CALLE DE HUERTAS
Overlook
CALLE HOSPICIO
CALLE DE CORREO
CALLE DE SAN FRANCISCO
Oratorio de San Felipe Neri
Mercado HOMOBONO
Iglesia de Nuestra Señora de la Salud
Templo de San Francisco
CALLE DE MESONES
PEPELLANOS
B. JUAREZ
BARRANCA
CALLE DE RECREO
Jardín Principal
La Parroquia
CALLE DIAZ DE SOLLANO
CALLE DEL RELOJ
CUNA DE ALLENDE
ALDAMA
Presidencia Municipal
HIDALGO
Parque Benito Juarez
CABALLERO BAEZA
CJON. DEL CHORRO

DR.
HERNANDEZ
Centro Cultural "El Nigromante"
Templo de las Monjas
Casa del Mayorazgo de Canal
Casa de Allende
CALLE DE JESUS
MACIAS
CALLE DE TENERIAS
CALLE NUEVA
CALLE DEL CARDO
CALLE DE INSURGENTES
CJON. DE LOS MUERTOS
PILANCON
BENEFICENCIA
SAN ANTONIO ABAD
CALLE DE LA CANAL
ZACATEROS
CALLE DE UMARAN
CJON. DEL CODO
ARBOLES
LADRILLERA
PILA SECA
CALLE ANCHA DE SAN ANTONIO
BAYONETA
Instituto Allende
AVENIDA GUADALUPE
To Train and Bus Station
CALLE DE ORIZABA
28 DE ABRIL
20 DE ENERO
LA PALMA
ALLENDE
SAN ANTONIO

The collage image is obvious, of course. Everyone knows that San Miguel is an art colony, and one rather self-conscious of the fact. But visitors standing at this spot have been known to fall in love with the town instantly and not always reasonably. And why not? This is the prettiest town in Mexico, although many others are more spectacular, imposing, or exotic. And despite recent growth and urban sprawl, it remains a small city, easy to see and manage.

San Miguel can be "done" in just a few hours by a zealous sightseer with a checklist. Indeed, a few marathon bus tours out of Mexico City offer just such a production-line schedule. However, the town will not reveal itself in a series of snapshots; much of its charm is subtle and indefinite, the whole being more than the sum of its parts. As a result, energetic folks who do not enjoy sauntering, lounging, or soaking up ambience may grow restless after a day or two here.

San Miguel is a winter haven for a few hundred refugees from the cold and snow of the United States and Canada. In summer it is a cool and convenient retreat for people from Texas and the Gulf Coast region. Many of these visitors from the north return year after year, renting houses or apartments or booking the same rooms in favorite hotels, staying a month or two, or even three. They become possessive of the town, as well as strong supporters of its cultural and charitable activities. Others, again mostly from the United States or Canada, retire to San Miguel to live on pensions and investments. A much smaller expatriate group actually works for a living, painting, writing, or running small businesses.

There are fears, usually expressed from a distance, that San Miguel has become Americanized. Indeed, on any given morning during mid-summer or mid-winter Americans seem to occupy the south side of the main plaza as surely as they do the Alamo. But travellers wishing to avoid other visitors have only to detour half a block to be solidly back in Mexico. Mexicans outnumber foreigners here by a hundred to one, and all the guest rooms in town would fit easily into a single resort hotel in Acapulco. San Miguel, despite superficial indications to the contrary, is as Mexican as cactus.

THE PLAZA AREA

Visitors standing on the south side of the main plaza (usually called *el jardín*) facing San Miguel's imposing parish church, La Parroquia, will find themselves surrounded by as well preserved a colonial town as there is. Despite the traffic and overhead power lines, its 18th-century character remains surprisingly intact, much of this due to the fact that San Miguel was declared a national monument in 1926. Since then, architectural change has been banned, signs regulated, neon forbidden.

At the same time, the preservation of the town is only in part the result of decrees. The 17th and 18th centuries saw the town grow wealthy from commerce and ranching, as well as from the tanneries that lined some of its streets. Eventually it changed its name to San Miguel el Grande (because it was by then the biggest San Miguel, of which there were more than a few, in the region) and assumed aristocratic airs. But civil upheaval and the Industrial Revolution brought ruin to the burghers of the 19th century. The silver in the surrounding region was mined out and the silver trains stopped coming; the tanneries found themselves unable to compete in mass markets because the town lacked sufficient water. Gradually, San Miguel was bypassed by the times. The old buildings were left standing because there was no need and no money to replace them; cobblestones were left in place by a town that could not afford repaving.

Today almost everything dates from the 1700s, with the exception of the French-influenced details from the turn of this century (the landscaping, benches, and bandstand of *el jardín,* for example) and an occasional sign of more recent prosperity. And since the town has never been reconstructed as a sort of museum, it has been saved from being self-consciously picturesque. In the long run, San Miguel's past misfortune has become the visitor's good fortune.

La Parroquia

At the edge of La Parroquia's atrium rises a bronze statue of Fray Juan de San Miguel, the barefoot Franciscan missionary who founded the town in 1542, naming it for his own patron saint, the warrior archangel. The full name of the town was San Miguel de los Chichimecas, prematurely honoring those Indians the friar intended to convert. As it turned out, the angel's protection was needed; this was wild country, and the Chichimecs proved so stubborn that Indians from Tlaxcala had to be imported to serve the needs of the Spaniards.

The settlement, located astride the silver trails, thrived. Prosperity, however, meant rebuilding; nothing remains of the 16th-century village. A stone church was erected, then replaced. The oldest walls of La Parroquia may date as far back as 1620, but most of it, except for the famous façade, was built 60 years later.

Today La Parroquia is the most photographed, most

painted church in Mexico, an astonishment of Neo-Gothic architecture gone mad—or Mexican. Ceferino Gutiérrez, a self-taught Indian stonemason, was commissioned in 1880 to create a new façade for the then-conventional church. In love with the Gothic architecture of Europe, he studied drawings, engravings, and postcards, admiring especially the cathedrals of Milan, Chartres, and Cologne. Though he was probably illiterate and knew nothing of drafting, Gutiérrez daily sketched his plans in the sand for workmen to follow, just as the great cathedral builders of Europe once had. The result is, in the truest sense of the word, fantastic. La Parroquia stabs the sky with its turrets and spires; everything is aimed heavenward. But that was the only aspect of Gothic style Gutiérrez grasped. The rest of his façade is massive, brooding, solid as a fortress.

Still, La Parroquia completely dominates the San Miguel landscape, just as its humble builder dreamed it would. Its heavy bells, the largest almost six feet high, give it added authority and act as a constant sound track for the town, sounding early Mass at dawn, ringing rosary, signaling events, arrivals, and departures. The slender clock tower next door, rebuilt by Gutiérrez to match his church façade, adds its own strong bell voice as it announces the quarter hours. (Visitors should be warned that there are about 150 public bells in town; all are rung on various occasions and sometimes all at once.)

The interior of La Parroquia is less interesting than its façade. There is, however, a remarkable life-size statue of Our Lord of the Conquest—made by Tarascan converts at Pátzcuaro in the 16th century out of cornstalks and an enduring orchid-bulb glue—in a chapel to the left of the main portal. This powerful figure is venerated by the *conchero* dancers, who perform their ceremonial dances in flamboyant costume, accompanied by shell instruments, at various religious festivals throughout the year. More than 100,000 *concheros* are scattered over a wide region that was once Chichimec country, but apart from the religious customs and ceremonial dances that glorify their ancestral heritage, most *concheros* lead ordinary lives. The wild dancing warrior with hair to his waist may be, under his wig, the short-haired bank clerk who changed your money earlier in the day.

The Birthplace of Allende

Across the narrow street that flanks La Parroquia to the west stands the birthplace of Ignacio Allende, the town's most famous citizen. This fine and well-proportioned mansion is now a museum open to the public. Allende himself was an aristocrat, but the "taint" of being born a *criollo*—a Spaniard born in Mexico—condemned him to second-class status in his own country. The Crown's discrimination against Spaniards born abroad gradually nurtured resentment and, eventually, rebellion. Allende, a career army officer, was one of the few trained military leaders among the insurgents and became their general, second in command only to Father Hidalgo. After the rebel forces disintegrated in 1811, he was captured, shot, and then beheaded by royalist forces. His beloved hometown of San Miguel el Grande was renamed in his honor by an independent Mexico in 1862.

Art Galleries

San Miguel's three leading art galleries are all within a block of Allende's birthplace. Around the corner at Umarán 1 is the **Josh Klingerman Gallery**; facing the side of the church at Cuna de Allende 15 is the **Galería Atenea**; and on the north side of *el jardín* at number 14 is the **Galería San Miguel**. The number of artists living in San Miguel has declined over the last dozen years, but the town remains the nation's second-largest art market, surpassed only by Mexico City.

Casa del Mayorazgo de Canal

The imposing Casa del Mayorazgo de Canal, now occupied by Banamex, the Bank of Mexico, rises at the north end of the block-long colonial arcade on the west side of *el jardín*. (To visit a colonial mansion in San Miguel, all you need do is step into a bank. There are five of them established in palatial quarters, all located on the street running uphill from the north side of the plaza.) The grand entrance to this 18th-century mansion is on Calle de la Canal, which heads downhill from the northwest corner of the plaza. The carriage doors seek to overwhelm the caller with the family Canal's importance: The eagle signifies its baronial status, the helmets indicate that ancestors fought against the Moors in Spain. (Two helmets here; both the husband and wife's families earned the distinction, and flaunted it.) The residence itself was built sometime around 1740 on top of an older structure, then remodeled some 50 years later. Supposedly, Eduardo Tresguerras did the restyling. Regardless, it is a fine example of the Mexican "severe" style: dark red walls, black wrought iron, white trim and woodwork. All such buildings—and there are many in Mexico—were either built or spruced up around 1800.

The owner of the house at the time of the War of Independence was Colonel Narciso de la Canal, commander of the local Spanish garrison. When the rebels, led by his neighbor Allende and Father Hidalgo, marched on the town, the colonel prudently kept his soldiers in their barracks. Later, when the possibility of his elevation to the rank of count was brought up, serious questions about his true allegiance were raised, and the title remained unconfirmed when the colonel died, under arrest, in Querétaro. His true role in the rebellion is still unknown, but posterity has granted him the title that was withheld in life: His family is always called "the Counts of Canal" in San Miguel de Allende.

Templo de San Francisco

The church of San Francisco, an elegant structure with a disturbing note, graces the street named after it, one block east of *el jardín*. The delicately carved façade, with its abhorrence of a blank spot, is pure Churrigueresque, its columns tapering illogically toward their bases. (Whenever you see this inverted column in Mexico you can instantly date the structure as having been built between 1720 and 1785; the odds against being mistaken are overwhelming.) This particular church was caught in a period of stylistic flux, however. Begun in 1779, its bell tower was still unbuilt when the shift to the Neoclassical swept the country. The always ingenious Tresguerras was brought in from Celaya to design a tower that would express the new style yet blend with the church's existing façade. Though he didn't quite manage this impossible task, he came close. The interior design is also mostly his, and features a nave bathed in light. The Enlightenment, which was late in coming to Mexico, is seen in the most literal terms here. The church of San Francisco, like many others of the era, was purged of its atmosphere of oppressive mystery.

Iglesia de Nuestra Señora de la Salud

A block to the north, the Plaza Civica fronts the church of Our Lady of Health. A gigantic seashell commemorating a mass baptism by sea water spans the entrance.

The interior boasts two unusual details. Panels of an old wooden altar in the right transept show Jesus the Good Shepherd ministering to his flock while some of the sheep are menaced by a unicorn. The oddity here is the portrayal of a New Testament parable in a Mexican church, where the miraculous usually reigns supreme. There are also four startling paintings of the classic virtues under the dome; while they're not exactly pagan, they're certainly not Roman Catholic, either.

The church itself was built early in the 18th century as a

chapel for the college next door, an institution radical enough to have educated several martyrs of independence, among them Allende. This is the only explanation for the odd decor of La Salud.

Oratorio de San Felipe Neri

A block west, the Oratorio de San Felipe Neri boasts silverwork designs chiseled into the stone of its façade. The designs are somehow appropriate, for San Felipe Neri stands in a neighborhood where pack trains from distant silver mines once halted for a night's lodging.

This otherwise ordinary church, San Miguel's largest, has two unusual features, neither immediately apparent. Attached to the building is the **Santa Casa de Loreto**. According to Catholic tradition, the house of the Virgin Mary was transported by angels to Loreto, Italy, where it still can be visited today. Here we have a replica of sorts, although some locals would have you believe it's the original. To enter this special sanctorum, walk to the left side of the altar, where impressive gates often bar the way; an attendant will usually fetch a custodian with a key.

The outer room, the Virgin's drawing room, contains statues of Manuel Tomás de la Canal and his wife, who paid for the chapel; they are buried underneath their statues. After going down a narrow hall lined with Oriental tiles (brought by the Manila galleons to Acapulco), you'll enter a dazzling chamber, the Virgin's bedroom, where even the stonework is gilded. The tile is Spanish Talavera, laid in 1735.

The other unusual feature of San Felipe Neri rarely seen by visitors is the **Indian entrance** on the east side of the church. To get there, go through the wooden gate, which is almost always open, at the front of the atrium. On the other side is the simple but beautifully carved entrance, with its Indian cherubs and plumes etched in stone. Originally, this was the portal of an older church that was taken from its humble congregation by legal trickery. In time, a grand new building was raised on the site by the rich *criollo* parishioners. Time has given the story a fittingly ironic ending: San Felipe Neri is once again the main church for the townspeople of San Miguel de Allende, whose ancestors once entered it through what is now the side door.

La Concepción and Bellas Artes

One block west of the main plaza, the convent and church of La Concepción, usually called "Las Monjas," dominates its neighborhood. Here the remarkable but unoriginal imagination of Ceferino Gutiérrez is again apparent. His façade for La Parroquia borrowed from several Gothic cathedrals, just as here he re-created the dome of Les Invalides in Paris—not exactly but quite obviously. The dome is a century old; the church goes back an additional hundred years.

Almost all of the massive former convent behind the church has been taken over by the government and turned into a school of the arts, part of the national system. Properly known as the Centro Cultural "El Nigromante," it is generally called Bellas Artes and is the focal point of the town's cultural life, especially for music. It boasts a magnificent patio, one of the most ambitious such designs in the country; as well, a small covey of nuns remains secluded in a corner of the building, squeezed between the church and the art center. Remarkably, their convent survived the battles and anti-clerical campaigns of the 1920s, and was perhaps the only one in Mexico not to be "opened" by revolutionary troops. The existence of this marooned little convent is still illegal, but nobody seems to care.

STAYING IN SAN MIGUEL

San Miguel has been receiving travellers since the early 17th century, when every week mule and burro trains arrived with silver ore bound for the capital. Today ancient inns line two streets, and the visitor may choose from a wide selection of hotels whose managements have a good idea of what foreigners want and expect.

Almost all the inns in town are small and have only two stories. (The town's single elevator is looked upon with suspicion.) There is no air-conditioning, but then it isn't needed at an elevation of 6,400 feet. It is best to have quarters within easy walking distance of the main square, as San Miguel distances are vertical as well as horizontal; the steep hill must be taken into account. A few otherwise good hotels are either too far out or too far up.

The ▶ **Casa de Sierra Nevada**, Hospicio 35, occupies four colonial houses, one a true mansion, that have been converted into rooms and suites. (One of the buildings houses the Sierra Nevada's health club facilities.) Some have patios, roof terraces, and fireplaces, and all are decorated with fine crafts and colonial-style pieces. The tone is refined and international (a former First Lady of the United States is a frequent guest), and the emphasis is on personal service and attention. Guests may have breakfast in the excellent dining room (discussed under Dining, below), on a verdant patio, in their own rooms, or on their terraces. No credit cards are accepted, but personal checks may be used by prior arrangement. The inn is near the center of town, slightly but not formidably uphill.

On the same quiet street, a step higher in topography but a decided step lower in price, is the well-named ▶ **Hacienda de las Flores**, a garden inn with restful lawns and a heated swimming pool. The hacienda has a modest entrance typical of San Miguel—noncommittal until you are fully inside—but then it opens onto a building and landscape designed to blend in with the colonial town. The hotel's intimate lounge centers around a fireplace, and the rooms, actually junior suites, are attractive, spacious, and have good views. Two meals are included in the daily rate. Children are welcome; credit cards are not.

Attracting the same type of knowledgeable clientele is the ▶ **Villa Jacaranda**, located a little farther from the plaza but on a level street at Aldama 53. The rooms and suites, some with private patios, are excellent, as are the classic films shown in the evening in a friendly lounge. The small heated swimming pool also has a whirlpool. (Villa Jacaranda's fine restaurant is discussed under Dining, below.)

▶ **La Puertecita**, situated near the crest of the hill on Calle Santo Domingo, is the town's newest, most luxurious inn and spa, pampering its guests with Jacuzzis, a game and billiard room, fireplaces, and private patios and terraces with magnificent views. Health and fitness are the watchwords here, with aqua-aerobics offered in an extra-large pool and in-house masseurs and masseuses; smokers should look elsewhere. Twenty-four-hour room service and excellent food are available on call, and hotel vans will take guests to the local restaurant of their choice—or anywhere else for that matter. La Puertecita is an outstanding inn, expensive but not overpriced.

▶ **El Patio**, another small hotel, offers its guests spacious colonial-style suites in the center of town on Calle Correo, a convenient but traffic-choked area just a few steps west of the post office. Its suites harmonize perfectly with the colonial ambience of San Miguel and its restaurant features Mexican cuisine in the same baronial building.

The ▶ **Villa Santa Monica**, on the south side of town at Calle Baeza 22, facing the Parque Benito Juárez, looks like the stage set for a Mexican operetta, complete with tile roofs, an arcaded patio, and a lovely garden. The rooms are cheerful and comfortable, but the restaurant, which serves only breakfast and lunch, is merely so-so. As well, the inn is just beyond convenient walking distance from the center of town, especially at night.

Generations of art students and vacationing teachers have

chosen the provincial surroundings at the ▶ **Posada de las Monjas,** two blocks downhill from *el jardín,* where the new section is nicer than the older part up front. The new ▶ **Hotel Monte Verde,** two blocks farther from the plaza, at Voluntarios 2, combines modern comfort with colonial decor, and has a flowering central garden and a good restaurant. The attractive rates make it worth the longer walk.

One of the best buys in town is the unpretentious but more than adequate ▶ **Casa Carmen,** located a few steps from the central post office on Calle Correo. Heated rooms encircle a pretty patio, and the attractive dining room caters to guests only, many of whom return year after year.

DINING IN SAN MIGUEL

Because of tourism and the presence of the foreign community, San Miguel's restaurants surpass those of neighboring cities in both quality and number. Still, regional fare of distinction is scarce here, and most of the better dining places emphasize "international" food, a cuisine that is sometimes a little hard to pin down.

The **Bugambilia,** Hidalgo 42, is an exception and has clung staunchly to a Mexican menu for three generations. The dishes are classical: *tinga, sopa Azteca,* steaming *caldo de res* with a chunk of chewy stewing beef, *chiles en nogada* sporting the national colors. There is also guitar music in the attractive patio of this former private home, which remains a bit rustic and nicely plain. Closed Wednesdays. No phone and no credit cards.

The expensive **Restaurant Casa de Sierra Nevada,** in the hotel of the same name at Hospicio 35, is characterized by flair and imagination. This is one of the best restaurants in the country, and because the elegant dining room seats only 32 (though other seating is available in the less formal patio), reservations are advised; there is also an intimate little bar off the far side of the patio. Soft classical guitar music; dress code evenings. Tel: (465) 2-1825.

The **Villa Jacaranda,** Aldama 53, also a hotel dining room, displays on its walls the various awards for excellence it regularly captures from travel magazines. The menu is international, the presentation and service meticulous. In addition to a cheerful main room with views of the patio, a glassed-in gazebo overlooks the leafy treetops of a nearby park. The atmosphere, food, and service justify the high prices.

Two blocks northwest of the plaza at Calle de Mesones 101, **La Hacienda de Pepe** is popular with San Miguel's foreign colony, especially for Sunday brunch. Its two rustic patios and handsome rooms resemble a movie set for *Ra-*

mona or *Zorro*. The menu includes traditional Mexican and international dishes.

La Vendimia, half a block north of the *jardín* at Hidalgo 12, serves a limited menu of international specialties in a fine old town house. Excellent food and service.

Restaurante El Correo, in a historic residence across from the post office at Correo 21, is a simple but quaint dining room and coffee shop. The varied menu, including numerous breakfast selections, is moderately priced. Tel: (465) 2-0151.

La Dolce Vita is a European-style coffee-and-pastry café, a place to browse through newspapers and magazines. Located on the second patio of Canal 21.

San Miguel tends to call it a night after a late supper. **Mama Mía,** a pizza emporium at Umarán 8, offers flamenco guitar music in a popular patio and various combos in a smaller bar. **Pancho and Lefty's,** Mesones 99, has a Texas saloon feeling, complete with a neon beer sign above the bar, and features changing entertainment: jazz, country and western, and combos. The town's discos cater to teenagers, although oldsters in their twenties do not arouse suspicion.

SHOPPING IN SAN MIGUEL

Metalwork, especially in tin and brass, is excellent in San Miguel, as well as a good buy. The town's weavers also offer fine quality, but the selection is more limited here than elsewhere. Furniture making in colonial or provincial style is a local tradition, and you'll also find a wide selection of embroidered clothing and a small but good choice of leatherware.

Two reputable places create wonderful items in silver: **Beckman,** Hernández Macías 115, and **David,** Zacateros 53.

There are galleries and boutiques all around the main plaza and in any street within a block of it. Others line Calle Zacateros two blocks west.

The **Casa Cohen,** Reloj 18, is the country's best maker of cast brass and also offers other items of more than usual interest. **El Pegaso,** a gathering place for coffee drinkers located across from the post office, displays carefully selected clothing and other unusual goods. The **Casa Canal,** at the corner of Canal and the main plaza, is a virtual museum of provincial furniture; it is also a boutique. Last but not least, novel and beautiful *objets d'art* from Mexico and elsewhere can be found at **Four Winds,** an unusual little shop of distinction at the corner of Calles Hospicio and Diaz de Sollano.

SPECIAL EVENTS AND STUDIES

Music Festivals and the Public Library

The frequent concerts and musical events in San Miguel range from soloists to symphony orchestras. The **Chamber Music Festival**, which features internationally known string quartets and offers master classes, is staged every August. Bellas Artes will be happy to provide information by mail (San Miguel de Allende, Guanajuato, Mexico 37700). A smaller but equally pleasing music festival is staged at Christmastime by a different sponsor. In addition, several theatrical performances are given each year, some in Spanish, others in English. Of course, art exhibits open with some frequency in this art colony.

On most Sundays at noon the **Biblioteca Pública** conducts a tour of local houses and gardens—an excellent opportunity to "see behind the walls." Not surprisingly, it's a very popular event. The library is on Calle Insurgentes between Hidalgo and Reloj.

Study Programs

For four decades special San Miguel schools have attracted students who are mostly English-speaking. The **Instituto Allende** on Calle Ancha de San Antonio offers a curriculum of fine arts, crafts, and Spanish. The School of the Art Institute of Chicago uses the Instituto's colonial-style campus for its study-abroad plan; students and teachers from the Rhode Island School of Design also come to San Miguel every winter. The Centro Cultural "El Nigromante" (Bellas Artes) offers classes in the arts and crafts, as well as some musical instruction. Two schools specialize in Spanish and related subjects only: The **Academia Hispano Americana**, at Mesones 4, is quite traditional in its by-rote approach; the newer **Casa de la Luna**, Cuadrante 2, is more innovative.

Around San Miguel

Hacienda Taboada

North of town is an area dotted with hot mineral springs bubbling from the ground. Naturally, spas and resorts have sprung up here, the most impressive being the ▶ **Hacienda Taboada**, 8 km (5 miles) north on the highway to Dolores Hidalgo. The hacienda offers an Olympic-size pool with geothermally heated water, 60 rooms done in Mediterranean decor, and all hotel services, as well as horseback riding and free transportation to and from San Miguel. Non-guests are admitted to the rather posh facilities every day from 9:00 A.M. until 6:00 P.M. Less costly and much less luxurious spas in the neighborhood (on the same highway as the Hacienda Taboada) include **La Gruta** and **El Cortijo**, both popular with the locals.

Santuario de Atotonilco

Nearby, but quite different from the picniclike gaiety of a spa, the hulking Santuario de Atotonilco is a repository of Mexican folk painting, offering a glimpse into a corner of Catholicism seldom seen. Although the main building was begun in 1754, a medieval grimness and chill seemingly centuries older pervade this sprawling maze of rooms and corridors. (Only the center section is open to the public.) Each year thousands of religious penitents trek to the shrine to attend "exercises," to cleanse themselves and be shriven. Little whips called *disciplinas* are available for those who want them, and discarded crowns of thorn are often found outside.

Inside, in room after room, walls and ceilings are frescoed with naïve but skillful murals charmingly executed. Never have pain, suffering, and penance been portrayed more cheerfully. Sometimes the themes of these murals stray from the religious: The naval battle of Lepanto, for example, appears on a chapel ceiling, and elsewhere legends mix freely with miracles. But the overarching theme is wickedness, remorse, and pain. Here you will confront the dark side of faith and be reminded of the days when saints mortified their flesh and starved themselves atop pillars.

The village of **Atotonilco** itself is also historically important, for it was here that Father Hidalgo seized the banner of the Virgin of Guadalupe and proclaimed her patroness and generalissima of the Mexican forces, an honor she unofficially holds to this day.

Celaya

The industrial and commercial center of Celaya lies 52 km (32 miles) south of San Miguel via Highway 51. In the center of this otherwise uninteresting city stands the masterwork of Eduardo Tresguerras, the **Templo de Nuestra Señora del Carmen**, which was erected in 1807. Tresguerras, as architect, sculptor, muralist, and decorator, created a light-bathed interior that proved it was possible to inject warmth into the usually severe Neoclassical style. In a mural depicting the

Judgment Day, the artist himself is shown emerging from a tomb, quite uncertain of his future.

Yuriria

Still farther south, 114 km (71 miles) from San Miguel over paved and pretty country roads (Highway 51 south to Salvatierra, then west toward Moroleón)—an easy one-day excursion or, alternatively, a stop on the way to Morelia (for which, see below)—lies the town and lake of Yuriria. The town is noted for its massive Augustinian monastery, which was begun in 1550 and completed in 1568. In the 18th century it was expanded to include a lofty cloister, buttresses, and a new main entrance. Today the building's impact is overwhelming, impressing the visitor as a prime example of the "fortified" religious centers of the early days of the colonial era. Several missionaries who were later martyred in Japan studied here while en route from Spain to the Far East. Ask to be admitted to the bell tower, which commands a sweeping view of the lake and countryside. But note: There are no especially worthwhile hotels or restaurants in the Yuriria area.

Viajes San Miguel, a travel agency in a courtyard at Diaz Sollano 3, almost on the corner of Correo, arranges local tours and explorations; they also handle national and international travel arrangements. Tel: (465) 2-2832.

THE CITY OF GUANAJUATO

For most visitors from north of the border, Guanajuato is little short of astonishing. With its narrow, tortuous streets that lose themselves in flower-bedecked plazas, unexpected balconies and bridges, and red-tiled roofs that lie level with the street above, few places in the world seem as exotic to northern eyes. Guanajuato both eludes and inspires description. Travellers speak of similarities to the hill towns of Italy, to southern Spain, even to the Aegean islands—all close to the mark but none quite hitting it. The fact is, Guanajuato retains a peculiar combination of Mexican and European qualities that is unrivaled.

It was once the second-largest city in Mexico and one of the wealthiest in the world—no place in Latin America could match it for the sheer display of its riches. The treasure that poured from its silver mines is legendary and beyond reckoning. The opulent structures left behind are mostly relics of two eras: the silver-mad 18th century, and just prior to the turn of our own century, when great new

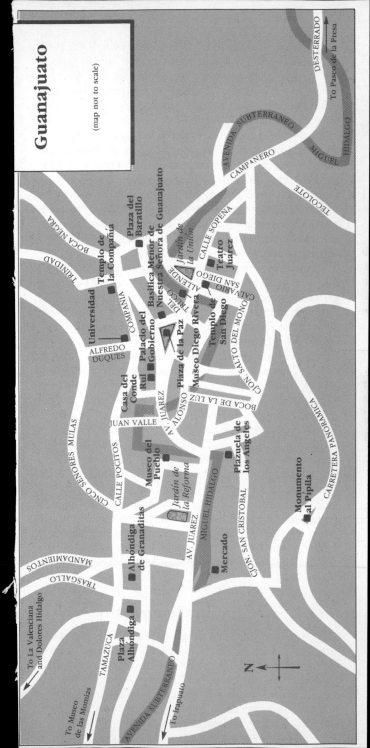

strikes again filled the local coffers. As a result of the Mexican fondness for different styles in both these periods, Guanajuato today is a mélange of the Spanish, Moorish, Italian, and French. The styles are not mixed. Instead, they stand side by side in happy defiance of each other, bewildering and wonderful all at once.

Guanajuato is sometimes offered as a one-day excursion from Mexico City. Certainly, you can cover the highlights of this compact city in a day, but even so it requires a sightseeing marathon. Instead, at least two full days should be allotted, and twice that amount would not be misspent. The city's monuments are impressive, but the greatest pleasure is derived from simply wandering among its picturesque plazas and fountains and getting lost in its colorful maze of streets and alleyways.

Visitors exploring the town will look in vain for an art gallery or good bookstore. Guanajuato, despite its claims to the contrary, has no intellectual climate to speak of—and this includes the university. In such matters, the citizens are quite unlike the elegant, imaginative buildings of their city. Never having been situated on a trade route, Guanajuato is a closed, provincial town clinging tenaciously to its old ways and, in some matters, to its self-satisfied isolation. The folk who live in this dramatic cityscape did not create it, and today outside support sustains it. (The state and national governments are the sponsors of the community's performing arts groups, for example.)

Guanajuato is also devoutly religious, its Catholicism of a conservative bent. You need look no farther than the **Cerro del Cubilete**, a looming mountain 13 km (8 miles) southwest of the city, for proof. Atop it, at what is reputed to be the geographic center of Mexico, towers a gigantic statue of *El Cristo Rey* (Christ the King) that dominates the great valley below it. This is not only a religious monument but a striking symbol of the will of the local people, who by a large majority resisted the national laws limiting the power of the clergy.

Around in Guanajuato

Guanajuato crouches in a gorge, hemmed in by rock walls. Although it's the capital of the state of the same name, a university town, and a busy city of some 75,000 people, it can be reached only by car or bus. If you come by car, after one initial detour (suggested below) your vehicle should be safely parked and then forgotten during your stay here. Guanajuato is truly an ordeal for drivers.

Marfil and the Hacienda San Gabriel de Barrera

Almost all traffic enters from the west, skirting the ghost town of Marfil. Once Marfil was rich beyond measure, a place where bullfights were staged in the private patios of mine owners' mansions and opera companies were imported to perform, but those days are long gone. Almost adjoining Marfil to the southwest is the Hacienda San Gabriel de Barrera, with its lovely gardens and French-inspired landscaping. The remaining estate buildings are of some interest, but the gardens outshine everything else in the neighborhood.

The Skyline Drive

At the edge of town, the **Carretera Panorámica**, a skyline drive that offers a spectacular introduction to the city, veers sharply to the right and is easy to miss. The road climbs steeply toward a titanic statue of El Pípila, a local hero of independence (his story is told below). At the statue, near stands heaped with souvenirs and junk, is a perfect place to view the magnificent gorge, the city, and the high hills with their fortified mines and scarred, rocky slopes—all this spread out below in a spectacular panorama.

Silver was the only excuse for building a city in this improbable place, but of silver there was plenty. In fact, the monarchs of Spain were deluged with silver for the better part of two and a half centuries, and fully half of it came from this inhospitable canyon. The first major lode was discovered in 1548—just 20 years after the town was founded—a bonanza that was only the beginning of its long and happy affair with the metal.

From the statue of El Pípila, the Panorámica winds eastward and down, debouching in a neighborhood known as **La Presa**, where the streets are lined with edifices financed by the city's last great windfall from silver, at the end of the 19th century. Many are sumptuously French Romantic and Italianate in design, and so grand it is hard to imagine them as formerly private homes. (They now serve as offices, public buildings, and apartment houses.)

Avenida Subterráneo Miguel Hidalgo

Just past this district is the entrance to the Avenida Subterráneo Miguel Hidalgo. Some years ago, to relieve traffic, the city utilized a number of mine tunnels and an old riverbed to create an underground thoroughfare that runs through the heart of the city. As a result of serendipity, the engineers also managed to create an unusual visual experience: The thoroughfare twists among the foundations of the town, its roof reinforced by a tangle of old mine cables embedded in concrete and stone. The effect is at once romantic and eerie, and will stay with the visitor long after the many meals eaten and shops visited are forgotten.

Avenida Miguel Hidalgo goes underground near the *mercado,* an area where a car or taxi becomes a definite encumbrance. The market, which bears an incongruous resemblance to an Italian railway station, offers a profusion of foods, goods, and gimcracks. The crafts mezzanine is worth the climb, if only for a view of the jumbled colors below. The merchandise offered here includes fake antique bells, machine-made cloth, and mass-produced figurines appropriate as prizes at a shooting gallery and little else. The sad truth is, there are no worthwhile crafts in Guanajuato and no surviving craft tradition to speak of.

The Cervantino

A block up the hill from the market is the broad esplanade behind the Alhóndiga de Granaditas, where every year the Cervantino, an international festival of performing arts honoring the master, Miguel de Cervantes, is staged. The festival, held in late autumn, once glittered with the stars of the music and dance worlds. In particular, during the six years (1976–1982) when Carmen de López Portillo was First Lady of Mexico, it enjoyed bountiful patronage; she even arranged the restoration and scrubbing up of part of the city to improve its setting. These days, though artists still come to the festival from a score of countries, it seems to have lost some of its glitter.

Short farces and skits from Spain, some by Cervantes, are performed by students during the Cervantino. These romps, called *entremeses,* are essentially mime shows and were written to be played as comic relief between the acts of Spanish dramas; the broad jokes are funny in any language, however.

ALHONDIGA DE GRANADITAS

The fortresslike Alhóndiga de Granaditas, one of the most prominent buildings in Mexican history, looms over the esplanade. Originally built as a granary, it served as a refuge for Royalist supporters when Hidalgo's rebels attacked the city in 1810. With the confrontation threatening to swing in favor of the Royalists, Juan Martínez, a miner from San Miguel who would be known to history as El Pípila, tied a broad flagstone to his back, and, so shielded, braved enemy fire to set the wooden doors of the granary aflame (an action that cost him his life). Rebels surged into the building, where a hand-to-hand struggle and, ultimately, a butchery of the Spaniards ensued. The few survivors retreated step by step to the roof, only to be slain there. But even this was not the end of the horror. Days later, after 247 unarmed Spanish soldiers had been imprisoned in the building, a screaming mob broke in and murdered them all.

The slaughter changed the public's perception of the uprising, with Spaniards throughout the country rallying in support of the Crown. When they finally recaptured Guanajuato, they retaliated with a bloodbath, killing every man, woman, and child they could get their hands on. If it hadn't been for a local priest, who stepped between the executioners and their intended victims holding aloft a cross as his only weapon, the massacre might have spread to other towns in the Bajío. As it was, the bloodshed in the Alhóndiga helped polarize Mexico for generations to come.

After the revolt ultimately failed, the heads of its leaders—Hidalgo, Allende, Jiménez, and Aldama—were sent back to Guanajuato and hung for ten years from iron hooks at the corners of the Alhóndiga. The hooks remain today.

A crafts museum has been set up in the building, its gaiety a welcome but odd note. In addition, Guanajuato painter Chavez Morado has dramatized the town's violent history in a series of powerful murals. There are also historical exhibits here, none of them especially fascinating, but one, a collection of small-town studio photographs that is ordinary at first glance, definitely worth closer inspection. It is a sweet and touching album of the city: newlywed couples stiff in their finery, awkward soldiers, and miners with their hair slicked down for the occasion.

Two Museums

Upon emerging from the Alhóndiga turn right and walk toward Calle Pocitos and the university. The building at Pocitos 47, now the **Museo Casa Diego Rivera,** is the house where the muralist Diego Rivera was born. The collection, not surprisingly, is meager, consisting of some old furniture and early Rivera practice pieces. What *is* surprising is not that the museum is modest, but that it exists at all—for years Rivera was persona non grata in his hometown. The town fathers despised the great painter for being an atheist, a leftist, and a mocker of the Church and society. Pious Guanajuato, which resisted the revolution Diego glorified, never forgave the sinner, and never had second thoughts about forcing his family, wicked liberals all, to leave the city. The little museum, needless to say, is of recent vintage.

The **Museo del Pueblo de Guanajuato,** nearby at Pocitos 7, was once the home of a noble Spanish family. On display here are a number of good provincial paintings of the colonial era, as well as works by Hermenegildo Bustos, a 19th-century talent.

The University Area

The many broad stairways of the **Universidad de Guanajuato** sweep upward toward a towering structure that is a less-than-happy mixture of Spanish colonial architecture and something else. The pale university building dominates a portion of the cityscape, an odd reversal of roles in light of the fact that the university has always been subservient to the interests of the city and its politicians. The school, in contrast, is tame and traditional.

Just to the east is the lovely **Templo de la Compañía**, an 18th-century Jesuit contribution to the city's beauty and an admirable example of Baroque architecture as it began to flower into the more elaborate Churrigueresque style. A block southeast the way widens into the charming, Italianate **Plaza del Baratillo**, where sunlight plays on a fountain Maximilian gave to a city that entertained him lavishly. Students live on the upper floors of the old buildings in this neighborhood, and much of the university's rather sedate social life is centered here: The University of Guanajuato produces some of the best *estudiantinas,* student musical groups akin to glee clubs, in the country. Students in the romantic beribboned costumes of Old Spain sing through the streets at least once or twice a month.

Jardín de la Unión

South of the Plaza del Baratillo is the Jardín de la Unión, one of the loveliest and most inviting little plazas in Mexico. As public squares go, this is a mere postage stamp, but the leafy low-branched laurels form a canopy that shades its pretty painted iron benches. On the southwest side of the plaza two adjacent buildings present façades exemplifying the richest architectural periods of the city's history: The exterior of the Teatro Juárez is a Neoclassical dream, while next to it rises, a little feebly, the weathered **Templo de San Diego**, an exquisite 18th-century Churrigueresque fantasy in stone. In different languages the two façades proclaim the same thing: the affluence of their builders.

Teatro Juárez

The Teatro Juárez is such a delightful building that only a curmudgeon would call some of it a little silly. The green columns of its façade, quarried locally, ascend majestically behind bronze lions. On the roof rest eight allegorical female figures, also bronze. Interestingly, these Hellenic ladies were the work of one W. H. Mullen of Salem, Ohio, and were purchased in the 1890s, an era when Mexico renounced all things Mexican.

The lavish interior is a marvel as well, its ceiling resembling a carpet out of the *Arabian Nights*. The stage curtain was reportedly copied from a backdrop at La Scala a century ago. Throughout the building the details and furnishings are ostentatious, overdone, and yet somehow perfect. And while the sightlines from the boxes of honor are so bad that half the stage remains obscured, no one seemed to mind; what mattered was that their occupants were royally displayed to the rest of the house.

Porfirio Díaz, "president" of the so-called republic from 1876 to 1880 and again from 1884 to 1911, attended the opening night here, arriving by special train with his whole cabinet and a good part of the capital's diplomatic corps. Across the street, in the Posada Santa Fé, there hangs today a painting of that special occasion. In it, the distinguished spectators are not looking at the Italian singers on stage, but, naturally, at each other.

Back outside, Calle Sopeña becomes Avenida Juárez and makes for an interesting stroll as it heads northwest and slightly downhill past the Hotel San Diego. Branching off it are the narrow alleyways and "pocket" plazas that give Guanajuato such character. No matter where you walk in the city, however, you'll probably notice plaques with the dates "1885" or "1905" on them; these indicate the high-water marks of disastrous floods that hit Guanajuato in those years. (The river has since been diverted.)

Plaza de la Paz

The Basilica Menor de Nuestra Señora de Guanajuato, opposite the Plaza de la Paz, was erected in 1671 and has suffered so many changes that little of distinction remains. Housed in one of its chapels, however, sits a statue of the Virgin Mary purportedly hidden in a cave in Spain after the Moors invaded in A.D. 714. The statue, rediscovered eight and a half centuries later undamaged by either time or dampness, was declared miraculous. It was bestowed on the city in 1557 by Philip II, who was grateful for the flood of silver originating from area mines. The plain wooden figure is enhanced by a gemmed gown and a golden diadem weighing almost five pounds.

On the far side of the Plaza de la Paz you'll find the handsomest **town house** in Mexico, once the palace of the conde de Rul, a Midas among millionaires. It should come as no surprise that the ubiquitous Tresguerras was the architect of this severe, august mansion, with its clean lines and near-perfect architectural balance. The stone, a soft rose color, was the best the area had to offer. (The handsome patio is usually open for inspection.)

The grace of Tresguerras's simple design is made all the more striking by the close juxtaposition of the green and grandiose **Palacio del Gobierno**, its ornate decoration proclaiming its own importance.

Callejón del Beso

The renowned Alley of the Kiss is a passageway and set of steps flanked by flowering balconies one block south of Avenida Juárez (turn onto Calle de Patrocinio at the charming Plazuela de los Angeles). A local legend tells of kisses stolen over balcony railings, a cruel father, and a girl whisked away to a convent.

Mummies and a Lake

The biggest indoor drawing card for visitors to Guanajuato is the **Museo de las Momias** (Mummy Museum), located next to the cemetery about half a mile west of the Alhóndiga. In fact, its turnstiles have proved to be the most profitable installation in town since the days of the first silver mine. About 60 "examples," as the cadavers are called, lie stretched out for inspection behind glass display cases. The exhibits are not mummies in the Egyptian sense, but corpses that have undergone a sort of tanning process due to exposure to chemicals in the ground before being dug up and thrust into show business. The museum is open daily, 10:00 A.M. until 6:00 P.M.

The **Presa de la Olla** is one of two dams that have created artificial lakes near town. Picnickers come for the shade and breezes at the lakes, and rowboats are available for rent. The park area is located at the southeast corner of town, at the end of Paseo de le Presa.

Silver Mines and the Silver King's Church

The **Valenciana Mine**, still operating and profitable, plunges 1,738 feet into the mountainside above Guanajuato. Old service buildings made of stone and tile remain, and visitors may look down a shaft whose mouth is supposed to represent the Crown of Spain. Far below, a black maze of tunnels twists and turns like the roots of a gigantic tree. Once the world's richest vein of silver, it yielded fully one-fifth of all the silver circulating in the world for nearly a century, bringing its owners, first the conde de Valenciana and then his son-in-law, the conde de Rul, unimaginable wealth.

Because it is an operating mine, visitors are not allowed to descend into the shaft of the Valenciana. Conditions and schedules for visits to other mines in the area change frequently; for up-to-date information, inquire at the state tourism office, located on the corner of Avenida Juárez and Cinco de Mayo. (Local guides will also have current information.) The Valenciana is located 4 km (2½ miles) north of town on the Dolores Hidalgo highway. Buses leave frequently from a spot near the municipal market; a cab costs the equivalent of $3 one-way.

Across the street from the Valenciana mine stands the church of the same name. Construction of the church was begun by the conde de Valenciana and continued by the conde de Rul, with a little compulsory help from their mine workers during the second half of the 18th century. In the course of construction silver dust and Spanish wines were added to the mortar, inspiring the comment that the count was not only bribing the Lord but "getting Him drunk at the same time." Regardless, the finished product reveals both wealth and superb craftsmanship. Connoisseurs of stone sculpture praise the elegant relief work around the church's main portal, the façade and interior carving, and the pulpit.

STAYING IN GUANAJUATO

Guanajuato's somewhat narrow range of hotels does not include any of Mexico's finest, and the difference between moderately priced hotels and budget accommodations is not a step but a plunge. Travellers trying to cut costs would be advised to do it in other cities rather than here.

The ▶ **Posada Santa Fé**, built in 1862, faces the lovely Jardín de la Unión, an ideal location from which to explore the city. Rooms vary, and the first one offered you should not automatically be accepted: The interior rooms, untouched by sun, seem positively polar on winter nights. The hotel, which is on the expensive side, is nonetheless gracious, and its stately public rooms are rich with the charm of Old Spain transported to Mexico.

The ▶ **Hotel San Diego**, across the square from the Santa Fé, is a little less expensive than its neighbor. Its better rooms have patios or balconies with views of the town, the rooftop terrace is inviting, and the cellar-style bar romantic (and lively at times). There's also a dining room with a fine view from the two tables at the corner window, though the vista is the only reason to eat here; the hotel is much better than the restaurant.

Although the ▶ **Hostería del Fraile** has 36 rooms, it feels more like an intimate pension. You'll need to prepare yourself for the precipitous stairs, and take note that the outside rooms tend to be noisy while the inside ones are cramped. Still, its excellent location at Sopeña 3, near the Jardín de la Unión, its reasonable rates, and its pleasing details make this converted 17th-century mint a more than satisfactory inn.

The more expensive and mostly newer hostelries are found along the Dolores Hidalgo highway that leads to La Valenciana. Guests without a car will have to depend on the bus or wait, sometimes a while, for a taxi to arrive after one has been called.

As its name suggests, the ▶ **Castillo de Santa Cecilia** is a castle, albeit more Disney than medieval. Spacious lawns, gardens, terraces, a heated pool, and a nightclub boost the rates for good rooms, though the hotel is more cheerful than its battlements would suggest.

The ▶ **Parador San Javier**, the largest of the hillside establishments, is a modern hostelry with colonial touches and boasts all the necessary conveniences of a high-quality inn. Some rooms have fireplaces, and there's a large pool, a disco, and a cocktail lounge as well. The place is a favorite of Mexico City residents who like to explore the provinces in style.

The ▶ **Motel Guanajuato**, like the Parador San Javier, offers its guests panoramic views from a perch high above the town. Modern and comfortable, as well as a little plainer and less expensive than its neighbors, it has a pool and quite a good restaurant.

On the opposite side of the city, about 2½ km (1½ miles) southwest of town on the Marfil road, the ▶ **Hotel San Gabriel de Barrera**, situated across a country lane from the famous gardens, is not cheap but is still an excellent value for those with a car who do not mind a ten-minute drive to the center of town. Everything is spacious at this former hacienda; the rooms, both public and private, are airy and bright; and the terraces overlook gardens and flowerbeds. There are tennis and swimming facilities as well.

DINING IN GUANAJUATO

Keeping in mind that a trip to Guanajuato is for attractions other than cuisine, visitors should expect sustenance, not delight, from the town's dining establishments. Guanajuato cares little about the capricious tastes of tourists, and the local cookery lacks flair and imagination as a result.

The sidewalk café at the **Posada Santa Fé** is happily situated so that customers can ignore the mediocre fare and concentrate on the scene in the Jardín de la Unión instead. Nearby on the same plaza, try the **Casa Valdez** for snacks, breakfast, and a hearty soup. The best buys here, however, are soda fountain items and postcards.

The **Tasca de los Santos**, Plaza de la Paz 28, presents a Spanish-style menu featuring *fabada* and paella. It's not outstanding, but the reasonable prices are some consolation. Tel: (473) 2-2320.

El Claustro, on the Jardín de la Reforma, one long block south and another block east of the Alhóndiga, is decked out like a Spanish tavern (Guanajuato seems to draw out the Spanish side of Mexicans), and is popular with students. Egg dishes are the safest bet here.

Other downtown eateries are pretty much alike. Order simply and be patient. At the hillside hotels your choices are better. The Motel Guanajuato runs the best, most reliable hotel kitchen in the region. The coffee shop at the Parador San Javier seems better than the dining room, perhaps because its simple surroundings keep expectations from rising too high. **Venta Vieja de San Javier**, across from the Parador, appeals more to the eye than the palate. The quality is not as high as the prices, but it offers more verve than most places. Tel: (473) 2-1434.

A bit farther from the center of town, two establishments offer cuisine that's a notch above the usual mediocre Guanajuato fare. **La Casserole**, in the suburb of Marfil at Arcos de Guadalupe 3, occupies a lovely roofed patio at the end of a cobblestone lane. French-owned and inspired, La Casserole artfully presents its Franco-Mexican cuisine from 1:00 to 4:00 P.M. only. Tel: (473) 2-2110.

The same management spreads a midday buffet (again, 1:00 to 4:00 P.M. only) in a colonial-era building across the street from the Valenciana church on the Carretera a Dolores Hidalgo. Of the two, the Marfil operation is the superior.

As in most things, Guanajuato is restrained when it comes to nightlife. The Castillo Santa Cecilia offers decorous dancing every night except Sunday, with a minimum charge designed to cover supper and the entertainment. **El Pozo**, the club in the Parador San Javier, presents fairly good late-evening entertainment in an unusual setting complete with built-in waterfall.

MORELIA

Morelia, the most stately and handsome of Mexico's cities, is like the Roman god Janus or certain masks on Mayan temples: It faces two directions at once. That's because Morelia is among the most Spanish of Latin American cities. It looks like Spain, and sometimes it even *feels* like Spain, which is unusual in Mexico. Yet almost in its backyard are the communities and culture of the Tarascan Indians. But despite its profuse craft markets, its patriotic nods to pre-Columbian culture, and even its geography, Morelia remains solidly colonial in appearance and Mexican in its style.

In recent years Morelia has burgeoned into a city of about half a million people, spilling over its old boundaries and creating a ring of suburbs, developments, and industrial zones that isn't of much interest to the traveller. Inside this ring, however, lies another world.

Founded in 1541 by Don Antonio de Mendoza, New Spain's first and greatest viceroy, and christened Valladolid in honor of his home town, the city was designed to be the center of government and religion for a vast area (the modern state of Michoacán, of which present-day Morelia is the capital, constitutes only a part of that region). The city grew slowly, however, and it wasn't until the middle of the 17th century that it truly started to flourish. Even then, the optimism and foresight of its architects and builders, who laid out their little provincial town with a practicality and spaciousness that are remarkable to this day (and must have been revolutionary more than three centuries ago), was amazing. The results are obvious to anyone who has spent time in Mexico's other colonial gems. Unlike most of its contemporaries, Morelia is not only well preserved, it actually works. Its plazas and public buildings accommodate modern-day crowds easily and efficiently, and its lovely streets even allow you to get around by car.

Around in Morelia

THE CATHEDRAL
The first glimpse you get of this old city is of the domes, towers, and pinnacles of its imposing yet graceful cathedral. Begun in 1640 but not completed until 1744, its design was intended to be Plateresque, a style of decoration based on silver plate. While a variety of architectural styles swept New Spain during the century of construction, the builders of

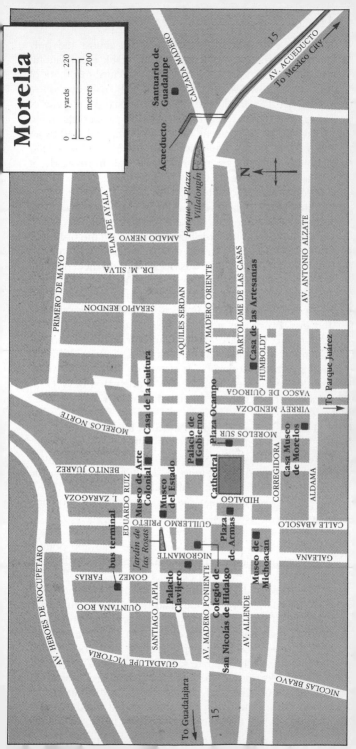

Morelia

0 yards — 220
0 meters 200

Santuario de Guadalupe

Acueducto

CALZADA MADERO

Parque y Plaza Villalongín

AV. ACUEDUCTO
To Mexico City

15

N

PLAN DE AYALA
AMADO NERVO
DR. M. SILVA
PRIMERO DE MAYO
SERAPIO RENDON
AQUILES SERDAN
AV. MADERO ORIENTE
BARTOLOME DE LAS CASAS
Casa de las Artesanías
HUMBOLDT
AV. ANTONIO ALZATE

Casa de la Cultura
MORELOS NORTE
Palacio de Gobierno
Plaza Ocampo
VASCO DE QUIROGA
VIRREY MENDOZA
To Parque Juárez

Museo de Arte Colonial
Museo del Estado
BENITO JUÁREZ
I. ZARAGOZA
EDUARDO RUIZ
Jardin de las Rosas
GUILLERMO PRIETO
Cathedral
MORELOS SUR
Casa Museo de Morelos
CORREGIDORA
ALDAMA

bus terminal
GOMEZ FARIAS
NIGROMANTE
Plaza Armas de
HIDALGO
CALLE ABASOLO

AV. HEROES DE NOCUPETARO
QUINTANA ROO
SANTIAGO TAPIA
Palacio Clavijero
AV. MADERO PONIENTE
Colegio de San Nicolás de Hidalgo
AV. ALLENDE
Museo de Michoacan
GALEANA

GUADALUPE VICTORIA
To Guadalajara
15
NICOLAS BRAVO

Morelia's cathedral stuck to their plan, almost the only builders in the country to do so. The result is a beautiful example of Baroque ecclesiastical architecture made out of trachyte, a brown volcanic rock warmed by rose overtones. Carved overlays and low reliefs, not to mention a number of broad, plain areas, accent the six statues around the main portal, and its two graceful towers are complemented by an exceptional dome. While it's true that Mexico is a land bubbling with domes, this one is special; from inside, it seems to float above the nave, giving an impression of height far greater than it actually can claim.

Although Morelia never became as rich from silver as its founders had hoped, the cathedral once boasted a communion rail made of the precious metal. In 1858 the bishop of Morelia refused to pay a war assessment, however, and as a result his precious railing was ripped out and melted down. But the church has other treasures: paintings by a number of outstanding colonial artists as well as what is perhaps the best pipe organ in Latin America—a treat for both the ear and eye. Every May a festival held in the cathedral takes advantage of this marvel, with organists from many countries coming to play. In fact, Morelia has a rich musical heritage: Among other distinctions, it claims the first conservatory founded in the New World. Today a celebrated boys' choir does its part to continue the tradition.

THE PLAZA DE ARMAS AREA

The idyllic Plaza de Armas (also called the Plaza de los Mártires, in honor of Mexico's slain patriots), a lovely square with a bandstand that is, in its modest way, as perfect as the adjacent cathedral, is the heart and hub of Morelia. This is the place to stroll, lounge, meet friends, and listen to band concerts.

Also inviting are the sidewalk cafés under the arcade across the street, where newspapers are read and politics discussed as students from the University of Michoacán, unusually purposeful for their age, hurry by.

The **Palacio de Gobierno**, the state capitol, faces the cathedral to the north. Although an 18th-century structure, it could be 100 years older. (Morelia seems always to have been wary of newfangled architecture.) Inside, murals by one of Mexico's outstanding painters, the locally born Alfred Zalce, dramatically illustrate scenes from Mexico's past.

Two blocks north of the cathedral and plaza, at the corner of Guillermo Prieto and Santiago Tapia, is the **Museo del Estado**, the state museum. The building itself and the murals inside are better than the displays, which include the complete stock of a Morelian pharmacy circa 1868, Tarascan jewelry, and other artifacts.

West and south of the plaza, on the corner of Allende and Calle Abasolo, an even better building houses the **Museo de Michoacán**. This former residence boasts beautiful Michoacán woodwork, starting with the front door. The arches are also unusually effective, as is the stairway. Once again, the structure, not the collection of historical items it houses, is the attraction here. Both museums are open daily except Mondays from 9:00 A.M. to 2:00 P.M. and again from 4:00 to 8:00 P.M.

A Hero of Independence

Three blocks east and a block south, at Avenida Morelos Sur and Aldama, is the **Casa Museo de Morelos**, the home of the hero for whom the city was renamed. Of all the early figures in Mexico's struggle for independence, José María Morelos was the most brilliant. Born in what was then Valladolid in 1765, he became a laborer on a hacienda as a young man. By almost starving himself to death he managed to make it through the Colegio de San Nicolás in his hometown and eventually became a priest. The revolt of 1810 was a call to greatness for Morelos, who emerged from obscurity to become the military genius of the rebellion. In a relatively short period of time, he raised, trained, and armed 9,000 men using captured equipment, and then gained control of virtually all of western and northern Mexico. Morelos, who stood barely five feet tall, cast a long shadow over Mexican history, both in his words and by his deeds, and Valladolid was renamed Morelia in his honor in 1828. The small museum (open daily except Mondays, 9:00 A.M. to 2:00 P.M. and 4:00 to 8:00 P.M.) is representative of a humble house of the hero's day.

Relics of the Colonial Era

Several impressive buildings are located along Nigromante a block west of the Plaza de Armas. The **Colegio de San Nicolás de Hidalgo** is the second-oldest college in the New World, and the oldest one extant. The patriot Father Hidalgo studied and taught here, as did Morelos and Agustín de Iturbide, who would later proclaim himself Emperor of Mexico. The University of Michoacán, which now occupies part of the old building, is a descendant of this venerable institution.

The 17th-century **Palacio Clavijero**, across the street from San Nicolás, houses a massive state library and industrial school, and boasts a magnificent patio that's a must-see for visitors. At the end of the second block heading north, you'll come to the lovely **Jardín de las Rosas**—named not for its abundant flowers but for the Templo y Conservatorio de las Rosas (Church and Conservatory of the Roses), the mellowed building across from this square. Once a girls' boarding school, it is now home to the Morelia Boys' Choir, whose singing can often be heard coming from this, the oldest music school in the Americas.

Three blocks east of Las Rosas stands the **Exconvento del Carmen,** now the government-sponsored **Casa de la Cultura**. Construction on the convent was begun in the late 1500s and continued for almost two centuries, producing a building of enormous proportions. The stairway and domed ceilings are especially noteworthy. Virtually next door to the former convent, the little **Museo de Arte Colonial** features an interesting series of displays, including a collection of religious figures made from cornstalks and sugarcane.

THE PLAZA VILLALONGIN AREA

The **Parque y Plaza Villalongín**, the most attractive strolling area in Morelia—high praise in a city where street after street vies for the attention of the visitor—is located about half a mile east of the cathedral on Avenida Madero Oriente. The small plaza itself is attractive, though a visitor can only marvel at the dreadfully kitsch sculpture of Indians and fruit here: The kindest word for it is memorable.

Beyond the plaza stands an **aqueduct** begun in 1785, an immense project designed to carry water more than a mile from the surrounding hills. Here you'll also find a shady promenade leading to the fanciful **Santuario de Guadalupe**, a church that's a bit of Morocco somehow Christianized and made Mexican. The neighborhood is woodsy, and a favorite Sunday spot for local families.

STAYING IN MORELIA

When it comes to accommodations, there isn't a great range of choices in Morelia, but comfort, charm, and—in one case—luxury are available.

The city is walled off to the south by the steep slopes of the Santa María hills. On their crest, reached from the city via Calle Galeana, is a quiet neighborhood with lovely views and two secluded hotels. Both establishments are located a little more than 3 km (2 miles) south of town, past the Parque Juárez and across the Periférico, the main highway. Calle Tangaxhuan winds up the hill.

With spectacular views of the city and the long valley in which it is situated, the ▶ **Villa Montaña** is one of the country's better inns. Its bungalow units have all the amenities you'd expect in a first-rate establishment, including fireplaces, and some guests spend a good part of the winter here even though it isn't an inexpensive haven. The inn's dining room is also outstanding (see below).

Across the road, the ▶ **Posada Vista Bella** is less luxurious and less expensive, but quite satisfactory. It also offers, in addition to its regular units, a number of apartments for weekly or monthly rental, and has a restaurant.

Downtown, just off the main plaza at Zaragoza 90, is the charming ▶ **Posada de la Soledad**, a former monastery that has been modernized with skill and taste. The patio garden, around which the hotel is built, is noted for its serene beauty. Not all of its 60 rooms are desirable, though; a few should be avoided because of kitchen noise, others because of lingering monastic chill.

The ▶ **Hotel Virrey de Mendoza** is Morelia's traditional choice for a good hotel on the plaza. Its style is colonial, the building old but recently remodeled and upgraded. The dining room under its covered central court is filled most nights.

The modern ▶ **Calinda Morelia Quality Inn**, 6 km (3½ miles) southeast of town on the Periférico opposite a shopping center, is well planned for comfort and convenience. Because its guests are more likely to be prosperous business travellers than tourists, its rates are designed for expense accounts, but the trained staff makes every effort to offer value for your money.

The cocktail lounges of the major hotels provide what entertainment the city has to offer, mostly piano music, with an occasional combo making an appearance.

You can also choose to stay in scenic Pátzcuaro, just west of the city (see the Western Highlands chapter) and make day trips to Morelia from there.

DINING IN MORELIA

The **Villa Montaña** keeps a fine restaurant and bar with a good wine selection. Non-guests should make reservations (small children are not welcome); Tel: (451) 4-0179. The menu is international—regional cookery appears to be taboo here.

Those who wish to sample the traditional dishes of the region will do well in the flowering patio or equally charming dining room of the **Posada de la Soledad**, just off the Plaza de Armas. Their special *sopa Tarasca* has the right zing, and the Pátzcuaro whitefish is delicate and flaky. Tel: (451) 2-1888.

Los Comenzales, a simple, low-priced patio restaurant two blocks north of the cathedral at Zaragoza 148, is devoted entirely to Michoacán and Mexican cuisine. Its fare is hearty rather than delicate, but the lengthy menu offers a good sampling of regional dishes. Try, for instance, *uechepos,* a slightly sweet cornmeal bread, or the little triangular tamales called *corundas. Ate Moreleon,* the most famous dessert item of the region, may appear in the form of any fruit paste, including pineapple, guava, mango, or papaya.

The **Restaurant Fonda las Mercedes** has an excellent kitchen, a colonial-style patio full of artwork and plants, and loads of charm. It is pleasant by day, enchanting by night, and the food is good enough to compensate for the slow service if you're not in a hurry. The restaurant is located three blocks west of the Plaza de Armas and half a block north at León Guzmán 47; Tel: (451) 2-6113.

The cafés under the arcade near the cathedral are better for snacks and sodas than for meals, but within their limits all are pleasing. Don't even think of trying to order when they're busy, however. Coffee or anything in a bottle will get to you; ordering anything else will be pressing your luck.

SHOPPING IN MORELIA

Morelia specializes in crafts from the various nearby Tarascan communities. Good quality can be found in a variety of stores, but the best choice is the fabulous popular arts market at the **Casa de las Artesanías**, two huge floors in the former Convent of San Francisco on Calle Humboldt crammed with items from all over the state. While buying here is not as exciting as going to a craft village and making your own discoveries, you probably won't find better bargains anywhere. The prices reflect real market value, and the selection is excellent. The only thing missing is the thrill of the hunt.

Michoacán lacquerware is an especially good buy here; the work is genuine and as lasting as this rather fragile craft can be. (In recent years there has been a lot of "forged" lacquerware—glossy auto paint sprayed on cheap wood—making the rounds. It takes a sharp eye and a bright light to spot the real thing.) On the other hand, you'll probably want to avoid the guitars; for those you must go to Paracho and search. (**Paracho**, noted for its woodcarvings and musical instruments, is a small town about 90 minutes west of Morelia via Uruapan, where you turn north on Highway 37 for 25 km/16 miles. While its specialty is guitars, other quality handcrafted string instruments are also available.)

The Monarch Butterflies

In an awe-inspiring migration, 100 million monarch butterflies make their way annually from Canada and the United States to winter (early November until late February) in Michoacán's forests of pine and oyamel trees. A visit to the groves at this time of year will be an unforgettable experience.

The most popular point of departure for the monarch sanctuary is the little mountain town of **Anganqueo** in eastern Michoacán, about 97 km (60 miles) east of Morelia via Highway 15, then a marked but unnumbered road going east from 15 just north of Zitacuaro. The groves are reached by an arduous climb up a steep path. The altitude will probably make it necessary for you to pause frequently along the way in order to catch your breath. Go slowly.

The scene that awaits you is worth the effort. On top, the trees are literally coated with monarchs; the muted sound you hear is the rustling of millions of wings.

If you make the trip from Morelia, plan to be on the road no later than 7:00 A.M. The experience is worth a leisurely trip, however. If you decide to take your time, you can stay overnight in clean but simple accommodations in Angangueo itself at the ▶ **Posada Don Bruno**. The famous old Hotel San José Purua, once a favorite for monarch watchers, now opens only erratically and cannot be counted on. On the western edge of Zitacuaro, about 20 km (12 miles) south of Angangueo, the rustic but comfortable ▶ **Rancho San Cayetano** has a good restaurant and pleasant rooms. The inn is situated five minutes west of Highway 15 on the paved road that leads to Presa del Bosque; posted signs will help you find its quiet location.

GETTING AROUND

Driving Down from the Border

The two routes discussed here both converge on San Luis Potosí, at the northern edge of the Bajío. The McAllen–Reynosa border crossing is especially popular with drivers coming from the U.S. Gulf Coast states. The Laredo–Nuevo Laredo crossing is the gateway to the most heavily travelled route to central Mexico. We will cover the first route in its entirety before turning our attention to the latter, which includes a brief discussion of hotels and restaurants in San Luis Potosí, and winds up in Querétaro.

Via McAllen–Reynosa

Although Reynosa has a few acceptable hotels, all the better choices are located on the U.S. side of the border in McAllen.

For years the route from Reynosa followed Highway 40 to China, Highway 85 south to Montemorelos and Linares, and then Highway 58 west to San Roberto, where it joined Highway 57. Nowadays, however, many drivers prefer going via Ciudad Victoria and Huisache Junction, a route that offers the advantages of a smoother road and lighter local traffic. Although most of the surrounding countryside hardly can be called scenic, it is more varied than the trip via Linares, and so it's the one described here.

Highway 97, the road to Ciudad Victoria, begins at the customs station in Reynosa. It's an adequate road, fairly fast, and heads due south through poor ranchland. At a cross-roads 107 km (66 miles) south of Reynosa, it is joined by Highway 101/180, which then branches off as Highway 101 some 32 km (20 miles) farther south. Stay on Highway 101 as it heads inland through Jiménez and a number of other small towns until it reaches the slightly more prosperous citrus country around Ciudad Victoria, the attractive capital of the state of Tamaulipas.

Three kilometers (2 miles) north of Ciudad Victoria you'll spot ▶ **Paradise** on the left side of the highway. While less heavenly than its name, Paradise is nevertheless a welcoming establishment, its cool, muted dining room the perfect antidote to the glare of midday. In addition to its attractive restaurant, the inn also offers modern, comfortable overnight accommodations.

Perched in the foothills of the Sierra Madre Oriental, **Ciudad Victoria** is a well-kept provincial capital with a number of handsome turn-of-the-century buildings. It's also your best bet for a lunch and/or gasoline stop; the roadside facilities between here and Huisache Junction, a 3½-hour drive to the southwest, are limited (although you'll pass two widely spaced Pemex stations along the way). In the center of town, facing the Plaza Hidalgo, stands the gracious ▶ **Hotel Everest**, with its cheerful, pleasant rooms, good dining room, and convenient coffee shop. On the same plaza, the ▶ **Hotel Sierra Gorda** is also a good choice for a meal (its kitchen specializes in regional cookery) or an overnight stay.

You'll notice that the surrounding hillsides become steeper as soon as you leave town heading south and west on Highway 101. (Road signs along this stretch say "Tula," which is not to be confused with the famed archaeological zone outside of Mexico City.) And, in fact, the first 62 km (38

miles) of the route follow a winding road that snakes along a
succession of ridgelines. The going is slow but not particularly hazardous, and you'll be rewarded by a measure of
coolness as you gain altitude. Gradually the ascent will level
off and you'll begin the almost imperceptible climb toward
the great *altiplano,* or central Mexican plateau, passing the
settlements of Tula, Colonel, and La Viga along the way.

At the junction of Highways 101 and 80, turn right and
follow the latter 58 km (36 miles) to Highway 57, the
principal north–south route into Mexico City. You'll begin to
see high mountains in the distance along this stretch, with
Cerro San Cristóbal, the tallest peak in the area, rising some
7,000 feet a short distance to the south.

Highway 80 veers sharply to the south as it joins Highway
57 just beyond the village of Huisache. From the junction of
the two you can follow Highway 57 through San Luis Potosí
and Querétaro into Mexico City. (For route and accommodations information in and around San Luis Potosí, see below.)

Via Laredo–Nuevo Laredo–Columbia

The route from Laredo/Nuevo Laredo to San Luis Potosí
and Querétaro is the most heavily travelled route to central
Mexico, and thus is the best maintained, has the most
frequent emergency service, and boasts the nicest tourist
facilities. For the most part, Highway 85/57 offers fast, easy
travel (although traffic can be slowed by tractor-trailer
trucks on certain two-lane stretches) all the way to San Luis
Potosí, some 756 km (469 miles) distant. The scenery, on
the other hand, is nothing to write home about.

There are plenty of decent accommodations in Laredo,
but many travellers prefer to clear border formalities and
spend the night in **Nuevo Laredo**, both to take advantage of
slightly lower prices and to ensure there are no delays in the
morning: Traffic tie-ups on the international bridges and
long lines at Mexican customs can get anyone's vacation off
on the wrong foot.

(A new and virtually traffic-free option involves the recently opened bridge at Columbia, Texas. The road to Columbia cuts west from Highway 35 about three miles north
of the Laredo city limits. The bridge and customs office are
located seven miles west of the cutoff, and the crossing is
remarkably fast and hassle-free. Before leaving the customs
area ask an officer to point out the road to Ciudad Anáhuac
and Lampazos; otherwise you're likely to end up on the road
to Nuevo Laredo.)

Set on attractively landscaped grounds 5 km (3 miles)
south of the International Bridge on Highway 85, ▶ **El Río**

Motel offers large, airy rooms smartly decorated with provincial furnishings and a restaurant noted for its Mexican specialties. The ► **Hacienda Motor Hotel**, 4 km (2½ miles) farther south on Highway 85, is of comparable quality.

The hotels in downtown Nuevo Laredo tend to be noisy and afflicted with a seedy border-town atmosphere. Students and other budget travellers often choose the ► **Hotel Siesta**, a plain but adequate establishment near the center of town at Ocampo 559. A little fancier and more expensive, if not noticeably better, is the ► **Hotel Reforma**, also downtown at Avenida Guerrero 822.

Leaving Nuevo Laredo on Highway 85, you will probably be waved through a customs checkpoint 18 km (11 miles) south of town. (When drivers are stopped, it's almost always to check for a car permit.) The surrounding countryside is flat and semi-arid, but the poor soil manages to support a few ranches raising sorghum. The only trees you'll see are Joshua trees, a relative of the century plant.

Toll Roads

Five toll roads, four of them quite new, are in operation between Nuevo Laredo and Mexico City. They are modern, fast, and so expensive that Mexicans joke grimly about "the new highway bandits." If you use toll roads all the way from the border to the capital, it will cost you about $60. Motorists unfamiliar with Mexican toll roads should note that the toll booths are often equipped with two sets of red/green signal lights. The upper light announces whether a lane is open; the lower light turns green after you have paid the toll.

Heading south, the first of these routes branches off Highway 57 a few miles beyond the checkpoint south of Nuevo Laredo. Like all toll roads in Mexico, it's marked "cuota." It rejoins the regular freeway, Highway 57, north of Monterrey.

The second toll road, clearly marked, is the Saltillo bypass. It returns to the regular freeway south of Saltillo.

It is more than 300 km (186 miles) to the third toll road, also clearly marked, which serves as the San Luis Potosí bypass. For travellers not visiting San Luis Potosí, it is the best way to avoid a great deal of traffic and delays.

The fourth toll road comes up 35 km (22 miles) north of Querétaro at the junction of Highway 111, the road to San Miguel de Allende. It rejoins Highway 57 north of San Juan del Río at the junction of Highway 120, the road to Morelia.

The final toll road begins south of San Juan del Río and continues almost all the way to the capital. Whereas the earlier routes were options, here you have no choice: There is no other practical way of getting to Mexico City.

The Old Route

Sabinas Hidalgo, 136 km (84 miles) south of Nuevo Laredo, is the only town of any size before you get to Monterrey. Next to a large Pemex station on the right is the Ancira Café and Curio Shop, adequate for bottled drinks, packaged snacks, and breaking up the drive. The Café Los Jacales, across the street, is in the same league.

As you get closer to Monterrey, mountains flanking the highway at some distance add a little variety to the scene. The most famous peak is Cerro de la Silla (Saddle Mountain), which comes into view about 186 km (115) miles south of the border.

At the 214-km (133-mile) mark approaching Monterrey you'll come to a bypass on your right marked with an unofficial sign reading "Saltillo." This two-lane road, which has almost no services and is choked with trucks, reportedly has a high accident rate, and because it's a winding route, making passing risky, it probably won't save you any time. It does, however, provide an alternative for drivers who dread going through an unfamiliar big city. (Those who decide to take this bypass should follow the signs for Saltillo; the exit is marked, but heed the signs carefully to make sure you're in the correct lane.)

Travellers choosing instead to spend time in **Monterrey** will encounter a huge, burgeoning industrial city, the third largest in Mexico and by far the most Americanized. (A former president of the Republic once angrily accused it of being more Texan in spirit than Mexican.) It's also an expensive city, and not a place for budget travellers to linger.

Two of the more pleasant accommodations in Monterrey face each other across Highway 85, just after it becomes Avenida Universidad, on the northern outskirts of the city. Those electing to stay at either place have a choice in the morning of continuing on through the city or backtracking 7 km (4 miles) to the bypass. The ► **Holiday Inn Monterrey**, Avenida Universidad and Calle 18 de Deciembre, is smart and moderately expensive, and offers good-sized suites, a large swimming pool, tennis courts, and a chic nightclub. The restaurant and coffee shop are also convenient for those passing through the city. Across the street, the ► **Royal Courts Motor Inn** is slightly less expensive, has a smaller swimming pool, and offers rather small but comfortably air-conditioned rooms.

The hotels in downtown Monterrey center around the Plaza Hidalgo. To get there, follow Avenida Universidad to the freeway and take the "Hidalgo" exit.

The ▶ **Hotel Ambassador** is one of the finest hostelries in the country. Built by the Westin Camino Real chain as a showplace for international business travellers, it is elegant right down to the details, and has a lovely and inviting garden swimming pool, a very good coffee shop, and the outstanding **Pavillon Restaurant**, a little corner of Paris in Monterrey. A dress code is observed, and the entrées are as expensive as you would expect in this luxury hotel. The ▶ **Ancira Sierra Radisson Plaza Hotel Monterrey** once saw Pancho Villa stable his horse in its lobby. Nowadays, the modernized Ancira retains an echo of its former Old World charm—a quality all too rare in Monterrey. While a little less costly than the Ambassador, it pampers its guests every bit as much.

Monterrey is connected to Saltillo by Highway 40, a good road that runs south and west for 85 km (53 miles) to its junction with the Saltillo bypass. **Saltillo**, just west of the bypass, is an attractive city with a few remaining colonial touches, but it doesn't really merit closer inspection unless you decide to stop for food and lodging, in which case it is less expensive than Monterrey and easier to explore.

The ▶ **Camino Real**, located 10 km (6 miles) southeast of town on Highway 57, offers very comfortable rooms and a range of amenities, including a well-managed restaurant. It is fairly expensive for the area, however. The much more reasonably priced ▶ **Posada San José**, on the opposite side of town, is a pleasing inn with a rooftop restaurant, a rooftop pool, and safe parking.

Highway 40 meets Highway 57 at a *glorieta* (traffic circle) north of town. In general, the latter is a fast road, but that's not the case as drivers navigate the curves and bridges immediately south of Saltillo. The road is subject to fogs here, and great caution must be exercised in such conditions.

Leaving the streams that generate much of this ground fog behind, the road plows through mile after mile of flat country dotted with cactus and ringed by distant mesas. Much of the area was a shallow sea in times fairly recent by geologic standards, and you'll get a real sense of travelling over a seabed encircled by the telltale rings of vanished shorelines. There is a Pemex station at San Roberto, 122 km (76 miles) south of Saltillo.

The cutoff to the ghost town of **Real de Catorce** is another 120 km (74 miles) south of San Roberto. For those who have an extra 5 hours for the excursion, it's a curious trip to a mountainside collection of mostly ruined buildings that was once a silver boomtown. There are, in addition, some simple restaurants and lodging houses in Catorce, although most visitors return to **Matehuala**, a little more than an hour's drive, for the night. Highway 57 bypasses Matehuala with no loss to travellers. However, many drivers bound for Mexico City, about a 7½-hour drive to the south, prefer to break the trip here, even though the choice of accommodations is better in San Luis Potosí, 178 km (110 miles) farther on.

On the Matehuala bypass, near a welcoming arch resembling a McDonald's sign, ▶ **Las Palmas** is the largest, most popular establishment. Its modern motel-type units are not overpriced, but its fairly good restaurant is. Las Palmas also has a large swimming pool, curio shop, and miniature golf course. The ▶ **Motel Hacienda**, a neighbor of Las Palmas, is much smaller but just as nice, with less of a truck-stop atmosphere. Its restaurant specializes in roast kid (*cabrito*) and other typically Mexican dishes. The ▶ **Motel Oasis**, also near Las Palmas, is economical and has a restaurant.

From Matehuala Highway 57 continues south through a barren and featureless landscape, with the Sierra Madre Oriental far to the east. Many of the roadside vendors you see will be selling snakeskins, while others offer caged birds fated to survive only briefly.

The town of **San Luis Potosí** lies west of the highway inside a ring of heavy industry. For those who have the time, its picturesque colonial center repays exploration.

Three very good motels are conveniently located on Highway 57. The moderately expensive ▶ **Cactus Motel**, 1 km (½ mile) southeast of the traffic circle, offers excellent accommodations, saunas, a good restaurant, and a lively nightclub. It recently became a Howard Johnson franchise and has been remodeled. The ▶ **Hostal del Quijote**, on the west side of the road, 5 km (3 miles) southeast of the traffic circle, is one of the better highway inns between the border and the capital. It also maintains a good dining room, coffee shop, bar, and discotheque. The ▶ **Motel Santa Fé**, 1 km (½ mile) southeast of the traffic circle, offers adequate accommodations at economical rates as well as an attractive garden, a pool, and a restaurant.

In the center of San Luis Potosí, two blocks west of the Plaza de Armas on Avenida Carranza, the ▶ **Hotel Panorama** offers first-class rooms and a full range of services. Also on Avenida Carranza, another two blocks west of the hotel, is **La Virreina**, one of the better provincial restaurants in Mexico.

While its Old World elegance is reminiscent of the turn of the century, diners in travelling clothes are made to feel welcome. The menu at La Virreina is international, but a variety of regional dishes will be prepared upon request.

South of San Luis Potosí Highway 57 is mostly a two-lane road until it meets Highway 110, 118 km (73 miles) distant. Signs pointing to the east read "San Luis de la Paz," to the west "Dolores Hidalgo." A right turn here will take you to San Miguel de Allende via Dolores Hidalgo, but this is neither the shortest nor the fastest way. For the shortcut continue south 15 km (9 miles) to the Los Rodríguez cutoff. A sign will point the way to San Miguel de Allende.

Querétaro lies 32 km (20 miles) to the south over Highway 57. On the northern outskirts of the city the bypass to Mexico City is a clearly marked left turn.

Querétaro

The most direct auto route from the capital is Highway 57, much of it a toll road. Count on the trip taking about 3 hours one-way. Daily rail service from Mexico City (approximately $10 one-way) leaves early in the morning and returns in the afternoon. Trains to all points leave from Mexico City's central station on Avenida Insurgentes Norte. Breakfast is included in a first-class ticket, a box lunch on the return trip. For attentive service, morning travellers should be at the dining room the moment it opens.

First-class bus service, which is faster than the train, is the usual choice for those not driving. There is good and frequent service from the capital to Querétaro, a major hub for almost all routes heading north and west, with about eight different buses leaving the D.F. every hour (fare approximately $6). The finest service, and the fastest, is offered by **ETN** lines (Tel: 5/368-0212) and **Primera Plus** (Tel: 5/587-5222). Both provide service to Querétaro from the capital as well as from Guadalajara. The fare is about double the first-class price. Buses depart Mexico City from the Central Caminero del Norte, also called the Terminal del Norte; the station is on Avenida de los 100 Metros, quite a way out on Insurgentes Norte. The metro stop for the terminal is Estación Terminal de Autobuses del Norte, more simply indicated on most system maps as TAN. Clearly marked city buses making limited stops also make the run to the terminal on Insurgentes.

Taking taxis is inexpensive and easier than trying to drive in Querétaro itself. Walking is also easy on the flat paving stones of this almost flat city. (Be sure to bring comfortable, thick-soled shoes, however.)

San Miguel de Allende

Until recently, the most direct auto route from the capital to San Miguel was Highway 57 via Querétaro. Motorists who choose this option should follow the signs for San Luis Potosí as they near Querétaro. The San Miguel cutoff is 25 km (15½ miles) north of Querétaro, and the entire trip should take about 3½ hours one-way.

Motorists wishing to bypass Querétaro should take the new toll road north of San Juan del Río, just past the junction of Highways 57 and 120. The route is clearly marked "San Luis Potosí–San Miguel de Allende," and rejoins Highway 57 at the San Miguel cutoff. The road shortens the driving time from the capital by approximately 20 minutes, and the toll is about $5.

One first-class bus leaves Mexico City every morning for San Miguel (fare approximately $8), arriving about 4 hours later. The line is **Tres Estrellas de Oro**; Tel: (5) 567-8157. **Primera Plus** (Tel: 5/587-5222) and **ETN** (Tel: 5/368-0212) buses, the best option but at about double the first-class price, depart each morning from the capital as well as from Guadalajara. Second-class bus service likewise departs from the capital's Terminal del Norte. Purveyors include Flecha Amarilla and Herradura de Plata. Both first- and second-class buses leave the D.F. every few minutes for Querétaro; San Miguel passengers failing to make a direct connection can go to Querétaro and change there.

There is little reason to have a car in San Miguel itself, but driving is the most practical way to explore the countryside. Car rentals are best arranged in Mexico City, however—rentals in San Miguel are uncertain and often unsatisfactory.

In town, comfortable thick-soled shoes are essential. Taxis are cheap and can be found near the *jardín* (they will seldom respond to phone calls).

Guanajuato

The relatively new international airport near León, 50 km (31 miles) northwest of Guanajuato, is serviced daily from Houston by Continental, from Los Angeles by Mexicana, and from Chicago three days a week by Mexicana. Aeroméxico offers a daily León–Los Angeles flight with a stop in Hermosillo. Taxis and *colectivos* are available to run visitors from the airport into Guanajuato; count on spending $17 for the former, $4 for a *colectivo*. Ground transportation to San Miguel and Querétaro, though more expensive, is also available. Cab fare to San Miguel de Allende will run about $50, but can be divided among as many as four passengers, depending on baggage. *Colectivos* cost about $7.

A car is a great convenience for getting to Guanajuato and a nuisance afterward (except for guests at the outlying hotels). Bus travel is the usual choice from Mexico City (see Querétaro and San Miguel de Allende above). **ETN** runs a deluxe bus to and from the capital daily. For reservations in Mexico City, Tel: (5) 368-0212; in Guanajuato, Tel: (473) 2-3134. Second-class **Flecha Amarilla** has more daily trips to Guanajuato than any other line; Tel: (5) 567-8033 or 8173. **Tres Estrellas de Oro** is better but offers less frequent service; Tel: (5) 567-8157. Buses to and from San Miguel de Allende arrive and depart frequently. From the capital or Guadalajara insist on a direct (*directo*) bus.

Stout walking shoes are a must. Taxi service is cheap, courteous, and as efficient as the cramped streets will permit. There are also bus tours of the city, although they're usually conducted in Spanish only. Hotels will arrange for guides if desired.

Morelia

Aeroméxico serves the Morelia airport daily from the capital. Car rentals are available at the airport, as are taxis and *colectivos*.

To reach Morelia by car from Mexico City follow Paseo de la Reforma through Chapultepec Park (west), staying on it as it becomes Reforma Lomas then joins Highway 15. The latter leads all the way to Morelia and is one of the most scenic routes in the country. For the last 103 km (64 miles), however, there are no roadside services; the last stop for gasoline and food is Ciudad Hidalgo. Allow 5½ hours for the drive.

Regular bus service from the capital originates at the Terminal del Norte. Destinations include Guadalajara, Guanajuato, Pátzcuaro, and, of course, points in between. Visitors travelling directly to or from the capital will want to go via Toluca, the fastest, most scenic route. The fare is approximately $17. The **ETN** deluxe bus runs between the capital and Morelia mornings and late in the afternoon, and costs about $34 one-way. In Morelia, Tel: (451) 3-7440 for reservations; in Mexico City, Tel: (5) 368-0212.

Train service to Mexico City (approximately $20) is available but not recommended. There is also daily rail service to **Pátzcuaro** (see the Western Highlands chapter), but buses are a more dependable alternative for this short trip (40 km/ 25 miles) to the west.

Morelia is mostly flat, and thus an easy city for walking. Taxis are cheap and plentiful, but fares should be settled in advance to avoid unpleasant surprises.

ACCOMMODATIONS REFERENCE

The rates given below are projections *for December 1993 through Easter 1994. Unless otherwise indicated, rates are for double rooms, double occupancy; the 10 percent VAT has been added. As rates are subject to change, it's always a good idea to double-check before booking.*

▶ **Ancira Sierra Radisson Plaza Hotel Monterrey.** P.O. Box 697, **Monterrey,** Nuevo León 64000. Tel: (83) 45-1060; Fax: (83) 44-5226; in the U.S., Tel: (800) 333-3333. $189.

▶ **Cactus Motel.** P.O. Box 393, **San Luis Potosí,** San Luis Potosí 78090. Tel: (48) 22-1995; Fax: (48) 22-0550. $50.

▶ **Calinda Morelia Quality Inn.** Avenida de las Camelias 3466, **Morelia,** Michoacán 58270. Tel: (451) 4-1427; Fax: (451) 4-5476; in the U.S. and Canada, Tel: (800) 228-5151. $102.

▶ **Camino Real.** P.O. Box 55, Carretera 57, **Saltillo,** Coahuila 25000. Tel: (84) 30-0000; Fax: (84) 30-1030; in the U.S. and Canada, Tel: (800) 228-3000. $133.

▶ **Casa Carmen.** Calle Correo 31, **San Miguel de Allende,** Guanajuato 37700. Tel: (465) 2-0844. $50 (includes two meals).

▶ **Casa de Sierra Nevada.** Calle Hospicio 35, **San Miguel de Allende,** Guanajuato 37700. Tel: (465) 2-1895. $139–$262.

▶ **Castillo de Santa Cecilia.** P.O. Box 44, Camino a la Valenciana s/n, **Guanajuato,** Guanajuato 36000. Tel: (473) 2-0485; Fax: (473) 2-0153. $78.

▶ **Hacienda de las Flores.** Calle Hospicio 16, **San Miguel de Allende,** Guanajuato 37700. Tel: (465) 2-1808. $131 (includes breakfast).

▶ **Hacienda Jurica.** P.O. Box 338, Carretera 57, northwest of **Querétaro,** Querétaro 76100. Tel: (42) 18-0022; Fax: (42) 18-0136. $139.

▶ **Hacienda Motor Hotel.** P.O. Box 682, **Nuevo Laredo,** Tamaulipas 88000. Tel: (87) 17-0000; Fax: (87) 17-0420. $69.

▶ **Hacienda Taboada.** Kilometer 8, Carretera a Dolores Hidalgo, **San Miguel de Allende,** Guanajuato 37700. Tel: (465) 2-0850; Fax: (465) 2-1798. $253 (includes all meals); $207 (includes two meals).

▶ **Holiday Inn Monterrey.** Avenida Universidad and Calle 18 de Deciembre, **Monterrey,** Nuevo León 66450. Tel: (83) 76-2400; Fax: (83) 32-0565; in the U.S. and Canada, Tel: (800) HOLIDAY. $131.

▶ **Holiday Inn Querétaro.** Carretera Constitución Sur 13, **Querétaro,** Querétaro 76010. Tel: (42) 16-0202; Fax: (42) 16-8902; in the U.S. and Canada, Tel: (800) HOLIDAY. $136.

▶ **Hostal del Quijote.** P.O. Box F-1893, **San Luis Potosí,** San

Luis Potosí 78090. Tel: (481) 8-1312; Fax: (481) 8-6105. $108.

▶ **Hostería del Fraile.** Calle Sopeña 3, **Guanajuato**, Guanajuato 36000. Tel and Fax: (473) 2-1179. $74.

▶ **Hotel Ambassador.** P.O. Box 1733, **Monterrey**, Nuevo León 64000. Tel: (83) 40-6390; Fax: (83) 45-1984; in the U.S. and Canada, Tel: (800) 228-3000. $177.

▶ **Hotel Everest.** Calle Colón 126, **Ciudad Victoria**, Tamaulipas 87000. Tel: (131) 2-4050; Fax: (131) 2-1443. $62.

▶ **Hotel Monte Verde.** Calle Voluntarios 2, **San Miguel de Allende**, Guanajuato 37700. Tel: (465) 2-1814. $53.

▶ **Hotel Panorama.** Avenida Carranza 315, **San Luis Potosí**, San Luis Potosí 78000. Tel: (481) 2-1777; Fax: (481) 2-5491. $78.

▶ **Hotel Reforma.** Calle Guerrero 822, **Nuevo Laredo**, Tamaulipas 88000. Tel: (87) 12-6250. $43.

▶ **Hotel San Diego.** P.O. Box 8, Jardín de la Unión, **Guanajuato**, Guanajuato 36000. Tel: (473) 2-1300. $62.

▶ **Hotel San Gabriel de Barrera.** Carretera Marfil, **Guanajuato**, Guanajuato 36000. Tel: (473) 2-3980; Fax: (473) 2-7460. $92.

▶ **Hotel Sierra Gorda.** Carretera 85 and Plaza Hidalgo, **Ciudad Victoria**, Tamaulipas 87000. Tel: (131) 2-2280; Fax: (131) 2-9799. $59.

▶ **Hotel Siesta.** Calle Ocampo 559, **Nuevo Laredo**, Tamaulipas 88000. Tel: (871) 2-4737; Fax: (87) 12-4737. $33.

▶ **Hotel Virrey de Mendoza.** Portal de Matamoros 16, **Morelia**, Michoacán 58000. Tel: (451) 2-0633. $83.

▶ **La Mansión Galindo.** P.O. Box 16, Carretera 5, Amealco exit, **San Juan del Río**, Querétaro 76800. Tel: (467) 2-0050; Fax: (467) 2-0100. $185.

▶ **Mesón de Santa Rosa.** Calle Pasteur Sur 17, Plaza de la Independencia, **Querétaro**, Querétaro 76000. Tel: (42) 14-5781; Fax: (42) 12-5522. $108–$139.

▶ **Motel Guanajuato.** P.O. Box 113, Carretera a Dolores Hidalgo, km 2.5, **Guanajuato**, Guanajuato 36000. Tel: (473) 2-0689; Fax: (473) 2-6883. $74.

▶ **Motel Hacienda.** Carretera 57, km 618, **Matehuala**, San Luis Potosí 78700. Tel: (488) 2-0065. $37–$44.

▶ **Motel Oasis.** Carretera 57, km 617, **Matehuala**, San Luis Potosí 78700. Tel: (488) 2-0742. $36.

▶ **Motel Santa Fé.** Glorieta Juárez, **San Luis Potosí**, San Luis Potosí 78090. Tel: (48) 14-4774; Fax: (48) 14-4784. $86.

▶ **Las Palmas.** P.O. Box 73, **Matehuala**, San Luis Potosí 78700. Tel: (488) 2-0001; Fax: (488) 2-1396. $68.

▶ **Paradise.** Carretera 180, **Ciudad Victoria**, Tamaulipas 87000. Tel: (131) 6-8181; Fax: (131) 6-7285. $55.

▶ **Parador San Javier.** Calle Aldama 92, **Guanajuato**, Guanajuato 36000. Tel: (473) 2-0626; Fax: (473) 2-3114. $92.

▶ **El Patio.** Calle Correo 10, **San Miguel de Allende**, Guanajuato 37700. Tel: (465) 2-1647; Fax: (465) 2-3180. $91.

▶ **Posada Don Bruno.** Calle Principal, **Angangueo**, Michoacán 61411. Tel: (725) 8-0026. $39.

▶ **Posada de las Monjas.** Calle Canal 37, **San Miguel de Allende**, Guanajuato 37700. Tel: (465) 2-0171. $51.

▶ **Posada San José.** Calle Manuel Acuña 240, **Saltillo**, Coahuila 25000. Tel: (841) 5-2303. $44.

▶ **Posada Santa Fé.** P.O. Box 191, Jardín de la Unión, **Guanajuato**, Guanajuato 36000. Tel: (473) 2-0084; Fax: (473) 2-4653. $84.

▶ **Posada de la Soledad.** Calle Zaragoza 90, **Morelia**, Michoacán 58000. Tel: (451) 2-1888; Fax: (451) 2-2111. $67.

▶ **Posada Vista Bella.** P.O. Box 135, Calle Galeana, Lomas de Santa María, **Morelia**, Michoacán 58090. Tel: (451) 4-0284; Fax: (451) 4-0284. $57.

▶ **La Puertecita.** Calle Santo Domingo 75, **San Miguel de Allende**, Guanajuato 37700. Tel: (465) 2-2250; Fax: (465) 2-0424. $129–$190.

▶ **Rancho San Cayetano.** P.O. Box 23, **Zitacuaro**, Michoacán 61500. Tel: (725) 3-1926. $46.

▶ **Real de Minas.** P.O. Box 77, Constituyentes Poniente 124, **Querétaro**, Querétaro 76010. Tel: (42) 16-0444; Fax: (41) 16-0662. $102.

▶ **El Río Motel.** Carretera 85, **Nuevo Laredo**, Tamaulipas 88000. Tel: (871) 4-3666; Fax: (871) 5-1232. $70.

▶ **Royal Courts Motor Inn.** Avenida Universidad, **Monterrey**, Nuevo León 66450. Tel and Fax: (837) 6-2017. $93.

▶ **El Señorial.** Guerrero Norte 10A, **Querétaro**, Querétaro 43700. Tel: (42) 14-3700; Fax: (42) 14-1945. $36.

▶ **Villa Jacaranda.** Calle Aldama 53, **San Miguel de Allende**, Guanajuato 37700. Tel: (465) 2-1015 or 2-0811; Fax: (465) 2-0883. $110.

▶ **Villa Montaña.** P.O. Box 233, Calle Galeana, Lomas de Santa María, **Morelia**, Michoacán 58090. Tel: (451) 4-0179; Fax: (451) 5-1423. $118–$195 (includes breakfast).

▶ **Villa Santa Monica.** Calle Baeza 22, **San Miguel de Allende**, Guanajuato 37700. Tel: (465) 2-0451 or 2-0427; Fax: (465) 2-0121. $178.

THE WESTERN HIGHLANDS

GUADALAJARA AND PATZCUARO

By Robert Cummings

Robert Cummings, a resident of Mexico for the past eight years, has written numerous travel articles as well as a novella, and is currently working on a novel.

The sophisticated residents of Mexico City have always looked upon Guadalajara as the overgrown village where their country cousins—friendly folk who strum guitars by day and perform hat dances by candlelight in a land of swaggering cowboys and blushing señoritas—live.

Everyone knows the stereotype is silly, but it persists because it bears a grain of truth. More than most large cities, Guadalajara *is* a collection of villages. There are strong neighborhood loyalties here, a sense of closeness to the parish churches, and, in the midst of modernity, a love of and yearning for the soil. Songs about *mi tierra,* "my land," and *mi ranchita,* "my little ranch," never lack for listeners and often bring a tear to the eye of these transplanted city dwellers. After all, this is the state of Jalisco, and Jalisco means ranches, cattle, and crops. There's a secret rodeo buckaroo lurking inside many a banker and attorney here, one that usually bursts forth as soon as the music starts.

Guadalajara is the chief metropolis of the Western Highlands and the gateway to the mountains that surround it on every side but the east. The grassy ranch country of Jalisco, from which Guadalajara drew its early wealth and cowboy traditions, crinkles into hills just south of the city, ridges that frame Lake Chapala, the largest and most northerly of the highland lakes.

Southeast of Chapala the forested mountains of Michoacán rise sharply, becoming the peaks that cradle Mexico's loveliest lake, Pátzcuaro. It was along these shores that the Tarascan civilization arose eight centuries ago; the area's mountain villages remain Tarascan to this day.

(Far to the west, and a world apart from Lake Pátzcuaro, Jalisco's booming coastal resort of Puerto Vallarta caters to sun worshipers from around the globe. See the Pacific Resorts chapter below for a closer look at it and some of its nearby smaller sister resorts.)

This crescent-shaped region, with spirited Guadalajara at one tip and colorful Pátzcuaro at the other, offers visitors some of Mexico's richest discoveries in colonial history, native crafts and cultures, and urban diversions.

MAJOR INTEREST

Guadalajara
Las Cuatro Plazas
Palacio de Gobierno
Cathedral
Museo Regional de Guadalajara
Teatro Degollado
Orozco murals at Instituto Cultural Cabañas
Mercado Libertad
Barrio de San Francisco
Mariachi music
Nightlife and entertainment
Ceramic centers of Tlaquepaque and Tonalá

Around Guadalajara
Barranca de Oblatos
Tequila
Lago de Chapala area

The Tarascan Country
Scenic beauty
Picturesque town and lake of Pátzcuaro
Tzintzuntzán colonial town and archaeological site
Craft villages around Pátzcuaro
City of Uruapan
Paricutín volcano

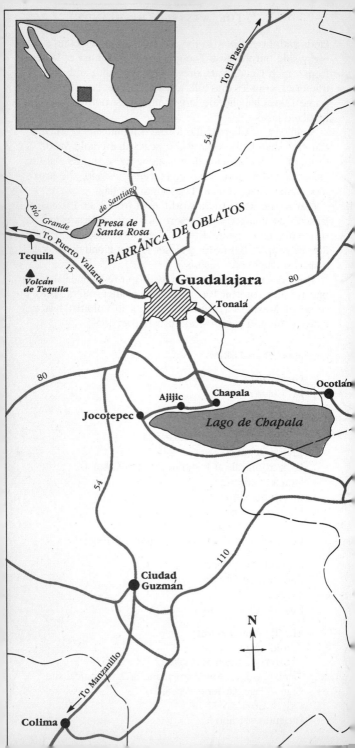

The Western Highlands

| 0 | miles | 25 |
| 0 | kilometers | 40 |

JALISCO

80

León

37

45

GUANAJUATO

Irapuato

To Mexico City

90

La Piedad

15

15

Zamora

MICHOACAN

Zacapu

15

To Capula

Quiroga

37

Lago de Pátzcuaro

Paracho

Janitzio

41

Tzintzúntzan

TZINTZÚNTZAN ZONA ARQUEOLÓGICA

Angahuán

Paricutín

Pátzcuaro

Uruapan

Opepeo

Río Cupatitzio

Santa Clara del Cobre

120

GUADALAJARA

Almost as populous as Chicago, Guadalajara is Mexico's second-largest city. But unless you're caught in rush-hour traffic, it's likely to feel much smaller. Maybe it's because there are no urban canyons, no skyscrapers, and even the moderately tall buildings are few and far apart.

It's true that there are more guitars per city block in Guadalajara than any other city would dream of listening to. And it's also true that despite the encroaching urban pressures and crush, these country cousins really are among the friendliest people in the Mexican Republic. Or perhaps it's just that they're the heartiest. In Jalisco it is sometimes hard to determine where heartiness ends and friendliness begins. The question becomes further confused by courtesy. The *tapatíos,* as the people of Guadalajara are nicknamed, are polite, smiling, and even courtly—insofar as the demands of surviving in the modern world permit.

Their style, however, can be confusing at times. You will be invited cordially, even enthusiastically, to "my house, which is *your* house," but you'll never learn the address. This is no more hypocritical than a friendly backslap at the club; it's merely a manner, a way of making life pleasant and gracious while staying safely uninvolved.

Perhaps *tapatío* cordiality, and the love of country values, is rooted in Guadalajara's unusually stable past. Founded soon after the Conquest on productive, gently rolling land, Guadalajara was bypassed by many of the storms of Mexican history. After some initial atrocities in the 16th century, ranch servitude here, though hardly an enviable condition, involved little of the suffering inflicted on native populations elsewhere in New Spain. The region also escaped the brutality of invasions, the social upheaval, and the violence that much of the country endured. Where other regions were forced to bow to sword and cross, Guadalajara had a chance to cultivate graciousness and romance—and it did so in abundance. Spain was remote, and life here casual.

Not surprisingly, its problems and dislocations have been more recent, a result of growth and industrialization. Guadalajara's major problem has been trying to reconcile its own explosive growth with its slow-paced, gracious traditions. Sometimes it manages to succeed; often it doesn't. In the spring of 1992 such a failure resulted in tragedy. Slipshod construction and maintenance by Pemex, the national petroleum company, caused a series of devastating blasts in a downtown residential area. The number of dead was large but indeterminate, perhaps 400. Some officials were arrested while others were expelled from office as the city struggled to rebuild and cope better with the hazards of industrialization.

For all that, Guadalajara remains a pleasant, livable, charmingly robust city.

Exploring Downtown

LAS CUATRO PLAZAS

The Four Plazas, which surround the cathedral on all sides, are at the heart of downtown Guadalajara. Realizing it must yield to modernization, the city has nevertheless made major efforts to preserve the traditional grace and dignity of its historic center. The large, impressive area set aside as a result occupies about a dozen city blocks.

Plaza de Armas and Palacio de Gobierno

A good place to start exploring is the Plaza de Armas, on the south side of the cathedral at the corner of Morelos and Avenida 16 de Septiembre. This is a small, formal park where nothing distracts from the ornate bandstand, forged in Paris at the turn of the century and today a fanciful reminder of the Art Nouveau style that Mexican travellers brought back from France. Concerts are held here every Thursday and Sunday evening, and it is truly a pleasant place to linger on a wrought-iron bench enjoying the almost perpetual spring of Guadalajara while studying the domes, towers, and balustrades of the cathedral.

On the east side of the plaza stands the stolid Government Palace, its 18th-century Baroque façade unusually severe. Inside is a dramatic mural by native son José Clemente Orozco that enfolds the viewer like a net. The subject is Father Hidalgo's abolition of slavery in Mexico, an act that was proclaimed from this very building.

The Cathedral

The **Plaza de los Laureles**, which fronts the cathedral to the west, takes its name not name from its laurel trees, but rather for the wreaths reserved for Mexico's heroes. Its fountain, bubbling in the sunlight, adds a touch of life to this public space of stone. The cathedral seems to stare at the plaza with its two big round windows. An ungainly building, it is said to embrace no fewer than 14 distinct styles in the hash of its architecture. But *tapatíos,* having grown up with it, love it and proudly show it off to visitors. Actually, the

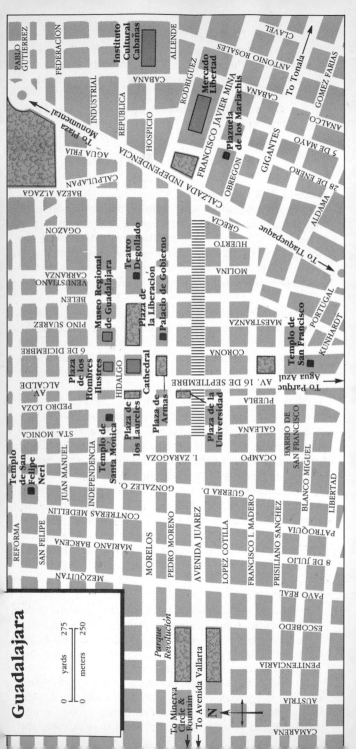

ponderous structure is seen to best advantage from Avenida Juárez at night, when the yellow lights on its towers impart a magic glow. Inside are a number of good paintings, especially *The Assumption of the Virgin* by Bartolomé Esteban Murillo, which hangs near the entrance to the sacristy.

In front of the cathedral you can hire a horse and carriage for $12 an hour or $23 for the standard tour of the neighborhood.

Museo Regional de Guadalajara

North of the cathedral a Doric rotunda graces the shady **Plaza de los Hombres Ilustres**. One block east, housed in a dignified 18th-century seminary building, is the Regional Museum. The highlights of the collection—and worth careful study—are the pre-Columbian figurines from the Western Highlands region. Fashioned by anonymous village sculptors, many are powerful representations of women at once fierce and compassionate; the animal figurines are also touched with genius. The second floor contains a collection of European paintings (mostly Spanish) assembled from the 19th-century collections of rich *tapatíos*. While most are not masterpieces, they are skillful and revealing of local tastes of the era. The museum is open daily except Mondays, 9:00 A.M. to 2:00 P.M.

Teatro Degollado

When you're ready to leave the museum, turn left and walk east along the **Plaza de la Liberación** toward the imposing 19th-century Teatro Degollado, another source of local pride. Inside are murals inspired by Dante's *Divine Comedy,* gleaming chandeliers, and a profusion of gold leaf. The theater is the home of the **Guadalajara Symphony Orchestra** and the **Ballet Folklórico** of the university. The orchestra is well worth hearing, the ballet a blaze of color. The dancers perform every Sunday at 10:00 A.M. except during Christmas and Easter weeks.

Orozco Murals

Continue strolling east through the long, narrow **Plaza Tapatía**, a model urban mall adorned with fountains and sculpture. The long thoroughfare is also a fitting buildup to perhaps the city's greatest treasure, the **Instituto Cultural Cabañas**, also called the Hospicio Cabañas.

Erected in 1801 as an orphanage, the building was the design of the talented Spanish architect-sculptor Manuel Tolsá, who was imported to head Mexico's first formal academy of the arts. While it's a fine and interesting building, no one pays much attention to it; the murals inside are what make it celebrated.

Working with a dark palette, chiefly grays and blacks befitting the atmosphere of its old chapel, José Clemente Orozco painted the frescoes inside in 1938 and 1939. Using details sparingly—a few thrusting lines portray a war horse, arrogant and apocalyptic, or what must be the sharpest barbed wire in the world, fangs of metal—Orozco managed to create a powerful protest against war and violence. The centerpiece of this breathtaking vision is his *Man of Fire,* painted on the interior of the dome high above. To be properly appreciated it should be viewed as the artist saw it. For this purpose, the institute provides benches so that visitors can lie down and gaze straight up. You needn't feel hesitant about this, but in case you do, the institute also provides mirrors; by all means use both methods. Either way, you'll feel as if you've come face-to-face with the gates to the inferno.

If you have time to see only one thing in Guadalajara, it should be this chapel.

MARKETS AND MARIACHIS

Just south of the Instituto Cultural Cabañas, facing Calzada Independencia, sprawls the **Mercado Libertad** (Liberty Market)—actually a complex of many markets of many types. Although no one should miss it entirely, don't expect too much.

Visitors to the market should search out its color and life rather than merchandise. While there are displays of local weaving, glass, and leather goods, most are not first rate, examining the goods is frowned upon, and the bargaining that goes on could serve as an example to sharks. (One exception is **Artesanías Méxicanos**, Locales 313–316 in the main building, with leather work of good quality and a few other items.) Serious buyers will do better elsewhere; serious hagglers for whom the hunt is worth more than the prize will think they've found paradise.

Plazuela de los Mariachis

At the southern end of the market is the old church of San Juan de Dios and, nearby, the famous "Mariachi Square." Here, at the many sidewalk cafés, customers may order drinks, food, and their favorite song. Day and night the musicians stroll among the tables or linger on the sidelines waiting to be hired. There is no charge for listening to what others have requested, but if you decide to become a patron yourself, ask the price in advance (this is not ordinarily a bargaining situation).

Mariachis are said to have originated in Guadalajara, and purists claim the city still has the best. Although they started out as string groups, featuring violins and a variety of guitars, these days their hallmark is brass. A traditional performance begins with a *sinfonía,* a gay little tune unconnected to the melody that will follow; this serves as an introduction, as well as the signature of that particular band. What follows is usually lusty and exuberant music, with hints of sadness and disappointment. While almost all mariachi musicians are accomplished instrumentalists, most usually are not talented vocalists. As a consequence, the mariachi tone is a little harsh, a little hoarse, and decidedly rough and masculine. The *gritos,* shouts often done in falsetto, are essential to a good performance.

Mariachi music is composed for streets, squares, and spacious patios. Open air is as characteristic of the performance as the mariachis' flamboyant adaptation of cowboy clothing. Customers are often part of the act, joining in or even performing solo, using the hired band as accompaniment. It's not unusual for a host, or even more frequently a guest, to leave a private party, drive to the square, and bring back a carload of mariachis to play for an hour—or a night.

Mariachi music is heard all over Guadalajara. Aside from the plaza, the best bands can be heard in nearby Tlaquepaque in the zócalo (El Parián) and at major Guadalajara hotels. (The nightclub groups tend to sweeten their tone.)

BARRIO DE SAN FRANCISCO

The Barrio de San Francisco, a corner of the downtown area five blocks south of the Plaza de Armas via Avenida 16 de Septiembre, is notable for two contrasting examples of ecclesiastical architecture, as well as for an old-fashioned garden that is both shady and welcoming.

The **Templo de San Francisco**, with a handsome Baroque façade that is at once ornate yet highly controlled, successfully combines Mexican Plateresque style with Flemish design elements. The twisting Salomonic columns are derived from the famous papal pillars at St. Peter's in Rome. The church, although remodeled in 1693, has stood here since 1554.

A modern street now separates the church from a smaller structure, the **Capilla de Nuestra Señora de Aranzazú** (Chapel of Our Lady of Aranzazú), to which it was once connected. The main altar and right secondary altar of the former chapel are sunbursts of Rococo gold leaf, fantastic and, in their very Mexican way, masterpieces of extravagance. The two churches, as well as half a dozen other structures now vanished, were part of a huge convent complex destroyed by the government's anti-clerical policies in the 1920s.

SPORTS AND SPECTACLES

The Guadalajara bullring, or **Plaza Monumental**, is famed for its great international stars and dazzling pageantry in the winter season. In warm Guadalajara, where early afternoon skies are almost always clear, it is important to get a seat in the shade, however. The bullfights are held on Sundays in the ring just off Calzada Independencia; take any "Independencia" bus northbound and tell the driver you want to get off at the Plaza de Toros.

During the summer the Sunday thrills are at the **charreada**, Mexico's version of a rodeo, where the beauty of the costumes and horses is almost as important as the skill of the *charros.* The stadium is located south of the downtown area near Guadalajara's **Parque Agua Azul.** The park, five minutes by taxi from the city's historic center, or 15 minutes on the Avenida 16 de Septiembre bus, is a favorite haunt of *tapatios,* and counts a bird sanctuary and miniature train ride among its diversions.

Cockfighting is a national passion, often an occasion for reckless betting, and not always to the taste of visitors. Matches are held on Sundays at noon and again at 7:30 P.M., with special fights on holidays. The Plaza de Gallos, site of these furious combats, is on Calzada de la Revolución, 1½ km (1 mile) past the Technological Institute. Take any bus marked "Tlaquepaque."

STAYING IN GUADALÁJARA

With beveled glass windows, lovely old paintings, well-chosen handwoven fabrics, the best local ceramics, and fresh flowers in every room, the elegantly colonial ▶ **Quinta Real Guadalajara** is the city's finest luxury hotel. In fact, presidents have actually stayed in its presidential suite. All this attention to detail and personalized service does not come cheaply, however. The Quinta Real is located at the corner of Avenida México and Boulevard López Mateos, about ten minutes west of the center of town.

The ▶ **Fiesta Americana Guadalajara**, one of the most luxurious and modern hotels in Mexico, has helicopter service from the airport to the roof, glass elevators, panoramic views of Guadalajara from every room, as well as a nightclub and a lively bar with music. Mexican businessmen like to stay here as much for the amenities as for the animated cocktail lounge. The Fiesta Americana is located on Minerva Circle, about 20 minutes west of the city center, but *colectivos* run frequently to the downtown area. (The hotel's fine restaurants are discussed below.)

The ▶ **Holiday Inn Guadalajara**, a little farther out at the Plaza del Sol, west of Minerva Circle, is a modern and attractive hotel complex with gardens, lighted tennis courts, a sauna and whirlpool, and all the other amenities of a first-rate operation. The music in the hotel's nightclub is an added bonus.

Popular with families and Mexicans travelling on business, the ▶ **Hotel Malibu**, a bit north of Minerva Circle, is a jumble of annexes and courtyards. Like its physical plant, the Malibu's furnishings seem to have been assembled at random by a couple of generations of managers, but the rooms are ample and have all the essentials.

Unfortunately, attractive hotels in the downtown area are the exception. The colonial-style ▶ **Hotel Francés**, behind the Government Palace at Maestranza 35, is the most charming, its cocktail lounge a cheerful gathering place offering music and an international flavor. Some of the inside rooms overlook air shafts, but guests who are lucky enough to get a room facing the street wax enthusiastic about the Francés. The rates are reasonable, and parking in a public establishment two blocks away is provided. The restaurant **El Molino Rojo**, on the first floor, is good for breakfast or lunch, but usually deserted in the evening.

The ▶ **Hotel de Mendoza**, centrally located a block northeast of the Teatro Degollado on tranquil Avenida Venustiano Carranza, offers airy, comfortable rooms and provincial decor with a colonial touch. While it is slightly more expensive than the Francés, the space and ventilation are better.

Situated on a hilltop overlooking Guadalajara, 6 km (3½ miles) south of the city on the road to Chapala, is ▶ **El Tapatío**. Winding up its third year of operation under new management, this high-tech health spa facility was built by the developers of the well-known La Jolla spa outside San Diego. The management claims that its staff outnumbers guests by two to one, which perhaps explains the astonishing dedication to massaging, exercising, and pampering that goes on amid the luxurious surroundings here. Packages are designed for week-long stays and bear price tags that reflect the personalized service guests receive.

DINING AND NIGHTLIFE
IN GUADALAJARA

Typically, Jalisco fare is ranch fare—hearty, rather plain, with the emphasis on meat and fowl. In fact, local cooks seem to have a patronizing attitude toward vegetables. An à la carte order in the typical Jalisco restaurant is apt to be a slab of meat, some tortillas, chile sauce, and nothing else.

Cabrito (roast kid) is a regional specialty, as is *birria,* a hearty dish with chunks of goat, pork, or mutton, and sometimes all three in combination. It is best barbecued, although most Guadalajara restaurants steam it. On the other hand, *carnitas* (chunks of roast pork), a staple in Mexico, are reputed to be superior here. Another local favorite is *pozole,* half soup and half stew, made with hominy and pork and topped with onions, lettuce, and radish slices.

For Mexican cuisine at its absolute best try **La Hacienda**, a smart and sophisticated restaurant in the Fiesta Americana Guadalajara (Tel: 36/25-3434). Its serious rival in this field is **Río Viejo**, a handsome Guadalajara town house romantically furnished with antiques at Avenida de las Américas 302, a few blocks north of Avenida Vallarta in midtown (Tel: 36/16-5321). With less atmosphere and lower prices, **Los Otates**, Avenida de las Américas 28, at the corner of Morelos, serves traditional Mexican food with few surprises (Tel: 36/15-0481).

Most fine restaurants in Guadalajara pride themselves on their European or "international" dishes. The two most elegant restaurants in town are French: **Lafayette** in the Hotel Camino Real, Avenida Vallarta 5005, near the Malibu, and **Place de la Concorde**, in the Fiesta Americana. There is a dress code at both. For reservations at Lafayette, Tel: (36) 21-7217; at Place de la Concorde, Tel: (36) 25-3434.

Less expensive **La Fuente** has a refined atmosphere, tables set with crystal and linen, and an international menu. A bubbling fountain serves as the centerpiece for this town house located in a pleasant neighborhood at Avenida Plan de San Luis 1899. You can get there by heading north from Minerva Circle on López Mateos and turning right at the Columbus Fountain. Jacket and tie are suggested for men; Tel: (36) 24-7946.

La Copa de Leche, in the center of town at Juárez 414, was for years considered the city's finest restaurant. It has since been surpassed by others but remains a traditional standby. Good Mexican food and other dishes are served on the second floor. There's a different menu downstairs, mostly seafood and steaks, the former better than the latter. Tel: (36) 14-5347.

Luscherly, at General San Martín 525 in a residential neighborhood off Niños Héroes (a main thoroughfare in the west-central part of town), has a Swiss chef who specializes in Continental cuisine, including snails and fondues. The decor is almost as impressive as the food: The intimate setting makes you feel as if you are dining in the home of a friend with impeccable taste. Reservations are a must; Tel: (36) 52-0509.

For nighttime entertainment and perhaps a taste of the region's famed tequila, the two most popular places are **El Parián**, the courtyard in the main square in Tlaquepaque (see below), and the **Plazuela de los Mariachis** near the Liberty Market. Both are authentic rather than fancy.

All the major hotels have bars with entertainment. The best show with traditional music (and, of course, a hat dance) is at the **Holiday Inn**. Its two rivals are **El Pueblito Cantina**, in the Hotel Hyatt Regency across from the Plaza del Sol on the southwest edge of the city; and **La Pergola**, in the Carlton Hotel, near Parque Agua Azul, a short distance south of the downtown area.

Atop the Hotel de Mendoza, in the center of town at Venustiano Carranza 16, you'll find the welcoming **El Compañario**, which offers twinkling panoramic views of Guadalajara and dancing after 9:00 P.M. Only couples and mixed parties are admitted, however.

Copenhagen is a cheerful spot to listen to a good jazz trio from 9:00 P.M. on. You can also dine here (paella is the house specialty), but a meal is not mandatory. You'll find Copenhagen in the center of town off Parque Revolución at Marcos Castellanos 140, near the university.

The **Hotel Francés** bar at Maestranza 35, one block south of Avenida Juárez, is inviting for its conversation, background music, and convivial atmosphere. The "disco" next door is actually a modest nightclub with live music for dancing or just plain listening.

SHOPPING IN GUADALAJARA

To find a wide range of crafts at fair prices, you should first visit the **Casa de las Artesanías de Jalisco**, a state museum and gallery devoted to the popular arts. Located in the Parque Agua Azul, at the southern end of Calzada Independencia, it offers a range of work and provides a basis for comparison.

In addition to the previously mentioned Artesanías Méxicanos in the Liberty Market, you might want to stop in at **El Charro**, Avenida Juárez 148, which has corralled a wild and woolly collection of cowboy and western clothes, from tooled boots to sombreros that could serve as parachutes. A few of the designs are outrageous, and the workmanship is excellent.

Good silversmithing, including jewelry, plates, trays, and ornaments, can be found at **Plata Mex**, Independencia 910.

El Instituto de la Artesanía Jalisciense, 10 to 15 minutes north of the central plaza area at Calle Alcade 1221, offers a better-than-average selection of clothing, glass, ceramics, and indigenous art.

Finally, **Calle Esteban Alatorre**, which begins at Calzada Independencia north of the Plaza Tapatía, is the center of a commercial neighborhood devoted to footwear of every size and shape, from hand-tooled cowboy boots to the latest designer fashions.

Tequila on Tap

An interesting demonstration of the tequila distilling process can be seen in Guadalajara at the big **Tequila Sauza bottling plant**, Avenida Vallarta 3273. Tours are conducted daily from 10:00 A.M. until 2:00 P.M., with courtesy samplings of the deliciously piquant drink offered to visitors. If you want to buy tequila to take home with you, remember that the smoothest varieties are those labeled "añejo" or "añejado" (aged).

To get to the Sauza plant, take the "Parque Vial" or "Plaza del Sol" bus from the Plaza de la Universidad to the far (west) side of Minerva Circle. Then walk a few blocks farther west on Vallarta. Because taxis are not expensive, however, it's probably more convenient to hail one westbound on Juárez and tell the driver you want to go to Tequila Sauza. For the return trip, taxis are easy to find outside the bottling plant or near Minerva Circle. (The town of Tequila, 57 km/35 miles from Guadalajara, is discussed below.)

Tlaquepaque and Tonalá

San Pedro Tlaquepaque (tlah-keh-PAH-keh) is no longer a separate town but a continuation of the city to the southeast. Once famed as a pottery village, much of it has been turned into a psycho-ceramic nightmare heaped with crimes against taste committed in clay. Three-fourths of the stuff is dime-store junk, both gaudy and fragile, with glazes that threaten lead poisoning. In the middle of this mess you can find some good pieces, but it requires perseverance.

Dark, unglazed pottery, thought of as a Oaxacan specialty,

is equally native to Tlaquepaque, and many pieces merit consideration. Good work is never glazed; the high sheen comes from a smothering process done in the firing: the darker and glossier the better. Shops and galleries in the pedestrian mall on Calzada Independencia have much the best offerings, and there's some imaginative work in metal and paper to be found here as well. The "antiques" on sale are also attractive, although usually manufactured last week. The **Ken Edwards** shop, Madero 75, presents the most appealing, whimsical earthenware in town.

At **Casa Canela**, Calzada Independencia 258, you'll find Talavera and Delft-inspired vases of remarkable quality—surrounded, of course, by garish ceramic souvenirs. The glassware is better than much of the pottery, and local glassblowers achieve some beautiful and rare shades of red. Casa Canela has some fine examples, in addition to crystal balls in delicate hues for gazing.

Some of the most attractive glass can be found at **La Rosa de Cristal**, Calzada Independencia 232, where you can also observe the fascinating, eerie world of glassblowing.

The **Museo Regional de la Cerámica**, Independencia 237, will give you an idea of what you wish you could find along the streets outside. Across the street is the gallery **Sergio Bustamante**, with sculptures in various materials, much of it imaginative. Bustamante, a native son of Tlaquepaque, now has shops throughout Mexico and is expanding into the States as well.

Tlaquepaque buses, so marked, run along Calzada Independencia with some frequency. By car, head south on Calzada Independencia Sur and turn left on Calzada Revolución. At the traffic circle keep to the left of the gasoline station and stay on Revolución. You'll see signs for Tlaquepaque ahead. A right turn takes you to the central plaza, El Parián.

Tonalá

Tonalá, a ten-minute drive south of Tlaquepaque, has managed to keep its integrity. Maybe it's because the town actually makes things rather than just selling them. Stoneware is especially good here, thanks to a recent tradition established by U.S. designers Ken Edwards (see above for his Tlaquepaque shop) and **Jorge Wilmot**. Wilmot's pieces, which are much more durable than the many imitations, are stamped with a "W." His studio is located at Morelos 80, not far from the church.

The **Bazaar El Caracol** boutique, Madero 19, specializes in cotton clothing and also offers metal work and archaeological reproductions.

Thursday and Sunday are market days in Tonalá, with displays of pottery overflowing the town square and filling the surrounding streets.

Buses to Tonalá run along Calzada Independencia and are clearly labeled. To get there by car, head east on Carretera los Altos and take the "Zapotlanejo Libre" exit.

AROUND GUADALAJARA

Barranca de Oblatos

The Barranca de Oblatos (*barranca* means "canyon") is an impressive 2,000-foot slash in the earth that has been cut by two rivers over the ages. In addition to its sheer beauty, it's interesting for the climatological changes that occur as the gorge deepens, with the heat and humidity becoming positively tropical by the time you reach the bottom. Fruits such as papayas flourish in the canyon, and are harvested for the markets back in Guadalajara. For those interested in taking the journey, a cable car makes the descent to the bottom and back.

The "Barranca" bus runs north along Calzada Independencia Norte to the canyon rim and the cable-car departure point. If you're driving, follow Independencia 11 km (7 miles) north until you reach the canyon (it's actually northeast but is marked "north"). Taxis, which are not expensive, are another option and can be hailed on Independencia; they're also available at the canyon for the return trip.

Tequila

The town for which the famous liquor is named lies 57 km (35 miles) northwest of Guadalajara. It is a typical country town with dusty streets, a slow pace, and friendly people, which may appeal to travellers looking for authenticity. Most, however, will find it does not warrant a special trip unless they're already passing that way on Highway 15, the coastal route that heads north to the Arizona border. In that case, it is worth a stop to tour one of the distilleries, which are usually open to the public until 2:00 P.M.

Tours can be arranged ahead of time through travel agencies in major Guadalajara hotels. A tour takes about half a day and usually includes lunch; the overview of the tequila-making process is more complete than that given drop-in visitors.

Lago de Chapala

It is an easy trip from Guadalajara—about an hour south by car or bus (see the Getting Around section below)—to Mexico's largest lake and its shoreline villages. The excursion merits a visit for those with the time, but be sure to explore Guadalajara first. The badly polluted lake, which is drying up at an alarming rate, is too dirty for swimming, almost useless for boating, and virtually devoid of fish. Only the magnificent views survive.

The town of **Chapala** has some attractive turn-of-the-century houses fronting the lake, worth a 30-minute walk or so. The villages farther west, Ajijic (ah-hee-HEEK) and Jocotepec, lost much of their innocence—and most of their charm—a generation ago, and now are advertised as places for "bargain retirement" and "bargain winter retreats." Actually, the bargains vanished at about the same time as the Chapala whitefish. Rentals and hotels here are expensive, and the restaurants and stores usually overpriced.

As almost everyone knows, a large colony of U.S. and Canadian retirees lives along the lake, enjoying the climate, the views, and one another's company. Over the years they've also established such things as an enterprising English-language community theater, a weekly journal, and a chili cookoff.

In Chapala the traditional place for a drink or lunch overlooking the lake is the **Beer Garden**, at the foot of the main street; it's the roofed terrace on the right as you approach the head of the pier. The view and drinks are fine, the food only so-so.

For a meal or even an overnight stay in the area the best choice by far is ▶ **La Nueva Posada**, in the dusty village of Ajijic, about a ten-minute drive west along the lake from Chapala. The bar and dining room offer pleasant views of the lake, and the guest rooms have a rustic charm.

Buses are reputed to run along the lakeside highway. Their reliability may be gauged by the large number of hitchhikers, both Mexican and foreign, you'll see thumbing their way between the villages.

PATZCUARO AND THE TARASCAN COUNTRY

The lakeside town of Pátzcuaro (PAHTZ-kwah-ro), situated just west of Morelia (see the Colonial Heartland chapter) about halfway between Mexico City and Guadalajara, is the spiritual capital of the Western Highlands region, and quite possibly Mexico's most purely Indian city. A city of almost 60,000 (at times it seems much smaller), it is, in the minds of many travellers, the heart of the most scenic corner of Mexico. For such people no other region equals Pátzcuaro and its environs for alpine beauty, and only the Mayan settlements in the southeastern part of the country rival it for exoticness. The Tarascan people themselves, often under even greater pressure to change than the Maya, have been almost as successful in preserving their traditional ways, their language, and their artistic heritage.

The Tarascans (also known as the Purépecha) are an ancient people. According to legend they were one of the tribes that migrated into the region with the Aztecs. When they paused at Lago de Pátzcuaro, so the legend goes, the Tarascans went into the water to bathe. The Aztecs seized the opportunity to abscond with the Tarascans' clothes, and so began the undying enmity between the two peoples. In time, gods, speaking through hummingbirds, commanded the Tarascans to build a city on the shore of the lake. It was a thriving center by the time the Spanish arrived, and somehow managed to survive the atrocities committed by the conquistadors—horrors that are remembered by the Tarascans to this day.

There is one archaeological zone of medium interest in the region, Tzintzuntzán, as well as some smaller cities. Volcano buffs may want to visit the desolate world left behind by the eruption of Paricutín, Mexico's youngest volcano. For the excursion minded, the semitropical city of Uruapan is less than an hour's drive away.

Some travellers also use Pátzcuaro as a base for visiting Morelia, a short journey to the east, preferring the lakeside town's serenity and lower prices to the bustle of the city.

Pátzcuaro is in high country, located at an elevation of 7,000 feet; a warm sweater is a necessity, as will be a windbreaker on many occasions.

Pátzcuaro Town

Pátzcuaro rambles down the slopes of several hills toward the big lake of the same name. Its steep red-tiled roofs jut out over carved beams, lending it a slightly Oriental atmosphere, while its cobblestone streets lead to the two plazas around which the life of the town revolves.

The **Plaza Chica** (Little Plaza) is the first one you see on arrival; it is officially named the Plaza Gertrudis Bocanegra, after a local heroine of the War of Independence. The municipal market, which has some good handicrafts alongside the fruits and vegetables, starts at the square's southwest corner. Like Indian markets throughout Mexico, it is commercial, bustling with life, rundown, and colorful. Facing it on the north is a 16th-century Augustinian church that now houses the drafty **Biblioteca Pública**. Inside you'll find a dramatic fresco depicting the region's history painted by Juan O'Gorman, one of Mexico's leading muralists in the middle decades of this century.

A block to the south lies the **Plaza Grande**, known formally as the Plaza Vasco de Quiroga. This spacious square serves as the community's outdoor living room, a place where towering ash trees at least a century old provide dappled shade as well as a stately reminder of the forests at the town's edge. There's also a sense here that the town is on its best behavior; all is quietly Tarascan, and the sidewalk cafés are pleasant rather than lively.

The Weekly Market

Friday is market day. Early in the morning Indians from the surrounding countryside pour into town to sell and buy. They walk, come by canoe, or lead burros loaded down with pottery, lacquerware, cloth, carved wood, and hammered metal. Many of the women wear the traditional skirt made of yard upon yard of homespun wool, a garment that can weigh as much as 30 pounds. Pleated accordion style, the skirts are gathered in back and held by a belt so that they spread outward like a fan. Their shawls, or *rebozos,* are often distinctive to a particular village. Women from the town of Paracho, for instance, favor a scarf with a brilliant fringe designed to resemble the plumage of a hummingbird.

The serape, carried folded during the day, is a masculine item. Serapes tend to be dark in Pátzcuaro, coarse in texture, and relieved by simple designs in red. Male fiesta wear, which you probably won't see at the market, is usually an intricately embroidered shirt complemented by a hat decked out with gay ribbons.

Tarascan jewelry is also handmade, usually out of hammered silver fashioned into hollow globes and a variety of other shapes; various shades of crimson beads made of lacquered wood are popular as well.

The Cathedral

A short walk uphill from the two squares and market is a spacious open area that was the town center centuries ago. In 1540 the Pope decreed that a cathedral be built in

Pátzcuaro, and grandiose plans were drawn up. Only a portion of the nave was erected, however, before a terrible earthquake struck the town, damaging the new structure. The bishop of Michoacán, alarmed by this turn of events, decided to move his see to Valladolid (now Morelia). Today, the cathedral, known as the **Basílica de Nuestra Señora de la Salud** (Our Lady of Health), remains standing as a relic of that bygone age, and still serves the local community. It also houses a revered image of the Virgin made out of corn paste. A bit farther to the south is the **Templo de la Compañía**, another church built in the 1540s.

Crafts on Display and for Sale

The **Museo de Artes Populares**, near La Compañía, was originally built in the 16th century as a Jesuit seminary. Today the museum inside is small but delightful, and boasts an antique kitchen, exquisite crafts, and a gracious patio. Open daily except Mondays, 9:00 A.M. to 7:00 P.M.

La Casa de los Once Patios (House of Eleven Patios), half a block east of the plaza fronting the cathedral, was once a Dominican convent and is now a hive of crafts workshops, studios, and salesrooms. The sheer volume of work on display—including lacquerware, woven goods, pottery, woodcarving, embroidery, lace, and metalwork (especially copper)—makes it worth a visit.

A *mirador* (lookout) on the shoulder of **El Estribo**, the extinct volcano that walls off the town to the south, offers spectacular views of the lake and its seven islands. To get there, follow the cobblestone road that twists sharply upward from the Plaza Grande for a distance of about 4 km (2½ miles); it ends at a small park, a nice spot for a picnic.

STAYING IN PATZCUARO

There are no deluxe hotels in Pátzcuaro, but there are several good places to choose from. The fanciest by far is the ▶ **Posada de Don Vasco**, a motor inn on the edge of town about 2 km (1¼ miles) north on Avenida de las Américas. It has a tennis court, cocktail lounge, what little nightlife the town offers, and a bowling alley (separate charge). As the most modern place in town, it is also the most expensive.

▶ **El Mesón del Gallo**, in the center of town adjacent to the Plaza Grande, is a smaller operation with a little pool and garden area. One drawback: The rooms can be cold in the winter.

The rooms of the cheerful ▶ **Hotel Los Escudos**, also on the main plaza, are not large, but all have fireplaces.

Easily the most charming of the local inns, the ▶ **Posada de la Basílica**, at Arciega 6 facing the cathedral plaza, is at once rustic and homey, with fireplaces and a big patio that lets in the winter sunshine. The management is similarly helpful and friendly.

DINING IN PATZCUARO

Whitefish, delicate and flaky, is the specialty here; ask for the *pescado blanco*. Trout (*trucha*) is always fresh. The *sopa Tarasca,* rich and spicy but not peppery, makes an excellent first course.

Local restaurants, almost all of them located in hotels or inns, tend to be small, adequate, and pleasant if not special. Service can be casual.

Los Escudos (454/2-1290), the dining room in the hotel of the same name, is satisfactory, as is its neighbor, **El Patio,** (454/2-0484), in the same category and also inexpensive.

The restaurant in the **Posada de la Basílica** (454/2-1108) offers a good breakfast and lunch as well as romantic views of the town—an almost Oriental panorama of steep tile roofs with quaintly upturned corners. A meal here will taste twice as good at a window table.

The restaurant in the **Don Vasco** (454/2-0227) is more elaborate than other dining rooms in Pátzcuaro—not because it offers better food, just a more attractive room. Traditional entertainment is presented twice a week, including the famous Tarascan Dance of the Old Men.

Lago de Pátzcuaro

This beautiful mountain lake is about 12 miles long from north to south, its irregular shoreline dotted with Tarascan villages. The scenery is made even more interesting by the islands that break the lake's surface.

The largest and most famous of these is **Janitzio,** easily identifiable by the colossal statue of patriot José María Morelos (who deserved something better than this ungainly stone heap) crowning its summit. The island itself is the favorite destination for launches leaving regularly from the Pátzcuaro pier. The boat trip is lovely, the destination dubious. Nowadays, Janitzio is utterly commercialized, one tawdry shop after another, their ranks broken only by risky eateries. The island was once justly famed for its annual Day of the Dead celebration on November 2, but it is now entirely a tourist event and a crush; worse than spoiled, it has become offensive.

Likewise, the colorful fishermen with "butterfly nets" who were once emblematic of the region have all but vanished, except for arranged appearances in front of tour groups.

Tzintzuntzán

On the other hand, the drive north on Highway 41 along the eastern shore of the lake is still a pretty trip. Tzintzuntzán (pronounced tsin-soon-SAHN, Tarascan for "place of the hummingbirds"), 21 km (13 miles) from Pátzcuaro, was once the capital of the ancient Purépecha people, ancestors of the Tarascans, who settled in Michoacán in the 12th century. When the Spanish arrived they estimated the population at 40,000—most of whom were soon liquidated or scattered.

Today the main points of interest are clustered around the southern entrance to the town.

Templo de San Francisco
The 16th-century church of San Francisco, mellow and splendid, was once the headquarters of Bishop Vasco de Quiroga, the most brilliant and sympathetic figure to emerge in New Spain in the decades immediately following the Conquest. After an outstanding career as a lawyer in the colony, a career that attracted the attention of Charles V, Don Vasco was chosen to mitigate the sufferings that recently had been inflicted upon the Tarascans. In order to employ the power of the Church in his task, Don Vasco took holy orders at a time when most men are ready to retire. He was 68 and a bishop by the time he arrived in Tzintzuntzán, and he quickly set about creating (or perhaps reorganizing) a communal and quite utopian society. As a result of his humane efforts, the bishop is still remembered as *Tata,* or "Father," by the people of the region.

Upon entering the huge atrium of the church you are immediately confronted by a reminder of the bishop— gnarled and venerable olive trees, planted by Don Vasco despite laws forbidding native production of olives. Also around the atrium are a number of small outdoor shrines, an echo of the long-ago times when the Tarascan people would purify themselves before entering their temples. The façade of the church is richly Plateresque, a beautiful example of the early handling of European themes by native artists.

Adjoining the churchyard is the studio of Luis Mandel Morales, an outstanding potter. His **Taller Alta Temperatura**, a ceramics workshop, is remarkable, if a bit hard to find. One of the small boys who frequent the church grounds will be happy to guide you to it for a tip.

Tzintzuntzán Zona Arqueológica

On the other side of the highway rise the heights that are now protected as the Tzintzuntzán archaeological zone. In 1500 the Purépecha people moved their capital from the vicinity of Pátzcuaro to Tzintzuntzán. Some construction at the site dates from this era, although much of it may be 200 years older. The zone is sometimes referred to as *las yácatas,* a Purépecha term for the five huge platforms that give the site its unique character. Unlike any other Meso-american temple bases, they are T-shaped, with short, rounded stems. The *yácatas,* which rise 40 feet above a cramped paved plaza, functioned as a sort of acropolis in the decades before the Spanish conquest.

The formidable hill with its massive structures proved no barrier to the Spanish invaders, however, for the inhabitants, like the Aztecs a few years earlier, were demoralized by astrological predictions and offered little resistance. Their last king, Tangaxoan, was strangled before the eyes of his terrified subjects, and so many women were raped or forced into concubinage that the Purépecha began to call the Span-iards "sons-in-law," *tarascue,* either ironically or as a sop to their own battered pride. The Spaniards, in linguistic confu-sion, thought *tarascue* was the name of the people they had just conquered—hence the still slightly opprobrious term "Tarascan."

Though the intervening years have not been kind to this "Place of the Hummingbirds," the temple platforms remain an impressive sight, the views of the surrounding country-side even more so. The village of Tzintzuntzán itself is not attractive, but displays of the inexpensive local pottery and ingenious crafts made from straw are worth examining.

Quiroga, a few minutes' drive to the north, is of interest primarily for its main-street shops, which feature the town's fine lacquerware and woven furniture.

Craft Villages

Villa Escalante, more commonly called **Santa Clara del Cobre**, is located 16 km (10 miles) south of Pátzcuaro. Bishop Quiroga introduced the art of coppersmithing to the region in the mid-16th century, and Santa Clara has thrived on it ever since. Here you'll find copper in every imaginable shape and form. There's also a little museum in town with prize-winning examples of the local specialty.

On the road to Santa Clara sits **Opepeo**, home to many skilled wood-carvers and furniture makers.

Capula, a 40-minute drive north and east of Pátzcuaro, is, like Tzintzuntzán, not an especially pretty village, but it does produce the most imaginative pottery in the region. To get there take Highway 15, which connects Quiroga and More-lia. The village is at the end of a side road heading north from the highway, about halfway between the two larger towns.

Uruapan

Uruapan (oo-roo-AH-pahn), a verdant semitropical city noted for its blossoms and luxuriant foliage, is located some 62 km (38 miles) west of Pátzcuaro, and the scenic drive from Pátzcuaro may be the best reason for visiting it. As the road descends from the 7,000-foot elevation of Pátzcuaro the scenery changes in only a few minutes from pine forests to lush hillsides checkered with coffee and banana plantations, as well as groves of lemon and orange trees.

At the northern entrance to town the **Parque Nacional Eduardo Ruíz** protects the headwaters of the Río Cupatitzio. Shady paths and rustic bridges make this a lovely place for a walk. At the end of the trail a cascade foams and seethes over rocks and ledges.

At the same end of town is a small museum that displays and sells local crafts, notably the lacquerware for which Uruapan is known. Another museum, located on the main plaza in a fine 16th-century building, features antique and modern Tarascan craft work.

Uruapan, despite its relatively fast pace, remains graciously provincial and still Tarascan enough to take pride in its local color; the annual fair, with locally produced crafts and toys, ranks among the best in Mexico, drawing a crowd during Holy Week.

STAYING AND DINING IN URUAPAN

The ► **Mansión del Cupatitzio** is a hotel in a converted and expanded hacienda overlooking the national park, about a ten-minute walk from the zócalo. The pool is well maintained, the restaurant satisfactory, and the rooms with park views the most desirable.

Downtown on the zócalo itself, the ► **Hotel Plaza Uruapan** occupies a parcel of land that is part of a shopping mall. Ask for a room on the top floor for views of the town and surrounding mountains from a private balcony. The bar, restaurant, and weekend disco are favorites with local business-people and commercial travellers.

La Pergola, a restaurant on the zócalo, is an unhurried spot with an extensive menu—though the broadly national dishes show the kitchen off to the best advantage.

Paricutín

Paricutín, the now-dormant volcano that raised havoc when it was born in a cornfield in 1943, is 39 km (24 miles) northwest of Uruapan. To get there, head north on Highway 37, the road to Paracho, for 18 km (11 miles), then turn left onto the road that leads to Angahuán. The village of Angahuán, where more Tarascan than Spanish is spoken, is at the end of the road about 19 km (12 miles) to the west. A guide—the most convenient way to see the volcano—will usually be waiting outside the village. If no guide is on duty, drive into the center of the village and someone will soon approach you. Just beyond town, but a little tricky to find, is the departure point for tours of the area, complete with a horse-rental stand and very basic overnight accommodations.

There is no access by car to the volcano itself, or to the villages it destroyed. Instead, it's a short ride by horseback (or a long hike) to the lava beds, a weird and lunar-like landscape. Of the first village, only part of the town church remains, the building buried in lava but the tower rising eerily above the blackness. Most visitors turn back after seeing this bizarre sight. To visit the crater itself requires an early morning start; the round trip, by horseback, takes most of a day. The ride to the village should not be daunting to inexperienced riders, however; the horses are gentle and know the routine.

Paracho

Paracho, the first town north of Uruapan past the turnoff for Angahuán, is famous for wood carvings, especially toys and miniature doll houses, and stringed musical instruments, especially guitars. Otherwise it has little to recommend it. None of its main-street cafés is particularly trustworthy or inviting, nor is any single guitar maker known as the best or most famous. Instead, musicians shopping here tend to spend hours visiting one shop after another, testing and comparing instruments as they go.

GETTING AROUND

Driving Down from the Border

The 1,520-km (942-mile) trip from El Paso–Juárez to Guadalajara requires careful planning, since acceptable overnight stops are not conveniently spaced. The average driving time, without stops, is 21½ hours, but that does not take into account possible dust storms, heavy rains, or snow in winter: This is a land of climatic extremes.

El Paso has a range of good accommodations, but drivers planning to go farther than Chihuahua the first day may want to have customs behind them before they start in the morning.

The fairly expensive ▶ **Hotel Plaza Juárez** is in the Pronaf Center in **Ciudad Juárez**, 3½ km (2 miles) south of the Bridge of the Americas at the corner of Avenidas Lincoln and Coyoacán. This is a gracious inn with a pool (heated in winter), a restaurant that serves spicy Mexican cuisine, a coffee shop with fast service, and a nightclub. The inexpensive ▶ **Motel Colonial Las Fuentes**, also on Avenida Lincoln, one long block closer to the bridge than the Plaza Juárez, offers good value for your money. The coffee shop next door is only adequate.

The **Paseo del Norte Restaurant**, located at 3650 Hermanos Escobar, not far from the Plaza Juárez, is an outstanding exponent of classic Mexican cuisine, with only a few concessions to the palates of Texans who cross the border to sample its fare.

From Ciudad Juárez, Highway 45 runs south across a semiarid slightly rolling plain pocked with scrub vegetation. The few settlements along this stretch offer little in the way of tourist amenities. About four hours after leaving Ciudad Juárez you'll reach the more hospitable area around the city of Chihuahua. (For Chihuahua information and accommodations, see the Copper Canyon chapter below.)

Highway 45 continues south from Chihuahua through ranchland that's fertile only in comparison to what precedes and follows it. About an hour and a half southeast of Chihuahua the town of **Ciudad Camargo** huddles on the plain at the junction of two rivers that seem to run dry more often than not. The ▶ **Motel Los Nogales**, at Avenida Juárez 404, is acceptable, if overpriced for lack of competition. The ▶ **Cabañas Santa Rosalía**, at the corner of Abasolo and Juárez, is less costly and has a restaurant.

At **Ciudad Jiménez** (often simply called "Jiménez"), 71 km (44 miles) south of Ciudad Camargo, Highway 45 turns west, and should be followed only by travellers bound for

Mazatlán. Others should continue south on Highway 49, the road to Torreón.

Though not much to look at, Jiménez begins to seem especially attractive when you take into account the fact that the next acceptable accommodations are nearly 292 km (181 miles) to the south in the so-called Triplet cities. The ▶ **Hotel Florido** is the best in Jiménez, though neither the hotel nor its restaurant is first class. The three other small inns in town will serve as ports in a storm.

Your goal the next day should be the attractive colonial city of Zacatecas, an 8- to 9-hour drive to the south.

From Jiménez, Highway 49 traverses another long stretch of infertile, windswept plain to the valley of the Triplet cities—Torreón, Ciudad Lerdo, and Gómez Palacio. Together the three are home to more than a million people. **Torreón**, little more than a century old and still unmellowed, was founded by British, French, and U.S. concerns active in dairy farming, mining, and smelting (today it is also a major transportation center). As a result, it is heavily North Americanized, and inevitably you will see the names of familiar fast-food restaurants lining the highway.

The ▶ **Hotel Gran Presidential Torreón**, with a restaurant, coffee shop, and pool, is the best the city has to offer in the way of roadside accommodations. To find it, follow Highway 40 5½ km (3½ miles) east to the large equestrian statue of Pancho Villa at the traffic circle, then 1 km (½ mile) west on Revolución and 2 km (1¼ miles) south on Paseo de la Rosita. You'll find the ▶ **Hotel Palacio Real**, the traditional gathering place for Torreón business executives and civic leaders, in the center of town facing the main plaza. The hotel is also the location of the city's two fanciest restaurants, **La Fuente** and **Café de Paris**, the latter not noticeably French.

Highway 49 joins Highway 40 in Torreón. From here you follow the combined route south some 100 km (62 miles) to the junction just north of the village of Cuencamé, where they go their separate ways. From the intersection, follow Highway 49 to Fresnillo and Zacatecas. (Highway 40 continues on to Durango, then becomes a rollercoaster through the mountains before it reaches the Pacific at Mazatlán.)

After passing through the picturesque old silver town of Fresnillo you come to Mexico's northernmost colonial city, **Zacatecas**, which has retained and restored much of its 18th-century charm and is well worth a leisurely inspection—if not an overnight stay. This old silver-mining town has some of the prettiest colonial buildings in Mexico, wrought from the pale pink stone quarried locally. Especially notable are the cathedral, built between 1612 and 1752; the Patrocinio

Chapel, which was erected on the summit of El Cerro de la Bufa, the mountain that dominates the town; and the graceful main zócalo. There's also the new **Museo Rafael Coronel**, in the Exconvento de San Francisco, which houses a collection of more than 1,000 Mexican masks collected by the well-known painter. The museum is closed Mondays.

Two of the newest hotels in Zacatecas are the ▶ **Paraiso Radisson Zacatecas** and La Quinta Real. The Radisson, across the street from the cathedral and the most convenient address for exploring the downtown area, incorporates the original façade of the restored colonial building it occupies. Some of its rooms have charming wrought-iron terraces and antique furniture. ▶ **La Quinta Real Zacatecas**, near the edge of town at Rayon 434, is an all-suites hotel built around what, until recently, was the oldest bullring in Mexico. It's a beautiful place and the service is excellent.

The ▶ **Hotel Aristos Zacatecas**, on a hilltop west of town off Highways 45 and 54, offers comfortable modern rooms and an adequate restaurant. Its finest feature, however, is the memorable vista of the city it affords. The ▶ **Hotel Gallery Best Western** is in town on Highway 45, at the corner of Boulevard López Mateos and Callejón del Barro. Pleasantly colonial in atmosphere, it has an indoor pool and a satisfactory restaurant.

From Zacatecas, Highway 54 continues south some 273 km (169 miles) through pleasant, temperate country to Guadalajara.

—*Robert Somerlott*

By Air

Several airlines fly directly between Guadalajara and the United States, including Alaskan Airlines, Aero California, American, Mexicana, and Aeroméxico. (Mexicana and Aeroméxico also offer frequent flights to Mexico City as well as other cities in the country.) From Guadalajara there are daily westbound flights to Puerto Vallarta. Transportation into the city from the airport is by *colectivo* (about $2) or rate-controlled taxi (about $12). Airport buses will also pick you up at your hotel and take you to the airport for departure. Car-rental agencies at the airport include Arrendadora de Automóbiles, S.A.; Albarran; National; Avis; Hertz; Budget; and Quick. All have offices in the city as well.

By Train

The only recommendable rail service to the capital is the night train, *El Tapatío,* which leaves Guadalajara at 7:55 P.M. and usually arrives in the capital the next morning at 8:10.

Passengers should avoid buying the cheapest ticket, which is misleadingly called "first class." True first class is called *primera clase especial.* A choice of roomettes and bedrooms is also available; the service is fair, the dining car adequate. The fare is approximately $45, one-way; expect to pay an additional $23 for a single sleeping compartment (*dormitorio*). *El Tapatío* arrives and departs in Mexico City from the central station on Calle Buenavista off Insurgentes Norte.

The *Del Pacifico* winds between Guadalajara and Mexicali on the U.S. border—a trip that takes about 33 hours. The fare is roughly $112, one-way; expect to pay an additional $23 a night for a single sleeping compartment. The only rail depot in Guadalajara is on Avenida Washington, 15 blocks south of the Liberty Market near the Parque Agua Azul.

In and Around Guadalajara
Except in the central historic district, distances in Guadalajara are too great to be covered easily on foot. Taxis are plentiful, however, and not expensive. An excellent bus system runs from the center of town to the Minerva Circle hotel area and beyond. There's also good bus service to Tlaquepaque and Tonalá, with destinations marked on each bus.

Although there is regular bus service to Lake Chapala, the problem is getting around once you're there. The trip is probably best made by car or tour bus. The outstanding tour-bus company is Panoramex, which calls at hotels throughout Guadalajara.

ACCOMMODATIONS REFERENCE
The rates given below are projections *for December 1993 through Easter 1994. Unless otherwise indicated, rates are for double rooms, double occupancy; the 10 percent VAT has been added. As rates are subject to change, it's always a good idea to double-check before booking.*

▶ **Cabañas Santa Rosalía.** Juárez y Abasolo, **Ciudad Camargo**, Chihuahua 33700. Tel: (146) 2-0214. $30.

▶ **Fiesta Americana Guadalajara.** Avenida Vallarta and López Mateos, **Guadalajara**, Jalisco 44100. Tel: (36) 25-3434; Fax: (36) 30-3725; in the U.S. and Canada, Tel: (800) FIESTA-1. $183.

▶ **Holiday Inn Guadalajara.** Boulevard López Mateos and Avenida Mariano Otero, **Guadalajara**, Jalisco 44100. Tel: (36)

34-1034; Fax: (36) 31-9393; in the U.S. and Canada, Tel: (800) HOLIDAY. $163.

▶ **Hotel Aristos Zacatecas**. Lomas de la Soledad, **Zacatecas**, Zacatecas 98040. Tel: (492) 2-1788; Fax: (492) 2-6908; in the U.S. and Canada, Tel: (800) 5-ARISTO. $83.

▶ **Hotel Los Escudos**. Portal Hidalgo 73, **Pátzcuaro**, Michoacán 61600. Tel: (454) 2-1290. $36.

▶ **Hotel Florido**. Avenida Juárez and 20 de Noviembre, **Ciudad Jiménez**, Chihuahua 33980. Tel: (154) 2-0186. $40.

▶ **Hotel Francés**. Calle Maestranza 35, **Guadalajara**, Jalisco 44100. Tel: (36) 13-1190; Fax: (36) 58-2831. $63.

▶ **Hotel Gallery Best Western**. Boulevard López Mateos and Callejón del Barro, **Zacatecas**, Zacatecas 98000. Tel: (492) 2-3311; Fax: (492) 2-3415; in the U.S. and Canada, Tel: (800) 528-1234. $93.

▶ **Hotel Gran Presidential Torreón**. P.O. Box 1010, Paseo de la Rosita and Diagonal de las Fuentes, **Torreón**, Coahuila 27000. Tel: (17) 17-4040; Fax: (17) 12-4968. $96.

▶ **Hotel Malibu**. Avenida Vallarta 3993, **Guadalajara**, Jalisco 45040. Tel: (36) 21-7888; Fax: (36) 22-3192. $93.

▶ **Hotel de Mendoza**. Avenida Venustiano Carranza 16, **Guadalajara**, Jalisco 44100. Tel: (36) 13-4646; Fax: (36) 13-7310. $100.

▶ **Hotel Palacio Real**. Calle Morelos 1280 Poniente, **Torreón**, Coahuila 27000. Tel: (17) 16-0000; Fax: (17) 16-8608. $85.

▶ **Hotel Plaza Juárez**. Avenidas Lincoln and Coyoacán, **Ciudad Juárez**, Chihuahua 32310. Tel: (16) 13-1310; Fax: (16) 13-0084. $98.

▶ **Hotel Plaza Uruapan**. Calle Ocampo 64, **Uruapan**, Michoacán 60000. Tel: (452) 3-3700; Fax: (452) 3-3980. $50.

▶ **Mansión del Cupatitzio**. P.O. Box 63, Calzada Fray Juan de San Miguel, **Uruapan**, Michoacán 64430. Tel: (452) 3-2060; Fax: (452) 4-6772. $72.

▶ **El Mesón del Gallo**. Calle Dr. José María Coss 20, **Pátzcuaro**, Michoacán 61600. Tel: (454) 2-1474; Fax: (454) 2-1511. $29.

▶ **Motel Colonial Las Fuentes**. Avenida Américas 1365, **Ciudad Juárez**, Chihuahua 32310. Tel: (16) 13-5050; Fax: (16) 13-4081. $70.

▶ **Motel Los Nogales**. Avenida Juárez 404, **Ciudad Camargo**, Chihuahua 33700. Tel: (146) 2-1247; Fax: (146) 2-4442. $35.

▶ **La Nueva Posada**. Calle Donato Guerra 9, **Ajijic**, Jalisco 49920. Tel: (376) 5-3395. $62.

▶ **Posada de la Basílica**. Calle Arciega 6, **Pátzcuaro**, Michoacán 61600. Tel: (454) 2-1108. $31.

► **Posada de Don Vasco.** Avenida de las Américas 450, **Pátzcuaro**, Michoacán 61600. Tel: (454) 2-0227; Fax: (454) 2-0262. $72.

► **La Quinta Real Guadalajara.** Avenida México 2727, **Guadalajara**, Jalisco 44100. Tel: (36) 15-0000; Fax: (36) 30-1797; in the U.S. and Canada, Tel: (800) 458-6888. $234.

► **La Quinta Real Zacatecas.** Avenida Rayon 434, **Zacatecas**, Zacatecas 98000. Tel: (492) 2-9104; Fax: (492) 2-8440; in the U.S. and Canada, Tel: (800) 458-6888. $185.

► **Paraiso Radisson Zacatecas.** Calle Hidalgo 703, **Zacatecas**, Zacatecas 98000. Tel: (492) 2-6289; Fax: (492) 2-6245; in the U.S. and Canada, Tel: (800) 333-3333. $130.

► **El Tapatío.** P.O. Box 2953, km 6.4 on Guadalajara–Chapala highway, Jalisco 45580. Tel: (36) 35-6050; Fax: (36) 35-6664; in the U.S., Tel: (800) 424-2440; in New York, Tel: (800) 431-2822. $152.

THE COPPER CANYON

RIDING THE CHIHUAHUA – PACIFIC RAILWAY

By Robert Cummings

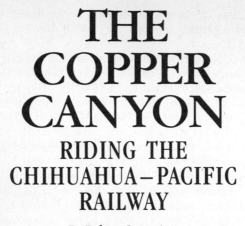

It has been called the most scenic railroad trip in the world. No doubt there are rivals and other claimants, but it's hard to name one. The Chihuahua–Pacific weaves, snakes, and climbs through as wild and spectacular a countryside as you are ever likely to visit. High in the Sierra Tarahumara of northwest Mexico, south of Ciudad Juárez and western New Mexico, the train skirts the brink of deep canyons, then rolls into the immense Copper Canyon (*Barranca del Cobre*) itself. Upon seeing it a rush of adjectives floods the mind: breathtaking, awe-inspiring, incomparable. In fact, four Grand Canyons could be dropped into this vastness, which is why it's sometimes called "the Grander Canyon."

There are two ways to do this trip. First—and the most popular way—is simply as an exciting rail journey. You get aboard at either end of the line and pass through a series of titanic canyons, getting out now and then to catch your breath and gape at the spectacular scenery that stretches as far as the eye can see. Then you detrain at the other end of the line, Chihuahua inland to the northeast, or Los Mochis, near the Sea of Cortés to the southwest. If the train keeps to schedule, the trip takes 13 hours, although 15 or more is not

To Ciudad Juarez
and El Paso
45

Chihuahua

To Ciudad
Juarez
10
28
*Laguna
Bustillos*

Matachic
*CAMPOS
MENONITAS*
16

Cuauhtémoc

C H I H U A H U A
Río Papagochic
*Laguna
de los
Mexicanos*

**Cascada
Basaseáchic**
San Juanito
Sisoguichi
Río Conchas

Caves of Chomachi
Creel
Lago de Arareco
Cusárare
Basihuare

S I E R R A
Divisadero
Bahuichivo
Cerocahui
*BARRANCA
DEL COBRE*
*Parque
Natural*

Río Septentrión
Río Urique
**Barranca
Batopilas**

M A D R E
▲ *Sierra
Tarahumara*

*Presa
Miguel
Hidalgo*
*Sierra
Mobinara* ▲
O C C I D E N T A L

El Fuerte

To Mexicali
S I N A L O A

Río Fuerte

N

Los Mochis
Topolobampo
15
To Mazatlan

To La Paz
MAR DE CORTES

**The
Copper
Canyon
Area**

0   miles   40
0   kilometers   60

unusual. Spending 13 to 15 hours, even in a comfortable coach, with stops too few and too brief, hardly does justice to the magnificence of the canyon, and totally omits the surrounding area, but if that's all your itinerary permits, by all means do it.

On the other hand, an unhurried trip with overnight stops is far better. The Copper Canyon can and should be considered as a short vacation destination of unusual interest and beauty, something more than an excuse for a spectacular train ride. Ideally you should allow three or four nights for exploring the canyon itself, not counting time spent in Chihuahua or Los Mochis. Even one overnight along the way is better than a nonstop trip, which may leave you tired and dazed from taking in too much scenic beauty at a single stretch.

If it is to be one overnight, consider either Divisadero, the halfway point of the trip and a very appealing town, or Creel, five and a half hours southwest of Chihuahua, and with more in the way of attractions.

A one-way ticket costs about $34 (first class is called "star service"), and there's a 15 percent surcharge covering unlimited stopovers in one direction. Although seats on the train are plenty comfortable, dining car service has been interrupted in the past; it's a good idea to inquire prior to departure whether it is necessary to bring your own provisions. There's also a good chance the train's heating system won't be working, so in cold weather you might want to carry a lap robe. Recently a number of new deluxe coaches have been added, but few things about the Chihuahua–Pacific are certain or permanent. At the frequent five-minute stops along the route vendors hawk hot coffee, cocoa, and soft drinks. Although the train runs year-round, the best time to see the canyon is October, after the rainy season but before the weather turns cold. March and April, before the spring rains and heat, are also good, but be sure to avoid Holy Week, when all facilities and attractions are crowded.

The Railroad

Gouged out of ancient rock, thrown across plunging gorges, and bored through towering mountains, this seemingly impossible route was the dream of Albert K. Owen, a visionary who longed for a railroad connecting Kansas City to Topolobampo on the Sea of Cortés, partly in order to service a utopian community he was building at what would be the line's southern terminus. Launched more than a century ago, it was an impractical idea, even for the Gilded Age, but

Owen sank large amounts of money into the project. The beginning and end of the line presented no problems; the land there was flat. But in between rose the formidable Sierra Madre.

Fortunes were devoured trying to make the link, until finally the best engineering and financial minds in the United States pronounced the railroad an impossibility. The enterprise was shelved and almost forgotten. Only the first section, from Chihuahua to Creel, was in use by 1914.

In the years after the Revolution Mexico gradually began to acquire ownership of her own railroads, and in 1939–1940 the government bought out the last of the foreign companies, among them the Chihuahua–Pacific. Mexican engineers studied and debated the ambitious project for 13 years before announcing their solutions to the daunting problems blocking the completion of the railroad.

The biggest one, of course, was the 160-mile stretch through the Copper Canyon, a land of rugged mountains and bottomless gorges inhabited only by the primitive Tarahumara Indians and a handful of missionaries. For eight years the construction work inched along. Thirty-nine bridges were built to span the chasms of the canyon and 86 tunnels were dug through its mountains. Finally, in 1961, the line was opened, making it possible to take what would soon be known as "the Train Ride in the Sky."

The Tarahumara

The railway did not replace a road; there were—and still are—very few through roads in the region. In fact, the surrounding countryside had been virtually isolated since the earliest days of its habitation. As a result, when the construction crews first encountered the local Tarahumara Indians, they found themselves among a Stone Age people.

The Tarahumara today's travellers encounter are a sturdy people with sharply defined features and long coarse hair, which the men wear bound in a headband. The men also wear rough white shirts and the *tapote,* a kind of loincloth. They are fabled runners who will hunt a deer by chasing it until the animal drops of exhaustion, and their strength is as great as their stamina. A favorite Tarahumaran game involves kicking a small ball while running a footrace; participants will run as much as 150 miles without a real rest, a feat of endurance that takes several days and nights.

Some of the Tarahumara still live in caves and follow the seasonal migration patterns of their ancestors: In summer they live on the high cliffs, but retreat to the canyon's depths—moving from colder to milder temperatures as they descend more than a mile to the bottom—as winter nears.

Taking the Train

First-class trains, known as *especiales,* make the trip daily in each direction, one southbound from Chihuahua, the other northbound from Los Mochis. They pass near Divisadero, but do not stop to exchange passengers. In other words, you'll have to wait about 24 hours at any stop along the line for the next train. And because the entire trip (without stopovers) takes longer than daylight lasts, you'll have to make a round trip to see everything in daylight. (Most travellers choose not to do this, although it can be a convenient plan depending on your next destination.) The best way to see the canyon is to take the *northbound* train, either from Los Mochis or El Fuerte, about 80 km (50 miles) to the northeast of Los Mochis. (You'll want to sit on the right side of the train for the best views.) If you must leave from Chihuahua and do the trip straight through, you'll probably be disappointed when falling darkness obscures the views while you're still in scenic country. The longer days of summer lessen this problem somewhat.

Los Mochis

Most travellers use Los Mochis, a modern agricultural center, as their boarding point. In 1903 an American named Benjamin Johnson built Mexico's largest sugar mill here and literally put the town on the map. Today Los Mochis is a prosperous but unexceptional community.

Those who want to linger in the area for an extra day or two may enjoy visiting **Topolobampo**, a small community on the coast 19 km (12 miles) south of town. The town was founded in the 1870s by Albert K. Owen, the same man who pioneered the Chihuahua–Pacific Railroad, and was envisioned as a socialist utopian settlement, grand in scale, noble in purpose. Today it is the eastern terminus for the ferry to La Paz, the capital of Baja California Sur, and offers day-trippers a pleasant beach, swimming, and abundant sportfishing opportunities. Excursions around the Bahía de Topolobampo can be arranged at the Hotel Santa Anita in Los Mochis. The scenic trip includes a visit to the **Roca de Farallón**, a low, wave-splashed outcropping of rock where sea lions come to breed. There are no recommendable accommodations in Topolobampo itself, but drinks and snacks are available at a number of places on the beach.

The ▶ **Hotel Santa Anita** in Los Mochis, part of the Balderrama hotel chain, offers comfortable lodgings at moderate rates. A five-story brick, glass, and steel structure, the hotel is best described as nondescript modern with a few Mexican touches and smallish rooms. Viajes Flamingo, a travel agency in the hotel, specializes in Copper Canyon excursions.

(If you are planning on staying overnight in the canyon, it is *essential* to have confirmed hotel reservations before you step aboard the train. Once en route your alternatives are limited; hotels are few and there is no way to get to the next town if the first one is fully booked.)

The train leaves the Los Mochis station at 6:00 A.M. If you have driven down from the States or from elsewhere in Mexico, hotels at either end of the line will arrange car storage. You can also have your car shipped from Los Mochis to Chihuahua. (The vehicles do not go on the passenger train but on a freight train that follows.) The cost is steep, however: about $250 to transport a compact model.

El Fuerte

An alternate boarding point is the town of El Fuerte. Founded as a mission in the 16th century, then a vigorous mining town in succeeding centuries, today it is a quaint colonial town located in the middle of good fishing and hunting country on the Río Fuerte. El Fuerte has the ▶ **Posada Hidalgo**, a sister hotel of the Santa Anita in Los Mochis. The former mansion of a local politician, this rustic provincial inn is filled with antiques and gay Mexican decorations, and offers a romantic, hacienda-like atmosphere. Officially, the train is supposed to leave town at 8:26 A.M., though it rarely does. The good news is that you won't have missed much by avoiding the Los Mochis–El Fuerte leg.

Into the Mountains

East of El Fuerte the train begins its long ascent into the Sierra Madre Occidental. The fertile coastal plains of Sinaloa soon give way to spectacular cliffs and buckled escarpments carved into a jumble of shapes by millions of years of wind and water. The whole complex is vast, a cluster of canyons of which the Copper is merely the greatest. As you look out the window of your coach or observation car, the surrounding peaks and mesas average nearly 6,500 feet above sea level. Several rise to 9,000 feet or more, soaring above gorges that drop completely out of sight. The most spectacular contrast of this sort is the upthrust of **Monte Mohinara**, towering more than 12,000 feet above the rocky canyon bottom. The canyon floor itself enjoys a semitropical climate, while the heights above are often snow covered.

At about 12:30 P.M., having crossed the state line into Chihuahua, you arrive in remote **Bahuichivo**. There is a short stop here for sightseeing; it is also the first possible overnight break in the trip—and a good one. The ► **Hotel Misión** in nearby Cerocahui, also part of the Balderrama operation, offers accommodations, food, guides, and a warm welcome to the back country. Situated in a quiet valley in the middle of inspiring scenery, the hotel sends a bus to meet the train (a trip of about 30 minutes), and pampers its guests with good food and service in a colorfully rustic setting.

Blessed with a gentle climate, the hotel's fertile valley is carpeted with apple and peach orchards. In 1690 Juan María de Salvatierra, the first European to see the region, was so enchanted that he established a mission here. Today Cerocahui offers riding, two mines open to the public, a sparkling waterfall, and lofty mountain peaks. In addition, guests can take a motorized excursion down to the lovely Río Urique or visit the mission school, where you'll meet the shy Tarahumara. The charm of the hotel is further bolstered in the winter months by the pot-bellied stoves used to heat it.

From Bahuichivo the train climbs through even more spectacular country, plunging into tunnels and seeming to fly over bridges. The illusion of flight is especially convincing when the bridge is narrower than the train and nothing but space can be seen between you and a stream hundreds of feet below; the sensation is exhilarating rather than frightening.

Divisadero, the halfway point of the trip, offers views so overwhelming that a 15- to 30-minute stop is made. The great canyon winds around a big bend in the river here, making it even more dramatic, and from a promontory you can see the opposite rim a mile away. Beyond that are still more peaks and mesas. The air is bracing, the whole prospect magnificent.

The ► **Hotel Cabañas Divisadero-Barrancas**, a five-minute walk from the train stop, perches on the very edge of a sheer cliff commanding views across the canyon and of a pine forest below. The log-and-stone building and rustic dining room would have an almost ski chalet–type atmosphere were it not for the wonderful, restorative sense of quiet. (Radios, TVs, and phones are conspicuously absent here as well as in the other hotels in the immediate area.) The hotel is fairly expensive, though well worth it, and its management will be happy to arrange trips to Indian villages, to a nearby waterfall, and into the canyon itself.

Creel

This logging town with a frontier ambience some five and a half hours southwest of Chihuahua is the next major stop. Situated high in the Tarahumara Mountains, the most forbidding part of the Sierra Madre Occidental, Creel straddles the track. Nearby, huge stacks of lumber await shipment, scenting the crisp mountain air with an aroma of pine.

Creel is known as the Indian capital of northern Mexico because of the concentration of Tarahumaras in the region. Roads, most of them quite rough, stretch out to all the major canyons from here, providing access to Tarahumaran villages, fantastic rock formations, a remarkable waterfall, mountain lakes, and old Jesuit missions.

EXCURSIONS FROM CREEL

Don't be put off by the words "tour" or "excursion" when used in connection with the places discussed below; there is nothing touristy, crowded, or spoiled about any of them.

The most difficult (albeit rewarding) trip from Creel takes you 140 km (87 miles) north and west to the spectacular waterfall known as **Cascada Basaséachic**. The Río Chinipas here plunges in eerie silence some 1,000 feet into the Barranca de Candameña—said to be the highest single-drop waterfall in North America. Hotels in Creel arrange excursions to the falls (travel time is about 4 hours each way), as well as to other natural attractions in the area. And though the hike from the edge of the falls to the canyon floor is a bit strenuous, the sight of the great silver ribbon of water tumbling past the sheer cliff face in a free fall is well worth the effort.

You should allow about 6 hours for the excursion to **Sisoguichi**, a Tarahumaran village located 29 km (18 miles) northwest of Creel. Although the modern village is centered around government medical facilities and a school, the trip is redeemed by the magnificent wilderness scenery en route, by a Jesuit mission founded in the mid-17th century, and by seeing the Tarahumaras themselves.

The **caves of Chomachi**, a system of mostly unexplored mountain caverns that once provided shelter for Apaches, begin about about 10 km (6 miles) northeast of Creel and extend over a considerable area, with the largest known cave in the complex measuring some six miles. A tour of the caves can take anywhere from 3 to 10 hours, depending on the amount of exploring you want to do.

A bit closer to town in the opposite direction, beautiful

Lago Arareco, a marvelous swimming and trout fishing hole located 7 km (4 miles) southeast of Creel, deserves at least a couple of hours of your time. In the same direction, the Jesuit mission of **Cusárare**, about 20 km (12 miles) south of Creel, remains more or less unchanged from the days of its founding in the 17th century. The interior, decorated with natural pigments made by the Tarahumara, is known for its life-size paintings of religious figures. Abandoned by the Jesuits in 1767, the mission has only recently been restored to its original function.

Another local attraction well worth your time is located outside the Tarahumaran village of **Basihuare**, 38 km (24 miles) south of town. Here you'll find a mountainside dotted with beautifully tinted outcroppings of rock, some soaring over 200 feet. These so-called "mushroom rocks" have, over the millennia, been eroded by the elements into fantastic shapes so that they appear to "sprout" from the side of the mountain.

The village of **Norogachi**, located 77 km (48 miles) southeast of the Creel station, is a worthwhile excursion on Sundays, fiesta day, when large numbers of Tarahumara from the surrounding area congregrate in the village center, lending it a distinctly pre-Columbian air.

Batopilas

Barranca Batopilas, the most beautiful canyon in the region, lies about 40 km (25 miles) farther south along the same road (118 km/73 miles from the Creel station). Although the trip is fairly arduous—taking almost 7 hours, one way, by Jeep, truck, or bus—the scenic rewards far outweigh any minor discomforts you may experience. The vegetation changes as the road descends some 6,000 feet to the bottom of the canyon, oaks and pines giving way to otate bamboo and Moctezuma cypress. The sheer cliff walls insulate this hidden land of ferns and wild roses, which flourish in the shadows of the precipices.

The remote village of Batopilas, which experienced a brief silver boom a century ago, is surrounded by crumbling haciendas, mining installations, and a late-16th-century mission church, its fallen walls betraying majestic proportions. The people of this mountain Shangri-la, both Tarahumara and their few Mexican neighbors, smile shyly and gravely in welcome.

The Parador de la Montaña in Creel (discussed below) will make arrangements for the trip as well as for simple overnight quarters (making this journey in one day is impractical). An even better choice is the ► **Copper Canyon River-**

side Lodge, a beautifully restored 19th-century hacienda surrounded by small tropical gardens in Batopilas itself. Owned and operated by the same people who run the Copper Canyon Sierra Lodge (see below), the Riverside Lodge offers its guests comfortable rooms decorated with claw-foot tubs, Oriental rugs, and Victorian antiques. Afternoon cocktails precede the family-style meals prepared by the lodge's own chef, and low-key entertainment is offered in the evenings. Most guests are booked for three nights as part of a nine-day Copper Canyon excursion offered by management, but overnight accommodations are made available to others when the lodge is not full. For contact information, see the Accommodations Reference list at the end of this chapter.

STAYING IN THE CREEL AREA

The stretch of road from Creel to Chihuahua is now paved and can be covered in a little more than two hours; in addition, small aircraft can be landed on a packed-earth landing strip outside of Creel. Many people from the United States drive to Creel, do some exploring, then take the train to the Pacific coast while their vehicle is shipped after them or stored in Creel to await their return.

In Creel the best hotel for your money is the ► **Parador de la Montaña**, a comfortable establishment close to the center of town. It has private baths (unlike some hotels in Creel), and a very good restaurant and bar. The ► **Copper Canyon Sierra Lodge**, about 30 minutes outside of town, is rustic but well equipped, with stone fireplaces in the guest rooms and a pleasant dining room. The lodge, which has been refurbished by new management, specializes in excursions to the region's many scenic attractions—as do most Creel inns—and provides bus transportation to and from the station.

Chihuahua City

If you board the train the next afternoon you'll arrive later that evening in Chihuahua, the capital of the state of the same name, and a large, thriving city in its own right. The cathedral here is a fine building, begun in 1724 but so often delayed by Indian wars that it wasn't completed until a hundred years later. The **Museo Histórico de la Revolución en el Estado de Chihuahua**, housed in the former home of the outlaw-patriot Pancho Villa at Calle 10 Norte 3014, has Revolution-related documents, arms, and photos, as well as the automobile in which Villa was riding when he was assassinated in 1923. The museum's tiny gift shop also has a list of Villa's 25 wives and 25 children. Villa, born Doroteo Aranjo, owes this memorial to his widow Luz Corral, whom he married and divorced four times, and who outlived her husband by 58 years.

Elsewhere in town, the collection of photos and farm implements of early Mormon and Mennonite settlers gathered in the **Museo Regional de Chihuahua** is completely at odds with the building that houses it, a 1910 mansion filled with Art Nouveau furnishings, a Louis XV dining room set, and an abundance of stained glass skylights and windows.

STAYING AND DINING IN CHIHUAHUA

There's a good selection of hotels to choose from in Chihuahua, the most luxurious and centrally located of which is the ▶ **Palacio del Sol**, at Avenida Independencia 500. Less expensive and also in the center of town, two blocks north of the zócalo at the corner of Avenida Independencia and Niños Heroes, is the good if unremarkable ▶ **Posada Tierra Blanca**.

In addition to the restaurants and coffee shops in its main hotels, Chihuahua has two noteworthy restaurants. Housed in a 19th-century brewery on Highway 45, two blocks north of the intersection of Juárez and Colón (at Juárez 3331), **La Olla de Chihuahua** serves up tastefully prepared steaks, seafood, and Mexican dishes (Tel: 14/16-2221). Just down the street at Juárez 3316 is the more elegant **Los Parados de Tony Vega**, a remodeled private residence with a good but fairly expensive selection of steaks and seafood (Tel: 14/15-1333).

GETTING AROUND

Aero California offers direct flights from Los Angeles and Mexico City to Los Mochis, Tijuana, La Paz, and Guadalajara. Aeroméxico flies from Tucson to Mexico City, Guadalajara, and Hermosillo; and from Mexico City, Guadalajara, Monterrey, Mazatlán, Los Mochis, Hermosillo, and Tijuana to Chihuahua. Aero Leo López (in the U.S., Tel: 915/778-1022; in Chihuahua, Tel: 14/15-4453) flies from El Paso to Chihuahua and from Chihuahua to Los Mochis.

A dozen major bus lines—including Transportes Chihuahuenses, Omnibus de México, Tres Estrellas de Oro, and Transportes del Norte—serve Chihuahua's Camionera Central, which is about 1½ km (1 mile) northwest of the city center at the corner of Avenidas Revolución and Progreso.

You need both a ticket and seat reservation for the Copper Canyon train. Information, tickets, and reservations can be obtained from: Jefe, Ferrocarril Chihuahua al Pacífico, Apartado 46, Chihuahua City, Chihuahua 31000; or Jefe, Ferrocarril Chihuahua al Pacífico, Los Mochis, Sinaloa 81200. It is easier, however, to deal with a travel agent than directly with the railroad.

In Los Mochis, **Viajes Flamingo** in the Hotel Santa Anita is helpful; Tel: (681) 2-1613; Fax: (681) 2-0046. In Chihuahua, **Quezada Tours** in the Palacio del Sol is good; Tel: (14) 15-7141; Fax: (14) 15-7606.

ACCOMMODATIONS REFERENCE

The rates given below are projections *for December 1993 through Easter 1994. Unless otherwise indicated, rates are for double rooms, double occupancy; the 10 percent VAT has been added. As rates are subject to change; it's always a good idea to double-check before booking.*

▶ **Copper Canyon Sierra Lodge. Creel,** Chihuahua 33200. Reservations: 1100 Owendale Drive, Suite G, Troy, MI 48083. Tel: (313) 689-2444 or (800) 776-3942. $160 (includes three meals).

▶ **Copper Canyon Riverside Lodge. Batopilas,** Chihuahua 33200. Reservations: 1100 Owendale Drive, Suite G, Troy, MI 48083. Tel: (313) 689-2444 or (800) 776-3942. $160 (includes three meals).

▶ **Hotel Cabañas Divisadero-Barrancas. Divisadero,** Chihuahua. Reservations: P.O. Box 661, Chihuahua City, Chihuahua 31000. Tel: (14) 10-3330 or 15-1199; Fax: (14) 15-6575. $140 (includes three meals).

▶ **Hotel Misión.** Domicilio Conocido, **Cerocahui,** Chihuahua. Reservations: Hotel Santa Anita, P.O. Box 159, Los Mochis, Sinaloa 81200. Tel: (681) 2-1613; Fax: (681) 2-0046. $135 (includes three meals).

▶ **Hotel Santa Anita.** P.O. Box 159, Calles Leyva and Hidalgo, **Los Mochis,** Sinaloa 81200. Tel: (681) 5-7046; Fax: (681) 2-0046. $94.

▶ **Palacio del Sol.** Avenida Independencia 500, **Chihuahua City,** Chihuahua 31000. Tel: (14) 16-6000; Fax: (14) 15-9947. $104.

▶ **Parador de la Montaña.** Calle Allende 114, **Creel,** Chihuahua 33200. Tel: (145) 6-0075 or, in Chihuahua City, (14) 15-5408; Fax (in Chihuahua City): (14) 15-3468. $65.

▶ **Posada Hidalgo.** Avendia Hidalgo 101, **El Fuerte,** Sinaloa 81820. Tel: (681) 3-0242; Fax: (681) 2-0046. $65.

▶ **Posada Tierra Blanca.** Avenidas Independencia and Niños Heroes, **Chihuahua City,** Chihuahua 31000. Tel: (14) 15-0000; Fax: (14) 15-8811. $70.

THE BAJA PENINSULA

By Jackie Peterson
with Susan Wagner and Candace Lyle Hogan

Jackie Peterson has worked as a feature writer for the San
Francisco Examiner *and* The News, *Mexico City's English-
language daily, and was the travel editor of the* Sacramento
Union *for 20 years. She lives in Mazatlán. Susan Wagner, the
travel editor of* Modern Bride *magazine for 10 years, has
worked on the staff of* Travel & Leisure *magazine and
written a series of guidebooks to Mexican resorts. She attended graduate school in Mexico and returns there frequently. Candace Lyle Hogan, a freelance writer and editor
currently living in New York City, has explored Baja California over the last 40 years from a home base in La Misión.*

Longer than the boot of Italy but far more isolated, the
Baja peninsula once beckoned only the hardiest travellers.
Most of them explored in four-wheel-drive vehicles, carried
spare cans of gasoline, and camped out. But that Baja is a
rapidly fading memory. Today, thanks to the transpeninsular
highway—Mexico Highway 1—which wends its way for
1,000 paved miles from Tijuana south to Los Cabos, you can
drive Baja's length in an ordinary passenger car.

Of course, in one short chapter we can't begin to mention
all the mile-by-mile details that a guidebook that focuses
solely on the peninsula might. But we can pique your
curiosity and perhaps tempt you into further exploration by
pointing out the highlights of the towns and resorts at either
end of the peninsula as well as of those scattered along the
length of Highway 1. If you have specific interests—off-
roading, fishing, birding, bicycling, or scuba diving—you

should be able to find guidebooks devoted exclusively to those subjects. (One excellent source for Baja material is John Cole's Book Shop, 780 Prospect Street, La Jolla, CA 92037; Tel: 619/454-4766.)

To avoid confusion about names, keep in mind that the Baja peninsula is divided into two states: Baja California and Baja California Sur. For the purposes of this chapter, we've divided the peninsula into three sections: the border zone (Tijuana, Rosarito, and Ensenada); the midsection (from San Quintín in Baja California to La Paz in Baja California Sur and including Cataviña, Guerrero Negro, San Ignacio, Santa Rosalía, Mulegé, and Loreto); and Los Cabos, "the Capes," at the southernmost tip of the peninsula (including the fast-growing resorts of San José del Cabo and Cabo San Lucas).

Late spring through late fall is the ideal time to visit the northern half of the peninsula. While the locals swear that the deadly storms and floods of early 1993 were a once-in-a-lifetime fluke, it does rain here in winter. (When in doubt, check the San Diego weather reports to get an idea of the conditions in the upper half of the peninsula.) Of course, the rainfall enables Baja's stubborn farmers and agriculturalists to scratch a living from the arid landscape; some do even better than that, as witness the vineyards around Santo Tomás and the lush farms in the San Quintín valley.

Then, too, the desert regions of the peninsula appear less bleak in the winter months. The slender *cirio,* the tuft-topped yucca, and the whiplike ocotillo, the tips of its branches seemingly dipped in bright red paint, take new strength from the limited moisture they receive at this time of year; elsewhere, wildflowers carpet the desert. January through March are also the prime whale-watching months in the bays and lagoons of the peninsula's midsection.

Winters in Baja California Sur, by contrast, are usually mild and dry. For sunseekers from Canada and the United States, the resorts at the southernmost tip of the peninsula offer pleasantly warm days and cool (but not cold) nights.

MAJOR INTEREST

The Border Zone
Sightseeing and shopping
Beaches
Spectator sports, including horseracing, bullfights, jai alai

The Midsection
Rugged natural beauty
Desert flora and fauna

Whale watching
Deep-sea fishing
Snorkeling and scuba diving
Nature tours

Los Cabos
Spectacular scenic beauty
Isolated resort hotels
Deep-sea fishing
Water sports, including windsurfing
Championship golf

If you travel the highway that stretches from Tijuana, just over the border from San Diego, south to Cabo San Lucas at the tip of the peninsula, you'll pass through 1,000 miles of rugged, sometimes forbidding terrain that is never less than spectacular and often is heart-stopping. This slender piece of land is only 30 miles wide at its narrowest point and no more than 145 miles at its widest. With the Pacific Ocean to the west and the long, narrow Sea of Cortés (known as the Gulf of California in the United States and Canada) to the east, a stunning beach or lovely seascape is never far away. The waters off Cabo San Lucas, where the two meet, are among the world's most fertile fishing grounds, their junction marked by a natural arch-shaped rock formation called El Arco.

People who haven't spent a lot of time on the peninsula tend to think of Baja as a huge cactus garden. Indeed, dozens of species of cacti and other plants—many of which cannot be found anywhere else in the world—flourish here, including 80-foot-high *cardóns,* the world's largest cactus, and the *damiana,* an herb alleged to possess curative and aphrodisiacal properties. Nevertheless, the Baja peninsula is the kind of place where smart visitors travel with a pair of binoculars at the ready. Around any corner you may come upon sea lions basking on the rocks offshore, gray whales frolicking in a bay, or fish jumping clear of the jade-green waters.

The indigenous people who lived here before the Conquest were unaware of the highly developed cultures that had flourished on the mainland before the arrival of the Spanish. Hernán Cortés himself came to the peninsula in 1535 and stayed searching for gold and pearls until 1537. By 1847 the United States had claimed Alta (Upper) California as its own, but Mexico's neighbor to the north decided not to acquire Baja, or Lower, California. In fact, except for the chain of missions built by the Jesuits, Franciscans, and Dominicans during the 1700s, the human imprint on Baja California is of relatively recent vintage.

It all started to change when Baja became a territory in 1931 and a state in 1952. (Baja California Sur became a separate state in 1974.) But until the Benito Juárez Trans-peninsular Highway (Highway 1) opened a little more than two decades ago, much of this immense desert wilderness remained an isolated backwater. Today Highway 1, though only two lanes, is a reasonably smooth ride all the way down. The peninsula is still sparsely populated, however, and much of its primitive natural beauty remains un-spoiled: Baja California is one of the few places in the world unmarred by vast road and rail networks, ports, or power lines. Though pockets of development are growing at the northern and southern ends of the highway, most of Baja is still heaven for naturalists and a world apart for the rest of us.

—*Susan Wagner*

TOURING THE BAJA PENINSULA

From Southern California, you can get a taste of a foreign culture, soak up expansive ocean views, and sample inexpensive cafés and curio shops along the highway by driving just a few miles south of the California–Mexico border. Anyone of a mind to experience Baja for the adventure rather than for margaritas, on the other hand, will head for Ensenada, 136 km (85 miles) from the border, and continue south on Highway 1 from there. By taking side roads, getting out of the car, and hiking off the beaten path you'll be able to explore areas where bobcats roam and eagles nest. But off-road venturing is not for the faint of heart: Baja is wilder than it seems, and its terrain and weather change by the hour. All the way down the peninsula are coves, caves, cliffs, and valleys waiting to be discovered, but it's a good idea to carry bottled water (canteens and a rattlesnake bite kit if you're hiking) and the means to repair your car should something go wrong. Travelling those 1,000 miles you'll pass through every kind of climate imaginable (and several land-scapes as well), from rainy tropics and dry desert to rocky mountains and sandy beaches.

A final word of advice: Because of Baja's remoteness visitors should bring plenty of cash or traveller's checks. Many fishing charters, meals, car rentals, and hotel accommodations still have to be paid for in cash, and patchy phone communications can make it difficult to get credit approval at those places that do accept cards.

THE BORDER ZONE

Crossing the California border into Baja is accomplished with a smile, a nod, and a slow roll—the border guards will simply be looking through your car windows to make sure you're just a tourist (and not an importer of major appliances or furniture). After they wave you along, follow the signs that say "Ensenada Cuota" (not Ensenada Libre) if you intend to bypass Tijuana for points south. Don't worry if your route along the outskirts of Tijuana seems circuitous; the signs will lead you south to the new road, Highway 1D, as opposed to the old road, Highway 1. (Most people refer to them as the toll [new] road and the free [old] road. The only toll booths on the Baja peninsula are the three located on Highway 1D between Tijuana and Ensenada; expect to pay about $7, one-way, for the trip.) Soon you'll begin to catch your first sea views, which become more spectacular the farther south you go.

Tijuana

The world's busiest border town sprawls over the hills and arroyos on either side of the Río Tijuana, extending westward toward the Pacific. In the past two decades the city's rapidly growing population (now estimated at a million) has overwhelmed its infrastructure and defied the best intentions of urban planners and government officials. As a result (and despite the devastating floods of 1993), amid plentiful public housing you'll still see acres of cardboard shacks clinging to the slopes above the river.

Nor has the growth been orderly. The downtown grid, centered by Avenidas Revolución and Constitución running north to south and Calles 1, 2, and 3 running east to west, deteriorates into a hodgepodge of unnamed streets and alleys as it extends outward over the rolling topography. Avenida Revolución soon curves to the east, then southeast, becoming Boulevard Agua Caliente. The latter more or less parallels the Río Tijuana for a number of blocks, with the two serving as unofficial boundaries of the so-called Río District (also called "the new Tijuana").

Notwithstanding ongoing efforts to clean it up, Tijuana remains the brash and gaudy border town of legend. The burros painted with zebra stripes still stand on various corners of Avenida Revolución, awaiting the tourists to pay to pose with them. Bazaars heaped with bright serapes, paintings on velvet, and tacky trinkets still blight the urban land-

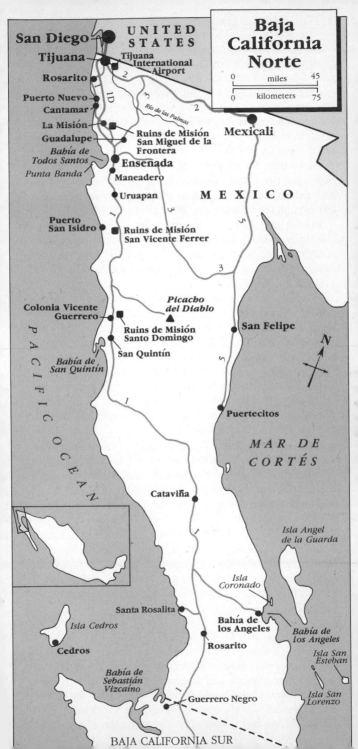

Baja California Norte

| 0 | miles | 45 |
| 0 | kilometers | 75 |

UNITED STATES

San Diego

Tijuana

Tijuana International Airport

Rosarito

Puerto Nuevo

Cantamar

La Misión

Guadalupe

Ruins de Misión San Miguel de la Frontera

Bahía de Todos Santos

Punta Banda

Ensenada

Maneadero

Uruapan

Puerto San Isidro

Ruins de Misión San Vicente Ferrer

Mexicali

Río de las Palmas

MEXICO

Colonia Vicente Guerrero

Picacho del Diablo

Ruins de Misión Santo Domingo

San Quintín

Bahía de San Quintín

San Felipe

PACIFIC OCEAN

Puertecitos

MAR DE CORTÉS

N

Cataviña

Isla Angel de la Guarda

Isla Coronado

Santa Rosalita

Bahía de los Angeles

Bahía de los Angeles

Isla Cedros

Cedros

Rosarito

Isla San Esteban

Bahía de Sebastián Vizcaíno

Guerrero Negro

Isla San Lorenzo

BAJA CALIFORNIA SUR

scape. Before you dismiss it, however, consider this: Beyond the insistent hustlers and chaotic congestion of the downtown area there are a number of worthwhile attractions.

Foremost among these (although certainly not for everyone) are Tijuana's two bullrings: **El Toreo** (Tel: 66/86-1510), located 3 km (2 miles) southeast of the downtown area on Boulevard Agua Caliente; and **Plaza Monumental** (Bullring-by-the-Sea; Tel: 66/80-1803), which lies 10 km (6 miles) west of downtown via Highway 1D. The bullfights alternate between the two venues during the May-to-September season, and tickets can be purchased in San Diego as well as at either ring; for information, Tel: (619) 232-5049.

During the same May-to-September season, *charreadas* (Mexican rodeos) are held almost every Sunday afternoon, rotating among several *charro* arenas. For the latest information on upcoming performances contact the Associación de Charros at (66) 81-3401.

Horse lovers of a different kind congregate at the **Agua Caliente Racetrack**, 5 km (3 miles) southeast of the downtown area on Boulevard Agua Caliente, where top-notch thoroughbreds run in season and greyhounds race the rest of the year. For information, Tel: (619) 295-7484. The racetrack borders on the **Tijuana Country Club**, a respectable layout located a few miles southeast of the downtown area on Boulevard Agua Caliente (look for the clubhouse a couple of blocks past the Grand Hotel Tijuana); Tel: (66) 81-7855 or 7863 for tee times and greens fees.

The **Centro Cultural Tijuana**, southeast of downtown at the corner of Paseo de los Héroes and Avenida Independencia, exhibits regional costumes and handicrafts from around the country. Open daily; Tel: (66) 84-1111 for hours and information on special events. Next door, the omnitheater screens a filmed tour of Mexico in English at 2:00 P.M. daily.

Last but not least, **Mexitlán**, a historic park featuring architectural highlights of Mexico in miniature, is located just a short taxi ride (or a long walk) south of the border (turn left at the first stoplight) on Avenida Ocampo between Calles 2 and 3.

STAYING AND DINING IN TIJUANA

In the Río Tijuana district near the racetrack, well beyond the range of walk-across visitors, the ▶ **Grand Hotel Tijuana** has accommodations and amenities the equal of most top-drawer hotels in the States. Its **Place de la Concorde** restaurant (Tel: 66/81-7000), open from 6:00 P.M. for dinner, offers formal dining and a pricey French menu. Across the street, and more typically Mexican in flavor, the ▶ **Hotel El Conquistador** offers rooms at half the rates of its high-rise neighbor, while its ▶ **Acapulco Bar** is said to be a favorite with *toreros* during the bullfight season.

For elegant, reasonably priced non-hotel dining, try **Los Arcos** (Tel: 66/86-3171), at Boulevard Salinas 1000, where a widely acclaimed chef presides over the kitchen—when he isn't flying off to Mexico City to prepare a state banquet for the president. A leisurely seafood lunch or dinner here traditionally ends with a flourish: A flower for the ladies and a courtesy round of brandy Alexanders for the table.

Other restaurants worth considering in the Río area include **Bocaccio's** (Tel: 66/86-1266), specializing in Italian cuisine, rack of lamb, and steaks; the informal, palapa-style **Mr. Fish** (Tel: 66/86-3603), where the filet of whitefish in a mustard-curry sauce is out of this world; and **Tour de France** (Tel: 66/81-7542), a moderately priced French restaurant housed in a mansion two blocks south of the Palacio de Azteca, where a smart local crowd dines surrounded by gardens and fountains.

Rosarito and Environs

If you end up skirting Tijuana on Highway 1D, the toll road, you'll soon encounter pockets of private homes and condos, with more under construction. There's a reason for the building boom: With the exception of a small beach just north of Ensenada, this entire area, from San Antonio del Mar to La Misión, south of Rosarito, boasts the best sand beach in the border zone.

ROSARITO

Located some 25 km (15 miles) south of the border, Rosarito has grown from a quiet fishing village known for its beaches and surf into the one major tourist destination between Tijuana and Ensenada. If your itinerary includes shopping for fine Mexican handicrafts, take the first Rosarito exit and turn onto Boulevard Benito Juárez, the town's wide, divided main drag. Almost immediately on the right, at Juárez 364, you'll pass **Touch**, whose large, tasteful selection of crafts includes talavera ware from Puebla, *nacimientos* from Guanajuato, and an impressive array of signed art pieces. Next door at **El Ultimo Tango**, proprietor Nelda Stokes specializes in hand-loomed textiles from Michoacán. You can purchase cloth by the yard or order it made up into bedspreads, tablecloths, and upholstered items.

Staying and Dining in Rosarito

Continuing south along Avenida Juárez you'll pass a variety of lodging, from tiny Hector's Motel, with just half a dozen rooms (during the season, about $25 a night; less during the off-season) to the monolithic Rosarito Beach Hotel (see below), at the southern end of the street. In between there's the sprawling ▶ Quinta del Mar Resort Hotel, with accommodations spread out among low-rise *casitas,* a high-rise tower, and an assortment of condominiums; the complex also has several shopping arcades and a number of restaurants.

A famous Prohibition getaway in its early days and later a hideout for such Hollywood stars as Lana Turner and Errol Flynn, the tile-and-wrought-iron ▶ Rosarito Beach Hotel retains a fair amount of nostalgic, if somewhat faded, charm. The complex includes Chabert's, the hotel's fine gourmet restaurant (dinner only, reservations recommended; Tel: 661/2-0211); tennis and racquetball courts; a swimming pool; and the Casa Playa Spa (Tel: 661/2-2687), which offers a range of beauty treatments as well as its own Mexican spa cuisine.

For a quick bite in less formal surroundings, head back into town and take your pick of the restaurants along Avenida Juárez. These include El Nido, a family-run steakhouse with branches in San Felipe, Mulegé, and Loreto; Las Olas for seafood; Los Panchos or Ortega's for Mexican food; Giuseppo's for pasta and pizza; and Los Pelicanos (Tel: 661/2-1757), a steakhouse on the beach at Calle Ebano 113. For a snack on the run, look for Manuel's or Sergio's, the best taco stands in town. At either place, a *quesadilla con carne,* with or without the hot salsa, will set you back about $2.

THE GOLDEN CORRIDOR

The 50 or so miles from Rosarito south to Ensenada comprise what developers have taken to calling the Golden Corridor. Here, one resort or condominium complex after another overlooks the shoreline. Many communities have sprung up along the old road (Highway 1), which more often than not serves as their main street.

Heading south on Highway 1 from Rosarito, watch for signs for El Calafia, a rambling hotel whose many terraces step down to a popular surfing beach below and whose cliffside restaurant serves good food in a romantic open-air setting. Tel: (661) 2-1581.

Puerto Nuevo, an enclave of 30 or so family-run restaurants specializing in seafood and the sweet, clawless Baja lobster, is farther down the road on the right. Frequent visitors complain that prices in Puerto Nuevo's restaurants keep rising while quality goes downhill, but if you want to give it a try your best bets are either **Ortega's** or the **Miramar**.

The next town you'll come to is **Cantamar**, with a gas station, a grocery store, a hotel, and a bakery or two. But mainly it's residential, a hamlet for locals and long-term vacationers. ATV buffs love the leviathan sand dunes here.

Hop onto the toll road at the next on-ramp heading south to enjoy the sea views, and keep an eye out for the rounded backs of frolicking dolphins and the spouts of gray whales. The whales migrate from their summer feeding grounds in the Bering Sea in October to their breeding grounds in bays halfway down the peninsula, arriving any time from late January into March. (The best time to see the whales close to shore is at dawn.)

Five kilometers (3 miles) south of Puerto Nuevo you'll see, off to the right, **Halfway House**. Named for its location halfway between Tijuana and Ensenada, this is the oldest bar and restaurant in the corridor, having been in operation for more than 60 years. It's very popular with surfers, who take respite here from the excellent waves at nearby Punta Mesquite, as well as photographers, who relish the ocean view from the house's garden.

LA MISION

A little beyond Halfway House, 30 km (19 miles) south of Rosarito and shortly beyond the kilometer 64 marker, you'll come to the La Misión exit. Turn left, and immediately on your left will be ► **La Fonda**, an oceanfront motel, bar, and restaurant known and loved by all. The food and drink here is good and moderately priced, the atmosphere easygoing. The staff is made up of locals, people who live in or near the charming valley of La Misión. The clientele consists of Americans and Mexicans who've known about the place a long time and keep coming back. As a result, accommodations in summer and on holiday weekends must be booked at least two weeks in advance. The rooms have a funky charm, and the ones with sea breezes will put you in mind of Key West and Hemingway. No less romantic is La Fonda's verandah, where you can eat or drink overlooking the beach from an umbrella- or tree-shaded perch.

If one or two quiet overnights is your plan and relaxed beach walks your pleasure—the ocean here is good for wading but not swimming—stay at La Fonda. With this as your home base, you can spend the rest of the day and evening exploring Ensenada to the south and still make the 56-km (35-mile) trip back to La Fonda with ease. And in the morning you'll wake up to the sound of gulls and the sight of pelicans knowing you've slept at a place that is part of local history: More than 30 years ago La Fonda was built by a Mexican citizen for his American wife, Eve Stocker, whose prickly proprietorship soon earned her the nickname "Cebolla" (the Onion).

Just a two-mile walk south along the beach from the motel is **Punta Piedra**, a rock formation that juts into the sea, forming an inviting little bay. If you're lucky you'll see dolphins teaching whales how to surf here. Plans for a hotel at Punta Piedra are in the offing, but for now the area remains relatively unspoiled. (You may have to pay to camp or park along the beach, but the price shouldn't be more than a few dollars or so. There's also a trailer park hookup nearby.) You can jog along the beach, explore the tidal pools, and sunbathe, but be careful when swimming: There's usually an insidious riptide. Ask at the motel about where to rent horses, which can be ridden inland a mile or two but not on the beach.

For organized recreation you can drive 12 km (7½ miles) south of La Fonda to **Baja Mar**, a Mediterranean-style resort offering golf, swimming, tennis, and bicycle rentals. The 1,600-acre resort, dormant until recently, has been taken in hand by Grupo Sidek, a Mexican mega-resort developer. Sidek has overseen the renovation of the golf course, rebuilt the clubhouse, and, as the centerpiece of its planned resort community, constructed a new hotel, the ▶ **Plaza Las Glorias**, a nouveau hacienda–style property with a central courtyard restaurant. In addition, more villas and condominiums (some available for rent) are being added to those that already overlook the golf course, and a second 18 holes, designed by Robert Von Hagge, is due to open sometime in 1994.

Ensenada

While the number of Americans living along the road to Ensenada sometimes makes it seem as if you've never left the States, things begin to feel more like Mexico as you approach this city of nearly 300,000. Located some 109 km (68 miles) south of Tijuana, Ensenada's fortunes have roller coastered ever since, in 1602, Sebastián Vizcaíno sailed the coast hereabouts and named the spot Ensenada de Todos los Santos (Big Bay of All Saints). But with the exception of a short-lived gold rush toward the end of the 19th century and, thanks to Prohibition in the United States, a mini-boom in the 1920s, prosperity has been elusive.

All that is changing, however. The big bay, which has been

a port of call since the days when Spanish galleons (and the pirates who preyed on them) stopped here on their way to and from the Orient, today harbors a sizable local fishing fleet as well as at least 50 cruise ships a month.

Leaving the new road (Highway 1D) at the third and final toll plaza, keep to the right for the descent into town and take the first right onto Boulevard Costero. (If you feel you need a map, you can pick one up at the visitors' center located at the intersection.) A bit farther on is the block-long Plaza Marina Ensenada, a new shopping/restaurant complex with a parking garage. As most of the downtown area has parking meters minded by vigilant meter maids, this is probably the best place to leave your vehicle while you have a meal or go shopping.

The waterfront area itself is clean and fairly bristles with energy. To your right as you face the Plaza Marina an alley leads to the fish market and its displays of fresh clams, crab, snapper, and smoked dorado. The sportsfishing boats are docked nearby; rates vary from vessel to vessel, and bargaining for a better rate is not unusual.

Shops specializing in high-quality Mexican crafts, leather goods, and furniture line both sides of the Costero as well as Avenida López Mateos, the next street up. Typical of the quality handicrafts you can expect to find is the selection at **Galería Ana**, Riveroll 122 (just off López Mateos). But there's much more to do here than shop.

Rowdy Mexican *charreadas* are staged almost every summer weekend on the *charro* grounds near the corner of Calle 2A and Avenida Blancarte, and bullfights are held at the Plaza de Toros on Avenida Sangines between Boulevard Lázaro Cárdenas and Avenida Cipres. Or you can tour the grounds and sample the wines of one of Baja California's most esteemed wineries, **Bodegas de Santo Tomás**, Avenida Miramar 666. Ensenada also hosts numerous sports and cultural events throughout the year, including bicycle races, yacht regattas, and the renowned Presidente-Sauza SCORE Baja 1000, North America's premier off-road-vehicle competition.

STAYING AND DINING IN ENSENADA

Nightlife has long been hot in Ensenada, and there are many good restaurants and hotels, with rates generally more affordable than those in the Los Cabos area. From top to bottom, however, Ensenada is fully booked on weekends. You can get information—and guarantee reservations at some hotels and motels—by calling the **Tijuana Baja Information Center** (in California, Arizona, and Nevada, Tel: 800/522-1516; in the rest of the U.S. and Canada, Tel: 800/225-2786; Fax: 619/294-7366).

Among the possibilities conveniently located in or near the tourist zone are the mission-style ▶ **Hotel La Pinta** and the ▶ **Ensenada Travelodge**. Also in town, the ▶ **Hotel Bahía** continues to be popular for its clean, carpeted rooms and balconies overlooking the bay. If, on the other hand, you want to get out of town for the night, try the ▶ **Estero Beach Resort Hotel**, 10 km (6 miles) south of Ensenada. The complex here includes tennis courts, horse rentals ($6 to $8 an hour), a campground, and a recreational-vehicle park.

Up-to-date information on the more than 200 restaurants in Ensenada can be found in its two English-language newspapers, the Baja *Sun* and the Baja *Times*. For elegant surroundings and excellent food, including tangy Mexican bouillabaisse, try **El Rey Sol**, an Old World French-Mexican restaurant honored by the International Seafood Fair and located at the corner of Avenida López Mateos and Avenida Blancarte. El Rey Sol's entrées are priced at a surprisingly moderate $10 to $15 per person; Tel: (667) 8-1733. The **Restaurant Bahía de Ensenada**, at the corner of López Mateos and Avenida Macheros, attracts a local crowd with its extensive menu of fresh seafood. In addition, tender ocean-fresh abalone, which is nearly impossible to find in the States anymore, still appears on the menus at **Haliotis** (Tel: 667/6-3720), Calle Defante 179; **Las Cazuelas** (Tel: 667/6-1044), the corner of Costero and Calle Sanguines; and **Cueva de los Tigres** (Tel: 667/6-6450), located 1½ km (1 mile) south of town at Playa Hermosa.

Ensenada's bars and cantinas are plentiful and popular. The most famous of them in the "drinking district" (Avenidas Gastelum and Ruíz) is **Hussong's**, which was still frequented by scowling *vaqueros* (cowboys) and Zapata lookalikes in the 1950s but is now crowded with young Southern California fun-seekers, bikers, and surfers. If you're just passing through, any café along the main drag will do for a quick snack or good Mexican beer; for fresh tortillas made before your eyes, head for the **Restaurant Las Brasas**, on López Mateos near Avenida Gastelum, where barbecued chickens are spit-roasted over an open flame.

Punta Banda

Before heading back to the States, take a side trip about 24 km (15 miles) southwest of Ensenada to Punta Banda and the area's most popular weekend attraction, **La Bufadora**, a tidal blowhole that makes a phenomenal groaning sound. From Ensenada turn west off Highway 1 right before Maneadero onto the road numbered 23. Along the way you'll pass the Baja Beach and Tennis Club, several campgrounds, and wooden stands where jars of chile peppers and olives are sold; La Bufadora is at the very end of the road.

— *Jackie Peterson and Candace Lyle Hogan*

THE MIDSECTION

The rugged, sparsely populated part of the peninsula begins a few miles south of Ensenada. Hotels, gas stations, and places to eat are less common here, though they do exist. Still, it's a good idea to top off a half-full gas tank when you see a Pemex station.

The highway wends south through foothills and flatlands (including the Santo Tomás vineyard region) for 182 km (114 miles) to the fertile San Quintín valley. Although visitor attractions along this stretch are limited, there are a couple of decent lodging choices in San Quintín itself. (El Rosário, some 58 km/36 miles farther south, has no recommendable hotels.) The more romantic of the two is the American-owned ▶ **Rancho Sereño Bed & Breakfast**, with just three guest rooms. If they don't have a vacancy, try the dependable ▶ **Hotel La Pinta**, one of a chain of hotels (formerly the Presidente hotels) built to accommodate motorists travelling on Highway 1.

CATAVIÑA

Just south of El Rosário you'll begin to see an odd-looking desert plant that resembles a prickly pole with thin top branches the size and shape of bent wire. *Cirio,* or "boojum," as English-speaking denizens of the peninsula have nick-named it, grows in a narrow belt extending as far as Punta Prieta, some 145 miles to the south, and nowhere else in the world (though a stumpier cousin is found in arid parts of Sonora). Other desert plants—*cardón,* ocotillo, fat elephant trees—poke up amid the fields of giant boulders surrounding Cataviña, eight hours' drive from the border and some 122 km (76 miles) south of El Rosário. Popular with mountain bikers and rock climbers, Cataviña also has a number of attractions and amenities that make it a good stopping point for motorists heading south on Highway 1. In addition to its photogenic rock garden–like setting (best captured in the soft light of early morning or late afternoon), these include a Pemex station, a small grocery store, a couple of cafés, and a ▶ **Hotel La Pinta** with a restaurant that serves an excellent *carne asada.*

Travellers who stop in Cataviña may want to backtrack some 30 km (19 miles) north to a decently graded road that leads inland a few miles to **El Marmól** (The Marble), a misnamed ghost town where onyx was quarried until the late 1950s. (On the way, some 4 km/2½ miles north of town, you can hike up an arroyo to see the cave paintings left by an ancient aboriginal tribe.) The main attraction in El Marmól itself is an old schoolhouse built entirely of onyx; be careful where you walk, though, as there are some deep, uncovered wells in the area.

CATAVIÑA TO GUERRERO NEGRO

Heading south on Highway 1 again, you'll come to a junction with a paved road after 104 km (65 miles). This road runs some 67 km (42 miles) east to the **Bahía de los Angeles**, on the Sea of Cortés. A place of breathtaking beauty, the bay attracts scuba divers, boaters, and anglers from all over the southwestern United States, most of whom bring their own gear. *Pangas* can be rented on the beach here, but overnight accommodations are limited to camping or staying at one of two hotels: a basic no-frills no-name establishment with only three rooms and the very comfortable 40-room ▶ **Villa Vitta Resort Motel**, where dinner the day of your arrival, three meals a day during your stay, and breakfast on the morning of your departure are included in the price of a room.

On Highway 1 from the junction with the bay road, it's another 128 km (80 miles) to Guerrero Negro, the next town of any size. Just two kilometers north of town you'll encounter a Sahara-like expanse of dunes—the northernmost fringe of the Vizcaíno Desert—extending westward toward the sea. Local families come here on picnics, the children amusing themselves by jumping and rolling down the hills of sand. You'll know you're on the outskirts of Guerrero Negro when you see the huge metal sculpture in the shape of an eagle. Marking the 28th Parallel, the border between the states of Baja California and Baja California Sur, the monument also is a reminder to set your watch ahead one hour; Baja California Sur observes mountain standard time.

GUERRERO NEGRO

An industrial town, Guerrero Negro proudly proclaims itself the world's leading producer of salt. Visitors from around the world who come here each winter to whale watch on the **Laguna Ojo de Liebre**, better known as Scammon's Lagoon, joke that they know where the salt for their margaritas comes from: Evaporating ponds layered with miles of the white stuff extend along both sides of the bumpy road leading to the lagoon.

Alas, there isn't much else to recommend Guerrero Negro except for a ► **Hotel La Pinta**, one or two basic motels, and two excellent seafood restaurants: **Mario's** and the restaurant at the **Malarrimo Motel**. Mario himself runs a travel agency on the side and will be happy to arrange tours to various off-road points of interest; Tel: (685) 7-0250. He also offers whale- and dolphin-watching excursions to Scammon's Lagoon or the Laguna de San Ignacio, to the south, as well as excursions by van and horseback to see pre-Hispanic cave paintings at the San Francisquito archaeological site in the mountains; the latter outing, an all-day trip, runs about $350 (with lunch) for a party of up to ten.

Whale Watching

Every winter, thousands of California gray whales migrate south from the Bering Sea to the warm Pacific waters off Baja, where they breed and give birth in the peninsula's protected bays. In February, as many as 1,000 of the giant mammals may congregate in Scammon's Lagoon at any one time, allowing visitors in *pangas* to see them at close range. It can be a stirring spectacle, as the entire lagoon comes alive with spouting, fluking males and protective cows overseeing the playful antics of their newborn calves.

SAN IGNACIO

From Guerrero Negro Highway 1 pushes south and east through the barren wastes of the Vizcaíno Desert to the lush oasis of San Ignacio, some 140 km (80 miles) distant. A paved road a couple of miles long leads off the highway and past shady palm groves to the town square and the Misión San Ignacio, one of the best-preserved missions on the peninsula. Founded by the Jesuits in 1728 in honor of their patron saint, the mission was completed by the Dominicans in 1786 after the Jesuits, discredited by their enemies in Spain, were expelled from Baja California.

In contrast to the bleak terrain along the highway, this mellow town with its pastel-colored buildings is both friendly and appealing. Staying overnight here at either the ► **Hotel La Pinta** or the basic ► **Hotel La Posada de San Ignacio**, half a mile south of the plaza at Calle V. Carranza 22, opens up the possibility of a whale-watching excursion to the Laguna de San Ignacio (located 48 off-road km/30 miles to the west) or into the mountains by muleback to see some of the hundreds of cave paintings in the area. La Posada's owner, Oscar Fischer, will be happy to arrange these expeditions, and nearby **Tota's**

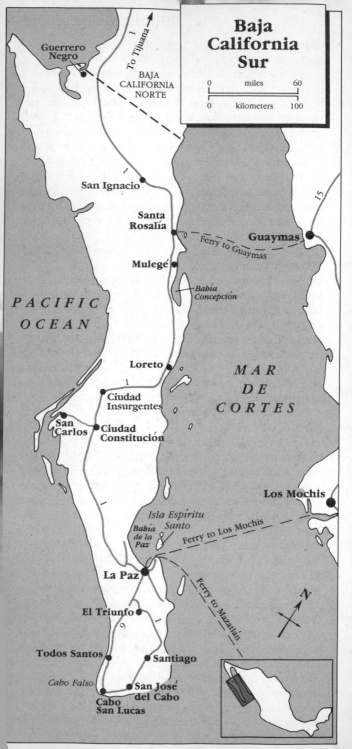

restaurant, which serves a well-prepared abalone entrée for $16, is the perfect place to rehash the day's highlights when you return to town.

SAN IGNACIO TO SANTA ROSALIA

Back on Highway 1: The road skirts the base of a mountain topped by three volcanic cones—Las Tres Virgenes—for the next 72 km (45 miles) before hitting **Santa Rosalía** on the Sea of Cortés. While quaint, the town is of little interest to visitors except as the Baja terminus for ferry service to Guaymas, on the mainland.

The French copper-mining concern that founded Santa Rosalía in the 1880s built a smelter on the plateau above the arroyo, wooden cookie-cutter houses for its employees on the flat below, and a port to ship the processed ore. Today its narrow streets are filled with impatient drivers ready to lean on their horns if you slow down to take a look. The main attraction in town is the Gustave Eiffel–designed **Templo Santa Barbara**, located three blocks west of the highway on a one-way street. Eiffel designed the termite-proof cast-iron church in 1884 thinking it would be erected in French West Africa. Somehow it ended up here, arriving disassembled in flats in 1895, whereupon it took local workmen two years to figure out how to rivet the pieces together.

Two blocks past the church is the **Panaderia Boleo**, which prides itself on its French breadmaking traditions. For accommodations your best bet is the ▶ **Hotel El Morro**, on the highway south of town. Or, even better, continue on to Mulegé, some 60 km (38 miles) farther south.

MULEGE

From Santa Rosalía Highway 1 veers inland and then back toward the coast, offering tantalizing glimpses of the Sea of Cortés before finally reaching another inviting date palm grove. The Misión Santa Rosalía de Mulegé was founded by Jesuits, their fourth on the peninsula, in 1705. The town, which is split by the Río Mulegé (actually an estuary fed by mountain springs), spills downhill from the road toward the sea. As you slowly drive past colonial-era buildings lining narrow one-way streets you're bound to feel the aura of serenity and well being that lures Americans and Canadians in some numbers here every winter. You won't see hordes of tourists, though. The few hotels in the area—the eight-room ▶ **Hotel Las Casitas**, with a walled entry patio and a small dining room; the ▶ **Vista Hermosa**, with sweeping views of town and the Sea of Cortés; and the ▶ **Hotel La Serenidad**, with an airstrip for fly-in fishermen—are fairly scattered. Las Casitas is located near the town plaza, while the Vista Hermosa is situated on a high bluff at the end of a dusty unpaved road 3 km (2 miles) east of town. La Serenidad is 4 km (2½ miles) south of town on the other side of the river, where you'll also find a number of RV parks popular with long-term vacationers. Still other visitors head a few miles farther south and camp on the beaches of the Bahía de la Concepción, the calm waters of which are ideal for fishing and diving. (The winter camping scene at Playa Cocos is especially convivial.)

Mulegé is a good base for a range of activities, including horseback riding, sea kayaking, fishing, mountain biking, and off-road tours to cave-painting sites. Your hotel can arrange any of these activities and will also be happy to prepare any fish you happen to catch (a service provided by virtually every hotel restaurant on the peninsula).

LORETO

This town 135 km (84 miles) south of Mulegé lacks its neighbor's cozy charm. Baja aficionados also complain that it's windswept. It does have a commercial airport, however, the only one serving the peninsula's midsection. The center of town, which is reached via badly rutted streets, has a sleepy look that belies Loreto's historic importance as the first permanent settlement in and capital of all the Californias. The site the Jesuits chose in 1697 for their mission did not prove fortuitous, however, and the mission was soon destroyed by floods. Fortunately, the town itself survived, and in 1750 the Franciscans rebuilt the Jesuits' mission church on the town plaza, where it stands to this day.

Staying and Dining in Loreto

Across the street from the mission, the new owners of the ▶ Hotel Plaza Loreto have redecorated its 29 rooms in an appealing colonial style. Other hotels line the seawall on the north side of town. The ▶ Hotel Misión de Loreto here offers basic accommodations and sea views as well as a convenient location next to a small marina.

Dining options in town include El Nido, for mesquite-grilled steaks; Caesar's, for seafood; and El Buey de la Barranca, for traditional Mexican dishes and handmade tortillas.

Local hotels can arrange off-road tours to San Javier, the peninsula's second-oldest mission; deep-sea fishing on the Sea of Cortés (during the summer high season); and boat trips to a number of offshore islands, where you can picnic, snorkel, dig for clams, or just unwind amid spectacular scenery. In winter fly-in visitors can rent a car for an all-day whale-watching excursion (via Ciudad Insurgentes) to Puerto López Mateos, at the northernmost end of the Bahía Magdalena.

Nopoló and Puerto Escondido

Loreto's airport, designed to accommodate hordes of tourists, was built in the 1970s during Mexico's oil boom, when the free-spending administration of President López Portillo sought to turn Loreto into another Cancún. A decade and a half later, the projected mega-resort at Nopoló, 8 km (5 miles) south of town, stands frozen in mid-construction. The Loreto Inn (formerly the Stouffer Presidente Loreto), the only luxury hotel between Ensenada and La Paz, sits on the beach by itself, a lonely reminder of grand ambitions gone awry. Paved streets, lined with light standards, lead nowhere; a still-playable golf course runs through acres of vacant house lots.

The same ghostliness pervades the marina at Puerto Loreto, 16 km (10 miles) south of Nopoló, where weeds poke through the pavement and a half-finished yacht club decays in the sun. ▶ **Tripui Resort RV Park**, located near the highway on the port road, is the only bright spot. In addition to a few motel rooms, it has a restaurant, a bar, and some recreational options, including fishing, golf, and hiking.

LORETO TO LA PAZ

About the only thing to break up the monotony of the final 345 km (215 miles) into La Paz, the capital of Baja California Sur, is the occasional glimpse of a desert plant. In winter you may be tempted to take the side road at Ciudad Constitución west to **San Carlos**, on the Bahía Magdalena. The trip takes about 45 minutes, one-way, most of it over pavement no better or worse than that of Highway 1. The bay, which is often glass-smooth in the morning, is another great place to watch whales; breezes can ruffle the surface in the afternoon, however, obscuring the clarity of the water and giving boaters a bumpy ride.

San Carlos itself is a village of 3,000, with unpaved streets and few amenities. Only the no-frills ▶ **Hotel Alcatraz**, owned by Coki and José Mendivil, can be recommended. (The row of pink casitas on the bay, for example, receives male guests by the hour.) Overflow guests in the busy winter season stay down the street in rental apartments owned by Coki's sister and brother-in-law, an American who can help with reservations if you don't speak Spanish.

In February and March local *panga* owners offer whale-watching excursions for about $25 per person. You'll find them hanging out on the patio that serves as the Alcatraz's restaurant-bar in the early evening. Coki and José also serve ocean-fresh seafood and shrimp that draws raves in several languages from the cosmopolitan crowd of whale watchers.

Back on Highway 1 after lunch the next day, you can easily cover the 208 km (130 miles) to La Paz before dark.

La Paz

Hernan Cortés himself founded a colony here in 1535, the main attraction for him being the oyster beds at the northern end of the Bahía de la Paz; the enterprise did not succeed. Subsequent attempts to settle the area failed in the face of hostile Indians, tenuous supply lines, epidemics, and hurricanes. A permanent settlement was finally established in 1811; 20 years later La Paz became the territorial capital of Baja California after a hurricane wiped out Loreto. Today it's a bustling city of 200,000, though hardly a big tourist town. As one Baja buff put it: La Paz is a staging area, a convenient jumping-off point for trips elsewhere.

The city sits on a mesa backed by foothills. With the exception of a confusing maze of angled streets in the center of town, La Paz is laid out in a neat grid with numerous one-way streets (not all of them paved). Though you'll feel as if you should be facing east, the city actually looks northwest to an endless series of fiery sunsets. The central business district clings to a steep hillside that ends at the *malecón,* a palm-lined promenade flanked by a seawall.

The city has no beaches and little in the way of shopping or tourist attractions. If you're passing through at the beginning or end of a tour of the peninsula, your best bet for entertainment will be talking to the characters who gather at **The Docks**, a Canadian-run restaurant and bar overlooking the marina, or at the restaurant in the **Hotel Lorimar**, a budget inn located one block from the *malecón*. You can also watch the world go by over a cold drink (but skip the meal) at **Terraza La Perla**, or walk the *malecón* at sunset to have dinner or a drink at the palapa-style **Paz-Lapa de Carlos 'n' Charlie**, yet another outpost of the ubiquitous Carlos Anderson chain.

STAYING IN LA PAZ
On the waterfront, the colonial-style ▶ **Hotel Los Arcos** wraps around a swimming pool set in a landscaped courtyard. Both it and the garden bungalows in its next-door annex, the Cabañas de los Arcos, have a handy central

location and an in-house travel agent to help you plan your activities. The hotel's **Restaurant Bermejo** (named for the reddish phosphorescent seas that sometimes appear on moonlit nights), with windows overlooking the bay, attentive service, and a menu of steaks, seafood, and Mexican dishes, is about as elegant as it gets in La Paz.

The 25 *casitas* at the ▶ **Hotel Posada de Engelbert** (as in Humperdinck, a co-owner) also overlook the bay, though from a less convenient location if you don't have a car.

Excursions from La Paz

Fishing is the main thing on everyone's mind here, but excursions to unpopulated, exquisitely beautiful islands in the Sea of Cortés like **Espíritu Santo**, with its own sea lion colony, also make for unforgettable day trips. Outings can be arranged through your hotel or one of the travel agents in town. Among the most reliable are **Viajes Perla**, 170 Cinco de Mayo, Tel: (682) 2-8777 or 5-3939; and **Viajes Lybsa**, at the corner of Alvaro Obregón and Degollado, Tel: (682) 2-6001.

You can also book one-day tours to Los Cabos and, from late January to March, to Magdalena Bay, for whale watching. Or you can rent a car and drive to either location at your own pace; the loop to Cabo San Lucas via Highway 19 and Todos Santos, returning via San José del Cabo on Highway 1, offers invitingly varied scenery, including desert flora, farmland, and seascapes.

Among the prearranged tours that depart from La Paz, **Baja Expeditions** (2625 Garnet Avenue, San Diego, CA 92109; Tel: 619/581-3311 or 800/843-6967) operates naturalist cruises into the Sea of Cortés from October through May. **Wild Rivers Expeditions** (P.O. Box 118, Bluff, UT 84512; Tel: 800/422-7654) runs educational trips into the surrounding desert to study its flora and fauna, as well as cave paintings in the area. Local travel agencies (see above) also offer off-road excursions in four-wheel-drive vehicles to empty beaches and isolated villages.

In addition, Grupo SEMATUR de California operates car ferries linking La Paz to **Mazatlán**, across the Sea of Cortés (about 18 hours; see the Mazatlán section in the Pacific Resorts chapter below for details). Its ferries also connect La Paz with **Topolobampo** (about 8 hours), the town next to the small city of Los Mochis, where interested parties can catch the spectacular Copper Canyon train (see the Copper Canyon chapter above). The ferry office in La Paz is located at Calle Cinco de Mayo, corner of Calle Guillermo Prieto; Tel: (682) 5-3833 or 5-8899. Schedules and rates are subject to

sudden changes, however, so it's best to call the office or
check with a travel agent several days in advance.

—*Jackie Peterson*

LOS CABOS

Los Cabos, the premier Baja California resort area, lies at the
tip of the peninsula where the Pacific meets the Sea of
Cortés. Highway 1, one of the most scenic seaside highways
in the world—and the location of most of the area's top-
drawer resort facilities—winds some 37 km (23 miles) between the region's two principal towns, San José del Cabo
and, to the southwest, Cabo San Lucas.

Vermilion mountains seem to rise out of the ocean itself
and, just behind them, endless terra-cotta–colored desert
landscapes stretch to the horizon. The visitor to Los Cabos
can rent horses or ATVs and ride for miles in the desert, or
take solitary strolls on beaches that extend as far as the eye
can see. Rock formations jutting out of the water and a
shoreline that is alternately craggy and gentle provide spectacular seascapes at every turn. **El Arco**, a towering arch-
shaped rock formation off the coast at Cabo San Lucas, has
become one of Mexico's scenic landmarks, and the pink
dawns and soft sunsets that bathe it are breathtaking.

Exquisite beauty lies under the water as well. The waters
off Los Cabos, one of the most fertile fishing grounds in the
world, teem with marine life and provide a stunning payoff
for scuba divers and snorkelers. (One of the deep underwater
canyons has been protected as a marine refuge.) More than
850 species of fish are said to live in these waters, and sharp-
eyed visitors can catch glimpses of some of them without
having to don scuba or snorkeling gear. Porpoises, whales
(between January and March), manta rays, and sea lions are
also frequently seen in the coastal waters hereabouts.

Before Highway 1 opened, this part of the peninsula was
accessible only by air or water. Most of the hotels were posh
fishing camps for wealthy sportsmen and Hollywood celebrities who could afford to arrive by private plane or yacht.
Even today Los Cabos is the kind of place where hotels list
private airstrips and fishing fleets among their amenities,
and fishing charts and boat-rental information feature prominently in the text of their brochures. The area has long been
known to those who love to fish as Marlin Alley; several
thousand blue, black, and striped marlin are caught here
every year. Swordfish, sailfish, dolphin fish, yellowfin tuna,
sierra (a large mackerel-like fish), black snook (a warm-

water pike), wahoo, roosterfish, and other species are also among the sportsfishing prizes here.

Not surprisingly, life in Los Cabos seems to accommodate a fishing schedule (though this is changing). Everyone gathers in local bars or around hotel verandahs in the late afternoon to watch the boats come in with their catches and to listen to the day's fishing yarns over drinks. Early-morning fishing trips mean that dinner is generally served early and that box lunches for the next day may be ordered along with the meal.

Fishing is no longer the sole activity, however. Seemingly overnight, Los Cabos has matured into one of the biggest stars on Mexico's resort map. Both towns have undergone successful face-lifts within the last few years, and the refurbished façades and new amenities are attracting great numbers of visitors. With a marina and new shops, restaurants, and discos in Cabo San Lucas, and a few boutiques and restaurants in San José del Cabo, non-anglers now have a wide range of options from which to choose—certainly enough to fill a week-long vacation. At the same time, many people come to Los Cabos to escape all the glitter, and it remains one of the few resort areas in the world where the natural beauty of the place is still its principal attraction.

The Los Cabos climate is ideal. The average annual temperature is 75° F, with hot days and cool nights (be sure to bring a light sweater or shawl). Some hotels used to close in summer when limited diesel-generated electricity ruled out the use of air-conditioners, but today most hotel rooms are air-conditioned and only the Twin Dolphin closes (for the month of September).

Many of the major hotels and activities in Los Cabos can be found on the new four-lane freeway between Cabo San Lucas and San José del Cabo. The majority of the hotels along the highway corridor are separated by vast parcels of land. Access to the various beaches is clearly marked by white signs with black letters and green symbols, and even those areas that have been fenced off for development are legally open to the public.

A final word about beaches. Though all are stunningly scenic, not all are good for swimming because of strong undertows. Ask at your hotel and follow their advice before you dive in.

San José del Cabo

San José del Cabo, the location of Los Cabos International airport, is the area's major banking and business center.

Though the population of the town is listed as 30,000, you'll probably wonder when you see it for the first time if everyone has "gone fishin'"—which, in all likelihood, they have.

The tranquil face of the town belies its relatively eventful history. San José del Cabo had its own mission and presidio in colonial times, when Cabo San Lucas was still a village inhabited largely by Pericue Indians. But the local priest was slain by marauding Indians, who then proceeded to discourage early settlers of the area from staying. Pirates, who plundered Spanish galleons arriving from the Philippines, were another thorn in the side of settlers.

Today, under the watchful eye of Fonatur, San José del Cabo is being transformed from a sleepy village into a busy little town. Shops and restaurants are situated in old pastel-colored buildings, and the private homes sprinkled among them have housed generations of families. Family names are often displayed on plaques by the door, and residents sit on the sidewalks chatting and watching passersby.

Visitors usually begin a walking tour of San José along Boulevard Antonio Mijares, which links the beachfront hotels to the south with the small downtown area itself. The boulevard is divided by a landscaped mall, and ends just past city hall at a small plaza with a fountain. Start at the open-air souvenir stalls on the east side of the boulevard and walk toward the plaza. You'll be passing San José's restaurant row and can study posted menus should you decide to return for a meal later. First up is **Eclipse**, a restaurant-disco, followed by **Calafia**, which specializes in pizza; the **Tropicana**, with only so-so accommodations but a lively bar scene in season; a second-story fast-food eatery; and an ice-cream stand with sidewalk tables. **Galería El Dorado**, a branch of a Cabo San Lucas shop featuring quality Mexican arts and crafts, stands on the corner. Directly ahead alongside the plaza is **Ivan's European** (Tel: 684/2-2218), which serves a variety of continental dishes, including Viennese schnitzel; **El Café Fiesta**, an indoor-outdoor coffeehouse; and **Damiana**, the town's finest restaurant, serving seafood and Mexican specialties in a garden setting; Tel: (684) 2-0499.

There are more restaurants on Calle Zaragoza, a narrow one-way street that runs past the foot of the plaza. As you stroll uphill past the church you'll find several restaurants within a block or so of each other. These include **La Fogata**, for grilled lobster and steaks; **Pietro** (Tel: 684/2-0558) for pasta; **Ah Jan**, a second-floor eatery with a Chinese-Mexican decor and Szechuan food; and **Señor Bacco**, a bar with live entertainment and Mexican snacks.

It's another couple of blocks up Zaragoza to Degollado,

the side street where the Posada Terranova (discussed below) is located. Back on Mijares, shops dominate the far side of the boulevard beyond city hall: **Hombres**, for men's sportswear; **Pa' Ella**, for women's resortwear; **Bye-Bye**, for women's casual wear; and **La Casa Vieja**, for casual wear and crafts. This is also where you'll find the **Iguana Bar & Grill**, the place for barbecued ribs and televised sports from the States. Tel: (684) 2-0266.

Down on San José's beach, birdwatchers take their binocs to the estuary next to the Stouffer Presidente hotel (the easiest access is through the hotel lobby to the beach, then a few yards to the left). As for swimming, only strong swimmers should attempt it along Playa Hotelera, the town beach. In fact, westward as far as Playa Costa Azul, at the km 29 marker, the waves are usually big enough to suit surfers, though **Playa Palmilla**, at km 26, is considered safe enough for children (it has tidepools to explore, too).

STAYING IN SAN JOSE

The European-style ▶ **Posada Terranova**, on Degollado between Zaragoza and Doblado, is a lovely small hotel with a dozen rooms, a tiny indoor restaurant and bar, and an open-air restaurant that's especially popular with locals and resident North Americans. Owned by a Mexican family of Italian descent, the Terranova is a charmer in an area where small hotels are the exception rather than the rule. It is definitely a "downtown" property, however, and thus about a ten-minute drive from the beach.

The ▶ **Stouffer Presidente Los Cabos**, at the southern end of Boulevard Mijares, is the first of about a dozen widely separated resort properties between San José del Cabo and Cabo San Lucas. But the Presidente is the place to stay if you want to be near the commercial district in San José (a five-minute cab ride) or the golf course (also a five-minute cab ride). The property itself resembles a Mediterranean-style village, with tiled walkways lacing the grounds and a large pool area that is usually the center of activity. The beach is just a few steps away. Rooms are spacious and very comfortable, and some have small sitting rooms and patios.

San José to Cabo San Lucas

The ▶ **Hotel Palmilla** has been the darling of knowledgeable resort travellers since the 1950s. Designed and built by Abelardo Rodríguez, the son of a former president of Mexico, it was the first luxury hotel in Los Cabos and is the only hotel in the area to have received the Mexican government's highest rating, Clase Especial Gran Turismo. The rooms and suites are large and comfortable, and most have balconies with an ocean or garden view. (Many also have patios where you can breakfast overlooking the ocean; ocean-view rooms cost a bit more.) Fluffy robes and giant towels add to the appeal of the large tiled bathrooms, and neither telephones nor TV sets are on hand to interrupt the reverie.

The Palmilla's personalized service (there are three employees for every guest here) begins the minute you step in the door. Not surprisingly, many guests return year after year (and request their favorite rooms), and a few have even married in the private chapel just up the hill. Tennis and paddle-tennis courts, horseback riding, and croquet are a few of the activities offered on the premises. The Palmilla also has its own fishing fleet, one of the best diving and water-sports centers in the area, and a beautiful uncrowded stretch of beach where good swimming and snorkeling conditions prevail.

As if all this were not enough, the Palmilla's owners have expanded their facilities by building a 900-acre resort on the property. The new resort has white stucco buildings with red-tile roofs, a tennis club, a shopping/entertainment complex, and a health spa. In addition, its 27-hole Jack Nicklaus–designed golf course offers unrivalled panoramas of mountains, desert, and ocean. Whether or not you golf, however, the Palmilla has a certain cachet and sophistication that other hotels and resorts in Los Cabos lack. For a perfect vacation in an idyllic setting, it's tough to beat.

Even though its driveway is marked by a tall freestanding gate in the middle of nowhere, **Da Giorgio's**, located a few miles west of the Palmilla, is hard to find. Standing atop a hill on the same side of the highway, this popular restaurant serves up homemade pasta, pizza baked in brick ovens, and a variety of other Italian dishes on an outdoor terrace or in a Mediterranean-style dining room.

Located almost midway between San José del Cabo and Cabo San Lucas, the 282-room ▶ **Meliá Cabo Real** resembles a small, futuristic city with all the creature comforts of home. Stone floors, a vaulted lobby, and tasteful decor that mixes pre-Columbian reproductions with Spanish touches lend the Meliá a certain stylishness often lacking in big hotels. A huge pool, two restaurants, three bars, and a water-sports center are just a few of its other amenities. Elsewhere on the premises, the new Cabo Real golf resort is taking shape around an 18-hole course designed by Robert Trent Jones, Jr. The layout of the hotel itself is designed to give its guests a feeling of wide-open spaces: The pool area, for example, is a five-minute walk from the lobby, and the hotel's beautiful beach (safe for swimming) is another few minutes' walk beyond that.

The ▶ **Hotel Cabo San Lucas**, about 8 km (5 miles) farther down the road in the direction of Cabo San Lucas, is sometimes referred to as "El Chileno" because it stands at the head of Punta Chileno. Situated on a 2,500-acre estate fronting a very pretty beach and the Bahía de Chileno, this massive facility bears the mark of the visiting fishermen who made it famous: Everything is built on a grand scale and has a solid, masculine look about it. (It also has its own private airstrip.) The rooms and suites are especially spacious, and all have beautiful views, either of the ocean or of the lovely gardens on the premises; some also have fireplaces. Of course, everyone gathers in the bar in the late afternoon to sip margaritas and watch the fishing boats come in, while the dining room, which overlooks the ocean and a palm-shaded pool flanked by native stone walls, is one of the most attractive in the area.

The hotel's fishing fleet is anchored minutes away, or if you prefer you can take advantage of shooting on the premises. As well, one of the most interesting boutiques in the Los Cabos area, offering a well-chosen selection of exotic treasures and jewelry from the Far East, is located in the hotel's lobby.

The posh ▶ **Twin Dolphin**, located on a bluff another few miles to the west, looks like a private sporting club with an unusual modern architectural style. Its comfortable rooms and bungalows, surrounded by desert landscape and a cactus garden, overlook the ocean, and graceful sculptures dot the property and stand guard over the pool. The bar, with its comfortable leather furniture, paneled walls, and soaring ceilings, resembles an old-fashioned gentlemen's club, and the dining room's high ceiling lends it a touch of elegance and formality.

The top-of-the-line facilities at the Twin Dolphin include an 18-hole putting green, two tennis courts lit for night play, a fishing fleet of eight boats, and two miles of marked nature trails. Service is truly personalized (the newest employee on the staff has been with the hotel more than seven years), and the sophisticated international resort crowd that can do without nonstop nightlife (and TVs and telephones) loves it here. The Twin Dolphin offers various meal-plan options, from European (no meals included in the room rate) to a full American plan (three meals a day), and is closed for the month of September.

The natural beauty of **Playa Santa María**, next to the Twin

Dolphin, is truly breathtaking. Vermilion-colored mountains tumble into the water at either end of the moon-shaped bay, and swimming and snorkeling conditions are almost always perfect. Watching the sun set from here is more than memorable. Bring your snorkeling gear, pack a picnic (but be sure to take your refuse with you when you leave), and make an unforgettable day of it.

Las Misiones, a condo/residential development that's still under construction, includes one of the area's most beautiful restaurants, **Da Giorgio's II**, situated on a promontory that affords a rare unobstructed view of El Arco and Lovers' Beach. The menu is weighted toward northern Italian specialties, and the restaurant itself is open to the air, with pool-framed multilevel walkways leading out to the point. Tel: (684) 3-2288.

Nearby, work continues on **Cabo del Sol**, an 1,800-acre resort that begins just past the Twin Dolphin and embraces Playa Barco Varado (Shipwreck Beach). Among its other amenities, the resort boasts the second Jack Nicklaus–designed golf course in Los Cabos. As of this writing, the front nine was ready for play, while the spectacular back nine, carved out of remote mountain terrain, was scheduled to open by early 1994.

Cabo San Lucas

Cabo San Lucas is a delight. In the old days the moneyed crowd that stayed at the posh hotels along the highway rarely ventured into the tiny village, but today it's busy and on the move, with the greatest concentration of shops, restaurants, and discos in the area. Old buildings around the plaza have been renovated and the plaza itself burnished to a grandeur it hadn't known previously. Victorian benches and lampposts, flowers, and an ornate bandstand now make it a pleasant place for watching the passing parade. Nearby, a marina with 340 slips for private yachts, a large hotel (the Plaza Las Glorias), condos, a shopping mall, and a pier for sightseeing boats give the entire downtown area a Mediterranean look and feel.

Nobody knows exactly how many people live in Cabo San Lucas. Part of the population comes and goes, spending late fall to Easter here and the rest of the year—including the sultry summer months—somewhere else. At the height of the winter season, though, locals estimate that at least 25,000 people call Cabo home.

A decade ago, of course, it was just another fishing village with a downtown section that occupied all of three blocks.

As the town grew, slowly at first and then more rapidly, streets that were extended into the hills surrounding the bay were laid out in a grid pattern while those downtown remained more or less untouched. Even today most of the streets downtown run at confusing off-angles while many are one-way (and some are unpaved). Almost all lack posted street signs. ("People don't go by addresses here," says one transplanted Canadian. "When we give directions, we tell visitors to count the blocks.") In other words, you'll want to bring a pair of comfortable shoes: Cabo San Lucas is a better town for strolling than for driving.

Even on a brief visit you can sense the energy that pervades the town. There's an aspect of this go-go spirit you should keep in mind, however: The developers who have fueled Cabo San Lucas's growth are time-share happy. A number of hotels—including the venerable Hotel Finisterra—have gone time-share or have added time-share annexes. As you walk around town you're likely to notice dozens of kiosks, many labeled "tourist information," staffed by overeager salespeople offering free meals, free water sports, a 50 percent discount on deep-sea fishing, or some such lure in exchange for a tour of their property and a hard-sell pitch. Be advised.

Around in Cabo San Lucas

As the highway from San José del Cabo enters San Lucas, it becomes Calle Lázaro Cárdenas and heads straight uphill toward the main plaza. If you veer left off Lázaro Cárdenas just past El Squid Roe you'll find yourself on Boulevard Marina, which edges the harbor. The part of town of greatest interest to visitors arcs around the Bahía de Cabo San Lucas in the shape of an open right hand. Using this analogy, the tourist zone starts at the Pemex station (the wrist), continues around the Cabo marina (sheltered by the thumb and palm), and ends in a turnaround near the Hotel Solmar (the fingertips). Many but not all of the hotels, shops, and restaurants are located on or near the marina; others face the bay south of the marina. A left off Lázaro Cárdenas about a block past the Pemex station brings you to the restaurants and hotels on **Playa Medano**, the town's clean, safe (for swimming) beach.

STAYING IN CABO SAN LUCAS

Right on Playa Medano, the pretty blue-and-white ▶ **Pueblo Bonito** is an all-suites condominium/hotel with a meandering pool that always seems to be crowded. Down the beach in the direction of town, the next large resort property is the 190-room ▶ Meliá San Lucas. An attractive Mediterranean-style complex, the Meliá offers smallish rooms with ocean views, a big pool just a few steps from the ocean, and breezy public areas, including two restaurants and two bars.

The ▶ Hotel Hacienda, at the far end of Playa Medano overlooking the marina, was one of the first hotels on the Cabo scene. Today it's popular with travellers who want to be near town (about a ten-minute walk around the marina) and aren't looking to spend top dollar. Though simply furnished, the rooms and suites here are comfortable, and the beach, where you can enjoy a variety of water sports, is right at your doorstep.

As you continue around the marina and up the hill: The ▶ Hotel Mar de Cortez, on Lázaro Cárdenas opposite the Giggling Marlin, is the place to stay if you're looking for economical accommodations in the middle of things. Locals call this clean, no-nonsense establishment the Mar De (pronounced MAR-day), and though it's strictly downtown, the newer part of the hotel is quite pleasant.

The rooms in the colonial-style ▶ Plaza Las Glorias, located on the marina across the street from Señor Sushi, are bright and pleasant, with cool tiled floors and rattan furniture. Most also have balconies overlooking the ocean. Guests who prefer to spend the day at the beach rather than at the pool (which is on the second floor of the hotel) are shuttled to Playa Medano by water taxi (a five-minute ride), and most of the area's fishing fleets and sightseeing boats are right outside the door or within easy walking distance.

Like a regal sentinel standing watch at one of the best locations in Cabo, the ▶ Hotel Finisterra perches atop a hill overlooking the harbor on one side and the exquisite expanse of sand at Land's End on the other. One of the first hotels in Los Cabos, the Finisterra offers the best of all possible worlds: It's within walking distance of the fishing fleets, restaurants, and shopping, yet still provides its guests with the feeling of being away from—or above—it all. Everything about it is sensible, solid, and first class, and the personalized service and faithful attention to details are not lost on its guests, who keep returning year after year. A drink at the **Whale Watcher's Bar** here is an established tradition.

Still catering to the fishermen who made it popular in the first place, the ▶ Hotel Solmar stands on a breathtaking beach farther out toward Land's End. The rooms here are breezy and comfortable, the restaurant and pool areas pretty, and the record catches on display in the dining room truly amazing. And though the beaches around Land's End are notorious for their dangerous surf and undertow, their breathtaking beauty more than makes up for the inconvenience of not being able to swim. Most hotel guests (or anyone else, for that matter) who spend the day soaking up the sun and exquisite scenery out this way will find it a day well spent.

(See also Villa Alfonso's, below.)

DINING AND SHOPPING IN CABO SAN LUCAS

Standing on the low hill at the eastern end of Playa Medano (the end farthest from Land's End), you can pinpoint the location of **Coconuts**, the beachside restaurant in the Club Cascadas condominium complex. In addition to its varied menu of meat, seafood, and pasta dishes, Coconuts has a great water-sports scene during the day. At night it's one of the most romantic spots in town, with soft candlelight and classical music backed by the sound of waves. Tel: (684) 3-0337.

Las Palmas, next door to the Meliá San Lucas, is locally famous for its lobster and abalone served in wine sauce, as well as for tasty hamburgers and light lunches, making it one of the most popular daytime gathering spots in the area. The best tables are on the sundeck overlooking the beach and afford panoramic views of the coast as well as the sometimes frenetic activity below (during spring break the restaurant sponsors a volleyball tournament that attracts more than 3,000 participants). Tel: (684) 3-0447.

Between Las Palmas and the Hotel Hacienda, Playa Medano is lined with rustic restaurants. **La Oficina**, a favorite breakfast spot along this stretch, also serves romantic dinners at tables right on the sand.

To find what many think is the most refined dining spot in the area, head over to the Marina Sol condominiums, just up the hill from Las Palmas, and look for **Villa Alfonso's**. Housed in an elegant colonial-style building, ▶ **Villa Alfonso's** bears the special touch of its owner, Alfonso Fisher, a native San Lucan and longtime restaurateur. The menu changes every night according to what is fresh or in season, and the presentation is impeccable. All dinners, which consist of seven courses, are prix fixe—about $30 per person before drinks and tip. Those who want to make an evening of it can arrive early and spend time in the Villa Alfonso's cozy bar or outside in its lush poolside garden. Of course, if you do there's a danger you'll fall in love with the place. Fortunately, Señor Fisher runs the only truly elegant bed and breakfast in town. Each of the 14 sumptuous rooms is decorated differently, and some have Jacuzzis. The restaurant is closed on Sundays; Tel: (684) 3-0739.

El Pavo Real (The Peacock), down the hill in front of the Marina Sol complex, is another of the handful of refined dining spots in town. The chef here is German, the entrées are served under a breezy palapa, and the elegant surroundings will encourage you to linger. Tel: (684) 3-1858.

Back on Lázaro Cárdenas across from the marina you'll find **El Squid Roe**, a two-story Quonset hut decorated with neon on the outside and typical Carlos 'n' Charlie's memorabilia on the inside. Though the place caters to a younger crowd, almost everyone drops by for a drink sooner or later, and the beat goes on until 2:00 or 3:00 A.M. In fact, party animals who start at the Giggling Marlin or one of the newer clubs in town invariably end the night with drinks and dancing here. Tel: (684) 3-0655.

You won't need a compass to find **Latitude 22**, in the same general area near the corner of Lázaro Cárdenas and Calle Morelos. A restaurant-bar popular with Anglo expats who have made Los Cabos home, Lat 22 keeps them happy by serving good, reasonably priced food—burgers, chile, Philly cheese steaks (the house specialty), and the like—amid a casual, well-worn decor that matches the look cultivated by many of the regulars at the bar.

The **Cabo Wabo Cantina**, up the street on Calle Zaragoza, is altogether different. Owned by Sammy Hagar, a member of the rock group Van Halen, it's a tastefully decorated nightspot with a good dance floor, a clublike decor, and a concert stage for performances by touring rock acts. Tel: (684) 3-1188.

The **Shrimp Bucket**, in the Marina Fiesta complex, is a branch of the popular Mazatlán restaurant. Seafood dishes dominate the menu at lunch and dinner, and the whimsical paintings will make you smile. Tel: (684) 3-2598.

The sleek terra-cotta-colored **Plaza Bonita**, across the way from El Squid Roe, houses a number of stores and restaurants, including **Dupuis** for decorative items and **Casual Affair** and **Dos Lunas** for resortwear; **Lukas**, the area's most sophisticated disco (no cutoffs here); and **La Terraza**, upstairs, which serves pizza, sushi, and a variety of Continental dishes. **Salsitas**, a lovely nouvelle Mexican restaurant run by the affable owner of Villa Alfonso's, is just around the corner in the same complex. You can dine (breakfast, lunch, and dinner) inside or out here and feel like a millionaire as you watch the yachts and sportsfishing boats come and go. Tel: (684) 3-1740.

Casa Roberto, in the Plaza Aramburo on Lázaro Cárdenas,

features a line of original sequined tee-shirts as well as resortwear and accessories for women. **Zen-Mar**, farther up the street, carries a good selection of folk art from the state of Oaxaca, some of it designed and made to order for the store.

The cavernous **Giggling Marlin**, overlooking the marina west of Plaza Aramburo, is an institution in Cabo San Lucas. The beer seems to flow from breakfast on, and once the sun sets there's usually a crowd dancing under the indoor palapa. In fact, it's the kind of place where anything goes: You can even have a photo of yourself taken while posing upside down like a hooked marlin. Tel: (684) 3-1209.

Temptations, one of the best stores in town for women's resortwear and accessories, is just behind the Giggling Marlin. The owners claim to stock the largest selection of hand-painted clothing in the state, much of it designed by California artist T. Jay, and the prices are significantly lower than what you'd pay for the same merchandise north of the border.

There's a cluster of good stores and restaurants on or just off Boulevard Marina in this neighborhood. Just off the boulevard, **The Shrimp Factory**—a branch of yet another popular Mazatlán eatery—has installed the same winning formula here: Customers order their crustaceans by weight and size, along with their choice of three delicious sauces. Brave customers wash it all down with a "Bulldog," a tequila-based house concoction. Tel: (684) 3-1147.

The **Río Grill**, a few blocks farther south, is a relatively new complex with a restaurant, bar, and tiny dance floor. The informal restaurant is under a palapa with shuttered windows, while the dance floor is under the stars. Tel: (684) 3-1335.

Señor Sushi, just beyond the Río Grill, is one of the most popular restaurants in Cabo San Lucas. In addition to being the area's best sushi bar, it also offers a mix of Japanese and Continental cuisine. And while the locals seem to congregate in the bar to watch televised sporting events from the States, others simply come to linger over a delicious meal and watch the passing parade. Boulevard Marina and Calle Guerrero; Tel: (684) 3-1233.

Capitán Lucas, one block south near the intersection of Boulevard Marina and Calle Hidalgo, embraces the nautical motif to the hilt. The restaurant has been built to resemble the prow of a boat, and, as a result, the ambience in its dining room is cozy and intimate. Diners who really want to enjoy the Continental dishes on its menu, however, should wait until the live music (which often drowns out all conversation) has gone home for the evening.

Heading north (uphill) on Calle Hidalgo in the direction of the town plaza you'll pass the **Mercado Mexicana**, filled with typical souvenirs. Look for the archway painted with flowers just before **Papi's** restaurant, home of the best cup of coffee in San Lucas.

Mama Eli's, on the plaza itself, carries a fine selection of decorative items, resortwear, jewelry, and accessories. On the far side of the plaza, Cabo's newest Mexican restaurant, **Mi Casa**, is housed in an old building that evokes the moneyed leisure and Old World graciousness of hacienda life. Innovative nouvelle dishes are the specialty here, and reservations are essential, especially on weekends; Tel: (684) 3-1933.

If good food in less formal surroundings is what you had in mind, head for **El Faro Viejo**, located in the trailer park of the same name just up the hill from the plaza at the corner of Calles Matamoros and Rosario Morales. (If it's your first visit, take a taxi: El Faro is in the heart of a residential section with unpaved roads and few street signs.) Blackboard menus for lunch and dinner change according to what's fresh at market, though you can usually count on a selection of meat and fish entrées. Whatever you choose, the food will be delicious and the portions hearty. Plan on arriving early for a drink in El Faro's lovely garden, complete with wrought-iron benches and Victorian-style lampposts. Reservations are necessary if you arrive after 7:30, but almost impossible to make; the restaurant doesn't have a phone, so you either have to stop by during the day or have your hotel do it.

There are several other good stores and restaurants along the boulevard as it skirts the marina on its way to the hotels near Land's End. **Nekri**, one of the most attractive stores in Cabo San Lucas, carries an especially good selection of folk art and decorative items. The main branch of **Galería El Dorado**, a few doors down, sells sculptures in a variety of mediums.

Last but not least, **El Galeón**, across from the ferry terminal and not far from the Hotel Finisterra, serves Italian and Continental cuisine, its Spanish decor—and owners—notwithstanding. The food is complemented by sweeping sea views and soft piano music in the evenings; Tel: (684) 3-0443.

Nightlife in Los Cabos

With new restaurants and clubs opening all the time, the early-to-bed reputation of Los Cabos is being laid to rest. Most hotels have live music in their lobby bars to get the evening off to a happy start. In San José del Cabo you can dance after dinner at the **Tropicana** and the **Iguana Grill**. **Eclipse**, downtown, and **Bones**, next to the Stouffer Presidente (open Thursday through Sunday), keep the beat going until well after midnight.

Of the two towns, Cabo San Lucas has the greater concentration of restaurants and nightspots. Those who like to have fun in a loud, informal atmosphere start off at the **Río Grill** or the **Giggling Marlin**, where you can drink, dine, and dance, then move on to **El Squid Roe**, where you can do the same after the others close. At some point during the evening you might also want to check out the action at **Picante**, in the Plaza Bonita, the self-styled "hottest nightclub in Cabo." For reservations, Tel: (684) 3-1744.

Those who like their evenings a bit more formal gravitate to the sleek setting of **Lukas**, across from Squid Roe, or the clublike atmosphere of the **Cabo Wabo Cantina**, where you never know what famous or semi-famous rock group might drop in. Even when the music is recorded, Cabo Wabo has one of the best dance floors in town, with comfortable chairs and tiny tables facing the stage and a snack bar outside on a pleasant patio.

Sports in Los Cabos

There are any number of sports options in Los Cabos, but fishing, whether for keeps or catch-and-release, remains a top attraction. If your hotel doesn't have its own fleet, here are a few outfits that can arrange anything from a 22-foot *panga* (skiff) to a fully equipped ocean cruiser.

- Los Dorados Fleet: (684) 3-1630
- Gaviota Fleet: (684) 3-0430
- Hotel Palmilla Fleet: (684) 2-0582
- Hotel Hacienda Fleet: (684) 3-0663
- Hotel Cabo San Lucas Fleet: (684) 3-0644
- Hotel Finisterra Tortuga Fleet: (684) 3-0366
- Hotel Solmar Fleet: (684) 3-0022
- Twin Dolphin Juanita Fleet: (684) 3-0522
- Pisces Fleet: (684) 3-0409 or 0249

Fishing fleets are moored either at their hotels or near the mouth of the marina in Cabo San Lucas. Prices range from $300 to $750 per trip, depending on the size and type of boat. Most hotels will be happy to help you get a group together. When booking, check to see if live bait and lunch are included.

Old hands at this game charter boats in advance. Most companies ask you to fax them a copy of the check you've mailed ahead of time. Those who sign up to compete in such well-known events as the Bisbee Blue Marlin Tournament (which usually is held in October) book boats as much as a year in advance.

The following establishments offer all-inclusive fishing packages in the East Cape area, about an hour and a half north and east of Cabo San Lucas (all telephone numbers are in the United States): the **Buena Vista Beach Resort**, Tel: (310) 943-0869; **Punta Pescadero**, Tel: (800) 426-BAJA; and **Villa Spacienda**, Tel: (510) 254-4123.

Canoeing, parasailing, snorkeling, windsurfing, jet skiing, and waterskiing are also available. If your hotel doesn't have the equipment, call Cabo Acuadeportes at the Hotel Hacienda, Tel: (684) 3-0117; Pisces Water Sports, Tel: (684) 3-0409 or 0249; Victor's Aquatics in the Hotel Posada Real, Tel: (684) 2-0155; or just head over to Playa Medano, where all kinds of equipment can be rented.

Bahía de Chileno (the location of the Hotel Cabo San Lucas), Punta Palmilla, and Playa Santa María (next to the Twin Dolphin) are the best places to snorkel. Scuba-diving excursions to multicolored coral beds, underwater caves, and the largest coral reef off the west coast of the Americas can be arranged through Amigos del Mar, Tel: (684) 3-0505, in the U.S., (800) 447-8999; Cabo Acuadeportes, Tel: (684) 3-0117; or the Hotel Palmilla dive shop, Tel: (684) 2-0582. The truly dedicated sometimes rent a boat and fish, scuba dive, and snorkel all in the same day.

The big hotels all have tennis courts. Horses—an exhilarating way to enjoy the truly spectacular scenery in Los Cabos—can be rented at Marco's Horse Rentals in front of the Hotel Hacienda or at the Stouffer Presidente in San José del Cabo.

Hunting trips for white dove and quail can be arranged through the travel agent at your hotel. Duck and goose shooting is also superb here.

Excursions from Los Cabos

One of the most popular excursions takes you by boat past hundreds of unconcerned sea lions to **El Arco**. Boats leave from the Cabo San Lucas marina, and the round-trip fare is about $7. You can also arrange for the boat to leave you at **Playa del Amor**, a stretch of sparkling white sand where you can dip your toes in the Pacific, walk a few yards up the beach, and then dip them in the Sea of Cortés (the boat will pick you up at a prearranged hour). If it's solitude you seek, however, don't do this on a Sunday or when a cruise ship is in town.

The East Cape Area

Any travel agency in Los Cabos can arrange trips to the East Cape area. One outing includes swimming and lunch at the **Rancho Buena Vista Hotel**, which also has bungalows and a large pool. Other excursions include the village of **Santiago**, where there's a small zoo full of animals indigenous to the area; the old lighthouse at **Cabo Falso**; the picturesque mining town of **El Triunfo**, where silver, gold, and zinc are still mined; a number of mission churches; and sunset cruises of the bay leaving from the Cabo San Lucas marina. Contact the travel agent at your hotel to arrange these and similar tours. Most will leave from your hotel lobby.

Whale Watching

The trimaran *Trinidad* (Tel: 684/3-1477) sails to whale-watching locations in season (January to March), as does a boat from the **Amigos del Mar** dive shop; Tel: (684) 3-0505.

Todos Santos

One of the most delightful trips you can do on your own involves renting a car and driving about an hour and a half north from Cabo San Lucas along the coast to the old sugar plantation town of Todos Santos. The desert countryside along the way is beautiful, and the combination of cactus forests backed by palm trees and the blue Pacific is especially breathtaking.

Once in Todos Santos you can visit the charming Hotel California (yes, the very one made famous in the Eagles' song) on Avenida Juárez, and enjoy a gourmet Italian lunch or dinner around the corner at the **Café Santa Fe**, a stylish and romantic restaurant owned by Enzo Colombo and his wife, Paula, an interior designer from New York. Salads are fresh from the garden and the lasagna is like none you've ever tasted before. The restaurant, which closes on Tuesdays, is on Marqués de León opposite the plaza. Reservations are advised; Tel: (682) 4-0002.

—Jackie Peterson and Susan Wagner

GETTING AROUND

Driving Down from the Border

Auto insurance, which is a must, can be bought along the San Diego Freeway or right before you cross the border;

U.S. insurance is not valid in Mexico. (See "Around Mexico by Car" in the Useful Facts section, above.) Car permits, mandatory for vehicles not bearing Mexican license plates, are *not* required for travel anywhere on the Baja peninsula. Posted speed limits are about the same as in the States, although some people often push 90 on the toll road (Highway 1D) in the border zone. Don't speed in town, though— sooner or later the *topes* (speed bumps) will nail you if the police don't first.

The transpeninsular highway is patrolled by the Green Angels, teams hired by the Mexican government to help motorists whose vehicles break down. And it's not unusual to see a friendly Mexican with a warm blanket appear out of nowhere to rescue a gringo. Of course, almost every Mexican male knows how to repair an American car—if only with tape and bailing wire.

Take extra gas if you're going to explore off-road. Although there are more gas stations along Highway 1 and near populated areas these days, unleaded gas and diesel fuel are not always available. Also take extra water for your car if it tends to overheat—it can get very hot along certain stretches of road.

The old road from the border to Ensenada, though *libre* (free) and beautiful, is full of twists and turns, often runs close to the edge of cliffs, is vulnerable to rock slides, and usually is occupied by slow trucks and limping, ancient cars. You'll need to take the old road to get off the beaten path, but the new road is just as beautiful, usually affords more breathtaking ocean views, and, regardless of the tolls, is the far better choice for getting from point A to point B.

Crossing back into the United States will take longer than coming in, although more gates have been opened recently. Border guards check for illegal aliens as well as contraband. It's a good idea to look them in the eye and state—before they ask you—your nationality, where you've been, and that you are returning only with those things you came with or bought—no fruits, vegetables, or pets.

—Candace Lyle Hogan

By Plane

The easiest way to get to Los Cabos is by plane. (All flights arrive at the Los Cabos International Airport a few miles east of San José del Cabo.) Aero California flies to Los Cabos from Los Angeles and Phoenix; Mexicana from Los Angeles, Denver, Mexico City, Guadalajara, Puerto Vallarta, and Mazatlán; Alaska Airlines from Seattle, San Francisco, Los Angeles, and San Diego; and United Airlines from Los Angeles.

Around in Los Cabos

Once you arrive in San José del Cabo you can either rent a car or take a taxi to your hotel. If renting a car, it's best to do so ahead of time or at the airport (Budget, Hertz, and others have desks there), as Cabo San Lucas is about 40 km (25 miles) distant. A *colectivo,* shared with others, will cost between $8 and $24, depending on the number of passengers.

Cabs, usually vans, can be called from most hotels. The average taxi fare for the 25-minute ride between San José del Cabo and Cabo San Lucas is about $26. There also are taxi stands at the plaza in Cabo San Lucas and in front of the church in San José del Cabo. The taxis in the latter are red and yellow; Cabo San Lucas taxis are blue or green and gray.

It's best to rely on cash or traveller's checks here, as credit cards are not accepted everywhere and stores that do accept them often charge extra to cover their costs. (MasterCard and Visa are the most widely accepted.) U.S. dollars can be used everywhere, but getting change for large-denomination peso or dollar bills is sometimes difficult. If you carry plenty of small bills, you should have no problem.

Remember: Baja California is on Pacific standard time (the same as Los Angeles and Vancouver), but Baja California Sur is on mountain standard time (the same as Calgary and Denver, and one hour earlier than Mexico City). Be sure to take this into consideration if you have to make a flight connection; airline representatives often forget to remind you.

ACCOMMODATIONS REFERENCE

The rates given below are projections *for December 1993 through Easter 1994. Unless otherwise indicated, rates are based on double rooms, double occupancy; the 10 percent VAT has been added. As rates are subject to change, it's always a good idea to double-check before booking. Because it takes about two weeks for a letter to reach Los Cabos, most hotel booking offices are located in the United States. Many hotels do not accept credit cards on the premises (you can use a card when booking in the U.S., however). Some have good swimming beaches, others offer them nearby; check with your travel agent if this is a concern.*

The Border Zone

▶ **Ensenada Travelodge**. Avenida Blancarte 130, **Ensenada**, Baja California 22800. Tel: (667) 8-1601; in the U.S. and Canada, Tel: (800) 255-3050. $66–$91.

▶ **Estero Beach Resort Hotel**. P.O. Box 86, **Ensenada**, Baja California 22800. Tel: (667) 6-6225; Fax: (667) 6-6925. $79.

▶ **La Fonda.** Tijuana–Ensenada Highway, km 59. Contact: P.O. Box 430268, San Ysidro, CA 92143. $55–$75.

▶ **Grand Hotel Tijuana.** Boulevard Agua Caliente 4500, **Tijuana**, Baja California 22420. Tel: (66) 81-7000; Fax: (66) 81-7016; in the U.S., Tel: (800) 343-7825. $118.

▶ **Hotel Bahía.** P.O. Box 21, Boulevard Costero y Alvarado, **Ensenada**, Baja California 22800. Tel: (667) 8-2101. $60.

▶ **Hotel El Conquistador.** Boulevard Agua Caliente 1771, **Tijuana**, Baja California 22420. Tel: (66) 81-7955; Fax: (66) 86-5433. $73.

▶ **Hoteles La Pinta.** Member hotels in Ensenada, San Quintín, Cataviña, Guerrero Negro, San Ignacio, and Loreto; contact: P.O. Box 120637, Chula Vista, CA 91912. In the U.S. and Canada, Tel: (800) 336-5454. $60–$65.

▶ **Plaza Las Glorias.** Tijuana–Ensenada Highway, km 77.5, **Baja Mar**, Baja California 22710. In the U.S. and Canada, Tel: (800) 342-2644 or (713) 448-2829. $85–$200.

▶ **Quinta del Mar Resort Hotel.** Boulevard Benito Juárez s/n, **Rosarito**, Baja California 22710. Tel: (661) 2-1644. $66.

▶ **Rosarito Beach Hotel.** Boulevard Benito Juárez s/n, **Rosarito**, Baja California 22710. Tel: (661) 2-1106. In the U.S., contact: P.O. Box 430145, San Diego, CA 92143; Tel: (619) 685-1259 or (800) 343-8582. $120.

The Midsection

▶ **Hotel Alcatraz.** Puerto Morelos y Puerto Vallarta, **Puerto San Carlos**, Baja California Sur 23740. Tel: (683) 6-0017 (Spanish), 6-0031 (English); Fax: c/o Ed Brennan, (683) 6-0019. $37.

▶ **Hotel/Cabañas Los Arcos.** P.O. Box 112, Paseo Alvaro Obregón 498, **La Paz**, Baja California Sur 23000. Tel: (682) 2-2744; Fax: (682) 5-4313; in the U.S., Tel: (800) 347-2252 or (714) 476-5555. $90.

▶ **Hotel Las Casitas.** Avenida Madero 50, **Mulegé**, Baja California Sur 23900. Tel: (685) 3-0019; Fax: (685) 3-0340. $35.

▶ **Hotel Misión de Loreto.** P.O. Box 49, Boulevard López Mateos, **Loreto**, Baja California Sur 23880. Tel: (683) 5-0048; Fax: (683) 5-0648. $60.

▶ **Hotel El Morro.** Highway 1 s/n, **Santa Rosalía**, Baja California Sur 23920. Tel: (685) 2-0414. $30.

▶ **Hoteles La Pinta.** Member hotels in Ensenada, San Quintín, Cataviña, Guerrero Negro, San Ignacio, and Loreto; contact: P.O. Box 120637, Chula Vista, CA 91912. In the U.S. and Canada, Tel: (800) 336-5454. $60–$65.

▶ **Hotel Plaza Loreto.** Paseo Hidalgo 2, **Loreto**, Baja California Sur 23880. Tel: (683) 5-0280; Fax: (683) 5-0855. $60–$70.

▶ **Hotel Posada de Engelbert.** P.O. Box 152, Playa Sur y Calle Nueva Reforma, **La Paz**, Baja California Sur 23000. Tel: (682) 2-4011; Fax: (682) 2-0663. $50.

▶ **Hotel La Posada de San Ignacio.** Calle V. Carranza 22, **San Ignacio**, Baja California Sur 23930. No phone. $25–$30.

▶ **Hotel La Serenidad.** P.O. Box 9, **Mulegé**, Baja California Sur 23900. Tel: (685) 3-0111. $53.

▶ **Rancho Sereño Bed & Breakfast.** Off Highway 1, **San Quintín**, Baja California Sur. Contact: Marcia Beltran, 1442 Hildita Court, Upland, CA 91786. Tel: (714) 982-7087. $50–$60 (includes full breakfast).

▶ **Tripui Resort RV Park.** P.O. Box 100, **Loreto**, Baja California Sur 23880. Tel: (683) 3-0818. $45; RV hookups, $16.

▶ **Vista Hermosa.** Camino al Puerto s/n, **Mulegé**, Baja California Sur 23900. Tel: (685) 3-0222. $55–$60.

▶ **Villa Vitta Resort Motel. Bahía de los Angeles**, Baja California Sur. Contact: Mrs. Brackamonte, 509 Ross Drive, Escondido, CA 92029. Tel: (619) 741-9583; Fax: (619) 489-5687. $50.

San José del Cabo

▶ **Posada Terranova.** Calle Degollado s/n, **San José del Cabo**, Baja California Sur 23400. Tel: (684) 2-0534 or 0902. $45–$55.

▶ **Stouffer Presidente Los Cabos.** Boulevard Mijares s/n, **San José del Cabo**, Baja California Sur 23400. Tel: (684) 2-0211 or 0327; Fax: (684) 2-0232; in the U.S. and Canada, Tel: (800) HOTELS-1. $180.

On the Corridor

▶ **Hotel Cabo San Lucas.** P.O. Box 48088, Los Angeles, CA 90048. Tel: (684) 3-0122 or 0123; in the U.S. and Canada, Tel: (800) 733-2226; Fax: (213) 655-3243. $160–$180.

▶ **Hotel Palmilla.** Carretera Cabo San Lucas, km 27.5, **San José del Cabo**, Baja California Sur 23410; or P.O. Box 1980, 4343 Von Karman Avenue, Newport Beach, CA 92660. Tel: (684) 2-0583; in the U.S. and Canada, Tel: (800) 637-2226; Fax: (714) 851-2498. $250.

▶ **Meliá Cabo Real.** Carretera Cabo San Lucas, km 19.5, **San José del Cabo**, Baja California Sur 23410. Tel: (684) 3-0967; Fax: (684) 3-1003; in the U.S. and Canada, Tel: (800) 336-3542. $174–$246.

▶ **Twin Dolphin.** 1625 West Olympic Boulevard, Suite 1005, Los Angeles, CA 90015. Tel: (684) 3-0259; Fax: (684) 3-0496; in the U.S., Tel: (800) 223-6510 or (213) 386-3940; in Canada, Tel: (800) 424-5500. $390 (includes all meals).

Cabo San Lucas

▶ **Hotel Finisterra.** P.O. Box 1, **Cabo San Lucas**, Baja California Sur 23401; or 4422 Cerritos Avenue, Los Alamitos, CA 90720. Tel: (684) 3-3333; Fax: (684) 3-0590; in the U.S., Tel: (800) 347-2252 or (714) 827-3933. $144.

▶ **Hotel Hacienda.** P.O. Box 48872, Los Angeles, CA 90048. Tel: (684) 3-0122 or 0123; Fax: (684) 3-0666; in the U.S. and Canada, Tel: (800) 733-2226; Fax: (213) 655-3243. $115.

▶ **Hotel Mar de Cortez.** P.O. Box 1827, Monterey, CA 93942. Tel: (684) 3-0032; Fax: (684) 3-0232; in the U.S., Tel: (800) 347-8821; in Canada, Tel: (408) 375-4755. $40–$50.

▶ **Hotel Solmar.** Avenida Solmar s/n, **Cabo San Lucas**, Baja California Sur 23410. Tel: (684) 3-3535; Fax: (684) 3-0410; in the U.S., Tel: (800) 344-3349; in Canada, Tel: (310) 459-9861. $158 (includes dinner).

▶ **Meliá San Lucas.** Playa Medano, **Cabo San Lucas**, Baja California Sur 23410. Tel: (684) 3-1000; Fax: (684) 3-0420; in the U.S. and Canada, Tel: (800) 336-3542. $246.

▶ **Plaza Las Glorias.** Boulevard Marina s/n, **Cabo San Lucas**, Baja California Sur 23410. Tel: (684) 3-1220; Fax: (684) 3-1238; in the U.S. and Canada, Tel: (800) 342-2644 or (713) 448-2829. $143–$198.

▶ **Pueblo Bonito.** P.O. Box 460, **Cabo San Lucas**, Baja California Sur 23410. Tel: (684) 3-1976; Fax: (684) 3-1995; in the U.S., Tel: (800) 262-4500 or (619) 275-4500; in Canada, Tel: (800) 654-5543. $135–$160.

▶ **Villa Alfonso's.** P.O. Box 3, **Cabo San Lucas**, Baja California Sur 23410. Tel and Fax: (684) 3-0739; in the U.S. and Canada, Tel: (800) 726-2226. $162.

THE PACIFIC RESORTS

By Patricia Alisau, Robin Lloyd, Mitchell Nauffts, Jackie Peterson, and Susan Wagner

Patricia Alisau, a resident of Mexico for more than 20 years, is a former Central American war correspondent turned freelance travel editor and writer. Her photographs and articles on Mexico have appeared in several European maga-zines as well as The New York Times, Newsweek, *and the* Chicago Tribune. Robin Lloyd has lived in Mexico for 17 years and is a correspondent for The News, *Mexico City's English-language daily, and for* Vallarta Today. *He is also the author of five books, and his articles and photographs have appeared in* Life, Time, *and* Newsweek. *Mitchell Nauffts also writes the Yucatán Caribbean Resorts section of this book, Jackie Peterson and Susan Wagner the Baja Peninsula section.*

Some of the world's most sophisticated resorts, not to mention some of its most scenic, are to be found on Mex-ico's Pacific coast. A combination of summerlike tempera-tures year-round, plenty of sunshine, broad sandy beaches, and lively nightlife has made these resorts, collectively, the country's major drawing card for international travellers. While those who want to combine a bit of archaeology with their sun, sea, and sand tend to congregate in the Caribbean resorts of the Yucatán peninsula, and sportsmen/sybarites who relish the comforts of home head for Los Cabos at the tip of the Baja peninsula, the international traveller looking for a mix of sun and fun, bustling activity, and peaceful surroundings is drawn to the exciting string of resorts that dot the Pacific coast from Mazatlán down to Huatulco. And though the personality of each of these resorts differs from those of its sisters, they all share one thing in common: Almost everything a visitor will want to see or do is located on or just off the coast road that runs through town.

We cover the Pacific resorts in geographical order, from Mazatlán in the north to Huatulco in the south. For driving down to one or more of these spots from the western United States, Highway 15 heads south from Nogales on the U.S. border and passes through Mazatlán on its way to Tepic, in the state of Nayarit. There, Highway 200 becomes the principal coastal route, linking the rest of the Pacific resorts all the way down to the Guatemalan border. (See the Getting Around section at the end of our coverage of Mazatlán for more information on driving down from the border.)

The Resorts

Mazatlán is the resort for those who put an emphasis on sports and would rather not worry about dressing up or doing anything too fancy. Besides being a commercial city in its own right, it's a hodgepodge of things to see and do, and although they're all here, you have to look to find them. If you want to arrange for a charter fishing boat or a wind-surfing lesson, the place is the El Cid Mega Resort's sports center on the beach; if you want to lie on a beach with plenty of company, head for the sand in front of the Playa Mazatlán or the Costa de Oro; if you like beaches that are quieter, put on your bathing suit and mosey over to the Camino Real; and if you don't want to see *anybody,* just travel north along Avenida Sábalo Cerritos and pick your spot. Mazatlán makes no demands.

Puerto Vallarta, perhaps the quintessential Pacific resort, combines the outgoing friendliness of a genuine small town with first-rate amenities. It's a favorite with discriminating travellers from the West Coast, who enjoy strolling around town before having dinner at one of its many charming restaurants. The shopping (including resortwear by nationally known local designers) is terrific as well, and a sprawling new marina complex has added an extra touch of glamour to the town that Taylor and Burton first put on the map. **Nuevo Vallarta**, just north of Puerto Vallarta, is a developing resort area with a long way to go.

The beautiful, remote Hotel Costa Careyes in **Careyes**, a small bay south of Puerto Vallarta, is all but out of business, at least for the time being. After it fell victim to the recession, its Italian owners decided to sell the 3,700-acre property. The land development company that built Puerto Vallarta's new marina complex is looking into buying the Careyes property, but the plans for its future are unknown. There is still a Club Med property at Careyes, however.

Tenacatita, a huge complex hidden away at the end of a winding road off the coastal highway to the south of Careyes, is another resort hotel on a small bay. It's a modern, comfortable place, ideal for those who wish to spend a few lazy days on a flat, sandy beach in the middle of nowhere.

Barra de Navidad, a few miles farther down the coast in the direction of Manzanillo, is a grown-up fishing village that has retained some of its charm despite the fact that, for the moment at any rate, it is stuck somewhere between what it once was and what it might yet become.

The kind of vacation you have in **Manzanillo**, due west of Mexico City, depends on your choice of hotel. Elegant Las Hadas (where much of the movie *10* was filmed) sits high on a hill like the regal dowager she is. Affluent travellers who want to unwind in a self-contained resort far from the madding crowd return here year after year. Other, less formal resorts line the road leading into town. Be forewarned, however: Nightlife and shopping are not the chief attractions of Manzanillo.

Ixtapa/Zihuatanejo, on the long stretch of coast between Manzanillo and Acapulco (but closer to the latter), is a laid-back version of Acapulco. With its "Hotel Row"—a string of soaring high-rise structures lining Palmar Bay—Ixtapa is a modern mega-resort. The old fishing village of Zihuatanejo, one bay to the south, attracts those who prefer a more casual atmosphere. In this friendly, charming little town (about four miles from Ixtapa over a paved road) you never have to wear anything more than cutoffs, a tee-shirt, and sandals—and that's the way the well-to-do international crowd that vacations here likes it.

Acapulco was the trailblazer of Mexican resorts. Today it's one of the world's most famous playgrounds and one of Mexico's larger cities and largest ports. The Las Brisas residential section in particular is a haven for sophisticated pleasure-seekers, movie stars, statesmen, and just plain folks who like to relax by day and party by night in the sprawling private villas overlooking the bay. Elsewhere in town, the wide variety of ethnic restaurants and shopping malls is hard to beat, as is the glittering array of discos.

Puerto Escondido and **Puerto Angel**, east of Acapulco and south of Oaxaca City, are slated for further development. For the moment they are mostly visited by young budget-conscious travellers, an international surfing crowd, and retirees who arrive in their RVs and don't need mugs for their beer. Still, the fishing and surfing *are* great, and neon lights and TVs scarce.

Last but not least is **Huatulco**, with its nine glorious bays. Amenities here include a sprawling Club Med, the deluxe Sheraton and Club Maeva resort hotels, a new Holiday Inn, and a growing number of stores and restaurants. Those expecting nonstop activity and nightlife at their doorstep are likely to be disappointed; it will take a few years for Huatulco to mature into a full-service resort. Those looking to get away from it all, on the other hand, may find Huatulco's combination of five-star hotels and unspoiled surroundings just what the doctor ordered.

—*Susan Wagner*

MAZATLAN

Mazatlán, on the Pacific coast due east of Baja California Sur's Los Cabos area, has one thing going for it no other major resort in Mexico can match: its proximity to the U.S. border. Located 600 miles due south of El Paso, Texas, it's close enough to the States to allow *norteamericanos* to fly down for long weekends, with Los Angeles just a bit more than a two-hour flight. Motorists with a longer stay in mind find that, thanks to recent highway improvements, they can make the drive from the Arizona border in about 10½ hours. As well, it is the only Mexican beach resort with an established language school, enabling those who want to learn Spanish or improve their skills to combine their studies with a seaside vacation.

A city that today numbers 500,000 residents, Mazatlán does not depend entirely on tourism for its well-being. In fact, it was a busy working seaport long before the tourists discovered its miles of sandy beaches. Still one of Mexico's leading ports (the largest between San Diego and the west coast of Panama), it receives frequent visits from cargo-liners, cruise ships, and ferries, to say nothing of the comings and goings of its own home-based shrimp fleet, the country's biggest—as a glance at any restaurant menu in town will reveal. Fortuitously situated at the mouth of the Sea of Cortés, it is also considered the deep-sea fishing capital of the mainland (more than 6,000 billfish are boated

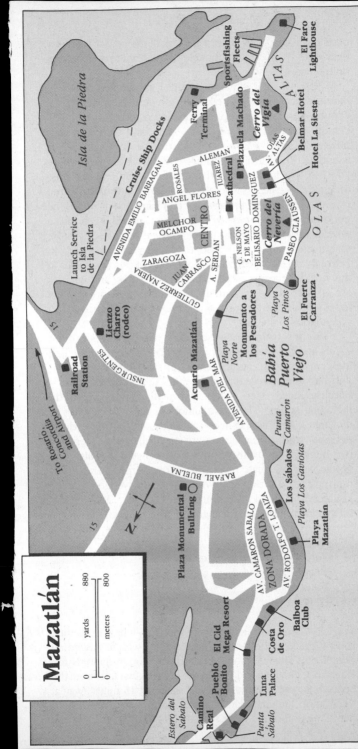

Mazatlán

0 yards 880
0 meters 800

Isla de la Piedra

Launch Service to Isla de la Piedra

Cruise Ship Docks

AVENIDA EMILIO BARRAGAN

Ferry Terminal

Sportsfishing Fleets

El Faro Lighthouse

Plazuela Machado

Cerro del Vigía

Belmar Hotel

Hotel La Siesta

AV. OLAS ALTAS

ALEMAN

ROSALES

ANGEL FLORES

JUAREZ

Cathedral

MELCHOR OCAMPO

CENTRO

ZARAGOZA

A. SERDAN

G. NELSON

5 DE MAYO

BELISARIO DOMINGUEZ

PASEO CLAUSSEN

Cerro del Nevería

O L A S

GUTIERREZ NAJERA

JUAN CARRASCO

Lienzo Charro (rodeo)

INSURGENTES

Railroad Station

To Rosario and Concordia and Airport

15

15

Monumento a los Pescadores

El Fuerte Carranza

Playa Los Pinos

Bahía Puerto Viejo

Acuario Mazatlán

AVENIDA DEL MAR

Playa Norte

Punta Camarón

RAFAEL BUELNA

Plaza Monumental Bullring

N

AV. CAMARON SABALO

ZONA DORADA

AV. RODOLFO T. LOAIZA

Los Sábalos

Playa Los Gaviotas

Playa Mazatlán

Balboa Club

Costa de Oro

El Cid Mega Resort

Pueblo Bonito

Camino Real

Luna Palace

Punta Sábalo

Estero del Sábalo

here every year) and is home to one of the country's largest breweries, Pacífico. And it's one of the few Mexican resorts on the national rail network.

In spite of their city's commercial importance, however, *mazatlecos* tend not to take life too seriously. The typical native, often bearing the features and coloring of his 19th-century forebears from France, Spain, and Germany, calls himself a *pata salada* (salty foot). The local attitude is friendly and informal. Mazatlán is the kind of place where you can live in cutoffs and go to bed early and not miss much. The musicians who play the bouncy, German-inspired music of the *banda tambora,* a brass band that moves to the perky beat of the *tambora* (bass drum), may launch into a tune in a parking lot (or anywhere else that moves them, for that matter) and set people to dancing on the sand. In February it's also the scene of one of the best *carnavales* in the world. Pageants, street dancing, fireworks, and parades are all part of the merriment as Mazatlán turns topsy-turvy for a week. (But be sure to reserve well in advance if you plan to join in the fun.)

A visitor's typical daily schedule here revolves around sports and the great outdoors. Mazatlán was one of the first Mexican resorts to attract visitors in substantial numbers—and has been successful at keeping them coming back—because there *is* so much of everything for everybody, including space. (There are almost 30 miles of beaches in the area.) Among the many activities offered here, duck, pheasant, and dove shooting are especially good (there are two hunts a day from October to April), and it is also one of the few Mexican resorts to allow surfing. The early-morning wave action at Playa Los Pinos, a wedge of beach just north of the 19th-century Fuerte (Fort) Carranza, has caused local surfers to nickname it "The Cannon."

MAJOR INTEREST
Zona Dorada resort-hotel area
Deep-sea fishing
Water sports
Hunting

The less-than-eventful history of Mazatlán—which in Nahuatl means "Place of the Deer"—is in keeping with its easygoing personality. The town was founded by the conquistador Nuño Beltrán de Guzmán in 1531. In the decades that followed, the Spanish garrison in the area was stationed 15 miles away at Villa Unión, and Mazatlán itself was merely a sentinel post. In the 19th century the troops of Napoleon III were based not here but at Malpica, a few miles due east, and gold and silver were mined farther inland near towns such as Rosarío, Copala, and Pánuco. In fact, the first municipal government here wasn't established until 1837.

But it was an event out of the Keystone Kops that finally put Mazatlán in the history books. In 1914, during the Mexican Revolution, General Venustiano Carranza's forces set out to destroy the fort on top of Icebox Hill (Cerro de la Nevería) with a homemade bomb fashioned from dynamite, stones, and nails packed in pigskin. Instead, the pilot overflew the target and the airsick bombardier dropped his charge on a downtown street—thereby earning Mazatlán the dubious distinction of being the second city in the world to suffer aerial bombardment (Tripoli was the first).

It wasn't until the 1950s, when it was discovered by deep-sea sportsfishermen, that Mazatlán truly came into its own, however. Happily, the emphasis on the outdoor sporting life has prevailed ever since.

Around in Mazatlán

The city and resort of Mazatlán together cover much of a 15-mile-long peninsula. Most visitors to Mazatlán congregate along the coastal strip that stretches from the old lighthouse on the southern tip of the peninsula to the new condominiums on the beaches to the north. The center of the action is the strip of high-rises between Valentino's Discotheque at Punta Camarón and the posh, private Balboa Club to the north—the Zona Dorada, or "Golden Zone."

The seaside hotels extending north from the Zona Dorada to the Camino Real are also popular. Large-scale development along here is imminent, however, with the construction of Marina Mazatlán in the former Estero del Sábalo well under way. Entrance to the marina is on the north side of Punta Sábalo, where the Camino Real hotel perches on a bluff overlooking the Pacific. The bridge that once connected the major hotel district to a sprinkling of resorts farther north has disappeared, and traffic now flows on a three-mile-long artery around the back side of the marina. The newly created channels here give boats access to the Marina El Cid, a mix of dockside homes and condominiums affiliated with the El Cid Mega Resort complex. A luxury hotel, retail shops, and a nine-hole expansion of the resort's golf course are also planned for this portion of the complex. As well, work is proceeding on the marina's centerpiece, an 800-slip yacht basin surrounding an island. Private homes, condos, hotels, shops, and restaurants are springing up along the waterfront to the north, along with 200 berths for smaller boats.

With these additions, the beachfront zone of greatest visitor interest is far more spread out than what you'll encounter at most Mexican resorts. As a result, the beaches in front of the Zona Dorada have an uncrowded feeling about them. (Many hotels also have roped-off areas on the beach to keep itinerant vendors from interrupting your siesta.) And, as is true of most resorts in Mexico, everything you'll need is on or just off the beach road, which changes names five times: At its southernmost point it is called Avenida Olas Altas, then sucessively becomes Paseo Claussen, Avenida Del Mar, Avenida Camarón Sábalo (north of Punta Camarón), and finally Avenida Sábalo Cerritos (north of the Camino Real).

At the far southern end of town sits the old lighthouse (second-tallest in the world after Gibraltar's), perched on a hill called Cerro del Crestón. To the east are berthed the fishing fleets.

El Centro, Mazatlán's downtown area (and a busy one by Mexican resort standards), is inland from Olas Altas and south of the Monumento a los Pescadores (Fisherman's Monument), the city's most famous landmark, which faces the Bahía Puerto Viejo on Avenida del Mar.

The curving strip of coastline that follows Avenida del Mar north from the old Carranza fort to Punta Camarón—the beginning of the Zona Dorada—was the resort-strip successor to Olas Altas. Now itself eclipsed by the Zona Dorada and points north, it still boasts a variety of restaurants, nightclubs, hotels, and motels.

We begin with the older parts of town.

OLAS ALTAS

This is where, in the 1940s, it all began. Back then celebrities such as Ernest Hemingway and Katharine Hepburn would watch the sun set into the Pacific from their rooms at the Hotel Belmar while their fans back in the States wondered where they had disappeared to. The fishing fleets were moored on the south side of Cerro del Vigía (Lookout Hill), and nothing but empty beaches, beaches, and more beaches spread out to the north. The somewhat seedy Belmar and the plain but clean ► Hotel La Siesta, on the waterfront nearby, are today funky and old-fashioned—La Siesta is the more appealing of the two—and remain popular with sportsfishermen who want to be near the fleets (you'll also find an older crowd of budget travellers here as well as students from the United States and Europe). These are not what anyone nowadays thinks of as resort hotels, however. La Siesta has a pleasant courtyard restaurant and a big paneled bar where fishermen gather to drink Pacífico from the local brewery. The beach, which is rocky here and sometimes pounded by fairly big waves, is just across the road.

While Olas Altas long since has lost its edge to the hotel strip to the north, visitors who want to stroll through the historic neighborhood behind the waterfront may well end up seeking a cold drink at a sidewalk table along the avenue. Or they may join those who have come specifically to eat at the one-and-only **El Shrimp Bucket**, the flagship restaurant of the ever-popular Carlos 'n' Charlie's chain, located in the Hotel La Siesta. Local businessmen, fishermen, and tourists alike flock to this place, especially at lunchtime, and the portions of fish, meat, and poultry are large—as are the drinks. No one comes here for a *quick* bite to eat: The Shrimp Bucket is all about animated conversation and hearty, drawn-out meals. (Dinner may be accompanied by live music, which can keep some hotel guests awake later than they would like.) For nonfishermen who want to see the day's catch on display, it's also a great place to stop in for a drink before heading over the hill to the pier. (And you can pick up a fisherman's box lunch here every morning at 6:00 A.M.)

While you're in the neighborhood, drive or climb the steep stairways to the heights of **Cerro del Nevería** (Icebox Hill) for panoramic views of the entire city. Originally a military observation point, the hill got its name in the days before electric refrigeration, when local fishermen would store their catch in ice-filled caves in its side.

OLD MAZATLAN

A daytime or early evening stroll around the historic downtown area, inland from Olas Altas, makes for an interesting counterpoint to the neon glitz of the Zona Dorada. The old part of town is undergoing a massive restoration, which, when completed, will make it pleasantly photogenic. Already many building façades sport new coats of paint and the general atmosphere has brightened considerably.

The jewel of the restoration is the 19th-century **Teatro Angela Peralta**, on Calle Carnaval a few steps from the historic Plazuela Machado (where outdoor art shows frequently brighten the scene on weekend afternoons). Originally called the Teatro Rúbio, the opera house was renamed for a famous Mexican diva who died of tropical fever during an appearance here in the 1880s. By turn it became a vaudeville, burlesque, and movie house, and ultimately fell into disuse 40 years ago when a hurricane blew off its roof.

Restoration of the Neoclassical theater began in 1987 and was completed in 1992. Though now air-conditioned, it retains features designed for the tropical theatergoer of yesteryear. The entry portico (which houses a second-floor gallery for occasional art exhibitions) leads to an open-air lobby. Inside the horseshoe-shaped house itself several tiers of balconies are edged by ornate wrought-iron railings designed for cross-ventilation. In addition to occasional appearances by touring groups, the theater hosts a range of events, from symphony and opera to rock and reggae, during Sinaloa's statewide cultural festival each November.

The **Museo Regional de Mazatlán** is housed in an old building at Sixto Osuna 76, a block east of Avenida Olas Altas. Assembled from the private collections of three prominent citizens, the museum exhibits are devoted to the ancient history of Mazatlán and the states of Sinaloa and Nayarit. The front gallery sometimes is given over to temporary art exhibitions. Open 10:00 A.M. to 1:00 P.M. and 4:00 to 7:00 P.M., Tuesday through Sunday.

Charming restaurants have sprung up around the neighborhood, joining the historic **Doney**, a block north at Calle Mariano Escobedo 610, where diners sample Mexican specialties in the roofed courtyard of a Spanish marquis' former home. Facing on the plazuela itself, at the corner of Calle Constitución and Heriberto Frias, is the **Café Pacífico**, a friendly bar offering light snacks and a pool table; **La Casa de Ana**, a vegetarian café at Constitución 515; the **Hostería de Pepe**, a Spanish restaurant at Constitución 519; and, one block farther east at the corner of Constitución and Avenida Juárez, the **Royal Dutch Café**, with a number of tables in a pretty garden courtyard. Proprietors Roelof Smeding and his wife, the former Alicia Cuevas, have converted the colonial-style Cuevas family home into an attractive café where foot-weary shoppers and sightseers can rest over coffee and pastry or a light lunch. The owners, newlyweds when they started up the operation in 1991, have recently expanded their kitchen to offer full-course lunches and dinners. Tel: 81-2007.

PLAZA REPUBLICA

Two blocks north on Juárez, the **Basílica de la Inmaculada Concepción** watches over the Plaza República, the heart of downtown Mazatlán. On Sundays between 5:00 and 7:00 P.M. the plaza is the venue for a free folkloric show featuring music, singers, and dancers. The cathedral itself, domed in blue and yellow tiles, is cool and imposing but of relatively recent vintage.

Continuing north on Juárez brings you to Fabricas de Francia, one of Mazatlán's leading department stores. The block-square **municipal market**, a block farther north on Juárez between Leandro Valle and Melchor Ocampo, is certainly worth a walk-through, although the predictable Mexican souvenirs you'll find usually can be bought elsewhere in less time, and for less money, than it takes to bargain for them here.

The **Centro de Idiomas**, three blocks west of Juárez at Calle Belisário Dominguez 1908, offers both group and private instruction in Spanish. Prospective students can show up any Saturday morning at 10:00 A.M. to take a proficiency test and then begin study the following Monday. In addition to Americans of all ages, the center attracts Europeans, especially the Swiss. Those who want intensive Spanish can arrange for homestays with Spanish-speaking families. For information, Tel: 82-2053.

FROM EL FUERTE CARRANZA TO PUNTA CAMARON

Avenida del Mar, the coastal strip along the Bahía Puerto Viejo, was the site of the first true resort action in Mazatlán. The palm-lined drive parallels Playa Norte, a three-mile crescent of sand that hugs the bay. (Be forewarned: The mostly local crowd hangs out on the southern quarter of the beach for a reason. A dangerous undertow—*resaca*—kicks in opposite the Aguamarina Hotel and extends north to Valentino's. The unpopulated stretch of sand is fine for strollers, but swimmers should avoid it.) Tucked amid private homes and apartments along the strand, a few popular restaurants draw lunchtime crowds (beginning around 1:30, with dinner starting around 8:00), but it's after dark when this area comes alive with bars, discos, and two nightclubs in older hotels—**La Guitarra** in the Hacienda and **Bar el Navegante** in the De Cima—that attract both locals and visitors.

El Marinero (Tel: 81-7682), a plain, family-style seafood place, has moved from its longtime location to a newer building a block and a half north at Paseo Claussen s/n. It still caters, however, to those who like good food but don't want to pay extra for ambience or decor. Popular with local residents for years, it shares its number one ranking as Mazatlán's favorite seafood restaurant with the even plainer

Mamuca's (Tel: 81-3490), Simón Bolívar Poniente 404; the latter is is so popular that its tables often spill onto the sidewalk.

Some of Mazatlán's most popular restaurants are located along the stretch of Avenida del Mar that runs from the Fisherman's Monument to Valentino's. Anyone who comes to Mazatlán soon hears about **Señor Frog's**, Avenida del Mar 255. The tongue-in-cheek mood is set by the life-size papier-mâché frog that greets guests as they enter the dining room. Cruise-ship passengers, some direct from the ship, arrive revved up and ready to party, and many stay right through lunch and into dinner. Consequently, you can forget about having a quiet conversation or sparking a little romance on most nights in season—and don't come at all unless you're prepared for rowdy fun and pranks. If you want to try the great ribs, chicken, or meat dishes without the hubbub, go for lunch. The tables just inside the door and in the seaside dining room next to the bar are the best for watching the action, but there's usually a line of eager revellers waiting to get in from 8:00 P.M. on. Tel: 82-1925.

A young crowd also frequents the **Toro Bravo Bar** up the avenue. Outside the line is always long, but once you get in you can join the group at the bar or take a spin on the mechanical bull.

The **Acuario Mazatlán**, one block east of Avenida del Mar at Avenida de los Deportes 111, offers those who don't scuba dive a look at the marine life inhabiting the waters around Mazatlán. Natural history films (in Spanish) are shown in the adjacent auditorium, and separate bird and sea lion shows are staged outdoors throughout the day. The small botanical garden, aviary, and zoo outside are also worth the time it takes to stroll through them. Open 9:00 A.M. to 7:00 P.M. daily.

Punta Camarón

The opulent Moorish-style complex at Punta Camarón looks like a movie set and houses two restaurants, a bar, a disco, and several other attractions. **Bora Bora**, a discotheque-bar on the beach level, fills two palapas lit by flashing colored lights. Next door is **Bali Hai**, a video bar that also serves light meals and snacks. Both draw a college-age crowd.

Upstairs, the multilevel **Sheik** has a reputation as one of Mazatlán's most elegant restaurants. The posh decor, spectacular views of the ocean, and soft piano music make it the kind of place you'll probably want to dress up for. The menu is Continental, and reservations are recommended. Tel: 84-1666.

If you find yourself in a dancing mood after dinner, head

next door to **Valentino's Discotheque**. Updated with shimmering mirrors and video screens a few years ago, this longtime favorite is one of Mazatlán's "hot" discos. There are separate areas for dancing to rock 'n' roll and touch dancing, a laser light show, and a game room where you can play pool or backgammon.

The sleek **Mikonos** piano bar, at the southern end of the complex, offers light snacks at tables inside or under the stars. The views of the coastline all the way to town are unforgettable, especially at night, and the piano music is the best in town, hands down.

THE ZONA DORADA

The "Golden Zone," an oval-shaped parcel of land bordered by Avenida Camarón Sábalo to the east and Avenida Rodolfo T. Loaiza to the west, encompasses the largest concentration of shops and restaurants in Mazatlán, as well as some of its prime resorts, all within steps of the town's most popular beach, **Gaviotas**.

Staying in the Zona Dorada

▶ **Los Sábalos**, a gleaming white stucco hotel just past the left turn onto Rodolfo T. Loaiza, sits in an oasis of green grass and rustling palms overlooking a meandering swimming pool and, beyond it, the sea. Its splashy setting and amenities such as clay tennis courts and a health club with saunas and Jacuzzis tend to compensate for the plain decor of its 185 units. Suites have wet bars and small refrigerators, and the palapa-shaded tables for patrons of **Las Gaviotas Bar** and the adjacent **Las Olas** restaurant offer striking views of the sunset. The young people who gather at **Joe's Oyster Bar**, well removed from the rest of the hotel's structure, enjoy their sunset views to the amplified sounds of rock 'n' roll.

The sprawling, 432-room ▶ **Hotel Playa Mazatlán**, one of the oldest and best-maintained beachfront hotels in Mazatlán, is half a block up the road on the same beautiful stretch of beach. With three restaurants, two large pools, and several shops, the Playa Mazatlán is considered one of the nicer hotels in town, and its beach is certainly one of the busiest. The rooms here are decorated simply but comfortably, with tiled headboards and night tables; not all have ocean views, however. The hotel's Mexican fiesta night is the best in town, and every Sunday at 8:00 P.M. its terrace bar and restaurant sparkle under a shower of fireworks.

Visitors who like the convenience of a kitchenette might consider one of the motels in the area. While the ▶ **Hotel Suites Las Flores**, about a block north of the Playa Mazatlán, may lack the lavish public facilities of its two neighbors, it does have cheerful deluxe suites with stove and refrigerator in the same price range. And then, at half the cost, there's the ▶ **Casa Contenta**. This small, truly special hideaway tucked between two larger motels at the north end of Rodolfo T. Loaiza has seven one-bedroom units and a large beachfront house suitable for eight guests, all delightfully decorated in Mexican colonial style.

Shopping in the Zona Dorada

Shopping should not be the main reason you come to Mazatlán. Most places feature quantity rather than quality, or cater to a crowd that likes to take home tee-shirts. The handful of shops and boutiques that offer a better selection of items are for the most part located in or near the Zona Dorada on Rodolfo T. Loaiza or Camarón Sábalo. (The siesta is observed by many of these shops between 2:00 and 4:00 P.M.)

Designer's Bazaar, at Rodolfo T. Loaiza 217 (with a branch in the Hotel Playa Mazatlán mall), specializes in resortwear, both casual and dressy, as well as decorative items with a flair. **La Carreta**, in the Playa Mazatlán mall, offers tasteful reproductions of antique furniture and a good selection of decorative items.

Hidden behind colonial-style arches, **El Viejo Mazatlán**, Rodolfo T. Loaiza 303, has a spacious showroom filled with ceramic pieces from Tlaquepaque and Tonalá, two of the country's foremost artisans' centers.

Indio's Gifts, Rodolfo T. Loaiza 311 (as well as at three other locations around town), is known for its attractive brass, leather, copper, and silver decorative items and jewelry, all beautifully displayed.

As you head north from Indio's, the first shopping arcade on the right has two shops of special note for gift buyers: **La Troje**, with small decorative objects, and **Fela the Flower Lady**, well back of the street, where you often find Fela Muñoz fashioning bright paper flowers while her husband, Ciro, sits outside at his workbench creating fanciful metal wall sculptures (schools of fish, flying birds).

On a side street at Avenida de las Garzas 1, **Si Como No** sells original artwork and antiques. If you continue past the gallery to the next corner you'll find the newest branch of **Pastelería Panama**, a popular local coffeeshop with tables inside and out.

For a substantial meal try **The Shrimp Factory**, on the corner of Rodolfo T. Loaiza and de las Garzas, where the assembly-line techniques perfected by Henry Ford are applied to the consumption of that delicious crustacean. Customers choose the size of shrimp and number of kilos they want, and then sit back and enjoy as their order arrives post haste with a choice of three sauces.

Maya del Pacífico, in the pyramid-like building at Rodolfo T. Loaiza 411, has leather goods and decorative items. Next door, a folkloric show featuring the flying *voladores* of Papantla is staged every night except Sundays in season (and on Tuesdays, Thursdays, and Saturdays the rest of the year). Dinner is included in the price of the show, about $30 per person. The **Mazatlán Arts and Crafts Center,** nearby at Rodolfo T. Loaiza 417, is a brick two-story colonial-style mall with some 20 shops.

When you get tired of shopping, you can head over to the **No Name Café** in the mall's patio for a light meal or quick snack, accompanied by pop music and sports highlights from several TV screens. Evenings, the culinary specialties include barbecued chicken and ribs. For a quieter luncheon respite head across the road to **Pancho's**, at the beach end of Las Cabañas shopping arcade, where you can munch a hamburger while perusing the wares of vendors parading by on the sand below.

FROM THE BALBOA CLUB
NORTH TO THE CAMINO REAL

On the beach side of the intersection of Rodolfo T. Loaiza and Camarón Sábalo, the private ▶ **Balboa Club** luxuriates in quiet, walled seclusion from its more boisterous neighbors. Exchange privileges from a club at home (say, the Bohemian or Metropolitan clubs in San Francisco or the La Jolla Beach and Tennis Club) or a letter from a member will get you a room or allow you entrance for a meal. Either arrangement must be reserved in advance.

Casa Loma, located uphill from the intersection at Avenida Gaviotas 104, is a two-minute ride from the Zona Dorada. With its elegant red-velvet-and-wood-paneled interior and its garden patio, this small restaurant is an anachronism, both in appearance and personality. The popularity of its Italian specialties has been proved over a dozen years, and people are still coming back. In fact, the place is so popular that the owners can afford to close it from June to October. Casa Loma is for those who like to dine early, however; closing time is 10:00 P.M. Tel: (69) 13-5398.

You can't miss the bright orange ▶ **Costa de Oro**, a large, modern hotel with two swimming pools, two restaurants, a bar, and tennis courts on the same pretty stretch of beach as the Balboa Club. Rooms are small but cozy, and some have balconies overlooking a garden. Only a few have ocean views, but the views from the public areas, especially the restaurant, go a long way toward making up for that lack. Another branch of **La Carreta**, one of the best shops in town for decorative items, is part of the complex, as is the restaurant-bar **Tequila Sunrise**, across the beach road.

▶ **El Cid Mega Resort**, about a block north of the Costa de Oro, is one of Mexico's largest and most complete resorts. Sprawling along both sides of Avenida Camarón Sábalo, it has everything from private homes and condos to a wide range of hotel accommodations (there are more than 850 rooms and 220 suites scattered among its two hotel buildings and tower). Most rooms have balconies and ocean views, but those overlooking the main pool also afford glimpses of the sea in the distance. Looking for a bite to eat? El Cid has 15 restaurants and three bars, as well as a discotheque, convention center, an 18-hole championship golf course, and Mazatlán's finest water-sports and racquet facilities (17 tennis courts; the only squash and racquetball courts in the city).

The **Caracol Tango Palace** here is a sleek, state-of-the-art nightspot for those who like to dance and stay up late. Built in a circular shape that gives the place its name (*caracol* means "snail"), this multi-million-dollar extravaganza looks like a set for "Miami Vice." The clientele is mostly young and well-to-do, but anyone is welcome as long as they dress the part, which means no shorts or cutoffs.

Los Arcos, under a gigantic palapa across the road from the northern end of El Cid, is popular with both visitors and locals. Mouth-watering marlin tacos, a great shrimp *ceviche,* and a decor featuring antiques from the colonial-era town of Concordia attract crowds throughout the day.

The 71-suite ▶ **Luna Palace**, a time-share hotel up the beach road a bit, offers amenities not found in most Mazatlán accommodations, including refrigerators, microwave ovens, and built-in hair dryers. Each unit also has a beach view.

The beautiful terra-cotta–colored ▶ **Pueblo Bonito**, another time-share hotel next door to the Camino Real, is one of the prettiest places to stay in Mazatlán. Its spacious rooms are tastefully decorated, and all have ocean views, large patios or balconies, color TV, and fully equipped kitchenettes.

The deluxe ▶ **Camino Real** stands apart from the other hotels in Mazatlán on its own promontory, Punta del Sábalo, overlooking the ocean at the northern end of the main resort area. The few extra minutes it takes to get downtown are compensated for by its many special features: You can wake up to birdsong and fall asleep to the sound of waves; it has its own tiny beach where swimming conditions are almost always perfect; and the atmosphere is pleasantly relaxing, thanks to the absence of itinerant vendors and gaggles of people watching the parasailers. Though the rooms are just average, clean and standard size, the public areas in the Camino Real are outstanding, and the attractive lobby bar is an especially good spot for watching sunsets.

It is unusual for a relatively small hotel like the Camino Real to have not one but two restaurants that rate so highly with the locals. The more formal of the two, **Las Terrazas**, is a candle-lit dining room offering Mexican and international specialties. **Chiquita Banana**, under a palapa downstairs, a few steps from the beach, is a lively place to lunch and an informal yet romantic place to dine and dance to the sound of waves and live music at night. For reservations at either, call the Camino Real switchboard at 13-1111.

Few restaurants in town are as elegant as **Señor Pepper**, across the beach road from the Camino Real. The candle-light and lace, polished wood and brass, and soft jazz music make it perfect for intimate conversation. The house specialties are juicy steaks grilled to perfection and lobster or jumbo shrimp. Open for dinner only. Reservations recommended; Tel: 14-0101.

Sports in Mazatlán

Mazatlán is made for sports enthusiasts. Almost every hotel has a water-sports center, and most will be happy to make arrangements for you. If yours doesn't, or won't, go to El Cid; theirs is right on the beach.

Mazatlán is the deep-sea fishing capital of the mainland, and the odds of catching something big here are stacked in the fisherman's favor. Striped marlin season runs from December through April; black marlin, May through June; sailfish, May through November. Tuna, dorado, bonita, yellowtail, and sea bass can be caught year-round. Boat rentals are available at most hotels or at the fleet headquarters just past Olas Altas. Among the best charter outfits here are the **Star Fleet** (Tel: 82-3878) and **Flota Faro** (Tel: 82-4977). Prices range from $180 to $260, depending on the size of the boat.

Scuba-diving and snorkeling excursions also can be arranged at your hotel. **Deer** (Los Venados) **Island**, just off the beach between the Playa Mazatlán and El Cid complexes, is one of the best places in the area for both activities. The island is about a 20-minute ride by water taxi (the "Super Pato" leaves from the water-sports center at El Cid every other hour between the hours of 10:00 A.M. and 2:00 P.M.), and equipment can be rented there as well.

Parasail rides and rental concessions for Hobie cats, kayaks, jet skis, and sailboards are available on the beach from the Hotel Playa Mazatlán to the El Cid complex.

Tennis players congregate at the Camino Real, Los Sábalos, and El Cid hotels (although the excellent facilities at El Cid are reserved for hotel guests and members only).

There are two golf courses in Mazatlán. The private **Casa Club** at El Cid features an 18-hole championship course that winds through the main hotel zone. The **Campestre Club**, a 20-minute drive via Highway 15 in the direction of the airport, is a nine-hole course open to the public. Greens fees at the latter are $18 for a double circuit (18 holes).

Hunting for duck, dove, and quail is another popular sport in the Mazatlán area. The bag limit is 20 birds per day, and there are two hunts (at $150 per hunt) daily from October to April. It costs an extra $44 for nonshooters. Contact the Aviles Brothers, Tel: 81-3728 or 6060.

Charreadas, Mexican rodeos, are staged at Lienzo Charro near the railroad station; watch for announcements around town. There is also a small bull ring in Mazatlán; the season runs from December 15 through April. Aficionados will want to ask when the better matadors are likely to appear, rather than taking a chance on less skilled apprentices.

Excursions from Mazatlán

Anyone who likes getting out of a resort and into the countryside for a change of pace can choose from a number of destinations around Mazatlán.

Rancho las Moras

The newest accommodation in the Mazatlán area is a restored hacienda salvaged from a long-abandoned tequila distillery at the base of the Sierra Madre foothills, about a 30-minute drive from the Zona Dorada. There's nothing workaday about this elegant guest ranch, however. Visitors who drive out (the ranch lies 15 km/9 miles east of Highway 15, the old road to Culiacán, on the road to La Noría) can opt for the breakfast ride-cookout ($30), the midday ride and lunch ($35), or stay overnight and have all their meals at umbrella-shaded tables overlooking the pool. Accommodations consist of a six-room inn and five separate *casitas* spread around the flower-filled grounds, all impeccably decorated with

Mexican antiques and handicrafts. Overnight guests also have use of the tennis courts and stables as part of the ranch's standard recreational program.

If you're staying in Mazatlán and want to have a leisurely lunch or dinner in rustic luxury, you can ask if the ranch is providing transportation when you call ahead to make reservations. Otherwise, you'll have to rent a car or hire a taxi. But whatever you do, don't show up unannounced: The security guard at the gate has orders to turn away anyone who is not on the day's guest list. Rancho las Moras has no telephone. For reservations and directions, call their office in the Zona Dorada at least a day ahead of your planned outing; Tel: 16-5044.

Concordia and Copala

As for the more conventional outings organized by tour companies, the six-hour country tour offered by most hotels includes two of the most picturesque villages in the area. Concordia, only an hour to the east, is centuries away in feeling. More than 400 years old, the town is today a crafts center where leather goods, wooden furniture, pottery, and tiles are made; most tours will allow you to watch many of the artisans at work.

Copala, in the mountains northeast of Concordia on Highway 40, is an old mining town with cobblestone streets and a history that dates back to 1571. The main reason to visit, besides the scenery, is a restaurant called **Daniel's**. More than two decades ago Dan Garrison accompanied his mother when she returned to her hometown to claim a family inheritance. They fell in love with the sleepy village and decided to stay. Mama Chavala, an excellent cook, put her skills to work and soon she and Dan had established a restaurant that eventually expanded to serve legions of diners. Although Mama Chavala is no longer alive, the Mexican-style food remains decent and reasonably priced; the pièce de résistance is the coconut-and-banana-cream pie, still made from mama's original recipe. To work off their meal diners usually stroll up the lane to the village square for a look out over the steep hillsides, many dotted with restored haciendas now housing artists and fugitives from Mazatlán's sultry summers. Daniel's also has a few rooms for customers unwilling to tackle the mountain road after dark. Tel: 85-4225.

Expect to pay roughly $40 per person for a packaged excursion to both Concordia and Copala, which will include lunch. The same tour by taxi costs twice that, plus the price of lunch for yourself and the driver.

Villa Unión

Located a few miles east of the airport, this town and its outlying agricultural developments are the focus of a relatively new farming tour. The first stop allows visitors to see the local church and public market in Villa Unión before heading out into the country. In winter, fields around the village of Walamo supply U.S. and Canadian markets with fresh chile peppers, tomatoes, corn, and a variety of other vegetables. The tour also stops at **El Refúgio**, an authentic working hacienda, before continuing on for a picnic at **El Milagro**, a palm-shaded retreat with a swimming pool and tennis court.

Rosarío

Rosarío, southeast of Mazatlán on Highway 15, is a large, modern town with a historic district that has been kept more or less intact. Founded in 1655, it's another of the mining towns where Mexico's wealth from silver and gold was and is visible. (The splendid altar in its cathedral is made of gold.) Stops along the way include the thermal springs at **Aguacaliente** and **Villa Presidio**, the latter the first settlement in the area. Expect to pay about $25 per person for this morning excursion.

Laguna de Teacapán

Touring the Laguna de Teacapán, farther south of Mazatlán, is an unforgettable experience. This long, narrow body of water stretches along the coast for nearly 60 miles, and has been likened to the Amazon because of the vegetation that grows along its banks. The tour includes stops at the thermal springs of Aguacaliente and the old mining town of Rosarío, a catamaran ride on the lagoon, and a break for lunch on a primitive, palm-lined beach. Allow eight hours for the tour; the cost is approximately $50 per person.

Boat Excursions

The 40-foot sailboat *Cosas Buenas* departs at 10:00 A.M. daily from the sportsfishing docks for a four-hour trip around the three islands (Venados, or Deer; Pájaros, Bird; and Chivos, Goat) off the coast before landing at Isla de los Venados for sunning, swimming, and lunch. This trip costs approximately $35 per person. A five-hour excursion by boat or catamaran to **Isla de la Piedra** (Stone Island), across from the Port of Mazatlán, is offered by several outfits through hotel tour desks. It runs about $35 per person and includes a tour of the harbor and some of the estuaries and a broiled seafood lunch at a beach restaurant. For one-third the cost you can take a launch ($1 round trip) from Avenida Emilio Barragan, near the foot of Avenida Gutierrez Nájera, walk or ride (for about 70¢) from the landing dock to the ocean side of the island (which actually is a peninsula), stroll along the beach looking for shells and sand dollars, then pick a lunch spot from the string of beachfront restaurants (from $5 to $8, depending on what's cooking and what you order). Horseback riding is available at about $10 an hour.

Finally, you can take a cruise of the bay on the motor yacht *Fiesta*. Cruises leave daily at 11:00 A.M. from the pier near the lighthouse, and tickets can be purchased from any hotel travel agent as well as at the company's office at José María Canizales 5. The cost is approximately $13.50.

These and other tours can be arranged in Mazatlán through **Marlin Tours** (Tel: 14-2690), although **Alitur** (Tel: 83-7777) also goes to Daniel's in Copala. Most hotels in Mazatlán will also be able to arrange excursions for you. (Check with your travel agent beforehand, however, as some tours are only offered in season.)

—Jackie Peterson and Susan Wagner

GETTING AROUND

Driving Down from the Border

The recommended entrance to western Mexico and the Pacific resorts is Nogales, Arizona–Nogales, Sonora. Travellers coming from Southern California will have a better trip if they stay on the U.S. side of the border until they reach Nogales. Mexican Highway 2, which begins in Tijuana and hugs the border for most of its distance, is a dubious choice because of its generally inferior condition and a shortage of services.

One popular itinerary calls for a short day from Nogales to Guaymas and a second, longer day to Mazatlán, allowing motorists to spend the night in attractive coastal locations. However, many travellers choose to bypass Guaymas the first day in order to avoid a long drive to Mazatlán on the second. This option saves more than an hour by skirting the traffic and congestion of Guaymas. Either way, more than half the 720-mile trip will be tedious driving through a seemingly endless landscape of brush and cactus, the scattered towns along the way raw in their newness and jerry-built to shelter a mushrooming population. Still, this route, Highway 15, has its charming moments, and toward the end of the journey it even has its charming hours. Travellers in a hurry to reach Mazatlán should carry picnic food, thus avoiding slow-service lunch stops.

The stretch from the border to **Hermosillo**, the modern capital of the state of Sonora and a pleasant place to take a break, takes a bit more than three hours, much of it through semi-arid, sparsely populated countryside (but with adequate services for motorists). In Hermosillo itself, a good, if not very fast, lunch stop is the **Restaurant Villa Fiesta**, which specializes in regional dishes from northwestern Mexico. To find it, look for Calle Yañez near the *glorieta* (traffic circle) at the northern outskirts of town. Turn right onto Yañez and go half a block. For those in a hurry, Highway 15 is dotted with U.S.-style fast-food restaurants, most of them clean and quick if not especially appealing.

Travellers looking for lodging in Hermosillo will find the ▶ **Fiesta Americana Hermosillo**, conveniently located on Highway 15 (Boulevard Kino 369) at the northern outskirts of town, to be the city's best hotel.

After passing through more unchanging countryside south of Hermosillo, Highway 15 reaches the Pacific at the old fishing port of **Guaymas** (135 km/84 miles), now a low-key beach resort that's especially popular with sportsfishermen.

About 6 km (4 miles) north of Guaymas you'll come to a Y in the road, with the left (southeast) route marked "Ciudad Obregón." This is the Guaymas bypass. Except for a short stretch between Navojoa and Los Mochis, this route is a four-lane highway all the way to Mazatlán. Whether or not you take the bypass, veterans of the trip recommend the toll (*cuota*) roads as the best choices, even though they are somewhat expensive. Figure on $70-plus in tolls for the entire U.S. border–Mazatlán trip.

For those not taking the bypass, the Guaymas highway continues inland through the old town; those who want a view of the sea or to spend the night must turn right on any of the side roads marked "Playas" or "Bahía San Carlos."

The ▶ **Hotel Playa de Cortés**, on lovely Bocochibampo Bay, is the traditional choice here, its reasonable rates reflecting the fact that, as a beach resort, Guaymas lacks the glamour of its cousins to the south.

Travellers looking for nothing more than a place to lay their heads at an economical price will find the ▶ **Motel Armida**, at the north entrance to the city, satisfactory. A notch down in both price and quality is the basic ▶ **Del Puerto**, at the corner of Yañez and Calle 19 in downtown Guaymas. It's simple and clean, with air-conditioning and a restaurant that specializes in seafood.

Those who arrive in Guaymas a few hours before the sun sets may wish to continue on to **Ciudad Obregón**, 125 km (78 miles) to the south. The land along this stretch is by nature desert, but irrigation has worked miracles in certain areas. Ciudad Obregón itself was founded in 1928 as the commercial and transportation center of this reclaimed agricultural region. Tortilla flat and rigidly geometrical in its layout, the city is a testament to bureaucratic lack of imagination. It does have a decent hotel, however. The plain and quiet ▶ **Nainari Valle**, on the highway at the corner of Alemán and Tetabiate, has, in addition to its modest rooms, a pleasant coffee shop and dining room.

Navojoa, older than Ciudad Obregón but of no more interest, is 68 km (42 miles) south over a stretch of road that is frequently choked with farm traffic. The best roadside inn in the area is the clean and air-conditioned ▶ **Nuevo Motel del Río**, located on the northern outskirts of town right off the highway.

From Navojoa, an interesting side trip, or even an overnight stop, is **Alamos**, the most picturesque town in this region. It's a 45-minute drive (55 km/34 miles) over a reasonably good road. Dating back to the earliest Spanish exploration of northwest Mexico, Alamos came into its heyday in the 18th century when gold and silver were discovered nearby. Its colonial buildings, many of them restored, are now protected by government decree. Alamos has also attracted a small foreign colony and become something of a vacation center. Its main export is the Mexican jumping beans harvested in the area.

▶ **Casa de los Tesoros**, an unusually appealing inn, occupies a former convent one and a half blocks from the main plaza. This charming hotel has fireplaces in every room and a friendly, festive atmosphere. On the main square, the ▶ **Hotel Mansión de la Condesa Magdalena** is another inviting colonial inn.

Alamos's old buildings and two romantic hotels supply the feeling of Mexico that most travellers hope for. The town is situated in Yaqui Indian country, and the natives, distinguished by their rugged profiles and jet-black hair, have preserved much of their traditional way of life.

As you continue south on Highway 15 from Navojoa, it's about a two-hour trip to **Los Mochis**, 163 km (101 miles) distant. (For information about Los Mochis see the Copper Canyon chapter.)

The best and fastest sections of the west coast highway connect Los Mochis with Culiacán, capital of the state of Sinaloa. After following Highway 15 south 85 km (53 miles) from Los Mochis to Guamúchil, you can switch to Sinaloa 1, a toll road, which runs about 100 km (62 miles) to the outskirts of Culiacán, where signs at a junction direct you back to Highway 15 or to the toll road leading to Mazatlán. As recently as 1988 the crime rate on Sinaloa 1 was alarming; even daylight banditry was reported. This situation seems to have been remedied by strong police action, however.

There is little to entice visitors into stopping in **Culiacán**, except perhaps for lunch at the ▶ **Motel Los 3 Ríos**, a very pleasant establishment just off the highway north of the bridge as you approach the city. The motel is on the left (east) side of the highway. It will also do as a comfortable overnight stop.

If you are continuing on, follow the signs for El Dorado and turn right past the toll gate onto the new Mazatlán toll (*cuota*) road, which will cut the last leg of the trip to an hour and 45 minutes. Highway 15, the old road, runs through the mountains and takes a good three hours to negotiate.

—*Robert Somerlott*

By Air

Service to Mazatlán is offered by Aeroméxico from Los Angeles and Tucson; by Alaska Airlines from Seattle, San Francisco, and Los Angeles; by Delta through its Los Angeles hub; and by Mexicana from Los Angeles and Denver, with good connections (via Mexico City) from New York and Chicago. Schedules vary according to season, with the greatest number of flights departing from December through April. Air charters, especially from November through April, connect Mazatlán with Minneapolis, Houston, Oakland, Seattle, and several cities on the U.S. east coast. For up-to-date information, consult a travel agent.

The Rafael Buelna Airport—where you'll find a number of car-rental agencies (Hertz, National, and Budget among them)—is some 15 miles (about a half-hour's ride) north and east of the hotel zone. Aside from renting a car or going by taxi ($25), *colectivos* are the only other option. If that's the way you decide to go, bite the bullet and be patient as yours drops off other passengers along the way.

By Train

Mazatlán is one of the few Mexican resorts you can reach by rail. Trains leave daily from Nogales and Mexicali on the U.S. border, with connections to Guadalajara and Mexico City. The *Tren Estrella* (Star Train) leaves Mexicali at 8:00 A.M. and arrives in Mazatlán at 8:00 the next morning. There's a brief layover north of Hermosillo as you wait for the train from Nogales (which leaves Nogales at 2:00 P.M.); then the two trains combined continue on their way to Mazatlán and, at the end of the line, Guadalajara. There is no dining car or sleeping accommodations; food is brought to passengers in their seats. The one-way fare to Mazatlán, including food, costs $40 from Nogales, $53 from Mexicali. (Add another $20 for the Mazatlán–Guadalajara leg.) For more information contact Ferrocarriles del Pacifico, 10 Avenida Carrera Internacional, Nogales, Sonora, Mexico; Tel: (631) 2-0024. The Mazatlán depot is at Avenida del Ferrocarril s/n, two blocks from the end of Avenida Principal. Tel: (69) 84-6710.

By Bus

You have to be careful about service designations when travelling by bus. For example, *primera clase* may or may not resemble anything truly first class. Moreover, the bus companies have begun to add such adjectives as *servicio plus, futura,* and the like. What you mainly want to know is whether it's express service or a milk run.

Currently, Elite (Tel: 81-3811), a bus line fairly new to northwest Mexico, provides the best service between Mazatlán and the border. (Don't confuse it with the deluxe executive bus service out of Mexico City.) While Elite's Servicio Plus Express between Mazatlán and Nogales (16 hours; $64.25) or Tijuana (27 hours; $75.50) costs a bit more than the Servicio Plus of its chief competitor, Tres Estrellas de Oro (Tel: 85-1736), it tends to be a cleaner and more comfortable ride. In Mazatlán, both arrive at (and depart from) the Central Camionera on the corner of Calles Ferrusquilla and Río Panuco.

Another possibility: Recently, Mexico's Ministry of Tourism has waged a campaign to lure operators of U.S. motorcoach tours into the country. If these efforts succeed, your travel agent may be able to fill you in on this type of tour to Mazatlán.

By Ferry

Ferries linking Mazatlán with La Paz, capital of the state of Baja California Sur, 235 miles to the west, depart at 3:00 P.M. daily except Saturday from both cities. The service is operated by the SEMATUR group, whose offices in Mazatlán are located at the terminal on Avenida Emilio Barragan, a block east of the sportsfishing fleet. Tel: (69) 81-2454 or 5236; Fax: (69) 81-7023 (include your fax number for immediate confirmation).

There are four categories of accommodations on the boats: *salon* (reclining seat); *turista* (two or four bunks in a cabin, with shared toilet and bathing facilities down the hall); *cabina* (a small, basic, but clean cabin with two berths and a private bath); and *clase especial* (a cabin with two berths, private bath, and separate sitting area). Either category with a private bath is recommended—and even at that you will want to bring your own supply of paper products. Fares for the 18-hour trip are per person, one-way: *salon,* $18.60; *turista,* $37.25; *cabina,* $56; and *especial,* $74.50. Vehicle rates depend on the length of the vehicle, and run from $136.50, one-way, for compact cars to $232 for motorhomes.

In Town

Once you're in Mazatlán, getting around is a breeze. With the exception of the Zona Dorada, most hotels in a given part of town are within walking distance of each other. Taxi rates are slightly higher here than in other resorts in Mexico, however, and there are no meters (rates are set by zone), so check the rate before you get in. (Most hotels will post the going rates on a placard outside the lobby.) If your destination is not a well-known landmark, call before you go and get the name of the nearest one.

Another option is to hop aboard a *pulmonía*—or "pneumonias" as the locals call them—jaunty little golf cart–like contraptions. These charge about one-third to one-half less than taxis, but be sure to check the rate before boarding (again, there are no meters).

It's also easy to get around town by bus. Stops, a block or two apart, are often sheltered to protect waiting passengers from tropical sun and heavy summer rains. The sign on the front of the bus, whether green (express), white and yellow (first class), or blue (second class), indicates its destination. "Centro" or "Basílica" buses run through the Zona Dorada and end up downtown; those marked "Sábalo Cerritos" head back to the hotel zone. The fare is about 35¢ for the air-conditioned express, about 30¢ for the others (ask at your hotel which coins to use). On any of them, just pull the cord for your stop.

Mazatlán is on mountain standard time (the same as Denver and Calgary), one hour earlier than Mexico City, year-round.

ACCOMMODATIONS REFERENCE

The rates given below are projections *for December 1993 through Easter 1994. Unless otherwise indicated, rates are for double rooms, double occupancy; the 10 percent VAT has been added. As rates are subject to change, it's a good idea to double-check before booking.*

► **Balboa Club.** P.O. Box 402, Avenida Camarón Sábalo s/n, **Mazatlán**, Sinaloa 82000. Tel: (69) 13-5211; Fax: (69) 13-3223. $210–$250 (includes three meals).

► **Camino Real.** P.O. Box 538, Punta del Sábalo, **Mazatlán**, Sinaloa 82100. Tel: (69) 13-1111; Fax: (69) 14-0311; in the U.S. and Canada, Tel: (800) 7-CAMINO. $125–$175.

► **Casa Contenta.** Avenida Rodolfo T. Loaiza s/n, **Mazatlán**, Sinaloa 82110. Tel: (69) 13-4976 or 9986. $50–$150.

► **Casa de los Tesoros.** P.O. Box 12, **Alamos**, Sonora 85760. Tel: (642) 8-0010; Fax: (642) 8-0400. $132 (includes three meals).

► **El Cid Mega Resort.** P.O. Box 813, Avenida Camarón Sábalo s/n, **Mazatlán**, Sinaloa 82110. Tel: (69) 13-3333; Fax: (69) 14-1311; in the U.S. and Canada, Tel: (800) 525-1925. $135.

► **Costa de Oro.** P.O. Box 130, Avenida Camarón Sábalo s/n, **Mazatlán**, Sinaloa 82110. Tel: (69) 13-5888 or 2005; Fax: (69) 14-4209; in the U.S., Tel: (800) 342-2431. From $87.

► **Fiesta Americana Hermosillo.** Boulevard Kino 369, **Hermosillo**, Sonora 83010. Tel: (62) 15-1112; Fax: (62) 15-5721; in the U.S. and Canada, Tel: (800) FIESTA-1. $121.

► **Hotel Mansión de la Condesa Magdalena.** Calle Alvaro Obregón 2, **Alamos**, Sonora 85760. Tel and Fax: (642) 8-0221. $55.

► **Hotel Playa de Cortés.** P.O. Box 66, **Guaymas**, Sonora 85450. Tel and Fax: (622) 1-1224 or 1047. $78–$106.

► **Hotel Playa Mazatlán.** P.O. Box 207, Rodolfo T. Loaiza 202, **Mazatlán**, Sinaloa 82010. Tel: (69) 13-4455 or 4444; Fax: (69) 14-0366; in the U.S. and Canada, Tel: (800) 247-5292. $80–$90.

► **Hotel La Siesta.** Olas Altas 11, **Mazatlán**, Sinaloa 82000. Tel: (69) 81-2640. $30.

► **Hotel Suites Las Flores.** Avenida Rodolfo T. Loaiza 212, P.O. Box 583, **Mazatlán**, Sinaloa 82000. Tel: (69) 13-5100; Fax: (69) 14-3422; in the U.S., Tel: (800) 452-0627. $72.

► **Luna Palace.** P.O. Box 411, Avenida Camarón Sábalo, Privada del Camarón, **Mazatlán**, Sinaloa 82100. Tel: (69) 14-6006; Fax: (69) 14-9666; in the U.S. and Canada, Tel: (800) 352-7690. $90–$165.

► **Motel Armida.** Avenida Serdán s/n, **Guaymas**, Sonora 85450. Tel: (622) 2-3050. $42.

► **Motel Los 3 Ríos.** P.O. Box 311, **Culiacán**, Sinaloa 80000. Tel: (67) 15-4040; Fax: (67) 16-4435. $90.

► **Nainari Valle.** Miguel Alemán and Tetabiate, **Ciudad Obregón**, Sonora 85000. Tel: (641) 4-0940; Fax: (641) 3-4194. $85–$124.

▶ **Nuevo Motel del Río.** Carretera 15 s/n, **Navojoa**, Sonora 85800. Tel and Fax: (642) 2-0331. $73.

▶ **Pueblo Bonito.** P.O. Box 6, Avenida Camarón Sábalo 2121, **Mazatlán**, Sinaloa 82110. Tel: (69) 14-3700; Fax: (69) 14-1723; in the U.S. and Canada, Tel: (800) 442-5300. $132–$198.

▶ **Del Puerto.** Calles Yañez and 19, **Guaymas**, Sonora 85450. Tel: (622) 4-3408. $25.

▶ **Rancho las Moras.** Avenida Camarón Sábalo 204, Suite 6, **Mazatlán**, Sinaloa 82110. Tel: (69) 16-5044; Fax: (69) 16-5045. $360 (includes all meals).

▶ **Los Sábalos.** P.O. Box 944, Rodolfo T. Loaiza 100, **Mazatlán**, Sinaloa 82110. Tel: (69) 83-5333; Fax: (69) 83-8156; in the U.S., Tel: (800) 528-8760. $95–$155.

NUEVO VALLARTA

Nuevo Vallarta, in the state of Nayarit 15 minutes north of Puerto Vallarta's international airport, started as an ambitious nautical-residential property about 15 years ago. The plan called for expensive hotels and condominiums built along artificial canals. A slow starter, Nuevo Vallarta accelerated a few years ago and is now the location of a newly developed tourist center overseen by the Cousteau Society. There are, in addition, two major hotels in operation here: Jack Tar Village, an all-inclusive chain operation, and the recently opened Radisson. A second Radisson is scheduled to open in the summer of 1993, while a Four Seasons Hotel and Resort is still in the planning stages.

Punta de Mita, the northern tip of the Bahía de Banderas (Bay of Flags), Mexico's largest bay (which Nuevo Vallarta shares with Puerto Vallarta), has become very popular with day trippers. Apart from a cluster of restaurants bordering the rocky beach, however, it has very little to offer in the way of attractions. Boats can be rented to visit the nearby Marietta Islands, about 20-minutes offshore, but there's no way to go ashore unless you swim from your boat. The older local fishermen swear there's a fourth island that mysteriously appears and disappears on foggy days—perhaps the same one on which Cortés is alleged to have buried his treasure. In fact, tourists still visit the islands with metal detectors in hopes of striking it rich, even though history tells us that the great conquistador never visited the area.

PUERTO VALLARTA

Puerto Vallarta, on the Pacific coast due west of Guadalajara, looks like a movie set: Sprawling white stucco houses crowned with red-tiled roofs and bougainvillaea spilling over their walls are stacked on a hillside overlooking the ocean. The tiny, compact town, complete with a bandstand and seaside promenade, nestles at the hill's base. There's almost always a perfect Pacific sunset over the Bahía de Banderas, with palm trees silhouetted against an orange-pink sky.

Puerto Vallarta, or "P.V.," has been the darling of the California crowd ever since Elizabeth Taylor and Richard Burton made headlines here in the early 1960s when he was filming *The Night of the Iguana*. Visitors love the easygoing way of life, which rarely requires getting dressed up, and though there are plenty of sophisticated facilities in and around town, Puerto Vallarta remains less citified than some of her sisters on Mexico's Pacific coast.

Like most Mexican resorts, P.V.'s coastal road threads its way into, through, and out of town past dramatically scenic cliffs, beaches, and rock formations. And because Guadalajara is only 385 km (239 miles) to the east, *tapatíos* (as Guadalajarans call themselves) love Vallarta, with many of the wealthy among them maintaining homes here. As a result of this influx, much of the land south of town and north to the Nayarit border is becoming over-developed.

MAJOR INTEREST

Small old town with cobblestone streets
Bahía de Banderas sunsets
Boat trips to isolated beaches

Unlike many of the resorts on the Pacific coast, Puerto Vallarta did not start out as a fishing village in the 1500s. Founded in 1851, P.V. is, in fact, a relative youngster by Mexican standards. It remained unknown to the outside world until the 1950s, when Mexicana Airlines began to offer regularly scheduled flights into town. In the 1960s, after Highway 200 was opened, linking it to the rest of the country, Puerto Vallarta became even better known.

The influx of visitors from the States and Canada began in earnest after Taylor and Burton catapulted Puerto Vallarta

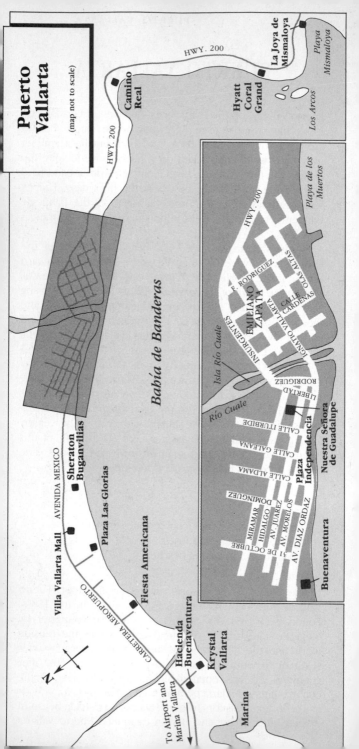

into the international spotlight. By the end of the decade, one area overlooking the Río Cuale—which divides the town into northern and southern halves—was even nicknamed "Gringo Gulch," in recognition of the many vacation homes that had been built by foreigners there. Today clusters of condos and time-share units are going up on both sides of the river and, as a result, vacationers and sometime residents are more widely dispersed than they were in the old days.

This development has not been without its drawbacks, the most obvious being the swarms of OPCs (Outside Personal Contacts) that buzz around visitors whenever they go into town. True, you'll be offered a variety of free gifts, free meals, and heavily discounted tours. But there's a price to pay: You'll be asked to attend a "presentation" at the particular time-share property, where a salesperson will extol the virtues of the property—and take a couple of hours of your valuable vacation time to do it. If you have an interest in the time-share concept, it might be worthwhile; otherwise, a simple "No, thank you" will get you off the hook.

Around in Vallarta

Getting around Puerto Vallarta couldn't be easier. Everything is built around the Bahía de Banderas, which extends from Punta de Mita in Nayarit south to Cabo Corrientes. The greatest concentration of hotels and two marinas are found north of the Río Cuale, in the direction of the airport. The major shops and restaurants as well as a few small hotels are located downtown. (You can walk safely anywhere in town, but rubber-soled shoes are a must. Hard, leather soles slip on the cobblestone streets and smooth sidewalks.) Just beyond Playa de los Muertos, the town beach south of the river, the coastal road begins to climb. Two major hotels—the Camino Real and the Hyatt Coral Grand—as well as numerous condominiums line the road all the way to Playa Mismaloya and beyond. On Mismaloya's beach you'll find the hotel La Jolla de Mismaloya. Vallarta's so-called "jungle restaurants" are situated off the road and up the hill to the east of Mismaloya, where *The Night of the Iguana* was filmed.

Sunsets in Puerto Vallarta are an event that shouldn't be missed. Purists like to watch them from places like El Set in the Hotel Conchas Chinas out on the highway south of town; Le Kliff, even farther out at Boca de Tomatlán; or Chez Elena in the Cuatro Vientos Hotel on the hill above Restaurant Row. Those who just want to enjoy the view without the benefit of food and drink can plop down on a bench along the seaside *malecón* (promenade).

NORTH OF DOWNTOWN

The approach to town from the airport passes through the busiest area in Puerto Vallarta. Most of the major hotels and shopping malls and many of the area's huge developments are spread out along this stretch of Highway 200, which here is called the Carretera Aeropuerto. New places to stay, shop, and dine continue to spring up all along the highway.

Marina Vallarta

The first sight in this new Vallarta to draw your attention is Plaza Marina, a huge air-conditioned shopping mall featuring such ubiquitous names as Denny's, Woolworth's, Price Club, and McDonald's. South of Plaza Marina the 442-acre complex called Marina Vallarta is on its way to becoming a city within a city, with luxurious private homes, condos, and a scattering of time-share properties. Marina Vallarta boasts one of the finest marinas on the Pacific coast, with many of its 400 slips frequently occupied by visiting mega-yachts. An adjacent property, also being developed, will include moorings for another 600 vessels.

Several major hotels have taken advantage of the access to a par-72 championship golf course, beach clubs, tennis clubs, and spas. Of these, only the three-story ▶ **Hotel Bel Air Puerto Vallarta** is not situated on the beach, but its many repeat visitors don't seem to mind (the hotel flanks the golf course instead). The air-conditioned rooms at the hotel, known to its admirers as the "Pink Hacienda," feature tile floors, hand-painted furniture, and original art, including masks by Sergio Bustamante, and its reasonably priced terrace restaurant offers one of the best menus in town.

Two of the other major hotels here, the ▶ **Meliá Puerto Vallarta** and the ▶ **Marriott CasaMagna**, have much in common. Each has a huge swimming pool, beautifully landscaped grounds, well-appointed rooms, and at least one very good restaurant. Both have the usual conveniences in the lobby as well, including car-rental and travel agencies, boutiques, and small stores for sundries. And both offer their guests the same tennis and golf privileges mentioned above. Because of their similarities, the choice becomes one of atmosphere and loyalty. The Marriott is managed by the parent chain, which is a joint investor with a Mexican cement manufacturing company. Inside the hotel there is no real feeling of Mexico: You could be in California or New York, an atmosphere that many guests find comforting. The Meliá, owned and operated by a Spanish group, strives for a blend of Mexico and Europe, which results in a feeling of Spain.

Apart from the hotels, Marina Vallarta is ideal for walking. A broad promenade surrounds the boat slips, and is flanked by a number of restaurants, stores, and, unfortunately, 7-Elevens. The best time to stroll is in the cool of the evening, when the lights of the buildings reflect on the water. You'll easily find the marina's landmark—the lighthouse at the **Royal Pacific Yacht Club**—and the bar up top is ideal for viewing the entire complex.

South of Marina Vallarta

Continuing south you'll come to the **city marina**. There will probably be a cruise ship alongside its single pier and perhaps one or two others anchored out in the bay. This is the marina where you board day cruises to beach hideaways or charter deep-sea fishing boats.

Favored by a fairly upscale clientele, the ▶ **Krystal Vallarta**, farther south, is one of Vallarta's top hotels. Built by the Gershenson family and run by them as the Posada Vallarta in P.V.'s early days, when it was *the* hotel in town, it was taken over by the Krystal chain after the elder Gershenson's death. Expanded in all directions, today it resembles a colonial village, with suites and villas (the latter perfect for families), cobblestone streets, beautiful gardens, and a fleet of electric carts to haul guests around in. Non-guests can get a taste of this elegance by dining alfresco poolside. The Krystal is also one of the few hotels in town that allows horseback riding on its beaches.

Tuesday and Saturday are Mexican fiesta nights at the Krystal. The hotel has its own bull ring a short distance away, and dinner is served buffet style at tables set up around the ring. Go hungry, because there's an extensive selection of Mexican dishes from which to choose and you can go through the line as many times as you like. The show itself, which includes mariachis, folk dances, lasso artists, and—the featured event of the evening—bullfighting, costs about $32. You needn't worry about the bulls: There is no blood and no killing.

Bogart's, a rather formal restaurant in the Krystal, is filled with fountains, shimmering mirrors, peacock chairs, and plants. The Continental cuisine is complemented by a number of Moroccan specialties, and soft piano music contributes to the romantic atmosphere. Make sure you bring a bundle of money, however; Bogart's is the most expensive restaurant in town. Reservations recommended; Tel: 4-0202, ext. 2609.

The Krystal has two other restaurants: **Tango** features Argentine steaks and decor, while **Kamakura** is strictly Japanese, complete with the dexterous *teppanyaki* chefs popularized by the Benihana chain. Both are open from 6:00 P.M. Tel: 4-0202, ext. 2620.

Christine, P.V.'s favorite disco, is also part of the Krystal complex. Though the discos in Vallarta are smaller and less flashy, with fewer videos and gimmicks, than those in other resorts, they're no less fun. Christine is still number one, in part because its competitors have gone out of business, but also because its laser lights, great sound system, and a variety of other features surpass those of her sisters in Ixtapa and Cancún. Christine's laser artists and audio-video experts show off at 11:30 each night when the disco opens. Before the hordes are turned loose on the dance floor, the kids in the control booth run every effect on the board, a spectacular show that lasts about ten minutes and is often accompanied by classical music. If you don't care for discos, at least go for the show: You can be in and out for the cost of just one expensive drink.

The owners of the Hotel Buenaventura (see below) bought and completely remodeled the defunct Hacienda del Lobo a number of years ago. Renamed the ▶ **Hacienda Buenaventura**, and located right next to the Krystal Vallarta, it's a colonial-style charmer wrapped around a large swimming pool. All 155 rooms of the Hacienda are tastefully decorated and air-conditioned, and have either small balconies or patios. The public areas are also quite attractive, and the hotel's pretty brick-ceilinged restaurant, Los Portales, is open for breakfast and dinner. Because the Hacienda is a short walk from the beach through the grounds of the Krystal, it's also very reasonably priced and an excellent choice for travellers on a budget.

The ▶ **Fiesta Americana** is popular with group travellers. The soaring seven-story lobby with its palapa-style roof immediately puts guests in a party mood, and the free-form pool with an island in its middle is the perfect place to have one. Better yet, every one of its well-appointed rooms offers a view of the bay (and those gorgeous Puerto Vallarta sunsets), and just about any water sport you can think of can be arranged on the beach in front of the hotel.

Also part of the Fiesta Americana complex are **Friday Lopez**, the only disco in town with live music, and **El Morocco**, one of the nicer restaurants in Vallarta. A chic and formal kind of place, with a Casbah-like setting and pretty Persian rugs, its specialties include lobster, red snapper, prime rib, steaks, and Moroccan dishes. Reservations are necessary; Tel: 2-2010.

Although it has undergone a series of name changes since it first opened, the sprawling ▶ Continental Plaza, down the beach from the Fiesta Americana, remains one of Vallarta's most popular hotels, especially for families travelling with children. Lots of planned activities in and out of the pool are complemented by a variety of theme nights. And with a John Newcombe Tennis Center on the grounds, it's also the best tennis/hotel facility in town. Three of the seven courts (some of which are lighted for night play) are under a roof, and though the courts are often crowded with guests it's easy enough for non-guests to reserve playing time.

The Villa Vallarta Mall, in the same complex as the Continental Plaza, makes for a pleasant shopping experience. Fiorucci and Mar y Mar, two of the best boutiques in town for women's resortwear, are here, as are Gucci and Cartier. In addition, just about any toilet article or sundry can be found at the air-conditioned supermarket on the street side of the mall. The Place Vendôme, P.V.'s most popular French restaurant, is located just outside the door. Locals are attracted by Place Vendôme's top-quality steaks, chateaubriand, and a variety of fish dishes. Open 6:30 to 11:30 P.M. Reserve; Tel: 4-0123.

Still farther south in the direction of town, the ▶ Sheraton Buganvilias is a nice enough hotel with six 13-story towers facing the ocean and beautifully landscaped grounds. Popular with travellers who feel comfortable with a name they know, the Sheraton has 500 air-conditioned rooms (many with balconies), a number of large meeting rooms, and a variety of stores off the reception area. It also has a family-run gourmet restaurant, Las Gaviotas, which serves up delicious Mexican and international cuisine with courteous service. Open for dinner only; Tel: 2-3000.

The ▶ Hotel Buenaventura is a little jewel of a place within easy walking distance of town. Everything about it is compact, clean, and efficient, yet the Buenaventura has a big-time-resort look and feel about it. It even has its own very pretty beach, with palapas and a palapa-style café as well as an excellent view of the more expensive hotels along the bay. The hotel is very popular with Mexican businessmen and European visitors, who like it for its harmonious mix of atmosphere and proximity to town—a bit of everything for those who have to be near the action.

The unhurried feel of the neighborhood between the Buenaventura and town along Avenida México eases visitors into the hustle and bustle of the congested downtown area. **Alfarería Tlaquepaque**, at the corner of Avenida México and República de Chile, looks as if it's an old garage but is in fact one of the few genuine souvenir shops in Puerto Vallarta. If you like looking for old-fashioned ceramic or glass knick-knacks, you'll love poking around this place. Christmas is a particularly good season to browse for decorations and unusual crèche figurines.

DOWNTOWN: THE NORTH SIDE

Roughly speaking, the north side of the downtown area (meaning north of the Río Cuale) encompasses everything from the point at which Avenida México hits the cobble-stones and becomes Avenida Díaz Ordaz (the seaside drive) to the river. Avenida Díaz Ordaz, the streets parallel to it—Morelos and Juárez—and the side streets between Calle 31 de Octubre and Calle Galeana constitute the main downtown shopping and dining district. The downtown area from Calle Galeana to the river also has some upscale shops and restaurants, but is largely commercial. This is where you'll find most of the airline offices and banks, as well as the open-air souvenir market. Much of the north side is tough on the ears and the feet. Its streets are too narrow for the number of vehicles using them, and the cobblestones don't make for comfortable walking. Still, no one seems to care.

Restaurant Row

Restaurant Row, which begins at Calle 31 de Octubre and extends along Avenida Díaz Ordaz to what was once the Océano Hotel, at the corner of Calle Galeana, is one of the most popular areas in town to shop, dine, and people-watch. Popular restaurants in this neighborhood include such old favorites as the **Red Onion**, **Il Mangiare**, **Mogambo**, and **Casablanca**. (There's also a branch of McDonald's here—P.V.'s second, and a source of much dismay to the more established restaurateurs.) It's not hard to make a choice; in Vallarta all the restaurants display their menus at the door. It's a good way to find out if they're serving the kind of food you're looking for at the prices you're willing to pay.

With its tried-and-true formula solidly in place at the corner of Díaz Ordaz and Domínguez, the **Hard Rock Café** has been a hit ever since it opened. If you've already been to a Hard Rock, you know what to expect: The rear end of a pink Caddy hovers near the entrance, the inside features lots of polished brass and rock 'n' roll memorabilia, the hamburgers and fries taste just like Mom's, and the shots of tequila will set you back about $3.50.

Although the Hard Rock is just two blocks south of the downtown area's former hot spot, **Carlos O'Brian's Pawnshop and Restaurant**, it doesn't seem to have taken any business away from the latter. Lines form around the block at both establishments more often than not (arrive before 7:00 P.M. to avoid them), and patrons drift from one to the other throughout the evening. If anything, O'Brian's still has the edge in ambience, with all sorts of odd things hanging from the ceiling and a variety of unusual seating arrangements. O'Brian's has long been a Vallarta landmark, and its status as a local institution remains soundly secure.

Las Palomas, on the corner of Díaz Ordaz and Calle Aldama, features simple Mexican meat and fish dishes. Decorated in colonial style, and open to the street and bay, it's a local favorite. (Try to wangle a table near the window in the bar; it's one of the better places in town to watch the sunset.) The small dining room on the other side of the bar is lit by candles at night. The quality of the food here often depends on the chef's mood, but the strategic location couldn't be better for those who like to people-watch. Tel: 2-3675.

El Panorama, a restaurant on the seventh floor of the Hotel La Siesta, high on a hill overlooking the *malecón* at Domínguez and Miramar, has it all, including a view of the bay and the hotel strip north of town that is nothing short of awesome. The food is consistently good and reasonably priced, and many of the dishes are prepared right at your table. Try the giant shrimp *flambé*—at almost a foot long (truly), they live up to their name. Open daily from 6:00 P.M. to midnight; the bar stays open until 3:00 A.M. Tel: 2-1818.

The former Océano Hotel, at the corner of Díaz Ordaz and Calle Galeana, across the street from the statue of a boy riding a seahorse (Puerto Vallarta's best-known landmark), is where everyone used to meet before it was turned into condominiums. Though its lobby bar is long gone, the colonial-style restaurant is still intact. Simple Mexican dishes and Continental cuisine are served in an informal atmosphere, and live music accompanies dinner in the evenings. Reasonable prices and a vantage point overlooking the street make it one of the best places in town to have breakfast or lunch—as well as to get a feeling for what the old days in P.V. were like. The new name of the restaurant is **Tequila**, but it will be a long time before anyone calls it anything other than the Océano.

Shopping Downtown

Dominating the downtown area is the cathedral (one of the most photographed in Mexico), **Nuestra Señora de Guada-**

lupe, completed in 1951 *sans* its unique crowned steeple. Added in the late 1960s, the steeple is said to be a copy of the crown worn by Mexico's Empress Carlota at her coronation in 1867.

Some of the most interesting shops in town are located close to the cathedral on Morelos and Juárez, the first two streets up from and running parallel to Díaz Ordaz. **Galería Uno**, Morelos 561, is one of the finest art galleries in the country. Owned by Jan Lavender, an American who has made Puerto Vallarta her home, the gallery sells paintings and sculpture by an impressive roster of Latin American artists. Visitors from around the world congregate here to see works by the likes of Manuel Lepe, Miguel Angel Ríos, and Colunga, and it is safe to say that every celebrity who comes to town visits at least once. (There's a branch of the gallery in the Marina Vallarta complex.) The Galería Uno print and poster gallery is in the Plaza Malecón, at the corner of Avenida Díaz Ordaz and Calle 31 de Octubre.

A block to the east, at Juárez 519, **Galería Pacífico** offers contemporary art and sculpture in a lovely patio setting. You'll find a permanent display of work by some of Latin America's finest artists here, as well as a gift shop with posters, art books, and the like.

St. Valentin, Morelos 574, is one of the best shops in town for handcrafted items, with bowls, platters, and other original tableware (along with whimsical folk art) from Oaxaca. Don't let the unimpressive façade deceive you; the collection of items inside is extensive. **Suneson's**, Morelos 593, carries pieces by the famous Taxco silversmiths Los Castillo in addition to a wide selection of other top-quality silver jewelry, and is one of the best such shops in town.

La Azteca, featuring a wide selection of 14- and 18-karat gold, is an extremely reputable family-run store, in business for more than 30 years. It's well located at Juárez 244. **Villa María**, at Juárez 449B, offers an exceptionally good selection of decorative and gift items.

Vallarta Mía, one of the more interesting boutiques in town, is on the south side of Aldama between Díaz Ordaz and Morelos. (There's no name on the door, and the narrow entrance is a few steps up from the sidewalk, so it's hard to find.) Necklaces and bracelets made from what look like the painted rubber rings of jelly jars, silver conch belts in all sizes, and other avant-garde accessories are among the items sold here.

Sucesos Boutique, featuring original all-cotton clothing for women, is at the corner of Libertad and Hidalgo, with several branches around town. Many of the fabrics are painted by hand at a commune high in the mountains, and Arizonan Toody Competello does a terrific job selecting unusual accessories and hand-painted objets d'art to round out the collection. The personalized service includes a wealth of information about where to go in town, what to do, and what to avoid.

THE BRIDGES

Downtown Puerto Vallarta is divided into north and south sides by the Río Cuale, which is crossed by two narrow bridges. Locals call the one nearest the bay, which is open to one-way traffic heading south, the "new bridge." The "old bridge," three blocks to the east, carries traffic going north toward the airport.

Agustín Rodríguez, running from one bridge to the other on the north side of the river, is the site of Vallarta's popular **flea market**, at the corner of Morelos and A. Rodríguez, near the new bridge. A covered mall with hundreds of small stores selling everything imaginable, this is the place to haggle. In fact, the local merchants love and expect it. They also win every time.

Farther down the street in the direction of the old bridge, at Agustín Rodríguez 267, is **Chef Roger**, one of Vallarta's finest, if not fanciest, restaurants, and easily its most difficult to find. Owner/chef Roger Drier took what had been a small hotel wrapped around a charming patio and miraculously converted it into a restaurant imbued with a Mexican-European-style intimacy. Miraculous, too, are his gourmet concoctions, which more than justify the restaurant's reputation among local aficionados of fine dining. Open for dinner from 6:00 P.M., daily except Sundays. Tel: 2-0604.

Isla Río Cuale

Paseo Río Cuale meanders through the parklike Isla Río Cuale under both bridges. If you have to go from one bridge to the other this is the place to do it. (Access to the little island is provided by a short staircase at either bridge.) The lush foliage down here also makes it the perfect spot to cool off on a hot day. The noises of the traffic above are subdued, and shoppers can browse to their hearts' content in the stalls and boutiques that line the promenade.

Le Bistro, one of Puerto Vallarta's most enjoyable restaurants, sits at the river's edge on Isla Río Cuale near the old bridge. Popular with affluent tourists and locals alike, Le Bistro's enameled walls and black-and-white floors give it a sleek California look. Soft candlelight at night, an imaginative menu, impeccable service, and mellow jazz music in the background all add to the experience. Be prepared to wait in line, however; Le Bistro does not accept reservations. Tel: 2-0283.

DOWNTOWN: THE SOUTH SIDE

The section of town south of the bridges is known as **Emiliano Zapata**. Jammed with good, inexpensive restaurants, interesting boutiques, small hotels, and trendy bars, the eight-block-square area is P.V.'s answer to Greenwich Village.

Playa de los Muertos

The main street, Olas Altas, starts at a central plaza and runs parallel to the beach. In the early days it served as Vallarta's "airport": Battered DC-3s with tourists on board would buzz the road in order to get the attention of the town's two taxis. The beach is Playa de los Muertos (Beach of the Dead), where, legend has it, sailing ships from Spain and Britain used to anchor to pick up their cargoes of gold and silver. On one tragic occasion 285 natives were massacred here after they demanded their fair share of the valuable metal they were hauling. A few years ago city officials tried to change the name to Playa del Sol (Beach of the Sun), on the theory that "Playa de los Muertos" wasn't likely to attract tourists, but the old name refused to die.

Today Playa de los Muertos is a lively spot that's a little on the grubby side but still popular with the locals. It's also crawling with vendors, who sell everything from dresses and tee-shirts to silver jewelry and puppets. The rule here is simple: Don't buy anything. You'll do much better in the stores nearby, which sell higher-quality merchandise at lower prices. Fortunately, the overwhelming majority of beach vendors are well-mannered, and after a firm but polite "No" they'll continue on their way looking grievously wounded but nevertheless resigned to your decision. If, on the other hand, you enjoy the sport of it, by all means give it a shot. Just remember you haven't bought a "bargain" at all. And, regardless of your attitude toward ritual haggling, definitely avoid the attractively designed and even more attractively priced rugs: After the first washing, you'll own an attractively designed placemat.

Restaurants on the South Side

The promenade along the beach is filled with restaurants, bars, and condominiums. You'll probably hear **Andale**, perhaps Vallarta's trendiest bar, before you see it—it's as popular as Carlos O'Brian's and the Hard Rock, and just as crowded with tourists, rowdy locals, and beach bums. The spirited dancing that characterizes the place fills the spaces between tables and is accompanied by lots of friendly pushing and shoving. But Andale's secret, safely removed from the crowds and noise, is its restaurant on the second floor. The portions are huge, the barbecue ribs fall apart at the touch of a fork, and the perfectly seasoned chicken is as good as any in town. Best of all, you can sit on the restaurant's small balcony overlooking Olas Altas and watch the revelers below from a safe distance.

Just a half block from Andale, at Francisca Rodríguez 130, across from the Hotel Marsol, is **Archie's Wok**. Archie was the late John Huston's personal chef for many years, and his tasty specialties include sweet-and-sour Singapore fish and *hoi soi* ribs. To guarantee the freshness of the fish, Archie sends his own boats out to do the fishing. It's a very unpretentious place and also has take-out service. Open 1:00 to 10:00 P.M.; closed Sundays. Tel: 2-0411.

A couple of blocks south of Archie's is **El Dorado**, a four-story condominium with a reasonably priced bar-restaurant right on the beach. More than a restaurant, El Dorado is a Vallarta institution and heavily patronized by longtime locals. The food, mostly typical Mexican dishes, is okay, but their chicken soup is as good as a blood transfusion. El Dorado opens around 7:00 A.M. and closes when it feels like it—usually early in the evening. Tel: 2-1511.

THE HIGHWAY TO MISMALOYA AND BEYOND

From El Dorado the street leads inland to a long flight of stairs. If you're in good shape, you can climb them to another street, which will bring you to the coast road, Highway 200.

In the Hotel Conchas Chinas, on the highway between town and the Camino Real, the funky, rustic-looking **El Set** is one of the best places in the Puerto Vallarta area to have a light meal and watch the sunset. It's also one of the oldest restaurants in Vallarta, and has an elevator to take you to its rocky beach, where you can explore the tidal pools. Tel: 2-0302.

The 337-room ▶ **Camino Real** is about ten minutes south of town by taxi but seems to be even farther, in part because there are no other hotels nearby. The trademark modern architecture of the Westin chain—in this case a stylish arc-shaped building with thick adobe-style walls and arches—and the lush vegetation enfolding the hotel make the complex all the more appealing to an upscale clientele of all ages. The Camino Real also boasts **La Perla**, one of the loveliest restaurants in Puerto Vallarta. After 22 years of serving oustanding international cuisine, La Perla recently made a dramatic switch to authentic Mexican food. The restaurant has been completely remodeled, and its walls decorated with the art of Sergio Bustamante, which may be purchased. What hasn't changed is the superior service, at prices you'd expect to pay in a top-notch restaurant. Reservations advised; Tel: 3-0123.

Farther south along the coast road the only points of interest are condos and a few restaurants. Among them, **El Coral**, the dining room of the Hyatt Coral Grand, is considered one of the town's finest, with exquisite table settings and a lovely view of the ocean. Frequented by discriminating locals and visitors, the Coral Grand satisfies those looking for good food served in a quiet, refined, air-conditioned setting. Dinner is accompanied by soft piano music, and on weekends there is dancing at the bar outside. Tel: 2-5191, ext. 1514.

The dark-orange-and-white complex split by the highway is the newish ▶ **Club Maeva Puerto Vallarta**. This latest addition to Club Maeva's all-inclusive resort properties includes 360 rooms and suites and a wide range of facilities for its guests. Half the property spreads out right on the beach; the remainder is just across the highway.

Mismaloya

Mismaloya, the locale that put P.V. on the map with the filming of *The Night of the Iguana,* is just before Boca de Tomatlán (about a 15-minute cab ride from the center of town), and these days is the site of a hotel/condo complex. The condo development, off the main highway, offers an excellent restaurant, fantastic views, and a 1960s-style disco with a waiter who moonwalks better than Michael Jackson. The young crowd finds it dull, but the older folks love it.

The hotel itself occupies most of the beachfront, and is easily reached by following the turnoff a short distance south of the condo units. ▶ **La Jolla de Mismaloya** is very attractive, with wide corridors and beautifully appointed rooms, some with small kitchens. (The façade of the movie hotel is still standing, but you have to climb a hill to reach it.) The hotel has managed to retain the original ambience of Playa Mismaloya without being obtrusive, and because it's so far out of town, every possible amenity and convenience has been provided, including three very good restaurants.

Additionally, there are two interesting restaurants deep in the jungle that are accessible by car (or taxi) from the village of Mismaloya: Chino's and Eden. (They're not hard to find as there's only one twisty road with signpost boulders pointing the way.) You'll find **Chino's** at the end of a bamboo bridge spanning the river, with a beautiful waterfall nearby where local youths will be happy to dive for you in exchange for a couple of dollars. The food is outstanding if you haven't already eaten and mildly interesting if you have. Beware the potent, overly garnished tropical drinks, however.

Continue on past Chino's and you come to **Eden**, which used to be the most primitive of the jungle restaurants, until Arnold Schwarzenegger and company arrived to shoot up some 40 acres of jungle during the making of *Predator*. They also blew up the original Eden in the process, and handsomely rewarded the owner with funds to rebuild it after they left. The food compares favorably with Chino's, but the restaurant is open only in the high season (the road is impassable the rest of the year).

Back on the main highway south of Mismaloya, on the bay side of the road, is **Le Kliff**, high atop a cliff overlooking Boca de Tomatlán, where the Río Tomatlán empties into the bay. Tablecloths and candlelight make this open-air restaurant a somewhat more formal spot for romance than some of its neighbors in the area, and the views of the sunset from here are truly out of this world. Tel: 2-5725 or 2733.

Chee-Chee, 1 km (½ mile) south of Le Kliff, is a reasonably priced Polynesian-style restaurant with so-so food and a splendid setting. A steep, winding bamboo staircase with a breathtaking vista at every turn leads down the overgrown hillside to the restaurant before continuing on to a swimming pool and a dock extending into the bay. (Women guests here often feel as if they should be wearing a Dorothy Lamour–type sarong.) The staircase, while a boon for photographers, is not for the weak of heart: People of all ages find themselves huffing and puffing on the way back up. Chee-Chee is open for lunch and an early dinner. Tel: 2-4697.

Chico's Paradise, just south of Chee-Chee, is perched above the Río Tomatlán, its giant boulders and flat rocks offering what seems to be an ideal spot for sunbathing. A word of caution, however: 11 tourists and two horses were swept to their deaths here within a two-year period. (The Río Tomatlán often swells with water high in the mountains and turns it loose without warning.) Chico's is also a prime example of what land developers can do to despoil the natural beauty of an area. The giant boulders now have rustic bridges built across them in a low-budget attempt to achieve a mini-Disneyland. And while the menu at Chico's is interesting, it's also a little on the pricey side. Your best bet is the black bean soup; try a bowl and you won't need to experiment with the drunken shrimp. Tel: 2-0747.

Sports in
Puerto Vallarta

Just about every water sport you can think of is available here, along with two other sports that you won't find at most other resorts: donkey polo and hunting.

Scuba-diving and snorkeling equipment can be rented in town or at most hotel beaches. Once you pick up your gear, head for Los Arcos, three small, uninhabited islands at the southern end of the bay, or Punta de Mita to the north (see Nuevo Vallarta, above). Any of these excursions can be arranged on the beach or at **Paradise Divers**, Olas Altas 443; **Divers de México** on Díaz Ordaz near Carlos O'Brian's; or at the **Dive Shop**, Díaz Ordaz 186.

Deep-sea fishing in the waters off Puerto Vallarta is also good. November to May are the months to catch sailfish, marlin, roosterfish, red snapper, snook, sea bass, tuna, and bonito. You can rent a boat through a travel agent, across from the Hotel Rosita downtown, or at the marina north of town on the airport road. Freshwater fishing excursions to the Cañon de Peña Reservoir, 112 km (69 miles) south of Puerto Vallarta, can also be arranged. If your hotel doesn't have a travel agent, head downtown or to the Krystal Vallarta.

Hunting excursions for wild boar, wild turkey, duck, dove, quail, and pheasant can be booked through **Aventuras Agraz**; Tel: 2-2969.

Before the new golf course at the Marina Vallarta opened, golfers had to make the 13-km (8-mile) trip to **Los Flamingos**, an 18-hole course that meanders around the inlets of a beautiful lagoon. Now both are popular, with condos and town houses beginning to sprout up around Los Flamingos.

Most hotels in P.V. have tennis courts. If yours doesn't, head over to the Plaza Vallarta, with its **John Newcombe Tennis Center**, north of town.

Sports buffs from the States who find themselves missing a daily diet of televised sports should check out **El Torito**, Ignacio Vallarta 290, south of the Río Cuale. You can pick up a schedule of games to be broadcast at the door—and with nine TV screens, you just might need it.

Excursions from
Puerto Vallarta

There are a number of excursions available for those who want to get away from the getaway of Puerto Vallarta. The following sailboat cruises leave from the marina and ferry terminal north of town.

Sailboat Cruises

The *Serape* or 60-foot *Vagabundo* will take you on a beautiful day trip south along the coastline to **Yelapa**, a Polynesian-style village with a beautiful white-sand beach, a number of thatched-roof restaurants, and a jungle waterfall that cascades 150 feet into a crystal-clear pool (the last is for the well-conditioned hiker only). The boats leave between 9:00 and 9:30 A.M. and return by 4:00 P.M. The *Serape* excursion (no lunch) will set you back about $16; for $27 the *Vagabundo* serves lunch and has an open bar.

The trimaran *Bora Bora* cruises to **Las Animas**, another beautiful beach south of Boca de Tomatlán, and one accessible by water only. Fishing en route and snorkeling once you get there are part of the fun. Plan on spending $30 for this six-hour excursion.

For about $45 the trimaran *Cielito Lindo* takes visitors to **Huanacaxtle**, north of P.V. in the state of Nayarit, a primitive fishing village fronted by a deserted beach where you can sun, fish, and sail.

The catamaran *Shamballa* sails to **Playa Quimixto**, yet another laid-back spot between Las Animas and Yelapa, for about $36.

There is also a sailboat excursion available to **Rincón de Guayabitos**, a primitive beach in the state of Nayarit. The day trip includes lunch, stops at small villages, and an exhibition of Huichol Indian art that consists mostly of whimsical "paintings" woven out of concentric circles of fine yarn.

San Sebastián

One of the more interesting excursions from Puerto Vallarta has as its destination the old silver-mining town of San Sebastián, 145 km (90 miles) inland via a narrow, twisty road that takes four hours to negotiate (or you can fly there in 20 minutes from P.V.'s airport).

San Sebastián was founded in 1607, and shortly thereafter became the proud provincial capital of the state of Jalisco. At one point during the colonial era it supported some 40,000 inhabitants, most of whom were kept busy refining ore into silver, which was melted down into ingots and transported by mule to the mouth of the Río Cuale, where it was loaded aboard ships bound for Spain.

Today the population is about 800, most of them agricultural workers, and there's very little in the way of organized activities for tourists. You can explore the abandoned silver mines or whoop it up with some of the locals at one of the town's many cantinas. Or you can play Trivia Quiz with Bud Acord.

A former Texan who has lived in Mexico for 22 of his more than 65 years, Acord literally rediscovered the ▶ **Hacienda Jalisco**, the former headquarters of the mining company that profited so handsomely during San Sebastián's heyday, and spent three years and half a million dollars converting it into a guest house, after which it became a favorite hideaway for the likes of John Huston, Elizabeth Taylor, Richard Burton, Peter O'Toole, and William F. Buckley, Jr. Huston, who had an eye for the finer things of life, once said, "Some day a movie company will find this place and the privacy will be gone." He was close enough: CBS has already shot stock footage here. For those who don't dally, there's still plenty of romance and privacy left.

The half-dozen rooms are arranged in pairs, with every other one sporting a fireplace. (In the winter it can get very cold, leading to some spirited bidding on the fireplace rooms.) The Hacienda also has a dining room, but most guests prefer to eat in the kitchen, where the coffee bushes grow right outside the window. The food is always good, but don't expect a menu: The meal consists of whatever the chef has a mind to cook. Room rates depend on the size of your group, the time of year, and how many people are in residence. Have a travel agent check before you commit.

Another thing to keep in mind: Pickup by plane at the end of your stay at the Hacienda is done Mexican style—that is, you may request a pickup time but not see the pilot and his plane until a day or two later. It's wise to allow some leeway if you're on a schedule.

If you'd like more information about the Hacienda Jalisco, check at the in-house travel agency in your hotel or contact one of the many travel agencies in town. **Viajes Horizonte**, in the lobby of the Fiesta Americana, is especially good when it comes to local tours of this nature. Tel: (322) 2-3888.

GETTING AROUND

The following airlines service Puerto Vallarta's Gustavo Díaz Ordaz International Airport from the United States: Aeroméxico offers daily nonstop service from Los Angeles and San Diego as well as daily flights from New York City (J.F.K.), Houston, New Orleans, and Miami via Mexico City. Mexicana offers daily nonstop service from San Francisco, Los Angeles, and Chicago; flights from Denver and Dallas–Fort Worth via Guadalajara; and from J.F.K. via Mexico City. Continental offers daily nonstop flights from Houston, and American Airlines flies nonstop daily from Dallas–Fort Worth. Alaska Airlines offers direct service to Puerto Vallarta from its hubs on the West Coast.

When you arrive at the airport, you'll find the trip through Immigration and Customs surprisingly smooth. After you collect your baggage, it's a good idea to change some of your money into pesos at the airport *casa de cambio,* where you'll get a much better rate of exchange than at your hotel. Change as much as you want to—you can always change it back again at the same *casa de cambio* when you depart. Keep some dollars, however; many of the restaurants and stores in town will offer a higher rate of exchange to their customers.

Don't look for a taxi at the airport: There aren't any. Mexico's airports are federal property and the government controls transportation to and from them. Taxis are allowed to drop passengers off, but they're prohibited from picking anyone up. Instead, you'll have to settle for a *colectivo* (a VW minibus). There's a ticket booth out front; the cost of the trip is preset by zone (it's about $10 from the airport to town). Passengers are loaded and dropped off at their respective hotels in sequence. If this forced "togetherness" doesn't appeal to you, or if you're interested in going directly to your hotel, you can opt for an *"especial"*; it's pricey, but for die-hard sun-lovers it will be money well spent.

Unless you're planning on leaving town frequently, there's no need to rent a car in Puerto Vallarta; the best way to get around is by taxi. Public buses tend to be dirty and crowded, but are also convenient and inexpensive. They stop every two blocks along the beach road and can be flagged down as well. Look for those saying "Pitillal," "Las Juntas," or "Ixtapa."

Guadalajara is a 5-hour drive over a good highway. The bus (first class) takes about 7 hours and costs about $18. The four bus stations in Puerto Vallarta are all on the corner of Insurgentes and Basilio Badillo, south of the Río Cuale.

—*Robin Lloyd*

ACCOMMODATIONS REFERENCE

The rates given below are projections *for December 1993 through Easter 1994. Unless otherwise indicated, rates are for double rooms, double occupancy; the 10 percent VAT has been added. As rates are subject to change, it's a good idea to double-check before booking. Puerto Vallarta is in the central standard time zone; the telephone area code is 322.*

▶ **Camino Real**. P.O. Box 95, Playa de las Ecstacas, **Puerto Vallarta**, Jalisco 48300. Tel: 3-0123; Fax: 3-0070; in the U.S. and Canada, Tel: (800) 7-CAMINO. $176.

▶ **Club Maeva Puerto Vallarta**. Carretera A. Barra de Navidad, km 4, **Puerto Vallarta**, Jalisco 48300. Tel and Fax: 2-2105. $220 (all-inclusive).

▶ **Continental Plaza**. P.O. Box 36B, Playa de las Glorias, **Puerto Vallarta**, Jalisco 48300. Tel: 4-0123; Fax: 4-4437; in the U.S. and Canada, Tel: (800) 882-6684. $120.

▶ **Fiesta Americana**. P.O. Box 270, Carretera Aeropuerto, km 2.5, **Puerto Vallarta**, Jalisco 48300. Tel: 4-2010; Fax: 4-2108; in the U.S. and Canada, Tel: (800) FIESTA-1. $198.

▶ **Hacienda Buenaventura**. P.O. Box 95B, Paseo de la Marina, **Puerto Vallarta**, Jalisco 48300. Tel: 4-6667; Fax: 4-6400; in the U.S. and Canada, Tel: (800) 223-6764. $66.

▶ **Hacienda Jalisco**. C/o Bud Acord, **San Sebastián**, Jalisco 48300. No phone. $35 (includes meals).

▶ **Hotel Bel Air Puerto Vallarta**. P.O. Box 81, Pelicanos 311, Marina Vallarta, **Puerto Vallarta**, Jalisco 48300. Tel: 1-0800; Fax: 1-0801; in the U.S., Tel: (800) 457-7676. $172–$193.

▶ **Hotel Buenaventura**. P.O. Box 8B, Avenida México 1301, **Puerto Vallarta**, Jalisco 48300. Tel: 2-3737; Fax: 4-6400; in the U.S., Tel: (800) 878-4484; in Canada, Tel: (800) 663-3141. $75.

▶ **La Jolla de Mismaloya**. Carretera A. Barra de Navidad, km 11.5, **Puerto Vallarta**, Jalisco 48300; or 301 East Colorado Boulevard, Suite 808, Pasadena, CA 91101. Tel: 3-0660; in the U.S. and Canada, Tel: (800) 322-2344. $215.

▶ **Krystal Vallarta**. Avenida de las Garzas, **Puerto Vallarta**, Jalisco 48300. Tel: 4-0202; Fax: 4-0222; in the U.S. and Canada, Tel: (800) 231-9860. $132.

▶ **Marriott CasaMagna**. Paseo de la Marina 5, Marina Vallarta, **Puerto Vallarta**, Jalisco 48300. Tel: 1-0004; Fax: 1-0760; in the U.S. and Canada, Tel: (800) 223-6388. $197–$209.

▶ **Meliá Puerto Vallarta**. Paseo de la Marina Sur, Marina Vallarta, **Puerto Vallarta**, Jalisco 48300. Tel: 1-0200; Fax: 1-0118; in the U.S. and Canada, Tel: (800) 336-3542. $182.

▶ **Sheraton Buganvilias**. Carretera Aeropuerto 999, **Puerto Vallarta**, Jalisco 48300. Tel: 3-0404; Fax: 2-0500; in the U.S. and Canada, Tel: (800) 325-3535. $154.

TENACATITA

If you've ever wanted to know what it's like to vacation in the middle of nowhere, this is the perfect place to find out—though it's hard to imagine you would travel to Mexico just to come here. The hotel Los Angeles Locos is aptly named—only "crazy angels" know where it is. Nestled on a beautiful bay off Highway 200, about 190 km (118 miles) south of Puerto Vallarta and 87 km (54 miles) north of Manzanillo, Tenacatita's lone hotel is announced by a few small signs along the road that point the way to the big red billboard at the turnoff to its access road. If you blink, however, you can miss them all.

MAJOR INTEREST

Superb bay and beach
Utter isolation

Though the choice to put a hotel on the graceful curve of this lovely bay was a sane one, it's the snaking mile-and-a-half-long access road through thick jungle that makes the whole prospect of the place seem crazy. The property, now managed by the Fiesta Americana chain and called the ► **Fiesta Americana Los Angeles Locos**, was originally built by a Mexican labor union that wanted to provide restful vacations for its members. (Shortly after this workingman's paradise was completed, the union had to turn it over to Fiesta Americana.) The result was a low-rise deluxe hotel with 200 rooms arranged around a central pool area. Most rooms overlook the ocean, and all have balconies, color TV, and comfortable rattan furniture. The hotel attracts Mexican families, Canadians on group tours, and more than a few U.S. travellers; to satisfy their palates, three open-air restaurants offer a choice of well-prepared Mexican and Continental cuisine.

Every imaginable water sport is available as part of the package as well. There are also four tennis courts lighted for night play and horseback riding along the wide, sandy beach. The lap pool is built around an island bar where the bartenders are happy to hand you a drink as you paddle by—a practice that tends to limit the number of laps you may have had in mind. A tiny disco with live entertainment (sometimes) is the only other distraction from the beauty and solitude in Tenacatita.

The hotel used to require a seven-night-minimum package, but due to demand the policy was changed to a flat day rate or split days pro-rated from $112 per person for a full day. While the price is fine if you plan to spend an entire day here, arriving in time for breakfast, the half-day offer is on the expensive side (how many laps can you swim and how many horses can you ride in half a day, with time out for meals?).

With all this and lots of favorable publicity besides, it was only a matter of time before private homes and condos began to appear on the hillside overlooking the hotel. If you are truly "seeking serenity in a remote paradise" (which the brochures promise to deliver), do it while the serenity and remoteness still exist.

GETTING AROUND

The hotel is about 60 km (37 miles) northwest of the Manzanillo airport and 190 km (118 miles) southeast of Puerto Vallarta. The taxi fare from the airport is more than the one-way plane fare to Manzanillo from Guadalajara, but you can always rent a car. For an additional charge of $22 per person, one-way, the hotel will send a *colectivo* to the airport to pick you up—perhaps your best bet (arrange in advance through the hotel or a travel agent).

—*Robin Lloyd*

ACCOMMODATIONS REFERENCE

The rates given below are projections *for December 1993 through Easter 1994. Unless otherwise indicated, rates are for double rooms, double occupancy; the 10 percent VAT has been added. As rates are subject to change, it's a good idea to double-check before booking. Tenacatita is in the central standard time zone; the telephone area code is 333.*

▶ **Fiesta Americana Los Angeles Locos.** P.O. Box 7, Melaque, Highway 200, km 20, **Tenacatita**, Jalisco 48980. Tel: 7-0220; Fax: 7-0229; in the U.S. and Canada, Tel: (800) FIESTA-1. Low season, $96; high season, $112.

BARRA DE NAVIDAD

Barra de Navidad (Christmas Bar) is well known to Mexicans, but the mainstream tourist has yet to discover it. The attraction here is sportsfishing; year-round catches include sailfish, dorado, tuna, and blue and black marlin. Visiting fishermen from north of the border favorably compare Barra to the Cabo San Lucas of 20 years ago.

MAJOR INTEREST

Fishing
Fishing-village atmosphere

The village of Barra de Navidad, 2 km (1¼ miles) off the main highway, is a quiet place built on a spit of land separating the ocean from a mangrove-lined lagoon. The cobblestone streets are narrow, dusty, crowded, and lined by row after row of open-air stores. The perfect, dark-sand crescent of a beach quarters a surprisingly large number of small hotels in the low- to moderate-price range as well as a number of excellent palapa-type restaurants, which attract customers from the posh Las Hadas complex 20 miles to the south in Manzanillo. One such restaurant, though nameless, sits on the east side of Calle Vera Cruz, a block back from the ocean. The restaurant is run by a charming woman named Esperanza, who opens her front door (most evenings), puts a few tables out on the sidewalk, and serves the best *pozole* imaginable. (*Pozolé* is a marvelous mixture of hearty beef stock, hominy, mixed vegetables, shredded pork, cabbage, and sweet, fresh onions served with stacks of corn tortillas.)

The ► Hotel Cabo Blanco, on the edge of town, looks like a posh country club and is part of a pretty, developed (for this part of the coast) complex called Pueblo Nuevo that also includes condos, the area's only tennis courts, a yacht club, and a canal that leads to the ocean. (Six steps will take you from the edge of the hotel swimming pool to the canal.) The hotel's fine restaurant is guaranteed to leave a smile on your face. Try a large bowl of the tortilla soup, which, preceded by a small green salad, is a meal in itself.

At the hotel's beach club, a five-minute drive from the hotel, waterskiing, scuba diving and snorkeling, windsurfing, or sportsfishing boat rentals can all be arranged.

After a few days you'll feel as if you know everybody in town. With this kind of hospitable atmosphere, it's only a matter of time before Barra de Navidad becomes a resort destination attracting the discerning traveller.

GETTING AROUND

It's essential to have a car in Barra de Navidad in order to get around. Cars can be rented at the airports in Puerto

Vallarta, Manzanillo (the closest air gateway, 13 km/8 miles to the south and east), or Guadalajara (see their respective Getting Around sections for further information).

—*Robin Lloyd*

ACCOMMODATIONS REFERENCE

The rates given below are projections for December 1993 through Easter 1994. Unless otherwise indicated, rates are for double rooms, double occupancy; the 10 percent VAT has been added. As rates are subject to change, it's a good idea to double-check before booking. Barra de Navidad is in the central standard time zone; the telephone area code is 333.

▶ **Hotel Cabo Blanco.** P.O. Box 31, Armada and Pueblo Nuevo, **Barra de Navidad**, Jalisco 48987. Tel: 7-0182; Fax: 7-0168. $72.

MANZANILLO

Manzanillo is the only Mexican resort to have become a movie star before it was a well-known destination. The movie *10* catapulted it onto the map with even more effect than the gala opening of Las Hadas, attended by celebrities from around the world, a few years earlier.

Before Las Hadas, Manzanillo was little more than a sleepy tropical port surrounded by fertile farmland. The few visitors who came here were likely to be deep-sea fishermen, and the biggest decision anyone ever had to make was whether to eat the large tangy oysters from the bay or the small sweet oysters from the Laguna Cuyutlán.

Highway 200, the road linking Manzanillo to Puerto Vallarta, about 260 km (160 miles) up the coast, opened more than 20 years ago, and things haven't been the same since. (In the interim, two more highways linking it to Guadalajara have been built, and a brand-new four-lane highway that will cut the driving time to three and a half hours is nearing completion.) With more than 20 miles of beautiful beaches, excellent weather (Manzanillo is on the same latitude as Hawaii), and a number of first-class hotels and resorts in addition to Las Hadas, Manzanillo is the perfect getaway for those who want to unwind in an exotic setting without the hustle and bustle of some of Mexico's larger vacation destinations.

MAJOR INTEREST

Las Hadas resort and marina

Manzanillo's fresh-faced appearance belies its importance: Connected by rail to cities throughout the country, it is one of the busiest commercial seaports in Mexico. It is also one of Mexico's major deep-sea fishing ports, and lies at the heart of one of the most fertile agricultural areas in the country—lush papaya, banana, and coconut plantations stretch for miles inland from the coast.

Cortés named the small settlement he found here for the beautiful blossoming chamomile plants of the surrounding area. Soon after, he established Latin America's first shipyard in order to build boats for the further exploration of New Spain and the Philippines. (He found the area so much to his liking, in fact, that he eventually retired here.) By the end of the 16th century Manzanillo was one of the New World's leading ports, with much of that activity revolving around trade with the Far East. But as Spain's fortunes in the New World declined, Manzanillo was all but forgotten by the rest of the world.

That all began to change in 1974, when Anteñor Patiño, a Bolivian tin magnate, unveiled the opulent Las Hadas resort. Other hotels and condominium complexes have followed, but, overall, the growth of Manzanillo as a destination for international travellers has been slower than that of other Mexican resorts.

Around in Manzanillo

The ten beautiful miles of the beach-fringed Bahía de Manzanillo run in a graceful curve from northwest to southeast. Downtown Manzanillo, where the major banks and airline offices are located, is at the southeastern end of the bay. Las Hadas is located to the north. The smaller, scallop-shaped Bahía de Santiago lies to the west of Las Hadas, with the two bays separated by the Península de Santiago. To the north and west of Santiago Bay are Playa de Oro, the finest black-sand beach in Mexico; the airport; and the coastal highway leading to Barra de Navidad and points north, including Puerto Vallarta.

For the most part, visitors confine themselves to the seven-mile stretch between Las Hadas and the downtown area. Pockets of development surround each resort complex in the area—among them Las Hadas, Club Maeva, Club Santiago, and the Hotel Sierra Radisson Plaza—but miles of relatively unspoiled beach lie between each busy pocket. Other attractions here are also spread out—so spread out, in fact, that it's best to rent a car if you plan on spending any time exploring; the roads in and around Manzanillo are good and getting around is easy.

FROM THE AIRPORT TO LAS HADAS

The ride from the airport to Las Hadas is a long (43 km/27 miles) but scenic one that passes through lush banana and coconut plantations. If excursions to nearby towns and villages are on your itinerary, this will be a good time to watch the road signs and get a feel for the lay of the land.

Although it's a bit off the beaten track at km 12.5 on Boulevard Costero Miguel de la Madrid, the coast road (about a ten-minute drive north of Las Hadas), **L'Recif** (The Reef) is worth checking out. Situated high on a promontory in the Vida del Mar condominium complex, this romantic restaurant offers spectacular views of the craggy coastline and terrific food prepared by a French-born chef. (The Sunday brunch here is legendary.) If you come for lunch, be sure to bring a camera and a bathing suit—there's a splendidly tranquil pool in a tiny garden on the premises where patrons can swim and sunbathe after their meal. Reservations recommended; Tel: 3-0624.

Santiago and Playa Miramar

What most visitors think of as Manzanillo starts at ▶ **Club Santiago**, on Playa Miramar (popular with bodysurfers, it's the first beach you'll see on the trip in from the airport). Club Santiago offers a variety of accommodations in a posh, country club–like setting, including one- to six-room beachfront villas, secluded cottages, and spacious condominiums. The huge pool has a shaded swim-up bar, and guests can dine on the beach at **Oasis**, a sleek, sophisticated restaurant under a soaring palapa that specializes in moderately priced French cuisine; Tel: 3-0937. The greatest attraction at Club Santiago, however, is the marvelous seclusion it offers.

The small but fast-growing town of Santiago itself is the location of the **Centro Artesanal Las Primaveras**, one of the best handicraft shops in the area (it doubles as a flower shop). You'll find it at Juárez 40, between the church and Camacho Supermarket, facing the highway.

To the south and east of Playa Miramar, following the curve of the bay in the direction of Las Hadas and town, the

Olas Altas and **Santiago** beaches are especially pretty and unspoiled.

Just down the road from Club Santiago in the direction of town, about a 20-minute drive from the airport, is the all-inclusive ▶ **Club Maeva Manzanillo**, a picturesque and self-contained resort hotel spread over 90 acres. The Maeva's blue-and-white villas, some capable of accommodating up to six people, cluster around the resort's beautiful gardens, and their no-nonsense interiors—bright blue tiles cover the floor and built-in couches and beds keep the living areas uncluttered—seem to have been designed with families in mind. The Maeva's villas are available by the day or week; when making your reservation, request a deluxe villa with a view.

Guests at Club Maeva tend to congregate around the pool, one of the largest in the country (the proprietors sometimes hold water-skiing exhibitions in it); a pedestrian walkway leads over the coast road to the beach on Santiago Bay. In addition, 4 of the 14 tennis courts are lighted for night play, and special activities for children are staged throughout the grounds. In fact, Club Maeva strikes the first-time visitor as a "user-friendly" playland where the whole family feels at home from the moment it arrives.

Playa La Audiencia

The ▶ **Hotel Sierra Radisson Plaza**, a newish deluxe hotel property designed by the architect of Las Hadas, stands on Playa La Audiencia, a graceful moon-shaped beach and bay at the the head of the Santiago Peninsula. La Audiencia got its name from a reputed meeting between Cortés and the local Indians—its only claim to fame besides its great natural beauty. Nestled in a protective inlet within the larger Santiago Bay, the beach is washed by the gentlest waves in Manzanillo, making it an ideal place to snorkel and swim.

The hotel itself is a towering 350-room complex with four lighted tennis courts, and numerous restaurants and bars. Rooms are large and tastefully decorated, and the impressive public areas are spacious and airy. Perhaps best of all, the developers of this huge hotel have not been totally insensitive to aesthetic considerations: The white walls and tile roofs of the complex lend it a vaguely Moorish look, and its striking architectural design complements the natural beauty of the bay.

LAS HADAS

It is entirely appropriate that *Las Hadas* translates as "The Fairies": The guests at this world-famous resort often feel as if they are vacationing in nothing less than an enchanted fairyland. The architecture of the ▶ Las Hadas Resort is a unique blend of Moorish, Mexican, and Caribbean elements combined to create a gleaming white stucco village perched on a hill overlooking Manzanillo Bay. And while Señor Patiño built the place to meet the high standards of his wealthy and discriminating friends, he also priced it so that others could enjoy the luxury and beauty that prevail here.

Everything at Las Hadas is on a grand scale, with the luxury built in from the ground up. Most rooms and suites have an ocean view, and some have large private patios. Inside, marble floors and tiled baths keep the spacious rooms and suites cool and inviting. (Las Hadas also offers rooms in its **Royal Beach Club**, complete with gorgeous views, deluxe amenities, and complimentary afternoon cocktails around the pool.) The two swimming pools are attractively decorated with mosaics, while the larger is crossed by a suspended bridge and has two landscaped islands in the middle of it. Exquisitely carved fountains dot the gardened walkways lacing the complex, and the small bay nearby is ringed by a lovely beach where beach attendants rake the sand and prepare white cabaña tents for their pampered guests. If you get tired of walking to the beach or the pool, a chauffeured golf cart (Las Hadas uses a noiseless model so that other guests won't be disturbed) will respond to your summons. Las Hadas also has a private 18-hole championship golf course.

The open-air **El Terral** (Tel: 3-0000), where Dudley Moore and Bo Derek shared a romantic dinner, is one of the charming restaurants at Las Hadas; **La Cartouche**, the piano bar/disco that also appeared in the movie, is where, during peak occupancy periods, you'll find the nightlife. The **Player's Club** at the Las Hadas marina, where live mariachi music livens up most nights, is also fun.

The 90-slip marina at the foot of the hill looks like a showroom for luxury yachts, and the condominium complex just across the seaside promenade, Marina Las Hadas, is managed by the hotel. The complex includes the **Marina Mall**, with its maze of shops, tiny restaurants, and outdoor cafés.

The Mediterranean-style ▶ **Plaza Las Glorias Manzanillo** is a picture-perfect luxury accommodation perched atop another steep hillside overlooking Las Hadas, the golf course, and Club Santiago. There are 85 "villas" with living room, bedrooms, and bath on the premises here, but you may opt for a traditional room if you wish. The rooms, most with large terraces, are bright and spacious, and the dining room offers a panoramic view and refreshing breezes by day and a romantic ambience with live music at night. The pool has its own swim-up bar and bridge (though it's not as big as the pools at Las Hadas or Club Maeva), and for guests who want to hit the beach, a shuttle bus runs between the hotel and Playa Santiago, a few minutes away. For those who would just as soon avoid paying top dollar and can survive without a beach right outside the door, the Plaza Las Glorias is one of the best lodging options in the area.

FROM LAS HADAS TO TOWN

Almost everything a visitor will want to see, do, or arrange can be found along **Playa Azul**, the seven-mile stretch of beach that rings Manzanillo Bay. With its gentle curves and gentler waves (more so the closer you get to town), Playa Azul has become a magnet for hotels and restaurants, which can be found on either side of the highway and become more concentrated as you near town. The dining establishments and discos along this stretch are as informal as they come—you're not likely to find the fast-track Mexico City crowd here. In fact, an older crowd of retired Americans seems to constitute the first shift at many of these places, though they fill up later in the evening with locals, especially on weekends. (Generally speaking, Manzanillo doesn't attract night owls, serious shoppers, or those who like to be "seen.")

El Vaquero Campestre, a garden-style restaurant in the Salahua neighborhood, across the main road and three blocks south of the Las Hadas turnoff at km 11.5, is a sister establishment of El Vaquero de las Brisas, a popular Manzanillo restaurant famous for its steaks and grilled meats. You enter this village-like oasis through a gate and follow a cobblestone path to a collection of palapas. Steak and meat dishes are the specialties, and on occasion there's music for dancing. Retired gringos seem to be especially partial to this one. Tel: 3-0475.

Popular **Juanito's**, at km 9.5 on Boulevard Costero Miguel de la Madrid, offers pretty colonial decor, typical Tex-Mex fare, and what many say are the best hamburgers, hot dogs, and American-style milkshakes in town. (They also will place long-distance phone calls for you.)

Papagayo's, at km 8.5 near the Cine Fiesta movie house, is an air-conditioned hangout popular with the locals. Seafood and pasta dishes are best here, and occasionally there is music for dancing between courses.

The moderately priced ▶ **Fiesta Mexicana**, on the beach across from the Restaurant Barra de Navidad, is a tropical charmer that's large enough to be comfortable but small enough to be friendly and cozy. Its rooms, decorated with floral prints and bamboo furniture, have a homey look, and the pretty pool with swim-up bar and dining area shaded by towering palms are the focal points of its layout. Its convenient location near a cluster of popular restaurants makes it even more of a bargain.

Farther south, at km 7 on Boulevard Costero, you'll come to the ever-popular **Carlos 'n' Charlie's Colima Bay Café**, one of a chain of unserious and much-loved restaurants started by the late Carlos Anderson. The prevailing attitude here is "Come in and join the fun"—although it's not as boisterous as some of its brethren in other Mexican resorts. If you like down-home cooking (barbecue ribs are the favorite) but hate loud fiestas, wait for a table out on the porch overlooking the water. Tel: 3-1150.

South of Carlos 'n' Charlie's on the coast road there's a cluster of good restaurants at the Crucero Las Brisas, or Las Brisas crossroads (marked by a life-size concrete sailboat). **Ostería Bugatti** was one of the first restaurants on the scene here and is still one of the most popular. Everyone likes the comfortable bar, the leaded-glass windows, and the piano music that accompanies dinner, while the cozy interior is a perfect complement to the food. Tel: 3-2999.

Willy's, on the beach at the end of Calle Benito Rincón Lopez, is one of the most popular places in town (along with Bugatti's and Oasis, in the Club Santiago complex). Tables spill out of the main building and its pretty porch onto a platform on the beach. Out front near the entrance savory meats are cooked over a charcoal grill, and elsewhere on the grounds a mini–street market keeps the same hours as the restaurant. Amid all this happy confusion, Chef Michele whips up delicious French cuisine and tasty tropical treats. Even with a reservation you'll probably have to wait, but with all the activity around, waiting is part of the fun. Tel: 3-1794.

El Vaquero de las Brisas (it's the place at the crossroads with a covered wagon on its roof) claims to serve the best meat in town. With its dark wood-paneled walls, red-checked tablecloths, and Wild West memorabilia, you'll think you've stumbled into a Colorado steakhouse. After you've chosen your steak by cut and weight, it is grilled to your specifications right at your table. It's a great idea, but the place does tend to get hot in the summer despite the air-conditioning. Tel: 3-1654.

If you stay to the right at the Las Brisas intersection, you'll soon enter the Las Brisas zone on Avenida Lázaro Cárdenas. The ▶ **Hotel La Posada**, across the road from the yacht basin (the place to charter fishing boats), is the kind of establishment where you can let it all hang out, relax in the sun on the beach with your favorite book, and enjoy the gorgeous Pacific sunsets over a cold drink without ever having to put on your shoes. People who have the time to travel through Mexico by car or RV love this place, and guests and locals alike stop here to enjoy the hearty, cooked-to-order American-style breakfasts and catch up on the latest gossip. Bart Varlemann, the owner, is an Ohioan who came to Manzanillo years ago, and he goes out of his way to make his guests feel right at home. (The bar works on the honor system.) La Posada is a cash-only operation.

DOWNTOWN

In the past there was little reason for visitors to head into downtown Manzanillo. Those who did usually visited the small **mercado municipal** (municipal market), where sundries and souvenirs are sold; shopped at the **Bazar El Dorado** in front of the main square; and ended up at the landmark **Bar Social**, Calle 21 de Marzo and Juárez on the zócalo (known here as the Jardín Alvaro Obregón), or the patio bar of the ▶ **Hotel Colonial**, Avenida México 100, for a drink and a bite to eat. Both are throwbacks to the days when Manzanillo attracted sportsfishermen and little else. Though the hotel's former elegance has faded (the once-ornate building now houses an appliance shop), it's still the only decent lodging option if you must stay downtown.

On the other hand, for those who enjoy local color, exploring downtown Manzanillo can be a treat. Streets that not too many years ago could only be described as seedy have been cleaned up, and the newly landscaped zócalo area invites tourists to relax and watch the passersby and commercial action that animate this busy port town. **Club Náutico**, a restaurant perched on stilts over the water, is a pleasant place for lunch or dinner.

Nightlife in Manzanillo

Nightlife and shopping in Manzanillo can be summed up in a few words: There isn't much of either. What little nightlife there is centers around the hotels, a few restaurants, and **La Cartouche** at Las Hadas (when it's open; call ahead to check; Tel: 3-0000). **Boom Boom** at Club Maeva and **Solaris** in the Hotel Playa de Oro (at km 15.5) are the most popular hotel nightclub/discos. Outside the hotels, three lively state-of-the-art discos on Boulevard Costero draw young (and young-at-heart) crowds. **Enjoy**, at km 16, is the largest of the three and has the standard laser lights and video screens. **Oui**, at km 9, is more intimate and ranks as the favorite among locals, while **Disco Bar de Felix**, at km 8.5, has the atmosphere of a bar in the States. Papagayo's and L'Recif, both discussed above, also usually have music for dancing.

Shopping in Manzanillo

As we've noted, Manzanillo is not a shoppers' paradise. Most hotels have one or two boutiques. The best collection of shops is in the Plaza Albina at Las Hadas: **Jaramar** for decorative items, **María de Guadalajara** for resortwear, and **Tane** for exquisite silver jewelry are three of the best here. The air-conditioned **Plaza Manzanillo**, at km 11.5 on the Boulevard Costero, has a number of good boutiques offering trendy resortwear and accessories, the usual fast-food restaurants, a couple of places where you can get your film developed, and a well-stocked supermarket. **Rubén Torres**, located in a snazzy glass structure on the beach side of the coast road at km 13, sells resortwear for men and women in a variety of bright colors. The **mercado municipal** downtown on Avenida Cinco de Mayo is the place to bargain for typical souvenirs.

Sports in Manzanillo

Manzanillo is yet another Pacific Coast paradise for sportsmen—though water-sport centers offering water-ski boats, scuba diving, and snorkeling trips are not as visible here as they are in other resorts. Windsurfing boards can be rented at the marina across from the Hotel La Posada, and the conditions at that end of the bay are usually gentle enough for even the greenest beginner.

Of course, fishing was the reason behind Manzanillo's early popularity and it remains one of its biggest draws. Sailfish and marlin (Manzanillo bills itself as the "Sailfish Capital of Mexico") are the prize catches, and November and December are the best months to catch them. Species such as sea bass, mackerel, giant tuna, and yellowtail are abundant year-round, with October through March being the busiest season. Your hotel will be happy to arrange a charter boat for you at the marina across the street from the Hotel La Posada; the price, ranging from $150 to $300, depending on the size of the boat, usually includes bait and tackle.

Most of the major hotels and resorts in Manzanillo have tennis courts. If yours doesn't, there are six at Club Santiago, four at the Hotel Sierra Radisson Plaza (all lighted), and 14 at

Club Maeva (four of them lighted) open to the public. Call in advance for reservations (see the Accommodations Reference list below for telephone numbers).

The **Laguna Juluapán**, northwest of Club Santiago, is a nature preserve and favorite haunt of visiting bird-watchers. Club Maeva allows horseback riding on its beach (and will supply the horses), and travel agencies in town and at the hotels will be happy to arrange scuba and snorkeling excursions.

Excursions from Manzanillo

Colima and Comala
Colima, about 100 km (62 miles) northeast of Manzanillo, is the capital of the small state of the same name, and is known for its geared-down pace and friendliness. Be sure to check out one of the folkloric or theatrical performances, staged year-round in its **Casa de Cultura**. The **Museo de las Culturas Occidentales**, part of the Casa de Cultura complex, houses the country's largest collection of the famous "dancing dogs of Colima," clay sculptures considered sacred by the local Indians, as well as other zoomorphic figures unearthed at nearby archaeological sites. The **Museo Regional de Historia**, at Hidalgo and Reforma, displays archaeological finds as well as handicrafts from the state of Colima; occasionally it also stages exhibitions of paintings by contemporary artists from the area.

Housed in an old building on Calle 27 de Septiembre at the corner of Regalado is the **Museo Universitario de Arte y Cultura Popular**, more informally known as the Museum of Dance, Masks, and Popular Art. It exhibits costumes worn for folkloric dances as well as other regional art, some of which is for sale. (None of these museums has display explanations in English.) Hours are usually from 8:00 A.M. to 2:00 P.M. and from 6:00 to 7:00 P.M., daily except Mondays.

In the nearby colonial town of **Comala** (15 minutes by car from Colima), visitors can choose from a good selection of painted furniture, pottery, and wrought iron at the **Mercado de Artesanías**. Your hotel or one of the travel agencies in downtown Manzanillo will arrange a trip to both Colima and Comala if you decide not to drive yourself.

Cuyutlán
More adventurous travellers can head for the primitive seaside town of Cuyutlán, about 50 km (31 miles) south of Manzanillo, most of the trip via Highway 200. The lagoon and beautiful unspoiled beach here are reason enough to

pack a picnic and make the trip, but the lucky visitor may reap a dividend: Every spring between March and May, especially as the moon waxes full, the beach here is subject to repeated visitations of the mysterious *Ola Verde,* or "Green Wave," a wall of water that sometimes reaches heights of 30 feet or more.

If your hotel does not have a travel agent, contact **Bahías Gemelas** at Las Hadas (you can also find them at km 10 on the Boulevard Costero); Tel: 3-1000 or 0204.

GETTING AROUND

You can drive good highways from either Puerto Vallarta or Guadalajara to Manzanillo or ride the bus. ETN buses leave Guadalajara four times a day. Although flying is by far the most convenient way to get here, most international carriers do not offer direct service to Manzanillo, which means travellers will be routed through either Mexico City or Guadalajara, with some connections through the former requiring an overnight stay. Two carriers that do offer "direct" service to Manzanillo are Mexicana and Aeroméxico. Aeroméxico offers daily flights from Los Angeles via La Paz, and Mexicana flies daily via Guadalajara (these stops do not require a change of planes). Flying time from Los Angeles is 4 hours.

The airport is a long ride—about 43 km (27 miles)—from the major hotels, so relax and enjoy it; the plantations you'll pass along the way are lush and lovely. There are a number of car-rental agencies right at the airport (Avis, Budget, Hertz, and National among them), as well as a few in town. A taxi from the airport will cost about $16; a *colectivo* will make the same trip for about $10.

Once you've settled in, taxis or rental car are the best way to get around. Taxis are plentiful and easy to hail; if you don't find one waiting outside your hotel door, ask the hotel to call one. There's also a taxi stand downtown across from the zócalo on Avenida Morelos. As is the case any time you decide to take a taxi in Mexico, establish the price *before* you get into the cab.

—Susan Wagner

ACCOMMODATIONS REFERENCE

The rates given below are projections *for December 1993 through Easter 1994. Unless otherwise indicated, rates are for double rooms, double occupancy; the 10 percent VAT has been added. As rates are subject to change, it's a good idea to double-check before booking. Manzanillo is in the central standard time zone; the telephone area code is 333.*

▶ **Club Maeva Manzanillo.** P.O. Box 442, Carretera Manzanillo–Barra de Navidad, km 12, **Manzanillo**, Colima 28200. Tel: 3-0141 or 0595; Fax: 3-0395; in the U.S. and Canada, Tel: (800) 431-2822; Fax: (914) 632-3496. $125 per person (all-inclusive).

▶ **Club Santiago.** P.O. Box 374, Carrizales s/n, Bahía de Santiago, **Manzanillo**, Colima 28200. Tel: 3-0413; Fax: 3-0768. Condos, $150; villas, $408 (up to eight people).

▶ **Fiesta Mexicana.** Carretera Manzanillo–Barra de Navidad, km 8.5, **Manzanillo**, Colima 28200. Tel and Fax: 3-1100. $71.

▶ **Las Hadas Resort.** P.O. Box 158, Rincón de las Hadas, **Manzanillo**, Colima 28200. Tel: 3-0000; Fax: 3-0430; in the U.S. and Canada, Tel: (800) 7-CAMINO. $292–$418.

▶ **Hotel Colonial.** Avenida México 100, **Manzanillo**, Colima 28200. Tel: 2-1080; Fax: 2-0668. $30.

▶ **Hotel La Posada.** P.O. Box 135, Calzada Lázaro Cárdenas 201–204, **Manzanillo**, Colima 28800. Tel and Fax: 3-1899. $72 (includes breakfast); no credit cards.

▶ **Hotel Sierra Radisson Plaza.** Avenida de la Audiencia, **Manzanillo**, Colima 28200. Tel: 3-2000; Fax: 3-2272; in the U.S., Tel: (800) 333-3333. $198.

▶ **Plaza Las Glorias Manzanillo.** Avenida del Tesoro, Fraccionamento Península de Santiago, **Manzanillo**, Colima 28200. Tel: 3-0812 or 0550; Fax: 3-1395; in the U.S. and Canada, Tel: (800) 635-8483. $117.

IXTAPA/ZIHUATANEJO

Ixtapa/Zihuatanejo, 208 km (129 miles) northwest of Acapulco, offers the best of two worlds. It is both old and new, and is really two destinations in one—visitors so inclined can get double their money's worth.

This resort duo, which spreads out along a 25-mile-long coastline characterized by scalloped bays and beautiful beaches, with Ixtapa to the west and north of Zihuatanejo, is somewhat difficult to describe. Ixtapa is sprawling and modern—it didn't even exist before the early 1970s—and is where most visitors stay, shop, and play after dark. Zihuatanejo dates to the 16th century and is where most visitors dine and play during the day, as well as where the area's business is conducted. The umbilical cord linking the two is a smooth, gently sloping four-mile highway with little in the way of development.

In addition to being one of the most relaxing resorts in the country, Ixtapa/Zihuatanejo also offers great value for your money. Experienced resort-goers will tell you that Ixtapa is particularly suited to parents with young children and disabled travellers because of the flat unbroken terrain of its beaches; it also has Acapulco's fine weather without that famous resort's crowds. (The average year-round temperature is 79° F, slightly cooler than Acapulco, and the best weather coincides with the high season, December through April. The rainy season stretches from June through October, but the showers usually wait until evening.) Those who like life in the fast lane, on the other hand, won't find it here. Instead, the ambience is laid back, giving you the feeling of being delightfully marooned in the midst of a tropical paradise.

MAJOR INTEREST

Relaxed resort pace with good shopping and dining

Ixtapa
Superior beach along hotel strip
Dining
Shopping
Nightlife

Zihuatanejo
Tranquil small-town atmosphere
Secluded beaches

IXTAPA

Ixtapa is a baby on the Mexican resort scene—but what a baby. Selected for development almost 20 years ago by the government computers at Fonatur, Ixtapa was built with the comfort and convenience of large groups of travellers in mind. This is one place where you can drink the water and not worry about the ice cubes (the hotel zone has its own water purification plant).

Around in Ixtapa

Ixtapa's two-mile-long hotel zone faces the Bahía del Palmar, which is edged by an expanse of flat beach known as Playa del Palmar. It takes about 30 minutes to walk the length of

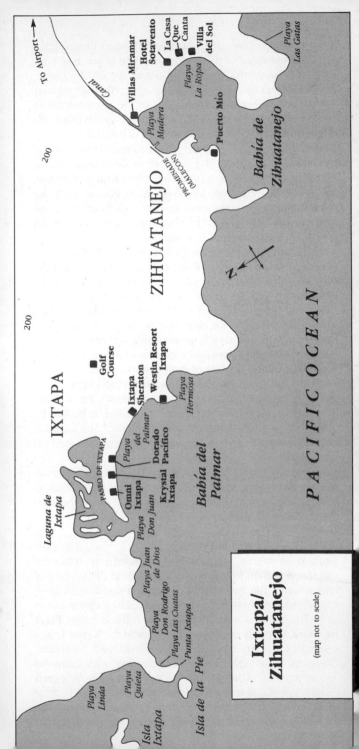

Ixtapa/Zihuatanejo

(map not to scale)

Paseo de Ixtapa (also called Paseo del Palmar), the road that serves as the spine of the hotel zone. The beach is at your back door along this stretch, the waves are usually gentle, and the water warm, so you can dive right in without shocking your system. It is also one of the few stretches of beach in the country that is lit for nighttime strolls (although you should stick to the section in front of the hotels).

The Ixtapa shopping district, easily accessible from any of the hotels in the zone, is a maze of modern malls on the inland side of Paseo de Ixtapa. The **Palma Real golf course**, an 18-hole Robert Trent Jones–designed course, is at the eastern end of the hotel zone, an easy walk from any of the major hotels here. (From the Sheraton you can walk to the first tee of the Palma Real in minutes.)

The coast is broken at the far (western) end of the hotel zone by the small mouth of the Laguna de Ixtapa and then continues in a westerly direction to Punta Ixtapa. This undeveloped western stretch of coastline is scooped out into coves and inlets and has a number of unspoiled beaches. **Playa Las Cuatas**, on the near side of the point, is a pretty beach with offshore rock formations that will remind you of Bermuda. The small moon-shaped **Playa Quieta**, in front of Club Med on the far side of Punta Ixtapa, is the departure point for the 15-minute boat trip to Isla Ixtapa (also called Isla Grande; see the Excursions section below). **Playa Linda**, the farthest beach from the Ixtapa hotel zone, is backed by trees that provide delicious (and welcome) shade. It's a perfect place for mid-week picnics, but gets crowded on weekends.

At the other end of Ixtapa, **Playa Hermosa**, a crescent-shaped beach in front of the Westin Resort Ixtapa hotel, is perhaps the prettiest of all the beaches in the area. (You have to enter through the hotel to get there, however.)

STAYING IN IXTAPA

Situated on its own promontory at the southern end of the bay, the ▶ **Westin Resort Ixtapa** is the crème de la crème of Ixtapa hotels. Big, breezy, and beautiful, it stands apart from the other hotels here not only in terms of its location but in its architecture as well. Built into the hillside above **Playa Hermosa**, its pretty crescent-shaped beach, the Westin Ixtapa resembles a vast expanse of bronze-colored bleachers. There are four freshwater pools, complete with fountains and an aqueduct (the six suites in the hotel have their own private pools), seven restaurants and bars, a disco, four tennis courts, and an indoor shopping area. But perhaps the outstanding feature of the Westin Ixtapa is the fact that even its smallest room has its own terrace-like balcony where you can dine under the stars, relax in a hammock, or read in a chaise longue. (Together, the room and the balcony have many of the amenities of a small cottage.) And yet, in spite of the hotel's size, you will never feel as if you're just one more guest of a big operation.

About a 15-minute walk to the west, the towering ▶ **Ixtapa Sheraton** heads the row of hotels that make up Ixtapa's hotel zone along **Playa del Palmar**. Newly renovated, the Sheraton is an attractive resort where efficiency and cleanliness are everywhere in evidence. Its soaring atrium lobby, glass elevators, mini-mall, and air-conditioned bar with live music all contribute to the home-away-from-home feeling that's a hallmark of this chain. And for golfers, the Sheraton is closer (within easy walking distance) to the Palma Real golf course than any other luxury hotel in the zone.

The ▶ **Dorado Pacífico**, one of the costliest hotels ever built in Mexico, is also one of the few privately owned hotels in the country. The lobby and public areas are cool and spacious, with marble floors and comfortable chairs in bright colors, and the butterfly-shaped pool with swim-up bar is just a few steps from the ocean. Inside, the contemporary polished-wood decor lends the Dorado Pacífico a plush, tropical feel. Even walking to and from your room is a treat. Hallways are punctuated by floor-to-ceiling picture windows, and the glass elevators look out upon the attractive lobby. All rooms have terraces and ocean views.

Everything about the ▶ **Krystal Ixtapa** is upscale, including Bogart's, a branch of the well-known chain of restaurants, and Christine, its dazzling disco (both are discussed below). Each room here has its own private terrace, climate control, and color cable TV, and there are five bars and restaurants as well as lighted tennis and racquetball courts on the premises. In addition, the Krystal's weekly Mexican fiesta night, which combines lively folkloric shows with traditional music, Mexican food, and rope tricks, is one of the best in town. (If you're not staying here, check with your own hotel for the day and time, as well as how to make reservations.)

The sprawling colonial-style ▶ **Omni Ixtapa**, at the far end of the beach, is one of the newest hotels in Ixtapa. Although austerely decorated, rooms here are spacious and equipped with the usual amenities; all have balconies with sweeping views. An attractive multilevel lobby, beautiful pool area, and half-dozen bars and restaurants add to its appeal, and its choice location is even more of an asset now that the marina at the mouth of the nearby lagoon has been completed. The marina is surrounded by pastel-colored villas and condominiums, and can accommodate 600 yachts. A shopping mall, an art gallery, and a disco are also among its amenities, and an 18-hole golf course skirting its perimeter should be ready for play by the end of 1993.

DINING IN IXTAPA

Almost all the major hotels in Ixtapa have one or more air-conditioned restaurants, but trying those outside your hotel is part of the fun of vacationing here.

Bogart's, in the Krystal Ixtapa, is easily the most outrageous restaurant in town. The experience begins on the sidewalk out front, where diners on their way to the front door pass between two flaming torches. The restaurant itself looks like a set from *Casablanca:* Everything—costumes, carved screens, peacock chairs, and more—could have been lifted from Rick's. A fountain dominates the center of the room, and soft music from a white piano provides the perfect accompaniment for a memorable dining experience. Dress up for this one, and be sure to reserve; Tel: 3-0333.

International fare and Japanese cooking come together under one roof at the Galería Ixtapa, across from the Dorado Pacífico, where **Le Montmartre**, one of Ixtapa's first restaurants, is downstairs and **Villa Sakura**, a little bit of Japan transplanted to Mexico's Pacific coast, occupies the second floor. Seafood with a French accent and juicy steaks without fancy sauces are the specialties at Le Montmartre, while at Villa Sakura waitresses in kimonos are the perfect complement to a menu that includes tempura, sushi, and *yakimeshi;* dishes can also be prepared *teppanyaki*-style at your table. Tel: 3-0692.

The hacienda-style **Lighthouse**, a five-minute taxi ride down the boulevard, boasts a nautical decor, a lovely flower garden, and the refined atmosphere of a stately home. Meat and fish dishes are its specialties, and after dinner you can climb to the top of the "lighthouse" for a panoramic view of Ixtapa and the bay. Tel: 3-1190.

Getting to **Carlos 'n' Charlie's** is like following the clues in a treasure hunt. (It's hidden away at the far western end of the hotel zone next to the Posada Real.) Once you find it, however, the ambience is pure barefoot vacation, the interior rustic Polynesian. The fun begins as soon as the front door opens around noon, and keeps rolling until the wee hours. The beach is a step away, so you can take a dip in the ocean or soak up the sun between courses at lunch, and after dinner you can dance in the tiny raised open-air disco overlooking the beach. Tel: 3-0085.

Coco's Beach Club, tucked between Carlos 'n' Charlie's and the Posada Real, is one of Ixtapa's best-kept secrets. It's the kind of restaurant where bamboo swings substitute for barstools and a secluded pool just over a tiny bridge in the garden outside allows diners to sunbathe as the spirit moves them. Don't be put off by the warehouse-like appearance of the place; once you've eaten here you'll want to come back again and again. Open for lunch and dinner. Tel: 3-1685.

An odd combination of colonial style and neon touches, **Los Mandiles** stands by itself behind the Magic Circus disco. Informality reigns with the beer-drinking crowd at the bar, however, and the Mexican food is wonderful. You can dine either inside or out on the porch. Tel: 3-0379.

Mac's Prime Rib, overlooking the boulevard on the second floor of Los Patios shopping mall, is one of the more popular places in Ixtapa. Owned by a former Mexicana Airlines pilot named McGregor, Mac's offers delicious meals in an attractive open-air setting and has one of the best salad bars in town. Mac's specialty? Prime rib from Montana and Nebraska, of course. Tel: 3-0717.

Dinner at **El Sombrero** (which is also in Los Patios) is an Ixtapa tradition. Maybe that's because the copper-accented decor is the perfect backdrop for the excellent Mexican-style seafood and meat dishes served up by the restaurant's German-born owners. And maybe not. Whatever the reason, El Sombrero has been packing them in ever since it opened. You'll want to reserve in season; closed Sundays. Tel: 3-0439.

Standing by itself on Paseo de la Roca, just past the Westin Ixtapa at the opposite end of the hotel zone, the **Villa de la Selva** is one of Ixtapa's most elegant restaurants. Tables in this former home of one of Mexico's presidents are placed a discreet distance apart on one of two terraces surrounded by lush vegetation. The candlelight, beautiful table settings, and soft piano music put the Selva a cut above the rest—and the prices don't reflect it. Come here to watch the sunset, stay through dinner, and enjoy one of the most memorable evenings of your life. You'll need a reservation, however; Tel: 3-0362 or 2096.

Although **El Faro** is the only place with a panoramic view of the entire bay, finding the restaurant on your own isn't easy. If you decide to drive, head for the Westin Ixtapa and take the right turn just before the entrance to the hotel. Then climb the hill to the condo development at the top called Club Pacífica. Parking is an adventure because of the steep incline of the parking lot, but the trip is worth it. The dining area opens to the sea breezes, and the spectacular view is accompanied by soothing piano music at dinner. Unfortunately, the mood of the chef has much to do with the quality of the food. For the moment the best way to enjoy the view here is to have a drink at the bar below the dining room. Closed Sundays.

SHOPPING IN IXTAPA

Resortwear is the purchase of choice here, with handicrafts running a close second. (Surprisingly few stores in Ixtapa carry the usual Mexican souvenirs.)

La Puerta, Ixtapa's original mall, is across from the Do-rado Pacífico hotel; newer malls have been built around and behind it. To help you sort it all out, here are a few of the shops to look for:

In La Puerta itself, **Galería Florence** has a good selection of paintings and sculpture for serious collectors. Aca Joe, Ralph Lauren, and Benetton, all stocked with goods made in Mexico; **Wanda Ameiro**, featuring the stylish designs of a well-known Mexican designer; **La Fuente**, one of the best shops in town for decorative items; and **Mic Mac**, which carries a well-chosen selection of resortwear, are also here.

Chiquita Banana, on the first floor of **Los Patios** mall, offers an especially tasteful assortment of decorative and gift items. The terra-cotta–colored **Plaza Ixpamar**, behind Los Patios, houses **El Amanecer**, with its small selection of folk art, and Calvin Klein (for men), among others. Of course, with many more stores in addition to the ones mentioned here, you're sure to discover your own personal favorites.

NIGHTLIFE IN IXTAPA

Ixtapa is the center of the area's nightlife. Though things wind down earlier here than they do in Acapulco, this former early-to-bed resort has nonetheless become popular with those who love late nights.

One of a chain of well-known discos, **Christine**, at the Krystal, is sensational. The crowd is generally well dressed and the place itself is attractive and exciting. Video screens, flashing lights, balloons, smoke, and other gimmicks are the rule, but they don't overpower conversations. Though the crowd for the most part is under 30, people of all ages feel comfortable here. In other words, Christine is worth the hassle at the door and the hefty cover charge—at least for an evening.

Near the Galería Ixtapa, **Magic Circus**, with its tiered, high-tech, Miami-disco look, also has a sophisticated atmosphere. Though its clientele is not quite as upscale as Christine's, it is every bit as fun.

Last but not least, **Euforia** is Ixtapa's newest discotheque. Again, the usual disco works prevail, but the pièce de résistance is a jungle "volcano," its periodic eruptions adding a certain suspense to the evening.

The hotels in Ixtapa occasionally feature international entertainers and hold Mexican fiesta nights on different days of the week (watch for signs at the various hotels or check at your own). In the off season, live music animates many a lobby bar.

ZIHUATANEJO

Zihuatanejo, a five-minute drive to the southeast of Ixtapa over a highway carved into the hills, is long on charm. Today a resort as well as a fishing village, the town dates back to the 1500s, when it was an important center for New Spain's trade with the Far East. (In Nahuatl *Zihuatan* means the "place of the women"; it is believed the Cuitlalteca tribe that lived here was ruled by matriarchs.) Until Ixtapa came along, however, Zihuatanejo was little more than a remote haven for adventurous budget travellers who loved the barefoot lifestyle it had to offer. Although it now serves as Ixtapa's commercial center and has a resident population of more than 30,000, Zihuatanejo has managed to hold on to its charm and small-town ambience.

The town nestles on its own bay, and the downtown beach, though sometimes sprinkled with seaweed, is shaded in places and friendly everywhere. Few tourists sun here, but the passing parade on the *malecón* is always fun to watch. Hotels, restaurants, and shops line cobblestone streets and alleyways. It's both easy and rewarding to spend a couple of days exploring Zihuatanejo—and you'll never have to dress in more than cutoffs and a tee-shirt to do it.

Around in Zihuatanejo

Scenic scalloped bays and inlets—some backed by hills and cliffs—link Zihuatanejo's three beautiful but very different beaches, all ringing the bay to the east and south of town. **Playa La Madera** is a broad, flat stretch of dark sand that begins just south of town. (What may appear on a map to be a short walk from town is in reality quite a hike: A channel forces would-be sunbathers into a 15-minute detour. Most people take taxis.) There's not much to see or do here, but a road behind the beach climbs a hill to such smaller hotels as the Catalina, Irma, and Sotavento; the Villas Miramar, one of

Zihuatanejo's coziest hotels, is at the bottom of the hill just across the street from the beach.

Along the curve of the Bahía de Zihuatanejo to the south, just a five-minute drive over a scenic, rolling road, is **Playa La Ropa**, perhaps the area's most beautiful beach and a favorite of international travellers. Named for the clothes that washed up on it after a long-ago shipwreck, the broad beach here and calm waters make this a favorite spot for a variety of water sports. La Ropa is lined with small hotels and bungalows, including the Villa del Sol and Fiesta Mexicana, about halfway down the beach. (In front of the Villa del Sol you can arrange your water-sport activities, especially water skiing.) **La Gaviota** beach club at the end of La Ropa is a great place to swim and grab a bite to eat.

Playa Las Gatas, still farther south, can be reached by a very rocky path from Playa La Ropa or by launch from the town pier. Swimming conditions are less than ideal due to the beach's rocky bottom, but it's a good beach for diving and snorkeling, and has a dive concession right on the sand. Tiny restaurants offer snacks and chairs for rent.

DOWNTOWN ZIHUATANEJO

Downtown Zihuatanejo has its share of funky stores, which slowly are being upgraded. You'll find an open-air souvenir market in front of the cathedral; **El Jumil**, on the *malecón,* has an excellent selection of exotic masks, and **La Zapoteca** offers a wide array of textiles from Oaxaca. **Coco Cabaña**, at the corner of Guerrero and Alvarez, past Coconuts, has the best selection of folk art in town.

The **Museo Arqueológico de la Costa Grande**, at the end of the *malecón,* houses a small, private collection of pre-Columbian artifacts in a charming stone building by the sea. It is worth a visit, if only to see the building and watch the sunset from the patio.

STAYING IN ZIHUATANEJO

▶ **Puerto Mío**, overlooking the Zihuatanejo marina, is on the far side of the small bridge at the western end of the town's *malecón* (just past the Hotel Tres Marías), a ten-minute walk around the bay from downtown Zihuatanejo. Everything about this place is intimate and tasteful. Most of its 21 suites (nine are located at the base of the hill; the rest are carved into the slope and accessed via a cable car) have a view of the bay. The tiled bathrooms are cool and pretty, and the dining room and large bar overlook a rocky, mite-sized beach.

The ▶ **Villas Miramar** is a small, colonial-style accommodation with a few charming rooms surrounding a small pool and a couple of additional suites across the street on Playa La Ropa. The guest-rooms have vaulted ceilings with fans, and the toilets and stand-up marble showers are in separate rooms. Clean, small, and friendly, the Villas Miramar is favored by seasoned resort-goers, so be sure to reserve well in advance.

▶ **La Casa Que Canta** is an 18-suite hotel on a cliff at the town end of Playa La Ropa, near the spot where La Ropa meets La Madera. The hotel's peaceful ambience (children under 14 are not permitted) and beautiful setting more than compensate for its location off the beach. The furnishings in the terracotta–colored suites (which are linked by winding paths) are handmade in the state of Michoacán. Two pools sit on different levels down the hill, and a meandering path leads to the beach and **La Sirena Que Canta**, a small restaurant with a popular sister establishment on the town *malecón*.

Shaded by lush foliage, a collection of simple bungalows known as ▶ **Las Urracas** sits a few steps from the beach. The problem here is finding the owner. Once you do, you're "in" forever, but whether you will is anybody's guess. We leave you on your own. Tel: (753) 4-2052.

Also some distance from town on Playa La Ropa, the ▶ **Villa del Sol** rates as one of Mexico's most charming small hotels and just one of two in the country to be awarded membership in the Relais & Châteaux organization. Built and run by Helmut Leins, a German engineer who came to Zihuatanejo more than 20 years ago, the Villa del Sol is marked by a heady combination of tropical opulence and European panache. Royalty, statesmen, and celebrities from around the world are among the guests who enjoy the hotel's spacious, split-level rooms and famous dining room. And for those who like to people-watch, the hotel's Bar Orlando, named after the bartender, is a popular watering hole for both guests and non-guests.

Guests staying at the Villa del Sol may want to rent a car to get to and from town; otherwise, the front desk will be happy to call a cab for you. (Sometimes cabs line up at the taxi stand on the corner to your left as you leave the hotel.) A final word of advice: The Villa·del Sol is the kind of place where loyal guests book their favorite rooms a year in advance. You just may want to do the same. Children are not permitted between November 14 and April 30.

DINING IN ZIHUATANEJO

Coconuts, in town at Pasaje Agustín Ramírez 1, is the essence of Zihua. Visitors like it and locals love it—the bar is a favorite hangout. If you want to find out who's in town and what they're doing, this is the place. Take time for a drink at the bar and then move over to a table under the stars (most of the restaurants in Zihuatanejo are open-air). You'll find as much company as you want here, or you can have a quiet, intimate dinner. Vegetarian and Continental dishes comprise the bulk of the menu, and reservations are advised, especially if you plan on dining late; Tel: 4-2518.

The restaurant at the **Villa del Sol** is open to the public. Under a large palapa and almost on the sand, it is especially lovely at dinnertime, when soft music and the murmur of waves accompany your meal. You'll want to reserve ahead, however (ask for a table on one of the lower levels of the dining room), especially on Fridays, when their Mexican fiesta night draws people from miles around; Tel: 4-2239.

There are, in addition, two pretty, informal restaurants on the hill between Playas La Madera and La Ropa, both with views of the bay. The **Bay Club** offers soft jazz in an outside patio/bar, as well as a Continental menu and soft candlelight in an upstairs dining room. The Polynesian-style **Kon-Tiki**, a little farther up the hill, has lots of bamboo and rattan, a menu featuring Mexican and international cuisine (as well as what many locals claim is the best pizza in town), and a spectacular view of the bay. It's also the place to go if you need a quick fix of televised sports from the States.

Al Andalus Expresso, also known as the Deli, is one of the most popular watering holes in town. Named after the famous Spanish luxury train, it has Pullman seats instead of chairs, a lovely garden for dining, and an outdoor café. It's also the place to catch up on all the local gossip. Great burgers, salads, pies, real espresso, and other U.S.-style treats keep locals and visitors coming back for more.

Other casual restaurants worth a try downtown include **La Bocana**, a family-style place popular with local businessmen, **La Sirena Gorda**, and **Casa Elvira**, the last two on the *malecón*.

Excursions from Ixtapa/Zihuatanejo

You can sail away aboard the 36-foot catamaran *Tequila* for a three-hour cruise of Zihuatanejo Bay (twice daily, November to May), with stops for swimming and snorkeling. The boat leaves from Playa Quieta, in front of Club Med in Ixtapa, at 11:00 A.M. and again at 5:00 P.M. To reserve, Tel: 3-0007.

Excursions to **Isla Ixtapa** leave from Playa Quieta at 10:00 A.M. and return at 3:00 P.M., and include a seafood lunch, snorkeling, and swimming. Once there, you can follow the path to Playa Naradero on the other side of the island, where you can sun and swim in front of **El Marlin**, the island's only restaurant. The cost of the excursion is approximately $16. Ferryboats also operate from Playa Quieta; the round-trip fare is approximately $4.

A coastal tour (offered by almost every travel agency in town) takes you to **Agua de Correa**, a typical fishing village untouched by time, and **Barra de Potosí**, a haven for birdwatchers, with a stop along the way for lunch and swimming. Coconut, mango, papaya, and lemon plantations line the road en route. Expect to pay about $26 per person.

All cruises and tours can be booked at your hotel, or with a local travel agent such as **Expoviajes de Ixtapa** (Tel: 3-0442) in advance.

GETTING AROUND

Mexicana offers daily flights from Los Angeles to Ixtapa via Guadalajara (no change of planes) and from San Francisco three times a week, also via Guadalajara. Aeroméxico flies from New York City's J.F.K. airport daily, with a change of planes in Mexico City, and three times a week from Houston with a stop in Mexico City but no change of planes. Delta offers nonstop flights from Los Angeles three times a week, and, during the season, Northwest flies nonstop charters from Minneapolis/St. Paul. The flying time from Mexico City to the Zihuatanejo airport is approximately 50 minutes.

Budget, Dollar, Fast (Jeeps), and Hertz all have desks at the airport.

The cost of a *colectivo* from the airport to the hotels in Ixtapa and Zihuatanejo is about $7 per person. Don't buy a round-trip ticket, however. Taking a regular taxi back to the airport will gain you some sun time.

You can drive to Zihuatanejo from Acapulco in about 3½ hours, with two stops for security checks along the way. The bus trip takes 4 to 5 hours. Estrella de Oro (Tel: 4-2075) and Estrella Blanca (Tel: 4-3477 or 4-3476) are the first-class lines.

It's about an 8-hour drive to Mexico City. (The best route follows Highway 200 along the coast to Acapulco, and then inland from there.) The bus to the capital—again, either Estrella de Oro or Estrella Blanca—takes 9 hours.

With a little effort you can walk just about everywhere in the Ixtapa hotel zone; buses make the run from the zone to downtown Zihuatanejo, with stops outside most hotels, but there is no set schedule.

Taxis are the easiest way to get around, and the major hotels have cabs waiting outside. The average fare from the hotel zone to Zihua is approximately $4; figure on $5 to Playa La Ropa. The taxi stand in Zihuatanejo is in front of the Canaima restaurant on Calle Juan Alvarez, which runs parallel to the *malecón*.

If you decide to spend the day at Playas La Ropa or La Madera, ask your cab driver to come back for you at an appointed time; or walk to the taxi stand behind the Fiesta Mexicana.

If you rent a car for the day, be sure to visit the opposite ends of the resort—Las Cuatas and Playa Quieta to the west of the Ixtapa hotel zone and La Ropa to the east of Zihuatanejo. The road from the Bay Club to La Ropa is one of the area's most scenic drives.

—Susan Wagner

ACCOMMODATIONS REFERENCE

The rates given below are projections *for December 1993 through Easter 1994. Unless otherwise indicated, rates are for double rooms, double occupancy; the 10 percent VAT has been added. As rates are subject to change, it's a good idea to double-check before booking. Ixtapa/Zihuatanejo is in the central standard time zone; the telephone area code is 753.*

▶ **La Casa Que Canta.** Camino Escénico a la Playa La Ropa s/n, **Zihuatanejo**, Guerrero 40880. Tel: 4-2722; Fax: 4-2006; in the U.S. and Canada, Tel: (800) 525-4800. $294–$402.

▶ **Dorado Pacífico.** P.O. Box 15, Paseo de Ixtapa, **Ixtapa**, Guerrero 40880. Tel: 3-2025; Fax: 3-0126; in the U.S. and Canada, Tel: (800) 44-UTELL; Fax: (402) 398-5484. $176–$184.

▶ **Ixtapa Sheraton.** Paseo de Ixtapa, **Ixtapa**, Guerrero 40880. Tel: 3-1858; Fax: 3-2438; in the U.S. and Canada, Tel: (800) 325-3535. $240.

▶ **Krystal Ixtapa.** Paseo de Ixtapa, **Ixtapa**, Guerrero 40880. Tel: 3-0333; Fax: 3-0216; in the U.S. and Canada, Tel: (800) 231-9860. $171.

▶ **Omni Ixtapa.** Paseo de Ixtapa 5A, **Ixtapa**, Guerrero 40880. Tel: 3-0003; Fax: 3-1555; in the U.S. and Canada, Tel: (800) 44-UTELL. $170.

▶ **Puerto Mío.** Paseo del Morro 5, **Zihuatanejo**, Guerrero 40880. Tel: 4-3624; Fax: 4-2048. $137–$402.

▶ **Villa del Sol.** P.O. Box 84, Playa La Ropa, **Zihuatanejo**,

Guerrero 40880. Tel: 4-2239; Fax: 4-2758; in the U.S. and Canada, Tel: (800) 223-6510. $308 (includes breakfast and dinner).

▶ **Villas Miramar.** P.O. Box 211, Playa La Ropa, **Zihua-tanejo,** Guerrero 40880. Tel: 4-2106; Fax: 4-2149. $81.

▶ **Westin Resort Ixtapa.** P.O. Box 97, Playa Vista Hermosa, **Ixtapa,** Guerrero 40880. Tel: 3-2121; Fax: 3-0751; in the U.S. and Canada, Tel: (800) 228-3000. $211.

ACAPULCO

Acapulco is still Mexico's most glamorous resort; its special brand of unabashed fun is unlike anything you'll find elsewhere. Other resorts may have scenic beauty and deluxe facilities, but it is the people of Acapulco, who go out of their way to make sure every visitor has a good time, that set it apart. And while daytime here is glorious—there are 360 days of sunshine every year—it is the nightlife that is truly legendary. No one ever asks what you did during the day, but seemingly everyone will exhibit an interest in what you did—or are going to do—after dark.

Despite the fact that the good times have been rolling since the 1950s, when the highway down from Mexico City opened and international flights began to arrive, what is now a fourth generation of waiters, boat boys, car attendants, and so on does not seem to have tired of the merriment.

Likewise, rumors of its imminent demise owing to pollution and a plague of itinerant vendors have proved to be premature. Well aware of the tough competition and fickle loyalties of the travelling public, Acapulco's city fathers initiated a cleanup campaign that continues to work. City streets and public buses are swept daily; the waters of the bay are cleaner than they have been in years; and vendors have been legislated off the beaches and relocated in sidewalk markets.

At the same time, Acapulco has been accused of welcoming only the young. The accusation is unjust. Anyone can have the time of his or her life here, whether the goal is to party or simply to relax. The trick is in knowing what you want and where to find it. Ninety-nine percent of the time Acapulco is the one Mexican resort that will have it.

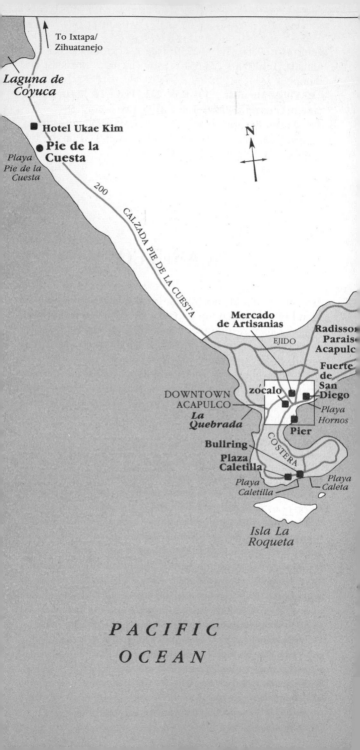

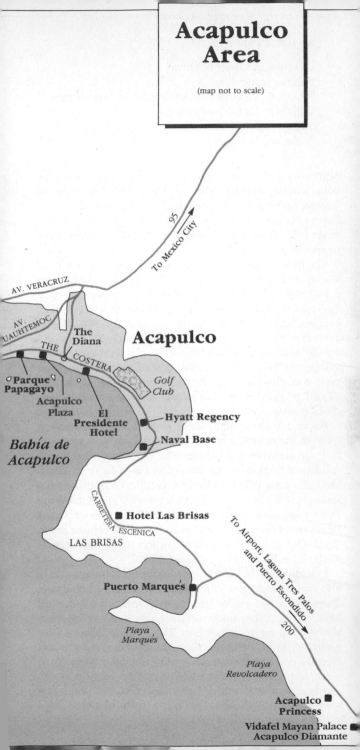

MAJOR INTEREST

Large-resort variety of activity
Legendary nightlife
Shopping, especially for resortwear and handicrafts
Cliff divers at La Quebrada
Sunsets and laid-back lifestyle at Pie de la Cuesta and
   Laguna de Coyuca

Acknowledged as one of the world's most beautiful bays, the Bahía de Acapulco has been compared with that of Rio de Janeiro, and it's easy to see why. The first glimpse of it, at Puerto Marqués as you come into town from the airport, never fails to take your breath away, regardless of how many times you've seen it.

The famous beaches ringing this beautiful bay come in all shapes and sizes, with rough or gentle waves, palapas or palm trees, utter seclusion or all the action you could want. Finding one that suits your own particular style is easy. The beaches between the Presidente and Acapulco Plaza hotels, as well as Playa Caleta and Playa Caletilla in Old Acapulco, are the most congested and lively. The rest are more tranquil and perfect for relaxing. No matter which you choose, however, you can count on the sun being strong; sunbathers should proceed with caution and be sure to use double doses of sunscreen.

For all the fun available here, those who seek a vacation far from the madding crowds can have it. If this is what you have in mind, rent a private villa in the posh Las Brisas residential section or stay at Las Casas de Villa Vera, on the grounds of the Villa Vera Hotel & Racquet Club. If you want serious privacy at more reasonable prices, you can stay at the Hotel Ukae Kim, in Pie de la Cuesta, or the Maeva Sunset Beach Hotel on Coyuca Lagoon and sun at places like Beto's Beach Club at Barra Vieja, off the airport road before it starts to climb Las Brisas hill.

In addition to being Mexico's liveliest resort, Acapulco is also one of its largest cities, with a year-round population approaching two million people. As a central cog in Spain's Mexico–Philippines trade route for almost 300 years, it has always been an important port. The Spanish galleons have given way to luxury cruise ships, but the area near the port facilities is still its commercial center (though it looks like a seedy tropical town). Fishermen mend nets on the beach and head out at dawn, and the same tacky souvenirs that were the resort's original take-home treasures are still sold at street stalls near the zócalo.

Great weather is Acapulco's ace in the hole. Sunshine is more dependable here than at other resorts, and the average annual temperature is 80° F. In fact, only the humidity varies noticeably from one season to the next. Locals consider it cold when they have to wear long-sleeved cotton shirts, and no one would be caught dead in a jacket, tie, or socks unless he were heading for a formal private party or one of the top hotel restaurants.

"The Season" runs from the middle of December to Easter (when the humidity is usually at its yearly low). But even in the rainy season—May to October—showers are short and usually fall at night; the foliage is at its most glorious then as well. Prices for everything go down after Easter, but the same kinds of fun and activities prevail year-round. At the end of May an international music festival draws artists and spectators from around the world. The only time things might slow down is late September or early October, when improvements are made in anticipation of the coming season, but this pause is imperceptible to most visitors.

Daily schedules follow those of most tropical places. If you want to conduct serious business, plan on doing it between 10:00 A.M. and 1:00 P.M. Lunch is eaten between 2:00 and 5:00 P.M., and dinner usually begins around 9:00 P.M., unless you're going to a private home, in which case cocktails normally are served around 10:00 and dinner at midnight. Discos are liveliest between midnight and 2:00 A.M. With this kind of schedule, it's worth resetting your internal clock to take advantage of it all.

Gourmet dining à la Paris or New York—or even Mexico City—is *not* an Acapulco trademark. If you like delicate food with intricate sauces, you won't find it here—or in any Mexican resort, for that matter. The best entrées are generally simple seafood and meat dishes with fresh tropical fruit for dessert. So unless you're dying for French, German, Italian, Japanese, Chinese, or Thai food, all of which can be found in Acapulco, when you select a restaurant you'll really be choosing an atmosphere to suit your mood.

When it's time to get ready for dinner, remember that in matters of dress Acapulco is one of the most relaxed places in the civilized world. You can wear a ballgown to breakfast, stay in your bathing suit until way past midnight, or walk around in an outrageous costume and no one will bat an eyelash. Anything goes, as long as you make an attempt to cover the important places. Well-put-together resortwear will get you in anywhere; the flashier it is, the faster you'll be accepted.

Finally, it won't take long to discover that Acapulco is a place where you can shop until 4:00 A.M. (Many discos and some restaurants even have stores where you can shop until dawn.) Competition from resorts such as Ixtapa and Cancún has forced retailers to upgrade both the merchandise sold here as well as the stores in which it is displayed. Acapulco seems to have risen to the challenge, and malls with good shops—the sparkling, air-conditioned Plaza Bahía is one example—are springing up all over town. The best buys are resortwear, handicrafts, and decorative items.

Around in Acapulco

A result of no conscious plan, Acapulco has developed into one pleasurable area after another.

The Vidafel and Acapulco Princess hotels are at the center of the action in the area lying between the airport and the bottom of the hill where Las Brisas presides. Travelling along this road, called the Carretera Escénica, is like reading a guidebook, with billboards announcing many of the most popular shops, hotels, and restaurants in Acapulco.

At the moment, the "Las Brisas hill" is one of the fastest developing areas of Acapulco, with a handful of new restaurants and an opulent disco having opened in the last few years. As a result, those renting or residing in the neighborhood or staying at the Westin Las Brisas no longer have to go into town to dine or dance.

"The Strip" begins on the far side of the hill at the naval base and Hyatt Regency, and extends around the bay to Papagayo Park. This is where you'll find the lion's share of malls, shops, restaurants, bars, and discos, with the section between the naval base and the Diana traffic circle being the liveliest. The greatest concentration of good stores is found on the Strip between the Presidente hotel and the Plaza Bahía mall, and a string of great seaside restaurants begins just past Sanborn's, a drugstore/cafeteria near the Presidente, extending west to the traffic circle itself.

Things settle down a bit between the underpass to the park and downtown Acapulco. The relatively tranquil old part of town, which first attracted visitors here, extends from and includes Isla La Roqueta, Playa Caleta and Playa Caletilla, the yacht club, and the bull ring.

Pie de la Cuesta, a beautiful, unspoiled stretch of beach near what used to be the airport, and Laguna de Coyuca are a 15-minute drive north and west of the old town over a winding and spectacular cliffside road.

FROM THE AIRPORT TO THE PUERTO MARQUES TURNOFF

As the location of several luxury hotels, numerous condo and time-share units, and the area's best golf course, the stretch of pancake-flat highway leading from the airport to the coast road gets more interesting with each passing year. Much of the excitement revolves around the ongoing development of **Acapulco Diamante**, a huge project encompassing the beachfront from the Acapulco Princess to Puerto Marqués bay and on up the hill as far as the Westin Las Brisas complex. When it's completed, the sprawling ▶ **Vidafel Mayan Palace Acapulco Diamante** here will have more than 1,000 rooms, most of them time-share. For now, the hotel's 368 junior suites (80 percent of which are time-share) are characterized by small sitting areas, kitchenettes, and views of lovely gardens or the Pacific. Distinctive features of the spread-out property include a lobby area and restaurant housed under soaring Mayan-style palapas, a winding swimming pool complete with waterfalls, and a nine-hole golf course scheduled to open by the end of 1993. With all this and more, the Vidafel qualifies as one of the best lodging bargains in Acapulco.

Many people who stay at the ▶ **Acapulco Princess** never venture off the premises. Built to resemble an Aztec pyramid, this bustling self-contained resort offers its guests an air-conditioned shopping mall, fresh- and salt-water pools, a broad beach (unsafe for anything but wading, unfortunately), horseback riding, several excellent restaurants (including the very French **Le Gourmet**), and a disco. With more than 1,000 rooms, it's also one of the largest hotels in the country. The Princess is typical of what makes Acapulco hotels different from others around the country. Most of the rooms are more spacious, the public areas larger, the pool areas bigger and more lavishly landscaped, and the range of services and facilities available more extensive than what you'll find in resort hotels elsewhere. And if, at times, it seems as if you're bumping into conventioneers with name tags on their bathing suits at every turn, it's still possible to find a quiet corner here.

As the coast road begins to climb west toward Las Brisas you'll get a glimpse of tiny **Puerto Marqués**, where pirates once hid from Spanish warships. Today the relatively undeveloped beach here is usually crowded with Mexican budget vacationers swimming or floating around the quiet bay in an inner tube or on a Sunfish. Spending a day away from other gringos can be a refreshing change of pace, but you might want to avoid it on Sundays (too crowded) and you should be prepared for the swarms of kids who try to hustle business (they're on commission) for the beachside restaurants.

Located five minutes west of the Puerto Marqués turnoff on Playa Pichilingue, one of the most beautiful beaches in the area, the new ▶ **Camino Real Acapulco Diamante** is as sophisticated a hotel property as Acapulco has to offer. Built into a hillside overlooking the ocean, the hotel has a sun-splashed Mediterranean look and feel about it, with the lobby on an upper floor and guest rooms spilling down the hillside toward the beautiful pool area. As is true of most Camino Real properties, attention is paid to the smallest details, from the chic international-style decor of each room to the meticulous landscaping of the grounds. As a result, many guests never leave the property, even though the Strip is only minutes away.

THE HILL BETWEEN LAS BRISAS AND THE HYATT REGENCY

This is one of the hottest areas in Acapulco today, and every time you look it seems as if there is something new to see and do here. Restaurants, shops, discos, even a new tennis club—all have been built within the last few years. And no wonder: The views of the bay are spectacular, and Las Brisas residents, though they usually entertain among themselves and seldom leave their enclave, are a natural target for ambitious entrepreneurs. This new crop of pleasurable distractions promises to restore some of Acapulco's original glamour, and at the same time get the really upscale crowd to leave their villas and enjoy Acapulco by night again.

Although you'll need patience and sometimes will have to bite your tongue over brusque treatment at the door, you'll probably be glad you dined at **Madeiras**. Their policy is "reservations only," however, and they're busy enough to enforce it. (In fact, those who want to be sure of getting a reservation often call from home before getting on the plane.)

Once you're in, dining here can be an especially pleasant experience, particularly if you reserve a table by the railing overlooking the bay. (Seating is on several levels, all open-air.) The menu, primarily Mexican nouvelle cuisine, changes frequently according to what's fresh at the market, and the four-course meals are prix fixe. There are usually several seatings each evening; if you opt for the later one at 9:30, you'll arrive at your favorite disco just as things are starting to heat up. Tel: 84-4378.

Miramar, a bigger place in the nearby La Vista mall, offers the same views of the bay as those from Madeiras. A slightly older crowd congregates here, which probably explains why the atmosphere in its open-air dining room is more formal. Give yourself time to have a drink in the bar before you head downstairs for dinner. Although every table has a view, ask for one by the railing when you reserve; Tel: 84-7874.

Mr. Frog's, also in La Vista, is a cool, moderately priced lunchtime getaway with a fine view, and an especially pleasant and informal place for dinner. Tel: 84-8020.

After dinner you might slip over to **Pepe's** cozy piano bar and sing along or grab the mike and belt out a number yourself. Pepe Valle, one of Acapulco's most popular restaurateurs, has put together a winning combination, with a bar downstairs overlooking the bay and a billiards room upstairs.

Extravaganzza is impossible to miss; in fact, the neon lights on its façade illuminate the entire hillside. Owned by Acapulco's disco king, Tony Rullan, this $4 million dazzler is as plush and sophisticated as they come, with a dance floor that overlooks the bay, a dramatic marble entrance, and a chic boutique. Occasional fireworks after midnight add to the outrageousness of it all. And at $15, the cover charge is still one of the best deals in town.

Smaller and plainer than its neighbor across the way, **Fantasy** is popular with a slightly less style-conscious crowd. Floor-to-ceiling picture windows afford revellers a spectacular view of the bay, and confetti, laser light shows, and fireworks are just some of the tricks used to keep the place jumping.

There's a special treat for serious art collectors just up the hill from this cluster of shops, restaurants, and discos. Sculptor Pal Kepenyes has designed a home for himself in which he exhibits his abstract bronzes. The house, a work of art in its own right, with an outdoor sculpture garden and a view that extends to Pie de la Cuesta, has been featured in the pages of *Architectural Digest.* The versatile Kepenyes, who also designs jewelry and objets d'art, can be visited by appointment; Tel: 84-3738 or 4738. It's more than worth the trip; call for directions.

Down the far side of the hill, **Kookaburra,** a small all-white charmer with great views of the bay, is additional proof of the canny genius of Acapulco restaurateur Carlos Hill, who also owns Hard Times on the Costera. Here, the view serves as the decor, and the informal atmosphere encourages customers to linger. Steaks, seafood, and barbecue are served indoors or out. Tel: 84-4418. The glass walls of air-conditioned **Italianissimo**, a few doors down, take full advantage of the spectacular view. The food, as you might expect, is Italian, and, as at Kookaburra, the under-the-stars ambience is what you come for. Tel: 84-3390.

The multilevel **Casanova**, owned by Mexican Arturo Cordova and his American wife, Pat, has added new style to the area across from the entrance to Las Brisas Resort. In fact, many residents and longtime visitors to Acapulco feel that this is the most elegant restaurant in town. Polished marble floors, exquisite flower arrangements, and tables inside or out on the balcony make dining on the Italian specialties here an unforgettable treat. Reservations two to three days in advance (in season) are advised; Tel: 84-6815.

A longtime favorite and one of the first restaurants in this area, **Los Rancheros** is located down the hill in the direction of the Strip but has the same spectacular view as the more expensive places higher up the hill. It offers standard Mexican fare in an informal setting, but until it gets a new chef you'll be better off sticking to the bar and dining elsewhere.

Staying in Las Brisas

Everything they say about the ▶ **Westin Las Brisas Resort** is true. Perched on the hill overlooking the bay, it has probably entertained more celebrities than any other resort property in the world. It's so exclusive, in fact, that guests have to wait at a reception building for the ubiquitous pink-and-white Jeeps to take them to their rooms. (Jeeps will also take guests to the resort's private beach club, **La Concha**, ten minutes away.) Many of the rooms (called *casitas,* or "little houses") have their own private pool, and the management makes sure each one gets fresh flowers every day. Morning rolls and coffee arrive through an unobtrusive window in one of the walls (so you can sleep as late as you like), and a fruit plate will be waiting in the mini-fridge when you come back after a day in the sun. Little things like this make Las Brisas one of the most relaxing and private resort hotels anywhere. (If you truly want to guarantee your privacy, check to make sure that your pool isn't visible from the *casita* above.)

In keeping with its exclusive character, Las Brisas does not allow non-guests to dine at most of its restaurants (there are five in all). Those who want to get a glimpse of this deluxe property, however, are welcome at their Mexican fiesta night, one of the most colorful events in town; at **El Mexicano**, overlooking the bay; and at La Concha's weekly "lobster night," in the hotel's posh beach club.

The Strip

The Strip is the heart of Acapulco. About 80 percent of the city's restaurants, discos, and boutiques are on or near it, and anyone who loves being in the middle of the action will want to stay in one of its hotels. Similarly, if you're looking to buy *anything* while you're in Acapulco, chances are you'll be able to find it here—even if it's tucked away among a host of other distractions.

Generally speaking, the Strip is the section of Avenida Costera Miguel Alemán (usually just called the Costera) that stretches along the bay from the naval base and the Hyatt Regency at the foot of Las Brisas hill west to the Radisson Paraíso Acapulco. The beaches fronting the Strip hop from sunup to sundown, and then the restaurants and discos take over and keep things going until dawn.

Until a few years ago this whole stretch was divided into unmarked pockets of action separated by private homes or empty tracts of land. Now, with breathtaking speed, almost all these homes have been or are being replaced by hotels and malls, and the empty lots are giving way to condos in anticipation of the completion of the new highway to Mexico City.

FROM THE HYATT REGENCY TO EL PRESIDENTE

The Hyatt Regency; Jimmy's and Flash Taco, two lively restaurants; and Baby O and the News, a couple of sensational discos, get the Strip off to a roaring start. All are clustered near the naval base, which is tucked away at the bottom of Las Brisas hill. The base is off limits to all but naval personnel, except when the *Cuauhtémoc,* Mexico's "tall ship," is in port.

The ▶ **Hyatt Regency** has a canny combination of qualities that enables it to be all things to all people. Financiers stay here when international bankers' meetings are held in Acapulco, and everybody else likes it because it's recessed from the highway and therefore quieter than some of the other hotels on the Strip. (The hotel grounds do abut the naval base, where maneuvers can get noisy—especially on a Sunday when you're trying to sleep late—so be sure to reserve a room on the beach side of the hotel.) A freshwater pool, a beach with good swimming conditions, and one of Acapulco's better shopping arcades make this a self-contained resort. It also has **La Cascada**, one of the best Mexican restaurants in town. Steaks, crepes, and flaming

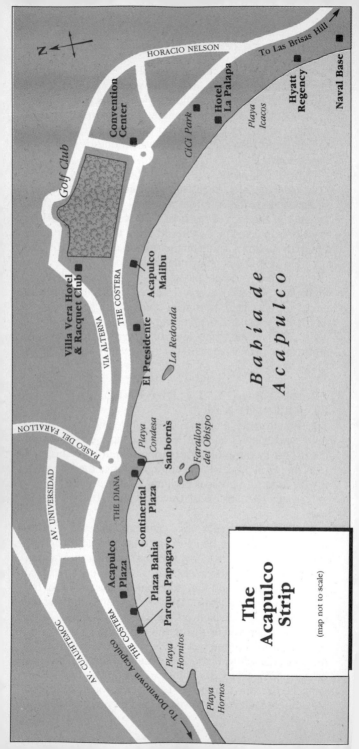

The Acapulco Strip

(map not to scale)

desserts are the specialties, and some form of live Mexican music as well as a friendly baby burro are usually on hand to keep things interesting. Tel: 84-2888.

Jimmy's, just a few minutes from the Hyatt, is an informal restaurant that serves light meals and snacks between rounds of backgammon or Loteria, a Mexican bingo game played with picture cards. Tel: 84-8918. Across the courtyard, **Flash Taco** is a sleek new taco place with an Art Deco look. Diners here have great views of the Baby O disco crowd across the street.

Acapulco disco-goers are accustomed to checking out two or three spots a night, and **Baby O** is always one of them. In fact, disco diehards invariably end up here to let their hair down after a warmup at, say, Extravaganzza. As a result, there's often a line at the door. The choice tables are on the dance-floor level, and of those the choicest are the banquettes against the wall and the "caves" at each side of the dance floor. Squeezing as many people as possible into a banquette or "cave" is the modus operandi, so don't wear anything you can't afford to wrinkle. Videos, electronic message boards, and other effects are part of every evening. If you happen to be in Acapulco at the end of February or beginning of March when their Pajama Party is held, don't miss it (even if you have to buy a pair of pajamas at the door).

The **News,** just beyond the Hyatt Regency, has managed to do something different. While other discos look small, this one is large and prides itself on its innovative special parties and events. On a good night the News packs in some 2,000 souls, but even then there's plenty of room for everybody. Two giant bars, a restaurant, and a "Champagne Room" (you have to buy three bottles of domestic champagne-style wine or one imported bottle in order to sit here) are part of the fun.

Cocula, down the Costera a bit in the direction of town at the sign of the sombrero, offers informal Mexican dining at its best. Have a drink in the unobtrusive air-conditioned bar under the steps (a secret the locals seldom reveal) while you wait for a table under the stars. The only view is of traffic on the Costera, but the do-it-yourself chicken and beef taco plates and the Bohemia beer more than compensate. Breakfast served at tables shaded by soaring palm trees is also lovely. Tel: 84-5079.

The ▶ **Hotel La Palapa,** a soaring structure on the beach behind the CiCi amusement park, is favored by Canadians and groups, and has nothing but small—truly small—suites. (It does have one of the best beauty salons in town for manicures and pedicures, however.) The pool is a few steps from the ocean, and the hotel itself offers tranquillity just off the beaten path at reasonable rates. For those who don't mind getting their elegance elsewhere, La Palapa is a good bet.

The dance floor of **Bananas Ranas**, a disco/snack bar for young trendies on the Costera in front of the Hotel La Palapa, is in a freight car that used to do service on the Acapulco–Iquala line. Also on the Costera, **CiCi**, a water-oriented park for children, is enclosed by a wall painted with blue-and-white waves. Inside you'll find a pool with a wave-making machine, water slides, and a dolphin show. The **Acapulco Convention Center** across the way is equipped to accommodate everything from operas to rock concerts; unfortunately, its beautiful gardens and buildings are rarely used. Watch the marquee for special performances.

A roomy **Hard Rock Café** has opened in the colonial-style Antigua mall, next to the CiCi amusement park (just look for the giant guitar). Inside, dark wood paneling, checked tablecloths, and the familiar Hard Rock menu make you feel as if you're in your favorite hamburger joint back home. The loud, live music at night inhibits conversation but does keep the dance floor energized.

Anna's and **Issima**, two boutiques with exceptional selections of women's resortwear and accessories, are located in the shopping arcade next door to the Hard Rock, while **Estebán**, a local designer, sells his California-style evening clothes and avant-garde streetwear out of a pretty shop opposite the Centro Deportivo, about five blocks farther west in the direction of town. (He also has an art gallery next door.)

The ▶ **Acapulco Malibu Hotel**, another of the town's best-kept secrets, is across from the Centro Deportivo on a nice stretch of beach. The Malibu is a time-share hotel; that is, it rents rooms when their individual owners aren't in residence. One of the very few small hotels on the Strip, it was built by a Texas millionaire and his partners, who intended it to be a chic hideaway in the midst of Acapulco's high-rise hotels and condominiums. The rooms are large and octagonal, and most balconies have a view of the ocean. With a cozy, family-style atmosphere and a friendly staff that will make you feel at home the moment you walk in the door, the Malibu is a refreshing change of pace from the larger, more impersonal hotels in town.

Tabasco Beach, a beachfront restaurant outside the Acapulco Malibu, is a pleasant spot for a quick breakfast, lunch, or drink; the tiny bar is also one of the better places in town from which to watch the sunset, though it is in need of some refurbishing.

At the corner of Avenida del Mar and the Costera, the **Café Pacífico** is popular with an older "in" crowd that favors the music of Barry Manilow, Neil Sedaka, and Englebert Humperdinck (who has been known to grab the mike and belt out a number here from time to time). When the entertainment celebs are elsewhere, Chacon, pet pianist of the expatriate crowd and those in the know, keeps toes tapping and vocal chords snapping with a seemingly inexhaustible repertoire of popular tunes.

La Mansión, a two-story hacienda-style steakhouse about ten doors down from the Acapulco Malibu, has a sophisticated big-city look that reflects the fact it's part of a Mexico City chain. Prime cuts of beef are cooked at your table; it's expensive but worth it. Tel: 81-0796.

Behind the Pizza Hut and up the hill, the very smart **Fiori** (formerly the Villa Demos) serves up Italian specialties in a pretty garden shaded by towering trees. Although it's a favorite with repeat visitors, reservations are not necessary.

Farther up the hill, **Alfredo's Tennis Club** and **Tiffany's Tennis Club** are both open to the public.

The ▶ **Villa Vera Hotel & Racquet Club** is the snazziest hotel on or near the Strip, and the sole small deluxe hotel in town. Only minutes inland from the Costera, it resembles a bit of Beverly Hills transplanted to Acapulco. The clientele ranges from serious tennis players (the tennis facilities are easily the best in town) to the well-heeled set seeking plush accommodations and privacy in a beautiful setting far from the crowds—but not so far that they can't partake of the action on the Costera. Every one of the 90 rooms is different (some have their own pools and many have large tiled tubs); the breezy dining room (Tel: 84-0333) has superb food and grand views of the bay; and the main pool is a favorite spot for the trendy singles crowd (it offered the first swim-up bar in the country). Water-sports lovers can also use the facilities at the Maralisa, the Villa Vera's charming sister hotel down on the beach, with a breezy, pleasant seaside restaurant of its own.

The hotel—which now includes Las Casas de Villa Vera, private homes on the premises available to rent—is owned by a young American woman who prides herself on running a first-class operation. Attention to detail is evident in everything, and guests are carefully looked after. The fact that everything—including the clientele (who apparently come here *after* going through a weight-loss program back home)—is easy on the eyes makes the hotel that much more appealing. As a result, a good percentage of Villa Vera's guests return year after year.

At the top of the hill behind the hotel, the Italian palazzo–style **El Campanario** offers Continental cuisine as well as 180-degree views of the bay and the city lights. It's a wonderful place for a drink, but when the restaurant gets crowded diners may have to call on their reserves of patience. By day, it's an oasis for people who like to relax around the pretty pool below the restaurant. The light lunch fare is tasty and the spectacular location seemingly puts you miles above the hustle and bustle of the Strip. Tel: 84-8831.

FROM EL PRESIDENTE TO THE DIANA TRAFFIC CIRCLE

This is Acapulco's epicenter, with the action really picking up as the Costera climbs toward the Presidente and Condesa del Mar hotels. **Rubén Torres**, **Franco's**, **Ethnics** (which features high-quality imports from Guatemala), **Dancin'**, and **Macarena Gutierrez** (with the best selection of bathing suits in town) are just a few of the "name" boutiques clustered along this stretch of highway.

Sanborn's, the drugstore/cafeteria that no one seems able to do without, is situated at the top of the rise. Only a handful of locals know that the best malted milkshakes in town are served in the downstairs restaurant.

Carlos 'n' Charlie's, the king of Acapulco's racous restaurants, is just across the street from Sanborn's. Unless you're a well-known celebrity, however, you'll probably have to stand in a first-come, first-served line to get in. Of course, that fact doesn't seem to deter anyone, and crowds of all ages and nationalities begin to arrive by car, taxi, and horse-drawn carriage as soon as the door opens at 6:00 P.M. The "Cluck, Moo, and Oink" items on the menu give you some idea of what to expect once you get inside, and waiters' pranks and jokes are an integral part of the total experience. In fact, nothing is serious here except the no-nonsense food. Fair portions of chicken, ribs, and fish are the most popular items, but with all the activity and people-watching going on, few customers pay attention to what they're eating. Stop in at the air-conditioned bar before dinner; chances are you'll stay longer than you planned.

The pink fortress-like structure behind and below Carlos 'n' Charlie's is the unusual **Galvez Club**; the club's imposing bar/restaurant is furnished with numerous colonial-era antiques, some of which are for sale. After dinner, history buffs will want to take a look at the Galvez family's collection of

Mexican Revolutionary memorabilia—weapons, uniforms, documents, portraits and drawings, and the like—all of it beautifully displayed downstairs in a private air-conditioned museum that is opened for special viewings upon request. Tel: 84-8182.

Acapulco Shalom, located a few doors farther down the Costera at the entrance to the Plaza Condesa mall, offers a tasteful selection of silver jewelry and decorative items (which they'll be happy to pack and ship for you), and is a great place for one-stop gift shopping.

The beachfront restaurants that have captured the hearts of Acapulco vacationers for years begin just west of Sanborn's. **Beto's Safari Bar** is popular with beer-drinking youngsters and budget travellers, but the open-air restaurant on the lower deck is another of the less well known delights in town. The prices at the restaurant are moderate and the food decent, and it's hard to resist the romance of a candlelight dinner under the stars with the Bahía de Acapulco just a stone's throw away. Ask for a table near the railing so you can watch the moonlight shimmer on the water.

Beto's, a separate establishment next door, is one of the oldest and best of these beachfront restaurants. Located at the bottom of a staircase leading down from the Costera, it somehow manages to look like the verandah of a private home. There are dining rooms on either side of the stairs and luncheon service under palapas on the sand (most restaurants along this stretch offer food service on the beach). Be sure to try one of the dishes here that are hard to find elsewhere: *quesadillas de cazón* (fried tortillas filled with baby shark meat), *pescado a la Talla* (marinated grilled fish), or red clams. Beto's also has live music for dancing if the spirit moves you. Tel: 84-0473. The left side of Beto's beach, **Playa Condesa**, is frequented by the local gay community.

Mimi's Chili Saloon (no beach service here) is a powder-blue hoot that promises and delivers dynamite two-for-one strawberry and mango margaritas at happy hour. In fact, everything at Mimi's, from the hot dogs and hamburgers to the potato skins and country-fried chicken, is designed to make you drool. All of which makes it the place to go when you're dying for American-style fast food and don't feel like McDonald's. Tel: 84-2549.

There's no restaurant on this planet quite like **Paradise**, a few doors down from Mimi's. One of the pioneers of Acapulco's special tongue-in-cheek style of fun, Paradise is the kind of place where anything can happen at any moment. A woman may find herself attracting admiring wolf whistles one minute, then have a lei of fresh flowers thrown over her head as a chimpanzee puckers up to give her a sloppy kiss the next. The live salsa and rock 'n' roll music gets everyone feeling friendly in a hurry (and out on the dance floor sooner or later), and heaven help you if they find out it's your birthday or anniversary—you just may be picked up, chair and all, and carried off to the bandstand to the great amusement of the other customers. The drinks are big, the palapas keep you cool, and the party lasts well beyond sunset. Hefty portions of lobster, shrimp, beef, and red snapper (*huachinango*) are the specialties of Paradise, and lunch is the busiest time; if a conga line to the beach starts to form, forget your inhibitions and jump in.

Sergio Bustamante, an art gallery a few doors down from Paradise on the opposite side of the street, sells a variety of whimsical papier-mâché animals and other sculpture inspired by that Mexican artist's work. **Martí**, everyone's favorite sporting-goods store, is nearby—look for the larger-than-life statue of an athlete—as are Ralph Lauren Polo (made in Mexico) and the "real" Acapulco Joe.

The Diana (as it is known), where traffic circulates around a fountain topped by a statue of the huntress with her bow, is one of Acapulco's busiest intersections. Highway 95, the old road from Mexico City, meets the Costera here, and it's the location of the only big gas station in town. (There are only three gas stations in the entire area: one at the bottom of the hill before the residential neighborhood of Las Brisas; the one here; and a third at the western end of town where the winding road to Pie de la Cuesta begins.)

FROM THE DIANA TO THE ACAPULCO PLAZA

Shanghai, a Chinese restaurant, is just down from the Diana in El Patio Mall, Acapulco's first shopping complex. Watch for it to move elsewhere, however, as rumors have it that the mall will soon disappear to make way for condominiums.

The **Galería Rudic**, one of Acapulco's top galleries, is a few blocks to the west on Vincente Yañez de Pinzón. It carries an extensive selection of paintings and sculpture by Mexico's best-known contemporary artists.

Located just beyond the Diana, the ▶ **Acapulco Plaza**, with more than 1,000 rooms and suites in three towers, a shopping mall with a variety of stores, four tennis courts, and two pools, is the biggest hotel on the Strip. And while its rooms and suites could use refurbishing, this is still one of Acapulco's top addresses. The rooms in the main tower here are the most convenient: Although the suites in the smaller towers have their own registration desk, they are a considerable distance from the hotel's restaurants and beach (something you'll notice if you leave your sunscreen behind). If you do end up staying in one of the smaller towers, try to avoid the west side of the Catalina Tower—the music from the lobby bar can make taking that all-important siesta a virtual impossibility.

Elsewhere on the grounds, **Maximilian's,** one of two "gourmet" restaurants in Acapulco (the other, Le Gourmet, is in the Acapulco Princess), is the only air-conditioned one on the beach (reservations advised; Tel: 85-9050); and **Los Arcos** is one of the few places in town where you can eat Mexican food in an informal, air-conditioned setting. Dark paneled walls and wooden furniture give the latter the look of a hacienda, and the make-your-own-taco platter is one of the best buys on the menu. The Oasis health club on the third-floor level of the hotel is just for adults, so you can tan, take a dip in the pool, get a massage, or simply relax in glorious peace and quiet.

The **Acapulco Plaza Mall** has two floors of good boutiques: **Marta Riestro, Henry, Esprit,** and **Pasarela** (for glitzy Mexican-style evening clothes and accessories) are a few of the better shops. Pasarela also sells beautiful (but expensive) hand-beaded dresses.

Papacito's Last Call, tucked away in a corner of the mall at street level, is one of a handful of places in Acapulco that can be enjoyed by the late-night crowd that doesn't like discos. The place has a modern look, with sofas where you can lounge and order drinks and snacks, and the Mexican folk art hanging on the walls was clearly chosen by someone with a sense of humor. The frozen margaritas are marvelous and the fajitas superb; the live music lasts until 3:00 A.M.

The Acapulco Plaza also has a sports center where everything from scuba diving to deep-sea fishing excursions can be arranged, and the hotel's beach is one of the best places to try the parasail rides for which Acapulco is famous.

The two-story **Plaza Bahía,** on the Costera a few doors down from the Acapulco Plaza, is the first and only air-conditioned non-hotel mall in town. Among the best shops here are **Baby O** and **Apasia,** for trendy resortwear and accessories; **Galería 10/10,** an art gallery; and **Bazaar,** which offers a varied assortment of souvenirs and objets d'art.

Acapulco off the Strip

THE UNDERPASS TO TOWN

After the Radisson Paraíso, located a bit to the west of the Acapulco Plaza, the Costera goes underground to accommodate **Papagayo**, a sprawling park with games for children and a cable car that connects it to the beach. The best thing about this piece of prime real estate, however, is the **aviary**, which is a wonderful place to keep cool on a hot day.

Super Super (with everything from shampoo to suntan lotion, food, wine, liquor, and film), Gigante, and Comercial Mexicana, the three best supermarkets in town, are just to the west of the Papagayo underpass and across the street from **Playa Hornos**, a palm-shaded beach beloved by Mexican vacationers, who rent beach chairs nearby and cool off in thatched-roof restaurants such as **Sirocco**.

You'll feel as if you're in France when you step into **Normandie**, on the corner of the Costera and Calle Malespina. This unassuming establishment has a time-tested reputation for excellent food. Fresh-from-the-market ingredients become imaginative appetizers and entrées, and the eclectic decor somehow manages to be relaxing. You can choose to dine on the patio or inside in air-conditioned comfort—but only for dinner, and only from December to Easter (it's closed the rest of the year). Tel: 85-1916.

The **Mercado Municipal**, five long blocks inland from the Costera, is one of the most colorful open markets in the country. Local residents depend on it for everything from food to magic potions, and strolling through its crowded aisles will give you an idea of what life in this tropical port is like behind all the glitz. The best spot to enter the market and begin your explorations is through the flower section. Ask your taxi driver to leave you at the corner of Ruíz Cortines and Diego Hurtado de Mendoza. If you drive yourself, look for the sign just past the Sol de Acapulco that reads "San Jerónimo, Pie de la Cuesta, Mercado." Turn right and get ready to sit: The narrow street is always congested, especially weekends. Park wherever you can just before Ruíz Cortines, and give the attendant a nice tip to watch your car.

Although not readily apparent, the market *is* divided into sections. If you're looking for something in particular, learn its name in Spanish and ask directions. Handicrafts and souvenirs are in the covered area next to the flower section toward the back. The market, where bargaining is part of the fun, is at its best in November and December, when whimsical Christmas-tree ornaments can be bought for pennies. Saturdays between 10:00 and 11:00 A.M. is prime time throughout the year. If you just want to have a quick look, go on a weekday morning around 10:00 and ask your taxi driver to accompany you inside.

The **Museo Histórico de Acapulco**, in El Fuerte de San Diego, overlooks the Costera from its hill above the cruise-ship pier. Despite its name, which means "place where the reeds were destroyed," Acapulco has had a relatively uneventful history. It became a shipbuilding center and an important port for Spain's Far East trade after the Conquest, and though pirates plundered its shores on occasion, no major war or uprising has ever disturbed the city.

After the Spanish departed in the aftermath of the War of Independence, Acapulco was all but abandoned for the next hundred years. In fact, it was only after the first road from Mexico City was pushed over the Sierra Madre del Sur in 1927 that Acapulco began to awaken. Highway 95, the first superhighway, was inaugurated in 1955, but the real fun began in 1964, when direct international flights began to bring a host of celebrities and jet-setters into town.

A broad staircase across from the cruise-ship pier leads from the Costera to the museum, where the story of the fort and the town's history are displayed in a series of air-conditioned rooms once used to store ammunition. The museum's clever design (created by experts from the Museum of Anthropology in Mexico City) is in many cases as interesting as the exhibits themselves. And though it only takes a few minutes to see everything, it's well worth a stop. The museum is open from 10:00 A.M. to 6:00 P.M., daily except Mondays.

DOWNTOWN

There are few good reasons for visitors to explore downtown Acapulco. It looks like any tropical port, complete with a zócalo and mandatory bandstand where concerts are held on Sundays; a church (Nuestra Señora de la Soledad) with a charming exterior; and some major banks and stores, including Woolworth's and branches of Sanborn's and Emil. If you want to change a large amount of currency, you'll save some money by doing it at one of the downtown banks. **Terraza de las Flores**, overlooking the plaza, is the best—and only— German restaurant in town; red cabbage, schnitzel, sauerkraut, and potatoes are among the delicious, rib-sticking items on the menu. Tel: 82-9413. **Paco's** is where you'll want to end up if succulent seafood is what you have in mind. Located in a busy part of town three blocks west of the cathedral on the road to La Quebrada, it's the kind of unassuming family-run place where the kitchen is in plain view of the customers and the decor changes once every three decades or so. For a taste of Acapulco the way it used to be at yesterday's prices, it can't be beat. No phone and no reservations.

The **Mercado de Artesanías**, sometimes called the Flea

Market, proffers the typical souvenirs you may already have found along the Costera. It covers several blocks of Calle Velásquez de León, behind the Woolworth's.

Fishermen mend their nets, much as they always have, across from the zócalo at the corner of Costera and Calle Iglesias. You can rent deep-sea fishing boats at Pesca Deportiva, opposite the zócalo next to the *muelle* (municipal pier).

OLD ACAPULCO

Old Acapulco—the peninsular area that includes **Playa Caleta** and **Playa Caletilla**, as well as **Isla La Roqueta**—looks much the same today as it did in the days when Acapulco was rehearsing for international stardom. This is changing, however. The pier between Caleta and Caletilla has been refurbished, and **Magico Mundo Marino**, the new aquarium here, is a wonderful place to spend a day. Besides the exceptionally well done marine-life exhibits, the aquarium has a pool with open and closed water slides for the kids, one of the breeziest restaurants in town, and a beach with good swimming conditions. There is also a concession on hand for jet skis and scuba-diving equipment. Avoid Sundays if you can, but don't miss it.

The aquarium is the departure point for the **Acapulco Zoo**, situated on Isla La Roqueta, making it one of the world's only island zoos (launches shuttle back and forth from 10:00 A.M. to 6:00 P.M. daily). Animals are kept in naturalistic state-of-the-art environments, and the many exhibits include a Serpentarium that climbs the slope of a gentle hill to the spot where Nene, a baby giraffe, munches serenely on nearby treetops. Visitors to the zoo can climb down and swim in tiny protected coves, or join the folks on the main beach. The more adventurous follow the mountainous path to Palao (see below under Excursions), a beachfront restaurant on the other side of the island with its own tiny beach.

Also in this part of town, back on the mainland, is the bull ring, **Plaza Caletilla**. The bravest bulls and greatest bullfights are usually not seen in the tropics, but Plaza Caletilla offers the best of any Mexican resort—largely because it has the largest potential audience. The season runs from December through Easter, but contests are staged sporadically. Seats by the railing (*barrera*), in the shade, are the best. Tickets can be arranged through your hotel or through any of the travel agencies in town.

The world-famous Acapulco *clavadistas* (cliff-divers) make daring leaps from a 100-foot-high cliff at **La Quebrada** in Old

Acapulco several times daily—once in the afternoon and two or three times at night. You can watch these spectacular athletes in comfort from the bar at the Hotel Mirador or, for a small fee, from La Perla, its nightclub. Or head for the steps in the cliffside park near the hotel. The "show" is free, but contributions are appreciated when the divers pass the hat. Ask at your hotel or call the Mirador for the times of the performances; Tel: 82-1111.

Pie de la Cuesta

Pie de la Cuesta and Laguna de Coyuca are for those who like their scenery without the crowds. The fishing village of Pie de la Cuesta is a great spot to visit on Sundays, and one of the best places to watch the sunset any day of the week.

The area is a scenic 15-minute drive north and west of downtown along Calzada Pie de la Cuesta. There's a turnoff leading to what was once the old airport road—now lined with ramshackle restaurants—after the road comes down out of the hills. If you've come to see the sunset, choose one of the restaurants on the beach side, rent a chair or a hammock, order your coco loco, and get ready for one of the world's finest shows.

The entire area is a world apart from the resort just over the hills to the south. Many children here still get to school by dugout canoe, and in some places at certain times of the year the waterways are made impassable by lily pads. The long, flat stretch of beach is unspoiled and beautiful, but the surf is too strong for swimming.

Laguna de Coyuca, across the street from the beach, is a nature preserve much loved by bird-watchers, fishermen, and filmmakers (*Rambo II* was shot here). It's also a water-skier's idea of heaven and the perfect place to learn how to drop one ski. **Tres Marías** and, especially, **Tres Palmas** are the local cognoscenti's favorite hangouts. Order your lunch when you first arrive and it will be waiting for you after you ski or swim. Whether you waterski or not, be sure to ask one of the boatmen to take you on a tour of the waterways at the end of the lagoon. "Broncos"—small motorboats for one or two—and inner tubes can also be rented.

If you fall in love with the place (a distinct possibility), you can stay overnight at ▶ **Ukae Kim**, an attractive and romantic 18-room hotel on the beach side. (If you're only coming out for the day, be sure to arrange with the taxi driver who brings you out to pick you up at an appointed time.) Reserve a room overlooking the ocean; the beds are on raised platforms so you can catch the view. There is also a small restaurant and beach club at Ukae Kim—all far from the crowds; non-guests can use the beach club for a small fee, which also gets you a towel and lounge chair.

Nightlife in Acapulco

For a touch of nostalgia, you can dine and dance at air-conditioned rooftop restaurants such as **Techo del Mar** in the Fiesta Americana Condesa hotel or **The Windjammer** (La Fragata) in the Radisson Paraíso Acapulco. Both have the feeling of days gone by and attract an older crowd that likes to dance cheek to cheek.

From time to time nightclubs such as **Banneret** in the Calinda Acapulco Quality Inn and **Numero Uno** in the Hyatt Regency feature floor shows with big-name entertainers. The Acapulco Convention Center also offers the occasional spectacle. Watch their marquees for announcements of upcoming events.

For the most part, however, when the sun goes down Acapulco revelers gravitate to its dazzling discos. Acapulco's discos rank as one of the resort's leading attractions, and you're definitely missing something if you don't go at least once. They're at their best between 12:30 and 2:00 A.M. on a weekend night. Otherwise, they're open every night of the year from 10:00 P.M. until the last customer goes home. Some discos have big crowds waiting, especially in season, but if you're well dressed and well behaved (and good at staring doormen down) you're likely to get in sooner than the rest. Once you're inside, tip the maître d' or waiter right away to ensure a good table and good service. If you can't get into the disco of your choice, try another one. Extravaganzza, Fantasy, Baby O, and the News are the current favorites, and are discussed above along with others.

Sports in Acapulco

Most of the bigger hotels have centers where you can arrange just about every imaginable water sport. In addition, water-skiing boats are available at most every beach, as are parasail rides. Jet skis can be rented by the hour on the beach behind Mimi's Saloon or at the aquarium. The beach behind Mimi's is also the place to rent Broncos (one- or two-person motorboats).

Windsurfers and sailboats can be rented on the beach behind the Hotel Malibu and Diana traffic circle. Scuba-diving and snorkeling excursions can be arranged at **Arnold Brothers** (Tel: 82-1877 or 0788) or **Divers de México** (Tel:

82-1398), both on the beach side of the Costera just before town. Surfing is not permitted on the beaches along the Strip, so diehards take their boards out to Playa Revolcadero, south and east of town just before the Acapulco Princess.

Fishing boats can be chartered through your hotel or at **Pesca Deportiva**, across from the zócalo near the municipal pier; Tel: 82-1099. Sailfish, marlin, tuna, mackerel, and snapper are all prize catches in the waters around Acapulco. Divers de México will be happy to arrange a spot for you on a boat shared by others.

The area's championship 18-hole golf course is next door to the Acapulco Princess hotel. Greens fees (with cart) are approximately $64 for hotel guests and $85 for non-guests. Tee times should be made at least a day in advance; Tel: 84-3000. The public is also welcome at the nine-hole **Club de Golf Acapulco**, on the Strip opposite the Hotel Elcano, where the greens fees run about $40 for nine holes and $50 for 18; caddies are an additional $11 for nine and $15 for 18. Tel: 84-0781 for tee times.

Excursions from Acapulco

The catamaran *Aca Tiki* takes guests on day and sunset cruises of the bay. The boat, which its owners claim is the world's largest sailing catamaran, leaves from the pier near the Fort of San Diego. Reserve in advance to avoid being disappointed; Tel: 84-6140 or 6786. Sunset cruises include drinks (Mexican brands), dinner, and a folkloric show.

Those who want to do it the way the locals do can sail around the bay on the *Fiesta Cabaret,* which goes out twice daily. The four-hour daytime cruise includes lunch and a stop at Playa Pichilingue for swimming and snorkeling; the three-hour moonlight cruise includes a buffet, your drinks, a show, and live music for dancing. Tel: 83-1550 for sailing times and reservations. Other options for getting out on the water include the *Bonanza* (Tel: 83-1803) and the *Hawaiiano* (Tel: 82-1217); each has its own pier (as does the *Fiesta Cabaret*) past town on the way to Playa Caleta.

Ferryboats take passengers from the Caleta pier to **Isla La Roqueta**, where you can visit the zoo and lunch at **Palao**, on its own tiny bay. Palao serves tasty, simply prepared seafood and meat dishes, occasionally accompanied by marimba music. After lunch you can take a dip or walk through the jungle, with breathtaking views of the ocean along the way. More energetic visitors can climb to the lighthouse. The main beach at La Roqueta, a favorite Sunday excursion for visiting Mexicans, is a ten-minute walk from the restaurant when the boardwalk is in good repair. Otherwise, it's about five minutes by boat.

GETTING AROUND

A number of international carriers link Acapulco to cities in the United States. While many flights are direct, few are nonstop, and often passengers will have to deplane and go through customs in Mexico City. Those carriers that do fly nonstop to Acapulco include Continental, which offers daily flights from its hubs in Newark and Houston, and American and Delta, which offer daily flights to Acapulco from Dallas–Fort Worth and Los Angeles. Aeroméxico (from New York) and Mexicana (from Chicago) offer daily "direct" service to Acapulco, with a stopover in Mexico City for customs.

Getting from the Acapulco airport into town is no cup of tea, either. Private taxis are available, but at about $20 per head. *Colectivos* cost half as much but usually make several stops for other passengers en route to your hotel. (Try to get a seat on the left side of the *colectivo* for the best views.) Your best bet is to call your travel agent or hotel before leaving home and arrange to be picked up by private car. If, on the other hand, you do take a *colectivo* or bus, buy a one-way ticket: Taxis taking departing guests *to* the airport usually cost a few dollars less than those making the reverse trip.

Acapulco is 416 km (258 miles) south of Mexico City. Driving down on the new superhighway, Highway 95, takes about 3½ hours, with the road spilling motorists onto the coast road in the neighborhood of the Acapulco Princess. The bad news is that once the tolls on the new highway are set, they may total as much as $80, one-way. Old route 95, with minimal tolls, takes about 5½ hours from the capital and ends on the Costera at the Diana traffic circle. Those who prefer a more scenic, leisurely trip travel the old "old road," making stops in Taxco and Cuernavaca. The trip takes 7 to 10 hours (depending on traffic), without stops, and no tolls are charged.

Buses—Estrella Blanca (the first-class line; in Acapulco, Tel: 86-3735) and Flecha Roja (Tel: 82-0351 or 2184)—operate several runs daily between Acapulco and the D.F. The trip takes at least 5½ hours. If you decide to do it, travel first-class—it's worth it.

Getting around Acapulco itself is a breeze. Taxis are the best choice now that there are parking meters on the Costera. If you choose to drive to the beach in a rental car, you'll have to come back every hour and plug 1,000 pesos into the meter. If you don't, zealous traffic cops will take your·license plate.

Taxis in large numbers cruise the Costera day and night. Fares are set by zone and are usually posted on placards outside hotel lobbies. An average point-to-point fare will cost in the neighborhood of $2 to $5. "Sitios"—those taxis that have paid for the privilege of standing in front of specific hotels—cost a bit more. Rates go up as the night progresses, but are generally far lower than rates back home.

City buses run from downtown to the naval base and beyond, but their schedules are erratic. The large yellow shelters with blue public phones are the stops.

—Susan Wagner

ACCOMMODATIONS REFERENCE

The rates given below are projections *for December 1993 through Easter 1994. Unless otherwise indicated, rates are for double rooms, double occupancy; the 10 percent VAT has been added. As rates are subject to change, it's a good idea to double-check before booking. Acapulco is in the central standard time zone; the telephone area code is 74.*

▶ **Acapulco Malibu Hotel.** P.O. Box 582, Avenida Costera Miguel Alemán 20, **Acapulco**, Guerrero 39868. Tel: 84-1070; Fax: 84-0994. $92.

▶ **Acapulco Plaza.** Avenida Costera Miguel Alemán 123, **Acapulco**, Guerrero 39868. Tel: 85-9050; Fax: 85-5493; in the U.S., Tel: (800) 626-0569. $145–$187.

▶ **Acapulco Princess.** P.O. Box 1351, Playa Revolcadero, **Acapulco**, Guerrero 39868. Tel: 84-3100; Fax: 84-8820; in the U.S., Tel: (800) 223-1818; in Ontario, Tel: (800) 268-7140; in the rest of Canada, Tel: (800) 268-7176. $285–$345 (includes breakfast and dinner).

▶ **Camino Real Acapulco Diamante.** Carretera Escénica km 14, Fracc. Pichilingue Diamante, **Acapulco**, Guerrero 39867. Tel: 81-2010; Fax: 81-2700; in the U.S. and Canada, Tel: (800) 344-3829. $165.

▶ **Hotel La Palapa.** Fragata Yucatán 210, **Acapulco**, Guerrero 39850. Tel: 84-5363; Fax: 84-8399. $94–$120.

▶ **Hyatt Regency.** Avenida Costera Miguel Alemán 1, **Acapulco**, Guerrero 39869. Tel: 84-2888; Fax: 84-3087; in the U.S. and Canada, Tel: (800) 233-1234. $215–$237.

▶ **Ukae Kim.** Pie de la Cuesta, **Acapulco**, Guerrero 39868. Tel: 60-0727. $60.

▶ **Vidafel Mayan Palace Acapulco Diamante.** Playa Copacabana, Fracc. Acapulco Diamante, **Acapulco**, Guerrero 36978.

Tel: 84-7595 or 62-0020; Fax: 84-5070; in the U.S. and Canada, Tel: (800) VIDAFEL. $150.

▶ **Villa Vera Hotel & Racquet Club.** Lomas del Mar 35, **Acapulco**, Guerrero 39690. Tel: 84-0333; Fax: 84-7479; in the U.S. and Canada, Tel: (800) 525-4800. $198–$275; $413 (villa with private pool).

▶ **Westin Las Brisas Resort.** P.O. Box 281, Carretera Escénica 5255, **Acapulco**, Guerrero 39868. Tel: 84-1850; Fax: 84-2269; in the U.S. and Canada, Tel: (800) 228-3000. $237 (shared pool); $347 (private pool).

PUERTO ESCONDIDO, PUERTO ANGEL, HUATULCO

Isolated from the outside world by the Sierra de Miahuatlán, and overshadowed by such glittering stars of the "Mexican Riviera" as Acapulco, Puerto Vallarta, and Mazatlán, the Costa Oaxaqueña remained a place outside of time well into the 1970s. Like their ancestors before them, the region's Mixtec, Zapotec, and Chatino Indians worried a living from the narrow shelf of land between the mountains and sea, or pulled their harvests from the sea itself. As far as the international jet-set was concerned, Puerto Escondido and Puerto Angel were just names on a map; Huatulco didn't even exist.

For a steady trickle of gringo fishermen and surfers, on the other hand, the region's empty beaches, big waves, and nominal cost of living represented the pot of gold at the end of the rainbow. That accommodations generally ran to palapas and hammocks, and a fancy dinner was considered the day's catch and a couple of *cervezas,* only added to its laid-back appeal.

As international tourism picked up in the latter half of the 1970s, things began to change. Fresh from its success in Cancún, Fonatur, the government agency in charge of tourism development, was given the go ahead to launch a state-of-the-art resort complex somewhere along the coast, and eventually settled on the tiny fishing village of Santa Cruz Huatulco. With the paving of Highway 200, the coast road, all the way to the Guatemala border in the early 1980s, the Costa Oaxaqueña was opened to growing numbers of Mexican vacationers, budget travellers, and the RV crowd. The lengthening of the Puerto Escondido airstrip and the completion of the Huatulco airport a few years later accelerated the region's transition from sleepy backwater to fledgling international resort destination.

Today the Oaxaca coast is poised between what it was and what the Mexican government is determined to see it become. Spring still brings a pall of smoke from burning fields, and sleepy hamlets dot the landscape; this is the state of Oaxaca, after all, where the roots of traditional Indian culture reach back thousands of years. And yet, the telltale signs of the 20th century—from the oil refineries of Salina Cruz to the satellite dishes and ATMs of Huatulco—clearly suggest what the future holds in store.

MAJOR INTEREST

Proximity of all three to Oaxaca City and surrounding pre-Hispanic ruins and handicraft centers

Puerto Escondido
Appealing mix of locals, expatriates, and sophisticated crowd of international travellers
Superior surfing at Playa Zicatela

Puerto Angel
Beautifully situated fishing village
Playa Zipolite

Huatulco
Spectacularly scenic coastline
Low-key resort atmosphere

Mindful of past criticism, Fonatur pledged to develop the **Bahías de Huatulco** (as Huatulco is officially known) with respect for the environment and sensitivity to the welfare of the local population. For the present, the four or five luxury hotels here, most of the good stores, and a championship golf course are concentrated around a beautiful bay backed by steep hills. No building may exceed six stories, and all must conform to a generic Mediterranean architectural style. Development in and around the other bays has been, and will continue to be, regulated. Throughout the 23-mile length and six-mile width of the resort zone large parcels of land have been set aside as nature preserves. If activities and social opportunities outside the hotels are still somewhat limited, the beauty of the setting is unforgettable. Fonatur is committed to keeping it that way.

Although Huatulco has been the chief beneficiary of

Fonatur's efforts, Puerto Escondido and, to a lesser extent, Puerto Angel—linked to each other as well as to Huatulco by Highway 200—are also feeling the impact of Fonatur's economic clout. With an increase in the number of visiting tourists and a quadrupling of its population in little more than a decade, **Puerto Escondido**'s days as a quiet fishing village and surfers' hangout have gone the way of the Woodie. While fishermen and surfers still roll into town in beat-up Beetles and campers, they're outnumbered these days by vacationing sun-lovers and the occasional celebrity looking to escape the fast pace of the bigger resorts up the coast. A small but colorful population of European and gringo expatriates, a dozen decent, relatively inexpensive restaurants, and a live-and-let-live attitude that seems to infect visitors and locals alike all help to explain Puerto Escondido's popularity with budget travellers and the knowingly untrendy.

Situated midway between Huatulco and Puerto Escondido at the southernmost point of the Costa Oaxaqueña, **Puerto Angel**, a rustic fishing village with accommodations to match, remains more or less what it always has been, despite a modest influx of well-heeled tourists. Inevitably, many of these tourists are discovering what for years was Puerto Angel's best-kept secret: Playa Zipolite, the most unfettered nude beach in Mexico.

For the moment, all three are ideal hot-weather destinations for those who can do without flash and glitter, and who don't mind packing it in early after a day at the beach. As often happens with good things, however, the word about these destinations—Puerto Escondido and Huatulco, in particular—is spreading. As a result, it's not unusual for the better hotels in either resort to be booked up to half a year in advance for the Christmas and Easter vacation periods, while the one singular accommodation in Puerto Angel is usually booked solid for the entirety of its ten-month season (July to the end of April).

PUERTO ESCONDIDO

Before it was "discovered" by surfers and budget travellers in the 1960s, Puerto Escondido was a quiet fishing village with a long, uneventful past. Today it's the kind of place that's big enough to have the amenities you expect to find in a resort—airport, car-rental agencies, a range of hotels and places to eat—but small enough so that people will usually remember your face, if not your name, the second time they see you. With a population of more than 50,000, all that is changing, however.

The first hint that "Escondido" offers something in addition to the usual beach-resort pleasures comes at its small but modern airport. For an hour or two every morning the hangarlike building here fills with a colorful crowd of board-toting surfers. Of course, surfing is serious business, and Puerto Escondido boasts some of the most serious surfing in North America. The "Mexican Pipeline," as surfers call the stretch of **Playa Zicatela** where the best waves break, is famous for its warm water and reliable "swells" (a sustained period of good waves). The perfectly formed waves are shaped by the configuration of the continental shelf, which rises abruptly from a depth of 300 feet to 30 feet just offshore. The town hosts two major surfing competitions a year, one in August—July, August, and September are the big-wave months—and another in November. Nonsurfers take note, however: Zicatela's pounding surf and dangerous riptides are not to be treated lightly. Strong swimmers will want to exercise caution; everyone else should confine their swimming to the town beach or the beaches west of town (see below).

Around in Escondido

Town is a few miles east of the airport via Highway 200, the coast road. West of the airport Highway 200 sweeps north and west in the direction of Punta Colorado and, eventually, Acapulco, in the state of Guerrero. If the developers have their way, **Playa Bacocho**, which stretches all the way from the airport to the point, will be thick with condominium projects and luxury hotels by the end of the decade. For now, it's a ruggedly beautiful but desolate stretch of sand pounded by heavy surf and patrolled by police during the day to discourage small-time *bandidos;* visitors will be wise to exercise caution when beachcombing there.

FROM THE AIRPORT TO TOWN

With the Pacific to your right, you'll pass Escondido's only gas station, a number of inexpensive motor inns, and various commercial establishments on the way into town. **Bacocho,** the spiffy-looking subdivision perched on a steep bluff about halfway between the airport and town, is home to a number of expatriate Americans as well as a sizable community of affluent Mexicans who have built second homes here. (Its popularity has spawned another residential area next door called Conjunto Esmeralda.) It is, in addition, the location of the Best Western Posada Real (see below), the lodging of choice for most tour groups and families despite its distance from the shops and restaurants that cater to tourists.

While the heavy surf makes Escondido's most spectacular beach too dangerous for swimming, there are a couple of smaller strands where the waves roll rather than detonate. Among these are **Playa Carrizalillo** and **Puerto Angelito**, located midway between the Bacocho neighborhood and town. (Small signs on the highway point the way. The former is reached by taking the right fork in the unpaved access road, followed by a short hike down a steep bluff. The left fork leads to a badly rutted road that spills rattled drivers and passengers onto the beach at Puerto Angelito.)

There are two beaches at Playa Carrizalillo, and because they're somewhat difficult to reach, rocky, and lacking amenities (it's a long, sweaty hike back up the bluff if you get thirsty), they're often deserted. The water is warm, however, and the waves perfectly manageable; the smaller of the two is also good for snorkeling. The beach at Puerto Angelito, a curving stretch of flat sand backed by a stand of palms and washed by gentle waves, is a popular spot, especially on Sundays, when local families arrive in numbers. Small concession stands here sell snacks and soda.

The main intersection in town is another 1 km (½ mile) east of the turnoff for Carrizalillo and Puerto Angelito. Though tourists seldom explore it, the dusty grid of streets laid out over the hillside to the left of this intersection is where most of Escondido's full-time residents live and conduct their business. The fastest-growing part of town, it's also where you'll find Escondido's two bus stations (Flecha Roja and La Gacela), as well as a number of very inexpensive restaurants. As none has yet to establish a reputation as anything other than adequate, however, your best bet is to ask around before striking out into the gastronomic unknown.

CENTRO

A right turn at the intersection (marked "Centro") will lead you down the hill to **Avenida Alfonso Pérez Gasga**, Escondido's main tourist zone, and Playa Principal, the town beach. Closed to vehicular traffic (parking is provided at either end of the street), the eight blocks of Pérez Gasga are lined with a dozen beachside restaurants, a number of shops offering well-designed resortwear and quality handicraft items—in addition to many more peddling the usual junk— and a couple of inexpensive hotels. Much of what passes for nightlife in Puerto Escondido is situated along this stretch as well, as are the Mexicana airline office, the Budget office, and the only banks in town—which visitors will be wise to avoid. (Most places in town accept American dollars; the Hotel Santa Fé and Art & Harry's Bar & Grill, at opposite ends of the Zicatela beach road, will cash traveller's checks.)

Playa Principal, a swath of brownish sand backed by palms and the above-mentioned restaurants and hotels, is a good family beach with little or no surf and plenty of room to spread out. The waves pick up where the beach curves around the bay in the direction of Playa Zicatela, a stretch of sand known as **Playa Marinero**, but rarely are they big enough to discourage swimming. In fact, from the "tadpoles"—junior surfers who have yet to develop the skill or muscle to tackle the giant waves on the other side of the rocks—at the far end of the beach to the never-ending parade of people, Marinero is the liveliest spot in Puerto Escondido.

PLAYA ZICATELA

Motorists headed for Playa Zicatela or the Hotel Santa Fé will want to continue through the main intersection on Highway 200. After passing an open-air market and a number of low-budget accommodations the road heads uphill. The turnoff signposted "Playa Zicatela," which also leads to the Santa Fé, will be to your right after the second set of speed bumps (look for the building with a painted "Bungalow Marinero" sign). Calle de Morro, the rutted road leading down the hill and around the Santa Fé to the bungalows and guest houses strung out behind Zicatela, has lately attracted the attention of the state government. In fact, the powers-that-be in Oaxaca City have decided to turn it into a paved, two-lane circuit with access roads at either end of the beach. (They've also allotted funds for the installation of a new sewer system here.) The idea is to improve—and increase—the flow of tourist traffic at this end of town, an objective that, if realized, will likely force the establishments catering to surfers to go upscale.

For the time being, the scene along Zicatela remains more or less what it has been for the last decade or so. The Hotel Santa Fé anchors the end closest to town, and is still the best accommodation in Escondido, if not the best the Costa Oaxaqueña has to offer (see Staying in Escondido, below). At the opposite end of the beach, the old Tres Ochos has been reborn as Art & Harry's Bar & Grill, a breezy hangout popular with expats and anyone with a similarly carefree approach to living (see Dining, Shopping, and Nightlife, below).

In between these two very different but equally hospitable establishments, visitors will find a dozen low-key accommodations dotting the hillside between the beach and the highway. Places like the Hotel Arco Iris, the Hotel Inés, and Rockaway Surfer Village have long been popular with fishermen, surfers, and budget travellers not especially choosy about where they sleep. Generally speaking, accommodations range from the very basic (bed and cold-water shower) to the not-half-bad (swimming pool, expansive views of the water), with rates in the $22-to-$32 range. As an added bonus, bibliophiles and Orange County Republicans can stop by the **Richard Milhouse Nixon Memorial Library** and browse its eclectic collection of paperbacks and memorabilia devoted to the 37th president.

More than just surfers enjoy the waters off Puerto Escondido. **Deep-sea-fishing** enthusiasts have known about the place for decades, with the fishing for tuna, sailfish, bonito, mahi-mahi, and roosterfish especially good in the spring. Boats—most of them open *pangas* (skiffs)—can be rented on the town beach or at the small marina at the western end of Pérez Gasga. Rates range from $15 to $17 per person, per hour, and should include your tackle.

Horseback riding on Zicatela is another popular option. During the high season you can usually find well-behaved nags for rent for about $20 an hour at the farthest end of Playa Marinero, or you can contact the **Viajes y Excursiones García Rendon** travel agency in the Posada Real (Tel: 958/2-0290, 0133, or 0394).

STAYING IN ESCONDIDO

There is one obvious choice here; indeed, some would say it's the only choice. The ► **Hotel Santa Fé**, located at the eastern end of Playa Marinero between town and Playa Zicatela, is far and away the best accommodation—at any price—in Escondido. Owned and managed by Californians Paul and Robin Klever (along with more than two dozen silent partners), the Santa Fé is a delightful change of pace from the impersonal, characterless luxury hotels that have come to dominate the larger Mexican resorts. And although the number of rooms has almost doubled since 1992, the Klevers have managed to preserve its special charm.

The Santa Fé's 44 rooms and eight bungalows are spread among a compact cluster of three-story Mediterranean-style buildings. Rooms are simply but tastefully decorated with regionally produced ceramics and textiles, and feature two double beds, large tiled bathrooms, ceiling fans, and air-conditioning. Most also have tiny balconies where guests can wile away the hours with a book or magazine. (There are no radios or TVs at the Santa Fé.) Palm trees and flowering plants surround the small pool area at the heart of the complex, which is where nonswimmers will want to cool off. (Nearby Zicatela is no place for dog-paddlers or little children.)

Even if you aren't able to book a room here—and they go fast, especially during the Christmas and Easter holiday periods—the restaurant at the Santa Fé is a wonderful place for a meal. The menu, though pricey by local standards, features an extensive selection of meat, fish, and vegetarian dishes, all expertly prepared and served with style. But the food is only part of the restaurant's appeal. The pretty palapa-covered dining room overlooks the pool area on one side and the endless expanse of the Pacific on the other. Off to the right, Escondido climbs a hill behind its palm-fringed bay, while down the beach to your left the surfers—as many as 30 or 40 at once if a good swell has moved in—do battle with waves that seem to have rolled in from Hawaii. When you tire of soaking up the view you can turn your attention to the always colorful parade that comes and goes on the beach below. And if that gets old, there usually will be two or three interesting characters sitting around waiting to strike up a conversation and buy you a beer.

Perched high on a bluff in the tidy Bacocho neighborhood west of town, the ▶ **Best Western Posada Real** promises more than it delivers. For what a room here costs you expect something special, but except for its pretty grounds and lobby, the Posada Real is disappointingly average. The drab motel-style rooms are equipped with air-conditioning, TVs, and little else. The hotel's restaurant is a little better, and can even be charming if you eat at a table under the *portales*. The hotel's location in semi-isolated Bacocho, on the other hand, will come as a disappointment to many, necessitating frequent trips in taxis. It doesn't add up to much, given the rather high room rates, and inevitably there seems to be a lot of grumbling among the tour groups that wind up staying here.

Located at the base of the bluff behind the hotel, **Coco's Beach Club**, a Polynesian-style restaurant fronted by a palm-shaded patch of lawn and an enormous free-form pool (open to the public), is probably the best thing about the Posada Real. Although pricey, Coco's is a nice spot for a light snack, afternoon cocktails, or an early dinner, and is especially romantic after the sun sets, when the jungle decor, flickering torchlight, and pounding surf enhance its splendid isolation.

The neighborhood's newest addition is the gleaming white Moorish-style ▶ **Aldea del Bazar**, about two blocks east of the Posada Real. Although it sticks out like a flashy white elephant among the plainer local establishments, the Aldea deserves a closer look. The 48 nicely furnished rooms have two double beds and views of the beach (although the hotel isn't on the beach) or the gardens. The bathrooms, equipped with hair dryers and bathroom scales, are the fanciest in Escondido, and color satellite T.V. should be installed by the end of 1993. There's also a bar/restaurant and a pool.

At the low end of the budget spectrum, there are a couple of lodging choices right in town on Pérez Gasga that are more than adequate. The ▶ **Hotel Las Palmas** overlooks Playa Principal and a pretty courtyard filled with palms and flowering shrubs. The two dozen glass-fronted rooms here are on the small side, but louvered doorways and ceiling fans add a touch of charm, and the hotel's patio restaurant facing the beach is a popular spot. The ▶ **Rincón del Pacífico**, right next door, is a virtual carbon copy of Las Palmas, with rooms a bit smaller, perhaps, and slightly less expensive.

DINING, SHOPPING, AND NIGHTLIFE

If first-rate accommodations are a little scarce in Puerto Escondido, unpretentious, reasonably priced restaurants are not. The same holds true for shopping: Serious shoppers will definitely want to spend a day or two in Oaxaca City, one of the country's leading handicraft and folk-art centers (see Getting Around at the end of this section). If, on the other hand, a few trinkets are all you're looking for, Escondido can take care of your needs. Unless otherwise stated, the establishments mentioned below are located on the pedestrians-only stretch of Pérez Gasga right in town.

At the west end of the street (the end farthest from the Santa Fé), the two-story **Nautilus** has a few tables downstairs and a palapa-covered terrace upstairs with great views of the bay; seafood, chicken, and beef dishes monopolize the menu, and the service is pleasant if not especially speedy. Across the street and up a few doors, the **Bazar Ticun-Uman** and **Bazar Tamar** offer nice selections of Guatemalan textiles as well as ceremonial masks from the states of Oaxaca and Guerrero.

La Luna, down the street toward the Santa Fé, fills its tiny space with a colorful assortment of bathing suits and inexpensive jewelry, while slightly larger **Bamboleo**, next door, has Escondido's most interesting selection of resortwear. On the same side of the street overlooking the beach and still more palms, **Da Ugo** is the spot for a romantic, candlelit dinner. It is affiliated with **Ostería Viandante**, a longtime local favorite next door that dishes out garlicky Italian specialties.

The freshest grilled seafood in town is served in the Swiss Family Robinson–style surroundings of the **Perla Flamante**, near the east end of the street. **Banana's**, at the far end of the closed-off section of the street, offers the usual burgers-and-nacho fare but does it well; it's also the place to watch televised sports events from the States.

After the ballgame, you might want to head over to **Tío Mac's**, across from Banana's, which most nights can be counted on to be the loudest—if not necessarily the most happening—place in town. The **Spaghetti House**, a casually rustic spot on the beach around the corner from Banana's, is popular with hungry surfers and travellers on a budget.

During the day sun-lovers on Playa Marinero gravitate toward **Liza's**, with its simple, inexpensive food served at tables right on the sand. And though locals love to complain about its prices, the **Santa Fé**'s breezy palapa-covered restaurant, a bit farther down the beach, manages to attract its share of them regardless of the hour. Especially good here are the *huevos mexicana* (made with fresh eggs), the deep dish–style enchiladas, the three-cheese lasagna, and their deliciously refreshing *limonada*.

The low-key establishments along the Zicatela beach road, which almost every visitor to Escondido checks out sooner or later, are the special preserve of surfers and the local expatriate community. Because novelty is a much-appreciated commodity in a place like Escondido, where one sun-drenched day seems to blend into the next, the newest establishments also tend to be the most popular. For now, the newest and most popular is **Art & Harry's Bar & Grill** (formerly Tres Ochos), at the far end of the beach. Under the watchful supervision of Patty, Jeff, and Pablo, Canadian ambassadors *extraordinaire,* Art & Harry's offers huge portions from a saloon-style menu; a half-dozen clean, no-frills rooms; and a full slate of social activities, including hotly contested dart competitions and a weekly Frisbee golf game. Pizza aficionados will want to check out **Cipriano's**, at the opposite end of the beach, where an amazing variety of toppings adorn pies baked in a wood-fired oven.

Of course, not everyone who comes to Puerto Escondido is content to spend the week in shorts, sandals, and a tee-shirt. For those who've packed an outfit or two, the flashiest disco in town is **Bacocho**, in the neighborhood of the same name, where a sometimes-stylish crowd of expatriate Americans and affluent Mexicans pays a $10 cover charge to dance the night away.

PUERTO ANGEL

Situated on a pretty little bay about an hour's drive south and east of Puerto Escondido (the trip involves one clearly marked turn), Puerto Angel is the kind of place where everybody knows their neighbors' business and visitors are welcomed cordially, if not enthusiastically. Long a favorite destination of globe-trotting budget travellers, in recent years this small fishing village has also begun to attract a growing number of well-heeled tourists. Even with the money that has poured into Huatulco and, to a lesser extent, Puerto Escondido, however, the region around Puerto Angel remains one of the poorest in Oaxaca. Adequate health care and public schooling are unavailable to most of its residents, while sewage systems and paved roads are virtually nonexistent.

As a result, the tourist "scene" here still rates two or three speeds slower than laid back, with accommodations ranging from simple and straightforward to rustic and communal. Daytime activities are pretty much limited to strolling around town, spending a few idle hours at a palapa-covered restaurant, hiring a *panga* for a few hours of fishing, or heading out to Playa Zipolite, that rare thing in Catholic Mexico—a beach where nudity is tolerated. For those looking to spend a night or two, there is one exceptional *posada* in town, in addition to a couple of barely adequate hotels and any number of modest guest houses with basic rooms (bed, fan, cold-water shower) for rent. After that, you're on your own.

The town climbs a series of rumpled foothills at the point where curvy Highway 175, here called Avenida Principal, meets the Pacific. (Highway 200, the coast road, is approximately 11 km/7 miles north of town via Highway 175.) The town pier and a small navy base dominate **Playa Principal**, the uninviting beach at the end of the road. From here you'll want to follow bumpy Boulevard Virgilio Uribe (don't bother looking for street signs) around the west end of the bay in the direction of Zipolite. Most of the businesses and guest houses in town are found on the hillsides or side streets to your right.

A few minutes' drive on Virgilio Uribe will bring you to a fork in the road. The right branch leads to Zipolite (see below). The left branch continues around the bay to the town cemetery and, just beyond it, **Playa Panteón**, the safest and most popular swimming beach in town. The two or three palapa-style restaurants on the beach here are more or less interchangeable, and can be relied on to produce tasty grilled seafood and poultry dishes. They're also your best bet for a meal in Puerto Angel as long as the prevailing breeze isn't carrying the aroma of untreated sewage.

Continuing up and over the hill in the same direction (follow the signs to the Hotel Angel del Mar), you'll come to what appears to be the end of the road. The cobblestoned drive branching off to the left climbs another steep hill to the Angel del Mar, a splendidly situated hotel fallen on hard times, while the sandy road to the right leads to Puerto Angel's best accommodation, the ▶ **Posada Cañon Devata**. Owned and operated by Mateo López and his American wife, Suzanne, the *posada* has ten rooms spread out among several buildings dotting the slopes of a lushly forested arroyo. Each room is unique in terms of size and decoration, and all have paintings by the multi-talented Mateo. Suzanne and Mateo's commitment to sixties-style communitarian values is evident throughout: The secluded complex has an open-air dining room where breakfast and a very reasonably priced set-menu dinner are served family-style; a small ecumenical chapel for private meditation; and a modest gift shop featuring locally made handicrafts and Mateo's paintings. It all makes for a delightful getaway—and a popular one at that. The Posada Cañon Devata is closed for the months of May and June and is usually booked solid the rest of the year.

PLAYA ZIPOLITE

Backtracking toward Playa Panteón and the right branch of the fork, you'll see a sign pointing the way to Zipolite. If you don't have a car, spend a couple of dollars for a taxi; the little community of Zipolite is about 4 km (2½ miles) west of town, and seems double that when you walk it in Puerto Angel's steamy heat. If you do have a car, prepare yourself for a bumpy ride. Where the unpaved road comes to a T you can turn left and, for a few dollars, leave your car with one of the local families; there are also a couple of very informal palapa-style restaurants at this end of the beach. Or you can turn right, following the road around an empty field and past a long string of still more palapa-style restaurants to a magnificent stand of palms, a spot that appeals to backpackers and travellers in camper-vans. Just remember: Falling coconuts can leave nasty dents in automobiles—and heads.

The beach here is a long stretch of coarse-grained sand backed by rustic palapas where you can pick up a snack and rent a hammock for the night. It's also a place where bathing suits are shucked with aplomb and strolling vendors go about their business unperturbed. Over the years Zipolite's cheap, no-frills digs and anything-goes atmosphere have made it the toast of budget travellers the world over. In fact, if not for the music, which has changed with the times, you might think the Summer of Love had never ended. Except that these days the peace-and-love attitudes of many Zipolite devotees seem tinged with a hint of desperation. Chalk it up to the lean-and-mean nineties, if you want; just don't leave your valuables unattended, and think twice before deciding to spend the night. One final caution: Swimming conditions here range from tricky to treacherous; even standing in waist-deep water you'll feel the tug and pull of enormous sheets of water. It's okay for cooling off, but you'll probably want to keep your feet firmly on the bottom.

HUATULCO

By the time its nine bays and 23 miles of coastline are fully developed early in the next century, Huatulco is expected to have a population in excess of half a million people, with enough hotel rooms to accommodate more than two million visitors annually. At the same time, tougher zoning regulations will curtail the kind of haphazard development that has characterized other Fonatur projects. In fact, more than half the acreage here will be left in its natural state in order to preserve the area's distinctive flora and fauna. Still, when all the concrete has been poured and the last nail pounded, Huatulco, like Cancún and Ixtapa before it, will personify the term "hotel culture."

All that lies in the future. For the moment, Huatulco (officially known as the **Bahías de Huatulco**) is an undeniably scenic but still somewhat limited and spread-out resort destination. Everywhere you look condominiums, additional commercial space, and new roads are under construction, but unless you've rented a car or are prepared to drop a few dollars on excursions, you're likely to find yourself running out of things to do after three or four days. This will change, of course, but for now most of the commercial activity and recreational opportunities are concentrated in or around three distinct locations: beautiful scallop-shaped **Bahía de Tangolunda**, at the eastern end of the resort zone; **Santa Cruz Huatulco**, the fishing village a few miles to the west that initially attracted Fonatur's attention; and **La Crucecita**, where the government initially relocated local people whose land had been expropriated for the Bahías de Huatulco project, and today developing an appealing identity of its own.

BAHIA DE TANGOLUNDA

The decision to site the first of Huatulco's luxury hotels on beautiful Tangolunda Bay was made early in the resort's planning stages. With its craggy outcroppings, golden-sand beaches, and jungle-covered backdrop, Tangolunda dramatically fuses the wild and the sublime, its raw beauty tamed yet somehow magnified by man's additions to the landscape.

Staying on Bahía de Tangolunda

Club Med opened its 500-plus-room ▶ **Club Med–Huatulco** in 1987, years before there was much of anything else here, and has watched as other big chains such as ITT/Sheraton and Holiday Inn followed its lead. This particular outpost of Club Med offers casita-style lodgings in low-rise buildings perched above the pounding Pacific. Each room has two double beds, a private bathroom with shower, and a terrace with ocean views; ingenious sliding partitions that allow for greater privacy are optional. Four restaurants, a dozen tennis courts, four different beaches, and three swimming pools are among the facilities scattered around this sprawling complex; free jitney service gets you from one end to the other. The major attraction for Club Med guests is sports, in this case water sports. Swimming, windsurfing, snorkeling, sailing, and fishing are offered along with a variety of motorized and self-propelled contraptions; club-owned boats also take guests to secluded, almost surreally beautiful beaches for picnics and other fun. And golfers are only five minutes by taxi from Huatulco's championship course (see below).

Located a couple of hundred yards to the east, the ▶ **Sheraton Huatulco** is a handsome example of the "coastal" architectural style that Fonatur has mandated for Huatulco. Rooms here are large and breezily attractive, if somewhat short on charm, with all the comforts you expect of a five-star hotel plopped down in the wilds of Oaxaca, including private balconies or terraces, color cable TV, servi-bars, and 24-hour room service. There are, in addition, a number of bars and restaurants in the hotel, including the wood-trimmed, candlelit **Casa Real**, where the set menu featuring different international cuisines changes nightly, and an expensive cafeteria that specializes in regional buffets. The Sheraton has a lively pool area, four tennis courts, an excellent water-sports center, in-house travel and car-rental agencies, and a couple of good boutiques. If you're planning a visit during the peak holiday periods (Christmas and Easter), you'll want to book six months in advance; July and August, when Mexican families head for the beach, are less crowded but still busy.

The buff-colored, red-roofed ▶ **Royal Maeva**, next door to the Sheraton, resembles its neighbor but, like Club Med, has an all-inclusive policy. All rooms come with private terrace or balcony, servi-bar, color cable TV, and 24-hour

room service. With three restaurants, four bars, a nightclub/
discotheque, tennis courts, a fitness center, a complete
water-sports center, and bilingual hosts to help keep things
lively, the Maeva offers the spirited atmosphere of Club Med
in plush, Sheraton-like surroundings.

The newest luxury hotel in Huatulco is the ▶ Holiday Inn
Crowne Plaza Resort, a series of two- and three-story buildings cascading down a steep hillside into lush gardens. The
hotel consists of 135 suites divided into three categories:
junior, executive, and master (the last with Jacuzzis). All
suites have two double beds, a private bathroom with tub/
shower, and a terrace with ocean views. Although the property is not on the beach, it does have a beach club for guests
across the street next to the Sheraton. Amenities within the
hotel include two restaurants, two pools (one on the
rooftop), a tennis court, a travel agency, and boutiques. Free
transportation is provided by cars and golf carts for getting
from one end of the complex to the other.

The modest reception area for the ▶ Club Plaza Huatulco,
the only alternative to the big hotels on Bahía de Tangolunda,
is tucked away on the ground floor of the Plaza Huatulco
complex, directly opposite the Sheraton and Maeva. The 13
large, tastefully decorated suites here have their own terraces
(a few with Jacuzzis), kitchenettes, marble-tiled bathrooms,
purified water taps, color satellite TV, and air-conditioning.
And while its public areas are limited to the reception area
and a small patio out back with a hot tub–sized swimming
pool, no one seems to mind. In fact, if you overlook the
shortage of decent views and a small problem with noise on
the terraces—the choice terraces either look out on the neon
palm trees of the discotheque next door or the perpetually
noisy air-conditioning plant of the Sheraton across the way—
the Club Plaza just might qualify as the best value in Huatulco.

Dining, Shopping, and Nightlife on
Bahía de Tangolunda

Although there's no denying the natural beauty of Bahía de
Tangolunda or the quality of the accommodations here,
visitors are likely to be a little disappointed by the dining
and shopping options available outside its hotels. For whatever reason, restaurateurs and boutique owners have been
slow to move into Tangolunda's two colonial-style commercial complexes, while a couple of those that have, including
Yalalag, the fine handicrafts boutique from Oaxaca City, have
thrown in the towel after a year or so. Still, there are a
number of decent options to explore—with more in La
Crucecita (see below)—for those willing to make the effort.

Visitors who wander over to the **Plaza Huatulco**, opposite the Sheraton and Maeva, will find a couple of small convenience stores; Solarium and O'Healey's, two of the newest restaurants in Huatulco; and **Sebastian**, silver specialists from Taxco whose designs are beautiful and whose prices put the shops in Santa Cruz and La Crucecita to shame. (Sebastian also has shops in Cancún and Taxco.) **Solarium**, owned by the same Puebla man responsible for the Club Plaza Huatulco (see above), specializes in fresh seafood served outside under a handsome wood-timbered ceiling. As of this writing, it's also the only place in the Tangolunda area that serves a reasonably priced breakfast. **O'Healey's**, which took over the pretty space formerly occupied by Don Wilo (now in La Crucecita), is owned by Juan Ruíz Healey, a well-known news personality in Mexico City, and offers a limited menu of chicken, beef, and pork dishes, along with live entertainment on occasion.

A staircase between these two restaurants leads upstairs to **Savage**, the only disco open to the general public at this end of the resort area. The $5 cover charge goes up to $13 when there's a live show, but the place is still dead until the nightly entertainment at the Maeva ends (about 11:30 P.M.), at which point it usually fills with a young, well-dressed crowd and stays hopping until the early hours of the morning.

The dining-out options improve somewhat in the **Punta Tangolunda** complex, located across the street a short stroll from the Sheraton. At the far end of the complex, **La Pampa Argentina** offers grilled South American beef served hot on a brazier under airy *portales*. It's a good gimmick, but the glowing brazier tends to raise the already-warm temperature at your table. The **Misión Fa-Sol** (closed during the off-season) and **Cavendish** are located back to back on either side of the complex a few steps up from La Pampa. The former specializes in seafood with a Spanish accent, while the latter is a quiet and fairly expensive establishment serving seafood and Continental cuisine. Both offer comfortable seating outside and attentive service.

The selection of shops is also better here, with a couple of boutiques proffering good beachwear and a branch of **Mic-Mac**, which sells unusual ceramics, hand-embroidered dresses and blouses, wall hangings, and brass ornaments. The care with which each piece is selected is revealed by the high quality of the merchandise.

Golf

The gently rolling and well-maintained **Campo de Golf Tangolunda** sprawls over both sides of Boulevard Benito

Juárez, the main road winding through the Tangolunda hotel zone. (The clubhouse is a very long walk or five-minute cab ride from the lobbies of the big hotels.) Now with 18 holes open for play, the course measures 6,400 yards from the white tees and 6,850 from the blue. Greens fees are $35, with a cart costing an additional $35. Caddies, when they're available, charge a very reasonable $15, and a set of rental clubs goes for $20. You'll have to pay with cash, however; the golf club does not accept credit cards. Tel: 1-0059.

BAHIA DE SANTA CRUZ

According to local legend the first Spaniards to explore the Costa Oaxaqueña in the 16th century erected a wooden cross on the beach here that no amount of effort by the natives could destroy. Eventually, after Spaniard and Indian alike had accepted it as a miracle, the cross was removed and broken up into six pieces, with one piece ending up in the possession of the Vatican and the other remaining in the local parish church in Santa María Huatulco, where it became an object of veneration. (The village of Santa María Huatulco, 34 km/21 miles west of the Bahías de Huatulco, is also where city hall and other municipal offices are located.)

Today the fishing village of **Santa Cruz Huatulco**, located a few miles west of the Tangolunda area on the Bay of the Sacred Cross, has been transformed into a small but bustling commercial district with four banks, a busy marina, a couple of decent hotels, a string of beachside restaurants, and a lovely zócalo. While visitors will find it merits an afternoon, its appeal as a destination in its own right is pretty much limited to budget travellers.

Although the colonial-style ► **Castillo Huatulco**, opposite the marina and a souvenir market, presents a charming exterior to the world, it's really just a motor inn in disguise. The public areas, especially the pretty pool with swim-up bar, are nicer than the rooms, which tend to be small and Spartan in decor, with tiny balconies, one-channel satellite TV, and bargain-basement linens. Then again, at about half what a Tangolunda room goes for, they can look pretty good. Throw in the usual four-star amenities, including tennis court, gym, and room service, and the Castillo Huatulco might pass muster for a night or two.

The two-story ► **Posada Binniguenda**, a few blocks down the street, is where everyone with business in Santa Cruz seems to stay. While the rather gloomy air-conditioned rooms won't win any interior-design awards, the Binniguenda does have a lovely patio with a fountain, a pretty swimming pool area, and a lively restaurant and bar. Guests at both the Binniguenda and the Castillo Huatulco have access to the no-frills beach at Bahía de Chahue (see below), with free shuttle transportation provided by the hotel.

Magic Circus, the other disco in Huatulco frequented by tourists, is located two blocks from the Posada Binniguenda; head for the water and look for the two-story building with the colorful mural painted on one of its exterior walls. No one is likely to mistake its small dance floor and sound-and-light effects for big-time flash, but the crowd here seems to like it that way, and the $10 cover charge is modest enough to allow the curious to decide for themselves.

The small Santa Cruz **marina**, opposite the Castillo Huatulco, is usually jammed with covered *lanchas* that take passengers on excursions to the different bays (see below). This is an option favored by the locals, and is often the most fun way to see the spectacular coastline in these parts. Prices are controlled by a local collective, and range from $10 to $30 per person, depending on the number of bays visited. During the rainy season, June through September, the seas can get choppy; visitors prone to seasickness will want to take precautions.

There are several seafood restaurants lining the tiny beach on the other side of the marina breakwater. One of them, the **Restaurant Francis**, a thatched-roof affair with a breezy view of the bay, is run by Ramon Gil, a restaurateur from Guerrero, who usually puts out a tub full of live clams for customers who like them au naturel. (The normal practice here is to sprinkle them with lime juice, salt, and chile sauce before sliding them down the hatch.) At lunchtime, the beach area in front of these restaurants comes alive with peddlers and food vendors. Often you'll see little girls dressed in their Sunday best selling such local delicacies as iguana-tail tamales and armadillo or snake tacos. (The girls' mothers will have made them fresh that morning.)

After lunch you might want to spend an hour or two poking around the nearby **Mercado de Artesanías**, installed in charmless concrete-and-metal stalls next to Santa Cruz Huatulco's lovely zócalo. Oaxacan and Guatemalan handicrafts predominate, but the selection is limited and prices are higher here than in Puerto Escondido.

LA CRUCECITA

A chaotic and sometimes intimidating place for visitors just a few years ago, La Crucecita (The Little Cross) today is a beehive of commercial activity with a pretty zócalo and, facing it, a handful of busy bars and restaurants offering choice seats on an always lively scene. (From the Tangolunda hotel zone, follow Boulevard Benito Juárez to the traffic circle at the head of Santa Cruz's main drag; La Crucecita is another 2 km/1¼ miles up and over the hill to your right. A more direct route between the two areas was completed in time for Holy Week visitors in April 1993. In addition, a new four-lane highway linking La Crucecita with the airport is scheduled for completion in the latter half of 1993.)

Visitors might want to start their exploration of La Crucecita with the obiligatory stop at the Anderson group's ½ **Carlos 'n' Charlie's**, tucked away in a modest storefront at the corner of Carrizal and Flamboyan, two blocks south of the zócalo. The usual menu (chicken, beef, and pork) and high jinks prevail here, although the atmosphere seems to be less fevered than at other outposts of the chain. The patio out back is an especially relaxing place to enjoy a late afternoon margarita. Tel: 7-0005.

On the zócalo itself (also called Plaza Principal), the **Cactus Bar & Grill** has added sushi to what was already one of the more ambitious menus in the area. If you prefer your seafood cooked, try the *camaron à la Mechin* (giant shrimp grilled in a sauce of olive, onion, garlic, pimento, and jalapeño); the *filete à la Farrah* (red snapper sautéed in a white wine-and-tomato sauce); or always tasty langosta. Tel: 7-0648.

Don Wilo, on the opposite side of the plaza, is a homegrown three-story affair with a sometimes-raucous bar on the top floor, a restaurant serving seafood and a few regional dishes on the middle floor, and a pizzeria on the ground floor. The inviting **Palma Real**, at the corner of Calles Gardenia and Ocotillo, entices with its green-and-white decor and shady *portales,* and serves up unspectacular though reasonably priced Mexican specialties.

For the best bargain in town, walk one street over to Bugambilias and head toward the plaza, where **El Fogon**, a barbeque chicken place on the corner, does a brisk takeout business serving half a broiled chicken with a stack of fresh tortillas (less than $4).

Though it has been upgraded in the last year or so, shoppers are likely to be disappointed by the merchandise in La Crucecita, which still runs to tee-shirts and bikinis. Far more satisfying is the **Mercado 3 de Mayo**, on Calle Guamuchil half a block from the plaza, with bright red tomatoes, saucy yellow mangoes, and pungent burgundy-colored chiles stacked in neat piles lining narrrow aisles. The state of Oaxaca is well known for its chocolate, earthen-baked corn tortillas (called *totopos*), and string cheese, which is sold as *queso Oaxaca* outside the state but is called *quesillo* here.

Oaxaca markets are also famous for their *herberas,* female herb sellers who seem to have a remedy for any ailment, even the evil eye. The Mercado 3 de Mayo usually has a few *herberas* on hand, but they don't appear regularly. If you'd like to get a closer look at these folk remedies and traditions, your best bet is to head for the market in Pochutla, just north of Puerto Angel on Highway 175, which has built a reputation on the potency of its herbs.

THE BAYS

No visitor to Huatulco should leave without first spending a day exploring some of its less developed bays and beaches. In addition to Tangolunda and Santa Cruz, three others are now accessible to visitors with cars: **Conejos**, due east of Tangolunda and lately the site of frenzied upmarket condominium development; **Chahue**, a wide crescent of sand situated between Tangolunda and Santa Cruz; and **San Agustín**, the westernmost and least accessible of the bays, only because the long unpaved road leading into it from Highway 200 becomes a quagmire in spots during the rainy season. (As a precaution to possible mechanical mishaps, it's probably a good idea to leave word with the front desk of your hotel before making a trip to San Agustín.) Conejos is for sightseeing only: Access to the small beach is restricted, and the surf much too rough for swimming. Chahue also catches its share of rough surf, though at times it's a wonderful swimming beach. San Agustín, the best of the three for swimming, has a modest collection of inexpensive palapa-style restaurants where you can grab a tasty lunch of grilled fish or shrimp.

For the moment the other bays and beaches in Huatulco can only be reached by water taxi, of which there are no shortage. Spots such as **La Entrega**, where a coral reef in shallow water is protected as a national park; **El Maguey**, where the warm, jade-colored water works like a tonic on frayed nerves and stressed-out psyches; and all-but-deserted **El Organo** are the essence of Huatulco. Boats depart from and return to the beach in front of the Sheraton daily, with the cost of such an excursion starting at $20 per person. Or you can head over to the **Santa Cruz marina**, opposite the Castillo Huatulco, where a local cooperative runs *lanchas* to the same beaches, usually for a few dollars less per person. Regardless of the option you choose, it will be a day you long remember. Don't forget to bring extra pesos to pay for snorkel equipment and a fresh seafood lunch at a beachside restaurant, as well as a hat and sunscreen: You'll be out for the better part of the day, and if you don't already know it you'll soon realize that the sun this far south can be hazardous to your health.

Excursions from
the Oaxaca Resorts

The most common excursion from any of these resorts is a trip to one of its sister resorts. Puerto Escondido is 370 km (229 miles) east of Acapulco via Highway 200. The turnoff for Puerto Angel (Highway 175) is another 74 km (46 miles) east of Puerto Escondido via the same highway, most of it straight and flat. Huatulco is 48 km (30 miles) east of Puerto Angel, again via Highway 200, most of it twisting and hilly.

Manialtepec and Chacahua

Day trips to Manialtepec and the national park at Chacahua are especially popular with travellers staying in Puerto Escondido. Located 15 minutes west of town via Highway 200, Manialtepec, a glassy lagoon encircled by mangroves, is a favorite nesting and feeding ground for pelicans, herons, egrets, ibis, and the occasional spoonbill and parrot. A couple of local families run two- to three-hour tours of the lagoon, which usually include a stop at the narrow barrier beach protecting its fertile waters from the saltier environment of the Pacific.

At Chacahua, a much larger lagoon complex some 74 km (46 miles) west of Escondido in the heart of the Oaxacan jungle, you're likely to see the same kind of birdlife as well as storks, flamingos, and the occasional alligator. Although *lanchas* are for hire at the little village here (where you can also grab a bite to eat at an open-air restaurant), most visitors choose to explore Chacahua's three lagoons with a tour. The best are run by Michael Malone and his wife, Joan Walker, from December through March under the name **Hidden Voyages Ecotours.** For further information about their tours—of which there are a variety, ranging in price from $35 to $45 per person—contact Turismo Rodimar, Pérez Gasga 905, Puerto Escondido, Oaxaca 71980; Tel: (958) 2-0734 or 0737. Another travel agency in town offering trips to Manialtepec and Chacahua is **Viajes y Excursiones García Rendon,** in the lobby of the Best Western Posada Real, Avenida Benito Juárez, Puerto Escondido, Oaxaca 71980; Tel: (958) 2-0290, 0133, or 0394; Fax: (958) 2-0458.

Done as day trips from Huatulco, Manialtepec and, especially, Chacahua, are long, tedious affairs involving too much time on the bus and not enough time viewing wildlife. Some outfits have offered them in the past, although their numbers are dwindling. Interested parties might try **Viajes y Excursiones García Rendon**, Manzana 31, La Crucecita, Santa Cruz Huatulco, Oaxaca 70900 (Tel: 958/4-0025; Fax: 958/4-0125); or **TurHuatulco**, in the lobby of the Hotel Flamboyant, Calle Gardenia at the corner of Tamarindo, La Crucecita, Bahías de Huatulco, Oaxaca 70989 (Tel: 958/7-0105 or 0113; Fax: 958/7-0121). Either outfit also will be happy to arrange a tour of the bays, a horseback tour of the Huatulco countryside, or deep-sea-fishing excursions.

Oaxaca City and Environs

Day and overnight trips to Oaxaca City—one of Mexico's most colorful Indian centers and a serenely beautiful colonial city in its own right—as well as the splendid archaeological ruins at **Monte Albán** and **Mitla** can be arranged through a travel agent. From Puerto Escondido and Puerto Angel, the 250-km (155-mile) trip can be made by car or bus (the latter a long, often hair-raising ordeal) via Pochutla and Highway 175, a truly spectacular two-lane road that snakes through the cloud forests of the Sierra Madre del Sur. (Highway 131, the direct road from Puerto Escondido, is unpaved for much of its length and prone to washouts and rock slides; avoid it if possible.) From Huatulco, Highway 200 to Highway 190, the old Pan-American Highway, is a longer (by about an hour) but also much less nerve-wracking route than either of the other two. Regardless of the route and your departure point, however, try to get an early start, especially during the rainy season. The coastal mountains attract moisture like a sponge; should you be on the road when the thunderheads let loose, you'll think you're driving through an automated car wash, with one critical difference: Car washes have guardrails.

For many people, flying from either Puerto Escondido or Huatulco will prove to be the more sensible option. Daily service to and from Puerto Escondido is handled by **Aeromorelos** (Tel: 958/2-0789 or 0734). The 40-seat propjet leaves Escondido at 10:35 A.M. and arrives in Oaxaca City an hour later, with the one-way fare approximately $62. **Aviacsa** (Tel: 958/2-0115 or 0150) also flies to Oaxaca City from Puerto Escondido, departing at 8:45 A.M. on Fridays and 4:35 P.M. on Sundays and arriving an hour and 15 minutes later; their one-way fare is also $62. **Aero Vega** (Tel: 958/2-0151) sends a nine-seater over the mountains every day at 7:30 A.M. and again at 9:30 A.M. if there are enough passengers waiting; the one-way fare is $55.

GETTING AROUND

International air service into Puerto Escondido and Huatulco (Puerto Angel does not have an airport) is infrequent at best, with most flights routed through Mexico City (Mexicana and Aeroméxico are the main carriers) or Oaxaca City (see the Oaxaca City chapter); the flying time in either case is just under an hour. There are, in addition, charter flights from Dallas–Fort Worth, with feeder service from cities around the United States for those staying at the Club Med in Huatulco. For further information, Tel: (800) CLUB-MED.

Because the daily plane *from* Mexico City to Puerto Escondido turns around and, an hour later, becomes the daily plane *to* Mexico City, the scene at the Escondido airport usually borders on mass confusion. VW minibuses (*colectivos*) are an inexpensive and popular form of transportation to the various hotels around town but tend to fill up as fast as they unload. A taxi is a better option and will only cost a couple of dollars.

The fare from the Huatulco airport to the hotel zone, a 20-minute drive, is $7.50. Cab fare between Huatulco and Puerto Escondido starts at $80, with drivers willing to carry up to four passengers; the fare from either to Puerto Angel is about half that. Taxis also can be hired by the hour for sightseeing excursions of the wild and beautiful coast in this region, but some ability to communicate in Spanish is recommended.

If you decide to rent a car—always an expensive proposition in Mexico, but the best way to get around—you can arrange to have it waiting at either airport, thereby avoiding the scramble for a cab or *colectivo* altogether. Budget and Hertz have desks at the Puerto Escondido and Huatulco airports, as well as downtown (though in the case of Huatulco, both outfits require confirmed plane reservations). Budget also has offices in the Posada Real hotel in Escondido and at La Crucecita and Bahía de Tangolunda in Huatulco. The Sheraton and Maeva in Huatulco also have car-rental desks, and both run shuttles to and from the airport, as does the Santa Fé in Puerto Escondido, with advance notice.

—*Mitchell Nauffts and Patricia Alisau*

ACCOMMODATIONS REFERENCE

The rate ranges given below are projections *for December 1993 through Easter 1994. Unless otherwise indicated, rates are for double rooms, double occupancy; the 10 percent VAT has been added. As rates are subject to change, it's a good idea to double-check before booking. The Oaxaca Resorts are in the central standard time zone; the telephone area code is 958.*

Puerto Escondido

▶ **Aldea del Bazar.** Boulevard Benito Juárez s/n, Fracc. Bacocho, **Puerto Escondido**, Oaxaca 71980. Tel and Fax: 2-0508. $90.

▶ **Best Western Posada Real.** Boulevard Benito Juárez, Lote 11, Fracc. Bacocho, **Puerto Escondido**, Oaxaca 71980. Tel: 2-0185; Fax: 2-0192; in the U.S. and Canada, Tel: (800) 528-1234. $94–$105.

▶ **Hotel Las Palmas.** Avenida Alfonso Pérez Gasga s/n, **Puerto Escondido**, Oaxaca 71980. Tel: 2-0230 or 0303. $44.

▶ **Hotel Santa Fé.** Calle del Morro, **Puerto Escondido**, Oaxaca 71980. Tel: 2-0170 or 0266; Fax: 2-0260. $70–$86.

▶ **Rincón del Pacífico.** Avenida Alfonso Pérez Gasga 100, **Puerto Escondido**, Oaxaca 71980. Tel: 2-0056 or 0193; Fax: 2-0101. $33.

Puerto Angel

▶ **Posada Cañon Devata.** C/o Mateo and Suzanne López, P.O. Box 74, **Pochutla**, Oaxaca 70900. No phone. Single or double, $20; bungalow, $30.

Huatulco

▶ **Castillo Huatulco.** P.O. Box 354, Boulevard Santa Cruz s/n, **Bahía de Santa Cruz**, Oaxaca 70989. Tel: 7-0051; Fax: 7-0131. $91–$127.

▶ **Club Plaza Huatulco.** Lote 23, **Bahía de Tangolunda**, Oaxaca 70989. Tel: 1-0027 or 0035; Fax: 1-0035. $149 (no additional charge for up to two children).

▶ **Club Med–Huatulco.** P.O. Box 154, **Bahía de Tangolunda**, Oaxaca 70989. Tel: 1-0033; Fax: 1-0101; in the U.S. and Canada, Tel: (800) CLUB-MED. Rates upon request.

▶ **Holiday Inn Crowne Plaza Resort.** Boulevard Benito Juárez 8, **Bahía de Tangolunda**, Oaxaca 70989. Tel: 1-0044; Fax: 1-0221; in the U.S. and Canada, Tel: (800) HOLIDAY. Junior suite, $149; executive suite, $187; master suite, $209.

▶ **Posada Binniguenda.** P.O. Box 44, Boulevard Santa Cruz s/n, **Bahía de Santa Cruz**, Oaxaca 70989. Tel: 7-0077; Fax: 7-0284; in the U.S. and Canada, Tel: (800) 336-5454. $90.

▶ **Royal Maeva.** P.O. Box 227, Boulevard Benito Juárez s/n, **Bahías de Huatulco**, Oaxaca 70989. Tel: 1-0000; Fax: 1-0220; in the U.S. and Canada, Tel: (800) 336-5454. $175 (all-inclusive).

▶ **Sheraton Huatulco.** Boulevard Benito Juárez s/n, **Bahías de Huatulco**, Oaxaca 70989. Tel: 1-0055, 0005, 0039, or 0052; Fax: 1-0113; in the U.S. and Canada, Tel: (800) 325-3535. $149–$165.

THE GULF COAST

THE STATES OF VERACRUZ AND TABASCO

By Robert Cummings

The coastal lowlands of Veracruz and Tabasco are wedged between the Bahía de Campeche (part of the Gulf of Mexico) and some of Mexico's steepest mountains. It is verdant, flower-filled country, with vanilla and coffee plantations perched on the low shoulders of mountains to the northwest, steamy rubber country to the southeast—the center of the first great Mesoamerican civilization, the so-called Olmec, which in the language of the Aztecs meant "the people of rubber"—and cattle ranches hacked out of the jungle in between.

The people of the region, with the exception of a pocket of Totonac Indians in northern Veracruz, share a number of qualities that set them apart from highland Mexicans as well as from the people of Chiapas and the Yucatán. The Caribbean influence is strong here, the impact of African cultures over the centuries more noticeable than in other parts of the country. Writers of popular songs delight in the area. *Veracruzanos* are reputed to be languorous but passionate, tolerant but fierce; these extremes often seem to resonate in the region's music, while its traditional dances can shift from courtliness to sudden abandon. It is also rumored elsewhere in Mexico that people from the Gulf Coast region are given to crimes of passion—an unsubstantiated rumor but one that makes them appear both dangerous and attractive. Katherine Anne Porter seemed to accept the notion of the archetypal *veracruzano* when she wrote, "They carry on their lives of alternate violence and lethargy with a pleasurable contempt for outside opinion." While she may have overstated the case, the people of the region do impress the visitor with their confidence and self-assurance.

Foreign travellers have never come to the Gulf Coast in great numbers, but Mexican vacationers, searching for bargains, beaches, and the exotic, swarm to the Gulf, where they quickly notice the regional differences. The coast dwellers are darker complexioned, they drink rum instead of tequila, and their speech is lisping and clipped. And where does that odd music come from?

MAJOR INTEREST

City of Veracruz
Lively zócalo scene
Fortress-prison of San Juan de Ulúa
Beaches
Fiestas

North of Veracruz
Mountain town of Jalapa
Ruins at Zempoala and El Tajín
Sportsfishing and scuba diving at Tuxpan

South of Veracruz
Lago de Catemaco scenery
Parque-Museo de La Venta in Villahermosa (Olmec
    sculpture)
Regional birds and lush vegetation

The historic port city of Veracruz, on the coast east of Mexico City, is the primary gateway for the Gulf Coast region. From Veracruz we consider the coast north as far as Tuxpan, and then south, including Lago de Catemaco, as far as the Villahermosa area in the state of Tabasco. Villahermosa is also the jumping-off point for the Palenque archaeological site and San Cristóbal de las Casas, the capital of the state of Chiapas (for both of which see the Mayan Mexico chapter).

You should be forewarned that the climate in this part of Mexico is intensely hot from May through September. In addition, in August the *nortes,* or "northers," common to the hemisphere arrive with little warning and drench the entire region, bending trees and sending the temperature plummeting in the process. Fine weather usually follows in the wake of a *norte.*

The best time to visit is from November through March. Even winter doesn't necessarily bring better weather, however—one reason the Gulf Coast's beach resorts have been eclipsed by their younger Pacific and Caribbean cousins.

THE CITY OF VERACRUZ

Veracruz, the most piquant of Mexico's cities as well as the most European of its ports, was nicknamed "Little Havana" in the days before Cuba turned forbidding. Actually, Veracruz was never so freewheeling, although it has always been a sailor's haven. To quote Katherine Anne Porter again, who had a bad time in Veracruz in her youth: "It is in fact to the passing eye a typical port town, cynical by nature, shameless by experience, hardened to showing its seamiest side to strangers."

In those days, maybe. Today, not really. Veracruz has been scrubbed up a lot in the last decade, enhancing its charm without lessening its zest. It is far more high-spirited than bawdy, and still a city flirtatious in every way.

Veracruz is also a town of balconies. Wandering down any street you'll be distracted and delighted by them—long and narrow, short and obtrusive, many embellished by orange and yellow flowers that are startling in their vividness when seen against the pale-colored walls typical of the city's architecture. From these balconies the women of Veracruz call to street vendors, summon their children playing outside, or simply dry their long black hair in the sunshine.

Exploring the City

PLAZA DE ARMAS

The zócalo, also referred to as the Plaza de Armas or Plaza de la Constitución, is a vibrant public space (except in the heat of the day when it may turn languid) set off by a lacy iron bandstand, slender coconut palms, and tropical flowers so vivid they seem unreal. Most of the area is closed to vehicular traffic, the better to saunter, promenade, or, at fiestas, to dance. Arcades shelter the cafés around the edges of the plaza, and a table here is an observation point for a never-ending show, of which the spectators themselves are a major part. The zócalo in Veracruz is a crossroads not only of the city but of the Caribbean and the world beyond. At any moment you might spot a group of Russian or Norwegian sailors, or maybe the polyglot crew of some ship registered in Liberia, wandering along shady arcades as French and Italian tourists, looking chic in their new tropical outfits, stop to check their maps.

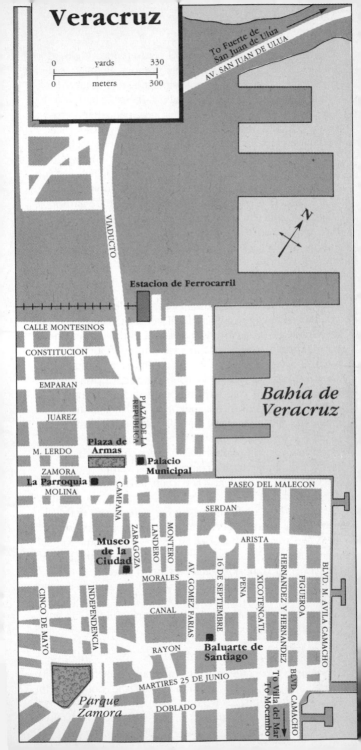

Veracruz

| 0 | yards | 330 |
| 0 | meters | 300 |

To Fuerte de San Juan de Ulúa

AV. SAN JUAN DE ULUA

VIADUCTO

N

Estacion de Ferrocarril

CALLE MONTESINOS

CONSTITUCION

EMPARAN

JUAREZ

M. LERDO

ZAMORA

La Parroquia

MOLINA

Plaza de Armas

PLAZA DE LA REPUBLICA

Palacio Municipal

Bahía de Veracruz

PASEO DEL MALECON

SERDAN

CAMPANA

ZARAGOZA

LANDERO

MONTERO

Museo de la Ciudad

MORALES

CANAL

RAYON

AV. GOMEZ FARIAS

16 DE SEPTIEMBRE

ARISTA

PENA

XICOTENCATL

HERNANDEZ Y HERNANDEZ

FIGUEROA

BLVD. M. AVILA CAMACHO

Baluarte de Santiago

CINCO DE MAYO

INDEPENDENCIA

MARTIRES 25 DE JUNIO

DOBLADO

Parque Zamora

To Villa del Mar
To Mocambo

BLVD. CAMACHO

Sidewalk Cafés

The row of cafés on Calle Miguel Lerdo (which is closed to traffic) begins with the venerable **Prendes**, the city's oldest restaurant and an ideal place to sip coffee or a bottled drink. While spending half an hour at an outside table here you can have your shoes shined, hear a marimba concert, purchase a hammock, test your strength, buy a lottery ticket, hear a recitation of patriotic poetry, admire the bunches of fantastic balloons sold by vendors in the plaza, or watch the world go by. On the other hand, if this sounds a bit overwhelming you can always retreat to the quiet of the dining room.

If Prendes, as proper as its elderly waiters are garrulous, seems too stiff, you can move down the row of cafés, taking a half step down the social ladder at every doorway. The voices gradually grow louder, the spirits flow more freely; the last watering place on the block, while not raunchy, is certainly déclassé.

Cutting back across the zócalo, circling the bandstand, and passing the vendors of gardenias and bubble-blowing pipes, you will come to the greatest local sidewalk institution of all, the **Gran Café de la Parroquia**, which faces the unpretentious parish church, now a cathedral. Here, at any hour of the day from 7:00 A.M. until 1:00 A.M., you'll find a noisy potpourri of *veracruzanos.* As patrons struggle to be heard over the din, waiters circle the café in pairs, one with a steaming pot of coffee, the other with hot milk. Spoons bang or tinkle on glasses as customers signal for milk to be added to their cups of black brew. "Coffee must be sweet, hot, and strong as love," *veracruzanos* will remind you at every chance. It is an old saying that applies to this colorful city as well.

The coffee is excellent. Then again, it has to be—many of the men who drink it here also grow it, pack it, or ship it by the ton. Others concern themselves with oil or beef deals, both major contributors to the region's prosperity. But not everyone arrives with a briefcase. Store clerks come to read their newspapers hurriedly, while students from the university gather to argue, joke, and plot their intrigues.

The Gran Café serves breakfast and snacks as well, but the coffee ritual is its chief drawing card. Endless cups of coffee and endless talk help pass the long hours until the sun goes down and the city cools off.

The Cathedral

The church across the street, La Parroquia, needs paint both inside and out, as do seemingly half the buildings in Veracruz. The salt spray from the sea only a block away has something to do with this, as do the city's torrential rains, *nortes,* and hurricanes. In a climate such as Veracruz's even the most vivid paint soon fades to a pastel color, and eventually to an indistinct gray. The church, which was dedicated in 1734, adds a softening touch of antiquity to the plaza but is not particularly interesting in itself—very few buildings in the city are. There is little in the way of art here outside of the art of living.

THE MALECON

The *malecón,* which starts two blocks east of the zócalo near a spot where crab sellers hawk their wares at the top of their lungs, is the city's long, winding shore drive. At the head of it, a long pier dotted with trashy curio shops and so-so seafood restaurants juts into the harbor. A monument nearby reminds the visitor that Veracruz was the first "European" city to be established in the Americas, as well as the site of the first democratic (European-style) assembly. For approximately $6.50 you can hop aboard a boat here for a tour of the harbor. (A trip to **Isla de Sacrificios** is worth making if you'd like to try the beach there. The island, a sandy, desolate little key, is 30 minutes by launch, and the going rate is between $6 and $10, depending on the boat. The destination itself isn't great, but the views of the city, the harbor, and the jungled coast are reason enough for going. Do not make the trip on a windy day, however.)

The pier is interesting by day, but especially romantic and colorful at night, when lovers and families go strolling, pausing to watch sidewalk artists, gape at jugglers, or listen to the ever-present troubadours.

As the *malecón* curves south it becomes Boulevard M. Avila Camacho, eventually leading to **Villa del Mar**, the most popular beach in the city and a good spot for sunning, wading, swimming, and playing games in the sand. The facilities are simple, but Villa del Mar is nevertheless inviting. There's also a public swimming pool here.

THE FORTS

There is little in the way of conventional sightseeing in Veracruz, certainly not enough to fill a day unless, in true *veracruzano* style, you spend an hour in a café before and after each attraction.

Fuerte de San Juan de Ulúa

One of the few sights in town, the fort of San Juan de Ulúa squats in the harbor like some grim, ugly curiosity. Although it looks close from the comfort of a café seat near the plaza, it's actually a long walk in the Veracruz heat. A taxi is a better idea, and it's easy enough to find one to take you back downtown once you've completed your explorations.

The castle was begun in 1528 on the island where Juan de Grijalva, the first Spaniard to land at what is now Veracruz, had come ashore a decade earlier. During the century that followed the fort did the town little good, as Veracruz became the victim of one raid after another by the likes of Drake, Hawkins, and Agromonte. The worst catastrophe occurred in 1683, when Lorencillo, a merciless buccaneer, captured the sleeping town. Its inhabitants were herded into the church and held there for four days—during which many died—while his men methodically sacked their homes.

In 1746, after other protective measures had failed, the entire town was encircled by a wall with seven gates—one of them reserved exclusively for use by the viceroy of New Spain. The illusion of security was just that, however. Although Veracruz managed to hold out for years during the War of Independence, thereby earning a measure of infamy as the last Spanish stronghold in Mexico, the seemingly impregnable gates and ramparts of San Juan de Ulúa itself fell easily to French bombardment in 1838 and were taken again by U.S. troops in 1846. They also offered little protection when U.S. forces landed once more in 1914, capturing Veracruz and killing nearly 200 Mexicans in the process—an incident known locally as the Massacre of Veracruz. (Although *veracruzanos* are too polite to mention it to visitors from the United States, they have not forgotten.)

When it wasn't being stormed by foreign invaders, this fierce-looking but impotent dinosaur did long service as a much-dreaded prison. High tides would sweep through the lower levels, forcing prisoners to stand with seawater up to their chins; such food as was provided would be lowered to prisoners by rope through manholes on the roof. Not surprisingly, incarceration here amounted to a virtual death sentence. Even today the atmosphere is dank and heavy, and while there are fine views of the city from the fort's roofs and battlements, an hour's visit is enough for most people.

Baluarte de Santiago

A much smaller and less interesting redoubt is found in the center of town at Calles Rayón and 16 de Septiembre, about six blocks southeast of the main plaza. This fortress, dedicated to Saint James and so known as the Baluarte de Santiago, is all that remains of the old city walls and gives the visitor an idea of Spanish defenses in New Spain. The cramped museum inside is of minimal interest.

The nearby **Museo de la Ciudad**, four blocks south of the

zócalo at Zaragoza 397, is worth a short visit. The sidewalk outside the museum is inset with tiles recounting the exploits of Cortés in this region—images that were borrowed from Aztec codices. The museum itself is housed in a gracious 19th-century building, and its interior, one of the best in the city, gives a sense of what life among the wealthy of Veracruz was like a century ago. An Olmec head, not one of the greatest, is displayed downstairs along with other artifacts and relics, including a number of wonderful clay pieces from the area. Upstairs, 26 life-size wax figures sport costumes typical of Carnaval (Mardi Gras) in Veracruz. If nothing else, it's a gaudy and alluring advertisement for this raucous fiesta. The museum is open daily except Mondays, 9:30 A.M. to 6:00 P.M.

Mocambo and Boca del Río

About 9 km (5½ miles) south of the zócalo, beyond Villa del Mar and just outside the city limits, stretch the sands of Mocambo, a better beach than Villa del Mar and a well-developed resort zone: In addition to its fine hotels (see below), chair and umbrella concessions dot the beach. Food and drink, including the locally famous *coco locos*— coconuts addled with gin—are also available. The clean, freshwater pool is open to the public.

Boca del Río, a fishing village still farther south, is a community doomed to be swallowed by the encroaching city before long. In the meantime there is swimming near the mouth of the Río Jalapa, although fishing remains the chief attraction. You might also want to check out one of the rustic open-air restaurants near the river for a fresh fish dinner.

STAYING IN VERACRUZ

Veracruz is a magnet for weekend vacationers from Mexico City. The climate and beaches may not compare to those of Cancún or Acapulco, but Veracruz is closer and a whole lot cheaper. Therefore, hotel reservations are *essential* if your stay includes a weekend. While the city has enough hotel rooms for something always to be available (except during Carnaval or Holy Week), the last rooms to go are also the most depressing.

First you have to decide between the beach and the plaza areas. The best hotels at either location are about equal in comfort. On the other hand, economy is much better practiced downtown. Whatever your choice, air-conditioning is a must year-round.

Downtown

The ► **Hotel Emporio**, centrally located on the harbor, is the traditional first choice. It offers balconies with most rooms, splendid views, three swimming pools, a restaurant, and a nightclub. In addition, the management is experienced and willing to help with boat rentals, fishing information, and tours of the region. It is expensive only by the standards of downtown Veracruz.

The ► **Hotel Veracruz**, practically facing the zócalo at the corner of Independencia and Miguel Lerdo, is a comfortable, pleasingly decorated full-service hotel. In terms of both quality and price, it's a notch above the neighboring hostelries on the zócalo and, considering its location, surprisingly quiet. The hotel was built a generation ago to be the city's most modern luxury inn. Time has left it a touch old-fashioned but still very inviting.

The ► **Hotel Colonial**, right on the zócalo, is the city's best value. Newer rooms, mostly in the front, rate better than the others, but the older ones have been modernized and aren't bad. Rooms up front come with zócalo noise and music, however, while the rear section is quiet. Many rooms are equipped with refrigerators, and all are air-conditioned. The Colonial also has a sidewalk café and an indoor pool.

On the Beach

The sprawling ► **Hotel Mocambo**, with terraces that seem to wander off to the sea, is the grande dame of the beachfront inns. The hotel offers a tennis court, three swimming pools, and lovely views of the Gulf from its rooms, mostly one- and two-bedroom suites on the beach. Best of all, like the Emporio, it is expensive only by local standards.

While the ► **Playa Paraíso**, on the beach near Boca del Río, is slightly more modern and luxurious than the Mocambo, it is also less gracious in style. Suites with one and two bedrooms overlook the beach, and the views of the Gulf are memorable. A bar and restaurant that stay open until 1:00 A.M. (when there are customers) offer a touch of nightlife in this otherwise quiet neighborhood.

DINING IN VERACRUZ

The word here is seafood, of course. The best-known regional sauce, *veracruzana,* is made from tomatoes, onions, olives, capers, garlic, and mild chile peppers. Cooking with fruits and the use of banana leaves as a wrapper are also common. Although the state is an important producer of cattle, local beef is usually not to the taste of foreign visitors.

Prendes, on the zócalo, is the traditional favorite, but a look at the unsanitary kitchen is enough to discourage anyone from ordering a meal here. (It is a good place for coffee or bottled drinks, however.) Tel: (293) 1-0241. Across the street from Prendes, **Restaurant La Moneda 1946** in the Hotel Veracruz offers fresh, steaming seafood with or without the spicy sauces of Veracruz. Tel: (293) 2-2916.

La Bamba, formerly Lorencillo, at Boulevard Avila Camacho near Rayón, overlooks the harbor. There's a South Seas touch to both the decor and the menu in this casually refined spot. Lunch will cost you about $17. Tel: (293) 6-0339.

Garlic's, about 1 km (½ mile) south of La Bamba on Boulevard Avila Camacho, also seems about to sail into the bay and draws an informally stylish crowd. A seafood platter will cost about $15. Tel: (293) 5-1034.

El Pescador, Zaragoza 335, serves fresh seafood, well prepared. The walls are planked to resemble the interior of a stateroom on an old luxury liner, and a collection of flotsam—kegs, belaying pins, nets, lanterns, and so on—further enhances the atmosphere. Tel: (293) 2-5252.

You'll find an exception to the usual Veracruz seafood menu at the **Submarino Amarillo** (Yellow Submarine), Boulevard Avila Camacho at the foot of Rayón. This upscale family restaurant is modeled after a typical U.S. steak house and features tender, thickly sliced steaks (about $10)—unusual in a region that range-feeds its cattle.

La Paella, located on the zócalo at Zamora 138, attracts travelling student types who appreciate the hearty set *comida,* usually four courses, at a thrifty price (about $7).

VERACRUZ NIGHTLIFE AND FIESTAS

Veracruz seems to wake up about an hour after the sun sets. That's when the zócalo begins to pulsate, couples drift toward the *malecón,* and the sidewalk cafés come alive. More formal—and costly—entertainment is provided at the Emporio, the Mocambo, and the **Torremar**, a resort hotel located on the beach near the Mocambo.

Veracruz also boasts the most famous **Carnaval** in Mexico. While not quite on the scale of the annual celebration in New Orleans, it remains happier, safer, and cheaper. The city turns delightfully mad, the floats are glorious, and the dancing never stops. Hotel reservations must be made, paid, and confirmed months in advance. Although the last three days are the climax of the celebration in Veracruz, most visitors try to arrive a week before Ash Wednesday.

After the fireworks of Carnaval, the city rests a little during

Lent, then explodes again during Holy Week. The Easter crowds here are enormous, and accommodation arrangements likewise must be made months in advance.

NORTH FROM THE CITY OF VERACRUZ

Buses will do for point-to-point travel to major destinations along the coast north of Veracruz, but you'll need a car if you really want to explore the region, an area much visited by Mexicans but seldom seen by foreign visitors.

The coast here is dotted with small, rustic beach resorts, especially between Nautla and Tecolutla. While it ought to be interesting—and often gives that impression from the highway—it isn't. It is a fisherman's paradise, however, and various annual tournaments are a major attraction of the region. Accommodations and restaurants are uniformly simple and economical.

Jalapa

Jalapa (pronounced hah-LAH-pah, and also spelled Xalapa) is an easy day's excursion from Veracruz (via Highway 140), or can be visited en route to or from Mexico City. Poised high above the Gulf in the foothills of the Sierra Madre Oriental, some 100 km (62 miles) northwest of Veracruz, Jalapa was once the site of a thriving pre-Columbian town. But it came into its own as Veracruz became Mexico's most important port. (It's also near one of the important coffee-growing regions of the state.) With its relatively temperate location, Jalapa offered escape from the tropical fevers that plagued the lowlands around Veracruz, and eventually became the capital of the state for reasons of health. Even after the old tropical diseases were eradicated in the lowlands, Jalapa remained popular because of its comfortable climate and scenic beauty. To this day its mountain breezes promise rejuvenation to sun-struck inhabitants of, and visitors to, the coast.

Here, where the easterlies off the Gulf collide with the Sierra massif, light rainfall is frequent and persistent—a local weather phenomenon known in Spanish as *chipichipi,* for its pattering sound. The abundant moisture, good soil, and mild climate of the region are ideal for plants of all kinds, and the town, as a result, resembles nothing so much as an open-air floral conservatory where blossoms seem to

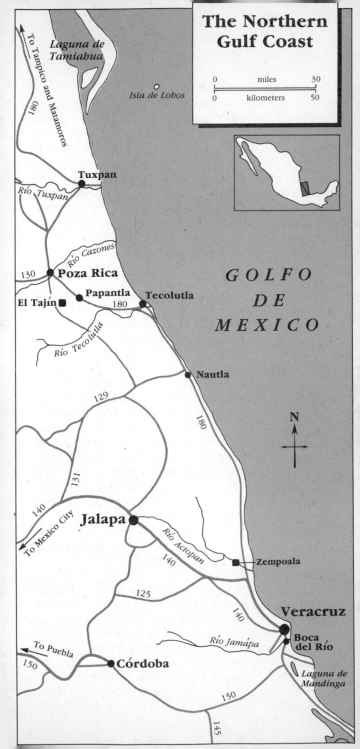

explode into vivid color. Jalapa is justly famous as the "Flower Garden of Mexico."

Museo de Antropología

It has also flowered in other ways. The University of Veracruz, in particular, has helped make Jalapa a lively cultural center famous for its theater, dance, and the best regional symphony orchestra in Mexico. In addition, the Museum of Anthropology, on the campus of the university, has a collection of pre-Hispanic art that is, according to many experts, second only to the national museum's vast collection in the D.F. Among its fascinating exhibits are a number of curious (and some think magical) wheeled "toys," smiling figurines of many different shapes and sizes, and a variety of ancient Olmec sculpture. There are, as well, three giant carved Olmec heads on the campus itself, which is located on the southwest edge of town just off the highway to Mexico City. Coming from Veracruz, stay on Highway 140, ignoring the "Centro" signs, until you come to Avenida Xalapa at the far end of town. Turn left, not quite making a U-turn, and then go straight. Like most museums in Mexico, this one is closed on Mondays.

Around Town

Although Jalapa, like Rome, was built on seven hills, it feels more like the older neighborhoods in Naples, with its sloping streets twisting sharply into hidden alleys and courtyards lined by pastel-colored houses. One of the greatest pleasures it affords visitors is simply wandering around its main plaza area and discovering such attractive spots as the lively and informal **Café Escorial** on Pasaje Enríquez. The nearby **Agora**, a center for the performing arts and favorite gathering place of students, is always busy with music, conversation, and the sale of records, tapes, and books.

The **Café Parroquia**, Zaragoza 18, is a popular eating and drinking place near the Hotel María Victoria downtown. It specializes in regional Veracruz cuisine.

Those who would like to spend more time in this delightful city should consider checking in at the very good and reasonably priced ▶ **Hotel María Victoria**, located in the center of town behind the government palace, or the older, somewhat rundown (and even more reasonably priced) ▶ **Hotel Salmones**, also centrally located on Zaragoza. Both have, in addition, clean and more than adequate restaurants. The huge ▶ **Hotel Xalapa**, downtown at the corner of Victoria and Bustamante, has air-conditioned rooms, parking, a nightclub, and a coffee shop descriptively named "24 Horas."

Zempoala

The ruins of Zempoala are only 4 km (2½ miles) west of Highway 180, and about 40 km (25 miles) north of Veracruz itself. It's an easy excursion from the city; if you have a car, a visit can be combined with a trip to Jalapa, or else as the first stop on a trip along the northern Gulf coast.

Zempoala was the first Indian city that Cortés and his men saw after their miserable bivouac on the beach of what is now Veracruz. The Spaniards were literally starving when they were befriended by Totonac warriors and led to this jungle city, and many of them initially mistook its gleaming stucco walls for silver. It was here that Cortés made his first friends among the native people, although the friendship between them would soon turn sour. But that still lay in the future when a delighted Bernal Díaz wrote in 1519: "We were struck with admiration. It looked like a garden with luxuriant vegetation." The local ruler, known to history as Chicomacatl and to the Spaniards as the "fat chief," welcomed the white men as allies against the Aztecs and presented Cortés with an obese bride—a lady whom Cortés "received with courtesy."

Today enough of the center of ancient Zempoala remains to give us an idea of pre-Hispanic life, although all but traces of its residential neighborhoods have long since vanished. It's clear, however, that it was the Totonac capital, a city of some 30,000 people who called it the "Place of Twenty Rivers" because of the many nearby tributaries of the Río Actopan, and that it rose to prominence about A.D. 1200 after Toltec warriors, advancing outward from the central highlands, pushed the Totonacs off their traditional lands and into this less fertile, less healthful region.

The base of its great temple, the **Templo Mayor**, is still in remarkably good shape. (When you multiply 13, the number of its tiers, by four, the number of its sides, you get 52, the mystical Mesoamerican number.) It was on these steps that Cortés had a violent encounter with Chicomacatl after the Totonac chief protested Cortés's decision to destroy the stone idols atop the temple base; Cortés held a blade to the chief's throat while his soldiers carried out the destruction.

The upper platform of the **Templo de las Chimenas** (Temple of the Chimneys), on the east side of the main plaza, offers the best view of the site; from here you can locate another temple and a path leading to it through a field of sugarcane. Known as the **Templo de las Caritas** (Temple of the Small Faces), its ornamental features have been badly eroded over time; still, it's worth the short walk, if only for the up-close look at a field of cane.

The whole area, shaded here and there by low, graceful palms, is open for roaming and exploration, and the small museum on the site is worth a glance.

Papantla and El Tajín

Some 185 km (115 miles) farther north, Highway 180 turns sharply inland near Tecolutla, and after about 20 km (12 miles) comes to Papantla, 225 km (140 miles) northwest of Veracruz in the heart of vanilla country. Vanilla plants are temperamental and demand endless pampering and coaxing. Until this century the world depended on the patience of Papantla's farm workers, mostly Totonac Indians, for this remarkable flavoring. Sadly, the discovery of inexpensive artificial vanilla extract all but ruined the economy of this corner of Mexico. There is still a demand for the real thing, however, so the vanilla farmers hang on.

Papantla also benefits from tourism, with visitors coming to see the archaeological zone at El Tajín, as well as to view the famous *voladores* (flying dancers). The dance, at once a religious rite and a beautiful spectacle, is performed every Sunday at noon in the zócalo. Four colorfully costumed men symbolically dressed as eagles and macaws leap from a tall pole to which they are attached by ropes tied to their ankles; 13 swooping revolutions around the pole bring them safely to the ground (the four fliers multiplied by the 13 revolutions create the sacred number 52).

STAYING IN THE AREA

Papantla is a charming little city, still countrified and quite Totonac. The zócalo is a small jewel; just up the hill from it a striking concrete relief sculpture depicting the history of El Tajín and the Totonacs adds an unusual aspect to the scene. The ► Hotel Tajín is the best of the town's several inns. You'll want to pay a little extra for air-conditioning, which is easily affordable at the hotel's modest rates. Its simple and straightforward restaurant puts out adequate meals.

Travellers bound for the archaeological site of El Tajín who prefer better accommodations can continue northwest past El Tajín to **Poza Rica** and the ► **Hotel Salinas**, which offers larger and better-appointed quarters as well as a more extensive menu. Unfortunately, this medium-size city is a raceway of traffic and, in addition to carbon monoxide, is often plagued by the smell of oil from nearby refineries. For travellers with cars it is perhaps a better idea to leave Veracruz early, take a quick look at Papantla, spend a few hours at El Tajín, and then continue on to the pleasant river town of Tuxpan (see below), which has a number of good hotels, for the night.

EL TAJIN

El Tajín, a bit west of Papantla, is the most spectacular pre-Hispanic center on the Gulf Coast and surely ranks among the finest archaeological sites in the country. Named for both lightning and the Totonac rain god, it was founded very early in the Classic era, about 200 B.C., and reached its zenith under the tutelage of Teotihuacán from A.D. 600 to 900. Toward the end of its history it came under the influence of the Toltecs, and was finally abandoned in the 13th century (considerably later than were most great Mesoamerican ceremonial centers).

Pirámide de los Nichos

The Pyramid of the Niches here is a startling sight, at once unexpected and strange. Emerging from the lush jungle that surrounds the site, it is not particularly lofty, like so many Mesoamerican pyramids, but its design nevertheless catches the imagination. Comprising six platforms, the pyramid is tiered like a wedding cake, with each of its sides covered by recessed rectangles, or niches, adding up to a total of 365—one for each day of the solar year (the exact number and their meaning are still debated). The pattern continues around the four sides of the pyramid, six layers of heavily outlined rectangles, dynamic and strong. The changing light of day constantly shifts the emphasis, creating different depths and shadows as the sun moves across the sky. Perhaps these openings are simply ornamental, a rhythmically repeated decoration—no one is really sure. What is clear is that builders throughout El Tajín's history were fascinated by niches, even though their use varied over time. One of the most common motifs was to use the niche as a frame for an important design element—the abstract serpentine image of the rain god, for example. Over the centuries, however, a significant change occurred in this approach. The early work is serene and confident; later relief sculpture, on the other hand, has a tense, even frantic quality, and sacrifice and self-mutilation begin to enter the picture.

Juego de Pelota Sur

This Toltec-inspired frenzy is most evident in the carvings from the South Ball Court, as well as in the details of a carved column now in the Tajín museum. The ball-court carvings, dating from about A.D. 1150, exhibit wild sculptural rhythms suggestive of an age of social turmoil, and feature the skeletal death god with ominous frequency. There is no established narrative in the six carved panels, nor even a prevailing theme. Some meanings are clear: Panel one illustrates human sacrifice in connection with the ball game; panel two has to do with blessed drunkenness and the native brew *pulque*; the third involves nature gods, including an eagle, and musicians playing shell instruments. Number four involves rain gods, while five and six depict initiation and consecration rites, including self-mutilation.

Tajín Chico

The complex known as New Tajin stands about 300 yards north of the main pyramid on slightly higher ground. The structures, unromantically designated "A" through "D," overlap and abut in many places, requiring careful observation to distinguish among the individual buildings. Edificio "C" is the most eye-catching, adorned as it is with niches and step frets in the manner of the main pyramid; it is a variation on the niche theme, however, and not a replica. Nearby is a ball court, one of at least 11 at this compact site.

A little farther uphill to the north and west is the **Edificio de las Columnas**, so-called because of an almost entirely vanished colonnade that once formed its façade. The columns' surviving drums are solidly banded with relief carving from the Early Postclassic era. The profusion of motifs and styles again suggests that El Tajín benefited from contact with many different cultures.

The Pyramid of the Niches is built over an older but similar structure that dates to about A.D. 300; archaeologists speculate that the more recent structure was built perhaps three centuries later, but the origins of El Tajín's early builders remain obscure. Fortunately, excavation continues at the site, and each year more of its mysterious but fascinating past is revealed.

Sometimes *voladores* perform their spectacular flying dance in the main plaza at El Tajín. For those lucky enough to catch such a performance, it is the perfect—not to mention original—setting.

Tuxpan

Tuxpan (TOOSH-pan), a pleasant fishing port rather recently made prosperous and prodded into the 20th century by the discovery of oil, lazes along a riverbank some 58 km (36 miles) northeast of Poza Rica. The feeling of an "oil town" is almost totally absent, with the exception of what amounts to a virtual second city built by the national petroleum company, Pemex, between Tuxpan and its beach near the mouth of the Río Tuxpan.

There are no attractions of particular interest to be seen here—although the colonial church and bridge are handsome. Nor is there much of anything to do other than saunter along the river admiring the palm trees and the view. For all its lack of specific attractions, Tuxpan is nevertheless quietly enjoyable, with much color and life on display in and around its two main plazas.

Launches serving as ferries ply the Río Tuxpan, affording a pleasant little boat ride with good views of the town. In the village on the opposite bank you'll find the Mexican-Cuban Friendship Museum, located on the spot from which Fidel Castro returned to Cuba in a fishing boat; the rest, as they say, is history. The boat is being restored (or perhaps re-created) for visitors, but only great admirers of Castro are likely to enjoy the museum, which consists almost entirely of early photographs of Fidel and his fellow revolutionaries.

The Tuxpan beach, **Barra del Norte**, is easily reached by bus or car from town. The beach has good sand and warm, shallow water; the facilities are simple but adequate. The strand itself resembles the more famous ones on Padre Island in Texas, long stretches of coarse but unpebbled sand and (usually) gentle water lapping the shore. (Industrial installations by Pemex neither pollute the beach nor seal it off.)

Tuxpan is perhaps best known for its **sportsfishing**, including the annual tarpon tournament held in June. Information is available at the Club de Pesca (Tel: 783/4-0406). In addition, the city is a good headquarters for excursions to **Laguna de Tamiahua** and **Isla de Lobos** north of town. The lagoon, separated from the Gulf by a narrow strip of hard sand, is an extensive, shallow basin. Isla de Lobos, a dot in the jade-green sea, lies just beyond the barrier. Divers planning on exploring either should bring their own equipment.

STAYING AND DINING IN TUXPAN

The ▶ **Hotel Sara**, the town's best, has tastefully decorated rooms with balconies and views of the town and river. The beds tend to be firm, even hard, so you might want to check this before registering. The Sara is about three blocks uphill from the center of town, and also has a cheerful restaurant.

On the main street a block above the river boulevard is the comfortable ▶ **Hotel Plaza**, older than the Sara and a bit worn but still a good buy. The Plaza's restaurant specializes in seafood and serves good breakfasts.

Fischer Restaurant, at the western edge of downtown facing the river, is Tuxpan's best restaurant, high priced but attractively situated. Tel: (783) 4-0271.

SOUTH FROM
THE CITY OF VERACRUZ

Travelling south and east along the coast from Veracruz you'll pass through green, level ranchland speckled with Brahman cattle. These pastures have been wrested from the jungle, and defending them is a never-ending struggle. Now and then the horizon is broken by mountains tumbling down toward the sea.

By car or bus, the trip around the Bahía de Campeche—as this southwesternmost part of the Gulf of Mexico is called—is both lovely and pastoral. But there are only two destinations of interest in the region: the Lago de Catemaco area and, farther east in the state of Tabasco, Villahermosa. For most travellers other towns along the route will be of little interest.

Catemaco

Both the town and lake are an easy one-day trip from Veracruz, lying just 145 km (90 miles) southeast of the city over a good road, Highway 180. There's also fast and frequent bus service to both.

The lake, created in prehistoric times by the eruption of a cluster of volcanoes, is an impressive body of fresh water some ten miles long. Two imposing volcanoes, **San Martín** and **Cerro Blanco**, both long extinct, rise to the north, forming a frontier of sorts: This is the northernmost extent of the tropical rain forest on the continent. Travellers will notice the change as they head southeast, with the greens becoming deeper and the timber taller as the miles tick by.

Lago de Catemaco, sometimes hailed as the most beautiful lake in Mexico, is certainly a contender for the title in a country where lakes are few. Although the town huddled on its western shore has some color and zest, it is not particularly attractive. Nevertheless, a walk along the tree-shaded lakeside promenade can be pleasant, even romantic. In addition, enjoyable boat rides are offered from the town dock. The charge is by the boat, not by the passenger, so it's cheaper to go with a group; people at the docks usually will be happy to have you join them. The trip affords expansive

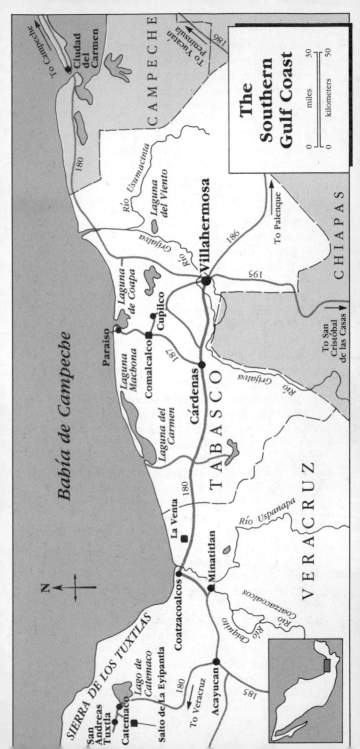

views of green highlands and mountains rising on every side, sloping pastures dotted with humped Brahman cattle, and waterfowl, especially egrets, wheeling in the sky or skimming the water. Seen from the lake the town is romantically transformed. Boats are allowed to approach the baboon colony established by the University of Veracruz on an island here, and if they're feeling sociable the baboons will make their way to the edge of the mangroves to look you over. Eleven other islands in the lake abound with vegetation, and lilies, hyacinths, and lotuses carpet its shallows.

Around Town

The **Iglesia del Carmen**, on the lake's eastern shore, is interesting for its collection of *milagros,* drawings and photographs about miracles experienced by pilgrims to this shrine. The most conspicuous pilgrims here, however, are the middle-class residents of Veracruz treating their families to a weekend at the lake. As a result, many of the hotels in town have kiddie water slides and such.

The ▶ **Gran Hotel Playa Azul**, located west of town on a gravel road facing the lake, has extensive lawns and its own dock, as well as a dining room. The rather modest accommodations are priced above value, and a car is necessary to get around. The rooms farthest from the driveway are the best.

For those without a car, the ▶ **Berthangel**, on the south side of the zócalo in town, is tidy and has pleasant balconies—about as well as you can do here despite the rather cramped quarters. It also has a coffee shop.

Mealtimes tend not to be joyful occasions in Catemaco. The small restaurants on the lakeshore offer limited menus of freshwater fish along with guitar music and lake views. Perhaps the best that can be said about the scene is that the Hotel Catemaco on the zócalo has good ice cream.

Not far from town are some beautiful waterfalls, one of which, **Salto de Eyipantla**, is truly spectacular. Before setting out, inquire about directions and road conditions; washouts are common, the mud often deep, and warnings rarely posted. The *tránsito* office, in city hall on the zócalo, will be happy to advise you.

Catemaco is the home of Mexico's "white magic" practitioners. Every autumn on a date determined by the lunar cycles, masks and skeletons are brought out in order to celebrate a reunion of sorcerers on the slopes of Monte del Cerro Blanco. Outsiders are most unwelcome at this native religious conclave, but the tradition inspires the youngsters of Catemaco to dress up and caper about as witches (*brujas*) regardless of the season—a surprising show for visitors, whether encountered in the town's streets, plazas, or along its back roads.

VILLAHERMOSA

The name Villahermosa means "pretty town," but most writers have begun their descriptions of the city by declaring the name deceptive, the place unpretty, even ugly. That declaration is no longer accurate; Villahermosa is beginning to live up to its name.

Located nearly 485 km (301 miles) southeast of Veracruz (via Highway 180), this once-sleepy Tabasco town boomed thanks to oil, a windfall prosperity that resulted in tacky overgrowth. In the 1970s the old rundown town was transformed into the modern rundown city. But since then Villahermosa has been consolidating its prosperity, building and remodeling. Unfortunately, inflation came with wealth, and Villahermosa remains one of the more expensive cities in Mexico.

Travellers to the region can get what they need here: attractive, if sultry, surroundings for those visiting the city's remarkable archaeological park-museum, its more conventional regional museum, and its zoo. Villahermosa is also a convenient gateway to Maya country, with **Palenque** less than a two-hour drive from the city (see the Chiapas section of the Mayan Mexico chapter below).

In addition, the many lagoons, rivers, and inlets nearby support an abundance of birdlife, attracting bird-watchers from near and far. The plumage of the tropical species that flock to the region is often gorgeous, and flamingos, toucans, and parrots make for a resplendent natural show.

In Villahermosa itself, café life centers on the Plaza de Armas, with the **Café del Portal** the traditional gathering place. Many blocks of the downtown area are closed to traffic, and visitors can stroll down streets lined with buildings designed in a simple but distinctive Caribbean style.

Around in Villahermosa

PARQUE-MUSEO DE LA VENTA

La Venta, the greatest of the Olmec centers, was established sometime after 1200 B.C.—at about the time of Moses—and reached its zenith around 600 B.C., becoming the fountainhead of art and culture in ancient Mesoamerica and predating the rise of the Maya by centuries. Everyone has seen pictures of the colossal Olmec stone heads sitting out in the jungle, but government officials felt that La Venta—about 80 miles west of Villahermosa in a swampy isolated area—and the two other major Olmec centers, San Lorenzo and Tres Zapotes, were too remote for most visitors. As a result, the great sculptures produced by this mysterious and surprisingly advanced culture were assembled and brought to an open-air museum in Villahermosa, the Parque-Museo de La Venta; smaller works went to the city's regional museum. (There is nothing of interest left at the original sites.)

Instead of simply setting out a row of statuary, a Mexican poet-savant by the name of Carlos Pellicer Cámara designed a "natural" environment in which these works might be seen as their creators had intended. Starting with a parcel of land along the **Laguna de las Ilusiones**, Pellicer created, in effect, an Olmec jungle.

The environment is perfect, at once a frame for and an extension of the sculpture. Monkeys scramble about in the trees; browsing deer look up, hesitate, then vanish into the thickets; the snarl of a jaguar (safely caged) underlines the fact that the Olmec were "jaguar people," with the great felines playing a dominant role in their religion and art. Small details have been considered as well. For instance, instead of directional signs, naked footprints that look as if they've dried in the cement walkways point the way.

Perhaps the best way to visit the park is simply to stroll through it, coming upon the huge heads, altars, and other great monoliths by surprise, gradually growing used to the "Olmec line" and concept of monumentality without worrying about specific meanings and relationships. Then walk through it a second time more slowly and, if possible, with the official guidebook and map in hand. These are sold at the entrance to the park, although the supply is not always reliable. With or without a guidebook, however, the monuments are compelling enough to repay careful scrutiny.

Of all the monuments in the park, Colossal Head #1 evokes the most comment. Carved almost 3,000 years ago, this single boulder was transported some 70 miles through the jungles to the original La Venta site—despite being over seven feet tall, measuring more than six feet in diameter, and weighing 44 tons. Yet according to experts the great stone was somehow moved without the help of wheels or draft animals.

You will read and hear endless speculation about the heads, especially the three magnificent examples in the park. Are they kings? Beheaded ball players? The simple truth is that nobody knows. Even the most thoroughly researched printed material contains much conjecture presented as fact. The carved altars, for example, may be something else—thrones, perhaps. Of course, visitors to the park are free to form their own opinions while contemplating the beauty and haunting power of these ancient stone sculptures created many centuries before the rise of Periclean Athens.

The Parque-Museo La Venta is open daily, 8:00 A.M. to 4:30 P.M. There is, in addition, a sound-and-light show every evening except Mondays and Wednesdays at 7:00 P.M.

MUSEUMS IN VILLAHERMOSA

The **Museo Carlos Pellicer**, named for the Tabascan poet-savant who was director of an older museum here, has one of the best regional collections in the country. Also, as an adjunct of the Centro de Investigaciónes de las Culturas Olmeca y Maya, or CICOM, it is the perfect complement to the Parque-Museo de La Venta. The museum is filled with artifacts from a variety of locations, but the emphasis—and the best collection—deals with the surrounding region: Olmec and Mayan objects, including beautiful copies of Mayan codices. You should allow about two hours for viewing its extensive displays of artifacts, maps, exhibits, and photographs. The Museo Carlos Pellicer is located on the banks of the Río Grijalva, just west of the Prolongación de Ocampe, an extension of Villahermosa's *malecón*. Tours begin on the second floor. Closed Mondays.

The **Museo de Cultura Popular**, at Zaragoza 810, displays a variety of Tabascan crafts, the most interesting of which are the masks and musical instruments used in native dances. A "modern" Chontal Mayan dwelling has been re-created using branches, logs, and thatch, and a conversation between two women has been recorded in the native Chontal dialect to give more authenticity to the dwelling. Plagued by errant husbands, the two women complain about the "lazy drunkards." Closed Mondays.

The **Casa de los Azulejos y Museo de la Ciudad**, at the corner of Avenida Juárez and 27 de Febrero, is a zany jumble of objects and ideas a young Scots-Mexican brought back from a grand tour of Europe in 1885. Housed in the family home (transformed by an Italian architect into something not entirely French, Italian, Persian, Moorish, or Gothic), the collection is supposed to illustrate the history of Tabasco—but that seems to be beside the point. Closed Mondays.

VILLAHERMOSA ZOO

Adjacent to the Parque-Museo de La Venta, and stretching along the esplanade bordering the Laguna de las Ilusiones, is a delightful public garden that is also home to the equally delightful Villahermosa Zoo. Here you'll find jungle animals and birds in a lush, tropical setting. The bands of monkeys, in particular, attract crowds of fascinated, wide-eyed children.

Behind the zoo runs the long esplanade with its lovely views of the palm-fringed lagoon—a perfect place to find the stray breezes that occasionally stir this tropical city.

The park-museum, zoo, and beautiful Laguna de las Ilusiones are grouped together on the west side of the city, occupying a broad area northeast of the prominent corner of Paseo Tabasco and Boulevard Adolfo Ruíz Cortines.

Day Trip to Comalcalco

The ruined Mayan city of Comalcalco, situated at the westernmost limit of Maya country some 55 km (34 miles) northwest of Villahermosa, was in pre-Hispanic times a satellite of Palenque. The first seven centuries of its life span, which covered the years A.D. 550 to 1250, comprised its greatest era. Comalcalco is somewhat of an oddity in that it was constructed of brick—the only important Mayan center so built. Though the site has been badly ravaged by time, some elaborate structures survive, as do some fine examples of stucco art inspired by Palenque.

While the site itself is only of medium interest, the drive through the surrounding cocoa-growing countryside, still inhabited by the Maya, will add a great deal of value to the excursion. Of the two routes you can take, the more interesting begins by following Villahermosa's main drag, Boulevard Ruíz Cortines, then turning north onto Avenida Universidad. Follow the signs for "Comalcalco via Nacajuca" and, a little later, a sign that says only "Nacajuca." Almost at once you will find yourself surrounded by cocoa plantations. A little past the halfway point to Comalcalco, 42 km (26 miles) from Villahermosa, stands the village church of **Cupilco**, a cheerfully gaudy example of folk art and decoration featuring a profusion of flowers and angels.

As you approach the modern town of Comalcalco, a sign indicates the ruins via a bypass north of town. Take the bypass. You'll be heading toward Paraíso before turning at the ruins access road, which is clearly marked.

Daily tours to Comalcalco leave from all the major Villahermosa hotels. It is also possible to take a bus to the access road, but this is usually an unappealing option due to the heat and overcrowding on the un–air-conditioned vehicles.

STAYING IN VILLAHERMOSA

The outstanding hotel here is also the city's newest, the ▶ Holiday Inn Tabasco Plaza, east of the Parque-Museo in a new residential/shopping district on Paseo Tabasco. One of the best operations in Mexico, it reflects Villahermosa's recent prosperity and burgeoning internationalism, with servi-bars, balconies, spacious rooms furnished with subtle good taste, and a swimming pool. The dining room is excellent for well-prepared regional and Mexican dishes as well as international-style entrées, and the bar features live entertainment. It all adds up to an elegant but relaxed hostelry, and a sterling, if expensive, addition to the Holiday Inn chain.

The ▶ Hotel Hyatt Regency Villahermosa, in the same fairly expensive price range, is also a decidedly first-rate hotel, with dining room, coffee shop, nightclub, and pool; located near the zoo at the corner of Ruíz Cortines, just off Paseo Tabasco.

The ▶ Hotel Cencalli, a comfortable establishment situated in a gardenlike neighborhood near the Laguna de las Ilusiones, offers its guests (mostly tourists) good rooms, attractive tropical grounds, and a swimming pool. The restaurant, with a bar and entertainment, is also recommended.

Located downtown at Calle Reforma 304 (part of the pedestrian mall closed to traffic), the ▶ Hotel Miraflores has air-conditioning, a bar, and a restaurant. This is a rare operation in Villahermosa—an inexpensive hotel that is still acceptable.

In the same economical category is the 60-room ▶ Hotel Ritz, a clean, adequate hostelry with air conditioning near the bus station at Avenida Madero 1009.

Because of a steady stream of business traffic, some of it international, Villahermosa's hotels are crowded and reservations absolutely essential.

DINING IN VILLAHERMOSA

The first choice for good food and service in town is the **Restaurant Gazebo**, the Holiday Inn Tabasco Plaza's serene but gleaming dining room. Tel: (931) 6-4402, ext. 848.

Overlooking the river in the same complex as the Museo Carlos Pellicer, **Los Guayacanes** is pleasant enough and serves good seafood. Tel: (931) 2-1530.

Capitán Buelo's riverboat restaurant serves lunch, in two sittings, on two separate trips; the first departs at 1:30 P.M., the second around 3:00. Go for the boat ride, not the food, although the meal is better and less expensive than you would expect from this kind of operation. You can catch the boat at the *malecón* and Zaragoza. Tel: (931) 3-5762.

Leo's, Paseo Tabasco 429, became so popular as a result of its efficient service, cheery informality, and substantial fare—beef and pork tacos, pastries, all-American hamburgers with fries, and the like—that a second branch has opened in Mérida. Tel: (931) 2-4463.

As noisy as the Caribbean music it's named for, **Guaraguao** seems to boil with crowds and tobacco smoke. But the *sopa de mariscos,* Mexico's answer to bouillabaisse, may be worth it. Salt- and freshwater specialties at moderate prices. Avenida 27 de Noviembre 947; no reservations. Tel: (931) 2-5695.

Los Pepes, centrally located at Madero 610, is the best of the open-air cafés and serves regional food at low prices. The ceiling fans help some, but nothing open to the outdoors is very appealing on a torrid Tabasco day.

GETTING AROUND

Driving Down from the Border

Most travellers heading down from the border want to cover the northeast corner of the country as quickly as possible; to avoid delay at the start of a long drive, consider clearing customs and spending the night in **Matamoros**, across the border from Brownsville, Texas, so you can set out early the next morning. (You should also be aware that during the rainy season, from May to October, travellers are at the mercy of summer downpours.) The modern ▶ **Hotel Gran Residential** is located on Matamoros's major street, Avenida Alvaro Obregón, at the corner of Amapolas. In addition to an inviting tropical patio, it has a good restaurant, a bar, and a nightclub; its prices are high by local standards, however. ▶ **La Casona**, in the center of town at Independencia 513, is merely adequate, its rates reasonable. Restaurant, bar, swimming pool.

From Matamoros you proceed south on Highway 101/180, traversing pancake-flat country bristling with scrub jungle. Twenty-nine kilometers (18 miles) south of San Fernando, Highway 101 swings to the southwest and Ciudad Victoria (and from there on to the central highlands). Southbound drivers will want to continue on Highway 180, which eventually becomes a toll road about 21 km (13 miles) north of Tampico.

Tampico, situated between the Gulf and a vast estuary, is a modern but sometimes makeshift city that has mushroomed in size with the growth of Mexico's petroleum industry. Relics of its previous incarnation as a resort—old decaying hotels near its beaches, a few waterfront bars—remain as forlorn reminders of a raffish past. Sadly, pollution has killed the fish that once drew sportsmen to its waters, and the oil refineries have overpowered the town's sleepy charm and driven out much of its other industry.

The first attractive hotel you'll see is the ▶ Posada de Tampico, 8 km (5 miles) north of the city on Highway 180. A 300-unit operation with satisfactory if expensive rooms and a clean, efficient restaurant, it's probably best as a convenient stop for lunch. The next establishment down the road, the ▶ Camino Real Motor Hotel, near the northern edge of the city on Highway 180, which here is called Avenida Hidalgo, is far more luxurious. The restaurant is also good and the coffee shop satisfactory, although not very fast. Less costly and more than adequate is the ▶ Hotel Impala, near the zócalo downtown, with a restaurant that serves very fresh and savory seafood.

Highway 180 heads due south out of Tampico over a new bridge that replaced an unreliable ferry which served the city badly for generations. The route passes through sparsely inhabited savannah and wetlands for 131 km (81 miles), until it reaches the village of Potrero del Llano, where Highway 180 joins Highway 127 and swings to the southeast for the final 42 km (26 miles) into Tuxpan.

—*Robert Somerlott*

Veracruz

All major airline service is via Mexico City. Mexicana is the chief carrier, with numerous flights to and from the capital daily; daily service to Los Angeles (with a Mexico City stopover); and occasional flights to San Francisco and San Jose (via Mexico City). The Mexicana office in Veracruz is on the corner of Serdán and Cinco de Mayo. Aeroméxico has two daily flights to and from the capital. Aerocaribe, a regional subsidiary of Mexicana, offers service to Cancún, Cozumel, and Villahermosa. Ground transportation to and from the airport is by taxi, *colectivo,* or rental car. A taxi costs about $8, the *colectivo* half that much. For the return trip from the city to the airport the *colectivo* is not always reliable.

Intercity buses arrive and depart from the Central Camionera, about 4 km (2½ miles) from downtown Veracruz and accessible by taxi or city buses running south on Avenida Cinco de Mayo. (They're marked "Camionera" in white paint on the windshield.)

First-class buses (the ADO line) depart almost every hour for Mexico City; the trip takes about 7 hours and costs about $14. Buses *from* the capital depart the Terminal de Autobuses de Oriente (TAPO) near the San Lázaro metro station. There is also good service from Veracruz to Lago de Catemaco, Villahermosa, Tuxpan, and Jalapa (which is on the northern route to Mexico City). There is, in addition, a special night bus to Mérida in the Yucatán, and another to Oaxaca. It takes about 14 hours to reach Mérida, a little less than 12 to Oaxaca. The fare to the former is approximately $31, while it's about half that much to Oaxaca. It is imperative upon your arrival in this busy terminal that you make a reservation for your next destination before heading into town.

Four trains a day run between Veracruz and the capital, two departing each city in the morning, one via Jalapa and the other via Córdoba. The trip takes about 12 hours. There's also a night express, with Pullman cars, via Córdoba that leaves both cities at 9:30 P.M. and arrives at the other end of the line at around 7:40 A.M. Travellers taking the night express have a choice of accommodations, and tickets should be purchased well in advance. The night sleeper, called the "Jarocha," offers the best service and costs about $40 from the capital.

The better highway to Veracruz from the capital is the southern (toll) route, Highway 150D, via Puebla and Córdoba. The alternate route, through Jalapa via Highways 140 and 129, is longer and slower. Both routes offer spectacular mountain scenery.

A choice of car-rental agencies is available in Veracruz, but none is of international reputation. Service at the airport and in the city is offered by Auto Laurencio, Autos Panamericana, Renta de Carros Veracruz, and Valgrande Rent a Car. Major credit cards are accepted. There is no real need to have a car in the city, however. Public transportation is fast and frequent, and taxis plentiful.

Villahermosa

Daily flights offered by Aeroméxico and Mexicana connect Villahermosa to Mexico City. Aerocaribe connects Villahermosa to Mérida, Cancún, Cozumel, and Oaxaca. Price-controlled taxis provide ground transportation from the airport to the city, about 10 km (6 miles) distant; the fare should be about $6.

The first-class ADO bus line links Villahermosa with Veracruz, as well as Mérida, Palenque, and San Cristóbal de las Casas in Chiapas. The trip to Mérida takes about 9 hours, with the fare about $23. The daily express bus to Oaxaca takes about 11 hours, with the fare about $26.

There is a Dollar Rent-a-Car office in the Holiday Inn

complex; otherwise, none of the city's dozen car-rental agencies is known internationally. Two of the larger are Arrendadora de Autos Usumacinta, at the airport and the Hotel Cencalli in town, and Tabasco Auto Rent, which is also at the airport and in town, the latter at the Hotel Calinda Viva, Paseo Tabasco 1201. Both offer a variety of models and accept credit cards.

Tour buses leave regularly for the archaeological zones of Palenque and Comalcalco, with pickup service at all the major hotels.

Highway 180 is the best road to Veracruz and points north and west; it also runs into Campeche and points east via the coast. Motorists heading east on this route, however, are dependent on the ferry at Ciudad del Carmen, and are therefore at the mercy of the weather. The inland route, Highway 186, is the more dependable route to the Yucatán Peninsula.

ACCOMMODATIONS REFERENCE

The rates given below are projections *for December 1993 through Easter 1994. Unless otherwise indicated, rates are for double rooms, double occupancy; the 10 percent VAT has been added. As rates are subject to change, it's always a good idea to double-check before booking.*

▶ **Berthangel**. Zócalo, **Catemaco** 95870. Tel: (294) 3-0007; Fax: (294) 3-0195. $35.

▶ **Camino Real Motor Hotel**. Avenida ˚Hidalgo 2000, **Tampico**, Tamaulipas 89300. Tel: (121) 3-8811; Fax: (121) 3-9226. $147.

▶ **La Casona**. Avenida Independencia 513, **Matamoros**, Tamaulipas 87300. Tel: (891) 6-3740; Fax: (891) 3-7375. $49.

▶ **Gran Hotel Playa Azul**. Carretera Sontecompan, **Catemaco**, Veracruz 95870. Tel: (294) 3-0001 or 0042. $43.

▶ **Holiday Inn Tabasco Plaza**. Paseo Tabasco 1407, **Villahermosa**, Tabasco 86040. Tel: (93) 16-4400; Fax: (93) 16-4569; in the U.S. and Canada, Tel: (800) HOLIDAY. $162.

▶ **Hotel Cencalli**. Carretera 180, **Villahermosa**, Tabasco 86040. Tel: (93) 15-1999 or 1994; Fax: (93) 15-6600. $82.

▶ **Hotel Colonial**. Zócalo and Calle Miguel Lerdo, **Veracruz**, Veracruz 91700. Tel: (29) 32-0193; Fax: (29) 32-2465. $42.

▶ **Hotel Emporio**. Malecón and Calle Xicoténcatl, **Veracruz**, Veracruz 91700. Tel: (29) 32-0020; Fax: (29) 31-2261. $120.

▶ **Hotel Gran Residential**. Avenidas Alvaro Obregón and

Amapolas, **Matamoros**, Tamaulipas 87300. Tel: (891) 3-9440; Fax: (891) 3-2777. $84.

▶ **Hotel Hyatt Regency Villahermosa.** Calle Ruíz Cortines and Paseo Tabasco 907, **Villahermosa**, Tabasco 86050. Tel: (93) 13-4444; Fax: (93) 15-5808; in the U.S. and Canada, Tel: (800) 228-9000. $125.

▶ **Hotel Impala.** Calle Díaz Mirón 220, **Tampico**, Tamaulipas 89300. Tel: (121) 2-0990; Fax: (121) 2-0684. $50.

▶ **Hotel María Victoria.** Calle Zaragoza 6, **Jalapa**, Veracruz 91000. Tel: (281) 8-6011; Fax: (281) 8-0521. $58.

▶ **Hotel Miraflores.** Calle Reforma 304, **Villahermosa**, Tabasco 86040. Tel: (93) 12-0022; Fax: (93) 12-0486. $45.

▶ **Hotel Mocambo.** P.O. Box 263, Carretera Mocambo, **Veracruz**, Veracruz 91700. Tel: (29) 37-1710; Fax: (29) 37-1660. $90.

▶ **Hotel Plaza.** Avenida Juárez 39, **Tuxpan**, Veracruz 61420. Tel: (783) 4-0738. $48.

▶ **Hotel Ritz.** Avenida Madero 1009, **Villahermosa**, Tabasco 86050. Tel: (93) 12-1611; Fax: (93) 12-1092. $46.

▶ **Hotel Salinas.** Calle Ruíz Cortines 1000, **Poza Rica**, Veracruz 93240. Tel: (782) 2-2347; Fax: (782) 2-9680. $30.

▶ **Hotel Salmones.** Calle Zaragoza 24, **Jalapa**, Veracruz 91000. Tel: (281) 7-5431. $25.

▶ **Hotel Sara.** Calle Garizurieta 44, **Tuxpan**, Veracruz 61420. Tel: (783) 4-0010; Fax: (783) 4-0018. $41.

▶ **Hotel Tajín.** Calle Domínguez 104, **Papantla**, Veracruz 93570. Tel and Fax: (784) 2-1062. $40.

▶ **Hotel Veracruz.** Avenida Independencia s/n and Miguel Lerdo, **Veracruz**, Veracruz 91700. Tel: (29) 31-2233; Fax: (29) 31-5134. $100.

▶ **Hotel Xalapa.** Calles Victoria and Bustamante, **Jalapa**, Veracruz 91000. Tel: (281) 8-2222; Fax: (281) 8-9424. $85.

▶ **Playa Paraíso.** Boulevard Veracruz Mocambo, Boca del Río, **Veracruz**, Veracruz 91700. Tel and Fax: (29) 35-5033. $103.

▶ **Posada de Tampico.** P.O. Box C-71, Highway 80, km 7, **Tampico**, Tamaulipas 89300. Tel: (122) 8-0515; Fax: (122) 8-0855. $144.

OAXACA

By Celia Wakefield

Celia Wakefield has lived in Mexico for many years, the past 17 in San Miguel de Allende, and travels extensively throughout the country. She has written articles for The Atlantic, Saturday Review, Newsday, *and* Punch. *She is also the author and photographer of* High Cities of the Andes.

The city of Oaxaca (wuh-HAH-kah) lies about 300 miles southeast of Mexico City geographically; in spirit it is a world away. There could be no more complete change from the frenetic traffic, bustle, and pollution of the capital than this lovely city in the Sierra Madre del Sur.

Some cities keep their essential character in spite of the passing of time. Although Oaxaca has mushroomed in size in recent years, it remains a semitropical oasis of quiet charm, a place where visitors return again and again to unwind in its gentle, springlike climate. Nobody seems to be in a hurry here, but there is always something to do—especially outside the city limits proper—whether it's visiting the native crafts villages for which the region is justly famous; exploring the magnificent archaeological sites at Monte Albán, Mitla, and elsewhere; or using the city as a gateway for vacations on the beaches of Puerto Angel, Puerto Escondido, or Huatulco (see the separate Pacific Resorts chapter for a more detailed look at these and other attractions).

MAJOR INTEREST

Oaxaca City
Main plaza and cathedral
Iglesia de Santo Domingo
Museo Regional del Estado, with finds from Monte Albán

Instituto de Artes Graficas de Oaxaca
Museo Rufino Tamayo
Museo de Arte Contemporaneo
Saturday market

Outside the City
Monte Albán
Mitla
Craft villages

OAXACA CITY

Oaxaca is easily reached by plane, train, bus, or car from Mexico City, though each of these may have its disadvantages: The seven-hour drive is through uninteresting country, the plane flight may be canceled for mysterious reasons, the train may be late, or the bus crowded. Any of these inconveniences will be forgotten, however, once this pleasant city is reached.

Oaxaca takes care of its guests in small but important ways. At the airport a *colectivo* van pulls up to carry passengers to their hotels for a minimal fee. (If it doesn't turn up instantly, wait for it; taxis charge five times as much.) A few years ago the city banned all vehicular traffic from the central downtown plazas. Now pedestrians amble freely under huge trees, rest in the shade on white wrought-iron benches, and listen to marimba music at the Rococo bandstand. Shopkeepers, passersby, and neighbors on park benches are liberal with information; old-fashioned courtesy has not gone out of style here.

How long will you want to spend in Oaxaca? There are several museums, churches, and markets to be explored, as well as two separate excursions to the important archaeological sites of Monte Albán and Mitla. Three days therefore should be the minimum. Travellers with special interests in crafts or archaeology will want to allow a day or two extra for visits to small weaving and pottery villages, or to the less well known archaeological sites at Cuilapán, Zaachila, Dainzú, Lambityeco, and Yagul.

A Cultural Crossroads
Oaxaca is a city of about 300,000 people nestled in a valley at an altitude of a little over 5,000 feet. Actually, there are three Oaxacas: the state, the city, and the valley of the same name. In conversation, "Oaxaca" may refer to both the city and the

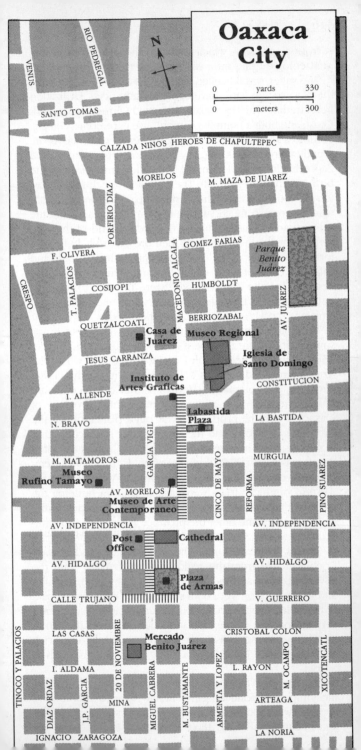

surrounding valley, which includes the craft villages and archaeological sites most visitors come to see.

The valley was inhabited as long ago as 9000 B.C. In time, the Zapotec Indians developed an advanced civilization here, trading with the equally advanced Olmecs on the Gulf Coast, and built a number of impressive ceremonial centers. Foremost among these was the great center of Monte Albán, founded around 800 B.C. by a pre-Zapotec culture. The Zapotecs, in turn, dominated the valley from around the birth of Christ to A.D. 800. Their eventual decline was hastened by the arrival of the warlike Mixtecs from the north, who did not so much subdue the Zapotecs as assume the reins of an exhausted culture. Toward the end of the 15th century the fierce Aztecs made their presence felt, building a fort in the center of the valley and controlling its trade and tribute. Details of these migrations and shifts in power are obscure, but the Zapotecs, who were the first to leave an imprint on the Valley of Oaxaca, survived, and theirs is the language most often heard in its markets today.

The Spanish appeared on the scene in 1521, but it was some years before they were able to subjugate the indigenous population and establish a city on the spot where the Aztec fortress had been. As W. H. Prescott wrote in his classic *History of the Conquest of Mexico:* "Cortes obtained a grant of an extensive tract of land in the fruitful province of Oaxaca, where he proposed to lay out a plantation for the Crown. . . . He soon had the estate under such cultivation that he assured his master, the Emperor, Charles the Fifth, that it was worth 20,000 ounces of gold." In 1529 the emperor gave Cortés the title of Marqués del Valle de Oaxaca.

The Dominican friars were instrumental in building the colonial city, and by 1575 there were 160 churches in the valley. At the same time, the province flourished economically. Silkworms were imported from Spain, and silk spinning was profitable until the China trade undercut it. Cochineal dye from the region was in demand until the advent of artificial dyes in the 19th century. Cattle ranching and wheat farming were both suited to the mild, dry climate of the valley. Oaxaca prospered, in part because it supported very few people. As the population increased over the centuries, however, the forests were cut down and the once-rich soil was eroded. Today Oaxaca is one of the poorest states in Mexico.

Oaxaca is also famous as the birthplace of two of Mexico's most important political figures. Benito Juárez, a full-blooded Zapotec, was prominent in the reform movement of the 1850s and instrumental in the 1860s in ridding Mexico of the foreign rule of Emperor Maximilian. In 1861 he became the first and (so far) only Mexican president of pure Indian descent, and since his death in 1872 has been revered as his country's Abraham Lincoln. The house where he worked as a servant in Oaxaca City is maintained as a small museum. Local legend has it that Juárez did not die but rather disappeared into a lake in his native town of Guelatao, from which he will emerge some day to lead his Zapotec tribesmen once again.

Porfirio Díaz, another *oaxaqueño,* rose to prominence from the other end of the social spectrum, having always known wealth and influence. Although he governed his country as president for 30 years, from 1876 to 1880 and again from 1884 until the second year of the Revolution in 1911, his accomplishments have not been so honored in Oaxaca, where he is usually thought of as a ruthless dictator not deserving of memorials—though you will find a street named in his memory.

Exploring Oaxaca City

PLAZA DE ARMAS

The Plaza de Armas, or zócalo, actually consists of two public squares, the large Plaza de la Constitución and the smaller Alameda de León, which is surrounded by the cathedral, a number of government buildings, and the post office. The cathedral, which was begun in 1553 and finally finished in the 19th century, is squat rather than soaring, solid rather than elaborate. It almost seems to huddle on its plot, its two flying buttresses ready to ward off the vicious earthquakes that have struck the city more than once. Nevertheless, the colonial clock on its façade still keeps good time.

The enormous main plaza is surrounded by arcades and café tables occupied from breakfast to late evening by people eating, listening to music, gossiping, reading newspapers, or simply nursing cups of coffee as they while away the hours. Jugglers entertain with brightly colored balls, guitarists tune their instruments. Native women, their *rebozos* worn turban-style, carry big flat baskets on their heads, balanced off-center in apparent defiance of gravity. Elsewhere, a small ragged boy recites a poem at the top of his lungs, stanza after stanza; payment is hoped for. For many, the best seats from which to take all this in are the tall chairs meant for shoe shines, spaced like thrones at the edges of flowerbeds and sidewalks. Business thrives. Except for running shoes, everything else seems to need a shine every hour or two.

The air in Oaxaca is soft, the climate mild, neither sultry nor cool (although a sweater or light jacket will come in handy in the early morning and evening). Against the sky over the zócalo float bunches of balloons arranged in the shapes of fanciful animals. The balloon vendors seem to float as well, wandering from spot to spot, seldom making a sale. Oaxaca's vendors in general are businesslike without being offensively pushy. They have apparently learned that "no" may actually mean "no," whether the prospective buyer is looking at a woven rug, an engraved machete, or a colorful necklace.

Iglesia de Santo Domingo and Museo Regional

The Iglesia de Santo Domingo, located five blocks north of the zócalo in an area free of traffic, was begun by the Dominicans in 1575 and finished about a century later; the Baroque façade was added another 100 years after that. The intricate ornamentation evident everywhere, however, makes it surprising it was ever finished at all. Dazzling golden scrollwork covers almost every inch of the interior, including the 11 chapels. Especially remarkable is the many-branched Tree of Jesse, a series of 35 detailed relief figures illustrating the lineal descent of Christ.

The **Museo Regional del Estado**, housed in the attached convent, has as its great prize the treasures from Monte Albán. Visitors who see nothing else in the city usually find their way to the **Tomb 7 collection**, discovered in 1932. The magnificent jewelry on display, dating from about A.D. 500, consists of gold, conch shell, turquoise, amber, obsidian, onyx, and glass worked into elaborate pieces by superb ancient craftsmen. (The filigree necklaces are often used as models for the jewelry sold in Oaxaca's downtown stores.) Like so much else in Oaxaca—the Rococo bandstand, the fine embroidery work, and the marimba music, with its extra trills and flourishes—the jewelry from Tomb 7 is above all elaborate and complex, suggesting that Indian craftsmen centuries ago originated the long artistic traditions of the region. The museum is open daily except Tuesdays, 10:00 A.M. to 6:00 P.M.

Instituto de Artes Graficas de Oaxaca

Oaxaca exerts a strong pull on its native sons; they often return, after they have become successful, to share their fame with their birthplace. A few years ago the painter Rufino Tamayo did just that by establishing a splendid museum of pre-Columbian art in Oaxaca. More recently, the artist Francisco Toledo opened a museum of graphic arts in the building that was his childhood home (he now lives in Mexico City) and filled it with hundreds of lithographs, aquatints, and silk-screened prints from his huge collection.

The museum, across the street from the church of Santo Domingo at Alcalá 507, opened in late 1989 under the auspices of the State of Oaxaca and the National Institute of Fine Arts. Its seven rooms surround a garden courtyard and are filled with an extremely varied collection, including works by the likes of Goya, Matisse, Picasso, and Rouault, as well as Mexican giants such as Rivera and Orozco. For every famous artist represented you'll also find something by one of today's emerging lithographers. Special exhibits from time to time only add to this first-rate museum's already considerable appeal. It is open 10:00 A.M. to 2:00 P.M. and 4:00 to 7:00 P.M., weekdays except Tuesday, and 11:00 A.M. to 5:00 P.M. on Sundays. Admission is free.

Museo Rufino Tamayo

A plaque in the Museo Rufino Tamayo tells the visitor, in less-than-perfect Spanish, French, and English: "This museum is dedicated to the millenary art which flourished in the area called now-a-days the Republic of Mexico, art entirely inspired (with the exception of Occidental Mexico) by Pre-Columbian religions and myths, which represents the deified forces of nature: the sun, the wind, the water, and a multitude of other natural phenomena. But if, in our time, the pieces exhibited in the niches of the museum impress its visitors, it is not for religious feelings, because the religions of ancient Mexicans, a long time ago have been forgotten. Rather they are moved by the aesthetic rank of the works, their beauty, power, and originality."

The plaque goes on to emphasize the point: "It is the first time that a Mexican museum exhibits the relics of Indian past in terms of aesthetic phenomena, in terms of works of art."

The pieces in this museum were assembled as a private collection by the late Rufino Tamayo, one of modern Mexico's most admired painters, and donated to the city of Oaxaca, his birthplace. Tamayo took care that the public would see the objects at their best: There are no catchall display cases of "black pottery from the valley" or "human figures, various" here. Instead, each piece has received careful consideration, is described individually, and is mounted against a background—light blue, perhaps, or rose or orange—that brings out its beauty. The museum, northwest of the zócalo at Morelos 503, is housed in an old mansion with a flower-bordered patio. Benches spaced around the patio are a good place to rest and admire the pre-Columbian figures of men playing musical instruments, the Colima dogs yapping in unison, a man in a coyote mask, or a fierce jaguar carved out of jagged volcanic rock. The Rufino Tamayo Museum is what a museum should be but often is not: a place for quiet contemplation and unhurried reflection. The Tamayo museum is open 10:00 A.M. to 2:00 P.M. and 4:00 to 7:00 P.M. weekdays except Tuesday, and 10:00 A.M. to 3:00 P.M. on Sundays.

Museo de Arte Contemporaneo

This is the newest of Oaxaca's museums, inaugurated in March 1992. Housed in a magnificent 16th-century mansion at Alcalá 202, it is "a cultural project dedicated to developing a greater awarenes of plastic arts from the State of Oaxaca as well as Mexico and other countries." The colonial building, with its fragments of original frescoes, has been restored beautifully, and some original doors and windows remain. Throughout, high-ceilinged rooms and a spacious patio form an imposing background for the works of contemporary Oaxacan artists. Several galleries are devoted to paintings by Rufino Tamayo, others to Francisco Toledo, Rodolfo Nieto, and Francisco Gutierrez. The museum also has a collection of rare 19th-century photographs as well as an extensive art library. Open daily except Tuesdays, 10:30 A.M. to 8:00 P.M.

THE SATURDAY MARKET

Outdoor markets are a way of life in Mexico, and the market in Oaxaca is one of the biggest and best known. Although it operates every day, it really comes alive on Saturday, when farmers, craftspeople, and merchants from the small villages of the great Valley of Oaxaca stream into town. D. H. Lawrence was so intrigued by the spectacle, in fact, that he devoted a chapter of *Mornings in Mexico* to it. In those days, some 60 years ago, Indians almost always travelled by foot or burro, arriving loaded with goods for sale or to barter. "A little load of firewood, a woven blanket, a few eggs and tomatoes," Lawrence wrote, "are excuse enough for men, women and children to cross the foot-weary miles of valley and mountain. To buy, to sell, to barter, to exchange. To exchange, above all things, human contact."

Today's participants are as likely to arrive by truck or ancient car as by burro or on foot. As well, the city has cleaned up and somewhat deromanticized the market. Food is no longer spread out haphazardly on the ground. Merchants are assigned stalls, and their wares are exhibited on wooden stands, shielded from the sun and rain by lengths of old canvas. What was once a wide-open area of color and activity has been turned into a maze of alleys (making it easy to get lost), with here and there an open patio. As is always the case in Mexican markets, the same types of goods are arranged near one another. Next to one sugarcane vendor is another sugarcane vendor and next to him yet another. There seems to be no special competitive atmosphere; instead, it's much like a department store where dresses or kitchen utensils are lumped together.

There is an endless variety of things to buy here, from shoelaces to coconuts. Still, for the visitor—especially one with a camera—the food area is by far the most interesting. All this food comes from the surrounding countryside, and is arranged artistically, best side visible, in small piles (*pilas*) of five, in mountains of gleaming color, or in bundles or baskets.

The food area may be splendid, but to get to it you have to walk through alley after alley of uninteresting pots and pans, tapes of rock music, bundles of men's pants, and stacks of automobile parts. Do not go to the Saturday market expecting a primitive Indian scene. Approach it, instead, as a remarkable chance to see how impressive a massing of objects can be: a hundred cold gray machetes, a thousand plastic shoes, a glittering mound of blood-red tomatoes, a barricade of papayas, a million dried shrimp in baskets shining golden in the sun.

One more word of advice: The market should not be visited in the early morning, despite the fact that this may be recommended to you. The vendors are still streaming into town then, and many of the stalls will not yet be open. The best time to go is about 10:30 A.M.

SHOPPING IN OAXACA

Oaxaca City is noted for the variety of its local crafts—serapes woven in muted colors and intricate patterns; unusual green and black ceramics; machetes with elaborate designs incised into their handles; delicate filigree jewelry. The serious shopper will have a wide selection from which to choose, and the way to go about it will depend on your personality and frame of mind. Anyone who loves to bargain will head for the market, where the first price mentioned is always far higher than the final one. The aficionado of cottage industries, on the other hand, will head for the outlying crafts villages. The best of these are **Teotitlán del Valle** (on the way to Mitla; see below) for weaving, **Atzompa** for green pottery, or **San Bartolo Coyotepec** for black. The black pottery, which is unique to the area, is left unglazed and fired in subterranean ovens so that the smoke colors the clay. Tours to these villages can be arranged in town as well as through the bigger hotels and travel agencies; there are also frequent buses from the second-class bus station at the end of Calle Trujano. For those with their own cars, these places are all a short ride from the center of town over good roads.

Anyone who dislikes discussing price will be best served in a shop, and Oaxaca has some good ones.

Yalalag de Oaxaca, at the corner of Avenida Morelos and Macedonio Alcalá, is excellent for black pottery and woven goods. Two shops on Alcalá, **La Mano Mágica** at number 203 and **Artesanías del Convento** at number 503, offer a wide variety of carefully selected merchandise, everything from ceramics and woven goods to jewelry and rugs, all of it good quality.

Casa Victor's, a long walk north of the zócalo at Calzada Porfirio Díaz 111, is housed in a 17th-century monastery that has been converted into a shop. The stark, battered building seems about to collapse, but the store boasts a large selection of woven goods, ceramics, and cut paper.

Specialty Shops

Some of Oaxaca's most interesting shops focus on specialty items. The **Cuchillería Alcalá**, at Alcalá 206, contains nothing but knives and swords handcrafted in the unique Oaxacan style, some embellished with mottoes. The hundreds of cutting blades here are suitable for everything from slicing a lemon to decapitating an enemy.

El Cactus, at Alcalá 401, specializes in wool rugs, with a variety of designs and sizes to choose from.

El Oro de Monte Albán, in the Palacio Santo Domingo, the recently renovated colonial-style shopping center on Alcalá, has specialized for more than 25 years in the art of manufacturing three types of traditional Oaxacan jewelry: colonial (based on colonial-period designs), filigree, and pre-Columbian (especially miniature reproductions of the jewels found in Tomb 7 at Monte Albán). Visitors are welcome to watch the craftsmen in the workshop across the street as they make the gold jewelry using the "lost" wax technique, a complicated, laborious process. Hot melted wax is poured into a rubber mold struck from a tin replica of the original design, and a plaster cast is made from the cooled wax impression. When heated in a kiln, the wax is "lost" into the surrounding plaster. The hollow cast then is placed in a centrifuge and connected to a crucible containing gold, which, when melted by a blowtorch, is forced into the mold. The shattered plaster cast reveals the delicate gold miniature, which is then cleaned in acid and trimmed; finally, a chain loop is attached.

Painted Animals

In the last few years the painted animals made by woodcarvers in the Oaxaca Valley have become known abroad, fetching astronomical prices in the United States. These whimsical, imaginative figures are carved from *copal,* a local hardwood, and painted in bright designs, mostly by carvers in three tiny villages close to Oaxaca City: Arrazola, San Martín Tilcajete, and La Union Tejalapan. Arrazola, home of Manuel Jimenez, the most famous of the local artisans, is at the base of Monte Albán. Your best bet is to take a taxi, since the driver usually will be able to locate the homes where carving is done (there are no conspicuous signs). The animals are less expensive in the villages than in Oaxaca, but some carvers may refuse to sell at all, saving their work for financially profitable export. If your trip to the source proves frustrating, check the usual folk art shops in Oaxaca. One such store, **Jimenez**, at Alcalá 407, carries Manuel Jimenez's work exclusively. You can purchase a crazy rabbit, a mermaid, a giraffe with a wonderfully elongated neck, or the Devil himself, for anywhere from $300 to $600, depending on size. Or you can purchase one of the wooden animals sold on the streets of Oaxaca by less well-known artists, many of which are quite inexpensive, ranging in price from about $10 to $30.

Clothing

Clothing shops in Oaxaca usually carry either traditional ethnic designs in *huipiles* (sleeveless garments resembling tunics), *rebozos,* and skirts (which, though beautiful in a Mexican setting, may seem out of place at home), or abandon the ethnic for international styles. At **Creaciones Lixhi-Tuu**, Alcalá 402, Interior 5, modern designs are created using handwoven cotton procured from villages in the Oaxaca Valley that is then decorated with delicate embroidery and drawn work. The result is a fine blend of traditional folk art and current fashion.

Finally, when you have done all your shopping and are wondering how to get it home, you can stop in at **The Open Door** office at Boca del Monte 108A, around the corner from the Presidente hotel. This answer to tourist prayers will pack and ship, translate and interpret, explain local business practices and customs, help with banking, phone calls, documentation, and anything else you need. Open Monday through Saturday from 9:00 A.M. to 12:30 P.M.; Tel: (951) 6-0403.

STAYING IN OAXACA CITY

The ▶ **Stouffer Presidente Oaxaca,** right around the corner from the church of Santo Domingo, is probably the most romantic, and certainly the most historic, hotel in Mexico. Originally the Convento de Santa Catalina (c. 1576), it was tastefully remodeled and converted into a hotel some years ago with no expense spared. Today it's a labyrinth of sunny, flower-filled patios and shadowy arcades surrounding a lovely, grassy pool area. The junior suites are decorated in rose or blue tile, with locally woven wall hangings. The single rooms tend to be a little monastic, perfectly adequate but not as nice as the doubles and junior suites. (Do try to avoid the rooms on the ground floor facing the street.) The building itself is a veritable museum, and offers its guests a tangible sense of Oaxaca's colonial past.

The food at the Presidente, on the other hand, is definitely international, with few traditional Mexican dishes on the menu. As one of the chain of Stouffer Presidente hotels it has the advantage of expertise from the capital, however, and may bring in a guest chef to supervise from time to time. The sauces, especially, are rich and elaborate, and everything is beautifully presented in a manner worthy of the hotel's colonial style. Romantic music provided by accomplished musicians at mealtimes further adds to the atmosphere of the past.

By Oaxaca standards the Presidente is expensive, but not by international or even national standards. It is especially popular with Europeans, so the atmosphere tends to be international, and the jeans-and-sandals set is made to feel welcome.

The ▶ **Hotel Victoria** sits high on a hill north of town at kilometer 545 of the Pan-American Highway (Highway 190). As it is not within easy walking distance of the zócalo area, its guests frequently fly down from Mexico City, then rent a car for the sake of convenience and sightseeing. There are two sections to the complex; the newer—and much the better— one features bungalows with slick pine furniture, walk-in closets, and refrigerators. The hotel's Mixtec-decorated restaurant caters to foreign tastes, with traditional Mexican dishes modified to suit North American palates. Looking out on the panoramic view of the valley, the diner here can enjoy what D. H. Lawrence described as the "gleaming, pinkish-ochre of the valley flat, wild and exalted...." The

Victoria also has a bar, disco, swimming pool, and is less expensive than the Presidente, though still high priced.

The ▶ **Fortín Plaza**, next door to the Victoria, features much white tile and marble, with Mixtec motifs. (The front rooms have the best views.) It also has a swimming pool and tennis courts, as well as a restaurant that specializes in seafood. Meals are served on a terrace overlooking the swimming pool, with soft tango music as an accompaniment from 4:00 to 8:00 P.M. every day except Sunday. Slightly less expensive than the Victoria, the Fortín Plaza nevertheless attracts affluent Mexicans from the D.F. as well as locally.

The moderately priced ▶ **Hotel San Felipe Misión Oaxaca**, in a new residential neighborhood five minutes north of the city by car, is an attractive, well-maintained member of the Misión chain of hotels. The rooms here are comfortable, if a bit bare, the lobby and public areas ample. It has all the usual amenities—swimming pool, bar, nightclub, convention hall —and the dining room and swimming pool overlook the city. The hotel also offers hourly courtesy transportation to and from downtown, a big advantage for guests who have not arrived by car. It's all a bit routine, not memorably different from hotels in other cities, but pleasantly far from the din of traffic. The Sunday brunch, lavish and well served, is worth going up the hill for even if you are not staying here.

The ▶ **Misión de los Angeles**, at Calzada Porfirio Díaz 102, is tropical, lazy, and spacious, with beautiful grounds ideal for strolling. The suites here have fireplaces and old-fashioned furnishings, and the hotel has a dining room, a nightclub, and, on weekends, a disco. The Misión appeals to an older crowd, many of them retirees from cold climates. It's in the same price range as the Victoria, but not quite as good.

The moderately priced ▶ **Calesa Real**, two-and-a-half blocks north of the zócalo, is a former colonial town house with 77 units and a central patio. The rooms are simple but charming, and there's a secure parking lot next door. The restaurant in the Calesa Real is the most Mexican of the hotel restaurants, in both atmosphere and menu, with few concessions to the tourist. The pork and chicken dishes are especially tasty, and the prices are moderate.

Located right on the zócalo, the ▶ **Hotel Señorial** also has a secure parking facility for guests (at the rear of the hotel). Behind its colonial façade is a modern, busy, and somewhat impersonal hotel. However, many visitors find it comfortable as well as convenient. The units vary greatly in size; the rates are moderate.

The ▶ **Hotel Las Golondrinas**, a small converted two-story home, is a good choice for the budget-conscious traveller. The 24 rooms here, all of which open onto garden patios, are clean and well kept, the atmosphere informal. Although there is no restaurant, breakfast is served. In fact, the hotel's only shortcoming is its slightly inconvenient location—about five blocks northwest of the main plaza.

The ▶ **Marqués del Valle**, next door to the cathedral, is an old favorite of budget travellers that recently has been completely redecorated in attractive style without sacrificing the amenities of a more gracious, bygone era: These include pleasantly spacious rooms and big old-fashioned bathtubs. And because the Marqués del Valle is right on the Zócalo, its café tables are a perfect spot from which to take in the endlessly fascinating zócalo scene.

The ▶ **Hotel Parador Plaza** is relatively new, having opened in 1991. Located near the zócalo at Murguia 104, it is decorated in a breezy modern style, with large and airy rooms. Its restaurant specializes in regional dishes.

DINING IN OAXACA CITY

Oaxaca has its specialties, among them tamales wrapped in banana leaves and its own version of *mole,* the chocolate-chile sauce more often associated with Puebla. Also notable here is the *comida corrida,* the fixed-price meal of several courses served during the midday lunch hour (a good way to get a well-balanced dinner from soup to dessert for a reasonable price).

In contrast to the hotel restaurants discussed above, the dining room at the **Hotel Monte Albán**, opposite the cathedral, is only mediocre. But the evening show of regional dancing here, despite its amateurism, is an excellent opportunity to see traditional dances from various towns in Oaxaca state staged with grace and enthusiasm. You'll be asked to pay a small admission charge; dining is not required.

Oaxaca has a handful of very good restaurants that are not in hotels. **Del Vitral**, listed in *Gastrotur,* a Mexican gourmet magazine, as "the best restaurant in Oaxaca and the southeast of Mexico," is a short walk east of the zócalo on Avenida V. Guerrero, where it occupies the second floor of a magnificent turn-of-the-century mansion. An imposing staircase leads up to a balcony, a dining room facing the street, and the "stained glass" room to the left. The stained glass, which gives the restaurant its name, runs along one whole side of the room, an enormous window decorated with fountains, cupids, and trees. It was created by European craftsmen for the wealthy Zorrilla family, whose descendants own the restaurant and have refurbished it. A pale rose decor, opulent draperies, and huge chandeliers are just some of its elegant touches. The menu leans toward the continental, with a few dishes inspired by old Oaxacan recipes. Tel: (951) 6-3124.

Las Chalotes, a couple of blocks east of the zócalo at Fiallo 116, is a first-rate French restaurant. The atmosphere is decidedly Gallic, the food excellent, the prices moderate. The usual French favorites—quiche lorraine, *boeuf Bourguignon,* and the like—are offered along with somewhat more adventurous choices such as warm goat's cheese salad or couscous. Tel: (951) 6-4897.

With a large indoor space as well as tables outside from which customers can watch the passing parade, **Terranova,** at Portal Benito Juárez 116, has brought new class to the collection of zócalo cafés. The food, often accompanied by an imaginative sauce, is consistently superior and always attractively presented. Open daily from breakfast through the evening. Tel: (951) 4-0533.

One restaurant that has been doing well for a good many years now is **El Asador Vasco,** located on the second floor of a building on the west side of the zócalo. It caters to a European crowd and serves steak, chicken, and fish as well as a few regional dishes. Try for a table overlooking the plaza; it's an expensive place, but you're paying partly for the view—as well as for the musicians who wander among the tables. Reservations are important in the high season; El Asador Vasco can get very crowded and rushed. Tel: (951) 6-9719.

The **Restaurante Bar Catedral,** one block north of the zócalo at Garcia Vigil 105, is pretty, airy, and comfortable, with tables set out in a small patio. The lengthy, reasonably priced menu emphasizes meat: eight different steak entrées along with chops and chicken; it's also a good place for the *comida corrida.* At night there is piano music. Tel: (951) 6-3285.

With its ostentatious decor and wide-ranging menu featuring everything from regional dishes to steak and pizza, **El Sagrario,** half a block from the zócalo at Valdivieso 120, is the closest thing to a night spot Oaxaca has to offer. Open noon to midnight daily. Tel: (951) 4-0303.

Under the same ownership as El Sagrario but considerably different in style, the **Santa Fe Restaurant,** Cinco de Mayo 103, claims to serve the "best Oaxacan mole" in town in addition to its more typical international specialties. Open daily from 8:00 A.M. to midnight, with piano music at dinnertime. Tel: (951) 6-9434.

The **Hostería de Alcalá**, Macedonio Alcalá 307, offers a varied menu that includes a number of Mexican specialties. Located in the patio of a renovated colonial mansion, it is a refreshingly cool place to unwind after a morning spent shopping in the attractive stores that line this street. Tel: (951) 6-2093.

There are very few good Chinese restaurants in Mexico, so it's both a surprise and a pleasure to find **Quing Long**, on the second floor of the new shopping complex on M. Alcalá, across the street from the church of Santo Domingo. The extensive menu embraces three styles of Chinese cuisine: Szechuan, Cantonese, and Hunan, with the emphasis on spicy Szechuan. Prices for individual dishes are high, but there are two reasonably priced set dinners on the menu. Tel: (951) 6-0232.

For a simple snack or light lunch in a quiet, restful setting try the **Cafeteria del Museo** in the back patio of the Museo de Arte Contemporaneo at M. Alcalá 202. The café is open during museum hours; closed Tuesdays.

OUTSIDE THE CITY
Monte Albán

At the majestic ruins of Monte Albán, 10 km (6 miles) south and west of the city, everything is enormous and austere, the ambience of the site enhanced by the sheer mass of the stone structures and the perspective lent by the surrounding mountains. As anyone who has ever visited Monte Albán knows, it's not surprising that people should come from all over the world with the express purpose of seeing the ruins. The groups of tourists who walk to and fro here are dwarfed by the scene; but then, so would be a crowd of thousands.

Monte Albán is the only pre-Columbian necropolis in Mexico. The hill on which it stands, 1,300 feet above the Valley of Oaxaca, was flattened and shaped by the original builders and then used as a base for the construction that ensued. Today buff-colored masses of stone—stairs, columns, platforms, colonnades, halls, and passages—surround the central plaza. Below ground are more than 200 tombs where the dead were buried along with their "companion sculptures" (meant to accompany them on their journey to the other world). The earliest writing (glyphs) yet discovered in Mexico was also found at Monte Albán.

Early Olmec Influence

The precise origins of this complex are uncertain. Construction of the site seems to have begun about 800 B.C., and it might have been an early outpost of the Olmec people; although no artifacts from that seminal culture have been found at the site, the presence of the flowing "Olmec line" in some of the sculpture suggests they had an early influence on local populations. The *danzantes* associated with the so-called **Templo de los Danzantes** (Temple of the Dancers), low relief sculpture carved out of hard stone, are the best-known relics from this period, and exhibit physical characteristics suggestive of the jaguar motif in Olmec art. The naked *danzantes* writhe and crouch in unnaturally contorted positions, and may represent individuals with medical problems or physical malformations. Or, since some seem to be marked with a flowery design on the interior of their thighs or on the abdomen, they may illustrate the practices of a primitive sexual cult. Still other scholars suggest that they represent prisoners who were ultimately sacrificed. In any case, they remain mysterious.

The period archaeologists call **Monte Albán II** began about 300 B.C., with a different group of Indians occupying the site and leveling the hilltop for the Great Plaza and the **astronomical observatory**, the arrow-shaped structure also known as Building J. The walls of Building J are inscribed with hieroglyphic inscriptions, probably recording the victories of Monte Albán's warriors in battle. The partly unroofed interior chamber may have been used for astronomical observations, although this is not certain.

Zapotecs and Mixtecs

About 400 years later the Zapotecs arrived and, over the next 800 years, created a brilliant ceremonial center, constructing, in the process, a huge patio surrounded by buildings. This period, known as **Monte Albán III**, was followed by years of decline, beginning about A.D. 1000. Although the reasons remain obscure, the decline was universal in Mesoamerica. Mixtecs from the north migrated into the Valley of Oaxaca at this time, a period known as **Monte Albán IV**, and began to build tombs at the site without displacing their Zapotec predecessors.

The last active period at the site, when it became a necropolis for Mixtec nobles, lasted from A.D. 1200 to the Spanish Conquest and is known as **Monte Albán V**. In 1932 **Tomb 7**, which dates from this period, was excavated, revealing the greatest haul of archaeological treasure ever found in Mexico. Today the gold necklaces, carved jaguar bones,

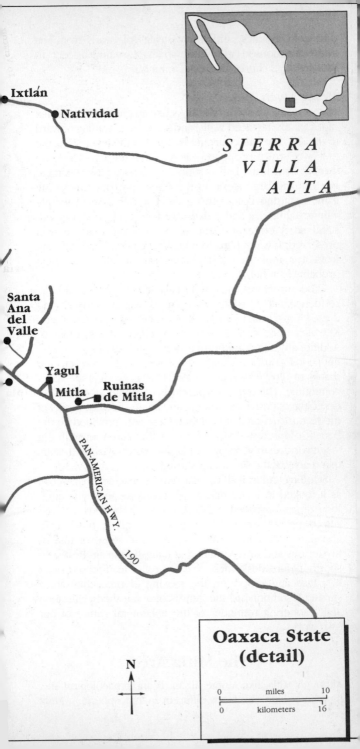

turquoise mosaics, and heavy strings of pearls from the tomb are housed in the Regional Museum adjacent to Oaxaca City's church of Santo Domingo.

Monte Albán Today

To the visitor Monte Albán looks like an enormous complex of flat patios, terraced walls, and stone steps leading upward to the sky. The **ball court**, in the form of the letter "I," is the first large structure apparent as you enter the area. The hoop through which the ball is supposed to have passed is missing, but the large stone in the center probably marks the game's starting point. Above the court is a small temple where dignitaries and judges presided, and tiers of grandstand seats on either side of the playing area are well preserved. It is not hard to imagine a contest here, differing from our modern sports events only in that the losers probably lost their lives as well.

Other structures include **El Palacio** (The Palace), a large residence with 13 rooms encircling a central courtyard, and those known rather prosaically as Buildings G, H, I, M, L, and P, which once served as temples, altars, and sanctuaries. Additionally, there are numerous mounds, tombs, and sunken patios. Much remains to be explored, however, and thanks to "Proyecto Especial 1992–1994," work at the site is continuing. The northern precincts of Monte Albán are undergoing extensive excavation, and an on-site scale-model of the reconstruction that is planned has been provided for the benefit of interested visitors. Slowly but surely, magnificent stonework, elaborate pyramids and courtyards, and stairs that reach for the sky are appearing.

Standing amidst it all you can almost imagine Monte Albán as it looked in its heyday, its platforms topped by temples long since collapsed, walls finished in brightly colored stucco, priests, warriors, and pilgrims walking busily here and there. Most impressive of all is the sense of history, mysterious and unrecorded, that hangs in the air. Best seen shortly before dusk, these massive relics lead most visitors to pause and reflect on the passing of time; they are a stirring testimonial to the genius of a vanished civilization and a sobering reminder of the ephemeral nature of our own world.

The Mitla Area

Although Mitla, like Monte Albán, is an archaeological site, the two couldn't be more different in atmosphere. At Mitla there is no feeling of vastness or isolation, for the ruins, close to a thriving village, are approached through an avenue of stalls where vendors urge serapes, *rebozos,* ceramics, and little pots of mezcal on every passerby. At the head of this avenue—really a dirt road—the ruins appear high on a hill, with a church to one side. Even at the entrance to the site wares are offered insistently.

To get to Mitla requires more time and effort than the 15-minute drive to Monte Albán. The daily tours from the Presidente, Victoria, and Marqués del Valle hotels, minivans of eight passengers with a trained guide, are your best bet. It's also possible to get there by bus, which gives you a chance to mingle with passengers who often speak an Indian dialect rather than Spanish and carry their children tenderly on their laps. (Children receive particular attention in Mexico. They are uniformly well behaved—except for some of the spoiled city kids—and seldom ill treated. Fathers seem to take as much practical care of them as mothers, and older children mind the younger ones. Charles Flandrau, who visited Mexico shortly after the turn of the century and wrote a classic account of his experiences, suggested that all children should be Mexican until the age of 15.)

THE ROAD TO MITLA

Along the 40-km (25-mile) road to Mitla (Highway 190, the Pan-American Highway) are turnoffs to Dainzú, Lambityeco, and Yagul (smaller archaeological sites), as well as the textile-craft villages of Teotitlán del Valle and Santa Ana del Valle. It would be easy to extend your visit to Oaxaca beyond three days in order to spend some time visiting any or all of them.

Every tour bus or taxi that heads out this way also makes an obligatory stop to see the **Tule tree** at Santa María del Tule. What kind of a tree warrants such attention? Well, it's a superlative tree, the oldest living thing in Mexico—2,000 years old, according to some naturalists. It's also an *ahuehuete* tree (*Taxodium mucronatum*), which is variously translated as a water cypress or sequoia. While they're larger in girth than redwoods in the States, they're not as tall. A smaller tree of the same species, known as *el hijo* (the son), grows nearby; it's only 500 to 600 years old. The older tree is usually surrounded by crowds of onlookers—foreign, Mexican, Indian, children as well as adults—staring with concentrated interest. But what else can be done with such a landmark? It's even too big to photograph, unless you're carrying a wide-angle lens.

The three archaeological sites would be more crowded than they are were it not for the ruins at Monte Albán and Mitla. **Dainzú,** which was an occupied village site as early as 600 B.C., boasts three large patios surrounded by building foundations, as well as 50 sandstone slabs bearing bas-reliefs of ball players in action that date from about 100 B.C. The small site of **Lambityeco,** which reached its zenith around A.D. 700, is noteworthy for its stucco busts of Cocijo, the Zapotec rain god, along with its portraitlike human heads. **Yagul,** a much larger site, has an acropolis comprising a cluster of tombs and palaces, most notably the Palace of Six Patios, as well as the ruins of a great fortress situated on the crest of a steep hill overlooking the site.

Textiles at the Source

The two crafts villages on the road to Mitla—**Teotitlán del Valle** and **Santa Ana del Valle**—produce some of the most elaborate handwoven textiles in Mexico. The *huipiles,* sleeveless tunic-like garments for women, are woven in complicated patterns on pale or colored backgrounds, and often have embroidered overlays and bright fluttering ribbons. Aficionados can even identify the town of origin: in Teotitlán del Valle, for instance, doves, fish, and flowers are combined in a variety of artful designs. Likewise, chemical dyes, not the primitive cochineal and vegetable dyes, are used to produce unusual shades of red, purple, and green. (The traditional dyes, though not as varied, are more vibrant.) The serapes worn by Zapotec men are less elaborate, although they're sometimes designed with strident patterns for sale to tourists. The most attractive are woven out of undyed gray or black wool, and feature figures of animals, birds, or abstract patterns in pale colors. Rugs are a specialty of Teotitlán del Valle, and you may be surprised to see designs copied from paintings by Picasso and other modern masters in addition to more conventional Oaxacan motifs. Originally taken from illustrations in an art book left in the village, the copies have proved to be as popular as the more traditional patterns.

If your time is limited, take the Mitla tour on a Sunday, when the town of **Tlacolula,** on the way, is crowded with buyers and sellers attending its weekly market. Wares from all the nearby villages are brought to town and then sold up and down the dirt road in front of the local church. Tlacolula is also a mezcal-producing center, and the neighborhood stores offer tiny glasses (your choice of sweet or dry) as a softening-up gesture. There's a Gypsy-like air to the Tlacolula market, and everyone seems to wear his or her brightest skirts, shirts, and shawls.

MITLA

Mitla was a shrine long before the extant ruins were constructed, and was probably inhabited 1,000 years before the beginning of the Christian era. The latest explorations here show that it probably emerged in its present incarnation during the period known as Monte Albán I, but its greatest development occurred later, possibly at the time of Monte Albán's decline, when it was rebuilt by the Mixtecs and dedicated to Mictlán, the Lord of the Underworld. It remained in full flower until relatively late, and was still active at the time of the Spanish Conquest.

Today the ruins (those that were not destroyed after the Conquest to build a sugar mill and churches) appear to be almost perfectly preserved, and seem designed for secular rather than religious use. Many of the structures date to about A.D. 1400. (Much older remains are still being explored in a larger area encompassing the town.)

The style of construction at Mitla also differs from that found at Monte Albán. There is no relief carving here; instead, all the decoration takes the form of geometrically abstract mosaics precisely cut and fitted into walls. The effect is akin to stylized embroidery, beige on beige, monochrome and repetitive, set in a surrounding area of sand-colored rock. Here and there the effect may be broken by a scarlet or bright blue flower that has gained a foothold in a crevice of the lattice-like patterns. In the courtyards enclosed by these elaborately worked walls are a number of heavy columns; put your arms around a certain column, legend has it, and the space between your hands will reveal how long you have to live.

To the left as you enter the village of Mitla is the **Museo Frissell de Arte Zapoteca** (open 10:00 A.M. to 5:00 P.M. daily). Formerly a private museum, it was started in the 1940s by Erwin Robert Frissell, a retired real-estate broker from Minneapolis to whom local farmers brought pottery unearthed in their fields. His collection of ceramic pieces arranged in chronological order is now the property of the University of the Americas and is open to the public. In the patio of the same building, which was Frissell's home, **La Sorpresa** (The Surprise) serves an excellent fixed lunch, while across the street a small cafeteria offers à la carte dishes.

CUILAPAN AND ZAACHILA

Two other sites off Highway 147, a side road heading south from Oaxaca, are worth visiting separately. At Cuilapán, in addition to a pyramid and Zapotec tomb, there's a handsome 16th-century monastery and church, both outsized and incomplete, with rows of columns waiting for a roof, enormous empty courtyards, and half-built arches. According to legend, the Dominican monks who initiated the project kept enlarging their plans, always thinking of something to add, never able to call it done. One day they welcomed a stranger in a carriage who offered to complete the project before cock crow the next morning if the abbot would sign a paper afterwards. Realizing this was the Devil, and that with the paper he would sign away his soul, the abbot rose in the night before the work was completed and made a cock crow, thus winning the contest. He kept his soul, but the monastery and church were never finished; the work was destroyed every night and, eventually, the Dominicans gave up trying.

Seven kilometers (5 miles) farther on, **Zaachila**, a small village and the last Zapotec capital in the valley, claims a huge unexplored pyramid that dominates the center of the town.

GETTING AROUND

Oaxaca is easily reached from Mexico City. (There are no direct international flights.) Both Mexicana and Aeroméxico make the 50-minute flight several times daily. There is also a night train with Pullman accommodations, with the fare ranging from $25 on up. Buses make the trip in 10 to 12 hours, and Highway 190, for those driving the 7 hours from the D.F. to Oaxaca, is a good one.

The beach resorts are a half-hour's flight from Oaxaca City. Puerto Escondido and Huatulco are served by Mexicana. Aeromorelos, Aviacsa, and Aero Vega. The fare to either is $75. Puerto Escondido can also be reached from Oaxaca City by car or bus over a spectacular, twisting mountain road, Highway 175, which plunges down the steep southern flank of the Sierra Madre del Sur and hits the Pacific coast at Puerto Angel. The direct Oaxaca–Puerto Escondido road, Highway 131, is still unimproved in places and better left to those in four-wheel-drive vehicles.

The city of Oaxaca itself is easily explored on foot. Taxis are always available near the cathedral, and rental cars can be obtained from Avis at the airport or from Hertz at Plaza Labastida (adjacent to the church of Santo Domingo).

Guided tours to the surrounding villages and archaeological sites leave from the Presidente, Victoria, and Marqués del Valle hotels. A *colectivo* from the Mesón del Angel (Mina 518) takes passengers to Monte Albán and picks them up later for the return trip to the city. Most cab drivers in town also will be happy to drop you off and pick you up again at an appointed time. (Note: Tomb 7 closes about an hour before the site itself does.) Taxis can be hired for about $12 an hour for trips to other sites and crafts villages.

The first-class bus station is at Niños Héroes de Chapultepec near Emiliano Carranza, but most buses to the surrounding villages leave from the second-class station across the railroad tracks at the end of Calle Trujano.

The train station is located on the west side of town on Calle Madero.

For the trip to the airport, seats in a van can be reserved at the office next to the Monte Albán Hotel or through one of the travel agencies in town.

When to go? The big tourist season is from January to March, but this is due as much to North Americans' desire to escape the snow as it is the belief that summer in Oaxaca is unpleasant. Summer *is* warmer, and there are brief tropical rains almost daily from June through September, but the altitude eliminates the sultry tropical heat you would expect at this latitude. If you decide to visit the city at Christmas time, be sure to make reservations well in advance.

There are a number of famous fiestas in Oaxaca, particularly the "Night of the Radishes," on December 23. This unusual celebration is marked by a competition among area villages to see which can fashion the most elaborate folk dance or creative depiction of a biblical story with figures made from the common garden radish. Another colorful fiesta that recently has attracted international attention features the Guelaguetza dances, honoring the ancient goddess of corn. The dates for the latter fall on two Mondays in July. Again, you'll want to book your accommodations well in advance, as Oaxaca's hotels are almost always booked for these festivals.

ACCOMMODATIONS REFERENCE

The rates given below are projections *for December 1993 through Easter 1994. Unless otherwise indicated, rates are for double rooms, double occupancy; the 10 percent VAT has been added. As rates are subject to change, it's always a good idea to double-check before booking.*

▶ **Calesa Real**. Calle García Vigil 306, **Oaxaca**, Oaxaca 68000. Tel: (951) 6-5544; Fax: (951) 5-9687. $46.

▶ **Fortín Plaza**. Pan-American Highway, km 545, **Oaxaca**, Oaxaca 68040. Tel: (951) 5-7777; Fax: (951) 5-1328. $79.

▶ **Hotel Las Golondrinas**. Calles Tinoco y Palacios 411, **Oaxaca**, Oaxaca 68000. Tel: (951) 4-2126. $30.

► **Hotel Parador Plaza.** Calle Murguia 104, **Oaxaca**, Oaxaca 68000. Tel: (951) 6-4900; Fax: (951) 4-2037. $64.

► **Hotel San Felipe Misión Oaxaca.** Calle Jalisco Sur 15, San Felipe del Agua, **Oaxaca**, Oaxaca 68020. Tel: (951) 3-5050; Fax: (951) 3-5744. $94.

► **Hotel Señorial.** Portal de Flores 6, **Oaxaca**, Oaxaca 68000. Tel: (951) 6-3933; Fax: (951) 6-3668. $54.

► **Hotel Victoria.** P.O. Box 248, Pan-American Highway, km 545, **Oaxaca**, Oaxaca 68040. Tel: (951) 5-2633; Fax: (951) 5-2411. $119–$152.

► **Marqués del Valle.** Portal de Claveria, **Oaxaca**, Oaxaca 68000. Tel: (951) 6-3198; Fax: (951) 6-6294. $63.

► **Misión de los Angeles.** P.O. Box 171, Calzada Porfirio Díaz 102, **Oaxaca**, Oaxaca 68050. Tel: (951) 5-1500; Fax: (951) 5-1680. $98.

► **Stouffer Presidente Oaxaca.** P.O. Box 248, Calle Cinco de Mayo 300, **Oaxaca**, Oaxaca 68000. Tel: (951) 6-0611; Fax: (951) 6-0732; in the U.S. and Canada, Tel: (800) HOTELS-1. $165–$198.

MAYAN MEXICO

THE YUCATAN PENINSULA AND CHIAPAS

By Robert Somerlott

"Whatever country this is, it is not Mexico."

So wrote journalist John Kenneth Turner after visiting the Mayan region at the beginning of this century, and he was by no means the first to express the opinion. It is an observation that springs more from the senses than from any single political or even economic fact. And yet, wars have been fought and lives sacrificed to support or discredit such a view. In the Yucatán, these are fighting words.

From the foreign visitor's viewpoint, the contrast offered by the Mayan region is simply another example of the Mexican republic's diversity. And what diversity it is! Anyone who spends time in the southeastern region of the country will soon understand what Turner meant. The people here call themselves *yucatecos,* not *mexicanos,* and, after 3,000 years of history, are heirs to a cultural legacy that, if not wholly independent, is quite different from that of the rest of the country.

To which a Mexican might well reply that Hawaii is part of the United States, as little as it resembles Vermont or Montana.

Even so, the sense that this is another world persists. Whereas most of Mexico is a topographical tumult, with rugged mountains plummeting down to lush valleys and, even in the most barren regions, distant ridges and peaks looming against the horizon, the tortilla-flat Yucatán Penin-

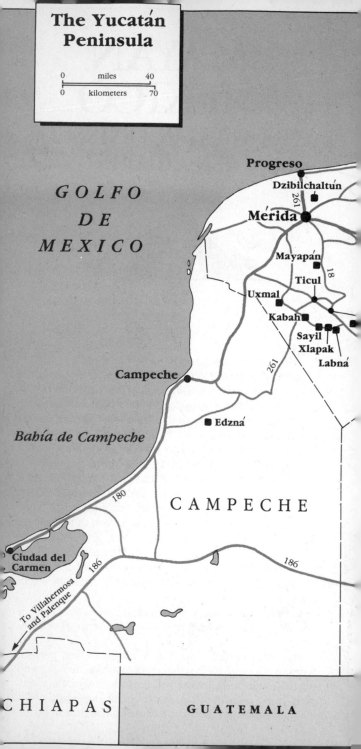

The Yucatán Peninsula

miles 40
kilometers 70

GOLFO
DE
MEXICO

Progreso
Dzibilchaltún
261
Mérida
Mayapán
Ticul
18
Uxmal
Kabah
Sayil
Xlapak
Labná
261
Campeche
Edzná
Bahía de Campeche
CAMPECHE
180
Ciudad del
Carmen
186
To Villahermosa
and Palenque
186

CHIAPAS   GUATEMALA

sula is so unbroken that normally insignificant hills are considered major heights. Likewise, to foreigners as well as the majority of Mexicans, the plant, animal, and bird life here is nothing less than exotic. Spider and howler monkeys romp— and sometimes rampage—through the trees (a howler monkey chorus is unforgettable). Brocket deer, which resemble tiny antelope, appear in clearings, then vanish, while parrots and parakeets flash gold, red, and green through the foliage. Where the topsoil is thick enough, tropical trees such as kapok, ebony, and rosewood flourish. Zapote trees produce not only the chicle used in chewing gum but also wood so strong and enduring that zapote beams still support the stones in Mayan temples after 1,000, and in some cases 2,000, years.

On the rim of the classic Mayan region to the south, in the state of Chiapas, in highland Guatemala, and in western Honduras, craggy sierras rear up to elevations of 13,000 feet. In the high, temperate valleys of such ranges the highland Maya still tend their corn (maize) patches, much as they have for centuries. And while this corner of the Mayan world outwardly resembles other parts of Mexico, its atmosphere is altogether different.

Still, it was not in these friendly highlands that the magnificent Mayan centers flourished. Instead, with few exceptions, the flowering of Mayan civilization took place in the lowland areas of the Yucatán Peninsula to the north, a flat, featureless limestone shelf covered with a thin veneer of soil and tangled with stunted vegetation. No rivers flow through the northern Yucatán; for water in the long dry seasons both men and animals must depend on natural wells, places where the limestone has collapsed, revealing underground water below. These life-sustaining ponds and concealed streams, called cenotes (from the Mayan *dz'onot*), were the single most important factor in the foundation of pre-Hispanic Mayan settlements.

The Yucatán was—and is—raw, calcareous land, newly liberated (in geologic terms) from the sea—and a sense of the sea still lingers. Yet from this meager, infertile soil sprang one of the most advanced cultures to appear in the Americas, as well as some of humankind's greatest achievements. The ruins of ancient cities and ceremonial centers here rival any the Old World has to offer, and strike modern eyes with their beauty and originality.

MAJOR INTEREST

City of Mérida (gateway to Uxmal, Chichén Itzá, and other Mayan sites)

The most important Mayan ruins
Uxmal
Chichén Itzá
Palenque (in Chiapas)

Smaller Mayan sites
Mayapán
Dzibilchaltún
Kabah
Sayil
Labná
Edzná (in Campeche)

San Cristóbal de las Casas and its environs in Chiapas

Besides these attractions (and in addition to the celebrated beach resorts of Cancún, Cozumel, and Isla Mujeres, which, along with the nearby Mayan sites of Cobá and Tulum, are covered in the Caribbean Resorts chapter), this region offers other delights: sparkling waterfalls, sweeping ocean views, mysterious caves, a score of lesser but fascinating archaeological zones, handsome native crafts, and colorful villages.

A World Apart

Although more than twice the size of the six New England states, the region that shares the Mayan heritage (including parts of Belize, Guatemala, Honduras, and El Salvador) is set apart from the surrounding area by mountains, jungles, and swamps. Even today, despite the advent of jet planes and high-speed highways, it is (or was until quite recently) a curiously isolated corner of the world. For the Maya themselves, of course, it simply was and still *is* the world. But outsiders living here have always felt this isolation.

"Yucatan is not an island," wrote Friar Diego de Landa in 1566, "but mainland. . . . It is not seen from ships until they come very close." The friar had to explain this even though he was addressing some of the best-educated men in Spain only a quarter of a century after one of the decisive battles of the Conquest had been fought on the site where the Mérida cathedral stands today. But because the region lacked silver and gold it had remained on the periphery of its Spanish rulers' collective consciousness.

Forty years earlier, Hernán Cortés, after conquering the

Aztecs, had rashly decided to traverse this country overland. The consequences of his decision, which were faithfully recorded by Bernal Díaz, make for one of the most grueling travel accounts of all time, a succession of days in which all the Spaniards seemed to do was slash, chop, stumble, sweat, and pray.

The wilderness was so dense and inaccessible, in fact, that they had to institute stern ordinances to keep their Indian converts (and labor supply) corralled. In 1552 Governor Tomás López decreed that "the Indians must not live off in forests, but come into the towns together ... under pain of whipping or prison." So came about the hundreds of villages in the region that travellers can still see, each with its own outsize church crumbling away.

The Maya Today

Prolonged assault on their language and customs notwithstanding, there remain about two and a half million native speakers of Maya today, the language fragmented into a dozen dialects that are not always mutually understandable. (University courses in Maya are offered by the state from time to time, but these seem to be token efforts.) Despite more than four centuries of persecution, the Maya have kept their ways surprisingly intact, contributing to a cultural gulf that still separates them from their Yucatec or "ladino" neighbors. (A *yucateco* is supposedly anyone native to the area, but the word often does not include the Maya—who are the most native of all. Instead, the Maya mysteriously call themselves *mestizos,* people of mixed blood, and describe all "Europeanized" folk around them as "ladinos." *Mexicanos,* a subgroup of the ladinos, are those who come from other parts of the country.) While the most obvious differences are in language and dress, religious differences, which are not instantly apparent, become clear on closer acquaintance.

Long treatises have been written on the distinctive Mayan way of life. Perhaps just one difference, concerning machismo, will illuminate the hundred other contrasts with mainstream Mexican ways. The Mayan male needs a woman to grind his corn and bear his children—he is incomplete without a wife. But he finds romantic love foolish and sexual conquest dishonorable. Success with several women would earn him no credit; in fact, Casanovas are considered contemptible. Similarly, a Mayan male is free to show affection to his wife in public without sacrificing his machismo; he has no need to display a masculine superiority or aloofness. At the same time, his dignity will not allow him the exuberant camaraderie most Mexican men enjoy with their male friends.

All of this is so different from the arrogant pride of mainstream machismo that the emotional understanding between the Maya and their neighbors is often tenuous. Some of the most basic words in life—"sex," "love," "honor," and "success"—become blurred in translation. As a result, the Maya and the more aggressive, acquisitive people around them have seldom communicated clearly except through violence. And although peace has long been maintained, the distance between them remains. For all that, the Maya are a friendly, gracious people with a lively curiosity about strangers.

Visiting Mayan Ruins

There are no real patterns to look for at ancient Mayan sites such as you might find in Gothic cathedrals or Turkish mosques, but a few features were frequently repeated. Whether or not traces of them remain will vary from site to site.

Often you will see stylized sculpted masks with long, trunklike noses representing the rain god or gods (*Chac* or *Chaques*). Sometimes, as at Kabah, the protuberant noses have fallen off and the great round eyes stand out as the main feature of these so-called *Chac* masks.

Some temples were situated with much thought given to astronomical or solar orientation (e.g., the Castillo at Chichén Itzá), so that certain patterns of shadow or light appeared on a critical day, such as the summer or winter solstice. Such effects can still be seen, although their frequency and impact are frequently exaggerated by on-site tour guides.

Originally, Mayan buildings, statues, and pavements were painted in brilliant colors that have now faded. The color red, often meant to connote death, was applied to tombs and other surfaces, such as paving. All central plazas were paved, as at Uxmal, and sometimes the entire central area of a site had a cement floor, as at Tikal (in Guatemala; see the Guatemala chapter below). The once-paved areas are now often planted with grass.

If you see a free-standing arch, as at Kabah, there's a good chance that a slightly raised road or causeway (*sacbeob*) once ran through it. Those temples that today appear squat usually had tall roofcombs to create the illusion of height.

A stable water supply was vital. A few sites, such as Copán (just over the Guatemala border in Honduras) and Palenque, were established near streams. Those that were not were almost always situated near cenotes, as at Chichén Itzá and Dzibilchaltún, or close to a system of reservoirs, as at Tikal.

MERIDA

Mérida, tropical and Caribbean, is the gateway for visits to Uxmal, Kabah, and some lesser but still fascinating ruins. It is also a possible headquarters for a day trip to Chichén Itzá (although it is much more satisfying to stay overnight at that magnificent site). Three days are enough to glimpse the highlights of the Mérida area. Five days are more reasonable, and a week is not too much.

Mérida has two nicknames, and both are clichés—"the Paris of the West" and "the White City." Neither is accurate, but both contain a germ of truth about this curious town.

From the beginning, the city, which was established in 1542, looked across flat country toward the sea. The markets for the raw materials taken from the jungle around it, including hemp and lumber, lay in Europe, not Mexico, and events in Spain loomed far larger here than the goings on in remote Mexico City. In the 19th century, when hemp exports brought great wealth to Mérida, the city sent its sons to Paris for cultivation; over time they brought back the French manners and styles that are still in evidence today. In fact, strolling or riding along Mérida's Paseo Montejo, its most elegant avenue, evokes not only France but far more the old French neighborhoods in Algeria. Here are the curlicues, fancies, and fripperies of both Paris and Tangier. Yet the "Frenchness" of Mérida is merely a patina; ultimately, the hemp barons adopted a style, not a civilization.

As to Mérida's reputation as "the White City," when the Spaniards first stumbled out of the jungle here they found a town called Tiho (the Mayan T'hó). This native settlement, which was constructed of gleaming limestone, impressed them as both splendid and lovely. So, with the perversity of their tribe, they promptly destroyed it. Francisco de Montejo the Younger, the chief destroyer, gazed upon the havoc his men had wrought and nostalgically recalled the white stone heaps of a Roman ruin near the Spanish town of Mérida. Hence the name of the new city that was built with the stone blocks of the old.

While the walls of Mérida are no longer uniformly white, the local people make up for it with their clothing. Mayan women billow like clouds in their *huipiles* (pronounced locally as "ee-pih-layz"), pale tunic-like dresses tipped by rainbows of embroidery. The men are usually clad in white trousers and loose white *guayabera* shirts. When the main plaza is thronged with scrubbed people in their scrubbed clothes, Mérida is still "the White City." (Like the Maya people, who always bathe more than once a day, Mérida takes pride in being "the cleanest tropical city in the world." Perhaps this is true, although the market area somewhat belies the claim.)

Around in Mérida

The appeal of Mérida does not lie in inspecting its local monuments. On heavily advertised city tours, guides struggle to fill up two or three hours, driving through gentrified neighborhoods, holding passengers captive at overpriced craft shows, and turning them loose on their own in the municipal market. It is far better, instead, to stroll the downtown area on your own or ride in one of the horse-drawn carriages that lend color to the city.

THE PLAZA MAYOR

The main square, variously called the Plaza Mayor, Plaza Principal, Plaza de la Independencia, and Plaza de Armas, is at the intersection of Calles 60 and 61, the geographic and commercial heart of the city. (Mérida, like most towns the Spanish built from scratch, was laid out as a grid: Odd-numbered streets run east and west, even-numbered ones north and south.) The spacious plaza, with its tall, dignified laurel trees, is the ideal place to linger and get accustomed to the tempo of the city. Like so many things in Mérida, even the laurels have a Caribbean connection. They were originally sent from India and were intended to embellish Havana. After they were salvaged from a shipwreck off the Yucatán coast, however, they were planted here. (*Yucatecos* have always been quick to snatch any gift from the sea.)

The cathedral, on the east side of the plaza, was begun in 1561 and is the oldest still in use in Mexico. Unfortunately, its age and size are its only real claims to distinction; as is the case with virtually all the extant colonial buildings in Mérida, it offers nothing special.

The 19th-century **Palacio de Gobierno**, on the north side of the main plaza, is noted for a series of dramatic murals by Fernando Castro Pacheco illustrating (in grisly detail) the history of the region. Three other works by the artist, decorating the main stairway, deal with more cheerful, Mayan subjects.

Casa de Montejo

The Montejo family—father, son, and cousin—and their successors were the Spanish conquerors (some would say plunderers) of the Yucatán. Their palace, built in 1549, originally occupied the whole south side of the square. Today the Casa de Montejo is greatly reduced in size and serves as a bank. Its façade, however, is the single colonial landmark in Mérida that merits careful inspection.

In 1841 John Lloyd Stephens, the modern discoverer of the ancient Mayan cities, strolled into Mérida's plaza, where this building instantly arrested his attention. As he later described the relief carving he saw that day: "The subject represents two knights in armour with visors, breastplates and helmets, standing upon the shoulders of crushed naked figures, probably intended to represent the conquering Spaniard trampling upon the Indian."

Stephens was accurate but kind. In actuality, the relief is one of the most arrogant representations ever commissioned for a private residence; the skill of the Mayan slave artists who did the carving only makes the whole matter worse. To see this relief is to see the brutal attitudes of the conquerors starkly revealed. Looking at it another way, you might say that even Diego Rivera, master propagandist for Indian rights, never created a more scathing indictment of the conquistadors.

Caryatid-like Amazons, fierce and busty, lurk at windows nearby, where they uphold royal escutcheons. Again, the stonework is as admirable as the idea is repellent.

The Conquest was neither as easy nor as complete as the Montejo façade would have it. The Maya resisted the Spaniards with greater fierceness and success than the Aztecs, at first repelling the invaders entirely, then battling for three years before their defeat at Tiho. Even then their acquiescence was no sure thing, and skirmishing went on for more than a century. In fact, the final surrender of the last rebellious band didn't come about until 1697, and resistance continued for years afterward.

Even as Stephens was studying the Montejo palace, trouble was brewing among the people who had been crushed by the conquering stone foot. In 1846 the Maya arose with such ferocity that only the cities of Mérida and Campeche held out, in what became known as the "War of the Castes." The terrified whites of the peninsula implored Spain, England, and the United States to accept the Yucatán as a colony. In 1848 a Mexican federal army came to the rescue, retaking the burned haciendas. Sporadic violence continued until 1901.

Mérida's Café Scene

On the opposite side of the plaza, a world away from the savagery portrayed on the façade of the Montejo palace, is the leisurely society of Mérida's sidewalk cafés. It's true that the city is a center of industry and commerce; somehow, things must get done. Yet in its cafés unhurried patrons who are obviously men of affairs have seemingly endless time for endless coffees served as *grecos*—triple strength with hot water on the side. Although the nearby streets bustle with scurrying people, haste is frowned upon here, and voices and gestures are modulated.

The **Parque Cepeda Peraza**, at the intersection of Calles 59 and 60, two blocks north of the cathedral, is another shady spot for lingering over coffee or a cool drink. It's also an international crossroads for archaeology buffs—many of them young and travelling on tight budgets—the kind of place where you can witness unexpected reunions of people who last saw each other in Cuzco or Crete. Tourists sit scribbling postcards, music echoes from a cantina in a nearby patio, and Mérida's only aristocratic church, the Iglesia de Jesús, mellows in the tropical sunshine.

PASEO DE MONTEJO

The Paseo de Montejo, which runs north from Calle 47, is lined with imposing homes and spacious gardens, a reminder of how patrician the rulers of this city have always been. Mérida is probably the only city in Mexico where old families trace their history not just to the Conquest, but to a specific conquistador. They have not intermarried with the Maya—although their men have certainly interbred. Nor have they formed marital alliances with the many immigrant Levantine merchants who dominate the city's drygoods business.

At the intersection of Calle 43 and the Paseo stands one of the most opulent and Rococo of the old mansions, now the local **Museo Regional de Antropología**. The collection of Mayan artifacts, including a variety of stunning jewelry, is excellent, while the building itself is a different kind of treat. Closed Mondays.

The **Museo de Arte Popular**, Mérida's very obscure craft museum, can be hunted down on Calle 59 between Calles 50 and 48, west of the plaza. The medley of flamboyant folk art includes looms, baskets, hammocks, textiles, and papiermâché Mayan figures disconcertingly reminiscent of outsize voodoo dolls. A government-run shop at the rear offers a good selection of reasonably priced items. Closed Mondays.

SHOPPING IN MERIDA

The city market, a short walk south from the main plaza, is a crowded, bustling, somewhat confusing maze of stalls and counters heaped high with the region's offerings. Articles made of henequen cord take a hundred different forms here, from the obvious, such as shopping bags, mats, and hammocks, to some quite surprising and imaginative neckties and belts. The rugs are both unusual and durable.

On the other hand, the best hammocks are made not from henequen but from linen, and are built to last a lifetime. Besides the usual one-person size, you can choose from matrimonial hammocks, family hammocks, and hammocks seemingly designed for community siestas.

Much of the embroidery on display is machine-made, yet so intricate that the method of manufacture hardly seems to matter.

Mérida is one of the great centers for Panama hats, but the best, unfortunately, are not displayed in the market. The city's most famous hat shop is **La Casa de los Jipis**, located on Calle 56 between Calles 65 and 67. Some of the hats here are among the best in the world, so don't be surprised if the prices seem high.

Gold filigree, crafted much as it was in pre-Hispanic times, is offered in many shops. Caution is advisable, however, for traditional Yucatecan gold work is only 10-carat, not 14 as is often claimed. In some shops true 14-carat gold is sold, for which you will be able to get a written or printed guarantee.

Guayabera shirts are a Mérida specialty and can be found in a score of shops. **Jack**, at Calle 59 number 505, has an especially large selection. The loose-fitting cotton *guayabera* is worn for its coolness, and you'll be disappointed if yours is warm because of the overuse of synthetic fiber, so buy carefully.

Finally, there are good craft and popular arts stores to be found at the entrances to major archaeological sites near Mérida; while the prices will be a little inflated, they won't be larcenous.

STAYING IN MERIDA

True to its name, the ▶ **Holiday Inn Mérida** conjures up a spirit of cheerful leisure. The service is excellent, and its large and well-maintained swimming pool is especially welcome after hours of exploring ruins. Located in a quiet flower-filled neighborhood just off the Paseo de Montejo, the hotel is convenient to fast transportation downtown. The clientele is international, as are the dining room, its two coffee shops, the cocktail lounge with entertainment, and the disco. It also has a lighted tennis court. Higher priced than other Mérida hotels, the Holiday Inn is still a top value.

At the corner of Calles 57 and 60, three blocks north of the plaza, the charming ▶ **Casa del Balam** mixes colonial and Mayan motifs in its decor. The rooms here, arranged around a leafy patio, are clean, spacious, and air-conditioned, with those on the top floor quietest. The pool is tucked away in a shady, restful garden, and the hotel also has a very pleasant bar and beautiful patio restaurant.

▶ **El Conquistador**, located in an expensive and busy commercial neighborhood halfway between the downtown area and the outskirts of the city, offers new and very good rooms and suites with private balconies overlooking the Paseo. Although it's more than walking distance from the center of town, transportation along the boulevard is good. El Conquistador also has an indoor pool and a restaurant.

▶ **El Castellano** is a modern high-rise on Calle 57 near the center of town, two blocks west of the main plaza. Rooms vary in size, but some of the best are on the upper floors, with panoramic views of the city spread out below. They are also quieter, almost hushed, than the rooms on the lower floors. The hotel has ample public areas, a pool, and a restaurant as well.

The ▶ **Hotel Dolores Alba** is a friendly, family-run establishment in a converted town house three blocks east of the main plaza on Calle 63. The rooms are basic, but the atmosphere is pleasant. Not all rooms are air-conditioned, however, and some are small. Get the best or go elsewhere; only the *good* accommodations here are a bargain.

Located a block northeast of the plaza at Calle 62, the ▶ **Hotel Colón** has enough charm to compensate for its rather plain rooms. Stay in the newer, air-conditioned wing if you can.

The ▶ **Gran Hotel** on the lively Parque Cepeda Peraza is a favorite of students and thrifty travellers of all ages. The interior of the old building is adorned with the owner's eclectic collection of antique sewing machines, phonographs, radios, and curios. Like the collection, the hotel is a relic of an earlier age, and despite the noise and reliance on ceiling fans, its guests seem to enjoy its personality.

DINING IN MERIDA

Yucatecan cuisine has little to do with the usual fare of Mexico, except for their common reliance on corn and chiles as basic ingredients. Marinades, seldom used in the rest of the country, add tantalizing, hard-to-recognize flavors to many dishes here. Foods prepared in a tangy orange marinade are a particular specialty. Likewise, the word *pibil* appears frequently on menus and refers to the traditional barbecue pits of the Maya (although *pibil* cookery in restaurants is usually done by steam). Chicken and pork (*pollo* and *cochinita*) so prepared are tender and succulent. Lime soup (*sopa de lima*) is a rich chicken broth made glorious with lime juice and spices, then garnished in a hundred different ways. Sometimes it has pieces of chicken, tortilla chips, chopped tomatoes, and onions (creativity is the soul of a good *sopa de lima*). Foods served *escabeche* have been soaked in a marinade of onions, vinegar, and whatever spices inspiration dictates. The Lebanese and Syrians have been settled in the Yucatán for so long that many of their national dishes have also become standard fare here.

Los Almendros, a traditional Mérida favorite, is located two blocks north and four blocks east of the Plaza Mayor at Calle 50-A number 493. A rather plain establishment, it nevertheless presents a fine sampling of Yucatecan cuisine at reasonable prices. For an introduction to the regional fare, the combination plate is a good choice, offering samples of about four selections. Here and in other regional restaurants you should treat the side sauces with respect; while the cookery is not especially fiery, the sauces can be molten lava. Tel: (99) 21-2851.

Rather more elegant (and expensive) is **Las Palomas**, on Calle 56 between Calles 55 and 53, a 19th-century Spanish-Moorish town house that has been converted into a very good restaurant serving Yucatecan and European dishes. Tel: (99) 25-5690.

The distinguished **Chateau Valentín** offers impeccable service and a tasty selection of international and Yucatecan offerings (although the regional fare has been somewhat adapted). Piano music adds to its elegant ambience. Calle 58 number 499. (This is in the Holiday Inn neighborhood, not downtown as its address might suggest.) It's expensive, and reservations are advised; Tel: (99) 25-5690.

The best Lebanese food in town is served in the hacienda atmosphere of **Alberto's Continental Patio**. Lunch and dinner from an international menu are served in this early-19th-century mansion, with the reasonable prices attracting local businessmen and more than a few tourists. Tel: (99) 28-5367.

For snacks, short orders, and good but rather standard desserts, **Leo's**, at Paseo de Montejo 460A and Calle 37, is modern, casual, and inexpensive.

EXCURSIONS FROM MERIDA

If your time is limited you *can* see Uxmal, Kabah, Sayil, and Labná in a one-day excursion, though it won't allow you to appreciate them fully. Uxmal by itself is enough to take in at one go; in a pinch it can be combined with Kabah. But that really should be the limit. (See the Getting Around section below.) Note, too, that all archaeological zones, regardless of size, are officially open seven days a week, though some may close "unofficially" on Mondays.

Mayapán and Ticul also can be combined in a one-day excursion. **Mayapán**, 51 km (32 miles) southeast of Mérida via Highway 18, flourished in the 13th and 14th centuries, and was an important Mayan city in the centuries leading up to the Conquest; unfortunately, not a great deal of it remains. Eleven kilometers (7 miles) south of Mayapán, the large village of **Ticul** is known for its handicrafts, especially its pottery and embroidery. Although both places are interesting, time should be allowed for them only after the major sites have been explored.

An excursion to the archaeological zone of Dzibilchaltún (see immediately below) certainly repays a half-day trip. But continuing north of Dzibilchaltún to the port town of Progreso is not worth the time or effort.

Most visitors skip the beautiful Mayan ruins at **Edzná**, a three-and-a-half-hour drive southwest of Mérida in the state of Campeche, because it does not fit conveniently into the usual itineraries. But devotees of Mayan ruins, provided they have extra time, will not want to miss the magnificent **Pirámide de los Cinco Pisos** (Pyramid of the Five Stories) and some newly excavated ruins there. While it's a convenient stop for drivers heading for the Yucatán from Villahermosa or Palenque, it will either require a day-long excursion or an overnight stay in Campeche, about 60 km (37 miles) northwest, for those coming from Mérida.

The most extensive, but least accessible, Mayan ruins are found at **Calakmul**, southeast of Edzńa near the Guatemalan border. Barely explored, but known to contain a large number of stelae, Calakmul was inhabited from about 1500 B.C. until nearly A.D. 1600. Entwined in dense jungle forest, the site may not be open to tourists for many years to come, as excavation is proceeding at a slow pace.

To sum up, the sights nearest Mérida, in descending order of importance, are the archaeological zones of Uxmal, Kabah, Sayil, Labná, Edzná, Dzibilchaltún, Mayapán, and, for handicrafts, Ticul. Magnificent Chichén Itzá is a possible one-day trip from Mérida, but is better left as an overnight (at least) excursion. On the other hand, it's an easy overnighter from either Cancún or Cozumel.

The Postclassic Mayan site of **Tulum** (too-LOOM), on the Caribbean coast, was a Mayan trading center from A.D. 1200 to 1450. Although it makes for a convenient excursion from Cozumel, and is easy enough from Cancún, it does not, in spite of its lovely setting, quite justify a five- to six-hour drive from Mérida itself. Those travelling between Mérida and the Caribbean resorts will find Tulum a delightful bonus, however (see the Caribbean Resorts chapter below).

Dzibilchaltún

Dzibilchaltún (tsee-beel-chal-TOON), just north of Mérida, is often hailed as the site of the longest continuous human occupation in the Western Hemisphere. A settlement sprang up here not long after 1000 B.C., and a Mayan village was still standing on the spot in A.D. 1580 when the Spaniards erected a church to aid in the conversion of the local inhabitants.

The site is extraordinarily large, complex, and important. Between A.D. 700 and 1000 this may have been not only the largest of all Mayan centers but the richest, supported by a flourishing trade in salt from the nearby coast. (Postclassic Dzibilchaltún covered an area as large as modern Washington, D.C.) The city declined dramatically after A.D. 1000, yet still managed to live on; in fact, modest buildings were being erected right up until the time of the Spanish occupation. Its past glories should not lead a visitor to expect too much today, however. The site is interesting and well worth exploring, but the beauty and glory have long since vanished.

Dzibilchaltún (the name means "place where there are inscriptions on flat stones") is easily reached from Mérida by car, taxi, bus, or packaged tour. A guide is helpful but not necessary. Allow two hours for inspecting the ruins and on-site museum. Drivers should take Highway 261 (the Progreso road) north from Mérida for 15 km (9 miles), then turn east and continue 5 km (3 miles) to the village of Xcunya. The site, which is closed to visitors on Mondays, is just south of the village.

Inside the entrance to the site a path leads past a small, well-restored temple known, in the sometimes arcane terminology of the archaeologist, as Edificio 38-sub. In classic Mesoamerican fashion, the fallen masonry of Edificio 38, a slightly newer temple that once covered the older building, is strewn around the surviving building.

A little farther on a sign points left (east) to the Temple of the Seven Dolls. The way is dotted with fallen and crumbling walls, and to the north rise a ruined platform and temple next to a good-sized building base, Edificio 36. A wide stairway faces south, commanding a view of the main plaza and the Spanish-built chapel with barrel vault huddling there, an incongruous and feeble architectural gesture dating from the 1590s.

Templo de las Siete Muñecas

Heading east, the rubble-strewn trail eventually passes a platform with a simple stela, then continues on to the famous Temple of the Seven Dolls (Edificio 1-sub), the most impressive structure at Dzibilchaltún. (The approach to the temple is over the remains of a *sacbeob*, one of the raised ceremonial roads the Maya built out of limestone and lime cement. Two such elevated roads are found at the site, both leading to the main plaza.) Other nearby structures, including a platform and stela, are all associated with the temple. Judging by the orientation of the stairways and these outlying structures, the temple itself seems to have been used for astronomical observations.

Built at the start of the Late Classic era (about A.D. 600), the temple was filled in not long after its completion and another building erected over it. The inner temple seems to have been forgotten for two centuries or more, but about A.D. 1300 the Mayan inhabitants of Dzibilchaltún tunneled down to the original temple floor and there cut an opening in the rubble. They then enshrined seven crude clay figurines in this pit, representations of human beings suffering various deformities. The tunnel was filled in, leaving a pipe or speaking tube (called a psychoduct) open to the outside world, apparently so the living could receive divine communication during healing rituals. (Similar tubes appear at a few Mayan sites, most notably at Palenque.)

The Cenote

From the Temple of the Seven Dolls return by the route you came; at the cutoff leading back to the entrance, turn left. A little farther on is the **Cenote Xlacah**, whose impressive surface area, more than 100 feet across, makes it one of the largest wells in the Yucatán and the most important in the ancient city.

The cenote, one of several in Dzibilchaltún, plunges 140 feet through the limestone amid a spacious but sadly ruined palace complex that was surely magnificent in its day. (One of its buildings contained 20 vaulted rooms.) Divers exploring the cenote have brought up skeletons, both bovine and human, one of them that of a Spaniard.

A collection of artifacts from the cenote are found in the small museum at the entrance to the site. In addition to these and the curious clay figurines from the Temple of the Seven Dolls, the collection includes hairpins, ornaments, and two beautiful fragments of Late Classic stelae.

UXMAL

The first U.S. traveller to visit this imposing ruined city south of Mérida was John Lloyd Stephens, who wrote in 1843, "We entered a noble courtyard with four great façades looking down upon it, each ornamented from one end to the other with the richest and most intricate carving... presenting a scene of strange magnificence."

Magnificence indeed! At Uxmal (oosh-MAHL) gigantic masks of snouted rain gods crowd upon one another in emphatic profusion, mosaics of amazing intricacy enfold whole buildings, and boldness of conception is combined with the most delicate masonry technique. Invariably, the visitor is struck by the deluge of carved symbolism applied to Uxmal's palaces, pyramids, and temples. At the same time, the decoration is daring and radical; potentially jarring combinations of geometric and floral patterns instead are magically combined to achieve a sublime harmony.

The prevailing architectural style at Uxmal is called "Puuc," a name taken from the Puuc hills, a series of low ridges that dominate this topographically monotonous region. Puuc architecture runs to thick walls decorated with thin stones set like mosaics. The most common motifs are the masks of the rain god Chac, often combined with diamond shapes; realistic representations of Mayan *na* huts; and geometric forms resembling Greek key decorations. The façades of buildings in this style are usually divided horizontally by a medial molding, with the top half given over to these ornate mosaics and the lower half left plain. Pure Puuc style is a Late Classic–era development, and is not confined exclusively to sites in the Uxmal area; in fact, lovely examples of it occur far to the south at Río Bec as well as to the northeast in the older buildings at Chichén Itzá.

The great center of Uxmal was rebuilt several times over the centuries, so it is impossible to date its structures with any exactness. Its zenith occurred between A.D. 600 and 900. The latest confirmed written date at the site is A.D. 909; its temples and courtyards were probably abandoned soon after that—for reasons that remain unknown.

Pirámide del Adivino

Near the entrance to the site rises the imposing Temple of the Magician. Constructed in five different stages, its exact function is unknown. (The name refers to a magical dwarflike figure in Mayan folklore.) A single mask on the temple suggests the influence of people from the central highlands. But the Toltecs, who greatly changed the architecture of the Yucatán, never occupied Uxmal; it remains pure Maya. Built in five separate stages, the unusual rectangular base of the pyramid is so rounded that it appears nearly oval. The three-room sanctuary atop it, with a few minor Mexican details on its west façade, offers a breathtaking view of the site and the surrounding jungle. In fact, anyone climbing the steeply pitched stairs of either the east or west façade quickly learns that, at Uxmal, pre-Columbian worshipers had to approach the gods with awkward humility, almost clambering upward.

Cuadrángulo de las Monjas

The Nunnery Quadrangle, immediately behind (to the west of) the Temple of the Magician, is often hailed as one of the most beautiful structures, or complex of structures, in the New World. The four buildings that compose it are a triumph of decoration in stone. The work is mosaic, but on a scale not usually associated with mosaic art. Individual pieces may be more than three feet in length and so heavy that one man could never have lifted them into place.

The four buildings of the Nunnery may have served as a residence for priests; at least that is the traditional theory. Modern explanations of its name, however, are illuminating, if no more accurate: It was so named by the Spaniards because nuns make lace and the stonework is lacy; or because the atmosphere within its walls suggests the serenity of a convent.

Casa de las Tortugas and Palacio del Gobernador

The **ball court,** just south of the Nunnery, seems to have been constructed to accommodate a small—doubtless elite—group of spectators. Raised on a huge man-made platform a bit farther south, the small and, at first glance, plain House of the Turtles is likely to be overlooked amid the grandeur of the rest of the site. Still, in its own sober way, the building is a masterpiece, at once pure in its proportions and discreet in its decoration (with a simple frieze of carved turtles adorning its upper ledge). The molding, especially, is beautifully managed, and the symbolism throughout is connected with rain and agriculture.

The Palace of the Governor, which takes its name from the crowned figure in the center of the structure, is located next to the House of the Turtles and dominates the site. Set upon a stone platform and built in three sections, it is regarded, like the Nunnery, as one of the masterpieces of Mesoamerican architecture. The designs on its façade were inspired by weaving and the decorative arts, and are combined with a variety of snakeskin patterns and representations of the rain god Chac (in total, some 20,000 mosaic elements were used in the frieze).

The three sections of the palace are joined by corbeled "arches." (Although not true arches in an architectural sense, they are as close as the Maya came to achieving that engineering feat and are often called "Mayan arches.") Corbeled arches such as these were created by gradually projecting stone blocks outward from each side until the arch came to a peak, but since these constructions did not support weight efficiently, the Maya would reinforce them with a beam near the top. Today, although many of the beams have fallen or rotted away, the holes cut for them remain.

Two sculpted works stand at the base of the broad stairway leading up to the palace—a two-headed jaguar on a small platform, perhaps a throne, and a phallic column that is an oddity in this otherwise classic Mayan site. (Phallic sculpture was rarely used to decorate lowland Mayan centers, although other examples are found at Uxmal, most notably serving as rainspouts. The theme seems to have been imported from the Veracruz area, where such work is not unusual. Plumed-serpent representations at Uxmal also suggest faraway influences that seem to have been introduced late and had little effect on the basic style.)

Other Structures at Uxmal

The **Gran Pirámide** (Grand Pyramid), a few steps west of the palace, is in poor condition, as is the small **Templo de las Guacamayas** (Temple of the Parrots) that sits atop it. The dedication here is to the sun. The pyramid is easy to climb, however, and affords both grand views and excellent photo opportunities.

A bit to the west is the ruined **El Palomar** (Dovecote). The nine triangular works of masonry that top it are fanciful Mayan roofcombs, which were often added to rather squat structures to create the illusion of height and grace. Like all of Uxmal, they were once painted in brilliant colors.

Three outlying groups of structures are in ruined condition, some of them little more than rubble. They include the Grupo del Norte (North Group), the Grupo del Cementerio (Cemetery Group), and the Casa de la Vieja (House of the Old Woman); beyond them lies the quite unerotic **Templo de los Falos** (Temple of the Phalli).

Uxmal is 77 km (48 miles) south of Mérida; take Highway 180 to Umán, then Highway 261 south. If your itinerary only allows for a one-day excursion, you should leave Mérida early in the morning so that any climbing you do at the ruins is over before the hottest part of the afternoon. (See the Getting Around section below.) In addition, every night a dramatic, well-designed sound-and-light show is presented: one just after sunset in Spanish, a later one in English. (The English version is usually too late for visitors returning to Mérida.)

STAYING AT UXMAL

There are a number of good hotels with restaurants if you decide to stay overnight at Uxmal, and all of them are helpful in arranging further exploration of the area. None is inexpensive, however.

Across the highway from the ruins, the ▶ **Hacienda Uxmal** is gracious, tropical, and colonial. Long verandahs, ceiling fans, and wicker furniture lend it a real hacienda feeling, and many people think it's the prettiest hotel in the Yucatán. Though expensive by local standards, the price of a room here would be a bargain almost anywhere else.

The ▶ **Villa Arqueológica Uxmal**, at the entrance to the ruins, follows the solid format of this chain, which is Club Med–connected but very unlike Club Med in personality. Cozy rooms, tennis court, bar, restaurant, pool, air-conditioning, and pleasant grounds.

The ▶ **Misión Park Inn Uxmal**, part of the Misión chain, is modern and comfortable, and all its rooms have air-conditioning. The better rooms also have balconies and striking views. Its popularity with tour-bus groups is an indication of its value, but it's less personal than the other hotels here. Located a mile from the archaeological zone.

Around Uxmal

Tours leaving from the Uxmal hotels cover Kabah, Sayil, Xlapak, Labná, and the Loltún caves in a day, though sometimes omitting the caves. Such a trip allows for a cursory glance at everything, but is far too rushed for true archaeology buffs, photographers, and anyone else who simply might want the time to absorb the strange and unusual things they will encounter.

A better trip would be: a full day at the Uxmal ruins, ending with a late lunch and perhaps a swim. Return to the ruins for the sound-and-light show in the evening and stay overnight at an Uxmal hotel. The next day return to the ruins to reexamine their memorable nooks and crannies, then go on to Kabah. A third day could be devoted to the other sights of the region, including the caves in the morning, and ending either at an Uxmal hotel or back in Mérida that afternoon.

KABAH

The fanciful ceremonial center of Kabah (kah-BAH), located on either side of Highway 261, lies approximately 22 km (14 miles) southeast of Uxmal. Visitors approaching the zone from Mérida and the north will suddenly see a remarkable structure rising above the low, spiky vegetation on the left side of the road. This is the famed **Palacio de los Mascarones** (Palace of the Masks), also known as the Codz-Pop (coiled mat) because of its vast array of masks with undulating noses, which vaguely resemble the curving lines of Mayan mats.

Even after the exuberant decoration at Uxmal, this structure comes as a surprise. The entire façade is covered with masks of the Mayan rain god Chac—row upon blank-eyed row, and mostly noseless now. Here is stone clamoring for rain, the most insistent statement made by any Mayan temple. The masks, like the decorative work at Uxmal, are in actuality large-scale mosaics: Each mask, of which there are some 250, comprises 30 separate carved and dressed stone elements. Obviously, the labor involved in running the "mask factory" must have been enormous. You will need a lot of imagination, however, to envision the palace in its former glory.

Kabah, which was contemporary with Uxmal, thrived from A.D. 600 to 900, when, for reasons unknown, it was abandoned. There are nine more or less excavated structures here, two of which are three-building complexes. One of the most intriguing is located across the highway from the Palace of the Masks: the arch, a white limestone structure standing stark and alone, is a beautiful work of corbeling that spans a distance of more than 15 feet. According to archaeologists, it once served as a monumental gateway to a *sacbeob,* or processional route, that ran all the way to Uxmal. These raised roads, of which there were more than a few in the region, were impressive achievements, cutting through dense jungle and crossing treacherous swamps. The Spanish, arriving more than six centuries after the arch was built, proved woefully inferior to the Maya when it came to building roads.

On the east side of the highway, about a quarter of a mile from the main cluster of ruins, is the **Tercera Casa**, often called the Temple of the Columns. A long ripple of carving, the temple is related artistically to the House of the Turtles in Uxmal, with both making extensive use of engaged columns as decoration. A front terrace once served to catch rainwater for a nearby cistern.

The soil around Kabah is ungenerous, yielding stingy corn crops to slash-and-burn farming, which the Maya practice today much as they did during the heyday of this ceremonial center. (At Kabah, Sayil, Xlapak, Labná, and other sites in the region, a high iron oxide content in the soil gives the crumbling structures a reddish tint that is especially noticeable in the early morning or late afternoon.) All the more reason, therefore, to stand in awe of the religious and cultural forces that fueled the Maya's magnificent impulse to build here and elsewhere in the Yucatán.

SAYIL, XLAPAK, AND LABNA

Three other interesting Mayan sites built in the Puuc style can be included in a trip from Uxmal.

Sayil (sah-YEEL) is a neighbor of Kabah. To get to this site, head south on Highway 261 for 5 km (3 miles), then turn left. This road, marked "Oxkutzcab" (oosh-coots-cahb), takes you to Sayil, 4 km (2½ miles) farther on. Road signs with the names of the sites make finding them a simple proposition.

The Sayil archaeological zone is famed for its **Palacio**, a terraced, 70-room, three-story structure. Though it is huge and massive, the lightness of its design counteracts any bulkiness, lending it instead a feeling of elegance and airiness. A broad stairway rises gracefully to divide the structure; elsewhere, round columns, well-spaced doors, and lovely friezes impart a pleasing rhythm to its lower floors. Among the site's curiosities are sculptures of the "upside-down god," which are variously described as diving, falling, or descending. The Chac masks and accompanying scrollwork are particularly beautiful. Carved stelae date from about A.D. 850, Sayil's heyday. Another stela, probably much older and perhaps not even Mayan, is an exaggerated phallic figure. Based on the ceramic evidence, the site, which was abandoned in the tenth century, seems to have been inhabited as far back as A.D. 200. There are several (out of several hundred) buildings accessible to the public; the rest are still locked in jungle.

Xlapak (shlah-PAHK) is 7 km (4 miles) farther along the

road to Labná and makes for a quick visit, since there remains only one temple at the site; it is an almost perfect structure, however. Three great stone masks dominate the center of the symmetrical, beautifully proportioned building—not rare but somewhat unusual in Mayan architecture. The structure dates from about A.D. 800.

The small but quite wonderful ruins of **Labná** are just 3 km (2 miles) east of Xlapak; there will be a sign indicating a parking area and path to the right. Four major structures survive here. The chief one, the **Palacio**, is almost 535 feet long at its base and two stories high. Besides the stern masks of the snouted rain god, you can see examples of the Mayan "hut theme"—a sculpted representation of what seems to be a thatched dwelling. (Another version of the hut motif appears on the remarkable **arch** south of the palace; see below.) A date corresponding to A.D. 862 is inscribed on the extended nose of one of the palace's rain gods, possibly the last carving done at the site before it was abandoned.

The Mirador, also rising south of the palace, displays an elegant roofcomb; the severe complex nearby is called the Edificio Este (East Building).

Also near the Mirador, the famous Labná arch, often called "La Puerta" ("the Gateway"), is a fantasy in stone. A corbeled arch is stepped up to an almost Gothic point and flanked by sculpted lattice-work and a small room on either side. This altogether delightful monument once connected two courtyards.

Labná was a major religious center, and probably an important market center as well, with a resident population that approached 3,000—an estimate partly based on the capacity of the 60 cisterns that were dug to supply it with water in the dry season. The most impressive remaining cistern, called a chaltun, collects rain in a catch basin on the terrace supporting the palace's second story and from there channels it into a covered pool below.

THE LOLTUN CAVES

These caves (*grutas*), a series of dramatic chambers and corridors honeycombing the limestone crust in this region, were known to ancient hunters, who left behind a variety of stone artifacts as well as the remains of animals they had killed, as early as 2500 B.C. Later on, the mysterious atmosphere, strange rock formations, and stalactites and stalagmites appear to have inspired a certain amount of religious awe among the Maya. Eventually, glyphs and steps were carved at the entrance, and a sculpted sentinel was placed nearby—a figure thought to date from 300 B.C.

Lights have since been installed in the caves, but only enough to illuminate the surroundings without compromising their mystery. You may enter only with a guided tour group, however. The tours, conducted in Spanish, leave from the entrance at 9:30 and 11:30 A.M. and 1:30 P.M., Tuesday through Sunday; allow two hours for the full tour.

The caves are 20 km (12 miles) east of Labná on the road to Oxkutzcab and can be visited as part of an excursion to Labná or when exploring Mayapán and Ticul.

Edzná

Edzná (edz-NAH), a jungle-besieged ruin in the state of Campeche, is more remarkable than beautiful. Although not one of the greatest Mayan ceremonial centers, it claims an honored place in the second rank.

A car is necessary for visiting the site, which is 225 km (140 miles) south and slightly west of Mérida via Highway 180 and Highway 261, the Campeche road. There's a well-marked turnoff to your left at kilometer 14, and it's another 19 km (12 miles) down this secondary road to the ruins. Travellers headquartered at Uxmal—which is the smartest (as well as the most comfortable) way to do it in terms of accommodations—face a slightly shorter trip of 148 km (92 miles) over the same highway. For those visitors staying in the nearby city of Campeche (discussed below), it's only 68 km (42 miles) distant, again via Highway 261.

Unlike most of the other Mayan ceremonial centers discussed in this chapter, Edzná is so little visited that travellers are likely to find only iguanas and howler monkeys frequenting the ruins. However, a spate of new archaeological work and restoration may soon change this. Until it does, you will find hardly anything remaining of what was once the pride of Edzná—an elaborate system of canals used for flood control and irrigation. Nevertheless, Edzná's attractions make it worth the trip.

The ceramic evidence seems to indicate that a village was founded here several centuries before the beginning of the Christian era. The city didn't reach its zenith until the Late Classic era, when most of the structures extant today were erected, often over older buildings. The fact that it stood at a major crossroads of trade no doubt accounts for its eclectic artistic style, which combines elements of the Chenes, Río Bec, and even Puuc styles, in addition to an elegant simplicity all its own. (Chenes is an ornate architectural style named for a Late Classic site in the Yucatán; the Río Bec style, so-called after a center in Campeche, features rounded towers meant to convey the illusion of height; Puuc style is characteristic of the northern Yucatán, most notably Uxmal.) The impression is of a cosmopolitan place open to new ideas and fashions.

After paying a nominal fee to enter the archaeological zone, you pass several sculpted stelae that merit inspection. A little farther on, past a temple platform and door columns, the broad stairway to the Gran Acropolis becomes visible. It is best to save it for last, however; instead, continue on down the path for 50 yards or so until you come to a low temple platform on your left. In front of it you'll find a number of beautifully carved stelae, now lying broken and scattered on the ground but still graceful.

Templo de los Mascarones

The Temple of the Masks, south of the Acropolis, is one of the oldest structures at the site, and dates to about A.D. 300. Masks of Itzamná, the sun god, are immediately recognizable by his plump, slightly bulbous face; the lips are pursed to emit invisible sunbeams, and his single emerging tooth symbolizes spring and, in a larger sense, the rekindling of life. The god displays a rare human touch at Edzná: He is cross-eyed, in the finest tradition of Mayan beauty.

The area on the opposite side of the Gran Acropolis, to the north, may have been the civil or administrative section of this urban center; its chief structure, the **Palacio de las Cuchillas** (Palace of the Knives), was named for the extraordinary number of these implements recovered from within and around the building. Four rooms of the palace have plaforms that may have supported beds.

About 100 yards west is a lonely arch. Dating to about A.D. 800, and thus newer than most of Edzná's monuments, it was built in the Puuc style, possibly by conquerors who overran the area at the time. The arch was the latter-day entrance to a raised road leading to the main temple.

Pirámide de los Cinco Pisos

The Acropolis, a complex structure with cascading stairways and a variety of civic and residential buildings, dominates the low jungle landscape. It, in turn, is dominated by Edzná's most imposing monument, the Templo Mayor, or Pyramid of the Five Stories, which rises 124 feet from its base to the tip of its partially ruined but still elegant roofcomb. Archaeologists have deduced only recently that the temple was built in such a way as to allow the rays of the setting sun to penetrate the interior on certain days in order to illuminate the figure of the Mayan sun god, Itzamná, located in one of the temple's four rooms. The phenomenon occurs every May 1, 2, and 3, the beginning of the rainy season; and again on August 7, 8, and 9, the start of the harvest, according to the Mayan calendar.

The Pyramid of the Five Stories displays a restraint unusual in Mayan architecture, its arresting effect achieved by the spacing of its five stories and multiple doorways in combination with the powerful stone undulations of its central stairway. The top story offers a splendid view of a number of recently restored buildings around the Main Plaza as well as of unrestored mounds in the jungle that seem full of archaeological promise. Especially striking is the well-proportioned seven-tiered temple base on the south side of the Acropolis.

In fact, all the nearby buildings give willing and able visitors an opportunity for unusual views of one another, as well as of the main temple. If nothing else, Edzná offers the challenge of a lot of climbing. Therefore, appropriate shoes are a must, and insect repellent is a blessing (as is something cold to drink that you can carry with you; if you can find him, the caretaker also sells cold sodas).

Campeche

Campeche, capital city of the state of the same name, is the closest overnight stop for visitors to Edzná. (It can also provide a break in the long trip from Mérida to Palenque or Villahermosa.) The city, which is made to seem romantic and colorful in travel brochures, proves less appealing in reality. Here is a typical Caribbean backwater, complete with rusting metal roofs, scraggly palms, and tropical swelter only occasionally relieved by cooling sea breezes—despite the claims of its boosters.

Colonial Campeche, constantly endangered by pirates, once crouched behind walls eight feet thick and bristling with *baluartes* (forts). The city is still studded with the remnants of these stone redoubts and ramparts, though they hardly evoke the ghost of Blackbeard. Two antique gateways to the city, La Puerta del Mar and La Puerta de la Tierra, also survive. The two chief examples of the city's modern architecture, on the other hand, have been aptly nicknamed "The Juke Box" and "The Flying Saucer" by the locals.

The **Museo de las Estelas** (Museum of the Stelae), in the Baluarte de la Soledad, displays a number of stelae carved by the Maya, while the limited **Museo Arqueológico** is housed in the Baluarte de San Miguel, facing the sea at the edge of the city. To get to the latter, take a taxi or drive 4 km (2½ miles) along the seaside *malecón* in the direction of Lerma, then turn left (uphill) at the Camino Escénica sign. The museum has a few artifacts from Edzná and some memorable funerary figurines from the island of Jaina, a Mayan burial place on a tidal islet off the Campeche coast.

To see a more eclectic collection—six rooms of curiosities ranging from fine Mayan jade jewelry to Spanish colonial art objects—search out the **Museo Regional de Campeche**, on Calle 59 in one of this modest city's better colonial houses. Closed Mondays.

STAYING IN CAMPECHE

The first choice for accommodations in town is the ▶ **Hotel Ramada Campeche** (formerly the Presidente), with balconies overlooking the Bahía de Campeche, a swimming pool and bar, and air-conditioning throughout. The adequate restaurant specializes in seafood, as it should in this fishing port.

Next door, and not quite as satisfactory, is the ▶ **Hotel Baluartes**, with many of its less expensive and slightly threadbare rooms overlooking not the sea but the parking lot. Restaurant, bar, and pool.

The ▶ **Hotel Lopez**, one block south and two blocks west of the zócalo on Calle 12, is a modest and inexpensive establishment popular with commercial travellers. Only the air-conditioned rooms are worth the price here.

CHICHEN ITZA

This sprawling ceremonial center thrusts itself up from the jungle about 120 km (74 miles) east of Mérida on Highway 180, not quite halfway to Puerto Juárez (Cancún and Isla Mujeres). Nothing in the Mayan world prepares the visitor for the architecture—dynamic, full of force and energy—here. The major structures at Uxmal authoritatively but serenely occupy the ground on which they rest. They are so self-contained it doesn't matter that they crowd each other; in a sense, they provide their own framing. But at Chichén Itzá the great monuments each seem to insist on—and get—their own space. As with skillfully executed stage sets, the illusion they create exceeds their physical dimensions. In fact, Chichén Itzá is so theatrical that dazzled visitors often call it perfect, the most beautiful of all the Mayan ruins. While no site is "perfect," what Chichén may lack in depth and subtlety it makes up for in drama.

Though it is quite easy to get lost at Chichén Itzá, literally as well as artistically, this does not mean that a guide is necessary. Most visitors will want to move at their own pace, taking time to form their own impressions; it is difficult to absorb a running commentary while trying to grasp the purely visual aspects of such alien and majestic surroundings. On the other hand, you might want to invest in a detailed guidebook to the ruins. The government handbook issued under the INAH (Instituto Nacional de Antropología y Historia) imprint, on sale at the entrance to the site, is invaluable.

Chichén Itzá (chee-CHEN eet-SAH) roughly translates as "place at the rim of the well of Itzá." Identifying the people known as the Itzá is not terribly important for fully appreciating the site. Knowing about the well, however, is crucial, for that is where the whole story begins.

The Well of Itzá

The northern Yucatán, for all intents and purposes, is without rivers or lakes. The torrential rains of summer disappear as quickly as they fall, running to the sea or vanishing beneath the limestone underlying the soil. Over the millennia this has created a huge and complex system of subterranean rivers whose life-giving waters are, for the most part, inaccessible. Here and there the limestone has caved in, creating the natural wells or sinkholes called cenotes. To the ancient Maya a cenote was literally the wellspring of life and a sacred gift from the gods.

The great cenote at Chichén Itzá, the **Cenote Sagrado** (Sacred Cenote), is the most awesome of these sinkholes, a gaping mouth in the earth roughly 190 feet in diameter and slightly more oval than circular. Sheer or undercut sides drop 65 feet or more to the surface of the water, which fills the hole to a depth of some 35 feet. The cenote is so unexpected and surrounded by such solitude that it would seem menacing even without the stories every visitor hears. It's not unusual to see people stand at the little temple platform on the rim, glance down at its murky waters, blink, and take a step backward.

In pre-Hispanic times the cenote was a magnet for Mayan pilgrims who came to this spot to implore or appease the rain god. Dredging in modern times has brought up a trove of sacrificial objects, including gold, silver, copper, polished jade, and, more grimly, about 50 human skulls, some of them belonging to young children. All this must be kept in perspective. The cenote was a center of sacrifice for at least 1,000 years: A victim every 20 years does not suggest that maidens were hurled into the depths seasonally, as some writers have imagined and certain guides still insist today.

The Toltec Influence

In time the mystique and sustaining power of the cenote impelled the Maya to erect a ceremonial center not far away, a center that flourished during the latter stages of the Classic period, from about A.D. 600 to 900. At that point the region was overrun by a people known as the Itzá, allies or perhaps cousins of the warlike Toltecs of the central highlands, whose great capital was Tula (they might even have *been* Toltecs; this is a subject for scholarly debate). At any rate, under their influence a new ceremonial center, strategically located between the Sacred Cenote and the older Mayan city, was built after A.D. 900.

Chichén Itzá, as it exists today, is a mostly Toltec-inspired creation built by Mayan skill and labor—"Toltec-Maya" is as good a term as any. Much of its drama derives from the Toltec imagery found at every turn: jaguars that are almost preternaturally ferocious, eagles devouring human hearts, snarling plumed serpents, low-relief portraits of great warriors. In fact, the Temple of the Warriors complex, with its intimidating colonnades, seems to have been lifted in its entirety from Tula. Toltec domination in the Yucatán was effective but brief, a case of "the flies conquering the flypaper." They were assimilated; they disappeared. Yet during their short tenure they revived the greatness of Mayan art, as Chichén Itzá attests.

Visitors to the site are often so eager to begin exploring that they forget to stop at the Service Unit located at the entrance. This is a mistake. You can get the latest orientation information there, as well as schedules giving the hours when certain temple interiors are open for inspection.

THE NORTHERN ZONE

The effect of the northern complex, more Toltec-Maya than purely Mayan, is instantaneous and powerful, so theatrical that the word "operatic" immediately suggests itself. Where other Mesoamerican ceremonial centers seem to have been constructed more for the benefit of the gods than for the impression they created on humans, Chichén Itzá is nothing less than a gigantic and obviously intentional show.

The Castillo

The Castillo, or **Pirámide de Kukulcán**, holds center stage. Kukulcán is the Mayan name for the Plumed Serpent, the Mexican priest-god folk hero who was also the Quetzalcóatl of the Toltecs and then the Aztecs. Besides being a temple the structure is a literal calendar in stone. Its original steps coincided with the days of the solar year, a type of symbolism not unusual in Mesoamerica; time cycles and months were numbered in terraces and panels. To this day, in fact, you can witness a curious byplay of shadows on the temple steps at the time of the equinox. Some observers claim to see a representation of a serpent during a precise 34-minute period in the late afternoon; others, watching the same thing, remain skeptical. In any case, the structure reveals a knowledge not only of architecture but of astronomy as well.

The pyramid rises in perfectly proportioned stone terraces of diminishing size, which contribute to the illusion of height. (The structure was built according to the tradition of placing one temple atop an older one after a 52-year cycle. The first Toltec religious structure here was dedicated to the sun.) Eager and heat-resistant visitors who have no tendency to claustrophobia can enter the pyramid and climb an irregular stairway to the top; there they will discover, besides a magnificent view, a rather crude but powerful jaguar sculpture, apparently a throne, cut from a single piece of limestone and painted with vermilion cinnabar. The bared teeth are made from white flint, the eyes from green jade (as are the large discs representing spots on the body). Access to this inner temple is limited to certain hours, and the schedule is by no means fixed; be sure to inquire at the entrance to the zone for the hours it's open to the public.

Juego de Pelota

Northwest of the Castillo lies the great Ball Court, the largest in Mesoamerica. There appear to have been various versions of this ceremonial game. Courts were always built in an I shape, thereby creating "end zones," and scoring at first may have involved cornering a hard rubber ball at either end. Later, stone rings were added to the side walls, and a player could win the contest by knocking or kicking (not throwing) the ball through one of these small hoops. The improbability of managing this is clear: A player who actually "scored" won all the clothes and jewelry worn by the spectators. It is often assumed, as a result of certain carvings, that those who lost the game were "sacrificed." This interpretation is Eurocentric, however; it's just as likely that the *winners* could have merited what was seen then as an honor.

Attached to the ball court, on top of the south end of the east wall, stands the small but massive two-story **Templo de los Jaguares**. Twin-plumed serpent columns, feathered and fanged, glare across the ball court as they support the entrance and roof. Murals of a procession have long since faded, but some carving endures: Warriors of the 12th century display their nudity, demonstrating that the Maya, or at least the Toltec-Maya, were not always puritanical. A steep staircase at the south corner provides passage to the lower temple and the remains of a sculpted jaguar, perhaps a throne, for which the temple is named.

Templo de los Guerreros

East of the main path leading to the Sacred Cenote, the Temple of the Warriors and the **Grupo de las Mil Columnas** (Group of the Thousand Columns) are second only to the Castillo in impressiveness and second to none in their fascination for visitors. In addition to comprising a huge complex of courtyards, platforms, terraces, and colonnades, the two signify a sharp change in the life of Chichén Itzá. Prior to their construction, small interior rooms were adequate to meet the needs of its inhabitants. At a certain point, however, there appears to have been a sudden demand for roofed areas and meeting halls protected from the rain— proof, according to some experts, that a large new military aristocracy had developed among the Toltecs. In fact, just such a warrior elite is depicted in full regalia in carvings throughout the site.

The so-called mercado (market), which rises about 200 yards southeast of the Castillo, was more likely a stone stage used for dance or theatrical performances. Just to the east of it efficient steam baths were built and no doubt used for both the ritual purification of priests as well as to accommodate the personal fastidiousness of the Maya.

Chichén Itzá seems to have been a gathering place rather than a continuously inhabited city, although it obviously could accommodate a large number of people. In addition to its many ceremonial buildings, there is a second cenote capable of supplying water year-round, as well as seven other ball courts (although not all were in use at the same time).

Over the years scholars have avoided public speculation about life at Chichén Itzá in its glory days. But one, Jacques Soustelle, has ventured to the edge of conjecture. Discussing the northern zone, Soustelle writes: "One is tempted to group the buildings ... under two headings: the religious and ritual center, with the great ceremonial ballcourt, the Temple of the Jaguars, and the sacrificial monuments; and the meeting place of the Itzá warriors ... whom one can imagine strolling through the colonnade and beside the pool on their way to the small ballcourt. The Temple of the Warriors, with the vast pillared hall before its façade, serves as a transition between the two centers, the one religious and the other secular, military and no doubt commercial."

Soustelle's speculations, whether wholly accurate or not, dovetail with the site's design and help a visitor to re-create the life that went on in the northern zone.

THE SOUTHERN ZONE

This area, called Chichén Viejo (Old Chichén), was the older ceremonial center that the northern Toltec-Maya zone replaced, and is built in the classic Mayan Puuc style, much in the manner of Uxmal (although Toltec embellishments were added to some of the buildings at a later date). While a fascinating and beautiful place, it does not have the instant impact of the northern group, in part because of its subtler architectural style, but mostly because the positioning of the structures does not result in the breathtaking vistas and contrasts that later Toltec planning afforded.

El Caracol

El Caracol (The Snail), with an interior stairway that spirals upward, is the most immediately striking structure in the neighborhood and was probably used by ancient stargazers. (Because a snail's shell is spiral-shaped, anything that winds upward—a road or stairway for instance—is likely to be called a *caracol* in Spanish.) In fact, the four apertures facing the cardinal directions at the top of the structure seem to confirm that it was constructed as an observatory. (Only three of the original apertures survive.) Although imposing and surprising, El Caracol is less than beautiful, inspiring Mayanist J. Eric Thompson to observe that the building "stands like a two-decker wedding cake on the square carton from which it came."

Edificio de las Monjas

Indisputably lovely, on the other hand, is the ruined Nunnery and its adjacent annex. (The modern name is simply a bit of Spanish fancy.) Unfortunately, in 1868 an eager archaeologist set off an explosive charge inside the Nunnery to speed his search and did irreparable damage to the structure.

The entrance to the annex is through the mouth of a stone monster. Such a door typifies the "Chenes" style, an ornate architectural style named for a site in the central Yucatán dating from the Late Classic era. Related to the Puuc style of Uxmal, Chenes is characterized by decorative doorways (variously defined as the gaping jaws of rain gods, earth monsters, and sky serpents), huge rain-god masks, ornamental scrollwork, and decoration below the medial molding.

Nearby, the exuberant decoration of the "church" reminds

viewers that the ancient Maya abhorred a design vacuum. Half a dozen other, lesser structures, each with its own mysteries, are scattered elsewhere around the area.

STAYING NEAR CHICHEN ITZA

The ▶ **Hotel Mayaland**, adjacent to the archaeological zone, is the traditional choice. However, its popularity with tour packagers has caused it to become increasingly noisy and crowded, and the too-heavy demands on the kitchen are often all too obvious on your plate. If you can somehow avoid the throngs, its bungalows are especially attractive, and most of the rooms are very comfortable (though a few seem cramped). Ask for a private balcony. Mayaland also has a pool, cocktail lounge, and a helpful staff skilled in making travel arrangements in the region.

The attractive ▶ **Hacienda Chichén** keeps its cottages open only in the winter and consequently relies on ceiling fans rather than air-conditioning. Rustic but gracious, it, too, is located in the archaeological zone. In fact, some of Chichén Viejo lies within the Hacienda's lovely gardens. Bar, dining room, swimming pool.

The fairly new and well-run ▶ **Villa Arqueológica Chichén Itzá** is on the East Access Road, just up the street from the Hacienda and Mayaland. As in all the branches of this Club Med–owned chain, the rooms are comfortable but far from spacious. The public areas, which include a pool, flower-filled patio, lighted tennis court, gift shop, and dining room that offers attractive, well-prepared food, more than make up for the somewhat cramped quarters.

The ▶ **Misión Park Inn Chichén Itzá**, in the nearby village of Pisté, is popular with families and tour groups. The atmosphere is vaguely colonial, the air-conditioning modern, and it has a swimming pool, adequate dining room, bar, and protected parking.

About 2½ km (1½ miles) east of the ruins, on the road to Valladolid, is the unpretentious ▶ **Hotel Dolores Alba**, with adequate accommodations at attractive prices. If air-conditioning is available (check first) it is worth the extra charge.

Some travellers, especially students, choose to stay in the small town of **Valladolid** itself, some 40 km (25 miles) east of Chichén Itzá. The town's attractions consist mostly of budget-priced hotel rooms and good bus service to the ruins. In addition, there are some colonial buildings here, as well as a cenote that is used as a public swimming pool.

▶ **El Mesón del Marqués**, on the Valladolid plaza, is a former colonial residence with a number of new rooms. Most of its rooms, old or new, are air-conditioned, and there is a pool and pleasant patio restaurant. A popular arts shop here offers a good selection of regional handicrafts. The ▶ **Hotel San Clemente**, also facing the plaza, has less character but is at least as comfortable as the Mesón del Marqués.

The Balancanché Cave

This is an adventure for the dedicated who don't mind squeezing and crawling through narrow passages. Visitors who were less than delighted by the interior stairways at Chichén Itzá will definitely want to skip it. Others may find it rewarding.

The subterranean passages of this complex contain sacred urns dedicated to the Toltec rain god, and are believed to have served as a refuge during times of invasion. As well, a pond at the end of a main passageway is home to blind fish. Cameras are banned, as are small children, the latter for good reason: The cave is eerie and tomblike.

Admission to the cave, which is about 5 km (3 miles) north and east of Chichén Itzá off Highway 180, is with a guide only; arrangements may be made at the cluster of buildings at the entrance to the cave.

PALENQUE

"The temples of Palenque . . . are exquisite rather than imposing; refined, rather than massive. They are quite content with the earth they stand on, and do not, like their predecessors, reach for the sky. Like precious jewels, they are beautiful and complete in themselves. The earlier gods, if they were gods, in the sculptures of Tikal, Copan and elsewhere seem to represent great natural forces, the forces that caused the maize to grow and the rain to fall; these gods here at Palenque are members of an elegant aristocracy that rules gracefully over the destinies of men."—Louis J. Halle, Jr.

The site at Palenque (pah-LEHN-keh), in the rain forests of northern Chiapas, is compact and remarkably harmonious. Although its structures do not all date from the same period, they are of a piece and share a common aesthetic tradition. Many people think this is the most beautiful cluster of pre-Columbian buildings in the Americas: To find its rivals you will have to travel to Greece, Turkey, or Southeast Asia.

For centuries Palenque was the proverbial "lost city in the jungle," known only through vague rumor and manuscripts that were as obscure as the city itself. In 1786, however, a

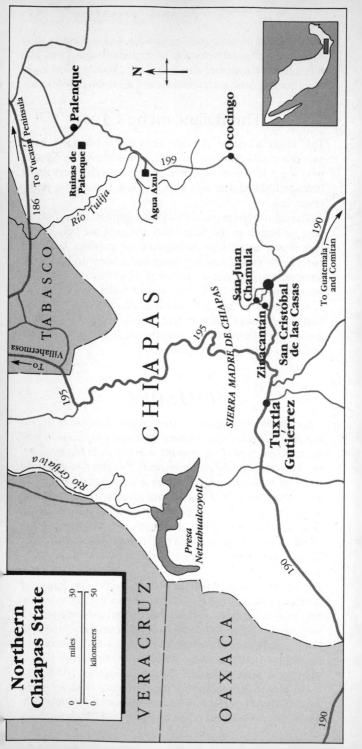

Captain Antonio del Río was sent to investigate. After weeks in the jungle he and his men found what they were looking for and immediately set about driving spikes into the stucco sculpture in order to hang their hammocks and armor. They also dug a quite useless trench, doubtless seeking treasure, then gave up after del Río had "discovered all that was to be found." The captain, while perpetrating this archaeological mayhem, observed that the natives were "sullen and suspicious." He was one of the rare visitors who did not like Palenque.

The two men responsible for focusing the world's attention on the ruined city were John Lloyd Stephens and his friend Frederick Catherwood, the English artist and architect. After hacking their way through the jungle with the help of native guides, the two stumbled upon the ruins in 1840 and were so delighted by their find that they fired the last of their gunpowder into the air.

Although the original name of this Mayan ceremonial center is unknown, we do know that it was the capital of a large Late Classic–era kingdom. The modern name, which was borrowed from the nearest town, means "palisade," and otherwise seems to have no connection to the ancient city that dominated this corner of the world with its knowledge and culture. When, near the end of its reign, some fortifications were built, it seems that Palenque was already doomed. It fell, for reasons unknown, in A.D. 800, the first great Mayan city-state to fail and be abandoned to the jungle.

EXPLORING THE RUINS

Today the ruins rest on a narrow shelf of forested land high enough to provide sweeping views of jungle, meadows, and, in the distance, flat savannah stretching toward the sea. It is, above all, a green world, with every shade from olive through emerald present. The site is also compact; there's no need to hire a guide. Stop at the information center at the entrance to inquire about hours and regulations, however, as well as to buy the official INAH handbook to the ruins. Once inside the zone, be sure to take your time. Not only are you in the tropics, but the subtleties of Palenque do not reveal themselves at a glance. If at all possible, allow two days for the site; the pleasure lies not only in seeing, but in absorbing and relating. Palenque is alien and distinctive even to travellers familiar with other Mayan sites. A good plan, therefore, is to use the first day for exploring the Palace, the Temple of the Inscriptions, and Temple XIII. The rest can wait for the second day.

El Palacio

Most visitors are drawn immediately to the Palace, readily identifiable by its four-story tower, leaving the structures on their right for later. A wise choice; the Palace is the best introduction to Palenque.

Much of this complex, which surmounts a huge rectangular platform, was the creation of Lord Pacal, the most famous ruler of Palenque. Ascending to power in A.D. 615 as a 12-year-old boy, he is said to have ruled until his death at the age of 80—a period that coincides with Palenque's most marvelous work. Augustus Caesar once boasted that he found Rome brick and left it marble. Lord Pacal's achievement was every bit as impressive: He found Palenque humble and left it magnificent.

Additions were made to the Palace by Pacal's son, Lord Kan Xul. Indeed, some of the finest reliefs here date from his reign, and the work merits close examination. Unfortunately, much of it has been eroded over the centuries and some destroyed. Visitors will need to do some restoration in their imaginations to appreciate fully the achievements of the Palenque stone carvers.

The landmark tower, which probably was used both for stargazing and keeping an eye on affairs on the plain below, is often called the **observatory**. The climb to the top, where you may be rewarded with a refreshing breeze stirring through the windows, is not difficult, and the views of the flat green world spread out to the horizon are unforgettable. From here it's also immediately apparent that only the central area of Palenque remains—or at least that is all that has been uncovered.

A new surprise awaits around every corner of the Palace complex—altars and thrones, hidden stairways, reliefs in stone and stucco. After a few hours you will even develop a sense for the unique Palenque line—smooth, serene, and quietly understated.

Templo de las Inscripciones

The Temple of the Inscriptions, adjacent to the Palace, perches dramatically above its green jungle backdrop on stone terraces stepped one atop another. Though beautiful in its own right, the structure is best known for the discovery made here in 1952 by the Mexican archaeologist Alberto Ruz Lhuillier. Noticing some holes in the temple floor and suspecting they were handholds, Ruz had a huge slab raised, which revealed a hidden stairway blocked with rubble. While the passage was being cleared, Ruz discovered the skeletal remains of five or six youths—apparently the sacrificial companions of a master who had been entombed beyond. But, of course, everyone knew that Mesoamerican pyramids and temples were never used as burial crypts. This wasn't Egypt, after all.

To everybody's surprise, a sepulchral vault was eventually uncovered, with the figures of the Nine Lords of the Night standing solemn watch in the chamber. When, after immense difficulty, the beautifully carved lid of the huge stone coffin was removed, Ruz found the skeleton of a large man as well as an extraordinary jade mosaic funerary mask. We now know, after decades of trying to decipher the ancient Mayan glyphs on the sarcophagus lid, that the bones are those of Lord Pacal. At the same time, Ruz made another interesting discovery: From the sarcophagus a sort of pipe, or hollow molding, wound up the stairs to the temple—apparently so that Lord Pacal could maintain postmortem communication with the world he had departed.

As was usual at that time, everything in the tomb was whisked off to Mexico City, where it is now on view at the National Museum of Anthropology. But the monolithic casket lid would not fit up the narrow, twisting stairs, and so it remains in Palenque, proof that the tomb was built before the temple.

Near the Temple of the Inscriptions is the much smaller Temple XIII (also known as the Templo de la Calavera, or Skull Temple), accessible by a hillside path from the top of the Temple of the Inscriptions, which means it isn't necessary to descend the steep steps of the Inscriptions, as most visitors do. This lesser temple is somehow connected with death; at least the main stucco decoration remaining portrays a death god. From here a short, steep path rejoins the main path from the entrance.

The Cross Group

A group of four temples, each distinctive but all related in style, is a good start for the second day's viewing. This group is located just southeast of the Palace across a narrow stream, and includes the Temples of the Sun, the Cross, the Foliated Cross, and Temple XIV. Such names as "the Cross" derive from European conjecture about sculpted forms found at the temples, and have no connection to the original names of the buildings, which remain unknown.

The small **Templo del Sol** is a treasure. Besides being valued for its lovely proportions, it contains a masterpiece, a carved panel of Pacal deified. The **Templo de la Cruz**, the tallest of this group, with a crumbling but still glorious roofcomb, almost seems to serve as a pedestal for the architectural element above. The **Templo de la Cruz Foliada** and the badly damaged Templo XIV nevertheless offer examples of beautiful carving. Considered as a whole, the quartet embodies the genius of Palenque, with the Temple of the Sun, especially, speaking volumes about its creators.

THE NORTHERN GROUP

North of the Palace complex are five structures that share a single base. Although they're in sad condition, the view of the surrounding plain from here is lovely, and it's still possible to imagine how they once might have looked. Nearby, the **Templo del Conde** (Temple of the Count), named for a German nobleman who lived in the structure for a time and made extensive drawings of the ruins in the early decades of the 19th century, is in slightly better condition. While this group is too damaged to be compared with its better-preserved neighbors, time spent lingering among the ruined structures will not be wasted: There's an ineffable atmosphere here that is likely to haunt you for years to come.

The small Palenque **museum**, located east of the Northern Group, while not extensive—the best of the site's artifacts has gone elsewhere—boasts some beautiful carvings, ceramics, and bits of stucco decoration.

STAYING AND DINING AT PALENQUE

Eight kilometers (5 miles) north and east of the archaeological zone is the town of Palenque. Seeing this modern settlement after visiting the ruins is enough to make anyone pessimistic about human "progress." Fortunately, there are far better accommodations closer to the site.

Staying at the ▶ **Chan Kah Cabañas**, a group of cottages about 4 km (2½ miles) from the ruins on the access road to the site, will enhance your visit to Palenque. The Mayan-style bungalows are so well designed and ventilated that ceiling fans provide enough cooling; there's also a stream-fed pool. Ask for a cottage near the river. The alfresco restaurant is just adequate.

The ▶ **Hotel Nututun Viva** has a beautiful, woodsy location on the river, 5 km (3 miles) south of town on the way to the ruins. Though some rooms are dark and damp, the two-story air-conditioned motel is comfortable and very popular, and the dining room has a delightful river view. While the Nututun Viva advertises swimming in the river, the rocks and shallow water make this an uninviting prospect.

Two of the hotels in town are geared to student and archaeological tour groups. ▶ **La Cañada**, with both cottages and rooms, has attractive grounds and a thatched-roof restaurant that's quite good. It's located on the street of the same name, just off Avenida Juárez, the main street, at the western end of town. The ► **Casa de Pacal**, facing the municipal park on Avenida Juárez, lacks charm but is modern, air-conditioned, and a good buy.

The ► **Misión Park Inn Palenque**, at the eastern end of town in a neighborhood known as Rancho San Martín de Porres, has lovely grounds and an attractive restaurant. Despite its rather small, sterile rooms, it is popular with tour groups and quite satisfactory.

At the other end of town, on the way to the ruins, the restaurant **La Selva** is a jungle fantasy mansion come true, a marvel of thatch, knotted twine, and polished wood. The menu is extensive, the food carefully prepared, and there's entertainment and dancing in the evenings.

(For directions to Palenque, see the Getting Around section at the end of the chapter.)

Agua Azul

Visitors to the Palenque area who have extra time, or who are driving on to San Cristóbal de las Casas, should stop at the lovely series of *cascadas* known as Agua Azul. To get there, follow the Ocosingo road 58 km (36 miles) south from the town of Palenque, then turn right onto the dusty side road, which requires patience and a bit of skill to navigate but is only 4 km (2½ miles) long.

At the end of the road, the waters of the Río Tulija swirl and plunge through a web of cataracts and rapids. You can follow the riverbank upstream past several foaming cascades, where the perpetual mist from the falls gives the foliage a special lushness and little rainbows form when the sun shines. In every direction the mountains of the Sierra Madre de Chiapas present a spectacular backdrop.

There's not much in the way of facilities at the little park, and the mist and dampness make it a less-than-ideal spot for picnics. (There are drier, more comfortable places farther from the tumbling, swirling water.) Nevertheless, it's an excursion well worth the time and effort. And the road from Palenque past the falls turnoff all the way into San Cristóbal de las Casas is extraordinarily scenic.

SAN CRISTOBAL DE LAS CASAS

The mountain-ringed city of San Cristóbal de las Casas is situated at the southwestern edge of Mexico's Mayan region, in the center of the state of Chiapas. Here, in the fastness of the Sierra Madre de Chiapas, the native settlements sprinkled throughout the region seem almost like outposts. And, in a sense, that's exactly what they are. Ages ago the highland Maya pressed no farther; they decided that their world ended here.

Most travellers will appreciate San Cristóbal as a stopover. Those bound by car for Guatemala from central Mexico should take the highland route, Highway 190, which goes through San Cristóbal, rather than the sultry and uninteresting Highway 200 along the Pacific coast: The scenery will more than make up for the extra distance. Likewise, motorists covering Mexico in a great loop from the Yucatán back to Oaxaca will also want to stop here. As a sole destination on what is a long journey, however, San Cristóbal is a dubious choice for most travellers. Still, a few will be enchanted by this odd, tucked-away town and will end up staying and exploring the surrounding region for as long as possible. The only way to tell which group you fall into is to make the journey.

The Highland Maya

The first signs that you're approaching San Cristóbal de las Casas appear along the roadside—groups or families of Maya gathering or carrying firewood, waiting for rides, plodding patiently toward unknown destinations. Physically these highland Maya look much like their cousins in the Yucatán: short, sturdy, dark, with rather coarse jet-black hair and expressive almond-shaped eyes. But their garb is noticeably different. This is cool country, after all. No gauzy *huipiles* for these women; instead, their clothing is dark and plain. It is left to the male to be the peacock, a role he embraces.

In fact, the different groups of the region can be distinguished by the costumes the men wear. The Zinacantecos, for example, stand out in their beribboned straw hats, pink-striped serapes, and scarves soberly checked in gray but trimmed with magenta tassels. Even in winter they are likely to be barefoot, although at times you'll see them wearing *huaraches* made from discarded automobile tires. The Chamulas, on the other hand, sport white hats big enough for a Hollywood cowboy; under these hats they wear a bright kerchief wrapped around the head for warmth in winter and used as a sweatband in summer, an accessory for all seasons. Their serapes, among the most beautiful in Mexico, are worn over white tunics and white knee pants, and are usually woven of thick wool left a natural or bleached white (although they are sometimes dyed black).

The ancestors of both these Mayan groups were quite possibly the builders of Palenque and other lowland centers in the Classic period. If so, they were probably dispersed and became refugees in the mountains after their magnificent cities were abandoned in the ninth and tenth centuries. They encountered the Spanish for the first time when Diego de Mazariego established San Cristóbal in 1528. His successor unleashed a reign of terror in the region, but the Maya's suffering abated after the arrival of the bishop of Chiapas, Bartolomé de las Casas, and 35 fellow Dominicans in 1545. The bishop was a vigorous and effective defender of Mayan rights and even managed to get some of the worst laws against them repealed. As a result, the town was renamed for him during the era of anti-clerical reform in Mexico in the 19th century, becoming simply "Las Casas"—a name that still is often used today.

The town held onto its isolation and old ways for centuries, its traditions more common to Guatemala than Mexico. Racial purity was maintained along with sharp class distinctions. Politically, San Cristóbal resisted independence, resisted union with Mexico, resisted *all* change. In 1890, as a punishment, the state capital was shifted to Tuxtla Gutiérrez, which subsequently outdistanced San Cristóbal in both size and wealth—though not in interest for travellers.

The racial and caste divisions are obvious even today in San Cristóbal. This is much more a city surrounded by Indians than an Indian city, and the easy cultural assimilation of Oaxaca or Morelia is virtually unknown here.

Around the Zócalo

The dark reds and oranges of tile roofs, steeply sloped to ward off the torrential summer rains, are what most visitors first notice about San Cristóbal. This is also a place of whites and pastels, pale lavenders warming to pinks. And everywhere, in any direction, you get a sense of distance and of being hemmed in by mountains.

The Zócalo
Situated on the north side of the zócalo, the old **cathedral** has a Plateresque façade and some antique statuary. The building dates from the 16th century, with later additions—a big structure but not a major one.

A very helpful government tourism office can be found on the south side of the zócalo, opposite the cathedral. Nearby is the 16th-century home of Diego de Mazariego, which is older than the cathedral but in the same style. (Today it houses the Hotel Santa Clara.)

There are pleasant strolls in every direction from the plaza; the destinations matter less than the cobblestone streets themselves, which are lined with quaint façades offering glimpses of gracious courtyards. The homeowners of San Cristóbal appear to have taken special pride in the ironwork decorating their houses; it is unusually good.

Templo de Santo Domingo

The 17th-century church of Santo Domingo, located five blocks north of the zócalo at the corner of Calzada Lázaro Cárdenas and Calle Nicaragua, is the finest colonial building in the region. Its style was borrowed from a number of 16th-century churches in Guatemala, and its interior is embellished by a masterpiece of a pulpit and some extraordinary gilded screens. Housed in the cloister of Santo Domingo is the small **Museo Regional**, which displays lacquerwork, native costumes, and an illustrated history of San Cristóbal.

Outside is a Mayan **market**; on a bright, sunny day a stop here leaves you with the impression of having walked into a rainbow of sparkling colors. The vendors, mostly women, wear delicately embroidered blouses, bold sashes, and, in their hair, yarn that is almost Chinese red. Their offerings include brocade and embroidery work, leather goods, hammocks, bags, and jewelry. Children, bright-eyed miniatures of the vendors, scamper and play among the displays.

Adjacent to the church is the **Sna Jolobil** shop and museum, run cooperatively by the local Maya. Prices seem slightly higher inside than out, but the co-op offers better quality. The museum is open mornings only.

The municipal market, north and east of Santo Domingo, is less interesting for its merchandise than for its customers: In every aisle appear faces that might have been models for the carvings at Palenque or Uxmal.

STAYING AND DINING IN SAN CRISTOBAL

Visitors in the winter will definitely want a room with a fireplace, an adequate supply of wood, and—equally important—sufficient kindling. All the hotels in town are colonial and provincial, and some are even rustic.

The ▶ **Posada Diego de Mazariegos**, an inviting provincial inn with ample rooms (some with fireplaces) arranged around large patios, occupies two converted colonial buildings a block north of the zócalo. The dining room is also the town's best restaurant. Added attractions include a bar, a coffee and pastry shop, and friendly service. Convenient parking, not easy to find in San Cristóbal, is provided.

The reasonably priced ▶ **Hotel Santa Clara**, right on the zócalo, is housed in the 16th-century Diego de Mazariego mansion and is charmingly decorated with tiles, iron work, and carved wood. The dining room is quite good, and there's a protected parking lot. The cold-water swimming pool is only for the hardy.

Not quite as good is the ▶ **Hotel Flanboyant**, centrally located two blocks north of the zócalo at the corner of Calle 16 de Septiembre and Primero de Mayo. All the rooms, which vary greatly otherwise, have fireplaces, and the hotel also offers a dining room and charming patio garden. (This is the former Hotel Español, enlarged and redecorated.)

Just southeast of town off Highway 190 is the inviting ▶ **El Molino de la Alborada**, a hacienda-style establishment with cottages. It's a small, intimate inn, with a fine kitchen to serve its guests. It also has a good stable—as well as an airplane landing strip. Although somewhat isolated, El Molino appeals especially to visitors with time to explore the countryside and the native villages, as well as those who simply want to relax. The rates are quite reasonable considering all that is offered.

San Cristóbal has no outstanding restaurants. The best food can be found in the hotels: Mazariegos, Santa Clara, and Flanboyant, in that order. **Madre Tierra**, a few blocks south of the zócalo facing the Templo de San Francisco, offers a good breakfast with a health-food accent, and also serves lunch and dinner. **El Fogón de Jovel**, Avenida 16 de Septiembre 11, features regional cuisine and evening marimba music in a patio that is as colorful as it is chilly after sundown. The **Restaurant Plaza**, on a second floor overlooking the main square, is well-situated for observing life in the zócalo; its best offering is coffee and rolls with a view.

Exploring the San Cristóbal Region

Casa Na Bolom, northeast of the zócalo at Calle Vicente Guerrero 31, is a small, privately run museum that serves as a center for visiting anthropologists and archaeologists investigating the area. It is owned and supervised by Gertrude Duby, herself an anthropologist (and photographer), and the widow of Frans Blom. The couple is celebrated for their efforts on behalf of the Lancandon Indians and the rain forest in which they live, as well as for their explorations and studies of the Chiapas highlands. Museum tours are conducted, and a donation is expected. In addition, maps of the surrounding countryside can be bought at Na Bolom, and the staff is generous with their knowledge of the region and its people. (El Molino de la Alborada is also helpful and expert in making excursion arrangements for its guests.)

Zinacantán and San Juan Chamula

Native villages, lovely lakes, and forested mountains—all lie within reach of San Cristóbal de las Casas. **Zinacantán**, 11 km (7 miles) west of San Cristóbal, and **San Juan Chamula**, 10 km (6 miles) northwest, are two of the more interesting rural centers of the highland Maya. In both places the inhabitants go about their business seemingly oblivious to the presence of curious tourists. Both villages absolutely forbid the taking of photographs in their churches—Zinacantán bans cameras altogether, and offenders are dealt with harshly. San Juan Chamula's church, built over a pyramid on the main square, is worth a visit if only to observe the rituals—which fall somewhere between Christian and pagan practices—enacted there. Reluctant to give up their traditional form of worship, the Chamulas compromised their religion in order to avoid annihilation by their Spanish conquerors.

There are no pews in the church; the faithful spread out across the floor to perform their healings. Scattered among the small groups are usually a chicken, lit candles, an egg, and a bottle of Coca Cola. According to one version of their beliefs, the "healer" passes the malady of the sick person to a chicken or egg, which then is taken outside and buried, thus trapping the disease. The Coke is sprinkled about like holy water.

The church, dedicated to Saint John the Baptist (father of Jesus Christ according to popular belief in Chamula), has no priest and holds no traditional Catholic Masses. Wooden statues of various saints have been banished to the back of the building in "punishment" for not saving another parish building that burned to the ground. Chamula policemen, dressed in traditional white tunics and pants, patrol the interior to make sure no photographs are taken. A modest admission fee is charged at the police station.

The Lacandon Region

The lakes of the **Lacandon Forest** are also accessible from San Cristóbal, though a fairly long trip by car; allow a full day. To get to the Lacandon area, drive to the town of Comitán, 86 km (53 miles) southeast of San Cristóbal via the Pan-American Highway. (The highway actually bypasses Comitán, a pretty little town with adequate cafés around its plaza.) Fifteen kilometers (9 miles) south of Comitán you'll come to the village of La Trinitaria, where you turn left onto the paved road that leads to **Lagunas de Montebello National Park**; the park lies 36 km (22 miles) farther on. After entering the park the road forks. Go left to the **Lagunas de Colores** (Colored Lakes), which are lovely, tranquil, and a startling sight with their contrasting colors.

Of the 16 lakes in the park, those off the right fork are not as accessible from the road. If you do take the right fork, after almost 16 km (10 miles) you'll come to **Dos Lagunas**, two especially beautiful bodies of water surrounded by forest. It is advisable to return to San Cristóbal for the night.

(Note: In 1993 the right fork to Lagunas de Montebello was being used as a logging road, heavy equipment making the dirt trail dangerous and impassable. Inquire locally before proceeding to the right [southbound]. If the road seems torn up, you should turn back at once and stick to the paved routes. Hiking, of course, remains possible.)

Horseback Riding

The San Cristóbal region is crisscrossed by bridle trails. Arrangements for renting horses may be made at El Recoveco, a shop on the San Cristóbal plaza. Reservations are taken at 7:00 P.M. for the next morning; information about trails and maps are also available. In addition, most local hotels will be happy to arrange horse rentals and provide relevant information.

Advice and help with excursions in the region can be obtained at the tourism office on the zócalo in San Cristóbal.

GETTING AROUND

Mérida

Mexicana Airlines offers flights connecting Mérida with Mexico City; it also flies, via Cozumel, to Miami. Aeroméxico links Mérida with Mexico City, Villahermosa, and Miàmi. Aerocaribe flies from Mérida to Cancún, Cozumel, Villahermosa, and Palenque (via Villahermosa). The Mérida airport is a ten-minute ride from the main plaza and is served by price-controlled taxis, which cost about $6. The inexpensive airport bus (marked "Aviación") departs from the corner of Calles 67 and 60, downtown.

All buses to other cities arrive and depart from the central terminal on Calle 69 between Calles 68 and 70. There is good first-class service to all major destinations, with ADO one of the larger and better lines.

The train from Mexico City, via Palenque, has sleeping

cars, but even so it is recommended only for travellers with endless time, patience, and fortitude.

Most Mérida hotels have travel desks or offices that are happy to offer options for exploring the area. These hotel services also tend to be more reliable than the little storefront agencies that pepper the city.

Bus tours are another dubious option and tend to be mass movers, highly regimented, and overly fast-paced. Any guided tour with more than seven passengers is also questionable. In fact, nothing larger than a station wagon or minivan is recommended. Private cars with guides are available at Sindicato de Guía; Tel: (99) 28-1794 or 25-3196.

A number of major car-rental agencies in Mérida serve visitors who prefer exploring at their own pace; expect prices considerably higher than in the United States and Canada. Public transportation by bus is available to all major sites; schedules can be obtained through hotels or at the tourism office, Teatro Peón Contreras, Calle 60 between Calles 57 and 59; Tel: (99) 24-9290 (the staff is most helpful).

Chichén Itzá

The first-class buses between Mérida and Cancún also serve Chichén, which is just off Highway 180. Most buses stop at the entrance to the ruins, while a few stop at the nearby village of Pisté, where taxis to the ruins are available. You can also use the sidewalk from Pisté to Chichén—about a 20-minute walk. Travellers arriving by bus or car from Cancún, Isla Mujeres, and Cozumel reach Chichén via the very good Cancún–Mérida highway. Chichén is about 200 km (124 miles) west of Cancún.

Palenque

The nearest large commercial airport is in Villahermosa, 151 km (94 miles) to the northwest. (Aerocaribe also services a recently opened landing strip in Palenque itself.) Car rentals are available in Villahermosa, and the ADO line offers good bus transportation to the site. (It's slightly more than a 2-hour drive from Villahermosa to Palenque.) Those with cars may wish to continue south on the beautiful mountain drive to San Cristóbal de las Casas after exploring Palenque. (See the Getting Around section for San Cristóbal below.)

For the adventurous, there is Pullman rail service to Palenque from Mexico City as well as from Mérida. The posted length of the trip from the capital is 24 hours—which seems to be more a speed record than the reality. The train sways and shimmies, and while the part of the trip through jungle is interesting, more of it is dull.

At Palenque, *combi* buses ply the road from town to the ruins with reasonable frequency, and taxis will respond to phone calls from area hotels.

For exploring the ruins, tennis or running shoes will do nicely; boots are not necessary. A sun hat and insect repellent are advisable.

San Cristóbal de las Casas

There is no commercial airport in the San Cristóbal area, but Tuxtla Gutiérrez, 93 km (58 miles) to the west, is serviced by regular daily flights to and from Mexico City. In addition, cars may be rented at the Tuxtla airport. There is minibus service from the air terminal to the bus depot, where you can catch the ADO bus for San Cristóbal. The road to San Cristóbal climbs steeply, so it takes about 2 hours to make the journey by car, a little longer by bus.

There is regular bus service from San Cristóbal to Guatemala City, with connections from there to most Guatemalan towns. The border is 172 km (107 miles) southeast of San Cristóbal. Buses also run regularly between San Cristóbal and Palenque, a distance of 207 km (128 miles). Travellers making the trip from Oaxaca by car should prepare for a very long day's journey: about 630 km (391 miles).

ACCOMMODATIONS REFERENCE

The rates given below are projections for December 1993 through Easter 1994. Unless otherwise indicated, rates are for double rooms, double occupancy; the 10 percent VAT has been added. As rates are subject to change; it's always a good idea to double-check before booking.

▶ **La Cañada.** Calle Merle Green 18, **Palenque**, Chiapas 29960. Tel: (934) 5-0102 or 0411. $45.

▶ **Casa del Balam.** Calle 60 466, **Mérida**, Yucatán 97000. Tel: (99) 24-8844; Fax: (99) 24-5011. $115.

▶ **Casa de Pacal.** Avenida Juárez 8, **Palenque**, Chiapas 29960. $28.

▶ **El Castellano.** Calle 57 513. **Mérida**, Yucatán 97000. Tel: (99) 23-0100 or 0621; Fax: (99) 23-0110. $90.

▶ **Chan Kah Cabañas.** P.O. Box 26, Carretera Ocosingo, km 31, **Palenque**, Chiapas 29960. Tel: (934) 5-0318; Fax: (934) 5-0489. $100.

▶ **El Conquistador.** Paseo de Montejo 458, **Mérida**, Yucatán 97000. Tel: (99) 26-2155; Fax: (99) 26-8829. $102.

▶ **Gran Hotel.** Parque Cepeda Peraza, **Mérida**, Yucatán 97000. Tel: (99) 24-7730; Fax: (99) 24-7622. $50.

▶ **Hacienda Chichén.** Zona Arqueológica, **Chichén Itzá**, or c/o Casa del Balam, Calle 60 466, Mérida, Yucatán 97000. In Mérida, Tel: (99) 24-8844; Fax: (99) 24-5011; in the U.S., Tel: (800) 624-8451. $128.

▶ **Hacienda Uxmal.** Zona Arqueológica, **Uxmal**, or P.O. Box 407, Mérida, Yucatán 97000. In Mérida, Tel and Fax: (99) 24-7142. $99.

▶ **Holiday Inn Mérida.** P.O. Box 134, Avenida Colón and Calle 60, **Mérida**, Yucatán 97127. Tel: (99) 25-6877; Fax: (99) 25-7755; in the U.S. and Canada, Tel: (800) HOLIDAY. $173.

▶ **Hotel Baluartes.** Avenida Ruíz Cortines 53, **Campeche**, Campeche 24000. Tel: (981) 6-3911; Fax: (981) 6-2410. $62.

▶ **Hotel Colón.** Calle 62 483, **Mérida**, Yucatán 97000. Tel: (99) 23-4355; Fax: (99) 24-4919. $55.

▶ **Hotel Dolores Alba.** Calle 63 464, **Mérida**, Yucatán 97000. Tel: (99) 28-3163; Fax: (99) 28-3167. $28.

▶ **Hotel Dolores Alba.** 2½ km east of the ruins on Highway 180, **Chichén Itzá**, Yucatán. In Mérida, Tel: (99) 28-3163; Fax: (99) 28-3167. $29.

▶ **Hotel Flanboyant.** Avenida 16 de Septiembre and Primero de Mayo, **San Cristóbal de las Casas**, Chiapas 29200. Tel: (967) 8-0045; Fax: (967) 8-0514. $82.

▶ **Hotel Lopez.** Calle 12 Norte 189, **Campeche**, Campeche 24000. Tel: (981) 6-3344. $27.

▶ **Hotel Mayaland.** Zona Arqueológica, **Chichén Itzá**, or P.O. Box 407, Mérida, Yucatán 97000. Tel and Fax: (985) 6-2777; in Mérida, Tel: (99) 21-9212; in U.S., Tel: (800) 235-4079. $130.

▶ **Hotel Nututun Viva.** Carretera Ocosingo, km 3, **Palenque**, Chiapas 29960. Tel and Fax: (934) 5-0161. $76.

▶ **Hotel Ramada Campeche.** Avenida Ruíz Cortines 51, **Campeche**, Campeche 24000. Tel: (981) 6-2233; Fax: (981) 1-1618; in the U.S. and Canada, Tel: (800) 854-7854. $113.

▶ **Hotel San Clemente.** Calle 41 206, **Valladolid**, Yucatán 97780. Tel: (985) 6-2208; Fax: (985) 6-3564. $31.

▶ **Hotel Santa Clara.** Plaza Principal, **San Cristóbal de las Casas**, Chiapas 29200. Tel: (967) 8-1140; Fax: (967) 6-0031. $46.

▶ **El Mesón del Marqués.** Calle 39 203 (zócalo), **Valladolid**, Yucatán 97780. Tel: (985) 6-2073; Fax: (985) 6-2280. $51.

▶ **Misión Park Inn Chichén Itzá.** Carretera Mérida–Cancún, km 10, **Pisté**, Yucatán 97752. Tel: (985) 6-2462 or 2513; Fax: (985) 6-2462; in the U.S. and Canada, Tel: (800) 437-PARK. $105 (includes two meals).

▶ **Misión Park Inn Palenque.** Rancho San Martín de Porres, **Palenque**, Chiapas 29960. Tel: (934) 5-0444; in the U.S. and Canada, Tel: (800) 437-PARK. $105.

▶ **Misión Park Inn Uxmal.** Zona Arqueológica, **Uxmal**, P.O.

Box 407, Mérida, Yucatán 97000. In Mérida, Tel and Fax: (99) 24-7308; in the U.S. and Canada, Tel: (800) 437-PARK. $105 (includes two meals).

▶ **El Molino de la Alborada.** P.O. Box 50, Periférico Sur s/n, **San Cristóbal de las Casas**, Chiapas 29200. Tel: (967) 8-0935. $32.

▶ **Posada Diego de Mazariegos.** María Adelina Flores 2, **San Cristóbal de las Casas**, Chiapas 29200. Tel: (967) 8-0513; Fax: (967) 8-0827. $81.

▶ **Villa Arqueológica Chichén Itzá.** Zona Arqueológica, Carretera Mérida–Valladolid, km 12, **Chichén Itzá**, Yucatán 97752. Tel: (985) 6-2830; Fax: (985) 6-2771; in the U.S., Tel: (800) 258-2633; in Canada, Tel: (514) 937-7707. $92.

▶ **Villa Arqueológica Uxmal.** Zona Arqueológica, **Uxmal**, or P.O. Box 449, Mérida, Yucatán 97000. In Mérida, Tel: (99) 24-7053; Fax: (99) 24-7023; in the U.S., Tel: (800) 258-2633; in Canada, Tel: (514) 937-7707. $82.

GUATEMALA

By Robert Somerlott

In the first installment of the *Star Wars* trilogy, Princess Leia flees to a hiding place in a remote galaxy somewhere on the nether edge of the universe. For the film's director the problem was where—on earth—could such an alien landscape be found? Eventually, he decided that the perfect background would be Tikal, the great ruined Mayan city hemmed in by the Guatemalan jungle, and at least a few viewers were startled to recognize the towering Temple of the Giant Jaguar when it appeared on-screen. The choice was brilliant. Until intergalactic travel becomes possible, Tikal is about as far removed from our own world as you can get.

To a lesser degree, the same can be said for much of Guatemala. In a world growing smaller and more homogeneous, Guatemala has managed to keep its character, its color, and its oddity. In a sense, a visitor here has an opportunity to sample time travel, to see a vanishing way of life—not everywhere in the country, of course, and perhaps not always for long. Still, there remains an element of fantasy in this picturesque land where reality has often been brutal.

For travellers who have become intrigued by the Maya in Mexico, a trip into Guatemala is a rewarding excursion. While the modern political boundary between the countries may separate two very different and sometimes antagonistic governments, in the Mayan view of time the separation is merely a recent development. The Maya recognize the frontier only as they are forced to. In the remote jungles straddling the border, people, ideas, goods, and news flow steadily in both directions. Despite a profusion of dialects and other differences, the indigenous folk are one people, far more like each other than akin to their Mexican, or ladino, neighbors.

The Mayan presence in Guatemala is strong. You will see

them everywhere, a flashing display of color, their embroidered and appliquéd clothing as flamboyant as the plumage of the country's tropical birds. They and, of course, the ancient monuments of their ancestors, are the chief reasons for visiting Guatemala.

MAJOR INTEREST
Mayan people and their crafts
Scenic beauty, including Lago Atitlán
Museo de la Ciudad de Guatemala (Mayan carvings)
Mayan ruins of Tikal
Mayan ruins of Quirigá and Mixco Viejo
Colonial city of Antigua
Boat trips on the Río Dulce

PLANNING YOUR TRIP

For a small country, Guatemala is unusually diverse in its scenery and climate. The terrain includes jungles, high mountains, temperate highlands, savannah, and a desert. Although it's about the same size as Ohio and almost half the size of the United Kingdom, such comparisons are misleading for the traveller—fully a third of the country is accessible only on horseback or by safari. Most of its attractions, with the exception of Tikal and the Río Dulce, cluster in the pleasantly cool highlands in the south, so you can see a great deal of Guatemala in a short time. Tours planned and sold by agents or airlines tend to be either five- or eight-day trips. Five days hardly offer time enough to cover the highlights, but an eight-day tour, whether packaged or independent, is not unreasonably crowded for sightseeing. Another day or two might be added for the Río Dulce or other out-of-the-way excursions.

Such tight scheduling allows little leisure for appreciating and absorbing this quite foreign land, however, and rules out some pleasant experiences—such as watching a sunset on Lago Atitlán for the second or third time or seeking out picturesque villages. Still, the colorful surface of Guatemala can be skimmed in a little more than a week, which is about what most travellers will choose to devote on a first visit. Inevitably, some of them, charmed by the country, will return for much longer stays.

(Not long ago many travellers hesitated to visit Guatemala because of guerrilla and army activities. The country is much more stable now; thousands of refugees have returned home, and thousands of visitors each year encounter no difficulties. The crime rate in the capital is about the same as in most of the world's large cities, and seasoned travellers who exercise caution should experience no problems.)

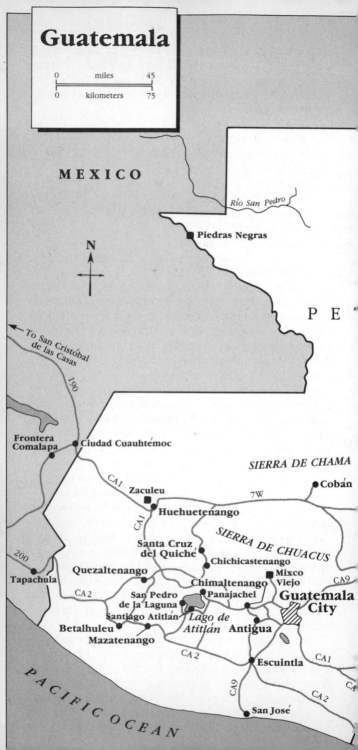

The Land

A great cordillera of lofty peaks and ridges thrusting south from Mexico forms the rugged backbone of Guatemala. Along the Pacific these mountains merge with an ancient chain of volcanoes that almost edge the ocean, leaving only a narrow shelf of lush tropical land broken by swift rivers pouring down from the highlands. No roads run along this coastal shelf; instead, all highways here lead inland and upland.

Higher up on the slopes lies coffee country—some of the richest in the world—and, higher still, long valleys wind among mountain peaks. Here are huddled the cities visited by most travellers: Guatemala City, Antigua, Panajachel, and Chichicastenango. Surrounding these are orchards of peaches and apples as well as truck farms and pastures. But above all, this is corn (maize) country. No slope seems too steep or discouraging for a Mayan farmer to plant this venerated cereal. The rainy season in the highlands lasts from May through October, but even in those months the climate is pleasant rather than sultry.

On the northern side of this mountainous spine, which begins a gradual descent to the lowlands below, are more coffee plantations. Soon, however, the land starts to fall away more sharply, and eventually becomes the wild, inhospitable region known as the **Petén**. Jaguars, often feeding on wild pigs, still inhabit this jungle, and bands of monkeys chatter and howl in the dense foliage.

The Petén is the root of the Yucatán Peninsula, a little less flat than the Yucatán proper, but just as tangled, torrid, and wet. It was here, where opportunities would seem poorest, that the Classic Maya raised their magnificent city of Tikal.

The Maya

Little is known about the first human inhabitants of Guatemala; the area's subsequent history, however, is linked to that of southeastern Mexico, for geographically it is the same region.

Mayan civilization was definitely established here before 300 B.C., flourished, like much of Mesoamerica, between A.D. 300 and 900, and then suddenly declined. No one knows why, though there is a lot of scholarly speculation (see the Bibliography).

In the highlands of Guatemala groups of seminomadic Indians appeared at various times, fought, mingled, and interbred with the local populace. The "pure Maya" of these highlands are a myth. Throughout its human history various Indians peopled Guatemala—as they still do—but the Maya were so dominant that it is simpler for the purposes of this discussion to group them all together.

When the Spaniards arrived in 1523, along with their Indian allies from central Mexico, they found a large population warring among itself. The subsequent conquest of the region was led by Pedro de Alvarado, an especially bloodthirsty and gold-hungry lieutenant of Cortés. The Spaniards, abetted by local treachery and feuds, not only defeated the Maya but also drastically reshaped their whole society. The educated ruling class of the Maya was annihilated; the surviving peasants were forced out of their rural dwellings and herded into Spanish-style towns that bore a strong resemblance to labor camps; Spanish Catholicism was imposed on the indigenous population, often with the aid of fire and the lash.

Mayan resistance, often passive but occasionally violent, proved to be more than a match for the Spanish. When native gods were officially abolished, the people simply renamed them after Christian saints. Here, as elsewhere throughout Mesoamerica, paganism and Catholicism ran like parallel lines, never meeting but always closely related and often indistinguishable.

Costumbre

The Maya maintained their identity, as they do today, through the force of tradition, which is summed up by the Spanish word *costumbre*. Although it usually translates as "custom," the word implies immeasurably more. *Costumbres* are not exactly at the heart of their religion; indeed, they are far less flexible than the Maya's faith. Perhaps the word "kosher" comes closest to conveying some sense of the power of *costumbre*.

After the Conquest, Spanish colonial society in Guatemala was divided into castes. For almost four centuries there existed a form of apartheid here, although it was somewhat diluted because Spaniards were neither as puritanical nor as consistent as the Afrikaaners have been. Guatemalan independence from Spain, achieved early in the 19th century, made little difference in the lives of most Guatemalans.

Today in Guatemala, blood and custom continue to serve as the basis for the division of society, even though the edges are a bit more blurred. The ladino segment of the population controls almost everything. Originally, the word "ladino" described someone who was crafty and cunning, a city slicker. Some Mayan people will tell you it still means that, although in everyday parlance it refers to all *guatemaltecos* who are "Europeanized." A ladino wears shoes, of course, and maybe a charcoal gray suit during business hours. Generally speaking, he is modern, regards mechanical and material progress as blessings, and admires novelties. Most ladinos are partly or entirely of European descent; skin color and features are important in Guatemala, although not as basic to classifying a person as proper shoes or a proper frame of mind.

In Guatemala, ladinos often tell you that an Indian is simply someone who chooses to call himself so. This pretense to equality, however, will not become a reality until the day all ladinos suddenly go blind. Guatemala is, above all else, a caste-conscious country. While there are no separate public facilities here, there are certainly separate bank accounts. Still, people on either side of this social and financial chasm are almost always courteous and gracious to visitors.

Guatemalan Food and Drink

Restaurant food throughout the country tends to be a blending of European and North American cuisine. In fact, you could travel extensively in Guatemala without ever suspecting the existence of a national cuisine. To sample local food you must therefore look for places advertising a *comida típica*. Such an establishment will usually call itself a *comedor* (eating place) rather than a *restaurante,* which sounds more pretentious to the ears of most Guatemalans.

Chuchitos are little tamales with a spiced meat stuffing; *pepian* is a fricassee with squash seeds in a rich, dark sauce; another unusual item is *guisquil,* a pearlike vegetable that grows on vines. *Pacaya,* also native to the country, is a vegetable with an unfamiliar, rather harsh tang. Bananas, fried, mashed, or prepared any number of other ways, play a major role in Mayan cuisine. Black beans, too, are prepared in various ways. Beef, except in expensive restaurants, is often tough, so it is usually cooked by simmering it in *guisados* (stews) or *caldos* (soup broths). Many foods usually considered Mexican are also standard in Guatemala, including enchiladas, guacamole, and *ceviche.* Corn tortillas are a national staple.

Local wines, usually concocted with grape concentrates, orange pulp, and the like, should not be considered; imported vintages are expensive, so ask about price before you order to avoid sticker shock later. Good Guatemalan beer helps to offset the lack of wine. Gallo and Cabro, both medium light, are the most popular brands, and higher-priced Medalla de Oro is not really better. Moza, a rich, dark beer, is excellent but not always available. Local rum and *aguardiente,* both distilled from sugarcane, are commendable, and the local vodka is smooth enough. The prudent will stay away from the native whiskey.

GUATEMALA CITY

La Ciudad de Guatemala may be the hub of the country and the seat of its government, but it is certainly not its heart. As the major transportation center of the country, the capital becomes the inescapable destination of most travellers. The best visit is a brief one; a day will do nicely, and even that is not necessary unless there's a delay involving your flight to Tikal. Hotels in Antigua and Panajachel will arrange to have a driver and car meet you at the airport, or you can rent a car at the airport, convert some currency, and be on your way, skipping the city altogether.

While this might make the capital sound like a dreadful place, it really isn't—except perhaps in rush-hour traffic or by the glare of neon at night. In fact, Guatemala City has good hotels and restaurants and three worthwhile museums. But then, they're probably not what you came to see.

Nor is the city the best jumping-off point for visits to the surrounding countryside. Both the attractive town of Antigua and the delightfully located lakeside town of Panajachel are better choices.

Guatemala City teems with more than two-and-a-quarter million people packed into a space never meant to accommodate such an onslaught. You can see some impressive buildings downtown, but beyond them spreads an ocean of urban sprawl. Likewise, parks too often are inundated by waves of hurrying humanity. The city's saving grace is that much of this humanity is Mayan, which enables you to see wonderfully expressive faces and, sometimes, the flair and flash of native costumes.

Around in the Capital

Tours of the city sold by hotels are of dubious value, mainly because much time is wasted on uninteresting monuments. Better to hire a cab by the hour at an agreed-upon price, or to take a series of cabs and be off on your own.

Before setting out you should know that Guatemala City is divided into 21 zones. A street address without a zone number is insufficient, as names and numbers may be repeated from zone to zone. Although addresses might sound complicated, they are logical and easy to find with a map.

Your exploration of the city should begin with the **Parque Aurora,** near the airport on the south side of the city, Zona 13, between 7 Avenida and 11 Avenida. Museums, a zoo, a racetrack, and an extensive handicraft market make this park a center of interest and activity.

Museo Nacional de Arqueológica y Etnología

The National Museum of Archaeology and Ethnology, often referred to by its old name, the **Museo de la Ciudad de Guatemala**, is housed in a modern gleaming white building. The architecture is totally Spanish-Moorish, which is odd because the museum's contents are almost totally Mayan. This is more than just an incongruity; it's also a telling comment about the divided nature of the country.

For all that, the museum's extensive collection of Mayan carvings, the largest in the world, is magnificent. One of its highlights is a throne from the jungle city of Piedras Negras. Masterworks in ceramics—masks, figurines, and a variety of containers and vessels—rival the priceless achievements in stone. Many of the objects on display were the accessories, the fittings and utensils, found at Tikal. Studying them here makes it easier to reconstruct that magnificent city in the mind's eye. The ethnological section of the museum, which is devoted chiefly to native costumes, is also interesting and well presented.

Other Cultural Attractions

Across the street, the **Museo de Historia y Bellas Artes** merits a short visit because of its fine interior, especially the main ceiling, and the paintings by Carlos Mérida; its historical section, however, is limited.

The **handicraft market**, located behind the Museum of History and Fine Arts, sells crafts from every part of the country. If nothing else, the prices here will give you a standard of comparison for shopping elsewhere; work of higher quality, especially fine weaving, can be found outside the capital. The colorful atmosphere and gay marimba music are the market's best offerings.

Except for its flamboyant native birds, the **zoo**, just north of the market, is nothing special.

Two other museums in the capital are also worth visiting. The **Museo Popol Vuh** occupies the sixth floor of a high-rise building known as the Edificio Galerías Reforma, Torre 2 (Zona 9 at Reforma 8). Its display of Mayan polychrome vessels, including a number of large burial urns, is dazzling.

The items were once in a private collection, and great care went into choosing every piece. All the Maya-inhabited regions of the country are represented, and although works created between A.D. 150 and 900 predominate, there are also earlier and later examples of the Maya's pre-Columbian artistry.

Quite different, but just as delightful in its own right, is the **Museo Ixchel del Traje Indígena**, where the textile arts of Guatemala, especially weaving and embroidery, are honored. The clothing on display in this museum is gorgeous, and the whole show so imaginatively presented that it rises far above the usual crafts display. In addition, this valentine of a museum is located in one of the city's better neighborhoods, 4A Avenida 16-17, Zona 10, about a 15-minute walk west of the Museo Popol Vuh.

If you have extra time, the **Relief Map** (*Mapa en Relieve*) in the pleasant Parque Minerva, Zona 2, may prove interesting. This is a sprawling rendering of the country, 125 by 250 feet, in somewhat exaggerated relief (the volcanoes, as shown here, would tower over Mount Everest in the real world). It's a painless and unusual geography lesson, and useful if you're about to set out to tour the country.

A number of city landmarks, though touted by guides and local advertisers, have little interest or charm. These include the grim National Palace, the Metropolitan Cathedral, and the National Theater—all of them, at best, just time fillers. Guatemalans are extremely proud of the municipal buildings in their Civic Center; these structures are modern, functional, and handsome.

Kaminaljuyú

The archaeological site of Kaminaljuyú, meaning "Hill of the Dead," is in Zona 7, off Calzada San Juan on 23 Avenida. Until recently this was the outskirts of the city; now it's a suburb. There is not a great deal left of the ancient center, which was founded before 1500 B.C., experienced its heyday between 300 B.C. and A.D. 200, then fell into irreversible decline over the next two centuries. With the exception of two modest complexes, almost everything was leveled in the course of building the modern city. Of the five stratigraphic levels at the site, the deepest and earliest is probably Olmec, followed by a stratum of Preclassic Mayan artifacts. The pronounced influence of Teotihuacán shows up in more recent strata.

Kaminaljuyú can be visited weekdays from 8:00 A.M. until noon and from 2:00 until 5:00 P.M. Bring a flashlight. The caretaker, who expects a small tip, will unlock the entrance to a tomb that is the site's most interesting feature. Further excavation proceeds by fits and starts nearby, with a number of promising finds of statuary and ceramic ware.

STAYING IN GUATEMALA CITY

The capital has good accommodations in all price ranges except the very cheapest, which are miserable. A room tax of 17 percent will be added to your bill, and will not always be announced in advance. You should inquire beforehand.

In an attempt to avoid congestion, which sometimes overtakes them anyway, the newer and more luxurious hotels are located outside the center of the city. The better neighborhoods are Zonas 4, 9, and 10. A hotel in Zona 1 is likely to be economical but noisy, and there is little advantage to being in this, the old central area.

Throughout the country national taste favors the sleek, streamlined, and unmistakably modern; the more North American the better. International travellers, on the other hand, seem to prefer more charm and less plate glass. Both types of hostelries are mentioned here.

The ▶ **Camino Real Guatemala** is excellent—as it should be for the prices it asks—and has a number of restaurants, three bars with live entertainment, tennis courts, a gym, and swimming pools in assorted sizes. (Guatemalan luxury hotels, by the way, put a premium on sports and body-conditioning facilities.) The hotel is located in an upper-class neighborhood in Zona 10.

The multistoried ▶ **Hotel El Dorado Americana**, a block of masonry and glass featured in tourism publications as representative of "modern Guatemala," has everything the Camino Real–Biltmore has—bars, restaurants, and swimming pools—only fewer of them. In other words, this is a fine international hotel, with prices to match. It's located in a good neighborhood, Zona 9, not far from the Tower of the Reformer, Guatemala's mini-version of the Eiffel Tower.

Expensive but less so than the Dorado or Camino Real, the ▶ **Conquistador Ramada** delights guests with its flourishing orchids in the lobby. While it has most of the amenities, it does not feature all the gym and sauna facilities of its somewhat more lavish competitors. It does have a good location in Zona 4, however, as well as a very good restaurant (discussed below), and is popular with European groups.

The ▶ **Hotel Plaza**, also in Zona 4; is straightforward and a couple of notches above basic at a moderate price. Ask for a room overlooking the swimming pool; the rooms facing the parking lot can be noisy.

In Zona 1, near the cathedral, the ▶ **Hotel del Centro** is rich in wood paneling and wrought iron; everything is hushed and gentle—except the streets outside (although the night traffic does eventually die down). The parking garage is convenient, the restaurant and carpets good, and it's not hard to imagine you've been transported to Spain. The location explains its bargain rates.

In the same moderate bracket, and with the same problems of noise and congestion due to its location in Zona 1, is the ▶ **Pan American**. In the Art Deco era the Pan American was the capital's leading hotel. Today, if some of its elegance has faded, it makes up for it with an abundance of comfort and charm. The hotel's restaurant is discussed below.

The ▶ **Posada Belén**, a quiet, friendly, and welcoming little inn (just nine rooms), is the city's best pension. Although it, too, is located in the center of town, in Zona 1, its street is spared the worst of the racket. The management is also happy to help with tours and excursions, and there's a library full of information about Guatemala.

DINING IN GUATEMALA CITY

The restaurant in the **Pan American**, though not exactly elegant, offers a good introduction to Guatemalan cuisine and also serves a variety of foreign dishes, good coffee, and fine pastries at modest prices. The waiters are decked out in traditional village attire, and the woven wall hangings are added attractions. Tel: (2) 26-8079.

The posh neighborhood around the Camino Real–Biltmore in Zona 10, **La Zona Viva**, or "lively zone," is where you'll find dining, dancing, and the cabaret world of Guatemala. While far from the equal of Paris or Rome, it is surprisingly chic for Central America. There are not many rich people in Guatemala, but those who have money seem to have a lot of it, and they spend it freely. They also all seem to know one another, and where they meet is New York, Paris, or here in La Zona Viva.

Le Rendezvous, 13 Calle 2-55, Zona 10, is a transplanted bit of Montmartre, more bistro than haute cuisine, and offering indoor or patio service. It's very good, very French, and fairly expensive.

The **Puerto Barrios**, at 11 Calle and 7 Avenida, Zona 9, is decked out like a Spanish galleon, but the seafood is much better than the pirate rigging would indicate. The steaks are good, the shrimp and lobster better. Tel: (2) 34-1302.

Martin's offers fare that is uncommon in Guatemala, including such items as frog's legs and rack of lamb. Broiled salmon, also served here, is an exotic item in Central America. Reasonable prices have helped keep this august establishment at 13 Calle 7-65, Zona 9, popular for almost two decades.

Located not in La Zona Viva but across the street from the Conquistador Ramada at Via 4, 4-36, Zona 4, is **Estro Armónico**. With a limited menu of seafood and meat dishes accompanied by light French sauces, it's as warmly provincial as its flickering hearth. And while less expensive than the better establishments of the more fashionable zone, it is not inexpensive. Tel: (2) 31-9240 or 32-0892.

The reasonably priced **Restaurant Altuna** is situated downtown in Zona 1, on Calle 5 between Calles 7 and 8. Paella and other Spanish classics are offered on the roofed patio of this charming colonial-style building, and the seafood is admirably fresh. Tel: (2) 51-7185.

All the leading hotels in Guatemala City have satisfactory restaurants. The best in the deluxe category, in the Ramada, is the **Restaurante de La Pergola**, which specializes in Italian cuisine. It also has style and panache. Tel: (2) 31-2222. Among the moderately priced hotels, the dining room of the **Hotel del Centro** is a good choice. The food isn't quite as Spanish as the decor, but the atmosphere is genteel and comfortable. Tel: (2) 38-1281.

TIKAL

Tikal, the grandest of the ruined Mayan cities, is nothing less than awe-inspiring. Here, in the tangled, almost impenetrable jungle of northern Guatemala you suddenly come upon the greatest human achievement of the Stone Age. For Tikal *is* a Stone Age creation, even though its magnificent structures were raised in the first centuries of the Christian era. Its builders used no metal tools, no draft animals, and no wheels (consequently, no pulleys). In order to accomplish these feats of engineering and construction, an army of laborers and artists had to be recruited, trained, and maintained not just for a few years, but for generations—an achievement as amazing as the buildings themselves.

To date, 3,000 buildings have been mapped near the Great Plaza of Tikal. Foundations of about 10,000 stone structures are known—impressive enough when read about, but mind-boggling when you are actually there in the jungle.

Tikal began to take shape around the **Gran Plaza** about 2,000 years ago on a site that probably was selected because it was higher than the surrounding swamps. The city reached its zenith of art and activity between A.D. 500 and 900, when it had at least 50,000 inhabitants. Then, suddenly and inexplicably, it was abandoned to the jungle.

Some dates at the site can be confirmed. Temple I, better known as the **Templo del Gran Jaguar**, bears a Mayan glyph corresponding to A.D. 741, which tests have confirmed as the probable date of construction. The steep, graceful temple, Tikal's most famous monument, rises a lofty 170 feet above the East Plaza and looms almost as high above the Great Plaza.

Nearby are plazas, terraces, and other buildings, including the tallest in the ancient Americas, **Templo IV**, which rises more than 212 feet from its base to the tip of its roofcomb, and even looks down on those giants of the jungle, the ceiba trees (which were sacred to the Maya).

Tikal is simply too vast and complex for a detailed discussion here. Those planning to explore the city should arm themselves with archaeologist William R. Coe's clear and definitive guide, *Tikal: A Handbook of the Ancient Maya Ruins,* published by the University of Pennsylvania Museum, Philadelphia, and in Guatemala by Editorial Piedra Santa. While it is usually available in English at the Tikal museum or in the town of Flores, it is safer to purchase it in advance. (For getting to Tikal, see the Getting Around section at the end of this chapter.)

STAYING AT TIKAL

Visitors have a choice of staying at the Parque Nacional Tikal itself; 30 minutes away by car on the lakeshore; or in **Flores**, the small capital of the Petén, an island town in Lago Petén Itzá that's connected to the shore by a causeway. Two other little towns, Santa Elena and San Benito, are located nearby on the mainland.

Accommodations at Tikal itself are Spartan and not always available. Despite the quality of these facilities, however, being a 20-minute walk from the ruins has its advantages. Besides the convenience, the jungle itself is an attraction. With its cacophony of bird and animal cries (especially at night), it seems to be a living, breathing entity. The experience has much to recommend it.

(Moonlight not only transforms the jungle but works magic on the ruins. Tikal is magnificent under a full moon, and although the zone is usually closed at night, exceptions are sometimes made. Spend a night or two if possible in Tikal or Flores. More extensive tours than the usual packages provide can be arranged here. In addition, a limited number of Jeeps are available for private exploring.)

A good, rustic choice right in the archaeological zone is

the ▶ **Jungle Lodge**, built to house scientists and leaders of the Tikal excavation team but now privately owned. The inn is clean and refreshing, with shaded verandahs and ceiling fans. It also has an adequate dining room, bar, and a friendly, helpful management. The rooms have walls so thin, however, you can hear conversations next door, and the electricity is turned off between 10:00 P.M. and 6:00 A.M. Still, you are right on the edge of the ruins, and free to wander at will.

Other small inns in the zone are uncomfortable and, in some cases, unsanitary.

The Flores/Santa Elena/San Benito area is an hour's drive from the Tikal archaeological zone, with good transportation available by bus or van. With one exception the better hotels in the area are adequate but not luxurious. There is a certain oddity, even simple charm, about these hotels, and you do not entirely lose the sense of being in the jungle.

The ▶ **Maya Internacional** is a collection of thatched, rather romantic cottages right on the water. The cottages are simple, clean, and comfortable, and the management will arrange tours of Tikal.

Also on the shore of Lago Petén Itzá, the ▶ **Camino Real Tikal** offers pleasant rooms, an attractive restaurant with satisfactory food, and the only real air-conditioning within 100 miles. The jungle setting, with views across the lake, adds charm; toucans may perch outside your window and spider monkeys at home in the tangled canopy are a fairly common sight. Some travellers may find its slick modernity at odds with the experience of exploring Tikal, and, of course, you sacrifice independent access to the ruins. The hotel does have car/Jeep rentals and offers guided tours to Tikal, about 30 minutes away by car.

If you have the time, boat rides on the lake are easy to arrange and an enjoyable way to spend an afternoon while you're in the area.

OTHER MAYAN RUINS
IN GUATEMALA

Any archaeological zone in Guatemala will seem a bit anticlimactic after Tikal, and in fact the sites that dot official maps are mostly of minimal interest, or else are too remote to repay the trouble involved in getting there. However, three other sites can be recommended to enthusiasts, with the obvious reservation: None is another Tikal.

Quiriguá

This lowland site (pronounced kee-rhee-GWAH) near the border with Honduras is famed for its carved monuments, some of the finest in the Mayan world. Though not a large site, with its extant buildings of only secondary interest, it is the location of the largest carved Mayan monolith known— Stela E, nearly 36 feet tall and weighing some 65 tons. Almost a quarter of this massive stone remains buried, and the narrative carving on it is fascinating. Scattered elsewhere around the site, a dozen smaller works boast equally intricate detailing.

Quiriguá is a little more than three hours from Guatemala City by car, about 206 km (128 miles) of that being paved road. Highway CA 9 heads northeast from the city to the vicinity of Los Amates, at which point you take a dirt cutoff for 3½ km (2 miles). You'll want to pack a lunch before heading out, including anything you might want to drink. (You can also visit Quiriguá on the way to the Río Dulce; see below.)

Mixco Viejo

Mixco Viejo (MEESH-ko VYEH-o), the capital of the Pokomam Maya, a warlike people who were eventually defeated by the conquistadors, was still a thriving urban center when the Spanish arrived in 1525, although it had been established many centuries earlier near the end of the Classic era. Today it's a beautiful site, and less well known than it should be. There are two Mayan ball courts here, one that's particularly impressive; a major temple structure; and a number of pyramids and platforms. Best of all, it's only 50 km (31 miles) north-northwest of Guatemala City, most of that over a paved road and the rest improved. You should allow an hour and a half by car for the drive—think of it as a good opportunity for a picnic and one of the prettiest short trips you can take in Guatemala. (If you decide to visit Mixco Viejo, make sure you have a reliable map with the two turnoffs marked by your hotel or the tourist office.) Bus travel to Mixco Viejo, on the other hand, is not a practical option.

Zaculeu

A trip to Zaculeu (sah-koo-LEH-oo), situated in Guatemala's far western highlands just outside the modern city of **Huehuetenango**, makes for a very long one-day excursion from Guatemala City, or a slightly easier one from Panajachel (see below). Huehuetenango (way-way-te-NAN-go) itself is

264 km (164 miles) northwest of the capital. Allow three and a half hours each way.

Occupied for at least 1,000 years before the arrival of the Spanish, Zaculeu's divided stairs, dance platforms, and other ruins show signs of Mexican influence. Structure I is an impressive stepped pyramid with a temple atop it. There is also a handsome ball court here. Of the more than 40 structures officially listed, most are only grassy mounds today. Although the site is interesting and the surroundings attractive, this is a trip for dedicated enthusiasts only—or for those seeking a good excuse to visit another region of Guatemala.

The ▶ **Hotel Piño Montano**, just outside Huehuetenango, resembles a motel, with a restaurant and pool in a garden setting. It's a simple but satisfactory establishment for those looking for a night's lodging near Zaculeu.

Travel agencies in the major hotels in Guatemala City offer regular tours to Quiriguá, Mixco Viejo, and a number of lesser sites. Clark Tours (see the Getting Around section below) also makes such arrangements and will be happy, in addition, to advise visitors about seeing Zaculeu, a site too remote to be included in most standard itineraries.

Copán

Located not in Guatemala but just across its eastern border in Honduras are the magnificent Mayan ruins of Copán, generally considered one of the half dozen greatest Classic Mayan centers. The trip is an ordeal, however, and casual travellers usually skip it. Archaeology buffs, on the other hand, will probably not want to miss it.

Copán ranks among the greatest and most beautiful pre-Columbian centers of Mesoamerica, and some authorities have hailed it as the highest intellectual and artistic achievement of the ancient Maya. For visitors the first stop in what is now a landscaped national park is the **museum** near the entrance, where information in English about the site may be obtained. You may also engage a guide here, an invaluable asset when visiting these complex and extensive ruins.

The Copán Valley, a fertile region at an altitude of 2,000 feet, is well watered by the Río Copán. The valley attracted the Maya long before the present age, and reached its greatness in the Classic era (dates on monuments indicate that the site's heyday extended from about A.D. 450 to 800). During this period temples, altars, and one of the finest ball courts in America were constructed. The ruler Smoke Squirrel, the next-to-last known monarch of Copán, ascended to power in A.D. 747 and built a gigantic stairway of 2,500 stone blocks carved with glyphs—the longest single pre-Hispanic inscription found to date, and a treasury of Mayan sculpture. The carved stone stelae at the site (which the Maya call "stone trees") are graceful and elegant, one monument after another proclaiming the genius of Mayan artists.

The highlights can be covered in about three hours; but, of course, the more time the better in this rare and beautiful place.

Bus tours from Guatemala City leave early and often return after dark. Unfortunately, much of this long day is spent in transit, with hardly enough time for the ruins themselves. Reliable service is provided by **Clark Tours**, 7 Avenida 6-53, Efidicio El Triángulo, 2nd floor, Zona 4, Guatemala City, C.A.; in Guatemala City, Tel: (2) 31-0213 to 0216; Fax: (2) 31-5916; in the U.S., Tel: (800) 223-6764. Clark is the most experienced provider, but the major hotels may have other good suggestions. The far better (and much more expensive) option is small-plane charter service, available through most large hotels and major travel agencies.

To visit Copán by car, take CA 9, the Atlantic Highway (see the Río Dulce section below). Turn south onto CA 10 near Río Hondo and follow it for 42 km (26 miles). You then turn left (northeast) onto Highway 21, a poor road, which will take you to the border of Honduras, 43 km (27 miles) farther on. There will be customs and immigration formalities at the border. Copán is another 13 km (8 miles) from the border via Honduras Highway 20.

The trip, which takes about four and a half hours from Guatemala City, can be combined with a visit to the ruins at Quiriguá to make a two-day archaeological excursion, with an overnight in Copán. The simple ▶ **Hotel Marina**, in the village of Copán on the main plaza, has adequate accommodations and a restaurant. The electricity is cut off at about 9:00 P.M., however.

ANTIGUA

Antigua, on first sight, reveals nothing of its former glory. It's a pretty town, 20 km (12 miles) west-southwest of Guatemala City, and is manicured and buffed for its many visitors, which it receives with a gracious nod. It's also decorous and proper, its residents quite aware that this is *the* (living) national showcase.

The wide cobblestone streets here are lined by colonial façades that you think must be old yet don't seem to have aged. These structures are, for the most part, single-story with red-tiled roofs, imparting a uniformity of height and style to some neighborhoods that makes them seem harmonious, if a bit monotonous. As a result, the profusion of flowering vines throughout the city adds a welcome touch of disorder. And everywhere you look the silhouette of a mountain looms in the background.

Because Antigua seems to have been created by a Latin American Norman Rockwell, with what some people see as a slightly artificial prettiness, many visitors find it difficult to fathom the cataclysmic past behind its genteel present. On the night of September 10, 1541, the original capital of Guatemala was obliterated by fire, followed by a terrible deluge of water released from the crater of a nearby volcano. The survivors dragged themselves to the apparently safe valley here and founded Santiago de los Caballeros de Guatemala, "Saint James of the Knights of Guatemala," as Antigua was then called.

The new capital, which was cradled in a valley dominated by three immense volcanoes, grew to become an important center of Spain's New World empire, second only to Mexico City and Lima in power. The city's business was to exploit—however ruthlessly—the whole Mayan region, and in so doing it became a metropolis of some 60,000 people.

Then the bad omens began. Several times in the early 18th century an irritable volcano by the name of Monte Fuego belched forth lava and ash, burying some inhabitants alive. Earthquakes set the town's massive arches trembling. According to contemporary accounts, Antigua descended into a vicious cycle of crime, violence, and oppression. There appears to have been a cruel Old Testament justice to what fate had in store for the town and its citizens.

In the summer of 1773 the earth came alive again and literally shook the city to death—not a quick death, but rather a prolonged agony that lasted more than a month, followed by week upon week of deadly aftershocks. Adobe walls melted under torrential rains, and plague soon haunted the ruins. The governor, believing the valley to be cursed, ordered an evacuation and removed himself and his capital to what is now Guatemala City, which was formally declared the new capital in 1776. (Exactly two centuries later the quake of 1976 would almost level *that* city.)

The archbishop fought the governor to save the old town but was himself forced to move. A few determined survivors nevertheless hung on among the ruins of Santiago. Gradually, a new town arose from the devastation; in the 19th century it began to prosper from the coffee trade and became known as Antigua Guatemala, "Old Guatemala."

Exploring Antigua

The town is laid out on a grid, with the north–south thoroughfares called *calles* (streets) and the east–west thoroughfares called *avenidas* (avenues). The point at which "north" (*norte*) becomes "south" (*sur*) and "east" (*oriente*) becomes "west" (*poniente*) is the cathedral on the south side of the plaza.

The tourist office, located on the south side of the plaza in what was once the Palace of the Captains-General, is manned by a most helpful and generous staff with access to up-to-the-minute information.

Sightseeing here is mostly a matter of inspecting ruins while you wander through tidy, quaint neighborhoods. Antigua has been preserved as a monument to earthquakes, and the city takes a perverse pride in these lingering echoes of destruction. The ruins, all dating from the 18th century, are impressive, though a little melancholy in the bright sunshine, and soon you begin to think of Shelley's Ozymandias. It's a fascinating, if not exactly jolly, way to spend time.

Start with the shell behind the present cathedral and continue around town—the remnants of ruin are everywhere. The **Monasterio de Santo Domingo** is worth a brief mention because it once was huge and fantastically rich. A silver statue of the Virgin here was reported to be the size of a tall woman, and a silver altar lamp was said to have been so weighty it took three men to raise it. (After one earthquake the Virgin was fruitlessly bribed with a crown of jewels.) At the corner of 2 Calle Oriente and 2 Avenida Norte, the **Iglesia y Convento de Capuchinas**, much of it still standing, affords memorable views from its roof.

The **Convento de San Francisco**, 7 Calle Oriente and 1 Avenida Sur, is an old rubble heap, but the adjacent **church** survived the frequent devastation and contains an extensive collection of votive paintings, signs, letters, and photos proclaiming the miracles performed by Brother Pedro de Betancourt, a 17th-century holy man entombed here. Those needing his intercession in their own affairs rap on the tomb to get his attention; the knocking is frequent, gentle, but persistent.

There are also two museums in Antigua. The venerable **University of San Carlos**, 3 Avenida Sur and 5 Calle Oriente, has an uninteresting collection of colonial objects, but the building housing it has a lovely patio. The nearby Museo de Santiago has little to recommend it other than its rough, almost medieval architecture.

STAYING IN ANTIGUA

Antigua's inns tend to be high priced for what they offer; nevertheless, the town is often short of rooms, so reserve ahead.

One reason for the town's popularity is its admirable location, which is excellent for staging excursions into south-central Guatemala. Knowledgeable guides and drivers are available in town, and attractive villages can be found nearby with their help.

The ► **Hotel Aurora**, conveniently located four blocks east of the cathedral, offers the best value in accommodations in Antigua, although it's not the most luxurious in town. This spacious old residence, built around a flower-filled patio, now houses a carefully run family operation and has all the necessities, but offers no public rooms or luxuries other than its own atmosphere and service. Breakfast can be ordered for an extra charge.

The ► **Hotel Antigua**, another colonial gem (at least in decor), is far more luxurious. Its beautiful lawns frame a swimming pool and a children's wading pool near nicely spaced bungalows, and the gardens' lovely but raucous parrots are rivaled in beauty only by the many rose bushes, trees, and hedges on the grounds. In addition, the dining room is cheerful and tastefully decorated. The hotel prides itself on its Sunday buffet, which is accompanied by music. Actually, Sunday, when it's crowded with day-trippers from the capital, is the least attractive day of the week here. Nevertheless, the Hotel Antigua is a rarity in Guatemala, and rare things tend to be expensive—but in this case not outrageously so. The inn is a five-minute walk south of the plaza on 8A Calle Oriente.

In the center of town on 5A Avenida Norte, a block north of the Parque Central, is the ► **Posada de Don Rodrigo**, a series of high-ceilinged rooms and a restaurant and bar clustered around several shady patios. This historic old residence is a little too heavy on shadowy atmosphere, but it is nonetheless a handsome inn. Only avid marimba-music aficionados should accept quarters facing the main patio, however—at least on weekends. There are also considerable differences in size, light, and ventilation among the room choices. No one section of the inn is best in its entirety, so look at the individual room offered before registering. The rustic dining room is colorful, but the food is unexceptional. The Posada is moderately expensive.

If you face the frequent scarcity of rooms in Antigua, you might choose the ► **Ramada Antigua**. To stay here is better than having to journey back to Guatemala City, and the hotel is not terribly overpriced. Still, this apricot-colored cube of cement at the edge of town gives the impression that several conventions are either just ending or threatening to begin. It is popular with the business and government crowd from Guatemala City, who enjoy the tennis courts and the illusion of being in North America. The Ramada is on the Ciudad Vieja highway at the southwest edge of town. (Its restaurants are discussed below.)

Scattered around Antigua are a number of modest pensions and rooming houses that accommodate travellers looking for economy over the long term and students studying Spanish in Antigua. (Antigua beckons language students of all ages, many of whom live with local families.)

DINING IN ANTIGUA

El Sereno, the most stylish restaurant in Guatemala, welcomes you with candlelight, crystal, and a lovely fountain. The food, which has gourmet aspirations, is French and international, with some transfigured native dishes. The restaurant is expensive but memorable. El Sereno's elegant entrance is found at 6A Calle Poniente 30; closed Mondays and Tuesdays. Reservations advised; Tel: (9) 32-0073.

Doña Luisa Xicotencatl seems to have something of everything, including a devoted following of students and young people from the capital. The courtyard is an especially convivial place, and a number of the tables upstairs offer striking views of the nearby volcanoes. You check off your choices on a long paper menu, which includes such fare as chile con carne, sausages, Reuben sandwiches, pies, and cakes. The food is fair, the atmosphere casual, the prices moderate. 4A Calle Oriente 2.

Located on Calle 4A one block west of the Parque Central, Welten serves up international-style cuisine (with an emphasis on pasta) in a pleasantly floral and ferny patio environment. Prices range from moderate to expensive.

Alom La Creación, in the Ramada, presents international specialties with a German emphasis. It's open evenings only from 7:00 until 11:00 P.M. but claims it won't turn you out until you're ready to end the night. Las Chimeneas, in the same hotel, is a standard operation, with piano music and (usually) good service that becomes rushed on weekends. Both Ramada restaurants are at the expensive end of the scale. Tel: (9) 3-2011 to 2015.

SHOPPING IN ANTIGUA

Tourist prices tend to prevail in Antigua, but you can find some good buys and fine merchandise here, especially at the **weaving market** located next to the Jesuit church, La Compañia de Jesús, 6 Avenida Norte and 4 Calle Poniente. Those searching for interesting textiles should also visit the nearby village of **San Antonio Aguas Calientes**, about 5 km (3 miles) to the east.

Jade is an Antigua specialty. The founder of the jade art and industry here is **Jades** (HA-dess), a large, beautiful shop at 4A Calle Oriente 34 (the building also houses a number of interesting working studios). Guatemalan jade is the real stone, by the way, and it's risky to buy it off the street unless you are highly knowledgeable; you can rely, on the other hand, on an establishment like Jades, which specializes in exquisite stones, finely set. The store has many other items of interest, including handwoven cloth and the best available coffee beans.

After checking out Jades, pause at the tempting candy shop on the opposite side of the street across from the gas station, where chocolate reigns in all its glory and many of its forms. This street, 4A Calle Oriente, also has several other worthwhile handicraft shops, all of them located between Jades and the main plaza.

Mayan women frequently come into Antigua to sell their work or their possessions on the streets. It's a mistake to turn away automatically; you just might miss the best buys in town.

LAGO ATITLAN AND PANAJACHEL

Half a century ago Aldous Huxley pronounced Lake Atitlán to be "the most beautiful of the world." Virtually every ad, brochure, and discussion of the lake begins with the great man's encomium. In fact, in the lakeside town of Panajachel you can find the Huxley quote printed in at least four different languages, at once challenging and offending countless travellers. (It seems that everyone has a personal candidate for "the most beautiful," and though the lakes are scattered from Finland to California, none ever seems to be Atitlán.)

Regardless of which is fairest of them all, Lago Atitlán, in all its changing moods, *is* unforgettably, hauntingly beautiful. This broad sweep of water, some 16 miles long and 11 miles wide, is framed by massive symmetrically shaped volcanoes whose eruptions created the basin in prehistoric times. The lake is relatively clean and remains good for water sports, but it is mainly enjoyed for its beauty, whether it's in the late morning, when a daily wind freshens and lightens its deep blue color, or in the early evening, when the rising mist tints it silver. At any time of day, lake watching is a local pastime.

A dozen towns and villages, predominantly Mayan and linked to each other by launches, hug the shoreline, although roads connect most places. (The Maya prefer to have their feet on the ground. They are neither fishermen, good swimmers, nor canny boat builders: *No es costumbre*. The lake is merely the limit of their cornfields. Accordingly, they do not create legends or sing songs about it, and its waters are not viewed as a resource.)

Panajachel

Of the lake settlements at Atitlán, the most interesting to travellers is Panajachel (pahn-ah-hah-CHEL), the only one with facilities for visitors. The town itself winds, sprawls, and ambles along the northeastern shore of the lake, as casual in its layout as it is in its approach to life. Being more Mayan than ladino, Panajachel has little of Antigua's tidiness, quaintness, and squared corners. There are no ruins, monuments, or museums here. Instead, the town draws visitors because of the beauty of its setting, the interesting variety of its people (both native and foreign), and the carefree atmosphere of easy living that prevails. As a headquarters for exploring the countryside, it is more centrally located than Antigua, and its accommodations are a better value.

Panajachel carries no heavy burden of history. There was a good-sized native population here when the Spanish marched into the region, but after one bloody battle the struggle was over, and only the resistance of custom and stubbornness remained to confound the conquerors. The town became a center for the Franciscans, who converted the local folk after a fashion. Otherwise, life, which chiefly meant raising corn, continued along its age-old path.

In our own century the lake has increasingly attracted tourists and vacationers. Day-trippers come from Guatemala City, travelling 115 km (71 miles) each way. Europeans, especially younger ones, also come in noticeable numbers, usually after visiting Tikal. (Many seem to be taking vague sabbaticals.) In addition, foreigners and wealthy people from the capital have bought or built homes here. These substantial holiday or retirement houses are planted comfortably between the commercial district and the shore.

There is also a small coterie of North American and European transients, mostly young, who maintain a 1960s lifestyle reminiscent of the vanished world of San Francisco's "Hashbury." You might call them "post-hippies," but the term somehow seems too emphatic. At any rate, they hang up their wind chimes, play their bamboo flutes, and contemplate the lake at sunset with great seriousness. The backpackers among them gaze uncomprehendingly at Mayan folk carrying loads in much the same way. (The Maya do it more efficiently; they have tumplines circling their foreheads to brace the burden.) A number of artists and writers are also drawn to the lake. While the mix of people is not homogeneous enough to be convivial, Panajachel is probably the liveliest little town in Central America.

Around in Panajachel

The town's center, like the lifestyle it encourages, is somewhat haphazard. Street names are rarely posted and frequently change. The heart of town can be found at the corner of Calle Principal, the main street, and Calle Santander, which runs toward the lake. Along Calle Principal you will find a slow-service bank, a peaceful enough pool hall, and a stand that sells delicious Topsy ice cream. The **Maya Palace** craft shop, an excellent store, is still operating even though the old hotel of the same name has become an office building. You'll also find a book exchange, a chocolate shop, and some restaurants and snack shops along the main street.

The evangelical church on Calle Principal is far livelier than the pool hall, in part because Protestant missionaries have flocked to Guatemala in recent years and enjoyed great success. The authorities seem to like this particular foreign import: The missionaries take a less jaundiced view of the Guatemalan government than the Catholic liberation theology movement. Politics aside, you'll probably be startled to hear "Rock of Ages" pounded out on an electric keyboard and backed by guitars as a fervent congregation sings along in Spanish and Mayan.

Walking down Calle Santander toward the lake, you pass several blocks of cloth displays. Visitors are invited, even urged, to inspect the wares but are not badgered. The overall effect is flamboyant and dazzling, and the quality often high—here and there you'll come across machine-made junk—but in the face of such a profusion of merchandise it is hard to concentrate.

The town's beach on the lake is a pleasant, busy place, but more for strolling than sunbathing, since much of it is gravel and dirt. The swimming is best in the morning before the breezes stiffen and turn the water choppy (there is better swimming nearby at the Hotel Visión Azul beach; see below). Still, you can always peruse the wares offered by perambulating vendors here as you enjoy a cool drink in one of the beach's open-fronted restaurants, or even take a boat ride.

Lakeside Villages

Instead of renting a boat, most visitors take the mail launch (really a passenger launch) across the lake to San Pedro de la Laguna and Santiago Atitlán. The roofed launch carries a couple of dozen people, mostly Maya, on each trip. Mayan women, who are often uneasy away from land, seem to draw comfort from hand-lettered signs posted by the captain: JEHOVAH OUR GOD IS UPON THE GREAT WATERS, one plaque announces in Spanish; another urges BE NOT AFRAID! Obviously, this is an evangelical boat.

San Pedro, sometimes the first destination, is also evangelical. Little wooden steeples poke at the sky, serving a town that was converted almost en masse before splintering into sects. Horses and mules replace men and women as beasts of burden here—definitely not *costumbre* and possibly the result of the new religion. Knotted wool rugs are a specialty of local artisans.

San Pedro's neighbor, **Santiago Atitlán**, is the largest and most colorful of the lakeside villages. Evangelical protestantism has made converts here, but many people combine Catholicism with adoration of a god called Maximón, represented by a stubby wooden figure smoking a cigar. Santiago is famed for weaving, embroidery on machine-made cloth, women's headgear called "halos" (to be worn wound around the head), and colorful shirts for men. The town market, though not a place to buy handicrafts, is nonetheless a colorful scene as the women, dressed in brilliant costumes, preside over their vegetable stalls. The parish church exhibits the starkness of Mayan temples, and is filled with strangely dressed statues of saints in village clothing. Inside, to the right of the main door, is a simple but touching memorial to villagers slain when the national army raided the town a decade ago.

About three hours should be allowed for lakeside exploring: a brief visit to San Pedro, about an hour in Santiago, and the rest of the time on the boat.

STAYING IN PANAJACHEL

The hotels in town will be happy to offer advice and help with nearby excursions, hiring guides or drivers, and bus schedules.

The ▶ **Cacique** (kah-SEE-kay) **Inn**, located near the southern edge of town on the Sololá road, a continuation of the main street, is a fine value. The rooms, which have attractive stone fireplaces, are grouped around a swimming pool and a well-kept garden; the dining room is probably the best restaurant in the area and serves international food with some local touches; and the inn itself is relaxed and very well run. In addition, you can walk from the Cacique to the center of town.

About a mile south of town past the Cacique Inn, the lovely grounds and gardens of the ▶ **Hotel Atitlán** feature topiary sculpture. The views from the hotel are also impressive, making the bar an ideal place for a drink at sunset. The dining room, with alamo beams, seems more stately than cheerful, however, and the food is only satisfactory. Individual rooms do not have fireplaces, and town is a long walk away. Still, the views and the serene, secluded surroundings make this handsome inn a fine choice.

The ▶ **Hotel Visión Azul** appears to have been carved out of the same coffee plantation as its neighbor, the Hotel Atitlán. This comfortable place, with lawns and a number of rooms offering panoramic views of the lake and surrounding mountains, is also simpler than its elegant neighbor, and therefore less costly. The beach is nearby, a short walk down a gentle hillside.

The ▶ **Rancho Grande Inn** is located in town, not far from the beach. The accommodations here are bungalows set in a garden, good but not special. A hearty cooked breakfast is included in the price. The only public room is the dining room at breakfast time, and the management is not especially helpful with information and arrangements. The attraction here is privacy and a fine location.

The ▶ **Hotel del Lago** overlooks the beach and was obviously designed with vacationers from Guatemala City in mind. Thick-pile carpets climb right up the sides of the bar, and the volcanic stone seems to come in a variety of designer colors. All the rooms have balconies and wonderful views of the lake, but the top-floor rooms are the best. The hotel also has a restaurant, nightclub, swimming pool, and two curio shops—and it is expensive.

The ▶ **Hotel Galindo**, on Calle Principal, proudly advertises its patio garden, which is a veritable jungle. Unfortunately, its rooms are small and far from bright, but it does have two things to recommend it: a location downtown and very low rates. The Galindo also rents out several lakeside cottages with kitchens.

DINING IN PANAJACHEL

All the dining spots in town are informal, and most of them at least a little rustic.

Although its menu is limited, the **Cacique Inn** has the most consistent kitchen in town (Tel: 9/62-1205). Of the other hotels, the **Atitlán** is really selling its surroundings more than its food, which is only satisfactory. The views are lovely, however (Tel: 9/62-1429).

La Fontana, on Calle Principal, offers Italian-style cooking, with indoor and outdoor service. Both the service and the surroundings are pleasing.

El Bistro (called El Patio by many locals), about halfway between the main street and the beach on Calle Santander, features lake bass, salads, chicken, and steaks. Tables are set up in a small dining room and an adjacent garden.

The murky **Last Resort**—it will take a few minutes for your eyes to adjust to the gloom—is mainly a bar. Late in the evening it draws a young (and sometimes not-so-young) international crowd. The food runs to such offerings as ribs and pizza, and the sandwiches are generous—a welcome surprise, because Guatemala is the land of the stingy sandwich and the scant taco. It's hard to find this place in daylight, however, even though it's just off Santander not far from the public school. At night look for a bulb burning outside, or trail a likely-looking patron (the clientele will quickly become identifiable).

The **Circus Bar**, in a Hansel and Gretel–style house near the center of town, also serves food, mostly snacks that are good enough as well as inexpensive, and has live music many nights.

Of late, several eateries have been tacked up along the beach. Most of them are breezy places where you can enjoy something cool while watching the lake and beach. One of them, **Los Pumpos**, is worth trying for lunch. The building is cobbled together out of split bamboo, thatch, and, it sometimes seems, glue. Hanging inside are stuffed fish, nets, oars, glass pendants, and all manner of flotsam. If the Swiss Family Robinson had opened a café, this would be it.

CHICHICASTENANGO

Despite the effects of increased tourism, Chichicastenango, about 20 km (12 miles) north of Panajachel, remains the quintessential Mayan town, at once a confluence of paganism and Catholicism, of folklore and ancient traditions culled from the entire highlands region. No numbers or names identify the cobblestone streets here—and it hardly matters. This is a small place, and everybody knows how to get everywhere; as a result, you will not need a hired guide.

The market tradition of Chichi, as the town is often called, dates back to the pre-Columbian era. People from a wide area have always come here to buy, sell, or trade. Others come merely to watch the transactions—not only foreigners but Mayan villagers themselves, for whom this is, and always has been, life and excitement. One writer described Chichi as "anthropology in action." The town, transformed by the market, is hardly worth visiting on other days, however.

The main market is held on Sunday, but preparations begin on Saturday afternoon (a smaller market is held on Thursday). Some visitors feel that the market is conducted for their benefit, that it's a craft show for tourists. And while it's true that ladino merchants are there to deal and give tourists what they want, another market, where cheap kitchenware, needles, dyes, and furnishings for primitive dwellings are sold, is operating for the townspeople at the same time. Your eyes should not be held entirely by those who want your attention; the sideshow is truly the main event. (It's not for nothing that the market tradition is centuries old. The merchants overprice their goods, usually asking about three times the amount they actually expect to get. Most sellers have a keen sense of humor, but after you've made your purchase you may feel they are laughing all the way to the bank over the price you paid.)

After checking out the market you should visit the local church, **Santo Tomás**. The rites here are not performances for the benefit of curious onlookers, and neither are they voodoo rituals. This is folk Catholicism, practiced with candles and overhung by incense. The chants, prayers, and costumes of the devout are strange, even alien, making Santo Tomás a grim place fraught with an almost palpable aura of belief in miracles and magic. (Taking photos inside the church is frowned upon by the natives, who can become very forceful in their objections.)

There's also a small **museum** of regional curios in town, nicely done, but it will occupy no more than half an hour of your time. The real museum is Chichi itself.

STAYING IN CHICHICASTENANGO

If you want to stay overnight you'll find the ▶ **Mayan Inn** to be outstanding. Although it faces the plaza, its terraces afford lovely views of the valleys around Chichi. The dining room is also very good, and the comfortable rooms are made charming and personal with a selection of antiques and native art. A marimba band plays in the patio on market days; its musicians are as good as everything else about this inn, which is well worth the fairly high tariff charged.

Slightly less costly but with less personality is the attractive and colonial ▶ **Hotel Santo Tomás**. It, too, has beautiful views and lovely grounds, and the comfortable dining room serves well-prepared food.

The ▶ **Posada Chugüilá** is, unfortunately, no better than the room you get, which may or may not have a private bath and can vary from cramped to spacious. Some have fireplaces; ask for one of those, even in a heat wave—they're the best the inn has to offer. The patio is comfortable; the restaurant serves hearty, rather heavy fare.

THE RIO DULCE

The relatively new Atlantic Highway (Carretera al Atlántico), designated CA 9, provides fast, easy access to a region of Guatemala that was, until recently, little known or explored by foreigners. Although the highway heads in a northeasterly direction toward the Caribbean coast, in the minds of most travellers it seems to go *down,* dropping in its course from temperate highlands to rain forest and the steamy tropics. The trip is usually made for one reason: to see the jungle and the somnolent Río Dulce as it meanders from Lago Izabal into the Gulf of Honduras and the Caribbean. (The river is also a possible stop on the way by car or bus to the ruins at Tikal.)

At minimum, this is an overnight trip from Guatemala City; driving time is a little more than four hours each way. Some travellers will wish to combine this excursion with a visit to the Mayan ruins at **Quiriguá** (see above), not far from the highway. (The Quiriguá turnoff is near the Texaco station at Los Amates, kilometer 205.)

For the Río Dulce, you continue on CA 9 past the Quiriguá turnoff until, just past the town of Morales, you reach the junction with the road to Fronteras, where you turn left (north). About 34 km (21 miles) farther on lies **El Relleno**, a small settlement at the water's edge—and not on most maps. There is a good general store here, Tienda Reed; Mrs. Reed, who speaks English, can help with car storage and advice. The local fire department (*los bomberos*) will also store and guard your car.

Once that is settled, all that's left is to hire a launch from among those you'll see moored nearby. In choosing a boat, be sure to select one with a strong motor. Some of the boats are underpowered, and although they manage the trip, what should be a leisurely excursion can become a slow boat to nowhere as the motor fights the current. You'll also want to agree upon a price in advance—it's usually not the first price suggested. The whole trip takes a little more than two hours, including a short stop at the **Castillo de San Felipe**, a 17th-century fortress built to fend off pirates. The boatman should understand that the castle stop is included in the price.

Downstream on the north bank of El Golfete, a broadening of the river that seems more like a tropical lake, is a reserve for those fantastic creatures, manatees (sea cows), which can weigh up to a ton. (Distant sightings of manatees by sailors may have been the origin of the mermaid legend.)

Soon the river narrows and then enters a gorge. Mangroves, their twisted, clawlike roots gripping the riverbank, line either side. Kekchi Indians have built a few primitive villages in the jungle here, their thatched huts with peaked roofs appearing every now and then in a clearing. But human intrusion into this region is, for the most part, barely noticeable, the silence broken only by the cries of a multitude of birds or a breeze rustling the tangled foliage.

With its cheerfully painted wooden houses and corrugated metal roofs, **Lívingston**, the small town at the mouth of the Río Dulce, gives an appearance of gaiety. But it's not really interesting unless you can stay long enough to become acquainted with its people, a mélange of Caribs, ladinos, Kekchis, Lebanese, Chinese, and East Indians.

The surrounding area has not been notably successful in promoting itself or its beaches—other Caribbean resorts outdo this narrow strip of coast in both facilities and atmosphere, nor is Lívingston cheap for what it offers—but there is good scuba diving, swimming, sailing, and fishing here.

STAYING IN THE RIO DULCE AREA

Perched on a hill above the boat landing in Lívingston, the luxurious and well-run ► **Tucán Dugu** is a striking building with white walls and tropical thatch. It also has a swimming pool and a beach. Jungle motifs and rich woodwork contribute to the exotic atmosphere of this expensive accommodation.

Upriver at the El Relleno–Río Dulce crossing, the ► **Turicentro Marimonte** is a good hotel and resort situated on the banks of the river. The Marimonte has a swimming pool and marina, and is popular with boating enthusiasts from Guatemala City. It also has a satisfactory restaurant.

About a mile downstream from El Relleno is the quite special ▶ **Hotel Catamarán**, situated on a small island in the river. The Catamarán caters to visitors who want to explore the Río Dulce and surrounding jungle, as well as those simply in search of a South Seas atmosphere in a relaxed environment. Its swimming pool and marina are well maintained, the food is good, and the rates are more than reasonable for such an attractive and unusual jungle inn. The Catamarán will also be happy to arrange for your transportation from the capital.

GETTING AROUND

Getting There

Citizens of the United States may obtain a Guatemalan tourist card, required by law, for a small fee by presenting proof of citizenship (passport, birth certificate, or voter registration) at airline check-in counters in the States, Guatemalan consulates, or border crossing stations; naturalized citizens may need their certificate of naturalization. British Commonwealth and Canadian citizens should apply in advance, with a passport and round-trip ticket in hand, at a Guatemalan consulate.

Entering Guatemala with an automobile requires an additional permit as well as proof of ownership. There will be a small fee for the permit, and still another for fumigating the tires of your car and squirting a whiff of something inside.

Entry Points for Motorists

There are three possible entry points into Guatemala from the north. Coming directly from Mexico by car, you can take either the lowland coastal route, Highway 200, through Tapachula, or the highland road, Highway 190, from San Cristóbal de las Casas, which crosses into Guatemala near Ciudad Cuauhtémoc. The highland route is cooler and much more scenic. If you choose the latter, you'll soon understand why Guatemala, with its pine-clad mountains and long auto tunnels, is sometimes called "North America's Switzerland."

A third possibility is to enter through Belize. This route should not be attempted in a conventional car, however; stick to four-wheel-drive vehicles with high wheel bases if you have your heart set on this option (even then, it will be a long, bumpy, exhausting trek).

By Air

Air service from abroad to Guatemala City, which has the country's only international airport, is frequent and dependable. Continental flies to the capital from Dallas, and American Airlines offers three flights a day from Miami and one a day from Dallas–Forth Worth. United offers one daily flight from Miami, and Mexicana offers a daily morning flight to Guatemala City from Mexico City. In addition, two airlines not widely known outside of Central America also deserve consideration. Aviateca, the Guatemalan national airline, flies to Guatemala City from Miami, Houston, New Orleans, Los Angeles, Mérida, and Mexico City, offering good service, an admirable safety record, and a thorough knowledge of its home country. At times it also offers reduced fares and attractive travel arrangements, including special rates on hotels and car rentals. Lacsa, the fine Costa Rican operation, flies to Guatemala City from New York and Los Angeles (with a stop in Cancún), and often lures passengers away from the bigger carriers with its discount fares. (Lacsa is a favorite with Latin American travellers.) Aerocaribe has three flights a week to Tikal (Flores airport) from Cancún. Aeroquetzal, a local airline, flies the same route.

Currency

The national monetary unit is the *quetzal* (ket-SAHL), named for the shy jungle bird beloved by the Maya. A quetzal is divided into 100 *centavos*. The currency is relatively stable; you should be able to change back to dollars or other major currencies without incurring startling losses. The present exchange rate is five and a half *quetzales* to one U.S. dollar.

The Guatemala City airport, La Aurora, is a convenient place to exchange currency—especially since banks in Guatemala can be quagmires of bureaucracy. Small denominations of U.S. dollars are generally accepted throughout the country. Hotels and the better shops almost always accept U.S. dollar traveller's checks.

Credit cards are accepted at establishments dependent on tourism, including the better hotels, restaurants, and car-rental agencies.

Local Time and Electric Current

Guatemala is on central standard time (the same as Winnipeg, Chicago, Dallas, and Mexico City), but does not change over to daylight saving time.

Electricity in Guatemala is supplied at 110 volts, alternating current, the same as in the United States, Canada, and

Mexico. The same type and sizes of sockets and plugs are also standard in all four countries.

Travelling in Guatemala

A rental car is a pleasure but not a necessity in Guatemala. You will find Avis, Hertz, Budget, Dollar, and National both at the airport and in Guatemala City. If you decide to rent a car from one of these outfits, make sure you're not paying double for insurance. Many credit-card companies cover such insurance, or at least a part of it, automatically (check with your own card-issuing company). Once you rent the car, stay with the attendant as it's being checked for damages prior to taking it; be sure that every dent and missing hubcap is properly noted, or else you may end up paying for them.

Those who wish to know more about packaged tours to Guatemala should contact **Clark Tours**, 7 Avenida 6-53, Edificio El Triángulo, 2nd floor, Zona 4, Guatemala City, C.A.; Tel: (2) 31-0213 to 0216; Fax: (2) 31-5919; in the U.S., Tel: (800) 223-6764. Clark is the oldest and largest company in the field. The international travel company **Wagon-Lits** may also have some attractive tours (Avenida Reforma 12-81, Zona 10; Tel: 2-31-3268; Fax: 2-34-6143), and **Aviateca**, the Guatemalan national airline, is usually helpful (10 Calle 6-39, Zona 1; Tel: 31-8222; Fax: 31-7401; in the U.S., Tel: 800-327-9832). Most hotels in the major cities will arrange for cars, drivers, and guides.

There is good, regular bus service from the capital to Antigua, Chichicastenango, and Panajachel. (Bus service to the Río Dulce region, on the other hand, is less than convenient, and the bus trip to Tikal is not only boring, it's an ordeal.)

First-class buses are your best bet. You can reach **Antigua** in an hour on the Preciosa line, 15A Calle 3-37, Zona 1. Buses depart hourly from 7:00 A.M. to 8:00 P.M., and a ticket costs about $3.50.

Panajachel service is provided by Rébuli, 20A Calle 3-42, Zona 1. Rébuli, a second-class line, offers regularly scheduled departures from 5:00 A.M. to 4:00 P.M., and charges $7 for a one-way ticket. Panajachel is a 4-hour journey one-way.

The **Chichicastenango** bus, also a 4-hour trip one-way, is for early risers. Buses leave at 4:30, 5:00, and 5:30 A.M., and the fare is about $7. Service is provided by Reinita de Utatlán, 20A Calle and 4A Avenida, Zona 1.

The 14-hour one-way endurance run that ends at Flores (**Tikal**) begins at 17A Calle 8-46, Zona 1. The line is Fuentes del Norte, and the one-way fare is $16; the bus goes via the **Río Dulce**, so it's possible to break up the trip. The stretch from Guatemala City to the river is the easy part (see below for more on Tikal).

Second-class buses, often antique school buses that were retired from service in the United States long ago, stop anywhere you can flag them down. Baggage goes on the roof; birds and animals travel inside with the passengers. Still, they are satisfactory, even an adventure, for good-humored travellers going a short distance. After a while, however, the pushing, crowding, fumes, and general slowness of the proceedings lose their charm.

In almost all Guatemalan towns buses arrive and depart from a central street near a main corner. Inquire locally.

Getting to Tikal

The easiest and most practical way for travellers to get to Tikal is by plane from Guatemala City. For a round-trip fare of $150, Aviateca offers regular morning and afternoon flights to the nearby town of Flores. From there you can get a bus, taxi, or *combi* to take you to a hotel or, if you so choose, the ruins themselves. A taxi will set you back about $46, a bus only $6. The largest hotel in the region, the Camino Real, provides courtesy transportation from the airport.

The ruins are also accessible by car, with the most common route starting in the capital and ending some 12 hours later. The least rugged vehicle available in Guatemala that is practical for the trip is a Suzuki model that looks something like a Jeep. Bus transportation over the same route is also available, but the inexpensive fare is no bargain when you figure in the day lost and the considerable discomfort (not to mention the boredom). An Aviateca flight is much the better choice.

Half-day tours of Tikal by Jeep or minibus, with air feeder service from the capital and lunch included (you return to the capital in the afternoon), can be arranged in Guatemala City. While this is better than nothing, it's hardly good enough. Not only will you be rushed at the ruins and miss much of what is best about them, you'll also miss the once-in-a-lifetime experience of nightfall and sunrise in the jungle. The tours also vary greatly in cost, ranging from $30 to $70, plus airfare. Clark Tours, Wagon-Lits, and Aviateca, discussed above, arrange tours.

Whichever option you choose, you should take a few items along with you: insect repellent, a sun visor or hat, a flashlight for viewing darkened chambers, and binoculars. The latter need not be especially powerful—the details you want to bring closer are not far away, just high overhead.

If you're arriving by plane and plan on going exploring as

soon as you get to Tikal, be sure to eat a good breakfast before departing the capital; food is not served on the flight.

ACCOMMODATIONS REFERENCE

The rates given below are projections for December 1993 through Easter 1994. Unless otherwise indicated, rates are based on double rooms, double occupancy; the 17 percent VAT has been added. As rates are subject to change, it's always a good idea to double-check before booking.

The international telephone country code for Guatemala is 502; the capital area code is 2. There are several other area codes within the country. In some jungle areas telegraph is the only way to contact hotels.

▶ **Cacique Inn.** Calle Embarcadero, **Panajachel**. Tel: (9) 62-1205. $58.

▶ **Camino Real Guatemala.** Avenida Reforma 14-01, Zona 10, **Guatemala City**. Tel: (2) 33-4633; Fax: (2) 37-4313; in the U.S. and Canada, Tel: (800) 228-3000. $190.

▶ **Camino Real Tikal.** Calle Flores Remate, **Tikal**. Tel: (9) 50-0204 or 0208; Fax: (9) 50-0222; in the U.S. and Canada, Tel: (800) 228-3000. $175.

▶ **Conquistador Ramada.** Via 5, 4-68, Zona 4, **Guatemala City**. Tel: (2) 34-1212 or 36-4691; Fax: (2) 34-7245; in the U.S. and Canada, Tel: (800) 854-7854. $122.

▶ **Hotel Antigua.** 8A Calle Oriente, **Antigua**. Tel: (9) 32-0288. $128.

▶ **Hotel Atitlán.** Camino a Sololá, **Panajachel**. Tel: (9) 62-1441; Fax (in Guatemala City): (2) 34-0641. $71.

▶ **Hotel Aurora.** 4A Calle Oriente 16, **Antigua**. Tel: (9) 32-0217. $42.

▶ **Hotel Catamarán. Río Dulce**. In Río Dulce, Tel: (9) 47-8361; in Guatemala City, Tel: (2) 36-4450. $47.

▶ **Hotel del Centro.** 13 Calle 4-55, Zona 1, **Guatemala City**. Tel: (2) 38-1519; Fax: (2) 30-0208. $54.

▶ **Hotel El Dorado Americana.** 7 Avenida 15-45, Zona 9, **Guatemala City**. Tel: (2) 31-7777; Fax: (2) 32-1877. $189.

▶ **Hotel Galindo.** Calle Principal, **Panajachel**. Tel: (9) 62-1168. $18.

▶ **Hotel del Lago.** Calle Rancho Grande, **Panajachel**. Tel: (9) 62-1555; Fax (in Guatemala City): (2) 37-1948. $123.

▶ **Hotel Marina.** González Bocanegra 100 ZP3, **Copán**, Honduras. Tel: (98) 39-3070; Fax: (98) 39-0957 (country code: 504). $65.

▶ **Hotel Piño Montano.** Pan-American Highway, km 259, **Huehuetenango**. In Guatemala City, Tel: (9) 64-1637. $39.

► **Hotel Plaza.** Via 7, 6-16, Zona 4, **Guatemala City.** Tel: (2) 32-7626; Fax: (2) 31-6824. $61.

► **Hotel Santo Tomás. Chichicastenango.** Tel: (9) 56-1061; Fax: (9) 56-1306. $76.

► **Hotel Visión Azul.** Camino a Sololá, **Panajachel.** Tel: (9) 62-1426; Fax: (9) 62-1419. $64.

► **Jungle Lodge.** Parque Nacional, **Tikal.** In Guatemala City, Tel: (2) 76-8775. $47.

► **Maya Internacional. Santa Elena**, El Petén. In Guatemala City, Tel: (2) 34-8136. $44.

► **Mayan Inn. Chichicastenango.** Tel: (9) 56-1176; in Guatemala City, Tel: (2) 31-0213; Fax: (2) 31-5919. $82.

► **Pan American.** 9A Calle 5-63, Zona 1, **Guatemala City.** Tel: 2-6807. $80.

► **Posada Belén.** 13 Calle A 10-30, Zona 1, **Guatemala City.** Tel and Fax: (2) 51-3478. $38.

► **Posada Chugüilá. Chichicastenango.** Tel: (9) 56-1134. $33.

► **Posada de Don Rodrigo.** 5A Avenida Norte 17, **Antigua.** Tel: (9) 32-0291. $98.

► **Ramada Antigua.** 9 Calle Poniente and Carretera a Ciudad Vieja, **Antigua.** Tel: (9) 32-0011; Fax: (9) 32-0237; in the U.S. and Canada, (800) 854-7854. $178.

► **Rancho Grande Inn.** Calle Rancho Grande, **Panajachel.** Tel: (9) 62-1554. $46.

► **Tucán Dugu. Lívingston.** Tel: (9) 48-1572; Fax: (2) 34-5242; in Guatemala City, Tel: (2) 34-7813. $83.

► **Turicentro Marimonte. El Relleno–Río Dulce.** In Guatemala City, Tel: (2) 34-4965. $78.

THE YUCATAN CARIBBEAN RESORTS

By Mitchell Nauffts

The Yucatán is among the most varied tourist destinations in Mexico. Depending on your itinerary, its bustling cities and remote rural villages, state-of-the-art luxury hotels and ancient Mayan ruins, vast swaths of jungle and strands of dazzling white sand can seem all-too familiar one day and utterly exotic the next. But then, the Yucatán has always been a world unto itself: Though part of the Mexican mainland, for much of its history it has been isolated both geographically and psychologically from the rest of the country. Even today, linked to the outside world by two-lane highways and international flights, it manages to remain apart, retaining some of the mystery of its long and fascinating past.

Archaeological sites that conjure up this ancient glory—Chichén Itzá, Uxmal, Labná, Kabah, Tulum, and Cobá among them—dot the map of the peninsula and tantalize travellers who have the time to make detours. Those who don't can still hear the ancient Mayan language spoken in the streets of the peninsula's towns and villages, see native women wearing the traditional *huipil* (a white shift with embroidered neck and hemlines), and eat such time-honored dishes as *poc-chuc* (grilled pork) and *pollo pibil* (chicken seasoned with *anchiote* and baked in a wrapping of banana leaves).

Like the subterranean rivers lacing the peninsula's limestone, the old ways and beliefs of the Maya run deep, hidden from the eyes of outsiders. And outsiders there are in abundance, as job-seekers from around the country and tourists from around the world continue to flock to Cancún by the tens of thousands. As a result, two-lane highways that were all but deserted a decade ago today hum with a steady flow of traffic, and even budget accommodations jump their prices come December 21. Likewise, at archaeological sites such as Chichén Itzá or Tulum, or natural aquariums such as Xel-Há (south of Cancún) or Garrafón National Park (on Isla Mujeres), the crowds can reach De-Mille-ian proportions by early afternoon. Which is not to say you won't find that deserted patch of palm-lined beach or perfect little cabana for two. You'll just have to look a little harder and be prepared to spend a lot more than you would have even a few years ago.

The Mexican portion of the peninsula comprises three states, each with its own distinct flavor: **Quintana Roo**, which covers the eastern third of the peninsula (including its long Caribbean coastline), and which these days is the area most obviously affected by the benefits and drawbacks of *turismo;* **Yucatán**, which takes in much of the northern third of the peninsula, including the colonial city of Mérida as well as two of the country's greatest archaeological sites, Chichén Itzá and Uxmal; and **Campeche**, the little-developed and infrequently visited state encompassing much of the western third of the peninsula. Travellers who plan to use Mérida as a gateway for the exploration of the many archaeological sites in the region will find it and the surrounding area covered in the Mayan Mexico chapter. The somewhat limited attractions of Campeche, both the city and the state, are covered in the same chapter.

The focus of this section, on the other hand, is the Caribbean coast of Quintana Roo, a sun-splashed region of powdery beaches and turquoise-blue water. A virtual terra incognita just 30 years ago, when it was still home to a scattered population of Mayan farmers and fishermen, jaguars, and the occasional *bandido,* the area today is so popular with international travellers that Mexican tourism officials are ready to rechristen it the Turquoise Coast. We begin our coverage with a look at **Cancún**, that monument to impersonal luxury and conspicuous consumption on the northeast corner of the peninsula, and then follow with a discussion of the **Cancún–Tulum corridor**, a onetime beachcomber's paradise that's getting its first taste of large-scale development. Next is **Isla Mujeres**, a small resort island off the coast northeast of Cancún that appeals to visitors looking for a low-key getaway. We end with a discussion of

Cozumel, Mexico's largest island and the site of some of the finest diving and snorkeling in the Western Hemisphere.

CANCUN

Situated off the northeast corner of the Yucatán peninsula, Cancún looks like Miami Beach, parties like Fort Lauderdale, and empties a visitor's wallet as quickly as New York City. Plucked from obscurity in the mid-1960s by Fonatur, the government agency charged with developing a new generation of modern beach resorts, it continues to grow after 20 years of pell-mell expansion and today attracts more than a million visitors annually. Many of them arrive with surprisingly reasonable package deals: Despite the government's stated intention to cap the number of hotel rooms at 20,000, Cancún recently surpassed the 22,000 mark, with still more rooms in the pipeline. In other words, if you're willing to settle for four-star comfort instead of five-star luxury, you'll almost never have to pay the rack rate. Don't be surprised, however, if the view from your room turns out to be less than postcard-perfect or the pool area is taken over by beer-drinking college kids and young singles.

None of which has much to do with the "real" Mexico, whatever that might be. But then Cancún never had much to do with the real Mexico—other than the fact it provides jobs for tens of thousands of real Mexicans. Instead, as the flagship of Fonatur's five mega-resorts, it was developed from scratch with an eye to the comfort and convenience of large numbers of tourists. Fonatur can pat itself on the back. Over the years Cancún has evolved into a kind of Disney World for hedonists, a place where drinking, dancing, and shopping take the place of rides; HBO and ESPN are beamed into every hotel room; and English is the lingua franca.

If it leaves many experienced travellers cold, Cancún does have charms that even its critics appreciate, including beautiful white-sand beaches, abundant bird and marine life, and more than 200 days of sunshine a year. For snorkeling enthusiasts it's one of the top sites in the Caribbean, while Cozumel, with some of the best snorkeling and scuba-diving in the hemisphere, is only a 15-minute flight (or a two-hour car-and-ferry trip) to the south. And for archaeology buffs, photographers, and the merely curious, it's the resort gate-

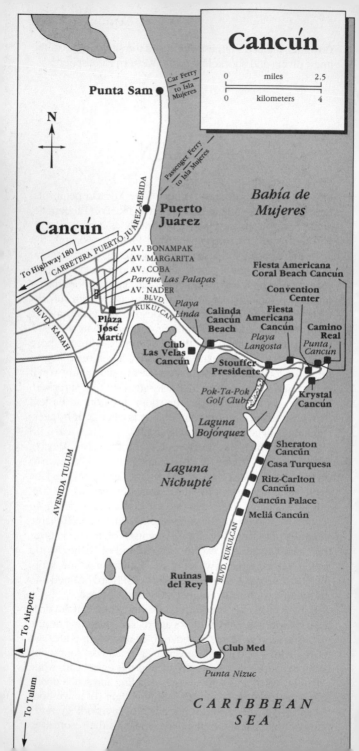

way to a number of fascinating sites, including Chichén Itzá, Tulum, and Cobá. (For a complete description of Chichén Itzá, see the Mayan Mexico chapter.)

MAJOR INTEREST

Cancún
Beautiful beaches
Luxury accommodations
Nightlife and shopping
Snorkeling
Ruinas del Rey

Cancún–Tulum Corridor
Funky beach town of Playa del Carmen
Natural aquariums at Xcaret and Xel-Há National Park
Diving and snorkeling at Akumal and Yal-kú
Beaches at Xpu-Há, Chemuyil, and Xcacel
Mayan ruins of Tulum and Cobá

The Zona Hotelera

Cancún's luxury hotels, many of its better restaurants, and most of its best boutiques are located in the *zona hotelera,* which stretches the length of a slender 14-mile-long island resembling the number seven. The island itself is connected to the mainland by two short bridges, one at either end of the "seven," and is washed by the Bahía de Mujeres to the north and the Caribbean to the east. To the west a huge saltwater lagoon system separates the island from the mainland. The unique geography of Cancún accounts for the two types of beaches in the hotel zone: those facing Isla Mujeres and the sheltered waters of the Bahía de Mujeres, and those exposed to the open Caribbean. The latter, with their soft white sand and brilliantly hued water, are especially beautiful but also subject to heavy, and sometimes dangerous, surf. Visitors are advised to pay close attention to the flag system employed by hotels on the Caribbean side of the island: A green or blue flag means it's safe to swim; a yellow flag means swim with caution; and a red or black flag signifies dangerous conditions, swim at your own risk.

From Cancún City to Punta Cancún

The hotel zone's main drag, Boulevard Kukulcán (from the ancient Mayan name for the legendary Toltec hero-cum-serpent god Quetzalcóatl), heads due east from Cancún City across the northernmost bridge on its way to Punta Cancún, at the "elbow" of the "seven." From there the boulevard swings south for the eight-and-a-half-mile run to Punta Nizuc, where it makes a final turn toward the mainland and crosses the other bridge before meeting up with Avenida Tulum (Highway 307), the road to the airport and points south. Virtually everything of interest in the hotel zone is located on, or just off, Kukulcán, with distances along the boulevard indicated by kilometer markers positioned on the malls dividing its four lanes of traffic. (Downtown Cancún City is km 0 and the bridge at Punta Nizuc is km 23.)

The hotels and commercial complexes strung out along the first few miles of Kukulcán, many dating back to the resort's early years, tend to be more modest in their pretensions than those built during the boom years of the eighties. Dense zoning and a mishmash of architectural styles combine to create a quasi–honky-tonk feel along the boulevard, while the informal restaurants in the area usually are more reasonably priced than those farther out on the island. In the same neighborhood, **Puerto Cancún**, an upscale marina and commercial complex, is under construction just east of the downtown area. Whether it eventually becomes the home base for the excursion craft and party boats that presently leave from the rather rundown **Playa Linda marine terminal**, next to the bridge, remains to be seen. In the meantime, Playa Linda is the place to catch the **Isla Mujeres shuttle**, which leaves for the Island of Women, a favorite day-trip destination, three times daily. (See the Getting Around section at the end of this chapter for shuttle details.)

The hotel zone begins to look almost residential as you near km 7.5 and the turnoff for the **Pok-Ta-Pok Golf Club**. The Robert Trent Jones–designed course is laid out on both sides of the boulevard and takes up most of one of the arms of land separating Laguna Nichupté from the smaller Laguna Bojórquez. Time-shares and expensive private homes line many of the fairways, and a small Mayan ruin overlooks the water on the 12th hole. (The course is open to the public; for greens fees and tee times, see the Sports in Cancún section, below.)

Two of the best beaches on the Bahía de Mujeres are located between the golf course and Punta Cancún. **Playa Tortugas**, which backs up to the Presidente, Calinda Viva Cancún, and Kin Há hotels, boasts bathtub warm water and a shallow, sandy bottom that extends out a good 50 yards before it drops off, making it perfect for kids and novice swimmers. **Playa Caracol**, situated beyond the Fiesta Americana Cancún hotel (and most conveniently reached by a sand track due west of the huge Fiesta Americana Coral Beach Cancún property), is a little wilder, with bigger waves and a degree of privacy—thanks to the rusting construction site behind it—that seems to promote topless sunbathing. Like all beaches in Mexico, Playas Tortugas and Caracol are owned by the government and open to the public. (The hotels overlooking them are under no obligation to provide service to non-hotel guests, however.)

Punta Cancún

The Punta Cancún area is the closest thing to a hub that you'll find in Cancún's otherwise far-flung hotel zone. This was the site of the first shopping mall on the island—today completely overshadowed by the upscale Plaza Caracol complex nearby—as well as a number of its original luxury hotels. Like fine wine, the Krystal, the Camino Real, and the Hyatt Regency have gotten better with age, in part because they've had to: The three-year-old Fiesta Americana Coral Beach Cancún here has set standards of luxury that will be tough to surpass. The addition, across the boulevard, of a state-of-the-art **convention center** (complete with 660-foot tower) on the site of the old center is further proof of the area's vitality, as is the nightly scene that unfolds along the shop-lined alleys of the Mayfair/Lagunas/Terramar/Caracol/Costa Blanca commercial complex.

Rounding the traffic circle at the point and heading south in the direction of Punta Nizuc you'll pass a long stretch of four-star hotels and time-share properties as well as a couple of busy marinas before reaching the **Plaza Flamingo** complex (see Shopping in the Zona Hotelera, below), at km 11, where Planet Hollywood has been packing them in since it opened in the fall of 1992. As recently as 1985 the long stretch of sand from here to Punta Nizuc was all but empty, with the Sheraton at km 12.5 the last of the big hotels before the dunes and scrub grass took over. Now the Sheraton is just one of a string of huge hotels lined up like battleships along the boulevard.

Generally speaking, the construction activity has been confined to the ocean side of Kukulcán, with most of the hotels set well back from the road and surrounded by expanses of lawn (or, in the case of the Meliá Cancún and Oasis hotels, executive-style golf courses). But with **México Magico**, a giant amusement park, under construction opposite the Sheraton, this too is changing. Stores and restaurants out this way, on the other hand, are scarce. (As a rule, the hotels south of the Sheraton—among them the Casa Turquesa, the Ritz-Carlton, the Cancún Palace, the Marriott Casa Magna, the Meliá Cancún, and the Fiesta Americana Condesa Cancún—are well beyond walking distance from the stores and restaurants in the Punta Cancún area.) The brand-new **Plaza Kukulcán**, south of the Sheraton at km 13, was built to redress this situation, and has in fact brought a measure of civilization to what had been a hotel wilderness. With its splashing fountains, liquid-nitrogen-cooled air conditioning, *faux*-Mayan decorative motifs, and acres of boutiques and snazzy restaurants, it's also a compelling argument for shopping malls as the real temples of our own consumption-obsessed age. (See Shopping in the Zona Hotelera, below, for more on Plaza Kukulcán.)

Ruinas del Rey

To see temples of a different kind—or what's left of them—continue south on Boulevard Kukulcán to the Ruinas del Rey, situated between kilometer markers 17 and 18 at the widest part of the island. (Watch for a sign on the lagoon side of the road.) The extant structures, which date to the Postclassic period (roughly A.D. 1100 to the early 16th century), form two main complexes: the **El Rey group**, which lends its name to the site and was itself named for the large sculpted head discovered here by the English archaeologists Channing and Frost around the turn of the century; and, to the south, the smaller, less elaborate **Pinturas group**, named for an interior mural fragment that no longer exists. Most of the structures are low platforms with the remains of what were once rows of columns, and are organized along two broad avenues. **Structure 2**, the site's only pyramidal mass, with rounded corners reminiscent of the two large pyramids at Cobá, squats on the northeast corner of the main plaza. (For a detailed description of Cobá, see the Cancún–Tulum Corridor section, below.) The most important structure here, **structure 3B**, is a few steps to the south on the same plaza, and appears to have been dedicated to the king or god for whom the site was named; if you look carefully you can still make out faint traces of mural painting on its façade and interior walls.

Alas, with a future as the centerpiece of the multimillion-dollar Westin-backed Ruinas del Rey complex—the last of the giant development projects slated for the island—the ruins' days as one of the least visited attractions in the hotel zone are numbered. For the time being a nominal entry fee gains you admission to the site, and INAH-sanctioned guides are usually on hand to give tours for an additional fee.

Punta Nizuc

You'll find the last group of hotels and condos in the hotel zone clustered farther south of the ruins in the vicinity of

Punta Nizuc (where, true to form, Club Med was the first hotel on the scene). Although conveniently located to the excellent snorkeling in the waters around the point, as well as the highway leading to Playa del Carmen and points south, these places are a *long* way from most of the stores, restaurants, and night spots in the hotel zone, and even farther from the affordable restaurants downtown. If you end up staying at one of them you'll want to think about renting a car for the duration of your stay; otherwise, be prepared to spend a lot of time on buses or money on taxis.

If you follow Boulevard Kukulcán west to Avenida Tulum and follow the latter north through downtown Cancún, you'll eventually come to **Puerto Juárez** (10 km/6 miles) and **Punta Sam** (15 km/9 miles). The former is the departure point for *passenger* ferries to Isla Mujeres, the latter the departure point for *automobile* ferries to the same destination.

In the opposite direction Avenida Tulum leads south to the airport and, in order, **Puerto Morelos** (the departure point for car ferries to Cozumel), **Playa del Carmen** (the departure point for passenger ferries to Cozumel), **Xcaret, Puerto Aventuras, Akumal, Chemuyil, Xcacel, Xel-Há,** and **Tulum**—all points of interest in what has become known as the Cancún–Tulum Corridor, for which see below.

STAYING IN THE ZONA HOTELERA

From a vantage point on the southernmost tip of Isla Mujeres, Cancún's *zona hotelera* appears to float on the horizon like a developer's vision of Emerald City: One high-priced ziggurat after another marches down the beach, with the density approaching Babylonian proportions around Punta Cancún. It's a sight that strikes terror in the hearts of budget travellers and intimidates just about everyone else. For starters, how does one choose from among so many hotels? And, if the main objective of a Cancún vacation is to maximize the amount of time spent on the beach or by the pool, does it really matter?

If money is no object, then it really doesn't matter. At the top end of the market—and in Cancún's hotel zone there is no bottom end—almost every hotel, including those we discuss, delivers the goods. Rooms are always comfortable, if not luxurious, and invariably come equipped with two double beds, color cable TV, and servi-bars; you should expect to pay a little extra to guarantee an ocean view. The hotels themselves all have multiple bars and grills, as well as one or two more formal restaurants for evening dining. Without exception all have attractive lobbies and pool areas, the latter usually dressed up with one or more gimmicks (e.g., imaginative configurations, waterfalls, island palapas). For the most part even location is not an issue: Taxis and an excellent public transportation system pretty much put everything within reach.

Which leaves the matter of price. During the high season a room for less than $150 a night is as rare here as a gringo without a sunburn. We've included the Calinda Cancún, one of the few establishments to offer such an animal, and recommend that you book well in advance for the high season. The same holds true for most of the hotels mentioned below, although less-than-80-percent occupancy at many of them has made advance reservations a less urgent priority outside the peak Christmas and Easter holiday periods. In fact, if you don't mind sharing the pool or beach with young singles in their twenties and families on vacation, the low season can be a great time to visit. Just remember that hurricane season in the Caribbean usually begins in late August and stretches into October.

From the Bridge to Punta Cancún

The ▶ Club Las Velas Hotel Cancún, on the lagoon just before the bridge, was one of the first deluxe hotels in Mexico to offer an all-inclusive program. (Prices include accommodations, meals and snacks, unlimited beverages, entertainment, use of all facilities, and tips and taxes.) A self-contained colonial-style village complete with tiled plazas, splashing fountains, and a profusion of bougainvillaea and hibiscus, Las Velas offers small but comfortable air-conditioned rooms in multi-story towers for one to three persons, or junior suites in two-story "villas" for up to four persons. The sprawling complex backs up to an arm of Laguna Nichupté, which here features jade-colored channels lined by mangroves—a watery maze ideal for exploring by kayak, canoe, or sailboat. Two pools and two small beaches, several restaurants (including one that stays open 24 hours), tennis courts, and a complete water-sports center round out the amenities. (Guests who want to swim in the ocean face a ten-minute walk to Playa Linda and the Bahía de Mujeres, on the other side of Boulevard Kukulcán.) The daily schedule of activities includes water sports, aerobics, and Spanish classes, and the clientele is a diverse mix of all ages and temperaments, from young singles to retirees. With plenty of opportunities to meet and mingle, everyone seems to get along, and many guests return year after year.

The 470-room ▶ Calinda Cancún Beach (not to be confused with the Calinda Viva Cancún near Punta Cancún), the first hotel on the island side of the bridge, is one of the better bargains in the hotel zone, which explains its popularity with groups and young singles. Rooms are pleasant if unspectacular, and come with color satellite TV, a choice of full- or king-size beds, and those harmless-looking but insidious contraptions known as servi-bars; the rooms in the tower next to the original building are much the better choice, however. When compared with the facilities at some of the theme parks masquerading as hotels elsewhere in the hotel zone, the Calinda's pool area and beach—the latter a flat stretch of sand lapped by the calm waters of the Bahía de Mujeres—may come as a bit of a disappointment. The Calinda also has two restaurants, a couple of bars, a complete water-sports center, tennis courts, and in-house car-rental and travel agencies. Its location opposite the Playa Linda marina, a busy terminal for excursion boats and the **Isla Mujeres shuttle**, is a bonus, as is its proximity to downtown Cancún and, in the opposite direction, the eating and drinking spots near Punta Cancún, both just five minutes by taxi from the hotel's lobby.

Situated a few hundred yards east of the golf course and within easy walking distance of the Punta Cancún area, the stylish, understated ▶ **Stouffer Presidente Cancún** was one of the first luxury hotels built in the hotel zone, and still attracts a well-fixed clientele, even though it's showing its age a bit. One of the reasons is the hotel's jewel of a white-sand beach, shaded by palms and facing an expanse of shallow, brilliantly colored water. With its two swimming pools, five Jacuzzis, shimmering swim-through waterfall, and mandatory swim-up bar, the pool area is no slouch, either. Don't coming looking for loud music or a rowdy pool scene, however—guests of the Presidente like their sun served up with plenty of peace and quiet. The hotel's standard-size doubles, all recently remodeled, are priced according to view, with lower-floor rooms facing the lagoon and parking lot the least expensive and upper-floor rooms overlooking the Bahía de Mujeres the most expensive. All guests receive a complimentary newspaper and coffee with their wake-up call, although only guests who spring for one of the 15 club-floor suites will be able to read their paper on a balcony; most rooms here don't have them.

The 281-room ▶ **Fiesta Americana Cancún**, located east of the Presidente opposite the Plaza Caracol complex, was the first of the chain's three hotels in Cancún, and the years—and an energetic management—have been kind to it. Every room here has its own terrace or balcony facing the Bahía de Mujeres, and all feature the chain's trademark rattan-and-pastel decor. The horseshoe-shaped Mediterranean-style complex cradles a pretty palm-shaded pool area dominated by a small island and palapa-covered restaurant. With loud (and often live) rock music piped through speakers in the afternoon, the pool and narrow beach are especially popular with groups of young people. And when guests tire of soaking up the sun they're literally right across the street from the greatest concentration of restaurants, bars, and stores in the hotel zone.

At the Point

The 11-story all-suite ▶ Fiesta Americana Coral Beach Cancún, on the Bahía de Mujeres almost at the point itself, is one of the newest and largest properties in Cancún. From the seven-story atrium-style lobby to the seemingly endless corridors with their handsome artwork and muted lighting, the Coral Beach strives for the grand effect—and usually pulls it off. The standard room here is a junior suite with marble floors, separate sitting and vanity areas, and a private bay-front balcony. (Although the views from the top-floor balconies are spectacular, guests with children should stick to the lower floors.) There are, in addition, 64 master suites equipped with in-room Jacuzzis and ten two-bedroom Caribbean suites. It's not until you start to poke around the premises, however, that the sheer size of the Coral Beach begins to sink in. Among the amenities are a 220-yard-long swimming pool, three swim-up pool bars, a handful of restaurants, an indoor tennis and racquetball complex, a health club and spa, a water-sports center, an upmarket shopping arcade, a barber shop and beauty salon, an indoor parking lot—well, you get the picture. In fact, with the new convention center under construction directly across the street, and the restaurants, bars, and stores of the Plaza Caracol complex a short stroll from the lobby, the Coral Beach just may be the premier accommodation in Cancún.

Surrounded on two sides by the pounding surf of the Caribbean, the low-slung ▶ Camino Real sits in splendid isolation a hundred yards east of the Coral Beach. A standard double in the main building comes with either a partial bay view or an ocean view (you'll pay a little more for the latter), a private balcony, and two doubles or a king-size bed; all rooms in the 16-story Royal Beach Club have balconies overlooking the ocean, as well as the usual complimentary club-floor services. Amenities spread out around the hotel's leafy grounds include a small saltwater lagoon stocked with some very large fish, a pretty pool area, four lighted tennis courts, a shopping arcade, an excellent restaurant, and a cozy palm-fringed beach facing the calm waters of the Bahía de Mujeres. (Although the coral creeps close to shore here, if you have the patience required to wade out to the end of the rock jetty this is one of the better places in Cancún to snorkel.) What the Camino Real's many repeat guests really like, however, is the privacy it affords: The hotel's sprawling layout and location at the point (only the hotels at Punta Nizuc are more secluded) make it easy to forget you're in Mexico's busiest beach resort, even as the Plaza Caracol area buzzes with activity just minutes from its lobby.

Everyone seems to stop in at the ▶ **Krystal Cancún**, across the street from the Coral Beach, sooner or later. Maybe it's because it has a certain mystique—or maybe it's just to have their picture taken in front of the *faux*-Roman colonnade that overlooks the hotel's narrow strip of beach. Then again, when the music starts to play in its lobby bars this is one of the liveliest spots in the hotel zone. Recently remodeled from top to bottom, the Krystal offers standard doubles with views of the lagoon—and a few, by request, with views of the ocean—along with the usual in-room amenities; none of the rooms has a balcony. For not a whole lot more you can enjoy the added perks of the Krystal Club, on the hotel's top two floors, with its own check-in/check-out area, complimentary Continental breakfast, canapes at the cocktail hour, and a small private swimming pool on the roof.

Of course, an integral part of the Krystal experience is a romantic dinner at **Bogart's**, its *Casablanca*-inspired restaurant, followed by an evening of dancing at **Christine**, its pricey, ever-popular discotheque; see the Dining in the Zona Hotelera and Nightlife in Cancún sections, respectively, for additional details.

From Punta Cancún to Punta Nizuc

Located a couple of miles south of Punta Cancún at km 12.5, the ▶ **Sheraton Cancún Resort and Towers** is a sprawling, self-contained resort property with a little something for everyone, including three swimming pools, six tennis courts, half a dozen restaurants, and a shopping arcade. The more than 700 rooms here are spread among three seven-story "pyramids" and an eight-story "club" tower. Standard doubles are located in the pyramids and come with the usual amenities; none has a balcony, however, and fewer than half have ocean views. (To get a balcony you'll have to spring for one of the suites, which have outdoor Jacuzzis and either an ocean or lagoon view.) The more expensive tower rooms all have balconies, as well as the usual club-floor amenities.

During the day the main pool is a beehive of activity—and a rowdy hornet's nest during spring break—but there are two smaller pools on the grounds where a quieter, family atmosphere prevails. The Sheraton's Caribbean beach is also one of the widest and most gently sloping around, with less of an undertow than other beaches on this side of the island. And for archaeology buffs there's an 800-year-old Mayan ruin located on a bluff at one end of the complex. Scholars speculate that it functioned as a lighthouse for the sea-going Mayan traders who plied these often treacherous waters in the late Postclassic period. While the federal government has declared it off limits to all commercial schemes, guests and non-guests are welcome to explore it.

After a few days in Cancún it becomes readily apparent that, with the exception of women's swimwear, a "big is better" philosophy informs everything from male pectorals to swimming pools. So when a new hotel bucks that trend it's worth a look. The gleaming ▶ Casa Turquesa, located just beyond the new Plaza Kukulcán, is one of the few accommodations in the hotel zone where small isn't a dirty word. The five-story stucco building boasts a grand total of 31 luxury suites in two categories: standard junior suites with garden-front views and a slightly larger, more expensive version overlooking the ocean. All are handsomely decorated one-room affairs with sitting areas, a range of five-star amenities (including VCRs and compact-disc players), and private Jacuzzis on the patio or balcony. The same kind of casual elegance prevails throughout the hotel, from its cozy piano bar to its very private Restaurant Bellevue to its Beverly Hills–style pool, where three often seems to be a crowd. And in its short existence the Casa Turquesa has hosted royalty both real (Prince Bernard of Holland) and celluloid (Sylvester Stallone).

The newest entry in Cancún's luxury-hotel sweepstakes is the 370-room ▶ Ritz-Carlton, Cancún, which debuted in the spring of 1993 and hopes to attract sophisticated travellers, regardless of age, with its unique brand of personalized service and attention to detail: Details like wrought-iron railings, louvered doors, marquetry-accented furniture, terry-cloth bathrobes, and a five-story atrium-style lobby with a stained-glass ceiling. Personalized service that includes 24-hour room service, baby-sitters on call, and a "camp" program for kids. At the Ritz, every room has a patio or balcony with a view of the Caribbean, every beach chair has a royal-blue cabana hood, and every other guest looks as if he or she stepped out of the pages of a fashion magazine. And all of this at a price that isn't much more—and in some cases is less—than what you'd pay elsewhere in the hotel zone.

The ▶ **Cancún Palace**, a quarter-mile south of the Ritz-Carlton, is a huge horseshoe-shaped hotel with more than 400 rooms and a multitiered pool area that always seems to be hosting a contest of some sort. In fact, unlike some hotels in Cancún, the Palace welcomes groups and prides itself on its lively pool scene. The music doesn't start until 11:30 A.M., but when it does the activity is nonstop: volleyball, water polo, bikini contests, tequila contests—you name it, the Palace will try it. The carnival atmosphere extends to two other attractions here as well: The Mini-Golf Palace, on the hotel's spacious front lawn, with 36 holes featuring waterfalls, reproductions of pre-Hispanic artwork, and mock-ups of the ruins at Palenque and Uxmal; and, now in its fourth year, the up-and-coming Cancún Jazz Festival, many of whose big-name stars perform on an open-air stage in the field next door to the hotel during the last week of May. (For more on the festival see the Nightlife in Cancún section below).

In pleasant contrast, the Palace's rooms and public areas are surprisingly attractive if not downright posh. There's a generous use of marble throughout, and every room has its own balcony, a pleasing peach-and-pastel decor, and large bathrooms with handsome wood trim. Seventy percent of the rooms face the ocean, and there's a variety of more expensively priced accommodations, from junior suites with Jacuzzis to luxurious penthouses. The hotel also is the home of **Los Golondrinas**, a casually intimate colonial-style dining room specializing in traditional Mexican dishes—something of a rarity in this fast food–crazy resort.

At km 16.5, the ▶ **Meliá Cancún** (not to be confused with its sister hotel, the Meliá Turquesa) is distinguished by its pyramidal Plexiglas roofline and a beautiful atrium lobby filled with soaring fluted columns, lush tropical vegetation, and the sounds of tropical birds. If the Spanish owners of this space-age château were hoping to create an oasis of civility in the middle of Cancún's vacation jungle, they've succeeded. The standard double, on the other hand, is something of a disappointment, modest in size and generic in decor, though each one has its own flower-bedecked balcony. (If money is no object, spring for one of the junior suites, which have separate sitting areas and two balconies.) Of course, with an 18-hole executive-style golf course right out front and a beautiful pool area out back, the Meliá's guests probably won't be spending a lot of time indoors.

DINING IN THE ZONA HOTELERA

As Cancún has grown so has the number of its restaurants, cafés, and fast-food places, both downtown and in the hotel zone. Other than to mention a few of the best—**Mediterraneo** (Tel: 83-0200) in the Stouffer Presidente, **Calypso** (Tel: 83-0100, ext. 8060) at the Camino Real, **Blue Bayou** (Tel: 83-0044, ext. 54) in the Hyatt Cancún Caribe, and **Ailem** (Tel: 83-2544) in the Meliá Turquesa—we ignore hotel restaurants in our coverage, if only because most can be counted on to deliver solid fare at top-drawer prices.

The restaurants discussed below fall into the moderate-to-expensive category (you're on your own for cheap eats). Casual wear is the norm unless otherwise noted. Phone numbers are listed (when available) so that you can call ahead for directions or to make reservations; the area code for Cancún is 98. (For coverage of the restaurant scene downtown, see the Cancún City section below.)

The Bridge to Punta Cancún

The best restaurant in the hotel zone will be familiar to experienced Cancún hands who used to frequent Maxime's and the under-appreciated Du Mexique, downtown. Alain Grimond Pages, formerly the owner of Du Mexique, bought the handsome residence that housed Maxime's for a dozen years and energetically set about remaking it. The result is **Grimond's**, a visual and culinary treat for lovers of fine food. M. Pages's urbane sensibility is evident throughout, from the front room with its peacock-patterned wallpaper, dark mahogany trim, and antique étagères, to the main dining room with its elegant white linens, muted lighting, and a single red rose on every table. Start your meal with a *salade de chèvre chaud* (warmed goat cheese on a salad bed) and follow it up with a seafood potage with fresh fennel or flamed lobster bisque with Cognac. Grimond's is one of the only restaurants in Cancún that serves duck (two different ways), beef tenderloin with *cuitlacoche* sauce, and veal medallions in a morel sauce. Seafood and lobster prepared a number of ways and outstanding desserts round out a menu that is both imaginative and reasonably priced. Dress up, come early, and enjoy a drink on the restaurant's beautiful terrace overlooking the Bahía de Mujeres, where reproductions of a 16th-century caravelle and sloop are on call for short catered excursions of the bay. Located off the boulevard on Pez Volador, just beyond the Hotel Casa Maya. Reserve; Tel: 83-0704 or 0438.

Everyone drops by **Carlos 'n Charlie's**, at km 5.5 on the boulevard opposite the Casa Maya, at least once while they're in Cancún, and no one seems to mind that the raised dining room gets hot or that the nachos-burgers-fajitas fare is a little pricey. But then, dinner is hardly the main event here. After a bite to eat most people head over to the open-air dance floor, either to watch or to become part of the boisterous scene. The (sometimes) live music keeps the place jumping until the wee hours, and a no-reservation policy prevails, so be prepared to wait in line, especially on weekends.

Jalapeño's, located at km 6.5, just before the turnoff to the golf course, is the kind of place where diners compete with the waiters to see who can make the most noise. Still, the seafood and Mexican specialties are better than average, and the kitchen stays open later than those at most restaurants in the hotel zone. Jalapeño's also offers an inexpensive all-you-can-eat breakfast buffet and a reasonably priced lunch menu. After dinner there's dancing to canned music during the week and live reggae music with a no-cover policy on the weekends. Tel: 83-2896 or 2682.

Plaza Caracol Area

The greatest concentration of restaurants in the hotel zone is found in the Mayfair/Terramar/Lagunas/Costa Blanca/Caracol complex just west of Punta Cancún. At the heart of this maze of glass-and-concrete the **Hard Rock Café** serves up rock-and-roll as religion to legions of young believers along with burgers, sandwiches, and fajitas. Lines begin to form long before the live music starts at 11:00 P.M., and the Hard Rock doesn't take reservations; go early to avoid the crush, or go for lunch and enjoy its dark, air-conditioned ambience in relative quiet. Tel: 83-3269.

For a completely different experience, head over to the pretty but partially unoccupied La Mansion–Costa Blanca mall, where two restaurants owned and operated by the same group have carved out niches for themselves. On the ground floor, the **Restaurante El Mexicano** offers mariachi and folkloric shows nightly, except Sundays, to go along with its pricey regional Mexican dishes (you're paying for the show). The mariachis play at 6:00 P.M., the folkloric ballet begins at 8:00, and there's live music and entertainment from 9:15 on. Tel: 84-1261 or 83-2220 for reservations, and ask for a table on the floor. Upstairs, **La Veranda**, an elegant room featuring wood trim and lots of glass brick, specializes in fresh seafood and quality prime rib at big-city prices. Open for dinner only. Reserve; Tel: 83-2122.

With its fine restaurants and upscale boutiques, the two-story glass-enclosed Plaza Caracol, right next door to the

Costa Blanca mall, has long been the pride of Cancún's promoters. (When it's fully occupied, the cavernous Plaza Kukulcán at km 13 will give it a run for its money.) The cozy, casually intimate **Casa Rolandi** here features Swiss-Italian cuisine prepared in a wood-burning brick oven. Specialties of the house include fish cooked in salt, charcoal-broiled lamb brochette, and goat with rosemary. It also has a good wine list. Reservations recommended; Tel: 83-1817.

On the Bahía de Mujeres side of the mall you'll find the upscale and ever-popular **Savio's**, a bright, airy café with a green-and-white decor, lots of plants, and umbrella-shaded tables under an atrium-style arcade. Refined northern Italian cuisine shares the menu with such appetizers as sliced salmon in a dill vinaigrette, quail-liver pâté, cèpes, and oysters Rockefeller. Open for lunch and dinner; reserve for dinner. Tel: 83-2085.

At the far end of the mall under the same arcade, trendy **Iguana Wana** gets your attention with black-and-white-checked tablecloths, lots of palm trees, and a video bar. In addition to steak, seafood, or nouvelle-style Mexican dishes, you can choose from a reasonably priced raw-bar/*tapas* menu featuring items such as mushrooms in garlic, crab-meat or conch fritters, and chicken wings. The recently instituted breakfast buffet here ($6.50 plus tax) is noted for its fresh ingredients (including stone-ground tortillas) and appealing presentation, and Iguana Wana is one of the better spots in Cancún for a late-night snack. Reserve for dinner; Tel: 83-0829.

At the Point

You'll find the original **Bogart's** on the far side of the Punta Cancún traffic circle in the Krystal Cancún (see the Staying in the Zona Hotelera section, above, for a description of the hotel itself). Though the restaurant is no longer unique (others have opened in Ixtapa and Puerto Vallarta), the layout of this Bogart's somehow makes it more appealing than its cousins. The decor is a Hollywood art director's idea of Moroccan, complete with peacock chairs, shimmering fountains, and live piano music. And while the prices are high, the service a bit snooty, and the food not always as good as it should be, Bogart's is worth trying all the same. You'll want to dress up and reserve. Tel: 83-1133.

For an altogether different experience head over to the **Hacienda El Mortero**, the Krystal's other "theme" restaurant, located a short walk from the hotel's lobby in the direction of Punta Nizuc. The ambience here suggests the gracious living of the colonial period, with the building itself a scaled-down replica of the 17th-century Hacienda El Mortero, in the northern state of Durango. Inside, crisp linens, pastel walls, and muted lighting enhance the stylish surroundings. The pricey menu features haute Mexican cuisine and a variety of international specialties, accompanied by the music of a polished mariachi band. It's not all that authentic but it is fun. Reservations recommended; Tel: 83-1133.

Plaza Flamingo Area

Two of the busiest restaurants in the hotel zone are tucked away on the southeastern corner of Laguna Bojórquez at km 10.5. Even though **Gypsy's Pampered Pirate** sits on stilts over the water, don't expect much of a view. Gypsy's customers are crowded together at closely spaced tables with only ceiling fans and open windows to keep them cool, and the simple menu is limited to fish, chicken, and lobster (the house specialty). The cramped quarters usually result in mediocre service, with dinner slow to arrive and quick to be cleared. Which leaves Gypsy's reasonable prices and twice-nightly flamenco show as the likely reasons for its continued popularity. The show (7:30 and 9:30 P.M.) lasts half an hour and is well worth the $2 admission price. Gypsy's also serves one of the cheapest ($4.95 plus tax) breakfast buffets in the hotel zone. Reserve for dinner; Tel: 83-2015 or 2120.

Lorenzillo's, right next door, advertises itself as having the largest palapa in the hemisphere. True or not, it's an impressive sight, soaring nearly three stories to its highest point and finished with wooden slats and peeled poles. The two-toned wooden floor of the restaurant is even more impressive, the whole thing rolling like a ship at sea. That's the good news. The bad news is that Lorenzillo's continues to survive—even thrive—on an inflated reputation. The service is courteous but brusque, the overpriced entrées adequately prepared but presented with little imagination. None of which seems to discourage the hordes of tourists who pack the place nightly. Reserve a table outside overlooking the lagoon (and the large fish cruising for scraps), but go early and plan to have a drink or two at the bar. Tel: 83-1254 or 83-3073.

The most elegant restaurant in the handsome Plaza Flamingo, a hundred yards or so up the boulevard, is **Seryna**, a quiet and expensive *teppanyaki*-style Japanese place with a sushi bar. Reserve for dinner; Tel: 83-2904 or 2995. In the same complex, **Pat O'Brien's**, an outpost of the New Orleans–based chain, has a smoky piano lounge and a lively open-air patio overlooking the lagoon. Its basic saloon menu features a tasty steak sandwich, brochettes, fajitas, and salads for under ten dollars, and the lounge is the only place in the hotel zone where you can listen to live jazz (on occasion). Tel: 83-0832.

At the far end of the Plaza Flamingo complex, **Planet Hollywood** continues to pack 'em in, making rich men of its already wealthy owners (Messrs. Stallone, Schwarzenegger, and Willis). The drill here is depressingly familiar: Teenagers and their mostly bewildered parents line up to gawk at mementoes of American popular culture and, occasionally, well-muscled celebrities celebrated by that culture (Messrs. Stallone, Schwarzenegger, and Willis). If you've memorized every episode of "The Brady Bunch" and think Bob Denver was the comic genius of his generation, you'll love it. Tel: 83-0527.

South of the Sheraton

Until recently non-hotel restaurants south of the Sheraton were few and far between. That has changed, however, with the inauguration of the hotel zone's newest state-of-the-art mall, Plaza Kukulcán, at km 13, so that guests of the big hotels out this way now have something more than beautiful beaches and long bus rides to look forward to. As of this writing there are two good restaurants here: **Splash del Caribe** (Tel: 85-3011), a Miami-style eatery with a video bar, stucco walls, lots of glass brick, great lighting, and a breezy terrace overlooking the boulevard and lagoon. A wonderful spot any time of day, the terrace is especially pleasant in the morning, when the restaurant offers a reasonably priced breakfast buffet. For something a bit more romantic try **Cenacolo**, a branch of the like-named restaurant downtown (see the Dining in Cancún City section below), which serves some of the best Italian food around in a setting oddly reminiscent of a Western saloon.

Captain's Cove, on the lagoon side of Kukulcán opposite the Fiesta Americana Condesa, Oasis, and Omni hotels (there's another branch on the beach between the Hotel Casa Maya and Club International), serves flame-broiled ribs and steaks and a good selection of seafood specialties in a pleasant dining room or out on a porch open to the lagoon. You'll want to come early for dinner: The Cove is an excellent spot for sunset watching, and they don't take reservations.

Restaurant Nizuc

Lastly, we mention this out-of-the-way place as a reminder of what Cancún was like 20 years ago and what the Cancún–Tulum Corridor was like as recently as six or seven years ago. The Nizuc is located just beyond the 22-km marker and the second bridge (just before the first bridge if you're coming from the airport or points south) on the Canal Nizuc, one of only two outlets draining the vast lagoon system between Cancún Island and the mainland. A simple palapa-style place with a few rickety chairs and tables set up on the banks of the crystal-clear canal, it offers a basic menu of reasonably priced seafood dishes and ice-cold beer. The extensive reef system at Punta Nizuc is just half a mile offshore, and there are flat-bottomed skiffs and skippers on hand (about $35 per hour for a party of four) if you want to make a day of it. There's also a small roped-off area with a sandy bottom here for people who want to swim. Take a cab and arrange to have it pick you up at an agreed-upon hour: The Restaurant Nizuc is a delightful place to spend a lazy morning or afternoon far from the madding crowds.

SHOPPING IN THE ZONA HOTELERA

Although it may come as a surprise to serious shoppers who haven't visited recently, Cancún's shops and boutiques in general, and those in the hotel zone in particular, have noticeably upgraded the quality of their merchandise over the last few years. Designer resortwear, leather goods and perfume, jewelry, and quality handicrafts are all widely available—at resort prices.

Plaza Caracol

Most people start their perambulations at the air-conditioned Plaza Caracol, where downstairs you'll find **Polo** by Ralph Lauren; **Aca Joe**, with the best-folded selection of resortwear in Cancún; **Gucci**; **Fila**; at least five silver shops, including **Sebastian** and **Sumire**; **Boutique Soqui**, for jewelry and well-known Mexican designer labels (Sucesos, Girasol, Judith Roberts); **Bally**, for shoes and handbags; **Toes**, for belts and sandals; **Marcela de Cancún**, with a small but well-chosen selection of handwoven blankets; **1800**, a small space packed with Guatemalan textile items and batik applied to casual wear; the **Orbe Galerias de Arte**, for fine-art prints and sculpture; and **Extra**, a five-and-dime with a little bit of everything, including archaeological guidebooks, makeup, suntan lotion, and a pharmacy. Upstairs, in addition to **Bellini**, a pleasant café under skylights, you'll find **Guess** by Georges Marciano; **Maria de Guadalajara**, for breezy, pastel-colored beachwear; **Popete's Fashion Place**, for colorful children's clothing; **Tikal**, for more Guatemalan textiles; and **Xaman-Ek** (The Bird Sanctuary), with a large selection of papier-mâché handicrafts (mostly birds).

La Mansion–Costa Blanca

Next door, the pretty but hard-to-find La Mansion–Costa Blanca mall offers some of the most interesting shopping in the hotel zone. **La Iguana**, right off the front entrance, has a good selection of lacquered platters and boxes from Olinala, in the state of Guerrero, among other handicraft items. The markup is fairly steep, but the sales clerks make up for it with their knowledge and helpfulness. Opposite La Iguana, **Mayan** has an unusual (and unusually expensive) selection of Mayan-style artifacts made from a variety of materials, including jade, onyx, mother-of-pearl, and obsidian. Off the mall's interior patio, **Mordo** (with outlets in the Plaza Caracol and Plaza Flamingo) has a large selection of Mexican-made leather boots, shoes, jackets, and Western-style accessories. And, tucked away in the farthest reaches of the mall, **La Galería** is the place for miniature limestone replicas of Mayan carvings—or etchings lifted from these exquisite creations—by the artist Gilberto Silva.

Plaza Flamingo

The neo-Mayan-style Plaza Flamingo, km 11 on the boulevard opposite the Continental Villas Plaza, offers visitors yet another good assortment of stores and restaurants. In addition to such well-known names as Guess, Gucci, Girbaud, Mordo (leather), Los Castillo (silversmiths from Taxco), and **Gold's Gym** (free weights for serious body builders), shoppers will also find the following of interest: **Arte Mexicano**, with a good selection of lacquered wood trays from Olinala as well as the usual assortment of mass-produced onyx, glasswear, and the like; **Original 60**, for hip resortwear made from colorful Guatemalan textiles; **Bond** and **Michel Domet**, for shoes; **Martí**, a sporting goods store that carries everything from bathing suits to fishing tackle; **La Casa del Habano**, for Cuban cigars; and **Kodak Express**, for film and a good selection of American magazines.

Plaza Kukulcán

At Plaza Kukulcán, km 13 on the boulevard, design motifs concocted by the ancient Maya have been applied to the latest construction techniques to create a lavish complex that is as much aesthetic experience as commercial enterprise. Though the mall is only partially occupied as of this writing, stores that have opened here include **Tikal**, a big bright outlet of the chain that fashions beach and casual wear out of Guatemalan textiles; **Genesis Boutique**, which uses beads, baubles, and miles of lamé to dress up evening wear for younger women; **Sybele**, with a slightly less flashy selection of evening wear; **USA Importacions**, which carries all your favorite name brands from home, at twice the price; **Coral Divers**, for all your scuba and snorkel needs; and **Aventura Mexicana**, which, under the skilled direction of José Magán and his girlfriend, Lidón Ibañez, purveys folk art and textiles of the American Southwest, including gorgeous—and expensive—Navaho blankets.

Cancun City

Downtown Cancún is no longer the rough-and-ready place it was in the early 1970s, when only 200 people—most of them construction workers—called it home. Today its resident population is closer to 300,000—spurred to a large extent by the lowest unemployment rate in the Mexican republic—and the city limits continue to expand to the north and west. What has been a boon for Mexican workers has also resulted in a bonus for tourists, as more and more of them head into town and discover, among the many lively bars and colorful street performers, some very good restaurants.

One thing hasn't changed over the years, however. For reasons known only to a higher authority, the downtown area is a congested maze of cul-de-sacs and traffic circles. Fortunately, many of the restaurants and bars catering to tourists are concentrated along or just off Avenida Tulum, the city's main north–south drag.

For years most of the tourists who came came into town ventured no farther than the row of restaurants strung out along Avenida Cobá, a continuation of Boulevard Kukulcán. These days that particular corner of the downtown area seems to be languishing, and only **La Dolce Vita**, a pretty Mediterranean-style trattoria at Cobá 87, continues to draw crowds. White wicker furniture, peach-colored linens, and waiters in black and white set the tone in the two rooms here, one a trellis-covered patio open to the street, the other an enclosed dining room with ceiling fans. The Italian specialties on the menu tend to be more nouvelle than home-style, though the chef sometimes uses garlic with abandon. You'll want to dress up a little and make reservations a day or two in advance. Dinner only. Tel: 84-1384.

The downtown hustle and bustle begins after you cross Avenida Nader heading toward Avenida Tulum. First up on the corner here is **Pizza Rolandi** (Tel: 84-4047), Cobá 12, serving breakfast, a variety of daily specials, and Cancún's best pizza. At the **Fish Market** (Tel: 84-4180) next door, customers choose their fish or lobster from iced-down displays and then watch as it's baked or charbroiled to their liking on the spot. **Risky Business**, around the corner, opens for happy hour at 6:00 P.M. but is usually dead before midnight. By 1:00 A.M. things are in full swing, and the partying continues until 5:00 or 6:00 A.M. **Mi Ranchito** (Tel: 87-3686), just up the street, serves breakfast from 8:00 A.M. (lunch and dinner, too), and offers the same kind of waiters' pranks and tacos-fajitas-burger fare that you'll find at the Anderson group establishments in the hotel zone.

Souvenir hunters may want to try their luck at the **Ki-Huic** market, just up the street on the same side of Avenida Tulum. Ki-Huic's maze of stalls has every trinket you'd expect to find, at prices slightly higher than you'd pay for them in other resorts. (Everything has to travel a little farther to get to this corner of the Yucatán.) Though by no means cheap, the best buys here are handmade, hand-dyed woolen blankets from Oaxaca. Just be sure the blanket you're about to pay $300 for is the genuine item. (Machine-made blankets tend to be flimsier and less tightly woven.) *Huipiles,* hammocks (usually machine made), and sisal bags are among the regionally produced items to look for.

Lined with inexpensive hotels and busy restaurants, the one-way side streets on the opposite side of Avenida Tulum have become crowded with budget-minded diners looking for a change of pace. In most cases reservations aren't needed (although we've included phone numbers for people who want to call ahead for directions). Among the more popular restaurants here is **La Posta**, Crisantemos 10, which serves Tex-Mex specialties and American-style cuts of beef in a setting that recalls Mexico's revolutionary past. Tel: 84-2105.

Don't let the relative lack of ambience at **Linus II**, across the street from La Posta at Crisantemos 8, put you off: All those tables full of Italian tourists must mean something. The owner, a restaurateur from Venice whose first Cancún eatery was Linus I (still in business up the street), puts a premium on quality at affordable prices. Which means you can get a simple tossed salad, a bowl of fresh homemade pasta with your choice of sauce (there are more than 20 listed on the menu), dessert, and an excellent cup of coffee for less than $10. The veal, lobster, and seafood entrées will set you back a bit more, as will selections from the modest wine list. It's all delicious, however, and the service is courteous and efficient. Tel: 87-1597.

Charming little **Cenacolo**, one block over at Claveles 26, bills itself as "the best-kept secret in Cancún," even though it's not that hard to find: Just take Claveles off Avenida Tulum and turn right at the corner. White stucco walls, sea-green linens, and soft music set the mood for the lovingly prepared northern Italian specialties that follow, among them *cappelletti verdi di ricotta burro-salvia* (green pasta hats stuffed with ricotta cheese), *agnolotti di pesce al salmone* (ravioli stuffed with fish and ricotta in a salmon sauce), and *tagliatelle all'aragosta* (homemade fettuccini in white wine sauce). Cenacolo also has a good selection of antipasti as well as a wine list with some Italian whites ($30) and one Italian red in addition to its domestic labels. Tel: 84-1591.

Don Emiliano, another block over at Tuliapanes 20, has been serving moderately priced seafood, meat, and Mexican specialties for a decade now. Maybe that's because it's not as noisy as some of its neighbors on the street, and on occasion strolling guitarists enhance its mellow dinnertime atmosphere. Tel: 84-4448.

Still farther off the beaten track but a longtime favorite nevertheless, **La Habichuela** (The Stringbean) offers a wonderfully relaxing atmosphere that's all too rare in this manically modern resort. Located down the block from the town square at Margaritas 25, two blocks west of Avenida Tulum, it has been around almost as long as Cancún has been a resort, and specializes in moderately expensive seafood, Yucatecan, and traditional Mexican dishes. This is a place you'll want to dress up for, and reservations are recommended. Ask for a table on the romantic garden patio, however, as the handsome wood-trimmed dining room is not air-conditioned. Tel: 84-3158.

Back on Avenida Tulum, **Pop**, next to city hall, sells toiletries and sundries imported from the United States at exorbitant prices; it's also the closest thing to an American-style cafeteria in greater Cancún, with a reasonably priced menu that includes hamburgers, milkshakes, enchiladas, and huevos rancheros.

Several shopping malls and a number of hotels popular with budget-conscious travellers—the Hotel América, on the southeast corner of Tulum and Cobá, is the nicest—have opened downtown in recent years. Generally speaking, their rates reflect the fact they're not on the beach, which can be anywhere from five to 20 minutes away by car or taxi, depending on the beach. But then, everything seems to be more economical downtown.

Nightlife in Cancún

With the exception of Acapulco, Cancún offers the willing visitor more nightlife than any resort in Mexico. The fun usually begins in the hotel zone, where most of the big hotels offer some kind of evening entertainment in their lobby areas. From there it's on to dinner and a floor show. The most lavish is staged at the Continental Villas Plaza, opposite the Plaza Flamingo, where Silvia Lozano's **Ballet Folclórico Nacional de México** holds forth nightly at 7:00 P.M. The price is $48 per person and includes dinner, drinks, tips, and the show. Tel: 85-1444, ext. 5706. Other dinner shows in the hotel zone include the mariachi bands and folkloric ballet at the Restaurante El Mexicano in La Mansion–Costa Blanca mall, and the twice-nightly flamenco shows at Gypsy's Pampered Pirate, on the lagoon side of Boulevard Kukulcán between Punta Cancún and the Plaza Flamingo.

Visitors who'd rather star in their own floor show have a choice of three state-of-the-art discotheques in the hotel zone, all of which stay open until the sun comes up. **Christine**, at the Krystal Cancún, attracts a well-dressed crowd with money to spend. **Dady'O**, located just beyond Christine at km 9.5 on the boulevard, is popular with a slightly younger, rowdier crowd. **Up & Down**, km 15.5 at the gigantic Oasis complex, appeals to both kinds of people: Upstairs, glass walls, dark wood trim, comfortable seating, and tuxedoed waiters create a casually elegant atmosphere that's perfect for conversation and touch dancing. Downstairs, computerized lights, a sonic sound system, and the world's largest fire extinguisher keep the mostly twentyish crowd charged up until the small hours of the morning.

There are, in addition, any number of less formal spots popular with hard-partying singles. Casual attire is the rule at these places, and many charge a small cover. The current favorite seems to be **Tequila Sunrise**, overlooking the Hard Rock Café and the open area at the heart of the Mayfair/Terramar/Lagunas/Caracol/Costa Blanca complex. (The courtyard-like area here functions as a sort of "quad away from campus" during spring break.) Other favorites include the aforementioned **Carlos 'n Charlie's**, with an open-air dance floor, taped rock 'n' roll, and the occasional live act; and the always jammed, always overheated **Señor Frog's**, with live reggae nightly. The last two are conveniently located next door to each other on the lagoon side of Kukulcán, opposite the Hotel Casa Maya.

Guests at the big hotels out past the Sheraton often start their evenings at **Sixties**, in the Marriot CasaMagna, where the deejay spins "classic" rock tunes from 6:00 to 10:00 P.M. nightly, before moving on to Carlos 'n Charlie's or "Froggy's." As things begin to wind down in the hotel zone, the truly dedicated jump in cabs and head downtown, where they usually finish the evening dancing to live reggae at **Cats**, Avenida Yaxchilán 12, or rock-'n'-roll favorites at **Risky Business**, Avenida Tulum 13A.

Sports in Cancún

Watersports

In addition to its an extensive lagoon system, Cancún faces the northern fringes of the second-longest coral reef in the world (extending from Isla Contoy, 30 miles north of the resort, to the Gulf of Honduras, off the coast of Belize). It's no surprise then that the resort is a nearly perfect destination for watersports lovers. Waterskiing, windsurfing, scuba diving, snorkeling, deep-sea fishing, jet-skiing, even kayaking—all can be arranged at the marinas scattered around the hotel zone. If your hotel doesn't have a water-sports center the following will be able to help:

Marina Aqua Ray (Tel: 83-3007, 1763, or 1773), next to Lorenzillo's at km 10.5 on the boulevard, offers a full range of services, from guided jet-ski tours of the bird-filled mangrove thickets rimming Laguna Nichupté ($35 per person) to waterskiing on the glassy waters of the lagoon itself ($65/hour). The **Royal Mayan Yacht Club** (Tel: 85-0641 or 3260), km 16.5 opposite the Omni Cancún and Royal Mayan hotels, is another full-service outfit renting everything from windsurfers ($60/day) to jet skis ($50/hour). **Marina Jet Ski** (Tel: 83-0766; closed Sundays), on the lagoon opposite the convention center, specializes in motorized equipment, from jet skis and waterski boats to flights on ultralights. **Krystal Divers**, at the Krystal Cancún (Tel: 83-1133, ext. 500), **Scuba Cancún** (Tel: 83-1011), opposite Vacation Clubs International, near the bridge, and the dive shop at the **Cancún Palace** (Tel: 85-0533, ext. 6201) will be happy to help with your scuba needs.

For snorkeling excursions to the reefs off Punta Nizuc—something every visitor to Cancún should do at least once—try the Marina Aqua Ray or Royal Mayan Yacht Club (see above); the **Marina Punta del Este** in front of the Hyatt Cancún Caribe (daily; Tel: 84-4551); or the yacht club at **Carlos 'n Charlie's** (daily; Tel: 87-4643, 84-5352, or 83-1304). In addition to getting you out to the reefs, all will be able to supply you with snorkeling equipment (for an extra charge).

Deep-sea-fishing boats can be chartered at most of the marinas listed above. Or try **Cancún Avioturismo** at the Casa Maya Hotel (Tel: 83-0315); **Sunset Tours** in the Sheraton (Tel: 85-0329, ext. 2020) or the Plaza Flamingo (Tel: 85-1113 or 1107); or the **Playa Linda marina**.

Tennis and Golf

Most of the big hotels have their own tennis courts. This being the tropics, however, court time is at a premium during certain hours of the day (early morning and late afternoon). Although it's rarely a problem, tennis players who want to avoid getting shut out should check their hotel's court-reservation policy when booking a room.

The golf boom has yet to be lowered on Cancún, though it's swinging this way: As part of the multi-million-dollar property it's constructing south of the ruins, the Westin hotel group is building a new championship course. In the meantime, the 6,700-yard **Pok-Ta-Pok Golf Club** at km 7.5 on the boulevard is a fine track, even if it tends to get burned out during the peak tourist season (which coincides with the driest time of the year). But then, as somebody once said, golf in the tropics is a game for mad dogs and Floridians. Greens fees are $50 per person; figure on another $30 for the cart. Generally speaking, you don't have to worry about reserving tee times, although it can't hurt. Tel: 83-1230 or 1277; Fax: 83-3358.

For those torn between the siren call of the links and Cancún's beautiful sand and water, the **Melía Cancún** and **Oasis** hotels have their own executive-style courses—a good way to get your fix of ball marks and bogies without sacrificing the better part of the day. For the Meliá, Tel: 85-1114; for the Oasis, Tel: 85-0867.

Horseback Riding

Finally, there's one outfit in the area that offers guided horseback tours of the tropical forest. At the **Rancho Loma Bonita** (Tel: 84-0861), located half an hour south of Cancún between Puerto Morelos and Playa del Carmen, visitors can choose between a five-hour jungle tour (one tour daily; departure time 8:00 A.M.) or horseback riding on one of the area's beautiful white-sand beaches (daily from 10:30 A.M. to 3:30 P.M. or 1:30 to 6:30 P.M.). The cost includes transportation to and from your hotel, the services of a bilingual guide, lunch, and beverages. For either tour it's recommended you bring a pair of long pants and tennis shoes; if you opt for horseback riding on the beach, be sure to bring a bathing suit and towel.

Excursions In and Around Cancún

Excursion boats of every size and shape ply the waters around Cancún, with the nearby island of Isla Mujeres their most popular destination. Many of these boats stop at El

Garrafón, a sadly overcrowded marine park at the southern end of Isla Mujeres, for a couple of hours of snorkeling before heading on to a beach-lunch rendezvous and a slate of loosely organized activities elsewhere on the island. It can be a diverting way to spend a day (the changing shades of water in the Bahía de Mujeres are reason enough to go), but only if you're prepared to spend the day with rowdy Americans in their twenties. (For more on Isla Mujeres, see the separate section below.)

The air-conditioned *Tropical Cruiser* (Tel: 83-1488) departs daily at 8:30 A.M. from the Playa Langosta dock (next to Vacation Clubs International) and returns by 3:30 P.M. Breakfast, free admission to Garrafón (they claim to be the first outfit to get there, a factor worth considering), use of snorkel equipment, and lunch at "Pirate's Village," a sort of beachside amusement park, are included in the cost, about $42 per person. The *Fiesta Maya* (Tel: 83-0389 or 1804) does much the same thing, departing daily at 10:00 A.M. from its own pier on Laguna Bojórquez near the Stouffer Presidente and returning by 5:00; the $45 cost per person includes breakfast, a buffet lunch, an open bar, and an hour and a half at Garrafón. The *Aqua II* (Tel: 84-1057 or 87-1909) departs daily at 9:00 A.M. from the Playa Linda marina (near the bridge) and returns by 4:00. The cost (about $50 per person) includes a Continental breakfast, buffet lunch, open bar, and stops at Garrafón and the island's only town.

For something a little different you can do the same excursion on a 60-passenger trimaran. The *Aqua-quin* (Tel: 83-1883 or 0100) departs daily from the Camino Real pier at 11:00 A.M. A buffet lunch, open bar, and snorkeling at Garrafón are included in the cost, about $40 per person.

The Isla Mujeres excursion can also be done after dark as a sort of theme party. The "Treasure Island" cruise departs every evening at 6:00 from the Playa Langosta dock. A sunset cruise across the bay is followed by a buffet dinner and dancing at Pirate's Village, with the boat returning to Cancún by 11:00 P.M. The cost per person is $50. For reservations, Tel: 83-1488. The same kind of evening with a Caribbean twist (different costumes, limbo contest, Afro-Caribbean dinner show) is offered on board the *Carnivale,* which departs from behind Fat Tuesday, on the boulevard at km 6, daily at 5:30 P.M., returning by 11:00. Again, the cost per person is approximately $50. For reservations, Tel: 84-3760 or 1395.

A more sedate version of the standard sunset cruise is offered on board the *Columbus,* a 62-foot motorized replica of the *Niña* that tools around the lagoon while its passengers enjoy an open bar and three-course dinner (featuring charcoal-grilled steak or lobster). The *Columbus* sails daily (except Sundays) at 4:00 P.M. from the Royal Mayan Yacht Club opposite the Oasis and Omni hotels, returning around 7:30, with the cost per person approximately $60. Reservations recommended; Tel: 83-1488 or 3268.

Isla Contoy

An excursion to Isla Contoy, a remote national park and bird sanctuary north of Isla Mujeres, affords those who take it the chance to see fauna above and below the water, as well as the scrubby *selva* of the northern Yucatán in a relatively undisturbed state. As an excursion from Cancún, however, it's a long haul there and back, with the time set aside for snorkeling and birding the first thing sacrificed when rough water lengthens travel time to the island. You'll get more of both if you do Contoy as a full day trip from Isla Mujeres (necessitating an overnight on Isla itself). If your travel plans won't accommodate an overnight on Isla Mujeres but you're determined to see Contoy, the 60-foot motor yacht *Contoy II* makes the trip daily (except Sundays), leaving from the Playa Linda dock at 8:30 A.M. and returning by 5:00 P.M. The cost of the excursion, about $66 per person, includes an open bar on the boat, snorkeling en route, and a full lunch on the beach. For reservations, Tel: 87-1909 or 84-1057.

Cozumel

A day trip to Cozumel, Mexico's largest island and a world-renowned diving and snorkeling spot, is another popular option. The standard travel agency package will provide round-trip transportation to and from your hotel, a few hours' snorkeling at Chankanaab Lagoon National Park, a few hours in the island's only town, a visit to a black-coral factory to see jewelry being made, and lunch for about $75 per person. Or you can explore the island on your own: Aerocaribe/Aerocozumel (Tel: 84-2000), the "air bridge," flies to Cozumel from the Cancún airport—a 15-minute flight—nine times daily. (For more on Cozumel, see the separate section below.)

Sunset Tours (Tel: 85-1113 or 1107) or **Intermar Caribe** (Tel: 84-4266), both with a number of offices around town and in the hotel zone, will be happy to arrange any of these cruises and/or excursions. Or you can contact the travel agent at your hotel. Both outfits also run day trips to the ruins at Tulum and the natural aquarium of Xel-Há (see below); the impressive Maya-Toltec ruins at Chichén Itzá; and the beautiful Late Classic ruins at Uxmal, with a stop in historic Mérida for lunch and sightseeing (see the Mayan Mexico chapter for more on Chichén Itzá, Uxmal, and Mérida).

THE CANCUN–TULUM CORRIDOR

Although it would take several vacations to see and do everything Cancún has to offer, not everyone is charmed by its flashy façade and materialistic soul. For many, Cancún is simply too familiar to be of interest; after a meal at Mc-Donald's and assorted encounters with friends of friends from home, they begin to crave something different, something a little more . . . authentic. It wasn't too many years ago that excursions to the Yucatán peninsula's ancient Mayan sites offered such an opportunity. And to some extent they still do, especially if you rent a car and take the time to explore along the way. These days, however, many of the better-known sites—Chichén Itzá and Tulum in particular—are thoroughly commercialized, their parking lots filled and their monuments overrun from midmorning on.

While the same is not yet true of the 80-plus miles of sand-fringed coast known as the Cancún–Tulum corridor, it will be soon enough. As recently as 20 years ago the corridor was a secret shared by a few thousand affluent divers, the occasional beachcomber who thought he'd died and gone to heaven, and the scattered Maya who called it home. Today, in contrast, the signs of *turismo* are everywhere. Billboards, commercial establishments and tourist attractions dot the side of the highway; the federal government is rumored to have targeted 28 sites for future development; and the whole area is on the verge of being marketed under a catchy new sobriquet: the Turquoise Coast.

But if the future of the Cancún–Tulum corridor is large-scale tourism, the present still revolves around beautiful uncrowded beaches, warm star-filled nights, and a diverse if funky mix of accommodations. Development pressures aside, the area as a whole is worlds apart from the luxury (and expense) of Cancún, and appeals to visitors left cold by the latter's soullessness. First-time visitors and day-trippers will discover that a full day is barely time enough to sample the area's many attractions. Better, instead, to plan on three days (making sure to book accommodations in advance)—and more if you decide to make day trips to places like Cobá, Sian Ka'an, and Cozumel.

Heading south out of Cancún, Avenida Tulum becomes Highway 307, a narrow two-lane road that follows the coast to the archaeological site of Tulum, 131 km (81 miles) distant. Although there is regular bus service between Cancún and Tulum (and points in between), service in the past tended to be erratic, leaving hardy travellers to broil under the Yucatecan sun. With two new bus lines servicing the corridor, however, the situation should start to improve.

Of course, a rental car gives you the freedom to explore the corridor's beaches and attractions at your leisure. If you do decide to rent—and most people do—remember to fill your tank before leaving Cancún; the only gas stations in the corridor are found right off the highway at Puerto Morelos, Playa del Carmen, and Tulum. And while on the road be sure to keep a sharp eye out for buses crowding the center line and disabled trucks.

Cancún to Playa del Carmen

The least interesting part of the corridor is the 36-km (22-mile) stretch between Cancún City and the town of Puerto Morelos. For lack of anything else to see, the modest little **Acuario Palancar**, on your left about 32 km (20 miles) south of Cancún, and, next door, **Croco Cun**, a crocodile farm-cum-zoo, may be worth a stop. Neither is especially interesting, although kids will probably get a kick out of the crocs. The owners of Croco Cun also keep a few monkeys, toucans, and pint-size deer on hand, and the small convenience store/snack bar out front serves breakfast from 7:00 A.M. on.

PUERTO MORELOS

The left turn for Puerto Morelos, the Yucatán's oldest fishing village, is another 2½ km (1½ miles) down the road. Like the highway itself, *turismo* has bypassed the town—at least for now. As a result, it's still a laid-back place filled with soft-spoken, genuinely friendly people. There's a small family-run shop on the main square with reproductions of Mayan jewelry and handicrafts from the Quintana Roo *selva* co-op and, on the beach, a pair of good, inexpensive seafood restaurants.

The handful of accommodations in town run the gamut from the clean, modest, family-run Posada Amor and the 12-room Hacienda Morelos to the low-key ▶ **Caribbean Reef Club** at Villa Marina, Puerto Morelos's only deluxe accommodation, on the beach south of the ferry pier. Though sparely furnished, each of the 22 units in this condo-hotel has a bedroom, dining room, hand-tiled kitchen, living room with sofa bed, and terrace or patio. Amenities include marble floors, central air conditioning, ceiling fans, and color satellite TV. The restaurant/bar overlooks a breezy deck with palapa-shaded tables and a small swimming pool, and guests have free use of the club's snorkeling equipment, wind-surfing boards, and Sunfish. Best of all, the resort is situated on a beautiful beach that stretches miles to the south with nary a soul or other structure on it.

As well, Puerto Morelos is the departure point for *car* ferries to Cozumel. "Car" in this case usually means trucks carrying supplies for the island; passenger vehicles are carried when and if space allows. The ferry makes the two-hour trip daily (weather permitting), and although officials insist there's no set schedule, the line starts forming as early as 5:00 A.M.

Just south of the turnoff to Puerto Morelos you'll see a sign and wrought-iron gate marking the entrance to the **Jardín Botánico Dr. Alfredo Barrera Marin**. Natural-history buffs as well as those simply looking to beat the heat are welcome to explore the almost three miles of trails and 150 acres of semi-tropical forest here. But be sure to bring insect repellent; the winged critters in this neck of the woods can be voracious. The gardens are open from 9:00 A.M. to 4:00 P.M. daily; admission is $2.50, and guided tours in English (about $5) can also be arranged.

The turnoff for **Rancho Loma Bonita** (Tel: 98/84-0861 or 0907), which offers horseback tours of the *selva* and nearby beaches—another way to get acquainted with the flora and fauna of the area—is 12 km (8 miles) farther down the road. (See the Sports in Cancún section above for details on the ranch's guided tours.)

PUNTA BETE

Backed by coconut palms and scrub jungle, the deserted beach at Punta Bete stretches for miles around a gently curving bay. In a world wired to a frantic beat, it's still a place where beachcombers can stroll for hours without seeing another footprint and nightlife is something that skitters around outside your cabana after midnight.

▶ **La Posada del Capitan Lafitte** and KaiLuum, two beachy getaways located next to each other at the end of a long, bumpy access road, have been fixtures here for almost 20 years. (The turnoff for both is marked by Lafitte's large masonry sign some 23 km/14 miles south of Puerto Morelos.) For years the basic Lafitte accommodation was a no-frills bungalow with private bath and a patio overlooking a small swimming pool. During the day the lineup of activities ran to reading, sand castle construction, and tan maintenance; in the evenings low-key socializing revolved around the bar and dining room. By 10:00 most guests were sound asleep. Not much has changed over the years, although Lafitte's management has begun to tinker with the formula. The older bungalows have been joined by five new quadruplex units offering an added measure of comfort, and the dining room has been enlarged. But the biggest change will be the addition, sometime in 1994, of an "activity complex" (marina dock and snack shop, sports shop, volleyball court, exercise room) at the southern end of the compound. While purists may groan when they hear the news, it's a good bet the expansion will enhance rather than alter the Lafitte experience.

Even bigger changes are in store for ▶ KaiLuum, the semi-legendary tent resort up the beach. Long rumored to be sitting on beachfront property coveted by developers, KaiLuum seemed destined to be a casualty of "progress." Much to the relief of its loyal clientele, an eleventh-hour agreement saved everything but its location: Starting May 1, 1994, KaiLuum will be located *south* of Capitan Lafitte, less than a kilometer from its present site. (Instead of turning left at the end of the access road, you'll turn right.) Otherwise, it will remain the same low-profile, low-impact resort people have come to love. The palapa-covered tents will still be set up on dunes overlooking the water; showers and toilet facilities will still be located in rustic bathhouses at either end of the compound; its famous three-course dinners will still be served by candlelight in a sand-floored dining palapa; and come sundown flickering kerosene torches will still transform it into the most romantic adults-only hideaway this side of Polynesia. (Light sleepers may want to steer clear of KaiLuum, where stiff onshore breezes have been known to rustle tent flaps all night, and the compound's east-facing orientation means the sun—and a good many guests—are up by 5:30 A.M.)

LUXE ON THE BEACH

Two of the most stylish accommodations in the Cancún-Tulum corridor, Las Palapas and Shangri-La Caribe, are located side by side some 15 km (9 miles) south of Punta Bete and a mile north of Playa del Carmen at the end of another long access road.

Now in its eighth year of operation, and managed by the same group that runs Capitan Lafitte and KaiLuum, the ▶ Shangri-La Caribe seems to have hit on the perfect combination of rustic charm and creature comforts. The semi-private compound (non-guests can drop in for lunch and/or drinks, and are welcome for dinner when space is available) features

50 beachfront bungalows and 20 additional units spread out among a number of one- and two-story garden units reserved for walk-ins. Each unit has twin double beds, a private bath, louvered windows, a handsome wood-accented decor, and a ceiling fan. Throw in a casually elegant thatched-roof restaurant (breakfast and dinner are included in the room rate), a couple of bars and a recreation palapa, a lovely pool and full-service dive shop, and a beautiful beach that stretches south to the village of Playa del Carmen, and it's easy to see why its mostly American clientele (with the occasional package tour from Europe) keeps growing. For the regular high season you'll want to book two to three months in advance; for the Christmas and Easter periods, at least five months. When reserving, try for one of the beachfront junior suites (numbers 1 through 5), which are slightly larger than the regular ocean-view units (numbers 7 through 36) and have unobstructed views of the water.

▶ **Las Palapas**, on the beach adjacent to the Shangri-La Caribe, bears out the old saw about imitation being the sincerest form of flattery. Now in its fifth season, Las Palapas has a more manicured look than its neighbor, with one- and two-story thatched-roof bungalows arranged in an orderly fashion around a grassy lawn and bocce court. (Las Palapas is German-owned and caters to a mostly European clientele.) The effect is something like *Robinson Crusoe* by way of the Grimm Brothers. The Spartan decor of the bungalows belies the touches that most travellers really appreciate: firm mattresses and pillows, powerful ceiling fans, and lots of hot water. The complex also has an elegant thatched-roof restaurant (no shorts or bathing suits here), a pool, and a recreation palapa. Again, you'll want to book months in advance for the high season, with the bungalows closest to the beach (numbers 1 through 4 and 26 through 28) the most desirable.

Playa del Carmen

Located 68 km (42 miles) south of Cancún, this bustling town is the point of departure for *passenger* ferries to Cozumel and, at first glance, not much more than that. (There are two ferry operations here; one makes the crossing to Cozumel in about 40 minutes, the other in half an hour. Boats leave frequently—more or less every other hour, on the half hour—with the fare the equivalent of $8.) But while it's true no one will mistake it for an oasis of glamour and luxury, Playa has become, thanks to its funky, kicked-back ambience and topless beaches, a very popular stop on the international backpacking set's endless-summer circuit as well as a busy port of call.

The town's two main streets are laid out at right angles to each other. Avenida Juárez, which runs perpendicular to Highway 307, is where the town's business and civic affairs are conducted. Avenida 5A Norte, the newly paved street running parallel to the coast, is the town's self-proclaimed "hotel and convention zone" and the location of most of the businesses that cater to tourists. First-time visitors who by-pass "Fifth Avenue" on their way to the ferry pier will wonder what the fuss is about. With the exception of the inviting porch of the colonial-style **Hotel Molcas**—a perfect spot to cool your heels and quench your thirst—you won't see much to tempt you into spending a night. (The huge Continental Plaza Playacar complex, for which see below, is another story.) Don't despair; almost everything of interest in Playa is located north and west of the plaza on 5A Norte.

There's a secure parking lot where you can leave your car for a night or three west of the bus depot at the corner of Juárez and 5A Norte (the water and Cozumel are to the east). Given the essentially footloose nature of Playa's foreign colony, the fortunes of commercial establishments seem to change as often as the tides. The open-fronted restaurants on the north side of the plaza are an example: In the last couple of years only **Mascaras**, serving tasty Italian specialties and pizza with inventive toppings at affordable prices, has hung on.

Back at the top of the hill, 5A Norte heads off to the right (the bus depot is on the far corner). Here, too, the names of restaurants change with some frequency, although the basic idea doesn't: fresh, inexpensive seafood served with cold beer and lots of hospitality. As you head north on 5A Norte, try **La Tarraya**, on the beach at the end of the first cross street, for a no-frills *muy auténtico* atmosphere; **Karen's Grill**, on the west side of 5A Norte between Calles 2 and 4, for live music (mariachi or marimba) and a party atmosphere stoked by swarms of cruise-ship passengers; or **Jimmy's Fajita Factory**, a hole-in-the-wall down the street, for sizzling kebabs, fajitas, and chicken tacos.

The new Rincón del Sol mini-mall, where **Sole Mio**, serving expertly prepared Italian specialties at lunch and dinner, is fast becoming one of Playa's top restaurants, is in the next block. The ever-popular **Flipper's**, across the street, and **Chicago**, on the northeast corner of the same intersection, draw attention away from the ordinariness of their food with entertainment—loud taped music in the case of the former, live sports via satellite at the latter. Both are fun, however, especially when a breeze is blowing through Chicago's open-air "upper deck."

Limones, still Playa's best restaurant, is down a set of stairs across the street from Chicago. Though you'll pay a little more here than elsewhere in town and, at dinnertime, will probably have to wait for a table, you won't regret it: The kitchen uses only the freshest ingredients, the service is first-rate, and the rock-garden ambience is charming. And Limones pours the best cup of coffee on the Turquoise Coast.

Restaurante La Lunada, the newest claimant to the best-cup-of-coffee crown, occupies a Swiss Family Robinson–style structure one block north of Limones on the same side of the street. Hickory-smoked meat, fish, and chicken entrées are the mainstays of the menu downstairs on the garden patio, while cool breezes, an eclectic cast of locals, and a great seat overlooking the passing parade on 5A Norte are the attractions upstairs in the second-story bar.

STAYING IN PLAYA DEL CARMEN

Playa has a well-deserved reputation as a budget traveller's oasis. For years, in fact, the abundance of inexpensive concrete-block motels and rustic cabana complexes helped give it the air of a sprawling youth hostel. Like everything else in the corridor, this too is changing, as the number of special—and not-so-special—accommodations grows along with the size of the town. In addition to the two properties mentioned above (see Luxe on the Beach), you can get a ring-side seat on Playa's biggest attraction—the parade of sometimes strange, sometimes wonderful people who pass through it—without sacrificing your comfort at either of the following.

The ▶ **Blue Parrot Inn**, on the beach three blocks north of Limones, has been popular with affluent beach bums from the West Coast and Europe for a decade now. Your choices here range from rooms with private baths in a two-story "hotel" to rustic bungalows with kitchenettes (and light housekeeping) right on the beach to a new two-bedroom cottage. Those with an affinity for "Margaritaville" decadence will feel right at home in the Parrot's **Dragon Bar**, where thong-style bikinis and gold cards usually outnumber surfer jams and baseball caps worn backwards. And the Parrot also has a breezy beachside restaurant, a full-service dive and windsurfing shop (windsurfing is taken seriously here), and a beach where topless sunbathing seems to be the rule.

Playa's newest accommodation is also its most conspicuously luxurious. The ▶ **Continental Plaza Playacar**, on the beach to the right of the ferry pier, is a sprawling Cancún-style complex with all the amenities old Playa hands traditionally have done without: private terraces or balconies, satellite cable TV, servi-bars, an Olympic-size pool, swim-up bars, and a shopping arcade. The idea, apparently, is to provide guests with the best of both worlds: the creature comforts of Cancún in a more "exotic" setting. The irony, of course, is that after a few more luxury hotels like this one are built, Playa del Carmen will be about as exotic as Cancún.

South of Playa

XCARET

The Postclassic Maya knew it as Polé (po-LAY); Miguel Quintana-Pali, its millionaire developer, calls it an "eco-archaeological" park; its critics call it a variety of other names. Located 4 km (2½ miles) south of Playa del Carmen and 72 km (45 miles) south of Cancún, Xcaret (shkar-ET) has been transformed in a few short years from a small, seldom-visited inlet alive with brilliantly colored fish into one of the major tourist attractions in the Cancún–Tulum corridor.

It's hard to fault Quintana's intentions. As the owner of the 250-acre property he could have turned Xcaret into an upscale condominium resort (see Puerto Aventuras, below). Instead, he spent $10 million (and plans to spend another $10 million) to create what one writer described as a theme park "composed of equal parts Tarzan, Huck Finn, and Mickey Mouse." In a largely undeveloped, historically poor region, that's a lot of bacon. Like Tarzan's Africa, Xcaret is lush with jungle flora, including a botanical garden full of rare native trees and plants. Like Huck Finn, visitors who pay the admission fee ($10) can experience the thrill of floating down a river—in this case a quarter-mile-long underground river blasted out of the area's subterranean limestone. And like the Disney folks, Quintana has burnished his theme park so there's nary a stone or palm tree out of place. The inlet from which Mayan pilgrims bound for Cozumel shoved off in the days before the Spanish arrived still teems with blue tangs, sergeant majors, and parrotfish; the dolphinar-ium has been set up as an educational program rather than an animal vaudeville act; and the remains of Polé are being excavated by staff archaeologists from the world-renowned Museum of Anthropology in Mexico City. And yet, as one might expect of a natural environment air-brushed of its warts and imperfections, there's an element of unreality about Xcaret that will leave some visitors scratching their heads and anxious to move on.

PUERTO AVENTURAS

Not everyone eager to escape Cancún's glitz and high prices will be enthusiastic about Playa del Carmen's scruffier charms. Those looking for something more upscale might want to take a look around Puerto Aventuras, a planned resort community located some 30 km (19 miles) south of Playa and 98 km (61 miles) south of Cancún. Well aware of the explosion in property values that occurred as Cancún grew from empty sand spit to mega-resort, the developers of this 500-acre parcel on the Bahía de Fatima—among them Pablo Bush, the legendary figure responsible for Akumal, the very first tourist attraction on the Turquoise Coast—set out to create their own upscale oasis. When it's completed, Puerto Aventuras will boast two marinas, an 18-hole championship golf course, and hundreds of villas and condominiums—all of it conforming to a grand master plan (including acreage set aside for an ecological reserve). As of this writing, there are two luxury hotels operated by the Oasis hotel group; a sizable commercial district with a number of expensive boutiques as well as a **Carlos 'n Charlie's**; the **Museo CEDAM**, a small but interesting dive museum established by Señor Bush to commemorate the exploits of his Underwater Explorers' Club; and a nine-hole golf course ($28 for 18 holes; $23 for a cart). And yet, the thing most likely to impress visitors from north of the border is the utter familiarity of it all.

XPU-HA

After the generic opulence of Puerto Aventuras, the beach at Xpu-Há (shpu-HA), about 2 km (1 ¼ miles) down the road, will come as something of a revelation. This is the Caribbean *norteamericanos* know from yellowed travel posters: a stretch of dazzling sand framed by turquoise water and palm trees rustling in the breeze. It's not a mirage—though the discreet signs on the highway can make it as difficult to track down. Persevere, and you shall be rewarded. Xpu-Há is a throwback to the days before bus tours and ecological theme parks descended on the corridor. The skiffs of working fishermen still bob at anchor just offshore, and the palapa-style restaurants on the beach are as likely to be filled with locals as tourists. Snorkelers (bring your own equipment) will want to hike north along the beach to Xpu-Há's beautiful lagoon, while anyone planning to spend a night or two at one of the modest beachside accommodations here should arrive early: Neither place takes reservations.

AKUMAL AND YAL-KU

With its wide beach, reasonably priced hotels and restaurants, and glorious barrier reef, Akumal has long enjoyed a reputation as the poor man's Cancún. (There are three separate turnoffs for Akumal from the highway. The first, and the one most visitors will want, is about 7 km/4 miles south of Puerto Aventuras and is signposted "Hotel Akumal." The second leads to the Hotel Akumal Cancún and its fine restaurant, for which see below. The third leads to Aventuras Akumal, a semi-private condominium development with a sometimes happening—for these parts—disco.) It's a distinction that must bring a perplexed smile to the face of Pablo Bush Romero, Akumal's developer and guiding spirit. It was Bush, after all, who, almost 30 years ago, offered his fledgling resort to a government agency looking to create an international tourist destination on the coast of Quintana Roo. Fonatur, the government agency, thanked him kindly and eventually settled on the barren sandspit that later became Cancún. The rest, as they say, is history.

A prime nesting spot for green and loggerhead turtles long before humans settled in these parts (Akumal means "place of the turtles"), today Akumal is a wonderfully relaxed hangout for divers, vacationing families, every type of beach bum, and budget travellers looking to spend a night or two in relative comfort. Days are spent exploring the coral formations offshore (there are good dive shops at either hotel); snorkeling through huge schools of fish in the Laguna Yal-kú (see below); or chatting up blissed-out strangers over a cold *cerveza.* And, of course, there's always the beach, a broad, seldom-crowded strand that's ideal for children or people with a fear of big waves: The reef at the mouth of the bay cuts down the waves while creating perfect snorkeling conditions. Evening activities, on the other hand, are pretty much limited (with the exception of the aforementioned disco) to leisurely dinners, quiet conversation, and moonlit walks on the beach—which is the way most people like it.

Though accommodations in Akumal are limited in comparison to Cancún (or Playa del Carmen, for that matter), they're more than adequate. The ▶ **Hotel Club Akumal Caribe** offers its guests a choice between traditional rooms in a three-story "tower" or plain but comfortable bungalows—the original accommodations for Bush Romero's Underwater Explorers' Club—equipped with air-conditioning, small refrigerators, and purified water bubblers. (They also have a variety of condominiums.) The two-story motel-style ▶ **Hotel Akumal Cancún**, just down the beach, has 130 rooms situated amid lush tropical vegetation and offers a wider range of facilities, including a pool, tennis courts, a gym, a complete water-sports center, and the breezily elegant **Restaurant Zasil**, which serves breakfast, lunch, and dinner under one of the biggest palapas in the corridor.

Both places are a longish walk (more than a mile) from the **Laguna Yal-kú**, which is often described as Xel-Há (see below) without the crowds. (There's a poorly marked turn-off for the lagoon north of the first Akumal turnoff; look for a ranch house with a windmill on your right as you're heading south. Or you can try to bluff your way past the security guard stationed around the corner from the Akumal Dive Shop.) Though only a quarter the size of Xel-Há, Yal-kú does in fact look like its more famous cousin. And, as at Xel-Há, it's fresh water from an underground source mixed with the warmer Caribbean that attracts the fish. In many places rocky shallows give way to barren sand flats, the latter created by the voracious appetites and tireless chomping of various species of parrotfish. The best snorkeling, however, usually is found in the narrow channel that cuts between the lagoon's back wall and a mangrove island, where schools of grunts numbering in the tens of thousands have been known to congregate for days at a time.

CHEMUYIL AND XCACEL

From Akumal, Highway 307 continues south past two of the best beaches in the corridor. In fact, the sign pointing the way to Chemuyil announces that it's "The most beautiful beach in the world"—a boast not without justification. Chemuyil isn't particularly dramatic, nor does it front a string of posh hotels; the only accommodations are a few sandy campsites behind the beach and a block-style condo-minium complex. What it does offer is acres of soft white sand fringing a beautiful bottle-shaped lagoon, a small palapa-style restaurant-bar, and friendly beach attendants who make it possible to spend the day here without lifting a finger. Happily, the fungus that wreaked havoc on the coco-nut palms behind the beach appears to have been licked, and Chemuyil is again on its way to being a shady patch of paradise—with the crowds to prove it. A weekday morning is the best time to come, while Sunday visits should be avoided altogether.

If Chemuyil *isn't* the most beautiful beach in the world, it's only because that accolade belongs to **Xcacel** (shka-CELL), located at the end of a short access road 5 km (3 miles) south of Chemuyil. The narrow, windswept beach here stretches around a crescent-shaped bay—the water is calmer, and the bottom less rocky, inside the point to your left—populated by a variety of marine invertebrates, including some impressive elkhorn coral specimens. And while the thatched-roof restaurant perched on a sandy bluff has gotten a little pricey (and is entertaining more tour groups), it's still hard to beat for its great views and end-of-the-world ambience. As well, there are 20 campsites behind the beach, along with clean rest rooms and cold-water showers, and a cenote hidden in the jungle south of the restaurant. Perhaps most interesting of all, however, is the turtle project that a mother-and-son team from Galveston, Texas, in conjunction with a Mexican biologist, has developed here.

It's human nature to want to improve on something that's already perfect; Xcacel seems unlikely to escape that fate. Those who like their sun and sand unadulterated by the trappings of civilization will want to experience Xcacel before the inevitable changes descend on it.

XEL-HA NATIONAL PARK

Xel-Há, just 4 km (2½ miles) south of Xcacel, is one of the best places in the country to see marine life. It's also one of the best places in the country to see other people, especially between 10:30 A.M. and 2:30 P.M., when it's not uncommon to count upwards of 30 tour buses in the parking lot. Still, this extensive lagoon system (fed by the largest creek on Mexico's Caribbean coastline) is undeniably beautiful, and if you get here early enough on a weekday you might even find an empty patch of sand.

It's the mixing of fresh water with the warmer waters of the Caribbean that accounts for the profusion of fish. Most of the fish, however, steer well clear of the schools of human beings. The best place to see them is along the ropes that divide the lagoon into "swimming" and "no swimming" areas, with visibility best on bright, sunny days. Unfortunately, bright, sunny days also mean people wearing sunscreens and suntan lotion, which come off in the water, clouding visibility and inhibiting the proper mixing of fresh and salt water. To prevent this from occurring, the custodians of the park now request that visitors wait until *after* they're through snorkeling for the day before applying lotion.

Visitors who arrive snorkel-less can rent equipment inside the park (admission about $5); a mask and snorkel rent for about $8, with the fins an additional $8. There are also two overpriced restaurants on the grounds in addition to a number of overpriced gift boutiques and souvenir stands.

Tulum

Tulum, the most visited and photographed archaeological site in the Yucatán, is the only extant example of a walled Mayan city—an architectural development that became necessary during the strife-torn Postclassic era. According to local legend, Mayan kings came to Tulum to vacation—and one look at the beautiful beach below this striking site makes it clear how such a legend was born. The truth, however, is somewhat less romantic. Thanks to its beach and strategic location opposite a gap in the reef that hugs the Quintana Roo coast, Tulum was well situated to handle the cargo-laden canoes that plied the coasts of the Yucatán in the centuries before the Conquest. In its heyday it probably housed a population of 600.

The turnoff for Tulum is 16 km (10 miles) south of Xel-Há; the archaeological zone itself is about half a mile east of the highway. The parking lot, which is usually filled with tour buses, is directly below the site. Tickets can be purchased in a booth to the left of the main entrance, where you'll find rest rooms as well. (Use the latter only in cases of dire need.)

The parking lot is surrounded by an assortment of open-fronted restaurants and souvenir stands; none is better than any other, and most are overpriced. Feel free to bargain for souvenirs, but don't forget that most of the stuff is mass-produced and usually can be bought elsewhere for less.

Although the surrounding countryside was populated as early as the Preclassic era, the Tulum that lies unveiled today dates back only as far as the Postclassic era (A.D. 1200–1521). It is an unusually compact site, containing more than 60 buildings, 20 of which are within the walls of the city. The site has not been completely excavated, and the partially buried rocks strewn around can make walking difficult, so be sure to wear sneakers or comfortable shoes that will not slip on hard surfaces.

El Castillo

The Castillo, the most impressive structure at Tulum, squats on a bluff overlooking some of the most beautifully tinted water in the Caribbean. According to experts, the Postclassic structure atop the platform served as a combined temple and priests' residence, although there is speculation that it might also have served as a lighthouse for coastal traders. And, indeed, just a few years ago, visitors who made the short but steep climb to the top were rewarded by sweeping views of the coastline to the north as well as the site's fortified wall and corner guardhouses. Unfortunately, the wear and tear caused by day-trippers from Cancún has forced the government to limit access to the structure; these days, the Castillo can be photographed but not climbed.

Templo del Dios Descendente

Of lesser stature but somewhat greater archaeological interest is the Temple of the Descending Gods, immediately to the left (as you're facing the sea) of the Castillo. The structure is named for the partially eroded relief of an upside-down figure—commonly referred to as "descending" or "diving"—recessed in a niche above the temple's sole doorway. Such reliefs were a fairly common decorative motif in the Late Classic and Postclassic eras, although their identities and significance varied from site to site and century to century. The god honored here is assumed to be Ah Macehcabob, the Mayan bee god, and as such is a cultural manifestation of the all-important role of commerce and trade in Postclassic Mayan society (honey being a valuable regional commodity then, as it is today).

Templo de los Frescoes

The other structure of note at Tulum is the Temple of the Frescoes, due west of the Castillo in the direction of the entrance to the site. A two-story building with a columned façade and a boxy, carelessly constructed temple set atop its first story, the Temple of the Frescoes is distinguished by a fairly well-preserved interior mural portraying a Mayan deity surrounded by bean pods and holding in its hands two images of the rain god Chac—a telling indication of the importance of adequate rainfall to the ancient Maya's prosperity. Here again, however, the huge number of tourists visiting the site has forced the government to rope the structure off from curious eyes and damaging camera flashes.

Strategies for Visiting Tulum

If you've rented a car, plan your itinerary so that you arrive at Tulum either first thing in the morning (before 10:00 A.M.) or toward the end of the afternoon (after 3:30; the site closes at 5:00). That way you'll avoid the worst of the crowds. (Generally speaking, this is good advice to follow at any of the archaeological zones in the northern Yucatán. During the high season in particular—from Christmas through Easter—they tend to get very crowded between the hours of 11:00 and 3:00—which can prove especially frustrating for amateur photographers in search of unobstructed shots.

This is also the hottest part of the day, when climbing pyramids can seem more like torture than vacation.)

Remember, too, that Cancún is a two-hour drive from Tulum. If you save Tulum for the end of the day and plan on heading back to Cancún for the evening, you're likely to end up driving most of the way in darkness—an unpleasant prospect at best. If Cancún is your ultimate destination, it's better to do Tulum first thing in the morning and then make your way back up the coast, stopping to check out Xcacel or Chemuyil, Akumal or Xpu-Há, Xcaret or Playa del Carmen in the afternoon.

Cobá

Archaeology buffs and travellers looking for an alternative to the increasingly overcrowded attractions along the coast will want to continue on to Cobá, 42 km (26 miles) northwest of Tulum over a paved two-lane road. The drive, especially in the late afternoon, is both interesting and beautiful, with lush jungle growth crowding the road on either side, an occasional toucan flying overhead, and tiny Mayan hamlets appearing out of nowhere just when you start to think that's exactly where you are.

Most travellers will drive through these hamlets as quickly as the *topes* (speed bumps) allow. Those with an eye for handicrafts will want to spend a few minutes inspecting the wares for sale at a roadside stand in the tiny village of **Macario Gomez**, 23 km (14 miles) northwest of the Coba turnoff. Jaguars, giraffes, *chumax* (a catlike fox indigenous to the Yucatán)—these and other species are hand-carved by machete from a single piece of soft wood, then given a fanciful coat of paint. The result is altogether different from, yet just as attractive and a whole lot less expensive than, the more familiar carved animals from the state of Oaxaca. And while the shops in Cobá carry a good selection of these locally produced handicrafts, it's much more satisfying to purchase them directly from the source.

As for the site itself, you'll need to stay overnight to explore it fully—Cobá is one of the largest, as well as one of the least explored, Mayan cities discovered to date. (Experts say it will take at least 50 years—and money the government doesn't have—to excavate it completely.) Again, such an itinerary will also allow you to explore the site in the late afternoon or first thing in the morning, thereby avoiding the oppressive heat of midday.

The ▶ **Villa Arqueológica Cobá**, a branch of the pleasant

motel-style chain run by Club Med, is situated on the shores of Lake Cobá, a five-minute walk from the entrance to the archaeological zone. With cozy rooms, potable tap water, and a pretty swimming pool to provide welcome relief from the heat and humidity of the *selva,* the Villa Arqueológica is a veritable oasis for travellers who insist on a modicum of comfort. The pricey restaurant on the premises serves regional Yucatecan specialties with a French touch, and the shady poolside bar is the perfect place to whet your whistle and strike up a conversation with a kindred spirit.

More adventurous gourmands can try one of the unpretentious restaurants in the village of Cobá, which straggles up from the northern shore of Lake Cobá. Of the lot, the most charming is **El Bocadito**, at the top of the hill as you enter town. Over the last few years El Bocadito has expanded in size and dressed up its folk-arty decor with tablecloths and linens. The extensive menu has everything from *huevos Mexicanos* and chicken tacos to *langosta* and barbecue-style Yucatecan specialties, with most entrées running a very reasonable $5 to $10. Elsewhere in town, mom-and-pop operations like the **Restaurant Caracol** and **Los Flamingos**, both just up the road from the entrance to the archaeological zone, offer inexpensive regional and Mexican fare in pleasant, no-frills surroundings.

THE RUINS

The ancient city of Cobá (*Cobá* means "water stirred by the wind") once extended over a large area dominated by two shallow freshwater lakes, Cobá and Maconxoc, and for a time in the Middle Classic period (seventh and eighth centuries A.D.) was one of the most important Mayan centers in the northern Yucatán. Ample proof of this is provided by the now-ruined causeway, or *sacbé,* that stretched west some 60 miles through the jungle from Cobá to Yaxuná. Such causeways (*sacbeob* in the plural) were constructed of double retaining walls and a core filled with broken stone that was plastered over to provide a smooth surface, and were an integral part of the city's ceremonial life as well as an important communication link to other Mayan communities. The remains of 50 such causeways have been found in and around Cobá, with the one leading to Yaxuná the longest discovered in the Yucatán to date.

Although the jungle reclaims structures almost as fast as they are cleared, the archaeological zone of Cobá is pervaded by an almost palpable sense of history—a feeling that's enhanced by the lack of other people exploring the site. The two principal structures here, the Iglesia, which is the centerpiece of the so-called Cobá complex, and the Castillo, in the Nohoch Mul complex, are situated roughly a mile apart; a third structure of interest, the Conjunto Las Pinturas, is situated approximately halfway between these two. Elsewhere, narrow pathways lead through thick vegetation to stelae in various states of decay; 32 stelae have been found at Cobá, 23 of which still bear some trace of carving.

El Castillo

The two pyramids are the main attraction at Cobá, and, despite their imposing height, can be climbed with relative ease. With its 120-step ascent, the Castillo, or Nohoch Mul pyramid, is the tallest pyramid in the northern Yucatán (slightly taller than the Castillo at Chichén Itzá). It is topped by a simple Postclassic-era temple decorated with a stucco relief of the diving god—an indication that the site was reoccupied by "Toltecized" Maya (perhaps the same people who built Tulum) centuries after the original Cobá culture collapsed. The 360-degree view from the top takes in a number of jungle-covered hillocks that poke their heads above the pancake-flat canopy; in many cases these are not hillocks at all but rather other structures that have not yet been excavated.

The Iglesia

The Iglesia, a few hundred yards from the entrance to the archaeological zone, is similar in design and construction to the Nohoch Mul pyramid, though not as well preserved. Nor are the views from the top as sweeping. The ceremonial center at its base (much of it cloaked in jungle) is far larger than the complex at the base of Nohoch Mul, however, suggesting that this pyramid was, in fact, the more important structure.

Conjunto Las Pinturas

Northeast of the Iglesia, in the direction of the Nohoch Mul complex, is the Temple of the Painted Lintel. The lintel above the doorway is indeed painted, in a style reminiscent of the frescoes at Tulum, which would seem to date the building to the Late Postclassic era. In the immediate vicinity of the structure you'll also find a number of altars, damaged stelae, and a stone phallus carved from a single stone.

Cobá probably won't strike everyone's fancy; the limited number of excavated structures, the distances between them, and the relative lack of tourist amenities will have some visitors wishing they were back in Cancún. But others will be charmed by the beauty and solitude afforded by the site, as well as by the chance to escape—if only for the night—the bonds of civilization.

ISLA MUJERES

Isla Mujeres, a small island eight miles north and east of Cancún, is the kind of place where cutoffs and a tee-shirt pass for formal wear and a video bar is a restaurant dining room with a portable color TV. It's the perfect resort for those who love the beachcomber's life, and despite recent changes—mostly in the form of higher prices and an influx of tourists—has so far managed to resist the glitzy path blazed by Cancún. Most visitors are content to take the ferry over in the morning, grab a bite to eat, go for a swim, and head back to the mainland before nightfall; others discover they could spend a week here. It all depends on your frame of mind and willingness to leave the comforts of home behind. The less you expect, the more you'll like this scruffy little oasis.

MAJOR INTEREST

Unhurried island pace
Playa Norte

In Town

The Spanish explorer Francisco Hernández de Córdova landed here in 1517 and named his "discovery" the Island of Women, after the statues dedicated to Ixchel, the Mayan goddess of fertility, he found. Except for occasional visits by the likes of Morgan and Lafitte, however, the island remained the almost exclusive preserve of its Mayan inhabitants until the Second World War, when the United States built a naval base here. A trickle of vacationers and divers followed in the 1950s, but it wasn't until Cancún started to boom in the 1980s that Isla Mujeres became popular as an international tourist destination.

The island itself is only five and a half miles long and half a mile wide. Its only town is situated at the northern end of the island, and most of its hotels, shops, and restaurants are

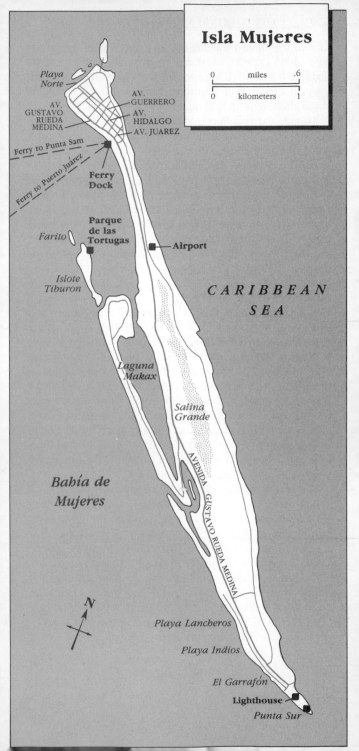

located within easy walking distance of one another. Otherwise, don't expect to find any neon lights, traffic jams, or nightlife here. In Isla Mujeres a visitor can go barefoot right through dinner, and lingering over drinks and a meal is about all there is to do at night.

Avenida Gustavo Rueda Medina is the main road on the island. In town, Avenidas Juárez, Hidalgo, and Guerrero run parallel to it; the major cross streets (from north to south) are López Mateos, Matamoros, Abasolo, Madero, Morelos, and Bravo. The zócalo and city hall are tucked away at the southeastern end of town; most of what action there is centers around the ferry dock and excursion-boat piers, farther to the west. As a rule, accommodations on the island tend to be clean, no-frills places where you change, shower, and catch some shut-eye. All are bargains compared to hotels in Cancún or Cozumel.

STAYING IN TOWN

The ▶ **Hotel Perla del Caribe**, at the corner of Madero and Guerrero, overlooks the Caribbean and a rocky shoreline. There are two types of rooms here: Those with ocean views and air-conditioning, and interior rooms with ceiling fans. (The hotel can get noisy after the bars and restaurants in town close, so a pre-registration room check is advisable.) And while the ocean on this side of the island is too rough for swimming, the Perla del Caribe does have a nice little pool, a small patch of sand, and a palapa snack bar. The same basic package minus the air-conditioning can be had for a little less at the Perla del Caribe II (formerly the Roca Mar), two blocks away at the end of Guerrero.

The ▶ **Posada del Mar**, at the candy-striped lighthouse just up from the ferry pier, offers good-sized rooms with ceiling fans and air-conditioning. Those on the second and third floors also have balconies affording views of the Bahía de Mujeres. The real draws here, however, are its public areas, which include a shady little pool area and a restaurant/ bar where patrons can sit in swings suspended from the ceiling, and its proximity to sand and water: There's an uncrowded beach right across the street, while Playa Norte (also known as Playa Los Cocos), one of the best beaches anywhere, is a five-minute walk to the north.

SHOPPING IN TOWN

The four-block stretch of Rueda Medina opposite the waterfront is crowded with shops selling casual wear, silver jewelry, and tee shirts. To find the more interesting buys you have to venture into town and explore its nooks and crannies. (Note:

Most shops on Isla close for the siesta.) **La Loma**, which sits on a hill at the corner of Morelos and Guerrero, all the way across town, has the best selection of Mexican handicrafts on the island, from Oaxacan black pottery and painted animals to lacquerware from Olinala to Guatemalan textile items and a wonderful assortment of masks. And though Isla is no longer the secret it was a few years ago, your chances of finding a bargain are better here than in Cancún.

At Hidalgo, one street over, the peach-colored **Casa del Arte Mexica** is a cool, elegant gallery filled with objets d'art inspired by ancient Mayan motifs. Batik wall hangings and clothing, limestone reproductions of the beautiful carvings from Palenque, and interesting jewelry make this one of the better boutiques on the island. A different kind of cultural legacy, that of Oaxaca's Zapotec Indians, is well represented by the beautiful quality blankets for sale at **Artesanías Arcoiris**, a plain little shop in the center of town at Juárez 3.

DINING IN TOWN

Eating out on Isla Mujeres is a decidedly casual activity; unless you're going to one of a couple of restaurants—Magaly's, in the Nautibeach complex, and Maria's, down island—you can leave the fancy duds and credit cards in your hotel room. **Pingüinos**, next door to the Posada del Mar (see above), is a sunny California-style café-bar with an even sunnier deck overlooking Rueda Medina. Reasonably priced burgers, sandwiches, and light entrées and a lively party atmosphere have made this one of the most popular spots in town. Open for lunch and dinner.

The main restaurant strip in the center of town is Avenida Hidalgo (the second street in from the water). The **Meson de Bucanero** here has two pretty dining rooms and a shady courtyard fronted by wrought-iron gates that's an especially pleasant spot for breakfast (daily, 7:00 to 11:00 A.M.); open till 11:00 P.M. Pizza cooked in a wood-fired oven is the thing at **Pizza Rolandi**, directly across the street, but you can also order steak, chicken, seafood, and any number of Italian dishes. Popular with noisy groups and kids trying to stretch their vacation dollars. For a somewhat more romantic atmosphere try **Gomar**, upstairs under a palapa at the corner of Hidalgo and Madero. Lobster and charbroiled steaks are the specialties here, and its second-story location puts patrons above the noise and fumes of Isla's ubiquitous mopeds.

Cocos Frios, Hidalgo 4, is the best place for not-so-fast food Isla-style. Pull up a seat (you'll need two hands), order a beer and the chicken tacos with cheese, and enjoy the show.

Any beach resort worth its salt needs a good müesli joint. Isla's is the charming **Café El Nopalito**, on Guerrero across from Ciro's (not-so-charming) Lobster House. A European-style breakfast featuring crepes, jam, fresh fruit, yoghurt, homemade breads, and, yes, müesli is served along with the island's best cup of coffee, espresso, or cappuccino from 8:00 A.M. to noon and again from 6:00 to 9:00 P.M.

Playa Norte

Fringed by rustling palms at the northern end of the island, Playa Norte is an easy ten-minute walk from the ferry dock. Just head north on Rueda Medina, turn right on López Mateos at the entrance to the Nautibeach complex, and then left on Hidalgo past the cemetery. Like a number of beautiful beaches along the Yucatán's Caribbean coastline, Playa Norte offers acres of satiny sand and warm, shallow water. It's the ultimate sandbox, and seems to have a liberating effect on the sunbathers who find their way here: After an hour or two of sunning and soaking, inhibitions—along with a surprising number of bathing suit parts—seem to fall by the wayside.

STAYING AT PLAYA NORTE

That visitors will love Playa Norte is a given. The hotel situation at this end of the island, on the other hand, is somewhat less certain. Perched on a rocky islet at the far end of Playa Norte, the Del Prado, Isla Mujeres's biggest hotel, finally closed after years of charging too much for too little. Since then, renovation of the property has proceeded in fits and starts—but mostly in fits. As of this writing the complex stands empty and unfinished, bigger and uglier than ever. Barring a massive infusion of capital from somewhere, it's likely to remain that way for the foreseeable future.

In pleasant contrast, the two-story ▶ **Na Balam** is a reminder that, sometimes, small and understated is every bit as appealing as big and flashy. Na Balam's 12 one-room junior suites are sparely furnished with king-size beds and sturdy wooden furniture. Each is equipped with a small refrigerator and ceiling fan (air-conditioning, available in about half the rooms and not usually necessary, should be requested when you make your reservation). All rooms have a small patio or balcony overlooking a sandy enclosure dotted with palm trees and, beyond that, Playa Norte. It's the little extras, however, that make this Isla's best accommodation: The grounds are leafy and lovingly maintained; the small dining room is as cozy as Mom's kitchen; the palapa-style bar has the best happy hour on the island; and the staff is always ready with a smile and a *buenos días*. Yes, its rates have gone up in the last 18 months—but then, in this corner of Mexico, whose haven't? The important thing is what hasn't changed: In an increasingly hectic, stress-filled world, Na Balam remains an oasis of charm and civility.

The other better-than-average lodging option at this end of the island is the ▶ **Nautibeach Condominium-Hotel**, at the far end of Rueda Medina just beyond the lighthouse. (The "naughty" in its name refers to the topless sunbathing on Playa Norte.) In addition to its pretty little swimming pool and handsome restaurant, Nautibeach has 34 two-bedroom units, 10 of which are rented to the public. All have kitchenettes and are pleasantly decorated, making them an especially attractive option for families on vacation. A minimum two-night deposit is required during the high season.

DINING ON PLAYA NORTE

Chez Magaly, the poolside restaurant in the Nautibeach complex, is the most elegant dining spot on North Beach, as well as the most expensive. Which makes the lack of imagination in the preparation and presentation of its seafood, meat, and Mexican specialties all the more puzzling. Still, the sunsets from its front porch are spectacular, and the talking parrot at the bar will be happy to chip in if conversation at your table starts to flag. Closed Mondays; Tel: 82-0259 for reservations.

Na Balam and Nautibeach anchor either end of Playa Norte. Between them are two other establishments worth checking out. During the day, **Las Palapas Chimbo's & Rutilo's**, on the beach at the northern end of Avenida Hidalgo, function as open-air seafood restaurants with laid-back service and ringside seats on the action. At night, Chimbo's becomes Isla's liveliest disco, with a happy hour from 9:00 P.M. to midnight and dancing until the sun comes up. Farther up the beach in the direction of Na Balam, **Buho's**, a onetime disco that was resurrected as a restaurant (breakfast, lunch, and dinner) after Hurricane Gilbert flattened it, offers a rather uninspired seafood menu, viewings of the latest video releases from Hollywood, and a wonderful palm-shaded patio that's perfect for sunset watching.

South of Town

South of town the island becomes hillier, with the vegetation along its main road (a continuation of Rueda Medina) low and scrubby. The airport, which cannot accommodate commercial jetliners, is located about a third of the way down the island on its eastern side. Almost everything else of interest is located on its western, or leeward, side, facing the calm waters of the Bahía de Mujeres.

The beaches on the way to El Garrafón park, at the southern tip of the island, are relatively unspoiled, although recent years have seen an increase in the number of makeshift souvenir stands and little open-air restaurants. **Playa Lancheros**, 5 km (3 miles) south of the ferry dock, gets its share of visitors in spite of its tacky ambience: Though the three giant turtles and one "sleeping" shark kept in underwater pens just offshore are meant to amuse curious daytrippers, the whole setup is more sad than appealing.

Of marginally greater interest is **Mundaca's hacienda**—or what's left of it—the newly landscaped path to which is located just before the turnoff to Playa Lancheros. According to legend, a sometime pirate and full-time slaver named Fermin Mundaca built the hacienda and surrounded it with beautiful gardens at great expense in order to woo an island beauty known as La Trigueña (The Brunette). La Trigueña had other plans, however, and married a local lad. The spurned Mundaca slowly went mad as his beloved bore her husband one child after another, and after he died his hacienda was left to the jungle.

In the opinion of many locals, **Maria's**, an elegantly rustic restaurant about a mile (1½ km) south of Playa Lancheros, is the best dining spot on the island. Lunch and dinner are served under a cozy palapa overlooking the water, and the French-inspired but reasonably priced food—seafood is the specialty of the house—earns raves. Maria's also has a few rooms to let, most of them cozy and quite attractive, if a bit musty. It's a good idea to phone ahead for reservations; Tel: 82-0130.

El Garrafón, a national underwater park at the southern end of the island, was once a snorkelers' paradise. Today, however, there are more people than fish—the park is usually packed with tourists who arrive in large groups (don't even think of going on Sunday)—and the small beach area has been turned into a miniature version of Coney Island, with dank dressing rooms, tacky snack stands, and overpriced snorkel concessions. The combination of people and protruding rocks makes it difficult to enter the water, and once you do you're likely to spend as much time dodging other snorkelers as looking at fish. If it's first-rate snorkeling you're looking for, try the wrecks at the mouth of the **Laguna Makax** south of town or, better yet, head over to Cancún or Cozumel; for a peaceful day at the beach, there are better choices elsewhere on Isla Mujeres.

From El Garrafón the road continues south for another quarter mile before it loops around and heads back to town along the windward side of the island. The narrow, rocky paths on your right cut through tangled undergrowth to the southernmost tip of the island and a partially reconstructed temple where native Mayan women worshiped the fertility goddesses Ixchel, Ixchebeliax, Ixhunie, and Ixhunieta long after the Spanish arrived in these parts. Today the views of the wave-tossed Caribbean to the east, Cancún (looking like a modern-day Emerald City) to the west, and the crashing surf below are well worth the short hike.

If you've rented a car or moped, you'll want to head back to town along the largely undeveloped windward side of the island. The road has been regraded and paved, and in spots the combination of green hillsides and craggy coastline—the limestone formations that hug the beach are a geologic phenomenon known as ironshore—will put you in mind of the northern California coast. Closer to town the windswept vistas give way to a gravel quarry and the town dump—a favorite haunt of egrets and other shorebirds. Take care along here: The small patches of sand on this side of the island are perfect for picnics or solitary sunbathing, but not good for swimming. It's better, instead, to head over to the protected beaches on the other side for any serious water activities.

COZUMEL

Cozumel is the kind of place you fall in love with without knowing exactly why. Observant travellers sense its uniqueness immediately, but the *source* of that uniqueness takes some time to figure out. Eventually you realize that the Mayan culture is more alive here than elsewhere, and that Mayan facial and physical characteristics are more prevalent. At the same time, the island, because it is an island, brings visitors into closer contact with the resident population, which seems to have a "live-and-let-live" attitude toward the divers, day-trippers, cruise-ship passengers, and others who make their way here. If you gear down to its own special pace, Cozumel will reveal itself gently and gradually; once it does, you'll want to come back again and again.

MAJOR INTEREST

Unsurpassed scuba diving

Snorkeling at Chankanaab Lagoon National Park and elsewhere

Strolling the *malecón* and back streets downtown

Unspoiled beauty of its windward coast

Although it's Mexico's largest island, measuring some 30 miles by 10 miles, Cozumel was isolated from the rest of the country until relatively recently. As a result, you'll still hear Mayan spoken with some frequency. Likewise, many of the local women still wear *huipiles*—not least because nothing beats the heat better. At the same time, Cozumel is the only place in Mexico where you're likely to see people wearing full wet suits in the zócalo. In fact, every other person here seems to have a diver's bag dangling over a shoulder, and advertisements for dive operators fill every local newspaper and guidebook.

The strong cultural contrast between the Mayan presence and the mania for water sports is a product of the island's colorful history. The Maya first settled Cozumel around A.D. 300, and by the Postclassic era it had become an important trading outpost as well as a pilgrimage site famous throughout the Yucatán for its shrines to Ixchel, the Mayan goddess of the moon and fertility. First Juan de Grijalva and then Cortés landed here in the years immediately preceding the Conquest, but it wasn't until 1543 that the Spanish gained firm control of the island. In the late 1500s the island's population was decimated by smallpox, and the few native survivors of the epidemic soon packed up and headed back to the mainland. After that tragedy, it was not until 1848 that Mayan refugees from the bloody War of the Castes began to slip back to their former island retreat. Cozumel remained isolated from the outside world, however, until the Second World War, when the United States built an air base on the island.

After Jacques Cousteau discovered **Palancar Reef** in the 1950s scuba divers began to arrive in numbers. Starting in 1959 they were joined by growing numbers of more conventional tourists after Fidel Castro, in one of his first acts as Cuban premier, shut down that island's booming casino business. Still, the modern tourist boom on Cozumel didn't begin in earnest until some 20 years ago, when the first hotel opened in Cancún.

Today Palancar Reef, off the southwestern coast of the island, is ranked among the top five dive sites in the world.

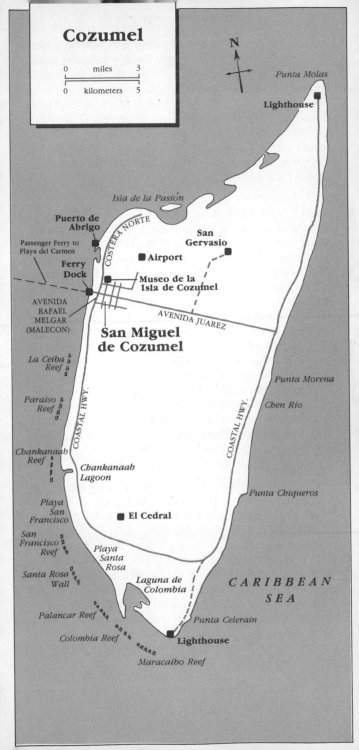

But Palancar isn't the only underwater attraction here. With visibility often exceeding 200 feet, virtually the entire southwestern quarter of Cozumel is surrounded by the kind of underwater reefs divers dream about. Best of all, there seems to be a reef for every level of diving expertise. Beginners can head out to inspect a sunken plane (put there for a movie shoot) in the "front yard" of the Hotel La Ceiba. At Palancar itself coral spires rise 60 to 80 feet from sloping reef walls, and deep canyons wind through spectacular gardens of coral and sponge.

AROUND THE ISLAND

In light of increasing competition from Cancún, about a dozen years ago the government decided to improve Cozumel's appeal to non-divers. Existing hotels were gradually refurbished and new investment encouraged, with dramatic results. Today the greatest concentration of hotels and condominiums is found at the northwest corner of the island, from the Meliá Mayan Cozumel south along the coast to the marina just north of town. The intersection of Avenida Juárez, the cross-island road (which here is open to pedestrians only), and the coast road is the undisputed center of activity on Cozumel, with the major restaurants, stores, and night spots all located within walking distance of the passenger-ferry pier. Several more luxury hotels, a handful of restaurants, some excellent beaches, and Chankanaab Lagoon National Park are located south of town, either right on or just off the coast road.

San Gervasio

A good deal less than half the island is inhabited; the pancake-flat northern half of Cozumel, most of it scrub jungle, is dotted with half a dozen small archaeological sites that are difficult to get to. Archaeology buffs will want to rent a Jeep or moped (or hire a taxi; drivers know the spot) to visit the Mayan ruins at San Gervasio (san her-BAH-see-oh), a recently restored Postclassic site situated in the middle of the northern half of the island. A self-guided tour to the ruins in the form of an easy-to-read map with brief descriptions of the various structures is available in town at, among other places, the Cozumel Flea Market, Avenida 5 Norte between Calles 2 and 4 Norte. Guides are also available at the site itself, though how informative they are depends a great deal on their mood. Find out beforehand if the guide you are about to contract speaks English; most do not. San Gervasio is closed Saturdays.

Cozumel's Windward Beaches

The beaches on the spectacular eastern side of Cozumel are, generally speaking, too rocky and rough for swimming, though there are exceptions. **Punta Chiqueros**, **Chen Rio**, and **Punta Morena** are three such spots, and offer an unspoiled and refreshing change of pace from the more crowded beaches on the island's leeward side. The secluded beaches stretching south from the paved island road to **Punta Celarain**, Cozumel's southernmost point, are also popular—especially with a clothing-optional crowd. Here and elsewhere on this side of the island, however, there are no lifeguards and very few people. In other words, if you get into trouble, help may be a long time arriving.

North of Town

STAYING NORTH OF TOWN

The ► **Meliá Mayan Cozumel** is one of the best hotel properties on the island. A large complex situated at the end of the coast road leading north out of town, it's a haven for well-heeled travellers who want to relax and don't care if they ever leave the premises. All rooms have balconies and ocean views, and the pool area and two restaurants are tastefully done. Its wide, palm-shaded beach is perhaps its most appreciated feature, however, especially among parents with children in tow. The Meliá Mayan is, in addition, a place where many of the island's pleasures "come to you." It stages great Mexican fiesta nights, for example, and a number of excursion boats leave from the pier off the beach.

Other, less elaborate properties, favorites of the island's visitors in the early days of its popularity, line the road—the Costera Norte—from the Meliá Mayan south into town. Most feature the kind of friendly ambience that only family-owned properties can offer. Guests are usually divers (or friends of divers tagging along with the group) who have been coming to Cozumel for years. The pink stucco ► **El Cozumeleño**, next door to the Meliá Mayan, is one such hotel. The rooms here are old-fashioned and quite spacious, as are the hotel's public areas, and those guests who aren't out diving or snorkeling usually spend the day lazing around the small but pretty seaside pool.

DINING NORTH OF TOWN

In contrast, restaurants at this end of the island are scarce. One of the few out this way is **La Cabaña del Pescador** (The Lobster House), a small family-run place well hidden behind lush vegetation opposite the Hotel Playa Azul. As its name suggests, La Cabaña del Pescador serves lobster—it's the only thing on the menu, in fact. The "lobster" in this case is actually *langosta,* a stringier, chewier version of its cold-water cousin, the Maine lobster, and the drill, like the menu, is straightforward: Customers choose their tails—*langosta* don't have claws—from an iced tray, and the tails are then priced according to weight (usually about $23 per person). The crustaceans are boiled while you enjoy a cocktail and are served, family-style, with bread and modest portions of rice and vegetables. Whether you're a *langosta* lover or simply want a fun dinner in cozy surroundings, it's an enjoyable way to spend an evening. But you'll want to arrive early—the Lobster House has only eight tables, and seating is on a first-come, first-served basis. Open 6:00 to 10:00 P.M. nightly.

Those who don't want to put quite such a dent in their wallets can wander over a small bridge in the same compound to the **Lobster House Grill**. Meat, fish, and *langosta* kebabs are the specialty here, and while the ambience isn't as rustically charming as the dimly-lit scene next door, your mood will brighten considerably when you get the check. No phone, no reservations.

Puerto de Abrigo, the small marina south of the Hotel Mara and just north of town, is where fishermen weigh and show off their catches at the end of the day. It's also the place to arrange deep-sea fishing expeditions.

San Miguel de Cozumel

San Miguel, a good-sized town with about 60,000 residents that seems to double in size every few years or so, is laid out in a grid. Avenida Juárez, the street that begins at the passenger-ferry pier and cuts east across the island, divides the town into northern and southern halves. Streets to the north of Juárez are even-numbered and ascend by twos. Those to the south are odd-numbered and also ascend by twos. Many of the best shops and restaurants are located along or just off Avenida Rafael Melgar, the seaside drive.

While on the subject, know that San Miguel is the kind of place that requires shoppers to *shop*. Resortwear and silver jewelry are the most popular purchases, with handicrafts running a close second, but jewelry and small sculptures made from **black coral** are the real prizes. Cousteau was the first to discover this type of coral, and it's extremely valuable because divers have to go to great depths to bring it up (it also takes 50 years to grow just one centimeter). **Roberto's**, at the corner of Avenida 5 Sur and Calle A.R. Salas, is one of the best places to shop for it.

NORTH IN TOWN

Los Cinco Soles, located "uptown" at the corner of Calle 8 Norte and Avenida Melgar in a beige colonial-style building, is the place to begin your shopping spree; from there you can work your way south. Behind the usual stacks of tee-shirts here you'll find an extensive selection of silver jewelry, pine furniture, clothing, and folk art by some of Mexico's most accomplished designers and artisans.

The patio of Los Cincos Soles is home to **Pancho's Backyard**, one of the few spots on the island where informal dining manages to be refined. The contemporary *faux*-colonial decor is easy on the eyes, the bar is a cool place to have a drink, and the menu features Mexican and Continental dishes prepared with health and fitness in mind. Closed Sundays.

One of the island's pleasant surprises is the enchanting **Museo de la Isla de Cozumel**, located between Calles 6 and 4 Norte on Avenida Melgar. Installed on two floors of a pink-and-white colonial-style building, the museum combines culture and cuisine in an attractive setting overlooking the sea. Permanent exhibits here include diving memorabilia and archaeological relics, while breakfast, lunch, and dinner are served upstairs on its balcony. The museum is open Saturday through Thursday, from 10:00 A.M. to 2:00 P.M. and again from 4:00 to 8:00 P.M. (Note: Most stores and restaurants in Cozumel observe the siesta.)

Aca Joe, everybody's unisex favorite, is on the corner of Melgar and 4 Norte; **Animal Fiesta**, right next door, has a charming selection of toys and children's clothing, all of it made in Mexico.

Already a downtown fixture on the corner of Melgar and 2 Norte, **La Concha** has expanded its selection of Mexican handicrafts without sacrificing its reputation for quality. Now open until 9:30 P.M. most nights, it remains one of the better boutiques on the island.

Carlos 'n Charlie's & Jimmy's Kitchen, a few doors down on Melgar, is one of Cozumel's liveliest spots. The young beer-drinking crowd comes revved up and ready to have a good time, and is helped toward that end by a jolly group of waiters: Picture Malcolm McDowell and mates in *A Clockwork Orange* crossed with Tom Cruise—wannabees and you'll know what to expect. The decibel level climbs as the hour gets later, so come early if a quick bite in relative peace is what you had in mind.

For a completely different atmosphere, climb the stairs to the **Café del Puerto**, in the Banpais building across from the municipal pier, where grilled seafood and Continental cuisine are served in an elegant art gallery–like setting overlooking Avenida Melgar and the plaza. The food and service are top drawer, the prices slightly less so. Reservations recommended; Tel: 2-0136.

Morgan's, around the corner and up a block on Avenida Juárez, is one of Cozumel's most romantic restaurants. Housed in the island's old customs house, its rich wood interior, muted lighting, and mellow atmosphere make it the perfect spot to linger over dinner with a special companion. Pricey but worth it. Reservations advised; Tel: 2-0584.

The **Sports Page**, around the corner at Avenida 5 Norte and Calle 2, functions as Cozumel's unofficial U.S. embassy, offering such services as the best dollar-peso exchange rate and the cheapest long-distance calls on the island. Burgers, chicken, Tex-Mex specialties, and a nonstop menu of major-league and college sports keep the place jumping—so much so that on the day of a big event you'll have to get here early if you want a seat.

As you head north again on 5 Norte you'll come to the **Cozumel Flea Market** and, next door, the **Batik Factory**, which between them have a good selection of handicrafts, including masks, blankets, and, of course, batik items. Across the street and up a few doors at the corner of 5 Norte and Calle 4 is the **Zermatt Bakery**, which serves pizza by the slice in addition to fresh pastries, doughnuts, and bread.

SOUTH IN TOWN

Back on Avenida Melgar opposite the municipal pier, **Las Palmeras** is a popular stop for the day-trippers and cruise-ship passengers that descend on the island. The drinks are great, the food only so-so, and there isn't a more convenient rendezvous spot on the island.

Donatello's, in the next block at Melgar Sur 131, is the best Italian restaurant on the island as well as one of the prettiest. The stylish tropical decor is enhanced by a scattering of antiques, and soft piano music accompanies your meal. After a drink at the spiffy bar, you can enjoy one of the specialties of the house either inside in air-conditioned comfort or outside on a small garden patio. And though you'll probably want to dress up a little, men need not wear jackets. Tel: 2-2586.

On the corner of Avenidas A. Rosado Salas and Melgar, **Pepe's Grill** manages to be informal and elegant at the same time, a rare enough combination in San Miguel. Steak, *langosta,* and grilled seafood are served downstairs in an intimate, wood-trimmed dining room or upstairs in a more conventional space overlooking the harbor and, in the distance, the lights of the mainland. Reservations advised; Tel: 2-0213.

La Choza, two blocks east of the waterfront at Avenida 10 Sur and Rosado Salas, is a local institution whose consistently good food, reasonable prices, and friendly service have earned it the loyalty of legions of tourists looking for something a little more *auténtico.* Success hasn't spoiled it—yet—although it has doubled in size of late, and as of this writing was getting ready to expand again. One of the best places on the island for breakfast. Tel: 2-0958.

Back on Melgar, four blocks south of the municipal pier, **Soberanis** is a branch of a Mérida steak-and-lobster restaurant that has been popular with knowledgeable travellers for more than 25 years. Lunch and dinner are served in a casual atmosphere that's made even more enjoyable by live music. Call ahead to make reservations; Tel: 2-0246.

Located at the southern end of town on the corner of Avenida Melgar and Calle 11 Sur, **El Acuario** is the nearest thing to a "theme" restaurant in San Miguel. The restaurant was once an aquarium (thus its name), and its steak and seafood entrées are served in a mahogany-and-glass setting that incorporates some of the old tanks along with expansive views of the water. The restaurant even keeps a number of large green turtles and dusky sharks in holding tanks out back.

Back-Street Dining Spots

La Misión, on Avenida Juárez between Avenidas 10 and 15, is recommended by every cab driver in town—which is why, in the evening, there's usually a line of tourists waiting for tables. It's a scene, for sure, but a fun one, and while you wait the drinks and guacamole are on the house. The menu is simple but extensive, with fish, shrimp, chicken, beef, and various flaming dishes the most popular. And while the room tends to get noisy (and warm) as it fills, no one seems to mind; in fact, most people seem to leave with a smile on their face and the phone number of a new friend or two in their pocket.

One of San Miguel's best-kept dining secrets is the garden patio at **Bon Appetit**, a deli-cum-restaurant at 621 Avenida 30, six cross streets back from the plaza via Avenida Benito

Juárez (a cab is probably your best bet). The prix-fixe dinner menu here ($14) changes according to market availability, and includes homemade soup, salad, and a choice of four inventive and usually delicious entrées. Lunch is a less formal affair, with deli sandwiches on homemade bread and the day's soups the usual offerings. Open 1:00 to 4:00 P.M. and 6:00 to 11:00 P.M., Monday through Saturday; open for brunch (11:00 A.M. to 1:00 P.M.) on Sundays. Reservations advised; Tel: 2-1681 or 0453.

The main streets running parallel to Avenida Melgar can be confusing to tourists, which is why so few of them bother to explore the area. One of the favorite stops for those who do is the **Restaurant El Moro**, whose inexpensive seafood and Mexican specialties have delighted visitors and locals alike for more than a dozen years now. You'll find it on the eastern edge of town at Avenida Bis Norte 75 #124. Tel: 2-3029.

South of Town

STAYING AND DINING

Set back from the road on six and a half acres, 3 km (2 miles) south of town, the ▶ **Hotel Villablanca Beach Club and Sports Complex** is popular with serious divers who have some money to spend (divers on a budget stay in smaller hotels in town). Standard rooms, which are spread around a couple of buildings on neatly landscaped grounds, come with large double beds, air-conditioning, sunken tile baths, color TVs, and refrigerators; the breezy master suites in a separate wing are popular with families that need a little more space. The real attraction here, however, is the management's knowledge of and preoccupation with Cozumel's favorite water sport. The hotel is conveniently located up the road from the Blue Angel Scuba School, one of the island's most reputable, and diving seems to be the topic of conversation on most guests' lips. Snorkelers need not feel left out: The Villablanca offers excellent snorkeling right across the street, and is just a short cab ride from such snorkeling hot spots as the Stouffer Presidente hotel and Chankanaab Lagoon National Park (see below).

A half-mile farther south, next to the Budget Rent-a-Car office, **Ernesto's Fajita Factory** serves what just might be the best fajitas in the Yucatán. In the old days Ernesto's customers sat on stools under an open-air palapa, their mouths watering as mounds of freshly sliced onions, chicken, beef, and pork were grilled to perfection. The portions were huge and the beer ice cold—a combination that, over the years, proved to be a winner. In the last few years Ernesto's has tripled in size and added another branch on Avenida Melgar south of the municipal pier. They've also expanded their menu to include breakfast, lunch, and dinner specials. The original gets the nod for atmosphere, but in either branch the basic principle remains the same: Come as you are and bring your appetite.

It's easy to see why many experienced Cozumel hands think the eight-story ▶ **Fiesta Americana Sol Caribe**, just down the road, is the best hotel on the island. From its glassed-in elevators to the beautifully landscaped pool area, the Sol Caribe is a top-notch luxury hotel. The cheery, light-filled rooms in the original building and a newish ten-story tower overlook either the water and mainland to the east or a flat stretch of scrubby jungle to the west (those rooms with a jungle view are considerably less expensive). Whichever side you choose, however, be sure to request a room on the higher floors—views from the first two floors are completely blocked by shrubbery.

▶ **La Ceiba**, next to the cruise-ship pier, is a pleasant, no-nonsense kind of place designed for divers. It has two restaurants—the seaside dining room is particularly good— a tennis court and pool, and a small stretch of beach dotted by palm trees and palapas. The simple rooms here reflect the fact that guests at La Ceiba spend most of their time underwater: The whole area north of Paraiso Reef is great for snorkeling, and there's even an upside-down plane wreck—put there during the shooting of a movie and later overturned by Hurricane Gilbert—right off the hotel's beach.

The sprawling ▶ **Stouffer Presidente Cozumel**, south of the Sol Caribe and La Ceiba at km 6.5 on the coast road, is an old Cozumel favorite and usually the first of the island's large hotels to fill up. The reasons are obvious. From its impressive driveway lined with a double row of palms to its casually elegant lobby to its sparkling pool area and gem of a beach, the Presidente delivers five-star luxury tempered by the languidness of the tropics. Rooms here are tastefully (though somewhat sparely) appointed with marble floors and white-cedar trim, two queen-size or a huge king-size bed, and a full package of amenities; most have a private balcony or terrace. The best are located in a separate beachfront wing and have their own private patios and a tropical garden ambience. The Presidente's gourmet restaurant, **Arrecife** (dinner only), is one of the best dining spots on the island, and **El Caribeño**, its pretty palapa-style restaurant, overlooks a dock where hundreds of brilliantly colored fish congregate. The snorkeling here is so good, in fact, that many guests never get around to checking out the island's other snorkeling hot spots. Throw in in-house car rental and travel agencies, lighted tennis courts, a complete watersports center, valet service, and live entertainment most evenings, and it all adds up to Cozumel's top-rated hotel.

The ▶ **Fiesta Americana Cozumel Reef** (formerly the Cozumel Reef Holiday Inn) is located midway between the Presidente and Chankanaab park—an excellent location for snorkelers, divers, and visitors who don't mind being some distance from the bustle of town. The large, well-equipped rooms here feature pretty pastels, rattan furniture, and small balconies overlooking the water. The hotel also has an open-air restaurant overlooking the water, a raised pool area, tennis courts, an in-house car rental agency, a branch of the full-service Pro Dive outfit, and a quarter-mile jogging trail carved out of the jungle. While not quite as luxurious as the Presidente, the Cozumel Reef nevertheless delivers all the comforts of home, and, as you'd expect from a Fiesta Americana property, does so with a fair amount of style.

PARQUE NACIONAL CHANKANAAB

Located about 15 minutes south of town, Chankanaab is a beautiful underwater marine park surrounded by shady botanical gardens. The swimming and snorkeling are truly wonderful (though things can get a bit crowded close to shore), and amateur botanists love the extensive gardens, not least because the more than 400 species of plants are clearly labeled. A replica of a Mayan hut in the middle of it all houses a small museum, and you can rent snorkel equipment on the beach. With a palapa-covered restaurant that serves lunch and appetizers from 10:30 A.M. to 4:00 P.M., Chankanaab is a great place to make a day of it.

SOUTH OF CHANKANAAB

If the crowds get a bit thick at Chankanaab, take your mask and fins down the road a half mile or so to **Playa Corona**, a laid-back (and usually empty) beach bar overlooking an underwater landscape populated by hundreds of sea fans and multitudes of tropical fish. One local publication calls the snorkeling and diving offshore here "a macro photographer's dream." We couldn't agree more.

Playa San Francisco, five minutes south of Chankanaab, is one of the best beaches on the island—no frills here, just blue-green water, coarse white sand, and a couple of modest beachside restaurants serving snacks and cold drinks. You can rent all sorts of water-sports paraphernalia on the beach, and there are a few gift shops and artisans' stalls on hand for those who can't let an afternoon slip by without doing a little shopping.

From Playa San Francisco the coast road swings east through miles of uninteresting scrub jungle. At km 16.5 Cozumel's newest accommodation, the sprawling ▶ **Diamond at Cozumel**, stands in stark contrast to the empty acreage surrounding it. The aim of this all-inclusive compound is to bring the island to your doorstep—not a bad idea given the resort's distance from town. Guests are plied with food and drink from the moment they step on the property, and the schedule of activities—everything from aerobic classes and scuba lessons to special theme nights— would intimidate a decathlete. No one will mistake Diamond's two-story thatched-roof "villas" for luxury digs—the rooms (four to a villa) are small and grimly decorated—but for active people who like the outdoors (the resort backs up to a gloriously empty stretch of Playa San Francisco) and the all-inclusive concept, Diamond at Cozumel is an attractive option.

THE WINDWARD COAST

The road finally hits the stunning windward coast of Cozumel a few miles north of **Punta Celarain**—the southernmost point of the island. On Sunday the lighthouse here is the scene of a fried-fish-and-beer bash, but those on mopeds or motorbikes will find the sandy track leading to the lighthouse difficult to negotiate. It's no problem in a rental car, on the other hand, and well worth the time it takes (about an hour round-trip, if you don't stop to sunbathe). The jungle scenery along the way is impressively varied, and the dune-backed beach is among the best on the island. There are even a few spots where it's okay to swim—although caution should be exercised at all times—and a few others where the swimwear of choice is a birthday suit.

Visitors who have rented mopeds or motorbikes should probably save Punta Celarain for another day. Instead, you can follow the paved road north along the coast, thrilling at the fabulous views of windswept sea and jungle. With a stop for lunch—the **Paradise Café** and **Mezcalito's**, small, funky beachside restaurants with grand views of the Caribbean, anchor either end of the coast road—it takes about three hours to circle the southern half of the island (less in a Jeep). You can also swim in protected coves at **Playa Chiqueros** and **Punta Morena**, both of which also have restaurants. The coast road eventually meets the cross-island road just north of Punta Morena. Would-be Indiana Joneses who want to continue their explorations north to Punta Molas, at the tip of the island, should look elsewhere for their thrills. The sand track leading to the point eats Jeeps for lunch, resulting in long hikes out of the jungle and astronomical towing charges.

Nightlife on Cozumel

Life after dark, like everything else on Cozumel, exists—but on a smaller scale than in Cancún or Acapulco. There are two discos on the island, neither especially elaborate, although the energy needed to keep the beat going until dawn (on weekends) is there. **Scaramouche**, the smaller of the two, attracts a younger crowd and is usually more raucous. **Neptuno**, with videos, lights, and other high-tech trappings, is more sophisticated. Both are on Avenida Melgar near the southern edge of town.

Mexican fiesta nights are held at the Meliá Mayan (Tel: 2-0411), the Sol Caribe (Tel: 2-0700), and the Presidente (Tel: 2-0322) hotels.

Sports on Cozumel

The world-renowned reefs off the southwestern quadrant of Cozumel teem with colorful marine life. What follows are brief descriptions of the best-known reefs, starting with those near the cruise-ship pier and moving south in the direction of Punta Celarain.

Paraiso Reef is actually a series of reefs that begins just south of La Ceiba and extends almost as far as the Stouffer Presidente. Situated about 200 yards offshore at an average depth of 40 to 50 feet, Paraiso is about a five-minute swim from the sunken plane in front of La Ceiba, and, at its southern end, is one of the best spots off Cozumel for night diving.

Chankanaab Reef, situated in 10 to 35 feet of water right offshore, is located just south of the lagoon of the same name. Like Paraiso, it is famous for its varied coral formations and colorful marine life, and it, too, is a good spot for night dives.

San Francisco Reef, a quarter mile long and situated in 20 to 60 feet of water, is located directly offshore from Playa San Francisco. The current that sweeps the wall here (depth unlimited) is less pronounced than at other underwater locations around Cozumel, which makes it a good spot for intermediate divers to practice their drift dive technique.

The **Santa Rosa Wall**, a dropoff that begins at about 50 feet and plunges into bottomless depths, is located due south of San Francisco Reef. After Palancar, Santa Rosa is Cozumel's second most popular dive spot, although a strong current is always a factor here; beginning divers will want to get their feet wet elsewhere before moving on to the Wall.

Palancar Reef, located about a mile offshore and stretching over three miles, is Cozumel's pride and joy; in fact, it's rated among the top five dive sites in the world. The northern end of the reef is situated in about 40 feet of water, with the wall dropping off to unlimited depths. Divers will encounter a fantasyland of bizarre coral formations, deep underwater canyons, winding ravines, and countless tunnels and passageways. Visibility sometimes extends as far as 250 feet, and most people who are lucky enough to explore it say there's nothing like it.

Colombia Reef, a few miles south of Palancar, is almost as beautiful as its neighbor. Situated in 60 to 80 feet of water, with a dropoff to unlimited depths, it comprises giant coral pinnacles riddled with tunnels, caves, and caverns. One local publication compares diving here to floating over the Rocky Mountains.

Maracaibo Reef, off the southern tip of the island, is located at a depth of 100 feet and has numerous crevices and caves. This is the most challenging of all the dive sites off Cozumel, and with travel time figured in requires a full day to explore.

The entire underwater area from the cruise-ship pier to Punta Celarain has been designated a marine refuge; collecting, breaking, or otherwise damaging the delicate corals and sponges is strictly prohibited. Dives can be arranged through one of the more than 20 operators on the island; underwater still or video cameras can also be rented at a number of places in town. Listed below are a few of the more reputable outfits:

- **Aqua Safari**: Daily trips to Palancar Reef, scuba lessons, snorkel gear for sale. Avenida Melgar 39a; Tel: 2-0101.
- **Blue Angel Divers**: Daily trips to Palancar, lessons, PADI certification, snorkel gear rentals. On the coast road near the Villablanca hotel; Tel: 2-1631 or 0931.
- **Caribbean Divers**: Daily trips to Palancar, lessons, equipment rental, night dives. Avenida Melgar 38b; Tel: 2-1145.
- **Dive Paradise**: Day and half-day trips for novice, intermediate, and expert divers; twilight dives.

Avenida Melgar 601 (near the Hotel Barracuda); Tel: 2-1007.

For a complete listing of Cozumel's dive operators, write: CADO, P.O. Box 414236, Miami Beach, FL 33141-0236.

Waterskiing can be arranged through the Stouffer Presidente. Hobie Cats and jet skis are available at the Meliá Mayan. Windsurfers can be rented at the Presidente, Villablanca, Cabañas del Caribe, Meliá Mayan, and Divers' Inn hotels. The Meliá Mayan, La Ceiba, and Cabañas del Caribe hotels have in-house dive schools.

Deep-sea fishing boats and sailboats can be rented at Puerto de Abrigo, the marina on the coast road a few miles north of town; Fax: 2-1135; in the U.S., Tel: (800) 253-2701.

No golf course has been built on Cozumel as yet, but there is a miniature course next to the Hotel Barracuda. Some hotels have tennis courts, although for the most part the same stiff breeze that keeps Cozumel temperatures pleasant has discouraged the serious development of tennis facilities.

Excursions from Cozumel

Travel agents anywhere in town will be happy to arrange the following excursions.

The usual tour of the island includes stops at Chankanaab Lagoon and the ten-acre archaeological site of San Gervasio; make sure that any such tour you sign up for includes both.

The *Bonanza* offers snorkeling trips to Paraiso and Palancar reefs, with a stop for lunch at Playa Santa Rosa, at the southern end of the island. Tel: 2-0563 to make reservations.

The catamaran *Zorro* takes you to a deserted beach on Isla de Pasión, off the northern end of Cozumel, for swimming, snorkeling, and a picnic. Lunch is sometimes caught along the way and prepared on the beach; the cost is approximately $50. Contact Fiesta Cozumel Holidays (Tel: 2-0831 or 0433) to make reservations.

You can also fly to Chichén Itzá—one of the greatest archaeological sites in the northern Yucatán—for the day (about $100 per person) or take a day-long trip to the beautiful walled city of Tulum, with a stop at the natural aquarium of Xel-Há (about $60 per person). Both trips depart at 8:30 A.M. (pickup at your hotel), with the Tulum trip returning by 2:00 P.M., the Chichén Itzá trip by 6:00 P.M. Contact Fiesta Cozumel Holidays (see above) or Turismo Aviomar (Tel: 2-0477) for further information.

GETTING AROUND

Cancún

American, Continental, United, Mexicana, Aeroméxico, Northwest, LACSA, and Iberia are the major international air carriers offering direct service to Cancún. American offers daily service out of its Dallas–Fort Worth and Raleigh hubs; Continental offers daily service from its Houston hub; United flies daily from Chicago and Washington, D.C.; Mexicana flies nonstop from Los Angeles, Dallas–Fort Worth, Miami, and New York, and direct (with a stopover in Mexico City) from San Francisco and Chicago; Aeroméxico offers nonstop service from New York (four times a week) and Houston (daily); and Iberia is now offering direct service from Miami, with service from New York and Los Angeles scheduled to begin in the near future. It's a 3½-hour flight from Chicago, Washington, and New York; 3 hours from Raleigh; 2½ hours from Dallas–Fort Worth; and 1½ from Miami. If Cancún is only one stop on your Mexican itinerary, arrange for it as part of your overall ticketing before you leave; individual domestic fares within Mexico can be costly.

Upon arrival in Cancún you must take a price-controlled taxi or a *colectivo* from the airport to your hotel. Tickets are purchased at a booth on your way out of the terminal, and cost anywhere from $8 for a *colectivo* to $30 for a private taxi. The length of the trip via *colectivo* (up to an hour) depends on the number of stops it has to make.

In Cancún buses run through the hotel zone along Boulevard Kukulcán until midnight. The downtown stop for the bus that returns to the hotel zone is across Avenida Tulum from wherever you got off. (A good bet is to stand across the street from the San Francisco de Assis grocery store and simply flag down the first bus that comes along.) If you see a bus coming, jump on. Otherwise, be prepared for a long wait; no apparent schedule is kept.

Taxis are always available outside hotels and the busier restaurants. If you don't see one in front of your hotel, walk down to Boulevard Kukulcán and flag one down. In either case, you may want to keep your eyes shut; many drivers here are new behind the wheel and view Boulevard Kukulcán as the tropical version of the course at Le Mans. Saying *"Más despacio, por favor"* will get them to slow down. If you're going anywhere other than downtown, check the price before getting into the cab.

The most difficult place to get a taxi is at the Puerto Juárez passenger-ferry terminal upon your return from Isla Mujeres. The law of the jungle applies here. Push to the front of the boat before it docks and prepare to disembark like a sprinter coming out of the blocks. When the gate opens, run—don't walk—to the road and grab the first available taxi. Unless you have extra reserves of patience, this is a situation where you simply can't afford to be shy.

Isla Mujeres

Direct flights to Isla Mujeres from anywhere convenient are virtually nonexistent; instead, most travellers fly into Cancún and then take the airport *colectivo* to the ferry at Puerto Juárez (about $20).

Passenger ferries operate out of Puerto Juárez, about 10 minutes north of Cancún City by taxi. *Car* ferries leave from Punta Sam, another 10 minutes north of Puerto Juárez. The trip from either to Isla Mujeres takes about 45 minutes. Schedules are rather informal, with a ferry leaving every other hour or so, and the fare is minimal. If you're bringing a car over, be sure to get to Punta Sam at least 45 minutes before the next scheduled departure; the ferry handles 25 cars on a first-come, first-served basis. If it's a rough day, the car ferry will give you the smoother ride.

A third ferry option to the island, the Isla Mujeres shuttle (no vehicles), leaves from the Playa Linda marine terminal opposite the Calinda Cancún Beach three times daily (9:00 A.M., 11:15 A.M., and 2:30 P.M.). The fare is $12 per person, round-trip, and includes beverages. For further information, Tel: 84-6656 or 6846.

The fastest and most exhilarating option is to take a "water taxi" (flat-bottomed skiffs powered by big Yamaha or Johnson outboards) from Punta Sam. The boats are usually operated by local teenagers, and on calm days can make the eight-mile crossing in about 15 minutes (only the strong of nerve—and stomach—will want to do this when the wind is up and the bay rough). Of course, you'll pay extra for the convenience—about $15 a head, one way, from Punta Sam, and $10 a head for the return trip.

The best way to explore Isla Mujeres itself is by taxi or rented moped. Mopeds can be rented at any number of places around town, including Cárdenas Moto Rent, Avenida Guerrero 105-A; Ppe's Moto Rent, Avenida Hidalgo 19; or Rente Una Moto, Avenida Rueda Medina 3.

It's easy to get around town on foot. To get out to El Garrafón or any of the beaches south of town, spring for the moped. The hills on Isla Mujeres are not particularly steep, but there are several and the trip by bicycle is tiring.

Cozumel

American, Continental, and Mexicana are the major international carriers offering direct service to Cozumel. American offers daily service from its Dallas–Fort Worth hub; Continental offers daily service from its Houston hub; and Mexicana flies direct (with a stopover in Cancún) from Miami, Los Angeles, New York, San Francisco, and Chicago (all daily), as well as Dallas–Fort Worth (four times a week).

Aerocaribe links Cancún and Cozumel with 15-minute flights that depart every other hour. It also makes the seven-minute flight to Playa del Carmen every other hour.

The car ferry from Puerto Morelos leaves early in the morning (the time changes from week to week), and is an option best left for travellers with plenty of time on their hands: Container traffic is given preference; the crossing itself takes two hours (and may not be made at all in rough weather); and once the ferry reaches Cozumel motorists have to wait what seems like hours for the last truck to clear the deck before they're allowed off.

A passenger ferry—either the Water Jet or the slower *Cozumeleño*—leaves Playa del Carmen approximately ten times daily, with departures at 5:30, 7:30, 10:15, 11:00 A.M., and noon, and 12:15, 2:30, 5:30, 6:30, 7:30, and 9:00 P.M. Note that schedules are subject to change, however. The fare is about $8.

Private taxis are the way to get from the airport to your hotel on Cozumel. If you're staying at the north end of the island, the trip takes about five minutes. Trips to the southern part of the island take longer but rarely exceed 15 minutes.

Taxis are also the best way to get around the island, although you have to be armed with patience; there aren't enough cabs to go around, so it's a seller's market. Taxi schedules also seem to center around drivers' appetites, with cabs tending to get scarce at lunch/siesta time and at night after 9:00 P.M.

Cars, Jeeps, and mopeds can all be rented in San Miguel, but you'll want to inspect the vehicle to make sure it's in working order before you sign the contract. You might also want to take your moped for a test drive to see whether you can handle it; loose sand or gravel on roadsides can cause serious accidents. Renting a Jeep or Volkswagen Safari is sometimes the better part of valor.

Public buses stop at the hotels along the coast road. Signs on the front of the often-rickety vehicles read "Hoteles," and though they are inexpensive, their runs tend to be sporadic.

ACCOMMODATIONS REFERENCE

The rates given below are projections *for December 1993 through Easter 1994. Unless otherwise indicated, rates are for double rooms, double occupancy; the 10 percent VAT has been added. As rates are subject to change, it's a good idea to double-check before booking. Cancún, Isla Mujeres, and Cozumel are in the central standard time zone. The telephone area code for Cancún is 98; for Isla Mujeres and Cozumel it's 987.*

Cancún

▶ **Calinda Cancún Beach.** Boulevard Kukulcán, km 4, **Cancún,** Quintana Roo 77500. Tel: 83-1600; Fax: 83-1857; in the U.S. and Canada, Tel: (800) 228-5151. $132–$143.

▶ **Camino Real.** P.O. Box 14, Boulevard Kukulcán, **Cancún,** Quintana Roo 77500. Tel: 83-0100; Fax: 83-1730; in the U.S. and Canada, Tel: (800) 722-6466. $250 (standard); $325 (tower).

▶ **Cancún Palace.** P.O. Box 1730, Boulevard Kukulcán, km 14.5, **Cancún,** Quintana Roo 77500. Tel: 85-0533; Fax: 85-1593; in the U.S., Tel: (800) 346-8225. $221.

▶ **Casa Turquesa.** Boulevard Kukulcán, km 13.5, **Cancún,** Quintana Roo 77500. Tel: 85-2924 or 1974; Fax: 85-2922; in the U.S. and Canada, Tel: (800) 525-4800. $308 (garden-front); $385 (ocean-view).

▶ **Club Las Velas Hotel Cancún.** P.O. Box 1614, Boulevard Kukulcán at Galeón, **Cancún,** Quintana Roo 77500. Tel: 83-2150; Fax: 83-2118; in the U.S. and Canada, Tel: (800) 223-9815 or, in New York, Tel: (212) 251-1800. $220–$290 (all-inclusive, garden or superior) or $300–$360 (junior suite).

▶ **Fiesta Americana Cancún.** P.O. Box 696, Boulevard Kukulcán, **Cancún,** Quintana Roo 77500. Tel: 83-1400; Fax: 83-2502; in the U.S. and Canada, Tel: (800) FIESTA-1. $242–$259.

▶ **Fiesta Americana Coral Beach Cancún.** P.O. Box 5-479, Boulevard Kukulcán, **Cancún,** Quintana Roo 77500. Tel: 83-2900; Fax: 83-3173; in the U.S. and Canada, Tel: (800) FIESTA-1. $325.

▶ **Krystal Cancún.** Boulevard Kukulcán, **Cancún,** Quintana Roo 77500. Tel: 83-1133; Fax: 83-1790; in the U.S. and Canada, Tel: (800) 231-9860. $187 (standard); $215 (club floors).

▶ **Meliá Cancún.** Boulevard Kukulcán, **Cancún,** Quintana Roo 77500. Tel: 85-1114; Fax: 85-1263; in the U.S. and Canada, Tel: (800) 336-3542. $271 (standard); $370 (junior suite).

▶ **Ritz-Carlton, Cancún.** Boulevard Kukulcán, km 13.5,

Cancún, Quintana Roo 77500. Tel: 85-0808; Fax: 85-1015; in the U.S. and Canada, Tel: (800) 241-3333. $253–$358; $468 (club floor).

▶ **Sheraton Cancún Resort and Towers**. P.O. Box 834, Boulevard Kukulcán, **Cancún**, Quintana Roo 77500. Tel: 83-1988; Fax: 85-0974; in the U.S. and Canada, Tel: (800) 325-3535. $209–$231 (double); $243 (tower); $330 (suites with Jacuzzi).

▶ **Stouffer Presidente Cancún**. Boulevard Kukulcán, km 7.5, **Cancún**, Quintana Roo 77500. Tel: 83-0200; Fax: 83-2602; in the U.S. and Canada, Tel: (800) HOTELS-1. $242–$302; $320–$363 (club floors).

South of Cancún

▶ **Blue Parrot Inn**. P.O. Box 64, **Playa del Carmen**, Quintana Roo 77710. Fax: (987) 3-0049. For reservations, contact: 655 West Wisconsin Avenue, Orange City, FL 32763. Tel: (800) 634-3547 or (904) 775-6660. $71 (hotel rooms, palapas); $93 (bungalow); $115 (bungalow with kitchenette); $137 (two-bedroom beachfront cottage); $208 (beachfront villa).

▶ **Caribbean Reef Club**. Villa Marina, **Puerto Morelos**, Quintana Roo 77000. Contact: P.O. Box 1526, Cancún, Quintana Roo 77500. Tel: (98) 83-2636; Fax: (98) 83-2244; in the U.S., Tel: (800) 3-CANCUN. $130 (attached "villas"); $90 (studios and mini-suites); $70 (standard rooms).

▶ **Continental Plaza Playacar**. Fracc. Playacar, km 62.5, **Playa del Carmen**, Quintana Roo 77710. Tel: (987) 3-0100; Fax: (987) 3-0105; in the U.S., Tel: (800) 88-CONTI. $165.

▶ **Hotel Akumal Cancún**. P.O. Box 28, Cancún, Quintana Roo 77500. Tel: (98) 84-2272; Fax: (987) 2-2567. $88.

▶ **Hotel Club Akumal Caribe**. For reservations, contact: P.O. Box 13326, El Paso, TX 79913. All reservations must be made through the El Paso office (the country code when dialing the United States from Mexico is "95"). Tel: (800) 351-1622; in Canada, (800) 343-1440. $100 ("tower"); $84 (bungalow).

▶ **KaiLuum**. C/o Turquoise Reef Resorts, P.O. Box 2664, Evergreen, CO 80439. No local phone; in the U.S., Tel: (800) 538-6802; in Canada, Tel: (303) 674-9615; Fax: (303) 674-8735. $98 (includes breakfast and dinner).

▶ **Las Palapas**. C/o Arrecife Caribeño, S.A. de C.V., P.O. Box 116, **Playa del Carmen**, Quintana Roo 77710. Tel: (987) 2-2977; Fax: (5) 379-8641 (in Mexico City). $157 (includes breakfast and dinner; full payment must be received 30 days before arrival).

▶ **La Posada del Capitan Lafitte**. C/o Turquoise Reef Resorts, P.O. Box 2664, Evergreen, CO 80439. No local phone; in the U.S., Tel: (800) 538-6802; in Canada, Tel: (303) 674-9615; Fax: (303) 674-8735. $140 (includes breakfast and dinner).

▶ **Shangri-La Caribe.** C/o Turquoise Reef Resorts, P.O. Box 2664, Evergreen, CO 80439. Tel: (987) 2-2888; in the U.S., Tel: (800) 538-6802; in Canada, Tel: (303) 674-9615; Fax: (303) 674-8735. $100–$140 (includes breakfast and dinner).

▶ **Villa Arqueológica Cobá.** P.O. Box 710, Cancún, Quintana Roo 77500. No local phone; in the U.S. and Canada, Tel: (800) CLUB-MED. $62–$75.

Isla Mujeres

▶ **Hotel Perla del Caribe.** Avenida Madero 2, **Isla Mujeres,** Quintana Roo, 77400. Tel: 7-0444; Fax: 7-0011; in the U.S., Tel: (800) 258-6454. $52–$76.

▶ **Na Balam.** Calle Zazil-Ha 118, **Isla Mujeres,** Quintana Roo 77400. Tel and Fax: 7-0446. $83 (includes breakfast).

▶ **Nautibeach Condominium-Hotel.** Avenida Rueda Medina, **Isla Mujeres,** Quintana Roo 77400. Tel: 7-0436 or 0259; Fax: 7-0487. $110 (two-night minimum).

▶ **Posada del Mar.** Rueda Medina 15, **Isla Mujeres,** Quintana Roo 77400. Tel: 7-0212; Fax: 7-0266. $50.

Cozumel

▶ **La Ceiba.** P.O. Box 284, Carretera a Chankanaab, km 4.5 **Cozumel,** Quintana Roo 77600. Tel: 2-0844; in the U.S. and Canada, Tel: (800) 877-4383; Fax: (800) 235-5892. $121.

▶ **El Cozumeleño.** P.O. Box 53, Playa Santa Pilar, **Cozumel,** Quintana Roo 77600. Tel: 2-0149; Fax: 2-0381; in the U.S. and Canada, Tel: (800) 437-3923. $128.

▶ **Diamond at Cozumel.** Playa San Francisco, Carretera Cozumel, km 16.5 **Cozumel,** Quintana Roo 77666. Tel: 2-3443; Fax: 2-4508; in the U.S. and Canada, Tel: (800) 858-2258. $110 (includes all meals, drinks, entertainment, taxes, tips, and non-motorized water sports).

▶ **Fiesta Americana Cozumel Reef.** Carretera a Chankanaab, km 7.5, **Cozumel,** Quintana Roo 77600. Tel: 2-2622; Fax: 2-2666; in the U.S. and Canada, Tel: (800) FIESTA-1. $187 (garden-view); $206 (superior ocean-view); $230 (deluxe ocean-view).

▶ **Fiesta Americana Sol Caribe.** P.O. Box 259, Playa Paraiso, km 3.5, **Cozumel,** Quintana Roo 77600. Tel: 2-0555; Fax: 2-1301; in the U.S. and Canada, Tel: (800) FIESTA-1. $151 (garden-view); $176 (deluxe ocean-view); $194 (tower ocean-view).

▶ **Hotel Villablanca Beach Club and Sports Complex.** P.O.

Box 230, **Cozumel**, Quintana Roo 77600. Tel: (800) DIVMEX; Fax: 2-0865; in the U.S., Tel: (800) 780-3949. $51–$68.

▶ **Meliá Mayan Cozumel.** Playa Santa Pilar, **Cozumel**, Quintana Roo 77600. Tel: 2-0411; Fax: 2-1599; in the U.S. and Canada, Tel: (800) 336-3542. $148 (standard); $170 (superior ocean-view).

▶ **Stouffer Presidente Cozumel.** Carretera a Chankanaab, km 6.5, **Cozumel**, Quintana Roo 77600. Tel: 2-0322; Fax: 2-1360; in the U.S. and Canada, Tel: (800) HOTELS-1. $215 (garden-view); $259 (partial ocean-view); $303 (full ocean-view); $655 (suites).

CHRONOLOGY OF THE HISTORY OF MEXICO AND GUATEMALA

The Beginnings

- **50,000 B.C.:** Wandering hunters and food gatherers cross into the Americas from present-day Siberia over a land bridge, long since submerged, that anthropologists have dubbed "Beringia." Little is known of these Stone Age peoples, but over the course of tens of thousands of years various racial types arrive and become diffused over both the northern and southern continents of the Americas.

  At Tepexpán, near Mexico City, the skeletal remains of a young woman have been discovered near those of a mammoth that was killed with flint-tipped weapons. This so-called Tepexpán Man has been dated to about 12,000 B.C.

- **9000 B.C.:** End of the Ice Age; large Pleistocene fauna such as mammoths and mastodons become extinct.

- **5000 B.C.:** Domestication of maize. After maize, squash, chile peppers, and beans become staples of the Mesoamerican diet—much as they are today.

- **2300–1800 B.C.:** Pottery is introduced; clay figurines begin to be fashioned.

The Preclassic Era

- **1800 B.C.:** Small villages are established in the Valley of Mexico (around present-day Mexico City), among them Ticomán, Copilco, Tlatilco, and Zacatenco. Many clay figurines are produced, especially fertility images of women.

- **1200 B.C.:** The **Olmecs**, an advanced people of mysterious origins, establish their first great ceremonial center, San Lorenzo, in the Gulf region. Subsequently, their influence spreads over much of Mesoamerica and becomes especially evident at Monte Albán, near present-day Oaxaca City. Jade carving, giant stone heads, and other major stone sculpture are produced.

- **800 B.C.:** The first structures that can be called architecture rise at Cuicuilco and Cerro de Tlapacoya, in the Valley of Mexico. The Maya establish themselves throughout the Yucatán Peninsula and the highlands of Chiapas—an area they occupy to this day.

- **700 B.C.**: The Maya, influenced by the Olmecs, build an elaborate ceremonial center at Uaxactún, in present-day Guatemala.
- **600 B.C.**: Olmec civilization reaches its apex at La Venta (in today's Tabasco). Hieroglyphs, numerals, and a calendar are developed.
- **500 B.C.**: In western Mexico, artisans create remarkable clay figurines.
- **300 B.C.**: America's first true urban civilization, Teotihuacán, begins to develop in the Valley of Mexico. In Guatemala construction begins at Tikal, where building will continue for the next 1,000 years.

The Classic Era

- **200 B.C.–A.D. 900**: Cities and ceremonial centers are established throughout Mesoamerica, in conjunction with a complex theology.
- **200–350**: The urban center of Teotihuacán covers six square miles and boasts more than 150,000 inhabitants in what is perhaps the largest pre-industrial city anywhere in the world. Centers in the Mayan region, on the Gulf Coast, and in Oaxaca continue to expand. Monte Albán, Palenque, Uxmal, and other centers are on the rise.
- **450–700**: The great Maya sites flourish. Teotihuacán remains a major commercial power, sending its traders as far as central Guatemala.
- **700–750**: Teotihuacán experiences irreversible decline. Eventually, internal dissension and other factors facilitate its destruction by nomadic invaders. South and east, however, other Mesoamerican cultures continue to thrive, even though their greatest years have been reached and passed. In central Mexico Xochicalco survives, spanning the Late Classic and early Postclassic eras. In Oaxaca Monte Albán is waning.
- **750–900**: The great Mesoamerican centers experience decline, collapse, and, most often, abandonment, for reasons still debated (see Overview).

The Postclassic Era

- **900–1200**: Semi-barbaric **Toltecs** migrate southward into the central highlands (where they came from remains unknown), supplanting older cultures while becoming civilized themselves. Their influence extends south as far as the Yucatán, where temples are built and the ancient cult of the plumed serpent is transformed and flourishes. Perhaps the best-known incarnation of the plumed serpent, Topiltzin-Quetzalcóatl, a priest-king, is supposed to have been born among the Toltecs in 947.

Another warrior people, the **Mixtecs**, move into the valleys near the ancient ceremonial centers of Cholula and Monte Albán. Their knowledge of metalworking—first gold, and then copper and silver—improves and spreads; as forms of writing are refined, they begin to record their history.

- **c. 999**: Topiltzin-Quetzalcóatl flees, promising to return. Warrior kings succeed him at Tula, the Toltec capital.

- **1325**: **Aztecs** (theories conflict as to their geographical origins) arrive in the central highlands of present-day Mexico and establish their capital, Tenochtitlán, on an island in Lake Texcoco. The settlement will evolve into what is today Mexico City.

- **c. 1400**: *Chinampas,* so-called floating gardens that improve agricultural efficiency, facilitate the Aztec domination of the central highlands.

- **1440–1500**: Aztec domination extends throughout what is now Mexico.

- **1502**: Móctezuma II is crowned god-emperor of the Aztecs. Disturbing omens punctuate his reign, seeming to foretell the return of the plumed serpent-god Quetzalcóatl.

- **1517**: The expedition of Hernández de Córdova sails along the Yucatán coast.

- **1518**: Juan de Grijalva, following up on Córdova's discoveries, explores much of the Atlantic coast of Mesoamerica and reports back to his king on its vast size. The population of the region at the time—a figure unknown to de Grijalva—is put at 25 million by modern scholars. Grijalva names the region New Spain.

- **1519**: Hernán Cortés, a Spanish adventurer, lands on a Veracruz beach with 555 soldiers and 16 horses—animals unknown and terrifying to the inhabitants. After a grueling march over the Sierra Madre Oriental punctuated by skirmishes with local tribes, Cortés and his men enter the island city of Tenochtitlán. Although initially welcomed as the returning serpent-god Quetzalcóatl, Cortés soon seizes Móctezuma and takes him hostage.

- **1520**: The ineffectual Móctezuma is slain (according to legend and the testimony of the conquistadors) by his own people, and the Spaniards are driven from the city.

- **1521**: Cortés, with an army of Indian allies, returns and besieges the Aztec capital. Eventually, Tenochtitlán falls to the invaders.
- **1523**: Pedro de Alvarado, Cortés's chief lieutenant, begins a prolonged conquest of what is now Guatemala.
- **1524**: Cortés kneels to welcome 12 Franciscan friars, who immediately set out to Christianize the country—a task they accomplish with astonishing speed.
- **1525**: Cuauhtémoc, Móctezuma's successor, is executed by the Spanish; he is the last Aztec emperor. Vast amounts of Aztec treasure are shipped off to Spain.

New Spain

The Spanish Crown moves quickly to exploit and evangelize its new colony. A caste system is established, with Spaniards born in Spain at the top; pure-blood Spaniards born outside the motherland, called *criollos,* next; people of mixed race, or *mestizos,* below that; and pure-blooded Indians, or *indios,* at the bottom.

Native art, which is viewed as diabolical, is ruthlessly destroyed. Weakened by plagues, Indian resistance collapses. The few surviving native painted books, called codices, are taken back to Europe; not a single pre-Columbian codex remains in its country of origin.

- **1530**: Construction of the National Cathedral in Mexico City begins.
- **1531**: Juan Diego, a humble Aztec convert, sees a vision of the Virgin on a hill north of Mexico City—a miracle that promotes the conversion of, and gives solace to, dark-skinned people throughout New Spain, because this Virgin is herself dark skinned.
- **1535**: Antonio de Mendoza is named the first viceroy of New Spain; he will establish the pattern for Spain's administration of its New World colony.
- **1542**: Enslavement of Indians is outlawed, only to be replaced by new ways of obtaining their forced labor.
- **1554**: A new mining process increases silver output. Silver pours into Spain's coffers for the next two and a half centuries, doubling the Western world's supply in the process.
- **1565**: A plot to establish an independent Mexican kingdom, to be ruled by Cortés's son, is nipped in the bud.
- **1571**: The Inquisition begins its work in Mexico City.
- **1651**: Sor Juana Inés de la Cruz, destined to become New Spain's greatest poet, is born.

- **1700–1800**: Baroque art and architecture are fostered by the Church. Ornate, fanciful architectural decoration—the Churrigueresque style—flowers, only to be supplanted by the Neoclassical style at the end of the century.
- **1767**: The Jesuits are expelled from the colony by royal order.
- **1776**: Earthquakes destroy the old capital of Guatemala (now Antigua). Guatemala City is founded three years later.
- **1808**: In Europe, France invades Spain, precipitating a crisis in Spain's New World colonies.

The Struggle for Independence

- **1810**: The Querétaro Conspiracy arises as patriots in the Bajío region discuss and partly plan an uprising designed to overthrow Spanish rule. At the same time, Miguel Hidalgo y Costilla, a priest from the obscure town of Dolores, raises the cry of independence and leads a ragtag army against the Crown. The struggle continues for 11 years.
- **1811**: Hidalgo and other rebels are defeated and executed. José María Morelos, Hidalgo's student and successor, continues the war but is himself captured and executed (1815).
- **1821**: Independence for Mexico is proclaimed by Agustín de Iturbide and Vicente Guerrero (though Spain withholds its recognition until 1836). Guatemalan independence is also proclaimed; its status in regard to Mexico is left unclear.
- **1822**: Iturbide establishes himself as "emperor," but is deposed the following year. After Iturbide's fall, Guatemala follows its own course.
- **1824**: Mexico drafts a democratic constitution, and Guadalupe Victoria is proclaimed president.
- **1833**: General Santa Anna is elected president. Over the next two decades this mountebank, who styles himself "His Serene Highness," will be in and out of power—to Mexico's great detriment.
- **1835**: Texas declares and wins its independence from Mexico.
- **1838**: France blockades and bombards Veracruz to collect outstanding debts owed by the fledgling Mexican government.
- **1846**: The United States invades Mexico.
- **1848**: The Treaty of Guadalupe Hidalgo results in Mexico ceding almost half its territory to the United States.

- **1854**: Santa Anna sells parts of what are now the states of Arizona and New Mexico to the United States in order to raise money for the suppression of liberal democracy in Mexico.
- **1855**: The bitter War of Reform, pitting liberals against the old establishment, breaks out. The Church battles against liberal reform.

Democracy vs. Dictatorship

- **1857**: A new constitution separating Church and State is adopted. Civil war continues and Church landholdings are seized. Pope Pius IX nullifies the Mexican constitution.
- **1859**: Benito Juárez, a full-blooded Zapotec Indian and liberal politician from Oaxaca, helps to draft the Reform Laws, which call for the nationalization of Church property, the closing of convents, and the liberation of religious expression. He is elected president two years later.
- **1862**: England, Spain, and France seize Veracruz to collect debts. Spain and England soon withdraw, but France invades and is defeated at the battle of Puebla—a military victory commemorated every year on May 5.
- **1863**: A second French invasion results in the capture of Puebla and Mexico City. Juárez flees north, while the Church and Mexican conservatives welcome the French.
- **1864**: The French and Mexican conservatives proclaim Austrian Archduke Maximilian Emperor of Mexico. War continues.
- **1867**: Royalist troops are defeated at Querétaro, and Maximilian is executed. Juárez is reconfirmed as president and enters the capital in triumph. He heads a liberal government until his death in 1872.
- **1871**: Liberals win military victory in Guatemala. Railroad construction begins.
- **1876**: General Porfirio Díaz is elected president.
- **1884**: Díaz, out of office four years, returns to the presidency and governs as virtual dictator until 1911. Dubbed the "Porfiriate," it is an era of foreign investment in Mexico, economic progress for the ruling class, and political repression.

Revolution and the Emergence of Modern Mexico

- **1910**: Francisco I. Madero, the son of a wealthy northern family, campaigns against Díaz for the presidency—

aided militarily by Emiliano Zapata—but is soon arrested. Díaz begins his eighth term in office.

- **1911**: Díaz, under pressure, resigns.
- **1912**: Madero is elected president. Invasion is feared as U.S. troops mass at the border.
- **1913**: General Victoriano Huerta stages a coup, and Madero is assassinated. Civil war breaks out and Huerta flees. In the south, Zapata leads an armed struggle for land reform.
- **1914**: U.S. troops seize Veracruz, killing nearly 200 Mexican defenders. In the north, Venustiano Carranza, an elderly landowner, forms a constitutionalist army. A power struggle ensues among Carranza, Zapata, and Pancho Villa, a peon turned general and warlord.
- **1915**: At the Battle of Celaya, troops of Carranza and General Alvaro Obregón defeat the forces of Villa and Zapata.
- **1916**: The United States recognizes the Carranza government. In retaliation, Villa raids Columbus, New Mexico. U.S. troops cross the border into Mexico.
- **1917**: Carranza is elected prèsident under a new reform constitution. In Guatemala an earthquake devastates the capital.
- **1921**: Gen. Alvaro Obregón, revolutionary hero, becomes president. He is later assassinated by a religious fanatic.
- **1920**: Guatemalan dictator Manuel Estrada Cabrera is overthrown after 22 years of calamitous rule.
- **1924–1928**: Labor unions become a strong institutional force during the presidency of Plutarco Calles. During the same period, the Church is more sharply restricted, and the old anti-clerical laws are once again enforced. *Cristeros,* religious militants in armed rebellion against this trend, are gradually suppressed. The Partido Revolucionario Institucional, or PRI, destined to become the dominant political force in Mexican life, emerges.
- **1934**: Lázaro Cárdenas is elected president. During his six-year term he nationalizes the railroads and petroleum industry (among other sweeping social and political reforms)—to the consternation of the international business community.
- **1940**: Avila Camacho wins an orderly election. Reform in the postwar period continues at a slower pace.
- **1945**: José Arévado becomes president of Guatemala and initiates democratic reforms.
- **1954**: In Guatemala, Colonel Carlos Armas seizes power

from duly elected Jacobo Arbenz with the help of the United States. Years of tumult follow.

- **1968**: The hosting of the Summer Olympic Games brings new prestige to Mexico; the favorable publicity is marred by the violent suppression of student demonstrations.

- **1973–1978**: Mexico rides a wave of prosperity, thanks to soaring oil prices in the wake of the OPEC oil embargo.

- **1976**: Great destruction is caused by an earthquake in Guatemala.

- **1982**: President López Portillo nationalizes the banking system; Mexico is thrown into economic crisis as oil prices worldwide plunge.

- **1985**: Mexico City is devastated by earthquakes.

- **1986**: Vinicio Cereza, elected president of Guatemala, institutes a struggle for peace and greater democracy.

- **1988**: Carlos Salinas de Gortari is elected president in the first hotly contested national election in modern Mexican history. Amidst charges of widespread fraud, opposition parties on both the right and left make inroads into PRI political dominance.

- **1989–1990**: President Salinas intensifies his political and economic reforms. The powerful oil workers union is brought under legal control.

- **1991–92**: Mexico, the United States, and Canada debate a free-trade pact that would create the world's largest economic union. Political reform and greater freedom of the Church is advanced under President Salinas.

- **1993**: Despite agreements in principle, free trade is far from becoming a reality, as Mexico struggles to build infrastructure and become competitive in a global economy.

—Robert Somerlott

INDEX

706